Iraq War

Iraq War

THE ESSENTIAL REFERENCE GUIDE

Brian L. Steed, Editor

BLOOMSBURY ACADEMIC
NEW YORK • LONDON • OXFORD • NEW DELHI • SYDNEY

BLOOMSBURY ACADEMIC
Bloomsbury Publishing Inc
1385 Broadway, New York, NY 10018, USA
50 Bedford Square, London, WC1B 3DP, UK
29 Earlsfort Terrace, Dublin 2, Ireland

BLOOMSBURY, BLOOMSBURY ACADEMIC and the Diana logo are trademarks of
Bloomsbury Publishing Plc

First published in the United States of America by ABC-CLIO 2019
Paperback edition published by Bloomsbury Academic 2024

Copyright © Bloomsbury Publishing Inc, 2024

Cover photos: Soldiers of the Iraqi National Guard in northern Iraq, November 2, 2004. (Johnny Saunderson/Alamy Stock Photo); U.S. President George W. Bush in the Oval Office of the White House, in Washington, DC, September 13, 2001. (White House Photo/Alamy Stock Photo); Portrait of Saddam Hussein, July 1982. (peter jordan/Alamy Stock Photo); U.S. Marines Corps from the 1st Battalion, 7th Marines (1/7), Charlie Company, Twentynine Palms, California. (USMC)

All rights reserved. No part of this publication may be reproduced or
transmitted in any form or by any means, electronic or mechanical,
including photocopying, recording, or any information storage or retrieval
system, without prior permission in writing from the publishers.

Bloomsbury Publishing Inc does not have any control over, or responsibility for,
any third-party websites referred to or in this book. All internet addresses given
in this book were correct at the time of going to press. The author and publisher
regret any inconvenience caused if addresses have changed or sites have
ceased to exist, but can accept no responsibility for any such changes.

Library of Congress Cataloging-in-Publication Data
Names: Steed, Brian L., editor.
Title: Iraq war: the essential reference guide / Brian L. Steed, editor.
Description: Santa Barbara, California: ABC-CLIO, 2019. |
Includes bibliographical references and index.
Identifiers: LCCN 2018034741 (print) | LCCN 2018035136 (ebook) |
ISBN 9781440858314 (ebook) | ISBN 9781440858307 (hard copy)
Subjects: LCSH: Iraq War, 2003–2011.
Classification: LCC DS79.76 (ebook) | LCC DS79.76.I735 2019 (print) |
DDC 956.7044/3—dc23
LC record available at https://lccn.loc.gov/2018034741

ISBN: HB: 978-1-4408-5830-7
PB: 979-8-7651-2028-6
ePDF: 978-1-4408-5831-4
eBook: 979-8-2161-0496-4

To find out more about our authors and books visit www.bloomsbury.com
and sign up for our newsletters.

Disclaimer
All opinions and suppositions expressed in this work are entirely those of the author and in no
way reflect the positions, opinions, or policies of the U.S. Army, the U.S. Department of Defense,
or any official or agency of the U.S. government.

For Psalm and Oliver and my other grandchildren yet unborn. I hope that understanding this war will make the world more peaceful by the time you take charge.

As always, for my wife and companion who inspires me daily.

Contents

List of Entries, ix

List of Primary Documents, xi

Overview of the Iraq War (2003–2011), xiii

Causes of the Iraq War, xxi

Consequences of the Iraq War, xxv

A–Z Entries, 1

Primary Source Documents, 269

Chronology of the Iraq War, 307

Recommended Bibliography, 319

List of Contributors, 323

Index, 327

About the Editor, 349

List of Entries

Al-Askari Mosque (Golden Mosque)
  Bombing (February 22, 2006)
Ambassadors to Iraq, U.S. (Chronological
  Order)
  John D. Negroponte (2004–2005)
  Zalmay M. Khalilzad (2005–2007)
  Ryan C. Crocker (2007–2009)
  Christopher R. Hill (2009–2010)
  James F. Jeffrey (2010–2012)
Arab Spring (December 18,
  2010–December 2012)
Arrowhead Ripper, Operation
  (June 19–August 19, 2007)
Atrocities, U.S.
  Haditha Incident (November 19, 2005)
  Mahmudiyah Incident (March 12, 2006)
Baath Party
Baghdadi, Abu Bakr al- (c. 1971–)
Bremer, Lewis Paul, III (1941–)
Bush, George Walker (1946–)
Bush Doctrine
Casualties, Operation Iraqi Freedom
Cheney, Richard Bruce (1941–)
Coalition Provisional Authority
Commanders, Multi-National Force–Iraq
  (or United States Forces–Iraq)
  (Chronological Order)
  Ricardo S. Sanchez (2004)
  George W. Casey Jr. (2004–2007)
  David H. Petraeus (2007–2008) (see
    Commander, CENTCOM entry)
  Raymond T. Odierno (2008–2010)
  Lloyd J. Austin III (2010–2011)
Commanders, U.S. Central Command
  (CENTCOM) (Chronological
  Order)
  Tommy Franks (2000–2003)
  John P. Abizaid (2003–2007)
  William J. Fallon (2007–2008)
  Martin E. Dempsey (2008)
  David H. Petraeus (2008–2010)
  John R. Allen (2010) (No Further
    Information)
  James Mattis (2010–2013)
Commands, U.S. and Coalition Military
  Multi-National Force–Iraq (United
    States Forces–Iraq)
  Multi-National Security Transition
    Command–Iraq (MNSTC-I)
  U.S. Central Command (CENTCOM)
Contractors
  Blackwater USA
  Halliburton
  Private Security Firms
Detention Operations, Coalition
  Abu Ghraib
  Camp Bucca
  Guantánamo Bay Detention Camp
Doctrine, Counterinsurgency
Doctrine, Insurgency
Fallujah, First Battle of (April 4–May 1,
  2004)

Fallujah, Second Battle of
    (November 7–December 23, 2004)
Garner, Jay Montgomery (1938–)
Global War on Terrorism
Hussein, Qusay (1966–2003)
Hussein, Saddam (1937–2006)
Hussein, Uday (1964–2003)
Insurgency and Opposition
    Badr Organization
    Fedayeen
    Mahdi Army
Interrogation, Coercive (Torture)
Iraq, Air Force
Iraq, Army
Iraq, History of, 1990–Present
Iraq, Navy
Iraq, Sanctions on
Iraq Study Group
Iraqi Freedom, Operation (2003–2010)
    Planning for Operations
    Air Campaign
    Coalition Ground Forces
    Coalition Naval Forces
    Ground Campaign
    Major Battles
    The Surge and the Awakening
Islamic State of Iraq and al-Sham (ISIS)
    Al Qaeda in Iraq
Karbala, First Battle of (March 31–April 6, 2003)
Kurds
Mosul, Battle of (November 8–16, 2004)
Nasiriyah, Battle of (March 23–29, 2003)
New Dawn, Operation (2010–2011)
Obama, Barack Hussein, II (1961–)
Oil
Phantom Strike, Operation (August 13, 2007)
Phantom Thunder, Operation
    (June 16–August 14, 2007)
Political Parties, Iraq
    Islamic Dawa Party
    Kurdistan Democratic Party
    Patriotic Union of Kurdistan
    Supreme Iraqi Islamic Council
Prime Minister, Iraq (Selected)
    (Chronological Order)
    Ibrahim al-Jaafari
    Ahmed Abd al-Hadi Chalabi
    Ayad Allawi
    Nuri al-Maliki
Reconstruction
Sadr, Muqtada al- (1973–)
Sadr City, Battle of (March 26–May 11, 2008)
Secretary of Defense, U.S. (Chronological Order)
    Donald Rumsfeld
    Robert M. Gates
    Leon E. Panetta
Secretary of State, U.S. (Chronological Order)
    Colin L. Powell
    Condoleezza Rice
    Hillary R. Clinton
Shia Islam
Sistani, Sayyid Ali Husayn al- (1930–)
Sunni Islam
United Nations Weapons Inspectors
U.S. Agency for International Development, Iraq
Viking Hammer, Operation (March 28–30, 2003)
Weapons, Insurgency, and Opposition
    Improvised Explosive Devices
Weapons of Mass Destruction
Weapons Systems, Coalition
    Mine-Resistant Ambush-Protected Vehicles
    Unmanned Aerial Vehicles
WikiLeaks
Wolfowitz, Paul Dundes (1943–)
Women, Role of in Afghanistan and Iraq Wars
Woodward, Robert Upshur (1943–)
Zarqawi, Abu Musab al- (1966–2006)

List of Primary Documents

Excerpt from Congressional Resolution Supporting the Use of Force against Iraq, October 16, 2002
Excerpt of the State of the Union Address, January 28, 2003
President Bush's Address to the Nation at the Start of Hostilities, March 19, 2003
Excerpt of President Bush's Remarks to the Crew of the USS Abraham Lincoln, May 1, 2003
Excerpt of Coalition Provisional Order Number 1, May 16, 2003
Excerpt of Coalition Provisional Order Number 2, May 23, 2003
Excerpt of Iraqi Constitution: Preamble and Basic Rights, October 15, 2005
Joint Statement by President George W. Bush and Prime Minister Nuri al-Maliki of Iraq, November 30, 2006
Excerpt of Field Manual 3–24: Counterinsurgency, 2006
Excerpt of Testimony of General David Petraeus to Congress, September 10, 2007
Excerpt of "Agreement between the United States of America and the Republic of Iraq on the Withdrawal of United States Forces from Iraq and the Organization of Their Activities during Their Temporary Presence in Iraq," November 17, 2008
Excerpt of President Obama's Speech at Camp Lejeune, February 27, 2009
Presidential Address on the End of Combat Operations in Iraq, August 31, 2010

Overview of the Iraq War (2003–2011)

The Iraq War (2003–2011) has its roots in the 1991 Persian Gulf War (also known as Operation Desert Storm) in which the United States, in conjunction with a coalition of forces from 35 countries, worked to expel Iraqi forces from Kuwait. Following the 1991 Persian Gulf War, the United Nations (UN) imposed sanctions on Iraq, calling for Iraqi president Saddam Hussein to destroy the country's arsenal of weapons of mass destruction (WMD). Over the next decade, however, Hussein repeatedly evaded attempts by UN weapons inspectors to ensure that the sanctions were enforced. Upon assuming the U.S. presidency in January 2001, George W. Bush and his administration immediately began calling for renewed efforts toward ridding Iraq of WMD—an endeavor that greatly intensified after the September 11, 2001, attacks on the World Trade Center and Pentagon.

In Bush's 2002 State of the Union Address, he castigated Iraq for continuing to "flaunt its hostility toward America and to support terror" and called the Middle Eastern nation part of "an axis of evil, arming to threaten the peace of the world." In the months that followed, the U.S. president increasingly spoke of taking military action in Iraq. Bush found an ally in British prime minister Tony Blair, but pressure from citizens of both countries pushed the two leaders to take the issue before the UN Security Council in the form of UN Resolution 1441, which called for UN weapons inspectors, led by Hans Blix, to return to Iraq and issue a report on their findings.

On November 8, 2002, the 15-member UN Security Council unanimously passed the resolution, and weapons inspectors began work on November 27. On December 7, Iraq delivered a 12,000-page declaration of its weapons program, an insufficient accounting according to Blix, and a month later Bush stated that "If Saddam Hussein does not fully disarm, we will lead a coalition to disarm him." Bush and Blair actively sought the support of the international community, but their announcement that they would circumvent the UN if necessary ruffled many nations' feathers, most notably drawing the ire of France, Germany, and Russia, all of which pushed for further inspections. Spain joined with the United Kingdom and the United States to propose a second UN resolution declaring Iraq to be in "material breach" of Resolution 1441. Although a small number of other nations pledged their support for military action in Iraq, only Australia initially pledged to commit troops to fight alongside British and U.S. forces.

Opting for a preemptive strategy instead of risking a potential repeat of the September 11 terror attacks—with the added specter of chemical, biological, or nuclear weapons—Bush and his advisers (principally Vice President Dick Cheney and Deputy Secretary of Defense Paul Wolfowitz) decided to act, unilaterally if necessary. Armed with a Central Intelligence Agency (CIA) report regarding Iraq's possession of nuclear and other weapons of mass destruction (the accuracy of which has since been called into question), Bush obtained a legal justification for invading Iraq when in October 2002 the Senate approved the joint resolution "Authorization for Use of Military Force against Iraq Resolution of 2002." In February 2003 Secretary of State Colin Powell addressed the UN Security Council with information based largely on the same flawed CIA report, but action was blocked by France, Germany, and Russia. Although Britain and 75 other countries joined Bush's "coalition of the willing" (contributing troops, matériel, or services to the U.S.-led effort beginning in 2003), the absence of France and Germany left his administration open to strong criticism for stubbornly proceeding without broad-based European support.

Bush's proactive rather than reactive strategy was viewed as a sea-change departure from that of his predecessor Bill Clinton, exposing him to further criticism. Condemnation was heaped on the president for attempting to conduct simultaneous operations in Iraq and Afghanistan with a force stretched thin by military drawdowns conducted during the Bill Clinton presidency. On the eve of the Iraq invasion U.S. Army Chief of Staff General Eric Shinseki told the Senate Armed Services Committee that an occupation of that country would require "several hundred thousand" troops, an estimate that, in hindsight, seemed prescient, but was sharply criticized in 2003 by Secretary of Defense Donald Rumsfeld and his deputy Paul Wolfowitz as "wildly off the mark."

Facing the disapproval of the British public, Prime Minister Tony Blair pushed for a compromise that would give weapons inspectors a little more time to inspect Iraq. However, with two permanent members of the Security Council—France and Russia—threatening to veto the resolution, the proposal was withdrawn. Undeterred by that set of events, or the Turkish government's refusal to allow coalition troops to use Turkey as a platform for a northern invasion of Iraq, Bush issued an ultimatum to Saddam Hussein on March 17 to leave Iraq within 48 hours or face military action. Hours before the deadline was to expire, Bush received intelligence information that Hussein and several top officials in the Iraqi government were sleeping in an underground facility in southern Baghdad called Dora Farms. Bush ordered a decapitation strike aimed at killing Hussein, which took place in the early morning of March 20. Dozens of Tomahawk missiles with 1,000-pound warheads were launched from U.S. warships in the Persian Gulf and the Red Sea. They hit their targets in Baghdad and were followed immediately by 2,000-pound bunker-buster bombs dropped from F-117 stealth fighters. The war had begun.

That same day (March 20, 2003) U.S.-led coalition troops (which included British forces plus smaller contingents from Australia and Poland) crossed the border from Kuwait into Iraq. The 297,000-strong force faced an Iraqi Army numbering approximately 375,000, plus an unknown number of citizens' militias. Armed with technology that included stealth bombers and precision-guided (smart) bombs, the coalition commenced its shock-and-awe campaign, designed to stun and demoralize the Iraqi Army into a quick surrender. Within a matter of days, the coalition had overtaken Basra, Iraq's second-largest city, as well as the port city of Umm Qasr and the city of Nasiriyah straddling the

Euphrates River. While Iraqi soldiers did not surrender with the same celerity as they had in the 1991 Persian Gulf War, nearly 10,000 Iraqi troops surrendered to coalition forces during those first days. Still, the coalition troops were caught unprepared by some of the Iraqis' guerrilla tactics, including faking surrenders and ambushing troops from the rear.

As the war began, two ground prongs struck north from Kuwait, while special forces and airborne forces worked with the Kurds in the north in a limited second front. The ground advance north was rapid. After securing southern Iraq and its oil fields, coalition soldiers began moving toward Baghdad; they secured an airfield in western Iraq and Hussein International Airport (immediately renamed Baghdad International Airport) with little difficulty. On April 5 and 7 coalition forces entered Baghdad where they destroyed many of Hussein's government buildings and palaces on the Tigris River. Six days later the United States declared the end of Hussein's regime. The vanquished Iraqi dictator was in hiding. One last hurdle remained, and by April 14 coalition forces accomplished it by capturing Hussein's hometown of Tikrit. Formal military action ceased, with fewer than 200 confirmed coalition deaths.

It is important to note the speed and success of this first month of Operation Iraqi Freedom—the Iraqi military was destroyed, and the Iraqi government was toppled in less than a month. The U.S.-led coalition captured a country the size of California faster than any land force in history.

In the weeks after the Battle of Tikrit, coalition forces began searching for WMD as well as Saddam Hussein and other top Iraqi officials. Although numerous caches of WMD were uncovered, the troops were unable to find an active WMD program. The lack of an active weapons program combined with the looting of historic treasures from Iraqi museums (which the coalition failed to protect) drew sharp criticism from those who opposed the coalition's presence in Iraq. Support for the war was further compromised by the fact that the search for Saddam Hussein took longer than anticipated. He was eventually captured in December 2003, brought to trial, found guilty, and executed on December 30, 2006. Although many Iraqi citizens and neighboring countries were very happy to see Hussein's regime toppled, many others protested the continued presence of coalition forces and the influence they had in the new Iraqi government.

Bush appointed L. Paul Bremer to govern Iraq through the Coalition Provisional Authority, whose stated aim was to reconstruct Iraq as a pluralistic democratic state. The ensuing occupation was plagued by violent resistance, which greatly hampered the economic and political reconstruction of the country, preventing international aid organizations from working in Iraq and discouraging badly needed capital investment. An interim constitution was signed in March 2004, and on June 28, 2004, sovereignty was transferred to the Iraqi people. On January 30, 2005, Iraq held its first open election in half a century, selecting a 275-member transitional National Assembly. Despite the withdrawal of several Sunni parties from the poll and threats of election day violence from insurgents, turnout was high. After two months of deadlock, on April 6 the new legislature elected Kurdish leader Jalal Talabani as president and Ibrahim al-Jaafari as prime minister. In April 2006 Talabani was reelected, and Nuri al-Maliki was selected to succeed al-Jaafari as prime minister. Maliki governed until September 2014, at which time a potent new insurgency, driven largely by the Islamic State of Iraq and Syria (ISIS), forced him to resign. The country continues to struggle with sectarian issues and associated violence.

Although Bush famously declared the end of major combat operations while aboard the U.S. aircraft carrier *Abraham Lincoln* on May 1, 2003, this declaration proved to be premature. Deadly guerrilla attacks against U.S. troops continued and increased. Although only 139 U.S. personnel and 33 British soldiers died during the invasion, nearly 4,500 Americans died thereafter in the insurgency that accompanied the occupation. In addition to the attacks conducted against coalition forces following the invasion, major violence broke out between Shiite and Sunni insurgents, causing many observers to begin calling the conflict a civil war.

In many ways, what is called Operation Iraqi Freedom or the Iraq War was two wars. The first was the war against the government and military of Saddam Hussein and lasted slightly more than three weeks. The second war was a fight against a variety of resistance and insurgent groups and lasted for more than eight years. The technological prowess of the West was clearly on display in that first war, and the regional and cultural ignorance of the West was on display in the second war.

The fighting in Iraq was supposed to change from combat operations to a short occupation and handover to a new Iraqi government. Actions with respect to the conduct of the Coalition Provisional Authority (CPA) impeded the possibility of such a transition if that possibility really existed at all. The transition turned into a prolonged occupation of a country that evolved into sectarian civil war. There are several reasons for the failure of the rapid transition plan.

First, the Iraqi governing councils, and later their elected representatives, had little control over the resources and organs of a state. The infrastructure of Iraq was in shambles. This was in part a result of combat action in the spring of 2003 and in part left over from the combat actions of 1991. Economic sanctions imposed on Iraq from 1991 until 2003 also played a role in the disarray and chaos of the Iraqi state. Saddam used what money he obtained during the sanctions to maintain his security and intelligence apparatus and make sure those most essential or loyal to him received the benefits of modernity—electricity, clean water, etc. Meanwhile, the Iraqi people, in general, suffered as their infrastructure degraded.

Second, those initially designated to be in the interim governing body were not respected by the Iraqi people as they were either seen as outsiders (exiles given power by the invaders) or as lackeys to the invading forces. To gain credibility it was almost necessary to be seen as opposing the Coalition Provisional Authority or at least not kowtowing to them in every action. Thus, nothing moved as quickly as expected. "Everything in Iraq is hard" became one of the most often repeated phrases by coalition soldiers and officials. It was said because it was true.

Third, there were several relatively rapid elections. No one governed for any significant length of time in Iraq until well into this period. This almost continuous hand over of authority from one to the next fostered a sense of corruption as a means of survival. Thus, little was really accomplished with the resources provided because those resources were often squandered or horded and then sent to out-of-country estates and banks for later use and benefit.

Fourth and most important, were the Bush administration decisions to dismiss Baath Party officials (essentially, Iraq's only trained administrators) and disband the Iraqi Army (which at one stroke dumped nearly 400,000 trained soldiers and potential insurgent recruits into the Iraqi general population).

The orders, known as Coalition Provisional Orders (CPA) 1 and 2, flooded Iraq with disgruntled, unemployed people and left the country rudderless. No one remained with the expertise or know-how to run the government and meet the basic needs of the people. In addition, lots of young, military trained people and nearly all those who were trained to organize and lead were suddenly without meaningful employment for themselves or their families. Their world was destroyed.

Following the departure of the CPA, the early governing officials experienced longer, though still short opportunities to govern. There was something of a sovereign government in Iraq. However, there was also growing violence. The violence coalesced and transformed. It began as simple banditry but became more ideological in nature with the bombing of the al-Askari shrine and mosque in Samarra and the rise of Al Qaeda in Iraq.

One of the biggest problems was the growing disconnect between the coalition's perception of what was happening and what was actually happening. It took time for the United States and other members of the coalition to comprehend the rise of a sectarian ideological struggle in Iraq. The U.S.-led coalition began to fall apart in 2004 with nine countries withdrawing their forces. The most famous of the withdrawals was the Spanish contingent who departed after the Madrid bombings in 2004. Two more countries departed each in 2005 and 2006.

General George Casey was tasked to get the Iraqi Army sufficiently ready to transition responsibility and depart within 18 months—or by January 2006. That did not happen as the violence only increased. General Casey believed that limited American participation and visibility would both encourage Iraqis to step forward and discourage attacks on U.S. forces.

Many in the Bush administration and Multi-National Force–Iraq (MNF-I) hesitated to call what was happening in Iraq a civil war, as if the term alone had power. Throughout the war in Iraq there were challenges with regard to labeling what was happening. Were the opposition "dead-enders" or "Ba'athists," or were they "opposition" or "insurgents"? No term was fully embraced until long after the term had become obvious. Many of the terms and labels had political overtones either in Iraq, the Middle East, or Washington, DC. Insurgents brought to mind Vietnam and the failures associated with that war. Opposition was reminiscent of Palestinians opposing the occupation of their territories by Israeli forces. For these reasons and others, word choice was challenging.

In 2007 the Bush administration implemented a troop surge in Iraq, increasing the troops present in Iraq by as many as 40,000. The additional forces temporarily reduced the potency of the insurgency. Nevertheless, by late 2008 the U.S. public's support for the Iraq War had plummeted. A status of forces agreement was subsequently negotiated between the U.S. and Iraqi governments that required U.S. combat troops to leave Iraqi urban areas by the end of June 2009 and leave the country entirely by the end of 2011. Soon after taking office in early 2009, President Barack Obama announced that most U.S. troops would exit from Iraq by the end of August 2010, with a smaller transitional force remaining until the end of 2011. The war was declared officially over by the U.S. military on December 15, 2011; by that time, more than 1 million members of the armed forces had served in Iraq, nearly 4,500 Americans had died in the conflict, and some 34,000 others were wounded in action.

Unfortunately, sectarian violence and radical Sunni Islamic extremism in Iraq increased after the U.S. military withdrawal.

These developments were aided by the policies of Maliki, whose government brutally repressed Iraq's Sunni population and shut it out of national governance. By January 2014, rebels associated with ISIS demonstrated significant influence in virtually all of Anbar Province, including Fallujáh, where U.S. forces had fought two bloody battles to save the city during the Iraq War. Within days, the Sunni rebels displayed control of the city of Ramadi, also in Anbar Province. The most significant event was the capture of the city of Mosul in June 2014 and the declaration of the caliphate by Abu Bakr al-Baghdadi. The situation underscored the inability of the Maliki administration to govern the country effectively. As the security situation worsened throughout much of 2014, calls for Maliki's removal from office intensified—both in Iraq and abroad. Finally, in September 2014 he reluctantly resigned and was replaced by the more level-headed Haider al-Abadi.

At that point, the Islamic State, or ISIS, had seized control of large portions of Iraq. By late summer of 2014 the United States was conducting airstrikes on Islamic State targets in Iraq, and in the fall of that same year U.S. forces returned to Iraq at the invitation of the Iraqi government. Their purpose was to train, advise, and equip the Iraqi Army in its fight against ISIS. Gradually over the next three years the territory claimed by the Islamic State was regained by the Iraqi military, and in December 2017 the government of Iraq announced the defeat of ISIS. That said, more than 10,000 American military personnel and security-related contractors remain in Iraq at the time of this book's publication.

Also of note with regard to the current U.S. role in Iraq is the change in perspective between the Obama administration and the Trump administration, which took over in January 2017. The Obama administration had as its goal the defeat of ISIS. The Trump administration has upped the ante by declaring a desire not only to defeat but to annihilate ISIS. In support of this aim, the Trump administration has indicated a need for continuing U.S. presence in Iraq for the foreseeable future with the goal being to provide stability and support in a post-ISIS environment.

Jerry D. Morelock, Brian L. Steed, and Lori Weathers

See also: Baath Party; Bremer, Lewis Paul, III; Bush, George Walker; Coalition Provisional Authority; Hussein, Saddam; Iraq, History of, 1990–Present; Iraqi Freedom, Operation; Islamic State of Iraq and al-Sham (ISIS); Prime Minister, Iraq: Nuri al-Maliki; United Nations Weapons Inspectors; Weapons of Mass Destruction

References

Atkinson, Rick. *In the Company of Soldiers: A Chronicle of Combat.* New York: Henry Holt, 2005.

Cavaleri, David. *Easier Said Than Done: Making the Transition between Combat Operations and Stability Operations.* Fort Leavenworth, KS: Combat Studies Institute Press, 2005.

DiMarco, Louis A. *Traditions, Changes, and Challenges: Military Operations and the Middle Eastern City.* Fort Leavenworth, KS: Combat Studies Institute Press, 2004.

Dodge, Toby. *Inventing Iraq: The Failure of Nation-Building and a History Denied.* New York: Columbia University Press, 2003.

Franks, Tommy, with Malcolm McConnell. *American Soldier.* New York: Regan Books, 2004.

Gaddis, John Lewis. *Surprise, Security, and the American Experience.* Cambridge, MA: Harvard University Press, 2005.

Gordon, Michael R., and General Bernard E. Trainor. *Cobra II: The Inside Story of the Invasion and Occupation of Iraq.* New York: Pantheon Books, 2006.

Gordon, Michael R., and Bernard E. Trainor. *The Endgame: The Inside Story of the Struggle for Iraq, from George W. Bush to Barack Obama.* New York: Vintage, 2013.

Murray, Williamson, and Robert H. Scales Jr. *The Iraq War: A Military History.* Cambridge, MA: Belknap, 2005.

Ricks, Thomas E. *Fiasco: The American Military Adventure in Iraq.* New York: Penguin, 2006.

Sanchez, Ricardo S., and Donald T. Phillips. *Wiser in Battle: A Soldier's Story.* New York: Harper, 2008.

Tripp, Charles. *A History of Iraq.* Cambridge: Cambridge University Press, 2007.

Wood, Trish. *What Was Asked of Us: An Oral History of the Iraq War by the Soldiers Who Fought It.* New York: Little, Brown, 2006.

Woodward, Bob. *Bush at War.* New York: Simon and Schuster, 2002.

Woodward, Bob. *Plan of Attack.* New York: Simon and Schuster, 2004.

Woodward, Bob. *State of Denial: Bush at War, Part III.* New York: Simon and Schuster, 2006.

Woodward, Bob. *The War Within: A Secret White House History, 2006–2008.* New York: Simon and Schuster, 2009.

Zinsmeister, Karl. *Dawn over Baghdad: How the U.S. Military Is Using Bullets and Ballots to Remake Iraq.* New York: Encounter Books, 2004.

Causes of the Iraq War

In the year and a half between the September 11, 2001, terrorist attacks on the United States and the invasion of Iraq in March 2003, President George W. Bush argued persistently for war. The president and administrative officials presented an array of justifications for war. Some of their reasons had been presented before, but the terrorist attacks on Washington, DC, and New York City gave them new urgency. The claim that Saddam Hussein possessed weapons of mass destruction (WMD) and had ties to terrorist organizations to which he might give these weapons persuaded an American public fearful of another attack that something had to be done about the brutal dictator. Persuasive though this argument ultimately proved, it hid a more complex reality. A mix of ideological and pragmatic motives lay behind the decision to invade Iraq. By themselves or even together, they probably would not have been compelling enough to persuade the American people that war could not be avoided. Only the terrorist argument could do that, but many experts believe that September 11 provided a pretext for a war that the administration had wanted all along.

U.S. Foreign Policy and the Middle East

During the second half of the 20th century, Iraq figured prominently in American foreign policy toward a crucial but volatile region of the world. That policy rested on three pillars. The United States wished to make certain that it and its European allies would have unfettered access to Middle Eastern oil. Western vulnerability to a cutoff or even a reduction of supply became painfully clear during the oil embargo following the 1973 Yom Kippur War. Americans experienced rising prices and gas rationing for the first time since World War II. Security for the state of Israel was the second pillar of American policy. With its technological superiority and nuclear arsenal, the Jewish state had proven a match for any combination of Arab countries in every war since 1948. The Yom Kippur War, however, had demonstrated Israel's vulnerability. Only a massive infusion of American military aid made possible victory over Syria and Egypt without resorting to the use of nuclear weapons, which the government of Golda Meier seriously considered. Israel's reliability as an ally, coupled with a strong Zionist lobby in the United States, has assured American support for the Jewish state. Preventing any state from dominating the region formed the final pillar of U.S. Middle Eastern policy.

The year 1979 proved transformative for American foreign policy. The overthrow of the Shah of Iran and his replacement by a fundamentalist religious state shocked both the U.S. foreign policy establishment and the Middle East. Within a matter of weeks at the end of the year, a mob overran the U.S. Embassy in Tehran, taking and holding hostages. At nearly the same time, the Union of Soviet Socialist Republics intervened in Afghanistan with tens of thousands of troops. These dramatic events caused President Jimmy Carter to declare the movement of oil from and through the Persian Gulf as a vital national security interest in his 1980 State of the Union Address. One could point to this statement as the moment in which U.S. involvement in the Middle East went from being benign and distant to being direct, controlling, and immediate.

Iraq figured prominently in achieving the three broad goals of free flow of oil, protection of Israel, and prevention of a single-state regional hegemony. Second only to Saudi Arabia in known oil reserves, Iraq could affect both the price and supply of oil. It was one of only two states large enough to dominate the region and could threaten Israel, particularly if Iraq acquired nuclear weapons. Iraq's importance in the balance of power equation became abundantly clear following the 1979 Islamic Revolution in Iran. Deprived of its longtime ally, the Shah of Iran, and concerned about Iranian belligerence following the American hostage crisis, the administration of Ronald Reagan reached a rapprochement with Hussein and armed him to wage war against Iran. The Iran-Iraq War (1980–1988) sapped the strength of both nations and ended in a bloody stalemate.

The Israelis had never trusted Saddam Hussein. In June 1981, they conducted a surprise attack to destroy a nuclear reactor in Baghdad for fear that it would produce weapons-grade uranium. By the end of the 1980s, Hussein had outlived his usefulness and become a liability. Hussein's use of poison gas against Iraqi Kurds in 1988 led to widespread international condemnation. While the expected development and use of weapons of mass destruction made the United States leery of the Iraqi dictator, they did not justify military action against him. That changed in August 1991 following Iraq's invasion of Kuwait.

The Persian Gulf War

On August 2, 1991, Iraqi forces invaded the small wealthy Persian Gulf state of Kuwait. Hussein accused the emirate of slant drilling into Iraqi oil fields. Perhaps because of miscommunication by acting ambassador April Glaspie, he believed that the United States would not act to reverse his fait accompli. Allowing the invasion to go unchallenged, however, would leave the brutal dictator in a position to threaten Saudi Arabia and dominate the Persian Gulf. The administration of George H. W. Bush amassed a coalition of more than 800,000 troops and drove the Iraqis from Kuwait in February 1991.

The president's aim had always been limited to driving the Iraqis from Kuwait. However, wartime rhetoric escalated to the point that Bush called on Kurds and Shiite Muslims to rise against the dictator. Unfortunately, they took him at his word, only to be slaughtered when expected U.S. support never materialized. For some members of the administration, especially Secretary of Defense Dick Cheney, the Persian Gulf War would be seen as an incomplete victory, a job that needed to be finished by removing Hussein from power.

In the decade following the Persian Gulf War, however, the United States pursued a policy of containment against Iraq. No-fly zones over the northern and southern regions of the country gave persecuted ethnic groups some protection. Occasional air strikes kept Hussein in check, and an embargo prevented him from rearming. Weapons inspectors sought to prevent him from gaining WMD until he expelled them. Hussein retained a firm grasp on power, but for the foreseeable future at least, he threatened none of his neighbors. American forces in the Persian Gulf region made sure of that.

Neoconservatism

National interest tempered by pragmatism drives foreign policy far more than does ideology. This fact explains why foreign policy changes little from one administration to the next. Under certain circumstances, however, ideology can exercise considerable influence. Such a situation occurred at the end of the Cold War. Convinced that the West, led by the United States, had won this titanic ideological struggle, a group of intellectuals and policy makers proclaimed what Francis Fukuyama dubbed "the end of history." Western liberal democracy represented the highest and final state of political development. All that remained was for it to permeate the globe. This philosophy spawned the ideological movement known as neoconservatism.

While many neocons had no political agenda, others advocated a more aggressive foreign policy to promote American values as well as American interests. The Project for the New American Century, a neoconservative think tank supported by many future members of the George W. Bush administration, was such a group. In 1998 several of its members, including Donald Rumsfeld and Paul Wolfowitz, sent a letter to President Bill Clinton calling for the removal of Hussein. For the neocons and the Bush administration, Iraq was to be a demonstration model, a bastion of democracy that would provide an example for the entire region. A year before the September 11 attacks Bush, then governor of Texas and U.S. presidential candidate, chastised Vice President Al Gore for the Clinton administration's decision to leave Hussein in power, clearly suggesting that were he elected, this situation would change.

The WMD Argument

Whether the neocons supported it or not, containment worked. Two no-fly zones, a robust U.S. presence in the Persian Gulf, and sanctions prevented Hussein from threatening any of his neighbors. A newly elected president would not be able to make a case for invading Iraq, never mind one who had won a highly controversial election by the narrowest of margins. Barring a dramatic change in circumstances, Bush would have a hard time making a case for invading Iraq. But September 11 provided an opportunity for an invasion that might not otherwise have occurred. The climate of fear following the terrorist attacks made it much easier to persuade the American public that even the possibility of Hussein possessing WMD that he might pass to terrorists was unacceptable.

Following the successful operation against the Taliban government in Afghanistan in the fall of 2001, the president and members of his administration launched a concerted and persistent campaign to persuade Congress and the American people of the need to invade Iraq. In his 2002 State of the Union Address, Bush identified Iraq as part of an "axis of evil" supporting terrorism around the world. His advisers revived interest in Hussein's nuclear weapons program, which most experts believed had been moribund since the end of the Persian Gulf War in 1991. Much of the evidence they presented was so suspect that the United Nations (UN), the North Atlantic Treaty Organization (NATO), and many of America's allies refused to support the war. Even the failure of the United Nations Monitoring, Verification and Inspection Commission, which reentered Iraq in November 2002, to find convincing evidence of an Iraqi nuclear program did not dissuade the Bush administration from its determination to invade Iraq.

Regime Change

For Congress and the American people, the threat of Hussein possessing WMD, however remote, seemed sufficient to justify war. The Bush administration still found it useful to put an altruistic gloss on the invasion, albeit one it believed. By the time the first bombs fell on Baghdad, liberating Iraqis from the tyranny of Hussein had become the mission dubbed Operation Iraqi Freedom. Not surprisingly, the name resonated with the philosophy of the neocons. Iraq would be an island of liberal democracy in a sea of Middle Eastern despotism. Bush's desire for regime change, voiced in a presidential debate with Gore, could now be achieved. Whether the invaders actually found WMD would be irrelevant if the mission succeeded.

Thomas R. Mockaitis

See also: Bush, George Walker; Cheney, Richard Bruce; Hussein, Saddam; Iraq, History of, 1990–Present; Iraqi Freedom, Operation; Oil; Secretary of Defense, U.S.: Donald Rumsfeld; United Nations Weapons Inspectors; Weapons of Mass Destruction; Wolfowitz, Paul Dundes

References

Dodge, Toby. *Inventing Iraq: The Failure of Nation-Building and a History Denied.* New York: Columbia University Press, 2003.

Karsh, Efraim. *Islamic Imperialism.* New Haven, CT: Yale University Press, 2006.

Makiya, Kanan. *Republic of Fear: The Politics of Modern Iraq.* Berkeley: University of California Press, 1998.

Murray, Williamson, and Robert H. Scales Jr. *The Iraq War: A Military History.* Cambridge, MA: Belknap, 2005.

Polk, William R. *Understanding Iraq: The Whole Sweep of Iraqi History, from Genghis Khan's Mongols to the Ottoman Turks to the British Mandate to the American Occupation.* New York: Harper Perennial, 2006.

Tripp, Charles. *A History of Iraq.* Cambridge: Cambridge University Press, 2007.

Consequences of the Iraq War

For the United States, the Iraq War (as discussed in this book) ended in December 2011 when the last U.S. forces left the country. There can be little doubt that the conflict has already had a profound impact on regional security, although this will continue to change over time. It also changed the nature and stability of the Iraqi state and that of some of its neighbors, most notably Syria. Since the withdrawal of U.S. troops, Iraq has descended into more sectarian strife and general violence. This development was made worse by Iraq's government under President Nuri al-Maliki, who largely excluded the Sunnis from any meaningful participation in Iraqi governance and in fact engaged in a campaign of repression against them. By 2015 Iraq's future remained very much in question, as radical insurgents with links to Al Qaeda and the Islamic State of Iraq and al-Sham (ISIS) seized by force almost all of Anbar Province and much of northern and western Iraq. Indeed, the nation once more stood at the edge of civil war and possibly sectarian-based dismemberment. Eight years of war also affected the United States itself. Indeed, the war's economic and security implications continue to unfold. Whether the struggle was worth its cost in blood and treasure will be debated for years to come.

Iraq and Regional Security

Any threat that Iraq posed to its neighbors was removed for the foreseeable future. Iraqi forces not destroyed during the invasion were disbanded during the occupation, and the army of police who largely replaced them have been retooled to deal primarily with internal security. The cost of rebuilding the country left little revenue for creating a military capable of offensive action, even if the international community were to tolerate it. At this time, Iraq almost certainly could not even defend itself from foreign aggression without U.S. assistance. The Iraqi government following the U.S. withdrawal had no weapons of mass destruction program.

However desirable removing the threat posed by Saddam Hussein may have been, it has had one undesirable consequence. Iraq was the only regional power with the population and resources to balance Iran. Since the 1950s the United States has played Iran and Iraq off one another, but weakening Iraq has enhanced the potential threat posed by Iran. While the United States became bogged down in a protracted Iraqi insurgency, fueled in part by Iranian aid to Shiite insurgents, Tehran was much freer to develop its nuclear program than it might otherwise have been. The rise of Iran created a more robust and aggressive Saudi Arabian foreign policy as demonstrated with incursions in Yemen and overt and covert measures directed to limit or weaken Iranian influence in the Middle East. The United States and Israel also stepped up rhetoric and actions in opposition to Iranian actions. Since late 2013, the United States, Russia, China, and several other world powers engaged Iran in negotiations designed to short-circuit its alleged nuclear weapons program resulting in a controversial Joint Comprehensive Plan of Action effective on October 18, 2015 and then abrogated by President Donald Trump on May 8, 2018. Preemptive military action against Iran by either the Americans or the Israelis could have serious consequences, not least of which might be an oil shortage and a spike in oil prices. Iraq may still regain its stature as a regional power, but that increasingly remote possibility does nothing to counter the threat of Iran attaining nuclear weapons.

A Fragile State

An invasion followed by eight years of internal conflict and a potent insurgency has, of course, profoundly changed Iraq. Far from the easy victory the George W. Bush administration promised, the war created a power vacuum filled first by lawlessness and then by an intractable insurgency. The resulting destruction of property and infrastructure, coupled with unemployment that topped 60 percent at its peak, caused the standard of living in Iraq to plummet. Resentment of Americans only fueled the insurgency. The conflict further damaged Iraqi infrastructure and delayed economic and social recovery. Indeed, the country is still struggling to rebuild and regain its prewar standard of living.

Operation Iraqi Freedom did deliver on its promise to remove Hussein from power and replace his brutal regime with a democratic one. Iraqi democracy is, however, still on very shaky ground. Because simple majority rule does not work in an ethnically divided state, the U.S.-led coalition facilitated the creation of a complex system of proportional representation and regional autonomy. These arrangements prevented Iraq from disintegrating into three separate states, as many feared at the height of the insurgency. The coalition led by Maliki and his successor, Haider al-Abadi, continued to grow weaker and govern less effectively, and ethnic and sectarian tensions threatened to tear the nation apart. The stated defeat of the Islamic State in early 2018 seems to have created a moment of possible national reconciliation. Even if Iraq can avoid a civil war and dismemberment, these problems threaten to keep the Iraqi state weak for years to come.

The U.S. Army

The U.S. Army entered Iraq with the same aversion to insurgency that it had harbored since the end of the Vietnam War. National security strategy eschewed direct involvement in counterinsurgency (COIN) campaigns, preferring to provide aid for internal defense, which could be handled by special forces. Regular soldiers received little education and training for unconventional warfare. The forces that invaded Iraq in 2003 did so with equipment and doctrine developed during the late 1970s. The best in the world at conventional war, these soldiers were woefully unprepared for the internecine complexity of internal security operations.

Fortunately, U.S. forces adapted quickly. The U.S. Army and the U.S. Marine Corps wrote a new counterinsurgency manual that embraced the lessons of past campaigns and the experiences of Iraq and Afghanistan.

Soldiers from armed units and even office clerks found themselves patrolling the streets of Baghdad and Fallujah. By the time of the Anbar Awakening, they had become considerably more adept at COIN. They had also adopted new equipment and undergone a reorganization from traditional divisions into flexible brigade combat teams far more capable of handling an array of threats across the conflict spectrum. In August 2010, at the end of Operation Iraqi Freedom, the U.S. Army produced a video titled *Did You Know* explaining the transformation since 2001 which included the following:

> Did you know? ... Ten percent of Soldiers serving in Iraq were equipped with modern body armor in 2003. Since then we have upgraded body armor nine times. Today every soldier in theater is equipped with the world's best body armor.... Prior to the war there were 194,000 Night Vision Goggles and 1,569 Thermal Weapon Sights in the Army. Today we have more than 575,000 Night Vision Goggles and 95,000 Thermal Weapon Sights. WE OWN THE NIGHT.
>
> Did you know? Prior to the war, Army Aircraft were not equipped to defeat Man-Portable Air Defense Systems (MANPADS) threats. Today, over 2,000 Army Aircraft are equipped with the Common Missile Warning System and, therefore, able to defeat all known MANPADS threats. In 2001 the Army had only thirty Unmanned Aerial Vehicles (UAV). Today, there are approximately 4,500. Stryker Brigade Combat Teams did not exist in 2001. Today the Army has fielded seven of them that have recorded over 22.5 million miles in combat. The Army commenced operations in Theater with primarily unarmored wheeled vehicles. To date, the Army has upgraded armor protection over twelve times and produced approximately 24,000 up-armored HMMWV's, over 1,000 Armored Security Vehicles, and over 18,000 Mine Resistant Ambush Protected (MRAP) and MRAP All-Terrain Vehicles (M-ATV). In 2003 the DOD's only small caliber ammo production facility, Lake City Ammunition Plant, was producing 400 million small caliber rounds a year. Today, Lake City is producing 1.6 billion rounds per year.
>
> Did you know? In 2001 we had a tiered readiness system which resulted in Guard and Reserve units being equipped to lower readiness levels than Active units. Today, next deployers—regardless of Component—are the equipping priority. Equipping requirements for like units are the same—regardless of Component. From WWII to the beginning of OIF/OEF, 52% of casualties resulted from "finding the enemy." Most KIA's occurred within one mile of the enemy. In OIF/OEF casualties were taken throughout the Force. Therefore, the Army needs the capability to find the enemy without a point man, kill outside the Close Combat Zone, and shrink the logistics footprint.

Following the withdrawal from Iraq in 2011, the U.S. Army contracted, but the rise of the Islamic State (ISIS) gave impetus for a force increase yet again. Operations in Iraq during Operation Iraqi Freedom and in the following fight with the Islamic State created a healthy debate over the U.S. Army's proper role in the 21st century. This debate will occur amid a general climate of fiscal conservatism and isolationism, as Americans have grown tired, for the time being at least, of foreign military adventures. Under these circumstances, the army might be expected to revert to the conventional mentality of the post–Vietnam War era. The publication of the U.S. Army's key doctrinal manual in 2018 reemphasized the importance of large-scale combat operations against a near-peer competitor. The idea is to be ready to fight against a country like Russia or China. This was produced even though the Army and Marine Corps continued to be fighting in Iraq and Afghanistan. The U.S. military must continue to train and plan for a host of contingency operations from midlevel conventional conflict through counterinsurgency.

Counting the Cost

Whether its long-term consequences will be for good or ill, the Iraq War has been an expensive war. A report by the Congressional Research Service published in March 2011 put defense expenditures for the conflict at $806 billion. Indirect costs, including reconstruction and veterans' benefits, have pushed the total to well over $1 trillion. Funding the war drove up the national debt and contributed significantly to deficit spending. The financial cost of the war must therefore be borne by Americans for years to come. Indeed, the deep economic recession that hit the United States and other nations beginning in late 2007 was likely made worse by America's deficit spending because the U.S. government had fewer fiscal options with which to counteract the downturn.

Although far lower than in previous wars, the human cost has been considerable. Between March 2003 and December 2011, the U.S. military alone sustained 4,448 killed and about 34,000 wounded. Improved medical care allowed perhaps three times as many wounded to survive than had done so in previous wars. Many of these wounded, however, suffered severe trauma and will need special care for the rest of their lives. In addition to the U.S. casualties, through December 15, 2011, a total of 318 coalition troops were killed, including 179 Britons. Also, the Iraq War claimed the lives of 139 journalists. More than 1,300 private contractors were also killed.

According to the Iraq Coalition Casualty Count, by 2011 an estimated 8,825 members of the Iraqi Security Forces had been killed in combat while fighting Iraqi insurgents. In 2013, a study conducted by U.S. university researchers estimated the total number of civilian deaths during 2003–2011 in Iraq to have been 461,000. This included deaths from all causes but related directly or indirectly to the ground war and the subsequent insurgency.

Whether any possible gain from the war is worth its cost in blood and treasure is both an academic and a moral question. Defenders of the war will argue that many more people might have suffered and died had Hussein continued to rule. Critics point out that the policy of containment was working and that since Hussein had a weakened military and no weapons of mass destruction, he threatened no one. The final assessment of the war, if indeed there is one, may depend on how Iraq turns out in the long run, and Iraq's future by 2018 still looked precarious.

In 2014 the Islamic State in Iraq and al-Sham seized and governed numerous cities in Iraq. During their attacks, the Iraqi security forces trained and equipped by the U.S.-led coalition performed poorly or completely broke and ran. This performance in the face of a nonstate actor served as a sobering reality check on claims of success from eight and a half years in Iraq. Though ISIS was effectively driven from most cities in Iraq by the end of 2017, it remains uncertain what will happen to Iraq as a result of ISIS. It seems clear that ISIS and the sectarianism that gave rise to the ideology supporting it was a direct result of the invasion and subsequent chaos created by Operation Iraqi Freedom.

Thomas R. Mockaitis

See also: Casualties, Operation Iraqi Freedom; Hussein, Saddam; Iraq, History of, 1990–Present; Iraqi Freedom, Operation: The Surge and the Awakening; Islamic State of Iraq and al-Sham (ISIS): Al Qaeda in Iraq; Prime Minister, Iraq: Nuri al-Maliki; Weapons of Mass Destruction

References

Gordon, Michael R., and Bernard E. Trainor. *The Endgame: The Inside Story of the Struggle for Iraq, from George W. Bush to Barack Obama.* New York: Vintage, 2013.

Murray, Williamson, and Robert H. Scales Jr. *The Iraq War: A Military History.* Cambridge, MA: Belknap, 2005.

"Operation IRAQI FREEDOM." Iraq Coalition Casualty Count, http://icasualties.org/Iraq/index.aspx.

"Operation IRAQI FREEDOM (OIF) U.S. Casualty Status." United States Department of Defense, http://www.defenselink.mil/news/casualty.pdf.

Wood, Trish. *What Was Asked of Us: An Oral History of the Iraq War by the Soldiers Who Fought It.* New York: Little, Brown, 2006.

Al-Askari Mosque (Golden Mosque) Bombing (February 22, 2006)

The Askariya shrine, also known as the Golden Dome Mosque, in Samarra, Iraq, is one of Shia Islam's most holy sites. The mosque holds the tombs of two ninth-century Shia imams, Ali al-Hadi and Hassan al-Askari (the 10th and 11th imams, respectively). On February 22, 2006, terrorists tied to Al Qaeda in Iraq (forerunner of ISIS) bombed the mosque, destroying the golden dome as well as the imams' tombs. This event unleashed a series of reprisal attacks on Sunnis in the Samarra area. The bombing of the mosque was the beginning of a sharp escalation in sectarian clashes in Iraq, which ultimately precipitated the U.S. military's troop surge strategy in 2007.

There were no fatalities in the actual attack; however, the day of the bombing, Shia and Sunni groups fought in Samarra. That sectarian fighting killed 20 people. The violence then spread throughout Iraq. The following day more than 100 people died in clashes, including several Sunni clerics. This began the most violent period of sectarian violence during the Iraq War. The terrorists who destroyed the dome disguised themselves in Iraqi military uniforms. They entered the shrine, subdued the guards, and then placed explosives in the dome.

In addition to housing the tombs of the two imams, the mosque was also the place where the Hidden Imam, a messianic figure in the Shia branch, left his followers in the ninth century. The golden dome, built in 1905, contained some 70,000 golden tiles. Many faithful believe that the Hidden Imam will return to the mosque and emerge from the crypt underneath the blue mosque that is next to the shrine. The association of these religious figures to the shrine and its adjacent mosque make this site key to Shia faith and identity. It has long been a place of pilgrimage and a vital part of Iraqi Shia culture.

The eight Al Qaeda in Iraq terrorists who executed the attack succeeded in their goal of instigating sectarian strife throughout Iraq. Although the violence began in Samarra with the burning of Sunni businesses, it soon engulfed the entire nation. By the end of 2006, more than 10,000 Iraqis had died as a result of the sectarian violence that began in Samarra. This violence was part of the reason for President George W. Bush's decision to increase the number of American troops in Iraq.

This bombing demonstrated the fragile nature of the relative peace that was in place by early 2006, as the attack struck a key aspect of Shia identity. The Shias retaliated with attacks on Sunnis. These clashes drove the two groups further apart, resulting in mass violence and complicating hopes of a relatively quick American withdrawal from Iraq. In June 2007, Al Qaeda in Iraq insurgents bombed the mosque again, destroying its two 10-story minarets. After extensive repairs, the mosque was reopened in 2009.

Gates Brown

See also: Iraq, History of, 1990–Present; Iraqi Freedom, Operation: The Surge and the Awakening; Islamic State of Iraq and al-Sham (ISIS): Al Qaeda in Iraq; Shia Islam; Sunni Islam

References

Hammer, Joshua. "Samarra Rises." *Smithsonian* 39(10) (January 2009): 28–37.

Worth, Robert. "Blast Destroys Shrine in Iraq, Setting Off Sectarian Fury." *New York Times,* February 22, 2006, http://www.nytimes.com/2006/02/22/international/middleeast/22cnd-iraq.html.

Ambassadors to Iraq, U.S. (Chronological Order)

An ambassador represents the head of state in a given country. In the case of the following entries, these ambassadors each represented the president of the United States to the nation of Iraq. Prior to 2004, there was a gap of 14 years in which the United States had no ambassador in Iraq. This gap in diplomatic relations was a direct result of the invasion of Kuwait by Iraq in 1990 and the subsequent state of conflict between the U.S. and Iraq from 1990 to 2004.

- John D. Negroponte, 2004–2005
- Zalmay M. Khalilzad, 2005–2007
- Ryan C. Crocker, 2007–2009
- Christopher R. Hill, 2009–2010
- James F. Jeffrey, 2010–2012

John D. Negroponte (1939–) (Ambassador from 2004 to 2005)

U.S. diplomat and the first director of national intelligence (2005–2007). John Dimitri Negroponte was born in London, England, on July 21, 1939. His father, Dimitri, was a Greek shipping tycoon. Negroponte attended elite schools in the United States, including Phillips Exeter Academy and Yale University, from which he earned an undergraduate degree in 1960. After attending Harvard University Law School for only a brief time, he joined the Foreign Service in 1960 and stayed with the State Department until 1997.

During his long career, Negroponte served in eight overseas posts in Asia, Latin America, and Europe. He also held a series of increasingly important positions with the State Department in Washington, DC. In 1981 he was appointed to his first ambassadorship in Honduras, a post he held until 1985. He subsequently served as ambassador to Mexico (1989–1993) and the Philippines (1993–1996). From 1987 to 1989 Negroponte was deputy assistant to the director of national security affairs in the Ronald Reagan administration.

Negroponte retired from the Foreign Service in 1997 and joined the publishing firm of McGraw-Hill as a senior executive. In 2001 President George W. Bush tapped him to become the U.S. ambassador to the United Nations (UN), a post he held until 2004. Negroponte worked at the UN to secure support for U.S. policies in the aftermath of the September 11, 2001, terrorist attacks and vowed not to bend to international pressure in the ensuing Global War on Terrorism. This stance did not always make him popular among his UN colleagues. In the run-up to the 2003 Iraq invasion, Negroponte was the Bush administration's reliable point man in dealing with the sometimes intransigent UN.

In April 2004 Negroponte was named ambassador to Iraq. He assumed his duties on June 30, when Anglo-American occupation forces turned sovereignty of Iraq over to the provisional government. Negroponte, who replaced Paul Bremer, was immediately faced with a rapidly expanding insurgency and the problems of stabilizing and rebuilding a war-torn nation.

A year later in February 2005, President Bush named Negroponte as the first director of national intelligence, a new cabinet-level position. Negroponte was charged with coordinating the work of all of the nation's intelligence-gathering services. As such, he was largely responsible for establishing the budgetary requirements of the new intelligence apparatus, which approached $40 billion by 2006. Negroponte's appointment was lauded by many who saw in him the required steadiness of a diplomat combined with the ability to organize and lead. Having worked under both Democratic and Republican administrations, he was seen as a relatively bipartisan public servant who could be counted on to do the right thing in the face of considerable political pressures.

Negroponte wasted no time in instituting needed reforms in the intelligence community and reorganizing the intelligence-gathering apparatus to make it far more efficient and less vulnerable to leaks and political infighting. Indeed, his policies earned high praise from both Congress and officials in the executive branch. In January 2007 Negroponte left his post to become deputy secretary of state, a position that he had long coveted and held until January 2009. After leaving public service, Negroponte accepted a teaching and fellowship position at the Jackson Institute of Global Affairs (Yale University).

Paul G. Pierpaoli Jr.

See also: Bremer, Lewis Paul, III; Bush, George Walker; Iraq, History of, 1990–Present

References

Draper, Robert. *Dead Certain: The Presidency of George W. Bush.* New York: Free Press, 2008.

U.S. Senate, Committee on Foreign Relations. *The Nomination of Hon. John D. Negroponte to be U.S. Ambassador to Iraq, April 27, 2004.* Washington, DC: U.S. Government Printing Office, 2004.

Zalmay M. Khalilzad (1941–) (Ambassador from 2005 to March 2007)

Afghani-born diplomat who served as the U.S. ambassador to Afghanistan (2003–2005), U.S. ambassador to Iraq (2005–2007), and U.S. ambassador to the United Nations (UN) (2007–2009). Zalmay Khalilzad was born in Mazar-e Sharif, Afghanistan, on March 22, 1951, a member of the Pashtun ethnic group. His family was among the elites of Afghanistan, and his father had served in the government of the last king, Mohammed Zahir Shah. Growing instability in Afghanistan contributed to Khalilzad's desire to emigrate. He first went to the United States as an exchange student in high school. Khalilzad subsequently attended the American University in Beirut, Lebanon, then a major educational center for the Middle East. He returned to the United States for graduate training in political science at the University of Chicago, where he earned his PhD before going on to teach political science at Columbia University from 1979 to 1989.

In 1984 the Council on Foreign Relations awarded Khalilzad a fellowship with the U.S. State Department. There he worked under Paul Wolfowitz, the director of policy planning and an Allan Bloom student who would loom large in neoconservative circles within the George H. W. Bush and George W. Bush administrations. When Khalilzad's fellowship ended he stayed on with the State Department, serving as an adviser on Afghanistan and the Middle East; given his background, he was particularly active in American policy vis-à-vis the arming of the mujahideen. In the George H. W. Bush administration, Khalilzad was made deputy undersecretary of policy planning at the Department of Defense.

Upon the election of President Bill Clinton in 1992, Khalilzad returned to the private sector, working for the RAND Corporation. He continued to teach and to participate in foreign affairs, writing on the role of the United States in international relations as well as potential challenges posed by the People's Republic of China for the United States. He also took consulting jobs with energy consortiums, advising them on the politics of the Middle East and Central Asia. Khalilzad also became one of the first members of the Project for the New American Century, which included numerous neoconservatives. The Project for the New American Century argued for the continuation of American preeminence within international relations that had existed since the end of the Cold War in 1991. In addition, the group strongly urged the maintenance of U.S. military strength as the foundation for American hegemony.

Upon the election of George W. Bush in 2000, Khalilzad returned to public service, heading the Bush transition team for personnel in the State and Defense Departments. Once the administration was in office, he became director for Southwest Asia, Middle East, and North Africa for the National Security Council. After the attacks of September 11, 2001, Khalilzad, given his background and training, was deeply involved in planning for the war in Afghanistan. On December 31, 2001, he became the president's special envoy to Afghanistan and held that post until November 2003, when he began serving as the U.S. ambassador to Afghanistan, a position he held until June 2005. In these positions, Khalilzad played a major role in guiding the new Afghanistan government and President Hamid Karzai in the successful oversight of democratic elections and in the first meeting of Afghanistan's *loya jirga*. He was also influential in overseeing relief and recovery efforts in Afghanistan.

In addition to his role in Afghanistan, Khalilzad became the ambassador at large for the free Iraqis in 2002, a key position in the run-up to the Iraq War. This post required Khalilzad to help expatriate Iraqis who wished to return to their nation and be active in a new regime, although his many duties in Afghanistan largely removed him from the bureaucratic battles over planning that took place within the Bush administration. In June 2005 Khalilzad succeeded John Negroponte as the U.S. ambassador to Iraq. In Iraq, Khalilzad oversaw the ratification of the Iraqi Constitution, the 2005 Iraqi elections, and the formation of a national government, among other duties. During Khalilzad's tenure in Iraq the insurgency continued to grow, however. In addition, intersectarian violence became an increasing problem, so much so that Khalilzad warned the Bush administration that these intersectarian conflicts might ultimately destroy the Iraqi state.

In February 2007 President Bush nominated Khalilzad to be the U.S. representative to the UN, and the U.S. Senate unanimously confirmed him in the post. He replaced the polarizing John R. Bolton, whose nomination had forced a showdown between the Democratically controlled Congress and the Bush White House. In the UN, Khalilzad continued to pursue the administration's stance toward Iran, which called for an immediate halt to its nuclear program, sanctions against Iran for failing to comply with the International Atomic Energy Agency, and support for a tribunal to be held in Lebanon to determine whether or not Syria was culpable in the assassination of former Lebanese prime minister Rafik al-Hariri. In general, however, Khalilzad struck a far more conciliatory tone than his predecessor. Khalilzad remains an active and influential figure in Republican foreign policy circles, particularly on issues involving Southwest Asia and the Middle East. He is president of Khalilzad Associates LLC, an international advisory consulting firm that chiefly advises firms seeking to do business in Iraq and Afghanistan. Khalilzad also is a counselor at the Center for Strategic International Studies and sits on a number of boards.

Michael K. Beauchamp

See also: Ambassadors to Iraq, U.S.: John D. Negroponte; Bush, George Walker; Iraq, History of, 1990–Present; Wolfowitz, Paul Dundes

References

Crews, Robert D., and Amin Tarzi, eds. *The Taliban and the Crisis of Afghanistan.* Cambridge, MA: Harvard University Press, 2008.

Khalilzad, Zalmay. *From Containment to Global Leadership? America and the World after the Cold War.* Santa Monica, CA: RAND Corporation, 1995.

Ryan C. Crocker (1949–) (Ambassador from March 2007 to March 2009)

Career U.S. diplomat. Ryan Clark Cocker was born on June 19, 1949, in Spokane, Washington. He attended University College Dublin and Whitman College in Walla Walla, Washington, from which he received his bachelor's degree in 1971. That same year he entered the U.S. Foreign Service. Crocker became a specialist in Middle East affairs, learning Persian and holding a wide variety of posts in the region. During 1984–1985 he studied at Princeton University, concentrating on Near East studies. Articulate, intelligent, and effective, Crocker moved quickly up the State Department's career ladder.

Crocker held diplomatic posts in Iran, Iraq, Egypt, Qatar, and Lebanon, among other nations, in addition to stints in Washington, DC. He served as the U.S. ambassador to Lebanon (1990–1993), Kuwait (1994–1997), Syria (1998–2001), and Pakistan (2004–2007). From August 2001 to May 2003 he held the position of deputy assistant secretary of Near East affairs in the George W. Bush administration. In January 2002, after the defeat of the Taliban regime in Afghanistan, the Bush administration sent Crocker to Kabul as interim U.S. envoy to Afghanistan. Crocker was charged with reopening the U.S. Embassy there.

After the major fighting was declared over in the 2003 invasion of Iraq, Crocker went to Baghdad in May 2003, where he served as the director of governance for the new Coalition Provisional Authority. He stayed in Iraq until August 2003. In September 2004 President Bush granted Crocker the rank of career ambassador, the highest-ranking ambassadorial position in the U.S. State Department. After being nominated for the position of U.S. ambassador to Iraq, Crocker was confirmed and assumed his new duties in Baghdad on March 29, 2007.

According to Karen De Young's biography of Colin L. Powell, in the autumn of 2002 Secretary of State Powell tasked Crocker and another official with drafting a memorandum outlining the potential risks of launching a war against Iraq. The result was a six-page report that stated unambiguously that ousting Saddam Hussein from power would likely lead to sectarian and ethnic turmoil. It also posited that the United States would face a long and expensive reconstruction effort in a postwar Iraq. The memorandum proved quite prescient.

In September 2007 Crocker was called upon to testify—along with General David H. Petraeus, commander of the Multi-National Force–Iraq—before the U.S. House and

Senate on the progress of the war in Iraq. While carefully avoiding any politically charged rhetoric, Crocker reported that Iraq remained a troubled and traumatized nation. He also stated that he believed that Iraqi officials would eventually take control of their own affairs but that this would likely take longer than anyone had envisioned or desired. Crocker continued in his role as ambassador to Iraq until February 13, 2009, having expressed his pleasure with the progress made in Iraq since between 2007 and 2009. On January 15, 2009, Crocker was awarded the Presidential Medal of Freedom for his service to the United States.

In January 2010, Crocker became dean of the Bush School of Government and Public Service at Texas A&M University. In April 2011, President Barack Obama nominated Crocker to the ambassadorship of Afghanistan. Crocker assumed the post on July 25, 2011, and remained in Afghanistan until July 13, 2012. In 2013, Crocker began serving on the Broadcasting Board of Governors. In December 2013, Crocker wrote an op-ed piece for the *New York Times* in which he argued that accommodation with Syrian president Bashar al-Assad might be the best way to temper advances being made by the Islamic State of Iraq and Syria (ISIS) and other extremist groups that threatened the stability of Iraq and Syria.

Paul G. Pierpaoli Jr.

See also: Bush, George Walker; Commanders, U.S. Central Command: David H. Petraeus; Islamic State of Iraq and al-Sham (ISIS); Prime Minister, Iraq: Nuri al-Maliki; Secretary of State, U.S.: Colin L. Powell

References

De Young, Karen. *Soldier: The Life of Colin Powell.* New York: Knopf, 2006.

Keegan, John. *The Iraq War: The Military Offensive, from Victory in 21 Days to the Insurgent Aftermath.* New York: Vintage, 2005.

Christopher R. Hill (1949–) (Ambassador from April 2009 to August 2010)

Career U.S. diplomat. Christopher Robert Hill was born on August 10, 1952. His father was also a career foreign service officer, which meant that he grew up around the world. Hill developed his reputation as an effective diplomat by dealing with major international crisis areas. Specifically, he worked with Richard Holbrooke as his deputy on the Dayton Peace Accords in 1995, which ostensibly ended the fighting in Bosnia. In 2005, Hill headed the U.S. delegation to the six-party talks focused on ending the North Korea nuclear crisis. Hill ended his foreign service as the U.S. ambassador to Iraq. He was nominated to become ambassador to Iraq in March 2009 by President Barack Obama.

Hill was sent to Iraq at a time of significant political turmoil. He was responsible to assist the Iraqi government in the conduct of national elections in 2009 and then the formation of a government resulting from those elections. As noted elsewhere in this work, the resulting government was highly contentious within Iraq and is blamed for conceding influence to Iran. As was true with Paul Bremer, Hill had no experience in the Middle East. and this seemed to play out in the quality of U.S. engagement to get a desired postelection Iraqi governing coalition.

Hill left public service to take the position as dean of the Josef Korbel School of International Studies at the University of Denver and then he became the chief advisor to the chancellor for global engagement and professor of the practice in diplomacy.

Brian L. Steed

See also: Bush, George Walker; Commanders, U.S. Central Command: David H. Petraeus; Islamic State of Iraq and al-Sham (ISIS); Prime Minister, Iraq: Nuri al-Maliki; Secretary of State, U.S.: Colin L. Powell

References

Al-Ali, Zaid. *The Struggle for Iraq's Future: How Corruption, Incompetence and Sectarianism Have Undermined Democracy.* New Haven, CT: Yale University Press, 2014.

Rayburn, Joel. *Iraq after America: Strongmen, Sectarians, Resistance.* Stanford, CA: Hoover Institution Press, 2014.

Sky, Emma. *The Unravelling: High Hopes and Missed Opportunities in Iraq.* New York: PublicAffairs, 2015.

James F. Jeffrey (1946–) (Ambassador from August 2010 to June 2012)

Career U.S. diplomat James Franklin Jeffrey was born in 1946 in Saugus, Massachusetts. He served from 1969 to 1976 as an infantry officer in the U.S. Army, including a tour in Vietnam. The majority of his foreign service career was spent in Europe with multiple assignments in Turkey. He served as the U.S. ambassador to Turkey from 2008 to 2010, immediately preceding his term of service in Iraq. He previously served in the Middle East in the U.S. Embassies in Kuwait City and Baghdad as the deputy chief of mission. He also served at the national level as a special adviser to the U.S. secretary of state for Iraq and as deputy national security advisor.

Jeffrey's tenure in Baghdad followed al-Maliki's accession to the position of prime minister for the second time and overlapped the withdrawal of U.S. forces in December 2011. He was the U.S. representative in country as the government in Baghdad became more and more sectarian.

Hill left public service and became a visiting fellow at the Washington Institute for Near East Policy and a member of various panels and councils to include the Council on Foreign Relations.

Brian L. Steed

See also: Commanders, Multi-National Force–Iraq: Raymond T. Odierno; Hussein, Saddam; Islamic State of Iraq and al-Sham (ISIS); Obama, Barack Hussein, II; Prime Minister, Iraq: Nuri al-Maliki; Secretary of State, U.S.: Hillary R. Clinton

References

Al-Ali, Zaid. *The Struggle for Iraq's Future: How Corruption, Incompetence and Sectarianism Have Undermined Democracy.* New Haven: Yale University Press, 2014.

Rayburn, Joel. *Iraq after America: Strongmen, Sectarians, Resistance.* Stanford: Hoover Institution Press, 2014.

Sky, Emma. *The Unravelling: High Hopes and Missed Opportunities in Iraq.* New York: PublicAffairs, 2015.

Arab Spring (December 18, 2010–December 2012)

The Arab Spring is a wave of prodemocracy uprisings that swept through North Africa and the Middle East beginning in December 2010. The protest movements—a mixture of both violent and nonviolent activities—were spurred mainly by dissatisfaction with local governments and economic inequalities that seemed to deepen after the global economic downturn in 2008. Essentially, the Arab Spring was propelled by a frustrated population contending with oppressive leaders, government corruption, and high levels of unemployment. The grassroots uprisings have had differing levels of success in each of the Arab nations.

On December 17, 2010, a Tunisian street vendor named Mohamed Bouazizi set himself on fire in the provincial city of Sidi Bouzid to protest police confiscation of his unregistered cart and vegetables. He died two weeks later, but the next day his act of self-immolation set in motion what would be the first of the Arab Spring's major movements, the Tunisian Revolution (2011). Angry about what happened to Bouazizi and frustrated with the lack of jobs in Tunisia, among other issues, hundreds of disgruntled young adults took to the streets in Sidi Bouzid on December 18, destroying shop windows and automobiles in their wake. The rioting gained momentum and soon spread throughout the country. By mid-January, autocratic Tunisian leader Zine El Abidine Ben Ali had lost control of the national military and dissolved his police state in favor of a more democratic process.

The success of the Tunisian protest movement encouraged civil dissidence in other parts of the Arab world. In early January 2011, an Egyptian man set himself on fire outside of a parliamentary building in Cairo after loudly criticizing the government. The Egyptian government was perhaps even more restrictive than that of Tunisia and had outlawed any form of public protest or demonstrations. However, despite government control over most media, people began connecting through such social media outlets as Facebook to orchestra massive demonstrations.

Although the government eventually cut Internet and text-messaging services, the seed was sown. Some 20,000 people gathered in Tahrir Square in Cairo on January 25, calling for an end to government repression in what was the beginning of the Egyptian Revolution (2011). After a bloody standoff between the military and a crowd of demonstrators that swelled to the millions, Egyptian leader Hosni Mubarak, encouraged to do so by the U.S. government, stepped down as president on February 11.

The Arab Spring demonstrations did not stop with Egypt. Soon, disgruntled citizens in other countries were stepping forward to voice their grievances against authoritative rule. Through most of 2011, prodemocracy protests ensued in such nations as Libya, Yemen, Bahrain, and Syria.

The results were not nearly as swift as what had occurred in Tunisia and Egypt. In Libya, dictator Muammar Qaddafi implemented a brutal crackdown on protests that began in February. However, the protests soon turned to an all-out rebellion. Over the next several months, rebel forces grew in scope and power until they controlled all of eastern Libya. As Qaddafi's military began forcibly taking back territories, the United Nations stepped in to call a no-fly zone in order to protect Libyan residents from air attacks called by their own leader. Aided by Western militaries, the Libyan rebels began setting up a transitional government in August 2011, but it was not until his death by rebel forces on October 20 that Qaddafi truly gave up all power.

In Yemen, large-scale protests began peacefully in February 2011 but turned ugly by early February as police and military led a violent crackdown on the demonstrators. Protests continued despite this hard-line stance, and longtime president Ali Abdallah Salih eventually agreed to leave office in November 2011 in exchange for immunity from prosecution over the violent tactics employed to quell the protests. Prodemocracy, antigovernment protests in Bahrain were complicated by religious tensions between the majority Shiite Muslim population and the Sunni Muslim ruling class.

Having lived with political uncertainty and strife since its independence in 1946, Syrian citizens were inspired to take matters into their own hands by the events that unfolded in Tunisia and Egypt. In March 2011, demonstrators took to the streets in what was a remarkably peaceful protest against the government. But the peace was not to last. Soon, Syrian president Bashar al-Assad violently retaliated with military force and martial law. Civil war erupted, and the United Nations called for Assad to face charges of crimes against humanity.

At the end of the year several nations, including the United States, formally recognized a rebel umbrella organization, the Syrian National Council, as the legitimate government of the people. However, Assad maintained his fight for power. Violent unrest and armed clashes continue.

As the Syrian Civil War has raged on, the death toll has continued to rise, but the level of unrest has made monitoring the war's impact extremely difficult. Even the United Nations has not issued a casualty estimate since 2016 (470,000). Despite the difficulty in obtaining accurate information, several groups continue to make an effort to monitor the grim effects of the ongoing conflict. Among these groups is an organization known as Syrian Observatory for Human Rights, which issued an estimate in March 2018 of 511,000 dead since the fighting began in March 2011. With the Assad regime still firmly in control at the time of this book's publication, it seems likely that the number of casualties will continue to climb for the foreseeable future. Sadly, the chaos and violence in Syria make maintaining an accurate death toll impossible.

In addition to these major uprisings, protests and demonstrations also took place in such states as Morocco, Iraq, Iran, and Jordan. Although the Arab Spring has brought with it powerful democratic change in much of the Arab world, the political future of many of these nations still remains uncertain.

Many argue that the existence and success of ISIS was a result of the vacuum of authority created by the Syrian Civil War, which began as an offshoot of the Arab Spring movements. It is difficult to separate the overthrow of Saddam Hussein and the occupation of Iraq from these broad, regional movements. It is uncertain that there were cause-and-effect relationships; however, there are certainly correlational connections between the Iraq War, the Arab Spring, and ISIS.

Tamar Burris

See also: Islamic State of Iraq and al-Sham (ISIS); Obama, Barack Hussein, II; Prime Minister, Iraq: Nuri al-Maliki; Secretary of State, U.S.: Hillary R. Clinton

References

Brownlee, Jason, Tarek Masoud, and Andrew Reynolds. *The Arab Spring: Pathways of Repression and Reform.* Oxford: Oxford University Press, 2015.

Dabashi, Hamid. *The Arab Spring: The End of Postcolonialism.* New York: Palgrave Macmillan, 2012.

Haddad, Bassam, Rosie Bsheer, and Ziad Abu-Rish, eds. *The Dawn of the Arab Uprisings: End of an Old Order?* London: Pluto, 2012.

Lesch, David W. *Syria: The Fall of the House of Assad.* New Haven, CT: Yale University Press, 2011.

Arrowhead Ripper, Operation (June 19–August 19, 2007)

Multi-National Force–Iraq assault against Al Qaeda in Iraq and other insurgents in and around the Iraqi city of Baquba during June 19–August 19, 2007. Baquba is located about 30 miles northeast of Baghdad. As a result of the Baghdad Security Plan developed in early 2007 and the American troop surge that accompanied it, Al Qaeda in Iraq and other Sunni forces withdrew from some areas of Baghdad and began operating in Diyala Province.

The insurgents, who belonged to the Khalf al-Mutayibin group, established a strong presence in Diyala Province and especially in Baquba, a city of some half million people. They made it the capital of their self-proclaimed "Islamic State of Iraq." Al Qaeda was determined to create havoc for the newly formed government of Iraq and to kill coalition troops attempting to gain control of the province.

On June 19, 2007, 10,000 U.S. soldiers, along with more than 1,000 Iraqi police and Iraqi military personnel, launched Arrowhead Ripper, an operation north of Baghdad to clear the region of Al Qaeda militants. Three U.S. brigades participated in the opening days of Arrowhead Ripper: the 1st Cavalry Division's 3rd Brigade Combat Team, commanded by Colonel David Sutherland; the 2nd Infantry Division's 4th Stryker Brigade Combat Team, commanded by Colonel John Lehr; and the 2nd Infantry Division's 3rd Stryker Brigade Combat Team, commanded by Colonel Steven Townsend.

For security reasons, Iraqi leaders were not included in the initial planning of Arrowhead Ripper, but as the operation progressed, the Iraqi 2nd Brigade and the 5th Iraqi Army Division played sizable roles. By the operation's end, the Iraqi 5th Army Division had particularly distinguished itself.

The operation began with a night air assault by Colonel Townsend's 3rd Stryker Brigade Combat Team, which led the effort to clear Baquba. As the operation unfolded, it quickly became apparent that Al Qaeda units, estimated to number more than 1,000 fighters, had dug in to stay. However, news sources reported that the leadership had fled in advance of the operation. In addition to Iraqi security forces (army and police), "concerned citizens" groups—also referred to as Iraqi police volunteers—cooperated with U.S. military personnel and Iraqi security forces in rooting out insurgents. The citizens' movement hoped to restore a measure of peace to the war-torn region. It was instrumental in finding and exposing the safe houses where Al Qaeda militants were hiding.

Fighting was fierce throughout Diyala Province but especially in Baquba, where Al Qaeda had essentially taken control of the city. Multinational troops, going house to house to capture or kill Al Qaeda insurgents, met heavy resistance in the early stages of the battle. As troops entered neighborhoods, they found schools, businesses, and homes booby-trapped with homemade improvised explosive devices (IEDs). The heaviest fighting during the operation occurred within the first four weeks.

American commanders had always believed that Al Qaeda was its own worst enemy, particularly in the way that it treated the locals. Thus, American leaders had anticipated help from citizens in the province, and when these citizens began to pass information as to the whereabouts of insurgents, it was clear that they were ready for Al Qaeda and its operatives to leave their province.

An important goal of Arrowhead Ripper was to prevent insurgents fleeing Baquba from escaping and reorganizing elsewhere. The attacking forces therefore set up a series of blocking posts to the northwest of Baquba in the Khalis corridor and south of the city near Khan Bani Saad to deny insurgents passage through these areas.

Coalition and Iraqi forces also conducted operations to disrupt enemy lines of communication and deny Al Qaeda any areas of safe haven. Following the initial push that cleared Baquba of insurgents, coalition forces began to reposition and destroy Al Qaeda positions northeast of Baquba in the Diyala River Valley. In spite of their attempts to contain Al Qaeda forces inside the area to prevent them from reorganizing elsewhere, many of the insurgents escaped capture and fled.

During the operation, which ended on August 19, the Al Qaeda leader in Baquba was killed, along with more than 100 other insurgents. An additional 424 suspected insurgents were taken prisoner. A total of 129 weapons caches were captured or destroyed, and some 250 IEDs were found and rendered inoperable, including 38 booby-trapped houses, which the military refers to as house-borne IEDs, and 12 vehicle-borne IEDs. Coalition casualties included 18 Americans killed and 12 wounded, 7 Iraqi army personnel killed and 15 wounded, 2 allied Iraqi militiamen killed, and 3 Iraqi police killed. Civilian casualties in the province were not accurately recorded, but an estimated 350 were killed, and many more were wounded. However, it was unclear if civilian casualties were a direct result of Multi-National Force–Iraq military actions or Al Qaeda members simply killing civilians who had helped their enemies.

One reason for the success of the operation was the newly formed Diyala Operations Center, established to coordinate coalition activities in the province. Through it, coalition forces, local police, the Iraqi military, and citizen informants sympathetic to the American military were all linked to one headquarters location. This enabled planners and leaders of the operation to react quickly to any situation, a scenario that the insurgents had not anticipated.

The surge in American troop strength in Iraq combined with operations such as Arrowhead Ripper forced Al Qaeda insurgents out of the cities of the Diyala Valley and broke their ability to sustain day-to-day attacks on coalition troops in the area. Success was also achieved in enabling government ministries to provide fundamental goods and services such as food, fuel, and displaced-persons services to Diyala Province. This enabled the local and national Iraqi governments to show that they could provide for their people and thus raise confidence in government authorities.

The U.S. troop surge begun in early 2007 and operations such as Arrowhead Ripper had great success in the Diyala Valley, with normal life beginning to reemerge by the end of the offensive. Schools, hospitals, and businesses were reopened in the relatively safer environment that came about as a result of the operation.

Randy Jack Taylor

See also: Commanders, Multi-National Force–Iraq: David H. Petraeus, Raymond T. Odierno; Iraq, History of, 1990–Present; Iraqi Freedom, Operation: The Surge and the Awakening; Islamic State of Iraq and al-Sham (ISIS): Al Qaeda in Iraq

References

Bensahel, Nora. *After Saddam: Prewar Planning and the Occupation of Iraq.* Skokie, IL: RAND Corporation, 2008.

Miller, Debra A. *The Middle East.* Detroit: Greenhaven, 2007.

Radcliffe, Woodrow S. *The Strategic Surge in Iraq: Pretense or Plan for Success?* USAWC Strategy Research Project. Carlisle Barracks, PA: U.S. Army War College, 2007.

Simon, Steven, and Council on Foreign Relations. *After the Surge: The Case for U.S. Military Disengagement from Iraq.* New York: Council on Foreign Relations, 2007.

Simons, G. L. *Iraq Endgame? Surge, Suffering and the Politics of Denial.* London: Politico's, 2008.

Woodward, Bob. *The War Within: A Secret White House History, 2006–2008.* New York: Simon and Schuster, 2008.

Atrocities, U.S.

Atrocity is defined as an extremely cruel, violent, or shocking act. Often the word "wicked" and the adjective "wanton" are included in the definition. The word comes from Latin, specifically Roman law, in which a father is warned against using his fatherly power to commit atrocious acts. Atrocity has no agreed on international definition. It tends to be used by the media in reporting events or actions that a particular network or reporter opposes or finds abhorrent. The events identified below, along with the treatment of some prisoners in the Abu Ghraib prison, were all identified as criminal acts under the Uniform Code of Military Justice. They also often get linked with the term "atrocity." It is worth noting that the Obama administration in its August 2011 Presidential Study Directive on Mass Atrocities (PSD-10) identified "preventing mass atrocities and genocide [as] a core national security interest and a core moral responsibility of the United States." In 2016, President Obama signed an executive order that defined mass atrocities as "large scale and deliberate attacks on civilians, and includes acts falling within the definition "genocide" as defined in international law and under U.S. domestic statute." None of the events identified as atrocities fit the definition of mass atrocities; however, it is important to recognize that the term is contentious and legally and politically debated.

Brian L. Steed

See also: Detention Operations, Coalition: Abu Ghraib

References

White House. Presidential Study Directive/PSD-10, "Presidential Study Directive on Mass Atrocities." Washington, DC, May 18, 2016, https://obamawhitehouse.archives.gov/the-press-office/2011/08/04/presidential-study-directive-mass-atrocities (accessed April 23, 2018).

White House. "Executive Order—Comprehensive Approach to Atrocity Prevention and Response." Washington, DC, May 18, 2016, https://obamawhitehouse.archives.gov/the-press-office/2016/05/18/executive-order-comprehensive-approach-atrocity-prevention-and-response (accessed April 23, 2018).

Haditha Incident (November 19, 2005)

The alleged murder of 24 Iraqi civilians in Haditha, in Anbar Province, on November 19, 2005, by U.S. marines of the 1st Squad, 3rd Platoon, K Company, 3rd Battalion, 1st Marine Regiment, 1st Marine Division. The incident gained international notoriety when it eventually became public knowledge, fueling critics' attacks on the conduct of the U.S.-led coalition's counterinsurgency operations in Iraq and raising charges that the U.S. Marine Corps had initially attempted to cover up the killings before reporters broke the story.

Domestic and international pressure to investigate the incident fully and to prosecute those involved gained increasing momentum, as public knowledge of the Haditha Incident in early 2006 coincided with other allegations of unnecessary violence against Iraqi civilians by U.S. military personnel during military operations elsewhere in the country. U.S. congressman John Murtha (D-PA) led congressional opponents of the George W. Bush administration in their strong criticism of the incident and the handling by the U.S. Marine Corps of its aftermath. Murtha's status as a former marine combat veteran of the Vietnam War has frequently made him the Democrats' point man in attacks on the Bush administration's handling of the Global War on Terrorism. Murtha was subsequently sued by one of the alleged marine participants in the Haditha Incident. Although several marine participants were eventually brought up on criminal charges for their roles in the incident, only one received criminal conviction. None of the eight marines were convicted of murder and none received jail for the accused crimes.

In November 2005 Anbar Province was one of the most dangerous places in Iraq, the heart of the Iraqi insurgency. The murders are alleged to have been in retaliation for the death of U.S. Marine Corps Lance Corporal Miguel Terrazas and the wounding of two other marines on November 19 after a four-vehicle U.S. convoy triggered the detonation of an improvised explosive device (IED) and came under attack by small-arms fire.

The U.S. Marine Corps initially reported that 15 civilians had been killed by the bomb's blast and that eight or nine insurgents had also been killed in the ensuing firefight. However, reports by Iraqi eyewitnesses to the incident, statements by local Iraqi officials, and video shots of the dead civilians in the city morgue and at the houses where the killings occurred contradicted the initial U.S. military version of events. Some of the Iraqi eyewitness reports were particularly compelling, such as testimony by a young girl who said that she saw marines shoot her father while he was praying. The vividness and detail of Iraqi eyewitness reports gave substantial credibility to their claims, making it virtually impossible for U.S. military authorities to ignore them. The Iraqi claims contradicting the official military report prompted *Time* magazine to publish a story alleging that the marines deliberately killed 24 Iraqi civilians, including women and six children.

Although *Newsmax* questioned *Time*'s sources for the story, claiming that the dead were known insurgent propagandists and insurgent-friendly Haditha residents, the U.S. military initiated an investigation on February 24, 2006. based on the *Time* report and the international outcry it generated. Led by U.S. Army Major General Eldon Bargewell, the investigation was charged with determining how the incident was reported through the chain of command. On March 9 a criminal investigation was also launched, led by the Naval Criminal Investigative Services, to determine if the marines deliberately targeted and killed Iraqi civilians. As *Newsweek* stated in a report on the Haditha Incident dated October 9, 2007, "the sinister reality of insurgents' hiding among civilians in Iraq has complicated the case" and was one of the main obstacles military investigators have faced in trying to determine if any Iraqi civilians were deliberately killed.

Marines on patrol in Haditha initially reported that one marine and 15 Iraqi civilians had been killed by an IED, whereupon insurgents opened fire on the marines, who proceeded to kill the eight or nine alleged insurgents. The U.S. Marine Corps subsequently reported that the 15 Iraqi civilians had been killed accidentally as marines cleared four nearby houses in front of the road where the IED had exploded in which they believed the insurgents were hiding and/or firing from. According to Iraqi accounts, however, after the IED explosion, the incensed marines went on a rampage, set up a roadblock, and first killed four Iraqi students and a taxi driver who were all unarmed and surrendering to the marines at the time. The marines then stormed the four nearby houses and killed numerous people (accounts vary as to the exact number), including perhaps as many as five women and six children. Details beyond that remain sketchy and changeable.

On April 9, 2007, one marine, Sergeant Sanick De La Cruz, was granted immunity from prosecution for unpremeditated murder in exchange for his testimony. He testified on May 9, 2007, that he and others, including his squad leader, Staff Sergeant Frank Wuterich, killed the four Iraqi students and the driver of a white taxi who were attempting to surrender. De La Cruz further testified that Wuterich then told the men under his command, including De La Cruz, to lie about the killings. According to De La Cruz, the five Iraqis, including the driver, had been ordered out of a taxi by Wuterich and himself after the marines had put up a roadblock following the ambush of the convoy.

Other marines, however, reported that shortly after the explosion of the IED they noticed a white unmarked car full of "military-aged men" arrive and then stop near the bombing site. Suspecting the men to be insurgents who had remotely detonated the IED, Wuterich and De La Cruz ordered the five men to stop and surrender, but instead they ran; they were all shot and killed. As reinforcements arrived, the marines began taking small-arms fire from several locations on either side of their convoy, and while taking cover they identified at least one shooter in the vicinity of a nearby house. Lieutenant William Kallop ordered Wuterich and an ad hoc team to treat the buildings as hostile and to clear them. They forced entry and shot a man on a flight of stairs and then shot another when he made a movement toward a closet. The marines say that they heard the sound of an AK-47 bolt slamming, so they threw grenades into a nearby room and fired; they killed five occupants, with two others wounded by grenade fragments and bullets. Wuterich and his men pursued what they suspected were insurgents running into an adjacent house. They led the assault with grenades and gunfire, in the process killing another man. Unknown to the marines, two women and six children were in a back room. Seven were killed. It was a chaotic and fast-moving action conducted in the dark in close-range quarters, causing accounts to diverge on the precise chronology and exact sequence of events.

After the firefight ended around 9:30 p.m., the marines noted men suspected of scouting for another attack peering behind the wall of a third house. A marine team, including Wuterich and Lance Corporal Justin Sharratt, stormed the house and found women and children inside (who were not harmed). They moved to a fourth house off a courtyard and killed two men inside wielding AK-47s, along with two others.

Thirty minutes after the house clearing, an intelligence unit arrived to question the marines involved in the operation. Shortly after the IED explosion, an unmanned aerial vehicle (UAV) flew over the blast area and for the rest of the day transmitted views of the scene to the company command headquarters and also to the battalion, regimental, and divisional headquarters. *Newsmax* reported that the UAV recorded marines sweeping the four houses for suspected insurgents and also showed four insurgents fleeing the neighborhood in a car and joining up with other insurgents. Based on Staff Sergeant Wuterich's account that in the first house he cleared he observed a back door ajar and believed that the insurgents had fled to another nearby house, it is possible that the four fleeing insurgents seen by the UAV were the same individuals who left through the back door of the first house that Wuterich and other marines were clearing. The UAV followed both groups of insurgents as they returned to their safe house, which was bombed around 6:00 p.m. and then stormed by a squad from K Company.

On December 21, 2006, in accordance with U.S. Marine Corps legal procedures, criminal charges were brought against eight marines for war crimes in the Haditha killings. Four enlisted marines (including Wuterich) were accused of 13 counts of unpremeditated murder, and four officers were charged with covering up their subordinates' alleged misdeeds by failing to report and investigate properly the deaths of the Iraqis. In 2007 the charges against three of the four enlisted marines were dismissed, and by the summer of 2008 the charges against three of the officers were dismissed; the other was found not guilty by court-martial. Kallop was never charged with a crime.

On June 17, 2008, military judge colonel Steve Folsom dismissed all charges against Lieutenant Colonel Jeffrey R. Chessani, the most senior officer to face charges, because the officer overseeing the Haditha investigation, Lieutenant General James Mattis, had been improperly influenced by legal investigator Colonel John Ewers, who was a witness to the case and later became a legal adviser to Mattis. The judge ruled that Ewers should not have been allowed to attend meetings and discussions with Mattis because Ewers's participation prejudiced and tainted the decision to charge and prosecute Chessani, who was accused of failing to report the incident and investigate the alleged killing of civilians by marines under his command. The U.S. Marine Corps has appealed the ruling to the Navy and Marine Court of Criminal Appeals, postponing indefinitely Chessani's case.

By June 17 the cases of six defendants had been dropped, and a seventh defendant was found not guilty. The sole exception was Staff Sergeant Frank Wuterich, the platoon sergeant implicated in the Haditha killings. On January 24, 2012, Wuterich was convicted of a single count of negligent dereliction of duty. He received a rank reduction and pay cut but avoided jail time. Many Iraqis expressed disbelief and voiced outrage that six years had passed and that no marines had been sentenced to prison, and there were threats to bring the case to international courts.

Wuterich insists that his unit followed the rules of engagement and did not purposefully attack civilians and that his squad entered the houses to suppress insurgent fire and pursue gunmen who had opened fire on them. He further asserts that the civilian deaths occurred during the sweep of nearby homes in which fragmentation grenades and clearing fire were used before entering the houses. Wuterich also said that his unit never attempted to cover up the incident and immediately reported that civilians had been killed in Haditha.

The Department of Defense has said that the rules of engagement in effect at Haditha prohibited unprovoked attacks on civilians, but this of course assumes that the marines knew that the homes were populated by civilians. In addition, marines are trained as a matter of combat survival to suppress enemy fire with overwhelming force, including the tossing of grenades into a room before entering. The lead investigator of the Haditha Incident has confirmed that some training the marines received conflicted with their rules of engagement and led them to believe that if fired upon from a house, they could clear it with grenades and gunfire without determining whether civilians were inside.

The Haditha Incident stands as a classic example of the profound difficulties and the immense potential for human tragedy encountered by conventional military forces engaged in combating an insurgency in which the insurgents' very survival depends on blending in with—and often becoming indistinguishable from—the local civilian population. Indeed, even when conventional forces win a tactical battle against insurgents, they risk incurring a more important strategic loss when they kill civilians (intentionally or accidentally) in the process. Inevitably, conventional forces conducting counterinsurgency operations are confronted by an unavoidable double standard: while being held strictly accountable for observing all of the internationally accepted laws of war, they must fight an enemy whose tactics principally rely on terror and indiscriminate killing of civilians and combatants alike. The very thought that Al Qaeda or other terrorist group leadership would conduct war crimes investigations for atrocities committed by its members as the U.S. Marine Corps has done in the wake of the Haditha Incident seems absurd; atrocities are the insurgents' main tactic, not aberrations occurring during the heat of battle.

The Haditha Incident also emphasizes that a conventional counterinsurgency force's major actions and policies must be in place in order to prevent or at least limit civilian deaths: effective training, strict discipline, individual accountability, rigidly enforced rules of engagement, and competent leaders at every level of command who remain totally involved in the conduct of all combat operations. Not even one of these critical elements can be lacking or ignored, as that raises the risk of a repeat of such incidents as occurred at Haditha.

Stefan Brooks

See also: Commanders, U.S. Central Command: James Mattis; Islamic State of Iraq and al-Sham (ISIS): Al Qaeda in Iraq; Weapons, Insurgency, and Opposition: Improvised Explosive Devices

References

Brennan, Phil. "New Evidence Emerges in Haditha Case." *Newsmax,* June 26, 2006.

Ephron, Dan. "Haditha Unraveled." *Newsweek,* October 29, 2007.

McGirk, Tim. "Collateral Damage or Civilian Massacre at Haditha." *Time,* March 19, 2006.

"What Happened at Haditha." Editorial. *Wall Street Journal,* October 19, 2007.

White, Josh. "Marine Says Rules Were Followed." *Washington Post,* June 11, 2006.

Mahmudiyah Incident (March 12, 2006)

Violent incident in which four U.S. soldiers from the 101st Airborne Division raped a 14-year-old Iraqi girl and killed her and her family on March 12, 2006, in Mahmudiyah, Iraq. Mahmudiyah is a rural enclave south of Baghdad. The four soldiers had left their post manning a checkpoint in order to commit the murders. After killing the girl, Abir Qasim Hamza al-Janabi, and her family (a total of four people were murdered), they set the girl's body on fire. This fire quickly spread to the rest of the house and alerted neighbors. The incident was initially suspected to be an Iraqi insurgent attack, a view that the perpetrators themselves had encouraged. However, Private First Class Justin Watt eventually came forward to voice suspicions about the role of American soldiers in the attack. Then the investigation shifted to the 101st Airborne Division soldiers. In response to the killings, there were several attacks by insurgent groups in Iraq that claimed that their actions were in retaliation for the rape and killing of Abir.

After the investigation and trial, two of the soldiers involved, Specialists James Barker and Paul Cortez, received 90 and 100 years in prison, respectively. Private Jesse Spielman received a sentence of 110 years for his role in the rape and killings. Private First Class Steven Green, the ringleader of the attack, was already out of the army when arrested for the crimes. He faced a civilian trial and in 2009 received a sentence of life in prison without the possibility of parole. Green's lawyers appealed the verdicts and sentence, but by 2011 they had run their course and were denied.

Gates Brown

See also: Detention Operations, Coalition: Abu Ghraib

References

Frederick, Jim. *Black Hearts: One Platoon's Descent into Madness in Iraq's Triangle of Death*. New York: Harmony Books, 2010.

Von Zielbauer, Paul. "G.I. Gets 100 Years for Rape and Killing in Iraq." *New York Times,* August 5, 2007, http://www.nytimes.com/2007/08/05/us/05abuse.html.

B

Baath Party

Political party that currently dominates Syria and was the leading party in Iraq from 1968 to the end of Saddam Hussein's regime in 2003. The Baath Party (Hizb al-Baath al-Arabi al-Ishtiraki) also has branches in Lebanon, Jordan, Sudan, Yemen, Mauritania, and Bahrain and enjoys support from some Palestinians. The Arabic word *baath* means "renaissance" or "resurrection." The party's fundamental principles have been Arab unity and freedom from imperialist control for all Arab states, personal freedom for Arab citizens, and support for Arab culture. The party also supported Arab socialist policies intended to eliminate feudalism but not private property. The Arab Socialist Baath Party of Syria explains its ideology as "national (Pan-Arab), socialist, popular and revolutionary," and its founding charter and constitution identifies its commitment to the "Arab Nation, the Arab homeland, the Arab citizen, the Arab people's authority over their own land and the freedom of the Arab people."

The Arab Baath Party, as it was originally called, grew out of an ideological and political movement in Syria, founded in 1940 in Damascus with the goal of revitalizing the Arab nation and society. The principal founders of the Baath movement and party were Syrian intellectuals Michel Aflaq, a Greek Orthodox Christian; Salah al-Din al-Bitar, a Sunni Muslim who studied at the Sorbonne in the early 1930s; and Zaki al-Arsuzi. The Arab Baath Party accepted Arabs of all religious backgrounds and ethnic groups.

The first Arab Baath Party Congress was held on April 4–6, 1947. Abd al-Rahman al-Damin and Abd al-Khaliq al-Khudayri attended that Congress, and on their return to Iraq founded a branch of the party there. This evolved into a small group of about 50 individuals, mainly friends and associates of Fuad al-Rikabi, who took control of the group in 1951. The Baathists in Iraq joined with other organizations that were in opposition to the monarchy. Baathism spread more slowly in Iraq than in Syria, with its candidates losing out to Communist Party candidates in many elections in the 1960s.

Meanwhile in Syria, in 1954 Aflaq and Bitar joined forces with Akram al-Hawrani, a populist leader who headed the Socialist Party. They adopted the name Arab Socialist Baath Party. The Baath Party found its greatest strength in Syria and Iraq, although it had branches all over the Arab world.

The Baath Party came to power first in Iraq and then in Syria in coups d'état in 1963. The coup in Iraq did not last out the year; however, during that time 10,000 leftists, Marxists, and communists were killed, 5,000 of these from the Iraqi Communist Party. Three years later, the Syrian and Iraqi parties split. Each was subsequently plagued by factionalism. Some disputes occurred as a result of Syria's union with Egypt in the United Arab Republic; others concerned a possible union of Syria and Iraq or ties with the Soviet Union and local communist parties as well as the Syrian Socialist Nationalist Party in Syria.

Rivalries between different factions of the Syrian Baath Party led to an interparty coup in 1966 followed by another one four years later that brought General Hafiz al-Assad to power. He headed a pragmatic faction that gained control of the military in contrast to a "progressive" faction that had pushed a more pervasive socialism and nationalizations and a harder line regionally. Asad remained in office until his death in 2000. His son, Bashar al-Assad, assumed leadership of the Syrian Baath Party and remains the president of Syria, although his leadership of the party and of Syria has been sorely tested by the ongoing Syrian Civil War, which began in 2011.

Saddam Hussein joined the Iraqi Baath Party at the age of 21 in 1956 and steadily rose in the party's ranks, first as a consequence of the Iraqi Revolution of 1958 and then as an assassin in the U.S.-backed plot to do away with President Abd al-Karim Qasim. Later after the Baath Party had regained power in a 1968 coup, Hussein served as vice chairman of the Revolutionary Command Council and then as president and secretary-general of the Baath Party.

The Baath parties of Iraq and Syria operated in associations in schools, communities, and the army and had workers' and women's associations, such as the General Association of Iraqi Women (al-Ittihad al-amm li-nisa al-Iraq). While the party ostensibly sought to expand membership to comprise a "mass party," in fact membership was tightly controlled. Nonetheless, party members wielded considerable power. Average Syrians and Iraqis could hardly conclude any official business without the intercession of a party member. In the military and in academia, it was nearly impossible to advance or be promoted without being a party member. In Iraq, the party claimed 1.5 million members, or about 10 percent of the country's population, in the late 1980s; however, only about 30,000 were bona fide party cadres. In Syria, Assad opened up membership so that by 1987 it was at about 50,000 people, and there were also some 200,000 probationary party members.

The Baath parties of both countries did not tolerate political challenges of any other group or party. They strongly opposed the Islamist movements that arose in each nation. Despite the dictatorial nature of the Iraqi government in this period, one notable accomplishment, in part facilitated through the party, was the serious effort to modernize the economy and society by promoting literacy, education, and gender equality. As a result, by the 1970s Iraq had a fairly high level of education. Hussein's disastrous war with Iran and then his invasion of Kuwait, which prompted war with the United States and a coalition of states, had a profoundly negative impact on the country and its economy.

The U.S.-led invasion of Iraq in March 2003 and the overthrow of Saddam Hussein led to an immediate ban of the Baath Party, the so-called de-Baathification, under U.S. and coalition occupation forces. Iraqis also attacked Baath Party offices all over the country. Some critics of the U.S. occupation policies in Iraq claim that U.S. administrator L. Paul Bremer's decision, approved by Washington, to bar all Baathists from government posts hopelessly hamstrung the government and fueled the Iraqi insurgency, which included some bitter and disenfranchised Baathists. Iraqi prime minister Nuri al-Maliki continued enforcing the ban on the Baath Party and extended rehiring only to those who were able to prove that they were forced to join the party. A related controversy emerged over the transfer of the Baath Party records to the Hoover Institution at Stanford University via an agreement with the Iraq Memory Foundation and with permission of Maliki. The seizure of these documents (which could reveal the precise status of connections with the party) has been protested by, among others, the director of the Iraq National Library and Archive and the acting Iraqi minister of culture.

In Syria, the Baath Party has had a great impact. Changes in landholding and commercial policies in the 1960s displaced earlier elites, but suppression of the Sunni merchants and Islamists, even after the Hama massacre, led to an Islamist revival that challenged Baath Party primacy. Although President Assad promised democratic reforms in 2005, virtually no change occurred. Since the civil war began in 2011, the survival of Assad's regime has trumped any efforts to reform Syria's political or economic systems.

In Lebanon, Bahrain, and other countries, the Baath Party retains a small presence. In Lebanon it held two seats in parliament in the 1990s, and the Iraqi branch also had a link in a group within the Palestinian Fatah organization. The Sudanese Baath Party operates underground as part of the opposition to the Sudanese regime and publishes a journal, *al-Hadaf*.

Stefan Brooks and Sherifa Zuhur

See also: Bremer, Lewis Paul, III; Coalition Provisional Authority; Hussein, Saddam; Iraq, History of, 1990–Present; Prime Minister, Iraq: Nuri al-Maliki

References

Batatu, Hanna. *Old Social Classes and New Revolutionary Movements of Iraq*. London: Al-Saqi Books, 2000.

Committee against Repression and for Democratic Rights in Iraq, ed. *Saddam's Iraq: Revolution or Reaction?* London: Zed Books, 1986.

Devlin, John F. *The Ba'th Party: A History from Its Origins to 1966*. Stanford, CA: Hoover Institution Press, 1976.

Heydemann, Steven. *Authoritarianism in Syria: Institutions and Social Conflict, 1948–1970*. Ithaca, NY: Cornell University Press, 1999.

Hinnebusch, Raymond. *Syria: Revolution from Above*. Florence, NY: Routledge, 2001.

Tripp, Charles. *A History of Iraq*. Cambridge: Cambridge University Press, 2007.

Baghdadi, Abu Bakr al- (c. 1971–)

Iraqi jihadist, terrorist, and militant leader of the Islamic State (formerly the Islamic State of Iraq and Syria) since 2010. Abu Bakr al-Baghdadi was born Ibrahim al-Badari on the outskirts of Samarra, Iraq, probably in 1971. He received undergraduate and graduate degrees—including a PhD in Islamic studies—from the Islamic University of Baghdad. Very little is known about Baghdadi prior to the Anglo-American invasion of Iraq in 2003.

Shortly after the fall of Saddam Hussein's regime in early April 2003, Baghdadi cofounded a militant Islamist group known as Jamaat Jaysh Ahl a-Sunnah wa-i-Jamaah (JJASJ). It was committed to expelling all foreign troops from Iraq and establishing sharia law in the country. Although the details of Baghdadi's activities remain rather murky until 2010, the U.S. Defense Department claims that he was incarcerated as a "civilian internee" at Camp Bucca (near Umm Qasr, Iraq) for much of 2004. He was released after a review board deemed him "unremarkable."

In 2006, JJASJ merged with the Mujahideen Shura Council (MSC), and Baghdadi served on its sharia committee. Later that same year, the MSC was renamed the Islamic State of Iraq (ISI), which functioned essentially as Al Qaeda's Iraqi satellite and was also referred to as Al Qaeda in Iraq. On May 16, 2010, Baghdadi assumed leadership of ISI. He immediately stepped up the group's terror activities in Iraq, including at least 23 attacks south of Baghdad during March and April 2011 alone. Upon learning of Al Qaeda leader Osama bin Laden's death at the hands of U.S. commandos in May 2011, Baghdadi pledged to perpetrate more acts of violence to avenge bin Laden's death. True to his word, Baghdadi engineered a spectacular series of suicide attacks throughout Iraq in the remainder of the year. In October 2011, the U.S. State Department listed Baghdadi as a designated global terrorist and offered a $10 million reward for his capture or death.

The departure of U.S. troops from Iraq in December 2011 seemed only to strengthen ISI's influence and reach. Meanwhile, the civil war that had begun in Syria earlier that year caught Baghdadi's attention. Before long, ISI had begun to extend its operations into Syria and was training and arming its militants so they could wage war against both the regime of Bashar al-Assad as well as other antigovernment rebels who did not subscribe to ISI's radical views. In 2013, Baghdadi changed the name of ISI to the Islamic State of Iraq and Syria (ISIS), in recognition that his reach now included swaths of Syria as well as Iraq. He also announced that the Syrian jihadist group Jabhat al-Nusra had allied with ISIS and would be formally incorporated into Baghdadi's organization. Meanwhile in Iraq, the ineffectual and corrupt government of Nuri al-Maliki appeared unwilling and certainly unable to stop ISIS's advance.

During 2013 and into 2014, ISIS made frighteningly rapid progress in capturing large portions of western and northern Iraq and northeastern Syria. By January 2014, ISIS had taken virtually all of Iraq's Anbar Province and appeared poised to advance on Baghdad. In the process, ISIS was also unleashing a violent holy war against any individuals who refused to accede to its demands. In February 2014 Al Qaeda severed all ties to ISIS, signaling that Baghdadi's campaign was too radical even for it. Fueled by money from wealthy private citizens in Qatar and Saudi Arabia as well as oil revenue from captured wells and refineries, Baghdadi envisioned imposing a worldwide Islamic caliphate under his personal direction.

On June 19, 2014, Baghdadi declared himself caliph of the Islamic State. Many Islamic nations, including those in the Middle East, were aghast with Baghdadi's audacity and merciless violence. Many Islamic scholars and religious leaders deemed the activities of ISIS as apostasy. In the late summer of 2014, the Barack Obama administration began assembling a multinational coalition aimed at defeating Baghdadi's organization. U.S. air strikes against ISIS in Iraq began in August; they were expanded into Syria the following month. In late September 2014 there were reports that he may have been injured in a coalition air attack and sought refuge in Mosul, Iraq. Since that time, he has remained reclusive and evasive. The Islamic State periodically releases audio messages from their leader but avoids live broadcasts because of the risk such tactics bring of disclosing the whereabouts of the most wanted man in the world. The last of these recordings was broadcast on August 2018. For now, Baghdadi remains at large.

Paul G. Pierpaoli Jr.

See also: Iraqi Freedom, Operation: The Surge and the Awakening; Islamic State of Iraq and al-Sham (ISIS): Al Qaeda in Iraq; Prime Minister, Iraq: Nuri al-Maliki

References

Andress, Carter, with Malcolm McConnell. *Victory Undone: The Defeat of Al Qaeda in Iraq and Its Resurrection as ISIS*. New York: Regnery Publishing, 2014.

"Injured ISIS Leader Abu Bakr Al-Baghdadi Flees Syria to Escape U.S. Air Strikes." *International Business Times,* October 1, 2014, http://www.ibtimes.co.in/injured-isis-leader-flees-syria-abu-bakr-al-baghdadi-arrives-mosul-after-escaping-us-airstrikes-610361.

Stern, Jessica, and J. M. Berger. *ISIS: The State of Terror.* New York: HarperCollins, 2015.

"20 Facts about Baghdadi, the Elusive ISIS Leader." *Fiscal Times,* September 9, 2014, http://www.thefiscaltimes.com/Articles/2014/09/09/20-Facts-About-Baghdadi-Leader-ISIS.

Bremer, Lewis Paul, III (1941–)

U.S. diplomat, career U.S. State Department official, and administrator of the Coalition Provisional Authority in Iraq (2003–2004). Lewis Paul "Jerry" Bremer was born in Hartford, Connecticut, on September 30, 1941. He received a BA from Yale University in 1963 and an MBA from Harvard University in 1966. Later that same year, he joined the Foreign Service and began his lengthy career as a diplomat.

Bremer's tenure with the State Department featured posts as an assistant to national security advisor and then secretary of state Henry Kissinger (1972–1976), ambassador to the Netherlands (1983), and ambassador-at-large for counterterrorism (1986). In 1981 Secretary of State Alexander Haig named Bremer executive secretary of the State Department, where he directed the country's round-the-clock crisis management and emergency response center.

L. Paul Bremer served as administrator of the Coalition Provisional Authority of Iraq from May 6, 2003, to June 28, 2004. Here he gives a speech at the Ministry of Education in Baghdad on April 3, 2004. (U.S. Department of Defense)

In 2002 in the aftermath of the September 11, 2001, terrorist attacks, Bremer was appointed to the Homeland Security Advisory Council. Considered an expert on terrorism, he spent much of his career advocating a stronger U.S. position against states that sponsor or harbor terrorists.

On May 6, 2003, after Iraqi forces had been defeated in the first phase of the war, President George W. Bush named Bremer U.S. presidential envoy in Iraq. In this role, Bremer became the top executive authority in Iraq as the administrator of the Coalition Provisional Authority. He was tasked with overseeing the beginning of the transition from the U.S.-led military coalition governing Iraq to Iraqi self-governance. Bremer was brought in to replace retired U.S. Army general Jay Garner, who had been put in place only two weeks earlier. Bremer's job, which began just five days after Bush declared that major combat operations were completed, was to serve as the top civilian leader of Iraq until such time that the nation was stable enough to govern itself.

Garner's leadership has been generally praised but was not without its problems. Under Garner's watch, looting of commercial and government buildings was rampant, including the alleged theft of priceless archaeological treasures from Iraqi museums. Iraqi citizens also faced growing problems with failing infrastructure and burgeoning street violence.

Bremer's first move was to increase the number and visibility of U.S. military police in Baghdad while making the reconstruction of the Iraqi police force a high priority. Bremer also pushed to speed up the rebuilding of Iraq's infrastructure and to make certain that government workers were being paid. Despite his efforts, however, violence—both sectarian and insurgent—continued to mount, causing Iraqis to become increasingly frustrated with the U.S.-led coalition. Bremer was also forced to postpone establishing an Iraqi-led transitional government.

Bremer is given credit for making some critically important decisions in his role as envoy. Among these were the removal of all restrictions against freedom of assembly, the suspension of the death penalty, and the establishment of a central criminal court. However, many were critical of some of Bremer's decisions, particularly his decision to disband the Iraqi Army and to remove members of Saddam Hussein's Baath Party from critical government positions. Bremer responded to his critics that there was, in truth, no Iraqi Army left for him to dissolve, as that task had already been accomplished by the war. He also claimed that his Baath Party purge was directed at only the top 3 percent of the party leadership. During his tenure, Bremer was also the target of numerous failed assassination attempts. At one point, Al Qaeda leader Osama bin Laden placed a bounty of 10,000 grams of gold on the diplomat's head.

Despite the violence and the assassination attempts, Bremer was able to achieve many of his goals. On July 13, 2003, the Iraqi Interim Governing Council, chosen from prominent Iraqis, was approved. On March 8, 2004, the interim constitution was signed after being approved by the governing council. Then on June 28, 2004, the U.S.-led coalition formally transferred limited sovereignty to the interim government. In a move that surprised many, Bremer left Iraq the same day. After his departure, U.S. ambassador to Iraq John Negroponte became the highest-ranking U.S. civilian in Iraq.

After leaving Iraq, Bremer embarked on several speaking tours and coauthored a book, *My Year in Iraq,* published in 2006. He is currently serving as chairman of the advisory board for GlobalSecure Corporation, a firm that deals with homeland security issues. In late 2010, Bremer became president and CEO of World T.E.A.M. Sports, a nonprofit organization; he stepped down in March 2012.

Keith Murphy

See also: Baath Party; Bush, George Walker; Coalition Provisional Authority; Garner, Jay Montgomery; Iraqi Freedom, Operation

References

Bremer, L. Paul, ed. *Countering the Changing Threat of International Terrorism: Report from the National Commission on Terrorism.* Darby, PA: Diane Publishing, 2000.

Bremer, L. Paul, with Malcolm McConnell. *My Year in Iraq: The Struggle to Build a Future of Hope.* New York: Simon and Schuster, 2006.

Ricks, Thomas E. *Fiasco: The American Military Adventure in Iraq.* New York: Penguin, 2006.

Bush, George Walker (1946–)

Republican Party politician, governor of Texas (1995–2001), and president of the United States (2001–2009). George Walker Bush was born in New Haven, Connecticut, on July 6, 1946, and grew up in Midland and Houston, Texas. He is the son of George H. W. Bush, president of the United States from 1989 to 1993.

The younger Bush graduated from the exclusive Phillips Academy in Andover, Massachusetts, and from Yale University in 1968. He volunteered for the Texas Air National Guard after graduation and became a pilot, although questions later surfaced about his actual service. He earned an MBA from Harvard University in 1975 and returned to Texas, founding Arbusto Energy Company in 1977. He then served as a key staffer during his father's 1988 presidential campaign and later became one of the owners of the Texas Rangers baseball team.

In 1994, Bush was elected governor of Texas. As governor, he worked with the Democratic-dominated legislature to reduce state control and taxes. In 1996 he won reelection, by which time he had earned a reputation as an honest broker who could govern in a bipartisan manner.

In 2000, having set records for fundraising and having campaigned as a "compassionate conservative," Bush easily won the 2000 Republican nomination for the presidency of the United States. His platform included tax cuts, improved schools, Social Security reform, and increased military spending. On foreign policy issues, he downplayed his obvious lack of experience but eschewed foreign intervention and nation building.

The U.S. presidential election of November 2000 was one of the most contentious in American history. The Democratic candidate, Vice President Al Gore, won a slim majority of the popular vote, but the electoral vote was in doubt. Confusion centered on Florida. Eventually, after weeks of recounts and court injunctions, the issue reached the U.S. Supreme Court. On December 12, 2000, a deeply divided Court halted the recount in Florida, virtually declaring Bush the winner. For many Americans, Bush was an illegitimate and unelected president.

As president, Bush secured a large tax cut in hopes that this would spur the economy, and he pushed forward Social Security reform. He and the Republican-controlled

President George W. Bush speaks to reporters in the Pentagon after he and members of his national security team were briefed on the latest developments in Iraq, Afghanistan, and the Global War on Terrorism, on January 4, 2006. (U.S. Department of Defense)

Congress also enacted a tax rebate for millions of Americans in the late summer and early autumn of 2001. That same year, with prodding from the White House, Congress passed the No Child Left Behind Act, a standards-based reform measure designed to build more accountability into public education. Although the measure won broad bipartisan support, it later was criticized for being too narrowly conceived and incapable of accounting for differences in the way children learn. Many also came to believe that the mandate was not properly funded, especially in poorer school districts. In 2003 Bush was successful in passing a prescription drug act for U.S. citizens over the age of 65, but the measure ended up being far more expensive than originally forecast. Many also criticized the plan for being too complicated and offering too many options.

The course of Bush's presidency was forever changed on September 11, 2001, when 19 hijackers associated with the Al Qaeda terrorist organization seized commercial airliners and crashed them into the World Trade Center and the Pentagon. The attacks killed nearly 2,700 Americans and 316 foreign nationals. Over the next few days Bush visited the scenes of the attacks, reassuring the public and promising to bring those responsible to justice. The catastrophe of September 11 seemed to bring legitimacy and purpose to Bush's presidency, although it tilted the economy further into recession.

On September 20, 2001, Bush appeared before Congress and accused Al Qaeda of carrying out the attacks. He warned the American people that they faced a lengthy war against terrorism. He also demanded that the Taliban government of Afghanistan surrender members of Al Qaeda in their country or face retribution. When the Taliban failed to comply, U.S. and British forces began a bombing campaign on October 7. Initially, the United States enjoyed broad international support for the Global War on Terrorism and its campaign to oust the Taliban from Afghanistan. Indigenous Northern Alliance forces with heavy American support, chiefly in the form of air strikes, handily defeated the Taliban and by November 2001 had captured the capital of Kabul. Taliban resistance continued thereafter, but the multinational coalition was nevertheless able to establish a new government in Afghanistan.

The Bush administration also sought to improve national security in the wake of September 11. A new Department of Homeland Security was created to coordinate all agencies that could track and defeat terrorists. In October 2001 at the behest of the Bush administration, Congress passed the so-called Patriot Act, giving the federal government sweeping powers to fight the Global War on Terrorism. Many Americans were uncomfortable with this legislation and feared that it might undermine American freedom and civil liberties.

In 2002, the Bush administration turned its attention toward Iraq. Intelligence reports suggested that Iraqi dictator Saddam Hussein was continuing to pursue weapons of mass destruction (WMD). When Bush demanded that he comply with United Nations (UN) resolutions seeking inspection of certain facilities, Hussein refused. Unfortunately, some of the intelligence dealing with Iraqi intentions and capabilities was faulty, and some have argued that the Bush White House pressured the Central Intelligence Agency and other intelligence services to interpret their findings in a way that would support armed conflict with Iraq. Still others claim that the White House and the Pentagon misled themselves and the public by reading into the intelligence reports more than what was actually there. By the end of 2002, the Bush administration had formulated a new policy of preemptive warfare (the Bush Doctrine) to destroy regimes that intended to harm the United States before they were able to do so.

In October 2002, Bush secured from Congress a bipartisan authorization to use military force against Iraq if necessary. Many in Congress believed that all means of international diplomacy and economic sanctions would be exhausted before the United States undertook military action against the Iraqis. Such was not the case, however, for the White House seemed intent on war.

By the beginning of 2003, a military buildup against Iraq was already taking place. However, Bush's efforts to create a broad multinational coalition failed to achieve the success of the Persian Gulf War coalition against Iraq in 1991. Nearly all of the forces were American or British, and the UN failed to sanction military action against Iraq as it had done in 1990. The virtually unilateral U.S. approach to the situation in Iraq greatly angered much of the international community and even U.S. allies. Such longtime partners as France and Germany refused to sanction American actions in Iraq, and relations with those nations suffered accordingly. To much of the world, the Bush Doctrine smacked of heavy-handed intimidation and hubris that simply circumvented international law whenever the Americans believed unilateral action to be necessary.

Military operations commenced on March 19, 2001, and Baghdad fell on April 9. At that point organized resistance was minimal, but manpower resources, while sufficient to topple Hussein, were clearly insufficient to maintain the peace. Rioting and looting soon broke out, and weapons stockpiles were pillaged by insurgents. Religious and ethnic tensions came to the fore between Sunnis, Shias, and Kurds. Far more American troops were killed trying to keep order in Iraq than had died in the overthrow of the regime.

Although Bush won reelection in November 2004 in large part because of his tough stance on the so-called Global War on Terrorism, support for the war in Iraq gradually waned, the consequence of mounting American military and Iraqi civilian dead, reports of American atrocities committed in Iraq, the war's vast expense, revelations that the White House trumped up or knowingly used questionable intelligence about Iraqi WMD, and general mismanagement of the war effort. Meanwhile, large budget deficits and trade imbalances piled up. Clearly, the failure to find WMD in Iraq undercut the stated reason for the attack, although Bush then claimed that the war was about overthrowing an evil dictatorship and bringing democracy to Iraq, a statement that was diametrically opposed to his insistence during the 2000 campaign that the United States should not undertake nation-building operations using the U.S. military.

The Bush administration was at first ambivalent toward the Arab-Israeli conflict, but with violence escalating, in August 2001 at the urging of Crown Prince Abdullah of Saudi Arabia, Bush issued a letter supporting the concept of a Palestinian state. September 11 and ensuing events in Iraq soon took precedence, however. Bush and his advisers realized that Arab support, or at least acquiescence, in his Iraq policies would be more likely if a peace process were under way.

On June 24, 2002, Bush publicly called for a two-state solution. He failed to outline specific steps but supported a process in which each side would meet certain criteria before moving to the next step. The result was called the Road Map to Peace. Bush agreed to work with the European Union, the UN, and Russia in developing it. This so-called Quartet developed a series of steps intended to provide assurances for each side but without involving the Israelis or Palestinians in its development.

The Road Map to Peace was unveiled in March 2003, just before the invasion of Iraq, but no details were announced. In June of that year, Bush arranged a summit conference at Aqaba, Jordan, involving Prime Minister Ariel Sharon of Israel and Prime Minister Mahmoud Abbas of the Palestinian National Authority. Progress on the plan stalled. The Bush administration's push for elections in the Palestinian-controlled West Bank backfired in January 2006 when these were won by the radical Hamas organization, which has called for the destruction of Israel and has continued to harass Israelis with random rocket attacks from Gaza and the West Bank. The peace process then ground to a halt. The Bush administration, faced with mounting American public dissatisfaction over the continuing American troop presence in Iraq, concentrated on that issue to the exclusion of virtually all other foreign developments.

Meanwhile, Bush suffered stunning setbacks at home. The White House was roundly denounced for its poor handling of relief efforts following Hurricane Katrina in the autumn of 2005 in which hundreds died in Louisiana and along the U.S. coast of the Gulf of Mexico. In the November 2006 midterm elections the Republicans lost both houses of Congress, and Bush was forced to fire Secretary of Defense Donald Rumsfeld, whose tenure had been rife with controversy. Many Americans placed the onus of blame for the Iraq debacle on his shoulders. The year before, Secretary of State Colin L. Powell had resigned because of sharp differences he had with the White House's foreign policy; he has since publicly regretted being taken in by faulty pre–Iraq War intelligence. By early 2007, Bush was besieged by bad news: plummeting approval ratings, a war gone bad in Iraq with no end in sight, and incipient signs that massive budget deficits fanned by Bush's spending and failure to veto appropriation bills were beginning to undermine the economy.

In January 2007 amid increasing calls for the United States to pull out of Iraq, Bush decided on just the opposite tack. His administration implemented a troop surge strategy that placed as many as 40,000 more U.S. soldiers on the ground in Iraq. Within six months the surge strategy seemed to be paying dividends, and violence in Iraq was down. At the same time, however, a growing Taliban insurgency in Afghanistan was threatening to undo many of the gains made there since 2001. Many critics, including a number of Republicans, argued that Bush's Iraq policies had needlessly diluted the U.S. effort in Afghanistan. But Bush was hard-pressed to send significantly more troops to Afghanistan because the military was already badly overstretched.

In the meantime, the White House's controversial policy of indefinitely detaining non-U.S. terror suspects, most of whom were being held at the Guantánamo Bay Detention Camp in Cuba, drew the ire of many in the United States and the international community. Although most of the detainees were supposed to be tried in secret military tribunals, few were ever brought to trial. Some observers have alleged abuse and mistreatment at Guantánamo, which further eroded America's standing in the world. More recently, several U.S. courts have weighed in on the detainees' status and have ordered that they be tried or released. In June 2008, the U.S. Supreme Court ruled that terror detainees were subject to certain rights under the U.S. Constitution. Even more controversial has been the use of so-called coercive interrogation techniques on terror suspects and other enemy combatants. A euphemism for torture, this has included waterboarding, which goes against prescribed international norms for the treatment of prisoners of war. The Bush administration at first insisted that it had not authorized coercive interrogation, but when evidence to the contrary surfaced, the administration claimed that waterboarding had been used on some suspects. The White House, and especially Vice President Dick Cheney, however, attempted to assert that the technique did not constitute torture.

Not all the news on the international scene was bad, however. After the departure of such neoconservatives as Rumsfeld and Deputy Secretary of Defense Paul Wolfowitz, Bush's foreign policy became more pragmatic and less dogmatic. Secretary of State Condoleezza Rice worked diligently to try to repair America's standing in the world, and she met with some success by the end of the administration. President Bush's 2003 Emergency Plan for AIDS Relief, a multibillion-dollar aid package to African nations hit hard by the AIDS epidemic, drew much praise in the United States and abroad.

By 2008, Bush's approval ratings were as low as any U.S. president in modern history. In the autumn the U.S. economy went into a virtual free fall, precipitated by a spectacular series of bank, insurance, and investment house failures and necessitating a massive government bailout worth more than $800 billion. Other corporate bailouts followed as more and more businesses teetered on the brink of insolvency. Unemployment began to rise dramatically in the fourth quarter of 2008, and consumer spending all but collapsed. The only bright note was a precipitous drop in the price of oil and gas, which had risen to dizzying heights in July 2008. Bush, a former oil man, and Vice President Cheney, who had also been in the petroleum-related business, had been excoriated for the run-up in energy prices, which certainly made the economic downturn even more severe. By the time Bush left office in January 2009, the nation was facing the worst economic downturn in at least 35 years.

The deep economic recession enabled the election of Democrat Barack Obama to the presidency in November 2008. He faced the daunting prospects of stabilizing the sinking economy, withdrawing all U.S. troops from Iraq, and reinvigorating the war in Afghanistan with an eye toward an American withdrawal from that country as quickly as possible.

Bush has kept an extraordinarily low profile since leaving office in January 2009. He has busied himself with building and organizing his presidential library, writing his memoirs, and participating in philanthropic work, including the Clinton-Bush Haiti Fund, which was created to help the residents of Haiti in the aftermath of a devastating earthquake in 2010. To his credit, Bush has steadfastly refused to criticize his successors in public, stating that to do so would not be "good for the country."

Tim J. Watts and Paul G. Pierpaoli Jr.

See also: Bush Doctrine; Cheney, Richard Bruce; Global War on Terrorism; Hussein, Saddam; Iraqi Freedom, Operation: The Surge and the Awakening; Obama, Barack Hussein, II; Secretary of Defense, U.S.: Donald Rumsfeld, Robert M. Gates; Secretary of State, U.S.: Colin L. Powell, Condoleezza Rice; Wolfowitz, Paul Dundes

References

Baker, Peter. *Days of Fire: Bush and Cheney in the White House.* New York: Anchor Books, 2014.

Daalder, Ivo H., and James M. Lindsay. *America Unbound: The Bush Revolution in Foreign Policy.* Washington, DC: Brookings Institution, 2003.

Singer, Peter. *The President of Good & Evil: The Ethics of George W. Bush.* New York: Dutton, 2004.

Woodward, Bob. *Bush at War.* New York: Simon and Schuster, 2002.

Woodward, Bob. *Plan of Attack.* New York: Simon and Schuster, 2004.

Woodward, Bob. *State of Denial: Bush at War, Part III.* New York: Simon and Schuster, 2006.

Woodward, Bob. *The War Within: A Secret White House History, 2006–2008.* New York: Simon and Schuster, 2008.

Bush Doctrine

The Bush Doctrine is a foreign/national security policy articulated by President George W. Bush in a series of speeches following the September 11, 2001, terrorist attacks on the United States. The Bush Doctrine identified three threats against U.S. interests: terrorist organizations, weak states that harbor and assist such terrorist organizations, and so-called rogue states. The centerpiece of the Bush Doctrine was that the United States had the right to use preemptory military force against any state that is seen as hostile or that makes moves to acquire weapons of mass destruction, be they nuclear, biological, or chemical. In addition, the United States would "make no distinction between the terrorists who commit these acts and those who harbor them."

The Bush Doctrine represented a major shift in American foreign policy from the policies of deterrence and containment that characterized the Cold War and the brief period between the collapse of the Soviet

Union in 1991 and 2001. This new foreign policy and security strategy emphasized the strategic doctrine of preemption, thus extending the right of self-defense to the use of force against potential enemies, attacking them before they were deemed capable of launching strikes against the United States. Under the doctrine, furthermore, the United States reserved the right to pursue unilateral military action if multilateral solutions cannot be found. The Bush Doctrine also represented the realities of international politics in the post–Cold War period, that is, that the United States was the sole superpower and aimed to ensure American hegemony.

A secondary goal of the Bush Doctrine was the promotion of freedom and democracy around the world, a precept that dates to at least the days of President Woodrow Wilson. In his speech to the graduating class at West Point on June 1, 2002, Bush declared that "America has no empire to extend or utopia to establish. We wish for others only what we wish for ourselves—safety from violence, the rewards of liberty, and the hope for a better life."

The immediate application of the Bush Doctrine was the invasion of Afghanistan in early October 2001 (Operation Enduring Freedom). Although the Taliban-controlled government of Afghanistan offered to hand over Al Qaeda leader Osama bin Laden if it was shown tangible proof that he was responsible for the September 11 attacks and also offered to extradite bin Laden to Pakistan, where he would be tried under Islamic law, its refusal to extradite him to the United States with no preconditions was considered justification for the invasion.

The administration also applied the Bush Doctrine as justification for the Iraq War, beginning in March 2003 (Operation Iraqi Freedom). The Bush administration did not wish to wait for conclusive proof of Saddam Hussein's weapons of mass destruction (WMD), so in a series of speeches, administration officials laid out the argument for invading Iraq. To wait any longer was to run the risk of having Hussein employ or transfer the alleged WMD. Thus, despite the lack of any evidence of an operational relationship between Iraq and Al Qaeda, the United States, supported by Britain and a few other states, launched an invasion of Iraq. In the end, after months of exhaustive searching, no active WMD program was discovered in Iraq. Likewise, no direct connections between the Saddam Hussein regime and Al Qaeda have ever been firmly established.

The use of the Bush Doctrine as justification for the invasion of Iraq led to increasing friction between the United States and its allies, as the Bush Doctrine repudiated the core idea of the United Nations (UN) Charter. The charter prohibits any use of international force that is not undertaken in self-defense after the occurrence of an armed attack across an international boundary or pursuant to a decision by the UN Security Council. Even more vexing, the distinct limitations and pitfalls of the Bush Doctrine were abundantly evident in the U.S. inability to quell sectarian violence and political turmoil in Afghanistan or Iraq. The doctrine did not place parameters on the extent of American commitments, and it viewed the consequences of preemptory military strikes as a mere afterthought. This could be most clearly seen in Iraq, which in 2006 was teetering on a full-blown civil war more than three years after the initial invasion. And by 2011, an Islamist insurgency in Afghanistan was steadily gaining ground, despite a major troop surge in that country that began in early 2010 under the Barack Obama administration.

Not surprisingly, the Obama administration, which began in January 2009, went to great lengths to distance itself from the Bush Doctrine. Obama sought to mend fences with disgruntled international friends and allies and emphasized the use of dialogue, diplomacy, and multilateral mechanisms to achieve foreign policy goals. When the Arab Spring swept through the Middle East beginning in late 2010, Obama was reluctant to use any force in the region, with the exception of air support (in concert with other nations) over the skies of Libya in 2011. Even amid irrefutable evidence that the Syrian government had employed chemical weapons to quash the civil war there in 2013, the Obama White House opted to engage the Syrian regime in an international plan to disarm it of such weapons rather than launch military strikes against it. Some criticized the avoidance of direct military engagement in Libya and Syria as perpetuating civil wars that may have been reduced with greater U.S. participation. Obama's detractors have argued that he backtracked too far from the preemptory Bush Doctrine and that his hesitant actions toward the ISIS threat allowed the group to ensconce itself in Iraq and Syria.

Keith A. Leitich

See also: Bush, George Walker; Cheney, Richard Bruce; Global War on Terrorism; Iraqi Freedom, Operation; Obama, Barack Hussein, II; Weapons of Mass Destruction

References

Baker, Peter. *Days of Fire: Bush and Cheney in the White House.* New York: Anchor Books, 2014.

Buckley, Mary E., and Robert Singh. *The Bush Doctrine and the War on Terrorism: Global Responses, Global Consequences.* London: Routledge, 2006.

Dolan, Chris J. *In War We Trust: The Bush Doctrine and the Pursuit of Just War.* Burlington, VA: Ashgate, 2005.

C

Casualties, Operation Iraqi Freedom

Casualties as a result of combat operations in Iraq during Operation Iraqi Freedom, which began on March 19, 2003, and ended on December 31, 2011, were a constant source of controversy, particularly in the United States. The quick and decisive victory won by the United States in the 1991 Persian Gulf War, which saw few American casualties, and the low initial American casualty count for the Afghanistan War, Operation Enduring Freedom, had conditioned U.S. citizens and politicians to expect a speedy and relatively easy victory in Iraq. Although the initial combat phase (March 19–April 30, 2003) produced few U.S. and coalition combat deaths, the subsequent insurgency led to several thousand more. Many responded to the mounting Iraqi Freedom casualty numbers with incredulity and calls for a full or total withdrawal of American troops from Iraq. Other nations with large troop deployments in Iraq—particularly Great Britain—experienced similar developments.

The U.S. Department of Defense provided a continuously running tally of American casualties. Its figures included numbers of American personnel killed in action and wounded in action in both official Operation Iraqi Freedom combat operations (March 19, 2003–April, 30, 2003) and postcombat operations (May 1, 2003–present). In the first phase of the war, 139 American military personnel were killed, and 545 were wounded. Total U.S. military deaths from both phases of Iraqi Freedom were 4,488 through the end of 2011, while the total number of American military personnel wounded in action during the same period was about 34,000. Of those wounded, a majority returned to active duty within 72 hours, classified as wounded in action, returned to duty. Each fatality milestone occasioned an outcry of opposition to the war, and when the casualty count topped 4,000 in the spring of 2008 and coincided with a particularly heated presidential primary campaign, these numbers became a source of even greater political controversy.

Air Force officers oversee the transport of coffins containing the remains of 20 U.S. servicemen killed during Operation Iraqi Freedom. The number of U.S. service members who were killed from 2003 to 2011 was 4,485; 4,555 were killed from 2003 to 2018. (U.S. Air Force)

In addition to the U.S. casualties, through December 15, 2011, a total of 318 coalition troops were killed, including 179 Britons. Also, the Iraq War claimed the lives of 139 journalists. More than 1,300 private contractors were also killed.

Although the Department of Defense makes information on U.S. casualties publicly available, precise figures documenting Iraqi casualties, both military and civilian, are more difficult to access, and nearly all figures come with caveats. Iraqi sources have reported that government agencies are not permitted to report the numbers of bodies buried daily. Credible sources indicate roughly 9,200 Iraqi combatant fatalities during the first phase of Operation Iraqi Freedom; estimates range from a low of 7,600 to a high of 10,800. According to the Iraq Coalition Casualty Count, by 2011 an estimated 8,825 members of the Iraqi Security Forces (ISF) had been killed in combat against Iraqi insurgents. The Iraq Coalition Casualty Count is one of the most thorough databases compiling this information, although the group does not provide numbers of wounded ISF personnel. Current and credible estimates of the number of insurgents killed are among the hardest statistics to obtain, because membership in those groups is both fluid and clandestine. According to calculations made in September 2007, the number of insurgents killed after the fall of Baghdad in April 2003 was 19,492; casualties continued to accumulate, although a reliably sourced updated estimate has not been released.

The number of Iraqi civilians killed during Iraqi Freedom has been widely disputed. The Lancet study of 2006, so called for its publication in the British medical journal of that name, was carried out by Iraqi and American physicians and researchers from al-Mustansiriyya University and Johns Hopkins University through a cluster survey of households where respondents had to show death certificates. The study estimated a total of 426,369 to 793,663 Iraqi deaths to that date. A third study by experts from the Federal Ministry of Health in Baghdad, the Kurdistan Ministry of Planning, the Kurdistan Ministry of Health, the Central Organization for Statistics and Information Technology in Baghdad, and the World Health Organization was carried out by the Iraq Family Health Survey (IFHS) Study Group (known as the WHO study in the media). The IFHS study estimated 151,000 Iraqi deaths from March 2003 to June 2006. The study actually presented a range of deaths from 104,000 to 223,000 for those years.

Other sources have estimated Iraqi civilian casualties from the war and sectarian violence as 600,000 to more than 1 million. The independent British-based Opinion Research Bureau estimated 1,220,580 Iraqis deaths by September 2007. Other than deliberate underreporting, some sources pointed to the suppression of statistics by the Iraqi government in the belief that to do so would compromise efforts to quell violence. In 2013, a study conducted by U.S. university researchers estimated the total number of civilian deaths (2003–2011) in Iraq to have been 461,000. This included deaths from all causes but related directly or indirectly to the ground war and subsequent insurgency.

Although there is great disagreement on the actual number of civilian deaths in Iraq, there is general agreement that the numbers were very high. Generally speaking, those who supported the war have denied the higher civilian casualty counts, while those who opposed the war held them to be valid.

The Iraq Coalition Casualty Count serves as a thorough clearinghouse for information on all coalition fatalities. During the period of official Iraqi Freedom combat

(March 19–May 1, 2003), 33 soldiers from the United Kingdom were killed; no other coalition nation suffered any fatalities during this phase of operations. The Iraq Coalition Casualty Count cites the following fatality numbers for other coalition nations as of the end of 2011, when the operation officially ended: Australia, 2; Azerbaijan, 1; Bulgaria, 13; Czech Republic, 1; Denmark, 7; El Salvador, 5; Estonia, 2; Fiji, 1; Georgia, 5; Hungary, 1; Italy, 33; Kazakhstan, 1; Latvia, 3; Netherlands, 2; Poland, 23; Romania, 3; Slovakia, 4; South Korea, 1; Spain, 11; Thailand, 2; Ukraine, 18; and United Kingdom, 179. The group does not provide wounded in action casualty figures.

A high suicide rate among U.S. military and veterans has become a special matter of concern. Although no clear answers for this have emerged, it has been attributed to extended tours, too little time off between tours, the nature of the conflict, circumstances at home, and other factors.

Periodic lulls in violence and the achievement of certain strategic objectives resulted in temporary decreases in the rates of injury and death, but the nature of the guerrilla-style low-intensity conflict that characterized the Iraq War and the sectarian conflicts that continue to plague Iraq mean that Iraqi casualties will continue to accumulate.

Rebecca Adelman and Sherifa Zuhur

See also: Iraqi Freedom, Operation

References

Baker, James A., III, and Lee Hamilton. *The Iraq Study Group: The Way Forward, a New Approach.* New York: Vintage Books, 2006.

Burnham, Gilbert, Riyadh Lafta, Shannon Doocy, et al. "Mortality after the 2003 Invasion of Iraq: A Cross-Sectional Cluster Sample Survey." *Lancet* 368(5945) (October 21, 2006): 1421–1429.

Capdevila, Luc, and Danièle Voldman. *War Dead: Western Society and Casualties of War.* Translated by Richard Veasey. Edinburgh, UK: Edinburgh University Press, 2006.

"Documented Civilian Deaths from Violence." Iraq Body Count, http://www.iraqbodycount.org/database.

Fischer, Hanna. "Iraqi Civilian Casualties Estimates." Washington, DC: Congressional Research Service, January 12, 2009.

Iraq Family Health Survey Study Group. "Violence-Related Mortality in Iraq from 2002 to 2006." *New England Journal of Medicine* (January 31, 2008): 484–492.

Mueller, John. "The Iraq Syndrome." *Foreign Affairs* 84 (2005): 44–54.

"Operation IRAQI FREEDOM." Iraq Coalition Casualty Count, http://icasualties.org/Iraq/index.aspx.

"Operation Iraqi Freedom (OIF) U.S. Casualty Status." United States Department of Defense, http://www.defenselink.mil/news/casualty.pdf.

Roberts, Les, Riyadh Lafta, Richard Garfield, et al. "Mortality before and after the 2003 Invasion of Iraq: Cluster Sample Survey." *Lancet* 364(9448) (October 29, 2004): 1857–1864.

Wood, Trish. *What Was Asked of Us: An Oral History of the Iraq War by the Soldiers Who Fought It.* New York: Little, Brown, 2006.

Cheney, Richard Bruce (1941–)

Politician, businessman, secretary of defense (1989–1993), and vice president (2001–2009). Richard Bruce "Dick" Cheney was born on January 30, 1941, in Lincoln, Nebraska. He grew up in Casper, Wyoming, and was educated at the University of Wyoming, earning a BA in 1965 and an MA in political science in 1966. He completed advanced graduate study there and was a PhD candidate in 1968.

Cheney, Richard Bruce

Richard Cheney served as secretary of defense (1989–1993) during Operation Desert Storm in 1991. He was vice president of the United States during 2001–2009. He was a prime mover behind the decision to invade Iraq in 2003. (White House)

Cheney acquired his first governmental position in 1969 when he became the special assistant to the director of the Office of Economic Opportunity. He served as a White House staff assistant in 1970 and 1971 and as assistant director of the Cost of Living Council from 1971 to 1973. He briefly worked in the private sector as the vice president of an investment advisory firm. In 1974, he returned to government service as President Gerald R. Ford's deputy assistant. In 1975, Ford appointed Cheney as White House chief of staff.

In 1978 Cheney was elected to the U.S. House of Representatives, serving six terms. He was elected House minority whip in December 1988. Cheney was known for his conservative votes: he opposed gun control, environmental laws, and funding for Head Start.

Cheney became secretary of defense on March 21, 1989, in the George H. W. Bush administration. In this position, Cheney significantly reduced U.S. military budgets and canceled several major weapons programs. In addition, in the wake of the Cold War he was deeply involved in the politically volatile task of reducing the size of the American military force throughout the world. Cheney also recommended closing or reducing in size many U.S. military installations, despite intense criticism from elected officials whose districts would be adversely impacted by the closures.

As secretary of defense, Cheney also provided strong leadership in several international military engagements, including the December 1989 Panama invasion and the humanitarian mission to Somalia in early 1992. It was Cheney who secured the appointment of General Colin Powell as chairman of the Joint Chiefs of Staff in 1989.

Cheney's most difficult military challenge came during the 1991 Persian Gulf War. He secured Saudi permission to begin a military buildup there that would include a United Nations (UN) international coalition of troops. The buildup proceeded in the autumn of 1990 as Operation Desert Shield. When economic sanctions and other measures failed to remove the Iraqis from Kuwait, the Persian Gulf War commenced with Operation Desert Storm on January 16, 1991. A five-week air offensive was followed by the movement of ground forces into Kuwait and Iraq on February 24, 1991. Within four days, the UN coalition had liberated Kuwait. Cheney continued as secretary of defense until January 20, 1993, when Democrat Bill Clinton took office.

Upon leaving the Pentagon, Cheney joined the American Enterprise Institute as a senior fellow. He also became president and chief executive officer of the Halliburton

Company in October 1995 and chairman of its board in February 2000.

Only months later, Republican presidential candidate George W. Bush chose Cheney as his vice presidential running mate. After a hard-fought campaign and a controversial election, the Bush-Cheney ticket won the White House in December 2000.

Arguably one of the more powerful vice presidents in U.S. history, Cheney endured much criticism for his hawkish views (he is believed to have strongly promoted the Iraq War) and his connections to the oil industry (Halliburton won several lucrative contracts for work in postwar Iraq). He also raised eyebrows by refusing to make public the records of the national energy task force he established to form the administration's energy initiatives.

Many people who knew Cheney personally have asserted that he became a changed man after the September 11, 2001, terrorist attacks. He became, they say, far more secretive, more hawkish than ever before, and, some say, even paranoid, seeing terrorists everywhere. As one of the principal promoters of the U.S. invasion of Iraq (Operation Iraqi Freedom), which began in March 2003, Cheney was well placed to receive the burden of criticism when the war began to go badly in 2004. As the subsequent Iraqi insurgency increased in size, scope, and violence, Cheney's popularity plummeted. Following the 2006 midterm elections, which caused the Republicans to lose control of Congress principally because of the Iraq War, Cheney took a far lower profile. When his fellow neoconservative Donald Rumsfeld, the secretary of defense, resigned in the election's aftermath, Cheney was increasingly perceived as a liability to the Bush White House, which was under intense pressure to change course in Iraq or quit it altogether.

Cheney did not help his approval ratings when he accidentally shot a friend during a hunting trip in February 2006, and the information was slow to be released. Even more damaging to Cheney was the indictment and conviction of his chief of staff, I. Lewis "Scooter" Libby, for his involvement in the case involving Joseph Wilson and his wife Valerie Plame Wilson, whose identity as a CIA operative was leaked. Some alleged that it was Cheney who first leaked the classified information to Libby and perhaps others, who in turn leaked it to the press. Cheney continued to keep a remarkably low profile. Beginning in 2007, a small group of Democrats in the House attempted to introduce impeachment proceedings against Cheney, but such efforts did not make it out of committee.

Since his retirement from politics in January 2009, Cheney has published a memoir and delivered a number of speeches, mainly to conservative groups. His precarious health has prevented him from taking on larger roles, but he was a consistent and vocal critic of the Barack Obama administration, even suggesting at one point that Obama's policies were making the United States less safe during the Global War on Terrorism.

Paul G. Pierpaoli Jr.

See also: Bush, George Walker; Global War on Terrorism; Iraqi Freedom, Operation; Secretary of Defense, U.S.: Donald Rumsfeld

References

Baker, Peter. *Days of Fire: Bush and Cheney in the White House.* New York: Anchor Books, 2014.

Nichols, John. *The Rise and Rise of Richard B. Cheney: Unlocking the Mysteries of the Most Powerful Vice President in American History.* New York: New Press, 2005.

Woodward, Bob. *Bush at War.* New York: Simon and Schuster, 2002.

Woodward, Bon. *Plan of Attack*. New York: Simon and Schuster, 2004.

Woodward, Bob. *State of Denial: Bush at War, Part III*. New York: Simon and Schuster, 2006.

Woodward, Bob. *The War Within: A Secret White House History, 2006–2008*. New York: Simon and Schuster, 2008.

Coalition Provisional Authority

Established on April 21, 2003, after Saddam Hussein's ouster, the Coalition Provisional Authority (CPA) was the head diplomatic and administrative office for the coalition occupation of Iraq. It was both an international body and an agency of the U.S. government. L. Paul Bremer, head of the CPA, would become associated with two of the most noteworthy actions of the early occupation: the de-Baathification policy and the decision to dissolve the Iraqi military. These two events ultimately spurred the insurgency in Iraq and affected the occupation throughout the remainder of the conflict. The CPA existed until June 28, 2004, when Iraq became a fully sovereign nation upon the authority's dissolution.

The CPA replaced the Office of Reconstruction and Humanitarian Assistance, headed by Jay Garner. The CPA had the approval of the United Nations (UN) Security Council through its resolutions 1483 and 1511, which recognized the occupation authority of both the United States and Britain. These resolutions made the CPA the official organization in charge of administering the occupation. Under U.S. law, the CPA derived its authority from the Emergency Supplemental Appropriations Act for Defense and for the Reconstruction of Iraq and Afghanistan, which was passed in 2003. This meant that the CPA had both international and U.S. authorization to create and implement policies to direct the actions of American and international forces in Iraq.

The CPA had direct oversight of many domestic departments, including the directors of oil policy, civil affairs policy, economic policy, regional operations, security affairs, and communications. In addition, the CPA had a general counsel consisting of a military staff, an operations support group, an executive secretariat, a strategic policy office, and a financial oversight group. It also had its own intelligence organization. Bremer had authority over the chair of the International Coordination Council, the body that organized humanitarian assistance from nongovernmental organizations and the UN.

One problem with the organization of the CPA was the lack of direct control over military forces in Iraq. Although Bremer was the senior U.S. civilian in the nation, he did not have any direct military authority. He could not order military forces to focus on any particular region or conduct any specific type of mission. He could coordinate or communicate his requirements, and although he was the head U.S. and international official in Iraq, he had no command authority. This meant that the CPA had difficulty achieving one of its major objectives, which was the provisioning of security, governance, economic, and essential services.

Iraqis did participate in the CPA, albeit in a limited fashion. The Iraqi Governing Council (IGC) acted as an advisory body to the CPA. The IGC could not veto legislation and initially functioned as more of a pro forma approval body. A point of concern was that Bremer's policies carried the full weight of law inside Iraq; this caused much frustration in the IGC. However, as the CPA's administration in Iraq continued, the IGC grew more confident and began to demand more input and authority over policies and laws considered by the CPA. This led to a deterioration of the CPA's efficiency but an increase in Iraqi sovereignty.

The first actions of the CPA included changes to the nation's currency, dissolution of the military, and elimination of Baath Party officials from most government posts. The two most problematic policies—the dissolution of the military and the de-Baathification policy—did not go through any Iraqi legislative process. The de-Baathification and dissolution of the military policies were the most far-reaching of the CPA policies and had serious second- and third-order effects on the future of the occupation mission in Iraq.

The decision to destroy the Baath Party came on May 16, 2003. This order was the first Bremer gave as head of the organization. The actual decision to remove party officials from government posts and destroy the Baath Party came from Washington. Douglas Fieth, head of the Department of Defense Office of Special Plans, drafted the policy. Supporters of the policy included Iraqi exiles, Shia groups, and Kurds inside Iraq. For these groups, the Baath Party represented the worst of the Saddam Hussein regime and was inextricably linked to the horror of his rule.

When Bremer announced the policy, he included a caveat that his office could issue exemptions. Many Sunnis feared that de-Baathification would turn into a sectarian program to remove Sunnis from government posts and other positions of influence. The de-Baathification policy also overlooked the reality of life in Iraq and the power of the Baath Party. Many Iraqis under Hussein had to join the party in order to keep their jobs, earn promotions in government service, or get hired for certain government positions. Although Bremer's authority allowed him to offer exemptions, this would prove difficult. If he was too lenient, the policy would not have the desired effect. If he was too hard, he would alienate many of the Sunnis in the country and drive them away from participation in a new Iraq.

The dissolution of the Iraqi military was the second of Bremer's most influential decisions. This policy immediately left approximately 400,000 people unemployed. It also discounted the almost cult-like status that the Iraqi military had in the culture of Iraq. The military was the body that protected the nation from Iran and protected the Arab world from the threat of Persian invasion. Under Hussein, the military was a force that unified the people of Iraq. Dissolving this organization was a blow not only to the almost half a million soldiers employed by it but also to the identity of Iraq as a nation.

The CPA was short-lived; it ended its existence on June 28, 2004, with the resumption of full Iraqi sovereignty. It then turned over authority to the Iraqi Interim Government. However, the CPA did not leave the new government of Iraq a smooth path forward as it struggled to deal with the budding insurgency and growing sectarian strife.

Gates Brown

See also: Baath Party; Bremer, Lewis Paul, III; Garner, Jay Montgomery; Hussein, Saddam; Iraq, History of, 1990–Present

References

Allawi, Ali. *The Occupation of Iraq: Winning the War.* New Haven, CT: Yale University Press, 2007.

Bensahel, Nora. *After Saddam: Prewar Planning and the Occupation of Iraq.* Santa Monica, CA: RAND Arroyo Center, 2008.

Sanchez, Ricardo, and Donald Philips. *Wiser in Battle: A Soldier's Story.* New York: HarperCollins, 2008.

Commanders, Multi-National Force–Iraq (or United States Forces–Iraq) (Chronological Order)

The same comments could be made here as in the entry on Commanders, U.S. Central Command (CENTCOM) as the role and expectation of a commander and the laws relating to senior officers in the U.S. military are the same. I direct a reader to that entry.

Command of Multi-National Force–Iraq (MNF-I) or United States Forces–Iraq (USF-I) did not follow any traditional or standard approach to command normally practiced by the U.S. military. General Casey was sent in to get the United States out of Iraq. General Petraeus was sent to deal with the "civil war." General Odierno was sent in to continue General Petraeus's policies while Petraeus took over CENTCOM. General Austin was sent in to close everything down.

The command was exclusively given to U.S. Army officers. It is safe to say that there was no initial intent to stand up the command from the inception of the invasion of Iraq. The idea was that the U.S.-led coalition would defeat Iraqi military forces, quickly establish an Iraqi-led government, and then withdraw from the country. It was only after it became clear that this plan would not work that the four-star command took form. It was created with the U.S. Army vice chief of staff taking command—an ad hoc commander for an ad hoc command.

The first commander discussed was not a commander of MNF-I at all, but he was the first commander of the ground combat mission postinvasion. All of the other commanders were designated as commanders of MNF-I or USF-I.

- Lieutenant General Ricardo S. Sanchez, U.S. Army
  May 15, 2003–June 4, 2004
- General George W. Casey Jr., U.S. Army
  June 4, 2004–February 10, 2007
- General David Petraeus, U.S. Army
  February 10, 2007–September 16, 2008
- General Raymond T. Odierno, U.S. Army
  September 15, 2008–September 1, 2010
- General Lloyd J. Austin III, U.S. Army
  September 1, 2010–December 18, 2011

Ricardo S. Sanchez (1951–) (Commander from May 15, 2003, to June 4, 2004)

U.S. Army officer best known for his command of coalition forces in Iraq from May 2003 to June 2004 (Operation Iraqi Freedom). Born on May 17, 1951, in Rio Grande City, Texas, Ricardo S. Sanchez began his military career in the Reserve Officers' Training Corps program at the University of Texas at Austin and Texas A&I University (now Texas A&M–Kingsville). A 1973 graduate of the latter institution, Sanchez was commissioned in the U.S. Army as a second lieutenant that same year. He served in both infantry and armor units early in his career. He was a platoon leader, an executive officer, an assistant logistics officer, and an operations officer. Sanchez's military education included both the Command and General Staff College and the U.S. Army War College. He also earned a master's degree in operations research and systems analysis engineering from the Naval Postgraduate School.

As a lieutenant colonel, Sanchez served in Operation Desert Storm in 1991 as commander of the 2nd Battalion, 69th Armor, 197th Infantry Brigade. His performance in the Persian Gulf War contributed to his early promotion to colonel in September 1994. From July 1994 to June 1996 he commanded the 2nd Brigade of the 1st Infantry Division (Mechanized) at Fort Riley, Kansas.

Sanchez then served as an investigator in the Office of the U.S. Army Inspector General Agency and in various roles at the U.S. Southern Command. After promotion to brigadier general in November 1998, Sanchez served as assistant division commander (support) of the 1st Infantry Division during 1999–2000. From July 2000 to June 2001 he was deputy chief of staff for operations, U.S. Army Europe and Seventh Army, Germany. During July 2001–June 2003 he commanded the 1st Armored Division, being promoted to major general in July 2002. Promoted to lieutenant general in August 2003, from July 2003 to June 2004 he was the commanding general of V Corps, U.S. Army Europe and Seventh Army, Germany, to include duty as commanding general, Combined Joint Task Force 7, Operation Iraqi Freedom.

With the rapid withdrawal of U.S. Central Command (CENTCOM) and its Combined Forces Land Component Command (CFLCC), Sanchez by default became the commander of Coalition Ground Forces in Iraq, the top military position in Iraq. This critical period after the end of major hostilities saw the emergence of the Iraqi insurgency, the deaths of Uday and Qusay Hussein, and the capture of deposed Iraqi president Saddam Hussein. The major challenges facing Sanchez were the reestablishment of essential services and basic security and ending the counterinsurgency. According to multiple sources, communications between Sanchez and L. Paul Bremer, head of the Coalition Provisional Authority, were strained and often nonexistent. This poor communication and lack of unified leadership is often cited as one of the contributors to the turmoil that followed the end of major conflict in Iraq. Compounding Sanchez's problems during this period was the fact that he was essentially a corps commander with little more than a corps staff yet was responsible for commanding an entire theater. With the vacuum created by the rapid withdrawal of the CFLCC, Sanchez was left with a staff that was nowhere near large enough for his responsible span of control or trained and experienced at the higher level of theater operations.

Despite progress in certain areas, this period of Iraqi Freedom was marked by a burgeoning insurgency, widespread lawlessness, and the challenge of detaining thousands of prisoners. The most glaring controversy during Sanchez's tenure was the prisoner abuse at Abu Ghraib prison. In September 2003 Sanchez approved in writing 29 interrogation methods authorized for use with Iraqi detainees. At the direction of CENTCOM, 10 of those methods were later repealed after having been deemed unacceptably aggressive. However, the actual methods employed at Abu Ghraib went beyond even what Sanchez had authorized, as evidenced by the graphic photographs that were ultimately seen on worldwide media. On January 16, 2004, Sanchez issued a press release announcing the investigation of "detainee abuse at a Coalition Forces detention facility."

Sanchez left his post in June 2004. Ultimately, several low-ranking military members were court-martialed over the abuse scandal, and Sanchez believed that he was denied his fourth star and was forced into retirement on November 1, 2006, because of it.

In 2008 Sanchez published his autobiography, *Wiser in Battle: A Soldier's Story,* a sweeping indictment of the handling of the

Iraq War by Defense Secretary Donald Rumsfeld and the George W. Bush administration. Sanchez now lives in Texas. In 2012, he hoped to run as a Democrat for an open U.S. Senate seat representing Texas but ultimately withdrew from the race for personal reasons.

Benjamin D. Forest

See also: Bremer, Lewis Paul, III; Coalition Provisional Authority; Commanders, Multi-National Force–Iraq: George W. Casey Jr.; Detention Operations, Coalition: Abu Ghraib; Iraq, History of, 1990–Present; Iraqi Freedom, Operation: Planning for Operations, Coalition Ground Forces, Ground Campaign, Major Battles; Secretary of Defense, U.S.: Donald Rumsfeld

References

Gordon, Michael R., and General Bernard E. Trainor. *Cobra II: The Inside Story of the Invasion and Occupation of Iraq.* New York: Pantheon Books, 2006.

Ricks, Thomas E. *Fiasco: The American Military Adventure in Iraq.* New York: Penguin, 2006.

Sanchez, Ricardo S., and Donald T. Phillips. *Wiser in Battle: A Soldier's Story.* New York: Harper, 2008.

George W. Casey Jr. (1948–) (Commander from June 4, 2004, to February 10, 2007)

U.S. Army general, commander of U.S. forces in Iraq (Multi-National Force–Iraq) during 2004–2007, and army chief of staff from 2007 until 2011. George William Casey Jr. was born on July 22, 1948, in Sendai, Japan; his father, a career army officer, was serving with the army occupation forces there. (His father, Major General George William Casey Sr., died in Vietnam in 1970 in a helicopter crash.) Casey spent his early life on army posts throughout the United States and Europe and graduated from Georgetown University in 1970, where he was enrolled in the U.S. Army Reserve Officers' Training Corps.

In August 1970, Casey was commissioned a second lieutenant in the army. During the next decade he served in a variety of command and staff positions. In 1980, he earned an MA in international relations from the University of Denver. Casey continued his military education at the Armed Forces Staff College, completing his studies there in July 1981.

Shortly thereafter Casey was ordered to the Middle East, where he worked with the United Nations Truce Observer Supervision Organization. From February 1982 to July 1987 he was assigned to the 4th Infantry Division based at Fort Carson, Colorado. In December 1989, he became a special assistant to the army chief of staff. He was then assigned as chief of staff of the 1st Cavalry Division at Fort Hood, Texas, where he later commanded that division's 3rd Brigade. In July 1996 he was promoted to brigadier general and sent to Europe, where he served as assistant commander for the 1st Armored Division in Germany and participated in the peacekeeping missions to Bosnia and Herzegovina.

In 1999 following his advancement to major general, Casey commanded the 1st Armored Division until July 2001. At the end of October 2001 he was appointed lieutenant general and took control of strategic plans and policy for the Joint Chiefs of Staff. In January 2003 he became director, Joint Staff of the Joint Chiefs of Staff. That October, he became vice chief of staff of the army and was advanced to four-star rank.

Casey became a major figure in planning for the U.S. response to the terrorist attacks of September 11, 2001, and for the 2003 invasion of Iraq. As director of the Joint Staff, he had been directly involved in the allocation of units and personnel for the Iraq operation. One of his assignments was the allocation of military personnel for administration in the occupied areas. In December 2002 with planning for the invasion in full swing, Casey ordered the formation of a follow-on headquarters for the postwar occupation but gave it few resources. It was in his capacity as director of the Joint Staff that Casey first encountered conflict over troop levels for the impending invasion, which occurred between the field commanders and Secretary of Defense Donald Rumsfeld.

Conditions in Iraq in the wake of the March 2003 invasion became central to Casey's fortunes. For all of his success, Casey had attracted little notice outside military circles. This changed when he was assigned to head the commission to investigate the abuse of prisoners by American guards at Abu Ghraib prison in late 2003.

In the summer of 2004, Casey was appointed to command U.S. and coalition forces (Multi-National Force–Iraq). By the time he took command the Iraqi insurgency was in full swing, but the coalition response had been hampered by fundamental conflicts over strategy and tactics between the civilian commissioner in Iraq, L. Paul Bremer, and the military commander, General Ricardo Sanchez. Casey soon established a cordial working relationship with the new American ambassador to Iraq, John Negroponte.

Such a relationship was needed in the desperate situation the two men faced in 2004. Casey was shocked to discover that there was no counterinsurgency strategy. He and Negroponte thus worked to develop a coherent approach to combating the growing attacks on American forces and the threat of civil war. Casey's strategy involved securing transportation infrastructure, containing insurgent violence by aggressively attacking insurgent bases, reaching out to Iraq's Sunni Muslims, and building up Iraqi Security Forces. Under Casey's direction, U.S. counterinsurgency operations took on a clearer direction, but violence in Iraq continued to escalate, and the war grew profoundly unpopular in the United States.

In March 2007, Casey turned over his command to Lieutenant General David Petraeus and returned to the United States to assume the post of U.S. Army chief of staff. Casey was cautious but noncommittal in his support of the troop surge implemented by the George W. Bush administration in January 2007. Casey also warned that U.S. Army resources were being stretched dangerously thin by the concurrent wars in Iraq and Afghanistan.

As army chief of staff, Casey engaged in a successful modernization program that permitted the U.S. Army to become more efficient and responsive to 21st-century challenges. He presided over a modest growth of the force, introduced troop rotations that had been used successfully by the U.S. Marine Corps, and improved the readiness and training of both the Army Reserves and the Army National Guard. Casey left his post on April 11, 2011, at which time he retired from active duty. He subsequently moved to his boyhood hometown in Massachusetts.

Walter F. Bell

See also: Ambassadors to Iraq, U.S.: John D. Negroponte; Bremer, Lewis Paul, III; Coalition Provisional Authority; Commanders, Multi-National Force–Iraq: David H. Petraeus, Ricardo Sanchez; Detention Operations, Coalition: Abu Ghraib; Iraq, History of, 1990–Present; Iraqi Freedom, Operation:

Coalition Ground Forces, Major Battles; Secretary of Defense, U.S.: Donald Rumsfeld; Sunni Islam

References

Casey, George. *Strategic Reflections: Operation Iraqi Freedom, July 2004–February 2007.* Washington, DC: National Defense University Press, 2012.

Gordon, Michael R., and General Bernard E. Trainor. *Cobra II: The Inside Story of the Invasion and Occupation of Iraq.* New York: Pantheon Books, 2006.

Ricks, Thomas E. *Fiasco: The American Military Adventure in Iraq.* New York: Penguin, 2006.

Woodward, Bob. *State of Denial: Bush at War, Part III.* New York: Simon and Schuster, 2006.

Woodward, Bob. *The War within: A Secret White House History, 2006–2008.* New York: Simon and Schuster, 2008.

David H. Petraeus (1952–).
See Commanders, U.S. Central Command entry (Commander from February 10, 2007, to September 16, 2008)

Raymond T. Odierno (1954–) (Commander from September 16, 2008, to September 1, 2010)

U.S. Army general who served as commander of Multi-National Force–Iraq (MNF-I) from 2008 until 2010 and served as U.S. Army chief of staff from 2011 until 2015. Born in Rockaway, New Jersey, on September 8, 1954, Raymond Odierno graduated from the U.S. Military Academy, West Point, in 1976 and was commissioned in the field artillery. During his career, he earned a master's degree in nuclear effects engineering from North Carolina State University and another

U.S. Army general David Petraeus commanded the Multi-National Force–Iraq during 2007–2008 and then commanded the U.S. Central Command (CENTCOM) from 2008 to 2010. He is credited with leading the surge of U.S. troops along with the implementation of a new counterinsurgency doctrine that turned the direction of the war. (U.S. Army)

in national security and strategy from the Naval War College.

Odierno's initial tours of duty took him to the Federal Republic of Germany, where he served as platoon leader and survey officer of the 1st Battalion, 41st Field Artillery, 56th Field Artillery Brigade, as well as aide-de-camp to the brigade's commanding general. Following completion of the Field Artillery Officer Advanced Course at Fort Sill, Oklahoma, Odierno was assigned to the XVIII Airborne Corps Artillery at Fort Bragg, North Carolina, where he commanded a battery and served as S3 in the 1st Battalion, 73rd Field Artillery. Additionally, upon completion of his master's degree in nuclear effects engineering, he served as arms control officer for the Office of the Secretary of Defense. During Operations Desert Shield and Desert Storm, Odierno was the executive officer of the 2nd Battalion, 3rd Field Artillery, and then held the same position in the Division Artillery of the 3rd Armored Division.

Following Desert Storm, Odierno went on to command the 2nd Battalion, 8th Field Artillery, 7th Infantry Division, during 1992–1994. After attending the Army War College and being promoted to colonel, he commanded the Division Artillery, 1st Cavalry Division, during 1995–1997. Following an assignment at the Army War College in Carlisle Barracks, Pennsylvania, he served as chief of staff, V Corps, U.S. Army Europe, and assistant division commander (support) of the 1st Armored Division, during which time he acted as deputy commanding general of Task Force Hawk, Albania. Upon promotion to brigadier general in July 1999, he became the director of force management in the Office of the Deputy Chief of Staff for Operations and Plans in the Pentagon.

From October 2001 to June 2004, Odierno commanded the 4th Infantry Division (Mechanized) at Fort Hood, Texas. Promoted to major general in November 2002, he deployed with his division to participate in Operation Iraqi Freedom from March 2003 to April 2004. Originally, the division planned to enter Iraq from the north through Turkey; however, the Turkish government refused permission to move the unit through its territory, and the division deployed into Iraq through Kuwait. Subsequently, the 4th Infantry Division acted as a follow-on force and conducted operations in the Sunni Triangle north of Baghdad.

In December 2003 Odierno's troops captured deposed Iraqi dictator Saddam Hussein. Despite this success, Odierno's area of responsibility, which centered on Tikrit and Mosul, experienced ever-increasing insurgent violence. Subsequently, some critics characterized as overly heavy-handed Odierno's attempts to suppress the growing insurgency through confrontational armed measures, thereby driving some Iraqis into the insurgent fold. He has since argued that these measures were justified, as similar tactics had been successfully employed to suppress radical insurgents, notably Al Qaeda in Iraq, in 2007.

Upon his return to the United States in August 2004, Odierno served briefly as special assistant to the vice chief of staff of the army. From October 2004 until May 2006, he was the assistant to the chairman of the Joint Chiefs of Staff, serving as military adviser to Secretary of State Condoleezza Rice. He was promoted to lieutenant general in January 2005.

In May 2006 Odierno took command of III Corps at Fort Hood, Texas, assuming command of MNC-I on December 14, 2006, the second most senior command position in Operation Iraqi Freedom responsible for implementing the campaign plan of the MNF-I commanding general. Shortly thereafter, General David Petraeus assumed command of MNF-I and implemented a thorough revision of strategy emphasizing counterinsurgency operations in conjunction with his rewriting of army doctrine on counterinsurgency.

In February 2007 Odierno launched Operation Enforcing the Law, also known as the Baghdad Security Plan. U.S. and Iraqi troops were dispersed throughout Baghdad and maintained a continual presence to establish security for its inhabitants through a system of joint security stations. His subsequent operations were aimed to deny Al Qaeda in Iraq its operational sanctuaries throughout the various provinces and to deny it an opportunity to regroup. The so-called Awakening Councils in Anbar Province aided these efforts.

Following rotation back to Fort Hood in February 2008, Odierno was selected to succeed Petraeus as commanding general of MNF-I. Odierno assumed that position on September 16, 2008, with promotion to full general. In that post, he was responsible for overseeing the continuation of the George W. Bush administration's troop surge strategy, which was credited with having significantly reduced violence and sectarian strife in Iraq, at least for a time. Odierno remained commander in Iraq when MNF-I was reorganized as the United States Forces–Iraq on January 1, 2010, and thus began to implement the gradual drawdown of American forces in Iraq, a process that was completed in December 2011. Odierno left Iraq in August 2010, at which time he became commander of the United States Joint Forces Command. On September 7, 2011, he became chief of staff of the U.S. Army, a post he held until his retirement from the army in August 2015.

Karl Lee Rubis

See also: Commanders, U.S. Central Command: David H. Petraeus; Doctrine, Counterinsurgency; Iraqi Freedom, Operation: Major Battles, The Surge and the Awakening; Islamic State of Iraq and al-Sham (ISIS); Phantom Thunder, Operation; Prime Minister, Iraq: Nuri al-Maliki

References

Kagan, Frederick W., and Kimberly Kagan. "The Patton of Counterinsurgency." *Weekly Standard* 13 (2008): 27–33.

Ricks, Thomas E. *Fiasco: The American Military Adventure in Iraq.* New York: Penguin, 2006.

Sky, Emma. *The Unravelling: High Hopes and Missed Opportunities in Iraq.* New York: PublicAffairs, 2015.

Woodward, Bob. *The War Within: A Secret White House History, 2006–2008.* New York: Simon and Schuster, 2008.

Lloyd J. Austin III (1953–) (Commander from September 1, 2010, to December 18, 2011)

U.S. Army general and commander of the U.S. Central Command (CENTCOM) from March 22, 2013, to March 30, 2016. Lloyd James Austin III was born on August 8, 1953, in Mobile, Alabama. He graduated from the U.S. Military Academy in 1975 and was commissioned as a second lieutenant. Austin was the 3rd Infantry Division Assistant Division Commander–Maneuver (ADC-M) for the 2003 invasion into Iraq. He later commanded Combined Joint Task Force 180 in Afghanistan. He maintained his Middle East focus as the CENTCOM chief of staff. He became the XVIII Airborne Corps commander and, in that position, became the Multi-National Corps–Iraq commander for 2008–2009. He returned to Iraq in 2010 to take over the position as the commander United States Forces–Iraq (USF-I) on September 1, 2010. This was a position he retained until the withdrawal of USF-I on December 18, 2011. Each of these command and staff opportunities gave him significant experience in conducting combat in the Middle East. Austin is the first African American commander of CENTCOM.

While serving as commander of USF-I, Austin oversaw the transfer from Operation Iraqi Freedom to Operation New Dawn on October 1, 2010—the end of combat operations in Iraq. At least this was the intended purpose of the change in operational name. Austin dealt with closing of hundreds of outposts and bases throughout Iraq and the transfer of all operational responsibilities from USF-I to the Iraqi Security Forces.

Austin was CENTCOM commander during the rise of ISIS in Syria and then the ISIS invasion into Iraq. He oversaw the initiation of Operation Inherent Resolve to fight ISIS in both Syria and Iraq. An infamous U.S. Senate hearing had Austin admitting that only four or five Syrian rebel fighters who had been trained were still operational. This admission spelled the end of the Pentagon-run program for training Syrian anti-ISIS fighters and a reemphasis on supporting Kurdish fighters in Syria.

Brian L. Steed

See also: Baath Party; Commanders, Multi-National Force–Iraq: Raymond T. Odierno; Commanders, U.S. Central Command: Tommy Franks, William J. Fallon; Iraqi Freedom, Operation: Major Battles, The Surge and the Awakening; Islamic State of Iraq and al-Sham (ISIS); Obama, Barack Hussein, II; Prime Minister, Iraq: Nuri al-Maliki; Secretary of Defense, U.S.: Robert M. Gates

References

Cockburn, Patrick. *The Occupation: War and Resistance in Iraq.* New York: Verso, 2007.

Gordon, Michael R., and General Bernard E. Trainor. *Cobra II: The Inside Story of the Invasion and Occupation of Iraq.* New York: Pantheon Books, 2006.

Ricks, Thomas E. *Fiasco: The American Military Adventure in Iraq.* New York: Penguin, 2006.

Commanders, U.S. Central Command (CENTCOM) (Chronological Order)

A commander is responsible for everything that happens or fails to happen within his or her command's purview. This military leadership truism means that the men explained below are responsible for the bulk of the fighting in Afghanistan and Iraq. By U.S. law, there is no permanent military rank above that of major general or two-star general. Each lieutenant general or general must be nominated for each position and approved by the U.S. Congress for the person to retain the rank. Typically, command of CENTCOM was for two years with some commanders being renominated for an additional two-year period. As will be noted in the entries that follow, this was not always the case. In two cases, the commander was the deputy commander elevated to be acting commander. In another case, the commander was essentially relieved of command. Command of CENTCOM typically rotated between the U.S. Army and the USMC. One U.S. Navy officer is on the list. Lieutenant General Allen is not included in the following entries as he was an acting commander and his subsequent assignments gave few opportunities to influence the fighting in Iraq.

- General Tommy Franks, U.S. Army
  July 6, 2000–July 7, 2003
- General John Abizaid, U.S. Army
  July 7, 2003–March 16, 2007
- Admiral William J. Fallon, U.S. Navy
  March 16, 2007–March 28, 2008
- Lieutenant General Martin Dempsey, U.S. Army
  March 28, 2008–October 31, 2008
- General David Petraeus, U.S. Army
  October 31, 2008–June 30, 2010
- Lieutenant General John R. Allen, U.S. Marine Corps
  June 30, 2010–August 11, 2010 (not included)
- General James Mattis, U.S. Marine Corps
  August 11, 2010–March 22, 2013

CENTCOM (U.S. Central Command) commander general Tommy Franks and his deputy, Lieutenant General John Abizaid, listen to a briefing on the progress of Operation Iraqi Freedom at CENTCOM's forward headquarters in Qatar. (CENTCOM Public Affairs)

Tommy Franks (1945–)
(Commander from July 6, 2000, to July 7, 2003)

U.S. Army general. Tommy Ray Franks was born in Wynnewood, Oklahoma, on June 17, 1945, and grew up in Oklahoma and Midland, Texas. After studying briefly at the University of Texas, Franks joined the U.S. Army in 1965 and went into the artillery. He served in Vietnam, where he was wounded three times. He attended the University of Texas but dropped out and joined the army after being placed on academic probation.

Franks later earned his master's degree in public administration at Shippinsburg University (1985), then graduated from the Armed Forces Staff College (1977). He also attended the University of Texas, Arlington (1970–1972), and in 1972 attended the USA Field Artillery Center at Fort Sill, Oklahoma. From 1976 to 1977, he attended the Armed Force Staff College, Norfolk, Virginia, and in 1984–1985 he attended the U.S. Army War College at Carlisle Barracks, Pennsylvania.

After advancing through the ranks, in the 1991 Persian Gulf War Franks was an assistant division commander of the 1st Calvary Division. He was promoted to brigadier general in July 1991 and to major general in April 1994. From 1994 to 1995 he was the assistant chief of staff for combined forces in Korea. Franks was promoted to lieutenant general in May 1997 and to general in

July 2000. After the September 11, 2001, terrorist attacks on the United States, he was named U.S. commander in chief for the successful Operation Enduring Freedom in Afghanistan. In 2003, he was the commander in chief of Central Command (CENTCOM) for Operation Iraqi Freedom, the invasion of Iraq.

Franks was a principal author of the plans for the ground element of the invasion of Iraq and was an advocate of the lighter, more rapid mechanized forces that performed so well during it. He designed a plan for the 150,000 American troops and for the few thousand coalition troops who would be under his command. His plan involved five ground prongs into Iraq, with two main thrusts: one by the 1st Marine Expeditionary Force up the Tigris River and one through the western desert and up the Euphrates by the army's 3rd Armored Division. The plan allowed for great flexibility, and even though CENTCOM advertised a "shock and awe" bombing campaign, in fact there was never any such intention, as Franks's plans called for a near-simultaneous ground and air assault.

When missiles struck Saddam Hussein's compound on March 20, 2003, ground forces moved into Iraq. Franks emphasized speed and bypassing cities and Iraqi strongpoints. Contrary to media reports that coalition forces were "bogged down" and had not occupied many cities, Franks maintained that this was by design: CENTCOM did not want the Iraqis to see demonstrated in Basra or Najaf the method and tactics by which coalition forces planned to take Baghdad.

The campaign was an unprecedented success, going farther and faster with fewer casualties, than any other comparable military campaign in history. This reflected what Franks called "full-spectrum" war, in which not only were the enemy's military forces engaged, but there were simultaneous attacks on computer and information facilities, the banking/monetary structure, and public opinion. Franks expanded the concept of command, control, communications, and intelligence (C3I) to include computers in C4I. For the first time, American forces operated in true joint operations, wherein different service branches could speak directly to units in other service branches, and featured true combined-arms operations, in which air, sea, and land assets were all simultaneously employed by commanders in the field to defeat the enemy.

Although many sources suggest that Franks was offered a position on the Joint Chiefs of Staff, he wanted to retire to be with his family and build his personal fortune. He therefore retired from the army on July 7, 2003, at the rank of full general and subsequently wrote his memoirs, *American Soldier* (2004). In 2003 Franks also established his own consulting firm, which specializes in disaster recovery. He has also sat on a number of corporate and nonprofit boards of directors, including those of Bank of America and the National Park Foundation.

Larry Schweikart

See also: Bush, George Walker; Commands, U.S. and Coalition Military: U.S. Central Command (CENTCOM); Global War on Terrorism; Hussein, Saddam; Iraqi Freedom, Operation: Planning for Operations, Coalition Ground Forces, Ground Campaign, Major Battles; Secretary of Defense, U.S.: Donald Rumsfeld

References

Cordesman, Anthony. *The Iraq War: Strategy, Tactics, and Military Lessons.* London: Center for Strategic and International Studies, 2003.

Fontenot, Gregory, E. J. Degen, and David Tohn. *On Point: The United States Army in Operation Iraqi Freedom*. Washington, DC: Office of the Chief of Staff, 2004.

John P. Abizaid (1951–) (Commander from July 7, 2003, to March 16, 2007)

U.S. Army officer and commander in chief of the U.S. Central Command (CENTCOM) from July 7, 2003, to March 16, 2007. John Philip Abizaid was born on April 1, 1951, in Coleville, California, into a Christian Lebanese family who had immigrated to the United States in the 1880s. He graduated from the U.S. Military Academy, West Point, in 1973 and was commissioned as a second lieutenant. Abizaid served initially in a parachute regiment as platoon leader before moving to the Rangers as a company commander.

Abizaid won a prestigious Olmsted Scholarship, which entitled him to study at a foreign university. After a year of training in Arabic, he enrolled in the University of Jordan–Amman in 1978. Political tension in Jordan resulted in the shutdown of the university, however, so Abizaid used the opportunity to train with the Jordanian Army instead. In 1980 he earned a master of arts degree in Middle Eastern studies from Harvard University.

Abizaid led a Ranger company during the U.S. invasion of Grenada in 1983. During the Persian Gulf crisis, he commanded the 3rd Battalion, 325th Airborne Infantry Regiment. In 1991 the battalion was deployed in northern Iraq during Operation Provide Comfort, which immediately succeeded the end of Operation Desert Storm. Abizaid subsequently studied peacekeeping at Stanford University's Hoover Institution and commanded the 504th Parachute Infantry Regiment of the 82nd Airborne Division before serving as assistant division commander of the 1st Armored Division in Bosnia-Herzegovina. Numerous staff appointments along the way included a tour as a United Nations observer in Lebanon and several European staff tours.

In 1997, Abizaid became commandant of cadets at West Point as a newly promoted brigadier general. There he played a major role in reforming some of the more egregious requirements of the plebe system. Promoted to major general in 1999, Abizaid assumed command of the 1st Infantry Division, which contributed troops to Operation Joint Guardian, the North Atlantic Treaty Organization campaign in Kosovo.

Abizaid's appointment as director of the Joint Staff brought with it advancement to lieutenant general. In January 2003 he became deputy commander of the U.S. Central Command, which had responsibility for covering 27 countries of the Middle East and Central Asia. During Operation Iraqi Freedom, which began in March 2003, Abizaid served as deputy commander (Forward), Combined Force Command. Abizaid succeeded General Tommy Franks as CENTCOM commander when the latter retired in July 2003. At the same time, Abizaid was promoted to full (four-star) general. When he took command of CENTCOM, insurgent violence in Iraq was escalating rapidly. Abizaid had already expressed reservations about poor planning for the postwar era in Iraq and the competence of Pentagon officials in charge of the arrangements. He believed that most Iraqis would not welcome a U.S. occupation of their country and that widespread terrorism and guerrilla activity would likely follow a U.S. invasion.

Abizaid used the opportunity of his first press conference to state that the United States was now fighting a classic guerrilla insurgency in Iraq, an opinion directly opposite the views held by Secretary of Defense Donald Rumsfeld, who bristled at Abizaid's comments. The contradiction quickly made headlines and resulted in Abizaid receiving a private reprimand from Rumsfeld.

Abizaid also disagreed with the decision by Paul Bremer, head of the Coalition Provisional Authority, to disband the Iraqi Army and advocated rehiring select Sunni officers. Abizaid was also critical of Bremer's de-Baathification policy. In addition, Abizaid realized that the U.S. intelligence apparatus in Iraq was in total disarray. On October 1, 2003, he issued orders reorganizing intelligence operations so that in the future all reports would be passed through a single intelligence fusion center.

During the summer of 2004, Abizaid informed his superiors that a military victory in Iraq was unlikely. Instead of pursuing an elusive victory, Abizaid favored a policy of shifting the burden of the war to Iraqi Security Forces and minimizing the U.S. presence. Abizaid also supported research into the situation in Iraq and on the Global War on Terrorism. However, publicly and in interviews with the press he presented an optimistic version of events, despite having privately expressed doubts. In keeping with his public optimism, Abizaid appeared before the Senate Armed Services Committee on March 16, 2006, and gave another positive review of progress in Iraq. During a break in the proceedings, Abizaid approached Congressman John Murtha (D-PA), a former marine who had been highly critical of the Iraq War, and indicated to Murtha that Murtha's views were close to his own.

Abizaid's retirement as head of CENTCOM was announced in December 2006. On March 16, 2007, he was replaced by Admiral William Fallon. On May 1, 2007, Abizaid retired from his 34-year army career to take up a post as research fellow at the Hoover Institution. In 2008, he became a member of the board of directors of RPM International.

Paul William Doerr

See also: Baath Party; Bremer, Lewis Paul, III; Bush, George Walker; Commanders, U.S. Central Command: Tommy Franks, William J. Fallon; Commands, U.S. and Coalition Military: U.S. Central Command (CENTCOM); Global War on Terrorism; Hussein, Saddam; Iraqi Freedom, Operation: Coalition Ground Forces, Major Battles, The Surge and the Awakening; Secretary of Defense, U.S.: Donald Rumsfeld

References

Gordon, Michael R., and General Bernard E. Trainor. *Cobra II: The Inside Story of the Invasion and Occupation of Iraq.* New York: Pantheon Books, 2006.

Ricks, Thomas E. *Fiasco: The American Military Adventure in Iraq.* New York: Penguin, 2006.

Woodward, Bob. *State of Denial: Bush at War, Part III.* New York: Simon and Schuster, 2006.

William J. Fallon (1944–) (Commander from March 16, 2007, to March 28, 2008)

U.S. Navy officer and commander of U.S. Central Command (CENTCOM) during 2007–2008. William Joseph "Fox" Fallon was born in East Orange, New Jersey, on December 30, 1944, and grew up in Merchantville, New Jersey. He was commissioned in the U.S. Navy through the navy's Reserve Officers' Training Corps program after graduating from Villanova University in 1967. He then completed flight training and became a naval aviator. Fallon later graduated from the Naval War College, Newport, Rhode Island, and the National War College, Washington, DC. He also earned an MA degree in international studies from Old Dominion University in 1982.

Fallon's career as a naval aviator spanned 24 years with service in attack squadrons and carrier air wings, during which he logged more than 1,300 carrier-arrested landings and 4,800 flight hours. It included combat during the Vietnam War and service in the Mediterranean, Atlantic, Pacific, and Indian Oceans in a number of different carriers.

Fallon's commands included Carrier Air Wing 8 aboard the *Theodore Roosevelt* deployed in the Persian Gulf during Operations Desert Shield and Desert Storm, during which he led 80 air strike missions into Iraq and Kuwait between August 1990 and February 1991; Carrier Group Eight (1995); and Battle Force Sixth Fleet as part of the *Theodore Roosevelt* Battle Group during the North Atlantic Treaty Organization combat Operation Deliberate Force (August 29–September 14, 1995) in Bosnia.

Fallon held numerous staff assignments. He also served as deputy director for operations, Joint Task Force, Southwest Asia, in Riyadh, Saudi Arabia; deputy director, aviation plans and requirements on the staff of the chief of naval operations in Washington, DC; assistant chief of staff, plans, and policy for Supreme Allied Command, Atlantic (his first flag officer position); deputy and chief of staff, U.S. Atlantic Fleet; and deputy commander in chief and chief of staff, U.S. Atlantic Command.

Fallon was promoted to full (four-star) admiral and became the 31st vice chief of naval operations, a post he held from October 2000 to August 2003. While serving in that capacity, he publicly apologized to the president of Japan following a collision between the U.S. submarine *Greeneville* and the Japanese fishing training ship *Ehime Maru* off the coast of Hawaii in February 2001. In 2002 Fallon asserted before the U.S. Senate Committee on Environment and Public Works that the ability to conduct military operations superseded obedience to environmental laws. He commanded the U.S. Fleet Forces Command (October 2003–February 2005) and the U.S. Pacific Command (February 2005–March 2007), where his approach to the People's Republic of China was less confrontational than previous commanders and was not well received by some American policy makers who favored a tougher stance toward China.

In March 2007 Fallon replaced U.S. Army general John P. Abizaid as the first naval officer to command CENTCOM. Fallon's tenure lasted only one year, from March 16, 2007, to March 28, 2008. Although the impetus for his abrupt retirement as CENTCOM commander is not disputed, its voluntariness is. Despite the fact that Fallon was publicly lauded by President George W. Bush and Secretary of Defense Robert Gates, Gates noted that Fallon's resignation was due in part to controversy surrounding an article by Thomas P. M. Barnett titled "The Man between War and Peace," published in *Esquire* magazine on March 11, 2008. In it, Fallon was quoted as having disagreements with the Bush administration on the prosecution of the war in Iraq and a potential conflict with Iran regarding its nuclear weapons program. The article portrayed Fallon as resisting pressure from the Bush administration for war with Iran over the latter's pursuit of nuclear weapons. Besides Fallon's rather open opposition to Bush's war policies, the admiral purportedly disagreed with General David Petraeus regarding Iranian covert exportation of weapons to Iraqi insurgents and the pace of future American troop reductions in Iraq. Many believed that Fallon was forced out principally because his superiors blamed him for the failure to halt Iranian weapons from entering Iraq.

Richard M. Edwards

See also: Bush, George Walker; Commanders, U.S. Central Command: John P. Abizaid, David H. Petraeus; Commands, U.S. and Coalition Military: U.S. Central Command (CENTCOM); Global War on Terrorism; Iraqi Freedom, Operation: Coalition Ground Forces, Major Battles, The Surge and the Awakening; Secretary of Defense, U.S.: Robert Gates

References

Barnett, Thomas P. M. "The Man between War and Peace." *Esquire,* March 11, 2008, 1–4.

Dorsey, Jack. "Navy Taps 2nd Fleet's Adm. William J. Fallon for 4-Star Pentagon Post." *Virginian Pilot,* September 7, 2000, 1.

Lambeth, Benjamin S. *American Carrier Air Power at the Dawn of a New Century.* Santa Monica, CA: RAND Corporation, 2005.

Martin E. Dempsey (1954–) (Commander from March 28, 2008, to October 31, 2008)

U.S. Army general and acting commander of the U.S. Central Command (CENTCOM) during March–October 2008. Born in 1954, Martin E. Dempsey began his army career when he was commissioned a second lieutenant upon graduation from the U.S. Military Academy, West Point, in June 1974. His first posting, from June 1975 to June 1978, was as a scout and platoon leader in the 2nd Armored Cavalry Regiment. In August 1982 Dempsey earned an MA degree in English from Duke University, and in 1984 he returned to West Point to teach English.

After earning a master's degree in military art and science in 1988 from the Command and General Staff College (Fort Leavenworth, Kansas), Dempsey served as a battalion executive officer in the 3rd Armored Division in Friedburg, Germany. As operations officer and then executive officer for the 3rd Brigade, he deployed with the 3rd Armored Division to Saudi Arabia in Operation Desert Shield and Operation Desert Storm (1990–1991).

In 1993 Dempsey was assigned as chief of the Armor Branch at the U.S. Total Army Personnel Command in Arlington, Virginia. He then earned another master's degree, in national security and strategic studies, at the National War College in Washington, DC, in 1995, the same year he was promoted to colonel. The next year Dempsey took command of the 3rd Armored Cavalry Regiment at Fort Carson, Colorado. He has served in numerous leadership positions at all levels, including assistant deputy director for Politico-Military Affairs Europe and Africa J5. From July 1998 to September 2001 he was a special assistant to the chairman of the Joint Chiefs of Staff in Washington, DC.

In 2001 Dempsey was promoted to brigadier general, and from September 2001 to June 2003 he served in Riyadh, Saudi Arabia, as a program manager and headed a U.S. effort to modernize the elite Saudi force assigned to protect the kingdom's royal family. From June 2003 to July 2005 Dempsey commanded the 1st Armored Division, and from June 2003 to July 2004 he served in Iraq in support of Operation Iraqi Freedom. During his time in Iraq he had charge of the Task Force Iron command, consisting not only of the 1st Armored Division but also, attached to it, the 2nd Armored Cavalry Regiment and a brigade of the 82nd Airborne Division. It was one of the larger divisional-level commands in the history of the U.S. Army. Dempsey's command tour coincided with the dramatic growth of the Sunni insurgency. He had charge of the Baghdad Area of Operations and received high marks for his handling of a difficult situation.

Dempsey redeployed his division to Germany and completed his command tour in July 2005. From August 2005 until the spring of 2007, he commanded the Multi-National Security Transition Command–Iraq with responsibility for recruitment, training, and equipping the Iraqi Security Forces. Promoted to lieutenant general on March 27, 2007, Dempsey became deputy commander of CENTCOM at MacDill Air Force Base, Florida. He served in that post until March 28, 2008, when he was named acting commander of CENTCOM, temporarily replacing General David Petraeus. On December 8, 2008, Dempsey was promoted to full (four-star) general and assumed command of the U.S. Army Training and Doctrine Command. On April 11, 2011, he succeeded General George Casey as chief of staff of the U.S. Army. On May 30, 2011, however, President Barack Obama nominated Dempsey to take over as chairman of the Joint Chiefs of Staff upon the retirement of Admiral Michael Mullen on September 30, 2011. Dempsey assumed the post on October 1, 2011, and he stepped down from the position on September 25, 2015.

Gary Lee Kerley

See also: Commanders, Multi-National Force–Iraq: Ricardo S. Sanchez, George W. Casey Jr.; Commanders, U.S. Central Command: William J. Fallon, David H. Petraeus; Commands, U.S. and Coalition Military: Multi-National Security Transition Command–Iraq, U.S. Central Command; Fallujah, Second Battle of; Iraqi Freedom, Operation: Major Battles, The Surge and the Awakening; Islamic State of Iraq and al-Sham (ISIS): Al Qaeda in Iraq

References

Ricks, Thomas E. *Fiasco: The American Military Adventure in Iraq.* New York: Penguin, 2006.

Schwartz, Anthony J. "Iraq's Militias: The True Threat to Coalition Success in Iraq." *Parameters* 37(1) (2007): 55–58.

Zelnick, Robert. "Iraq: Last Chance." *Policy Review* 140 (2006): 3–6.

David H. Petraeus (1952–) (Commander from October 31, 2008, to June 30, 2010)

U.S. Army officer, commander of the Multi-National Force–Iraq (2007–2008), and commander of the U.S. Central Command (CENTCOM) (2008–2010). Born on November 7, 1952, David Howell Petraeus grew up and graduated from high school in Cornwall, New York. Petraeus graduated 10th in his class from the U.S. Military Academy, West Point, in 1974. Commissioned a second lieutenant of infantry, he graduated from Ranger School and served as a platoon leader in the 1st Battalion, 509th Airborne Infantry, in Italy. As a first lieutenant he served as assistant battalion operations officer, and as captain he served as company commander, battalion operations officer, and then commanding general's aide-de-camp, all in the 24th Infantry Division (Mechanized).

From 1982 to 1995 Petraeus served in a progression of command and staff assignments, with alternating assignments for both professional military and civilian academic education. He graduated from the Army Command and General Staff College in 1983, after which he attended Princeton University's Woodrow Wilson School of Public Affairs, where he earned a master's degree in public administration in 1985 and a doctorate in international relations in 1987. His doctoral dissertation dealt with the U.S.

Army in Vietnam and the lessons learned there.

Petraeus returned to West Point as an assistant professor of international relations and then was a military fellow at Georgetown University's School of Foreign Service. In 1995 he was assigned as the chief operations officer of the United Nations mission during Operation Uphold Democracy in Haiti.

Petraeus's commanded assignments included the 3rd Battalion, 187th Infantry Regiment, 101st Airborne Division, during 1991–1993, and the 1st Brigade, 82nd Airborne Division, from 1995 to 1997. He was promoted to brigadier general in 1999.

Petraeus's first combat assignment, now at the rank of major general, came as commander of the 101st Airborne Division (Air Assault) in Operation Iraqi Freedom in March 2003. The division engaged in the Battle of Karbala and the Battle of Najaf as well as the feint at Hilla. Petraeus later oversaw the administration and rebuilding of Mosul and Niveveh Provinces. Subsequently, he commanded the Multinational Security Transition Command–Iraq and North Atlantic Treaty Organization (NATO) Training Mission–Iraq between June 2004 and September 2005. Petraeus's next assignment was as commanding general of Fort Leavenworth, Kansas, and the U.S. Army Combined Arms Center, where he exercised direct responsibility for the doctrinal changes to prepare the army for its continued efforts in Afghanistan and Iraq. He also coauthored *Field Manual 3–24, Counterinsurgency.*

On January 5, 2007, Petraeus, now a lieutenant general, was selected by President George W. Bush and later unanimously confirmed by the U.S. Senate to command the Multi-National Force–Iraq. Petraeus took formal command on February 10, 2007, replacing Lieutenant General George Casey. The Petraeus appointment was the keystone in Bush's troop surge strategy in Iraq designed to bring an end to the mounting violence there and to bring about peace in Iraq. Many welcomed the change in command but also remained skeptical that Petraeus could reverse the violence in Iraq.

In April 2007 Petraeus was tasked with reporting to Congress the progress of the Bush administration's surge strategy, begun that January, and met stiff and sometimes combative resistance. To his credit, however, Petraeus deftly handled the pressure and stated confidently that the strategy, given time, would show positive results. At the same time, he firmly argued against setting a timetable for the withdrawal of ground troops from Iraq. In July he submitted to Congress his first progress report, which was positive and upbeat. It met with derision, however, because it did not appear that Iraq was any more secure than it had been in January. His September 2007 report cited progress on the military and security fronts but admitted that the political climate in Iraq remained troubled. The September report drew sharp criticism from some Democrats and the antiwar lobby, compelling a bipartisan group of congressional representatives and senators to sponsor resolutions—which eventually passed—that condemned the recent attacks on Petraeus. Petraeus was promoted to four-star rank in December 2007.

By early 2008, defying high odds and most critics of the war, the surge strategy appeared to be paying off, as violence had fallen off markedly in the last quarter of 2007. Talk of troop drawdowns, however, were still subject to interpretation, as the possible numbers being cited would account mainly for the surge, meaning that troop strength in Iraq would remain unchanged from January 2007, even after troop reductions.

By the spring of 2008, however, Petraeus could point to a significant reduction in sectarian and insurgency-based violence in Iraq. In addition, the Iraqis themselves seemed increasingly willing and able to take over security and police tasks. As a result, U.S. and coalition troop withdrawals accelerated throughout 2008, and violence in Iraq hit four-year lows. Petraeus was largely hailed in the United States for his efforts at undermining the Iraqi insurgency, and because of this President Bush tapped him to command CENTCOM. Petraeus took command on October 1, 2008; General Raymond Odierno succeeded him as commander of the Multi-National Force–Iraq.

During congressional hearings, Petraeus was careful to point out that talk of victory in Iraq was still premature; instead, he viewed the situation with a great deal of realism, suggesting that an Iraq that is "at peace with itself, at peace with its neighbors, and has a government that is representative of—and responsive to—its citizens" might be considered a victory. As the head of CENTCOM, Petraeus became responsible for U.S. military operations in 20 nations, including Egypt and Pakistan as well as the ongoing conflicts in Afghanistan and Iraq.

On June 24, 2010, the same day that he removed General Stanley A. McChrystal as commander of U.S. and NATO forces in Afghanistan, President Barack Obama tapped Petraeus as McChrystal's successor, thereby sending a signal that there was no change in U.S. Afghanistan policy. Then on April 28, 2011, Obama nominated Petraeus to become the new director of the Central Intelligence Agency. Confirmed by the Senate on June 20 in a vote of 94 to 0, Petraeus was sworn in on September 6.

On November 8, 2012, however, Petraeus, who had been married for 37 years, submitted his letter of resignation with the admission that he had engaged in an extramarital affair. Since his resignation, Petraeus has held teaching positions at the City University of New York (CUNY) and the University of Southern California. He also serves on several corporate and organization boards in addition to engaging in occasional consulting work. In the fall of 2013, he was named a nonresident senior fellow at Harvard University's John F. Kennedy School of Government.

Marcel A. Derosier

See also: Ambassadors to Iraq, U.S.: Ryan C. Crocker; Bush, George Walker; Commanders, Multi-National Force–Iraq: Raymond T. Odierno; Commanders, U.S. Central Command: William J. Fallon, Martin E. Dempsey; Commands, U.S. and Coalition Military: Multi-National Security Transition Command–Iraq, U.S. Central Command; Iraqi Freedom, Operation: Major Battles, The Surge and the Awakening; Islamic State of Iraq and al-Sham (ISIS); Prime Minister, Iraq: Nuri al-Maliki

References

Atkinson, Rick. *In the Company of Soldiers: A Chronicle of Combat.* New York: Henry Holt, 2005.

Day, Thomas L. *Along the Tigris: The 101st Airborne Division in Operation Iraqi Freedom, February 2003–March 2004.* Atglen, PA: Schiffer, 2007.

Fontenot, Gregory, et al. *On Point: The United States Army in Iraqi Freedom.* Annapolis, MD: Naval Institute Press, 2005.

John R. Allen (1953–) (Acting Commander for 42 days from June 30, 2010, to August, 11 2010) (No Further Information)

James Mattis (1950–) (Commander from August 11, 2010, to March 22, 2013)

U.S. Marine Corps (USMC) general and commander of the U.S. Central Command

(CENTCOM) from August 11, 2010, to March 22, 2013. James Norman Mattis was born on September 8, 1950, in Pullman, Washington. He graduated from Central Washington University in 1971. He enlisted in the USMC in 1969 and was commissioned as a second lieutenant in 1972. He became the 26th secretary of defense and only the second to require an exception to U.S. law to take the position within seven years of retirement (the first being George C. Marshall, the third secretary, from September 21, 1950, to September 12, 1951) upon his assumption of the office on January 20, 2017. Mattis commanded combat units in Operation Desert Storm (1st Battalion, 7th Marines), Operation Enduring Freedom (Afghanistan) (7th Marine Regiment, Task Force 58, and 1st Marine Expeditionary Brigade), and Operation Iraqi Freedom (1st Marine Division). Each of these commands gave him significant experience in conducting combat in the Middle East. They also each presented specific challenges and some controversies. After commanding in Iraq, Mattis went on to command key USMC and joint assignments culminating in his command of U.S. Central Command (CENTCOM). He took over from General Petraeus following the relief of Lieutenant General McChrystal in Afghanistan that caused General Petraeus to relinquish command and replace McChrystal. Lieutenant General Allen was acting commander in the interim between Petraeus and Mattis and became Mattis's deputy—the first time a unified command had a USMC officer as commander and deputy. This was not the first time Mattis made USMC history.

In the initial planning and deployment to Afghanistan, Mattis commanded Task Force 58, a U.S. Navy task force making it the first time a USMC officer commanded a U.S. Navy task force in combat. Afghanistan had some controversy for Mattis. He denied helicopter support for medical evacuation of U.S. and Afghan troops wounded by an inadvertent B-52 strike. Several of the personnel involved blamed the decision for soldiers dying of wounds once Mattis was nominated for secretary of defense in 2016.

Mattis commanded the 1st Marine Division in Iraq as it advanced north to Baghdad. Later, his division was a critical combat element in both battles of Fallujah in April and November 2004—Operations Vigilant Resolve and Phantom Fury, respectively. His service in Iraq also had controversy. The most significant was the May 2004 bombing of a wedding party and Mattis's dismissal of the event by questioning if it had actually been a wedding party.

Despite the controversy, Mattis was generally well respected within the USMC and throughout the military-political establishment. He is viewed as an intellectual and thoughtful commander who regularly visited marines in combat situations. This reputation as a hard-fighting and deep-thinking commander is attributed to his nomination and overwhelming approval as the secretary of defense. The vote was 98–1 in a time of significant political polarization.

Brian L. Steed

See also: Commanders, U.S. Central Command: David H. Petraeus; Commands, U.S. and Coalition Military: U.S. Central Command; Fallujah, First Battle of; Fallujah, Second Battle of; Iraqi Freedom, Operation: Planning for Operations, Coalition Ground Forces, Ground Campaign, Major Battles, The Surge and the Awakening; Islamic State of Iraq and al-Sham (ISIS); Prime Minister, Iraq: Nuri al-Maliki

References

Cockburn, Patrick. *The Occupation: War and Resistance in Iraq.* New York: Verso, 2007.

Gordon, Michael R., and General Bernard E. Trainor. *Cobra II: The Inside Story of the Invasion and Occupation of Iraq.* New York: Pantheon Books, 2006.

Ricks, Thomas E. *Fiasco: The American Military Adventure in Iraq.* New York: Penguin, 2006.

West, Bing. *No True Glory: A Frontline Account of the Battle for Fallujah.* New York: Bantam, 2006.

Commands, U.S. and Coalition Military

The U.S. military arrived in Iraq as an invading combat force led by a U.S. Army corps headquarters—V (US) Corps stationed in Germany. Once the invasion was complete, the headquarters changed its name to become Combined Joint Task Force 7 commanded by a U.S. three-star general. It was the senior command for all coalition military forces operating in Iraq for the first year from May 2003 to June 2004. This command was superseded by Multi-National Force–Iraq (MNF-I) commanded by a four-star general. MNF-I remained the command designation until 2010, after the withdrawal of the British Army contingent, and it was renamed United States Forces–Iraq (USF-I).

Throughout the existence of MNF-I/USF-I the command consisted of numerous subordinate elements. The primary combat element was Multi-National Corps–Iraq (MNC-I), which commanded all of the ground combat elements in country and Multi-National Security Transition Command–Iraq (MNSTC-I), which was responsible for the fielding and training of the Iraqi Security Forces. A final significant command focused on detainee operations. Over the course of the eight years in Iraq, several specialized commands existed. One of the most prominent was the Joint Improvised Explosive Device Defeat Organization (JIEDDO), which was designated to deal with the development and evolution of IEDs across all combat theaters (including both Iraq and Afghanistan).

What follows are more detailed discussions of the key commands. Please note the ranks of commander for various commands. Greater rank does not necessarily mean greater performance, but one thing it always means for a military organization is greater value placed on that organization.

Multi-National Force–Iraq (United States Forces–Iraq)

U.S.-led military command of coalition forces in Iraq, established on May 15, 2004. The Multi-National Force–Iraq (MNF-I) was created ostensibly to combat the growing Iraqi insurgency, which began in earnest in late 2003 and early 2004; the MNF-I replaced Combined Joint Task Force 7, which had been in operation from June 2003 to May 2004. On January 1, 2010, the MNF-I was reorganized and renamed United States Forces–Iraq. This followed the withdrawal of most coalition troops from Iraq between 2008 and 2010 and the signing of the U.S.-Iraq status of forces agreement in December 2008. U.S. troops left Iraq in December 2011, ending the mission of the United States Forces–Iraq.

Commanders of the MNF-I were Lieutenant General Ricardo Sanchez (May–June 2004), General George W. Casey (June 2004–January 2007), General David Petraeus (January 2007–September 2008), and General Raymond Odierno (September 2008–January 2010). The MNF-I was tasked with bringing the growing Iraqi insurgency to an end but was largely unsuccessful in that effort until the George W. Bush administration placed General Petraeus in command and implemented a troop surge that placed as many as 40,000 additional U.S. troops on the ground in Iraq beginning in early 2007.

The troop surge strategy seemed to have worked for a time, as violence fell off markedly beginning by early 2008; Petraeus was given much of the credit for this development. At the same time, the so-called Anbar Awakening groups in Iraq also helped to curb sectarian and insurgent violence. General Odierno, while acknowledging that the surge provided strengthened security forces, credited a change in counterinsurgency strategy more than the surge itself for reducing the level of violence. Referring to it as an "Anaconda strategy," Odierno explained the strategy as a comprehensive approach that had success in, among other areas, cutting off insurgents from their support within the Iraqi population.

After its inception, the MNF-I overwhelmingly consisted of U.S. troops; the second-largest deployment was from Great Britain. The size of the MNF-I was fluid, but on average it contained around 150,000 combat-ready personnel, the vast majority of whom were American. The troop surge brought the total closer to 180,000 by early 2008, but that number dwindled steadily as troop withdrawals began that same year. Working with the MNF-I but not falling under its direct command was the United Nations (UN) Assistance Mission–Iraq, which provided humanitarian aid and observation, and the North Atlantic Treaty Organization (NATO) Training Mission–Iraq, whose goal was to train Iraqi security, police, and military personnel. The major component parts of the MNF-I were the Multi-National Security Transition Command; the Gulf Region Division, U.S. Corps of Engineers; Joint Base Balad; the Multi-National Corps–Iraq; the Multi-National Division–Baghdad; the Multi-National Division–North; the Multi-National Force–West; the Multi-National Division Center; and the Multi-National Division–Southeast.

In addition to battling the Iraqi insurgency and other indigenous violence, other goals of the MNF-I included support and aid to the Iraqi government, reconstruction efforts, specialized training of Iraqi military personnel, intelligence gathering, and border patrols. The December 2008 status of forces agreement between the U.S. and Iraqi governments stipulated that all U.S. troops be withdrawn by December 31, 2011. Under the terms of this arrangement, U.S. troops vacated Iraqi cities by July 31, 2009. The Iraqis concluded similar agreements with other coalition forces that still maintained a presence in Iraq. Numerous nations supplied troops to the MNF-I, many of whom were withdrawn by the end of December 2008. The participating members and the size of their deployments included the United States (145,000 troops as of December 2008), Great Britain (4,000 as of December 2008), Romania (500 as of December 2008), Australia (350 as of December 2008), El Salvador (300 as of December 2008), and Estonia (40 as of December 2008).

Those nations that participated but were withdrawn prior to December 2008, listed here with peak deployment numbers, included South Korea (3,600), Italy (3,200), Poland (2,500), Georgia (2,000), Ukraine (1,650), Netherlands (1,345), Spain (1,300), Japan (600), Denmark (545), Bulgaria (458), Thailand (423), Honduras (368), Dominican Republic (302), Czech Republic (300), Hungary (300), Azerbaijan (250), Albania (240), Nicaragua (230), Mongolia (180), Singapore (175), Norway (150), Latvia (136), Portugal (128), Lithuania (120), Slovakia (110), Bosnia-Herzegovina (85), Macedonia (77), New Zealand (61), Tonga (55),

Philippines (51), Armenia (46), Kazakhstan (29), Moldova (24), and Iceland (2).

To entice potential coalition partners to join the MNF-I effort, the U.S. government offered a plethora of financial aid and other incentives. Because the invasion of Iraq had not been sanctioned by the UN, the United States found it more difficult to convince other nations to become involved in the postwar stabilization effort in Iraq. Some nations and previously close allies refused to take part in the mission, despite U.S. promises of financial and other rewards. The United States reportedly offered Turkey up to $8.5 billion in loans if the country sent peacekeeping troops to Iraq; Turkey, which had forbade the use of its bases during the March 2003 invasion of Iraq, demurred. France and Germany refused any participation in Iraq. Some countries, such as Great Britain and Australia, were offered lucrative private-contractor business that would help fuel their economies. The Bush administration, however, refused to acknowledge that there were any quid pro quo arrangements in the assembling of international forces in Iraq.

Paul G. Pierpaoli Jr.

See also: Commanders, Multi-National Force–Iraq: Ricardo S. Sanchez, George W. Casey Jr., David H. Petraeus, Raymond T. Odierno, Lloyd J. Austin III; Commands, U.S. and Coalition Military: Multi-National Security Transition Command–Iraq; Iraqi Freedom, Operation: Planning for Operations, Coalition Ground Forces, Ground Campaign, Major Battles, The Surge and the Awakening

References

Cockburn, Patrick. *The Occupation: War and Resistance in Iraq.* New York: Verso, 2007.

Gordon, Michael R., and Bernard E. Trainor. *The Endgame: The Inside Story of the Struggle for Iraq, from George W. Bush to Barack Obama.* New York: Vintage, 2013.

Keegan, John. *The Iraq War: The Military Offensive, from Victory in 21 Days to the Insurgent Aftermath.* New York: Vintage, 2005.

Multi-National Security Transition Command–Iraq (MNSTC-I)

Training the Iraqi military and police forces was stated to be the ticket out of Iraq for the U.S. military. To accomplish this, the Coalition Provisional Authority established the Coalition Military Assistance Training Team in 2003 commanded by a two-star general. That team was later consumed in a much larger organization called the Multi-National Security Transition Command–Iraq commanded by a three-star general in 2004. The list of commanders for MNSTC-I is illustrative of the usefulness of the command in developing leaders even if the command itself was often underresourced. In 2010 the command was redesignated as advising and training under the Deputy Commanding General for USF-I or in military abbreviation DCG A&T. The commanders for MNSTC-I were Lieutenant General David Petraeus (June 2004–September 2005), Lieutenant General Martin Dempsey (September 2005–June 2007), Lieutenant General James Dubik (June 2007–July 2008), Lieutenant General Frank Helmick (July 2008–October 2009), Lieutenant Michael Barbero (October 2009–December 2010), and Lieutenant General Michael Ferriter (did not command MNSTC-I but served as DCG A&T) (December 2010–August 2011).

The command and later DCG A&T expanded the initial envisioned role of training a specific number of units to include doctrine, organization, training, maintenance, leadership, personnel, and facilities for both military and police forces for the entirety of Iraq. The need for this was a result of the Coalition Provisional Authority orders 1 and 2 that removed the ability for Baath Party members to work for the new government and the disbanding of the Iraqi Army and security force personnel, respectively. Once that was done, it was a requirement that the coalition must attract, create, and employ the replacement force.

The MNSTC-I commander was "dual-hatted" as the NATO Training Mission–Iraq commander, which meant that he coordinated U.S., coalition, and NATO activities in developing the Iraqi Security Forces.

Brian L. Steed

See also: Commanders, Multi-National Force–Iraq: George W. Casey Jr., David H. Petraeus; Raymond T. Odierno, Lloyd J. Austin III; Commands, U.S. and Coalition Military: Multi-National Force–Iraq; Iraqi Freedom, Operation: Planning for Operations, Coalition Ground Forces, Ground Campaign, Major Battles, The Surge and the Awakening

References

Broadwell, Paula. *All In: The Education of General David Petraeus*. New York: Penguin Press, 2012.

Gordon, Michael R., and Bernard E. Trainor. *The Endgame: The Inside Story of the Struggle for Iraq, from George W. Bush to Barack Obama*. New York: Vintage, 2013.

Robinson, Linda. *Tell Me How This Ends: General David Petraeus and the Search for a Way Out of Iraq*. New York: PublicAffairs, 2008.

U.S. Central Command (CENTCOM)

One of 10 unified U.S. combatant commands responsible for U.S. military planning regarding some 20 nations, stretching from the Horn of Africa through the Persian Gulf states to Central Asia. The U.S. Central Command (USCENTCOM, usually referred to as CENTCOM) has its primary headquarters at MacDill Air Force Base in Tampa, Florida, and a forward headquarters at Camp al Sayliyah (2002–2009) and al-Udeid Air Base (2009–present), Qatar, to handle the demands of operations in Iraq and the Middle East.

The Ronald Reagan administration established CENTCOM on January 1, 1983, to deal with growing instability in the Middle East following the Islamic Revolution in Iran and the Soviet invasion of Afghanistan, both in 1979. Policy makers were worried that the Soviet Union or one of its client states would invade oil-producing nations and deprive the Western powers of access to this vital resource. CENTCOM was built from the assets of the Rapid Deployment Joint Task Force. Its first commander was General Robert C. Kingston. The original intent was that CENTCOM would not be based in the region and would rely on political allies to provide facilities on an as needed basis. As such, CENTCOM to this day is not assigned combat units but instead consists of five component commands that are assigned forces from their parent service as the mission requires. These include the U.S. Army Forces Central Command, U.S. Central Command Air Forces, U.S. Marine Forces Central Command, U.S. Naval Forces Central Command, and U.S. Special Operations Command Central.

CENTCOM engaged in its first combat mission in August 1990, when Iraqi forces invaded and occupied Kuwait. In Operation Desert Shield, CENTCOM commander general H. Norman Schwarzkopf supervised the deployment of forces to Saudi Arabia to deter Saddam Hussein from advancing into

Saudi Arabia. With a broad international consensus and the assistance of Saudi Arabia's logistics facilities, in Operation Desert Storm CENTCOM led the invasion of Kuwait and Iraq in February 1991 with a nine-division multinational force. The Iraqi Army was ejected from Kuwait in short order, but President George H. W. Bush decided to terminate the war without toppling the Hussein regime. For the next 12 years, CENTCOM contained Hussein's power by maintaining a permanent ground presence to the south of Iraq and enforcing no-fly zones in the north and south of the country.

Since the terror attacks of September 11, 2001, CENTCOM has become the central front in the Global War on Terrorism. In the late autumn of 2001, CENTCOM successfully toppled the Taliban government in Afghanistan as part of Operation Enduring Freedom to destroy the Al Qaeda organization. Two years later in March 2003, CENTCOM launched Operation Iraqi Freedom and ended the rule of President Saddam Hussein. During the course of Operation Iraqi Freedom, in order to support further stabilization and counterterrorism operations in these countries and the region as a whole, CENTCOM operated several joint and multinational subordinate commands: Multi-National Force–Iraq, Multi-National Security Transition Command–Iraq, Combined Forces Command Afghanistan, Combined Joint Task Force–Horn of Africa, and Joint Task Force Lebanon.

On February 7, 2007, the U.S. Army announced that a U.S. Africa Command would be organized and would take responsibility for CENTCOM's African portfolio, which included Djibouti but not Egypt. Almost all of Africa had been under the European Command (EUCOM). EUCOM retained both Israel and Turkey. CENTCOM is currently responsible for U.S. security interests in Afghanistan, Bahrain, Egypt, Iran, Iraq, Jordan, Kazakhstan, Kuwait, Kyrgyzstan, Lebanon, Oman, Pakistan, Qatar, Saudi Arabia, Syria, Tajikistan, Turkmenistan, the United Arab Emirates, Uzbekistan, and Yemen. The area of responsibility also includes the international waters of the Red Sea, the Persian Gulf, and western portions of the Indian Ocean.

James E. Shircliffe Jr.

See also: Global War on Terrorism; Iraq, History of, 1990–Present

References

DeLong, Michael, with Noah Lukeman. *Inside CENTCOM: The Unvarnished Truth about the Wars in Afghanistan and Iraq.* Washington, DC: Regnery, 2004.

Eshel, David. *The U.S. Rapid Deployment Forces.* New York: Arco, 1985.

Contractors

One of the most significant transformations in armed conflict evident in the Iraq War was the increase in private security and intelligence contractors. The U.S. government made conscious choices to contract a lot of the logistics and soldier support issues rather than keep it in the uniformed military. This was an ongoing process from the beginning of the all-volunteer force in the mid-1970s until the present. What changed after Operation Desert Storm and then increased following the attacks on September 11, 2001, was the privatization of security and intelligence.

Representative Henry Waxman of California stated in a U.S. House of Representatives Committee on Government Reform hearing:

Over the past 25 years, a sophisticated campaign has been waged to privatize

Government services. The theory is that corporations can deliver Government services better and at a lower cost than the Government. Over the last 6 years, this theory has been put into practice.

The result is that privatization has exploded. For every taxpayer dollar spent on Federal programs, over 40 cents now goes to private contractors. Our Government now outsources even the oversight of the outsourcing.

... Privatizing is working exceptionally well for Blackwater. The question for this hearing is whether outsourcing to Blackwater is a good deal for the American taxpayer, whether it is a good deal for the military and whether it is serving our national interest in Iraq.

The first part of that question is cost. We know that sergeants in the military generally cost the Government between $50,000 to $70,000 per year. We also know that a comparable position at Blackwater costs the Federal Government over $400,000, six times as much ...

Blackwater charges the Government so much that it can lure highly trained soldiers out of our forces to work for them. [Defense Secretary Gates] is now taking the unprecedented step of considering whether to ask our troops to sign a non-compete agreement to prevent the U.S. military from becoming a taxpayer-funded training program for private contractors.

The point of the hearing was to question the role of Blackwater USA and its personnel in the killing of 17 Iraqi civilians at a traffic circle in Baghdad on September, 16, 2007.

Representative John F. Tierney from Massachusetts made the following comments about the role of contractors in the same hearing:

The all-voluntary professional force after the Vietnam War employed the so-called Abrams Doctrine. The idea was that we wouldn't go to war without the sufficient backing of the Nation.

Outsourcing has circumvented this doctrine. It allows the administration to almost double the force size without any political price being paid. We have too few regular troops and if we admitted that and tried to put in more, the administration would have to admit it was wrong in the way it prosecuted this war originally. It would have to recognize the impact on drawing forces out of Afghanistan.

If we call up even more National Guards or Reservists, then it would cause even more of a protest among the people in this country that are already not sold on the Iraq venture. If we relied more on our allies, they would have to share the power, share the decision making and share the contract work. So private contractors have allowed, essentially, this administration to add additional forces without paying any political capital.

... Figures by one account are some nine individuals a week losing their lives in the service of private contracting that are not counted in the figures of casualties reported to the American people.

In fighting groups like Al Qaeda and other nonstate actors one of the ways that nations have responded is through the use of their own nonstate actors—contractors.

See also: Commanders, U.S. Central Command: David H. Petraeus; Doctrine, Counterinsurgency; Iraqi Freedom, Operation: Coalition

Ground Forces, Major Battles, The Surge and the Awakening; Islamic State of Iraq and al-Sham (ISIS): Al Qaeda in Iraq; Phantom Thunder, Operation

References

Blackwater USA Hearing. Given before U.S. House of Representatives Committee on Government Reform, October 2, 2007. Washington, DC, https://www.gpo.gov/fdsys/pkg/CHRG-110hhrg45219/html/CHRG-110hhrg45219.htm (accessed June 17, 2015).

Frontline: Private Warriors. Producer: Martin Smith. PBS, 2005.

Prince, Erik D. Prepared Statement as part of Blackwater USA Hearing. Given before U.S. House of Representatives Committee on Government Reform, October 2, 2007. Washington, DC, https://house.resource.org/110/org.c-span.201290-1.1.pdf (accessed June 17, 2015).

Prince, Erik. *Civilian Warriors: The Inside Story of Blackwater and the Unsung Heroes of the War on Terror.* New York: Penguin Group, 2013.

Scahill, Jeremy. *Blackwater: The Rise of the World's Most Powerful Mercenary Army.* New York: Nation Books, 2007.

Blackwater USA

Private U.S.-based security firm involved in military security operations in Afghanistan and Iraq. Blackwater USA (now known as Academi) was one of a number of private security firms hired by the U.S. government to aid in security operations in Afghanistan and Iraq. The company was founded in 1997 by Erik Prince, a former Navy SEAL, wealthy heir to an auto parts fortune, and staunch supporter of the Republican Party. He serves as the firm's chief executive officer (CEO). The firm was named for the brackish swampy waters surrounding its more than 6,000-acre headquarters and training facilities located in northeastern North Carolina's Dismal Swamp.

Details of the privately held company are shrouded in mystery, and the precise number of paid employees is not publicly known. A good number of its employees are not U.S. citizens. Blackwater also trained upwards of 40,000 people per year in military and security tactics, interdiction, and counterinsurgency operations. Many of its trainees were military, law enforcement, or civilian government employees, mostly American, but foreign government employees were also trained here. Blackwater claimed that its training facilities were the largest of their kind in the world. Nearly 90 percent of the company's revenues were derived from government contracts, two-thirds of which were no-bid contracts. It is estimated that between 2002 and 2009, Blackwater garnered U.S. government contracts in excess of $1 billion.

Following the successful ouster of the Taliban regime in Afghanistan in late 2001, Blackwater was among the first firms to be hired by the U.S. government to aid in security and law enforcement operations there. In 2003 after coalition forces ousted the regime of Iraqi president Saddam Hussein, Blackwater began extensive operations in the war-ravaged country. Its first major operation in Iraq included a $21 million no-bid contract to provide security services for the Coalition Provisional Authority and its chief, L. Paul Bremer. After that, Blackwater received contracts for several hundred million dollars more to provide a wide array of security and paramilitary services in Iraq. Some critics—including a number of congressional representatives and senators—took issue with the centrality of Blackwater in Iraq, arguing that its founder's connections to the Republican Party had helped it garner lucrative no-bid contracts.

Erik Prince, chairman of the Prince Group, LLC, and Blackwater USA, holds up a picture showing the affect of a car bomb while testifying during a House Oversight and Government Reform Committee hearing on Capitol Hill, October 2, 2007, in Washington, D.C. The committee was hearing testimony from officials regarding private security contracting in Iraq and Afghanistan. (Mark Wilson/Getty Images)

Although such information was never positively verified by either Blackwater or the U.S. government, it is believed that at least 30,000 private security contractors operated in Iraq between 2003 and 2011; some estimates claim as many as 100,000. Of that number, a majority were employees or subcontractors of Blackwater. The U.S. State Department and the Pentagon, which both negotiated lucrative contracts with Blackwater, contended that neither one could function in Iraq without resorting to the use of private security firms. Indeed, the use of such contractors helped keep down the need for even greater numbers of U.S. troops in Iraq and Afghanistan. After Hurricane Katrina smashed into the United States at the Gulf of Mexico in 2005, the U.S. government contracted with Blackwater to provide security, law enforcement, and humanitarian services in southern Louisiana and Mississippi.

In the course of the Iraqi insurgency that began in 2003, numerous Blackwater employees were injured or killed in ambushes, attacks, and suicide bombings, including the killing and hanging of four corpses outside Fallujah in the lead up to the First Battle of Fallujah. Because of the instability in Iraq and the often chaotic circumstances, some Blackwater personnel found themselves in situations in which they felt threatened and had to protect themselves by force. This led to numerous cases in which they were criticized, terminated, or worse for their actions. Because they were not members of the U.S. military, they often fell into a gray area, which sometimes elicited demands for retribution either by the American government or Iraqi officials.

Loose oversight of Blackwater's operations led to several serious cases of alleged abuse on the part of Blackwater employees. One of the most infamous examples of this occurred in Baghdad on September 16, 2007. While escorting a diplomatic convoy through the streets of the city, a well-armed security detail consisting of Blackwater personnel and Iraqi police mistakenly opened fire on a civilian car that it claimed had not obeyed instructions to stop. Once the gunfire began, other forces in the area opened fired. When the shooting stopped, 17 Iraqi civilians lay dead, including all of the car's occupants. Included among the dead was a young couple with their infant child. At first there were wildly diverging accounts of what happened, and Blackwater contended that the car contained a suicide bomber who had detonated an explosive device, which was entirely untrue. The Iraqi government, however, faulted Blackwater for the incident, and U.S. Army officials backed up the Iraqi claims. Later reports stated that the Blackwater guards fired on the vehicle with no provocation.

The Baghdad shootings caused an uproar in both Iraq and the United States. The Iraqi government suspended Blackwater's Iraqi operations and demanded that Blackwater be banned from the country. It also sought to try the shooters in an Iraqi court. Because some of the guards involved were not Americans and the others were working for the U.S. State Department, they were not subject to criminal prosecution. In the U.S. Congress, angry lawmakers demanded a full accounting of the incident and sought more detailed information on Blackwater and its security operations.

To make matters worse, just a few days after the shootings federal prosecutors announced that they were investigating allegations that some Blackwater personnel had illegally imported weapons into Iraq that were then being supplied to the Kurdistan Workers' Party, which has been designated by the United States as a terrorist organization.

These incendiary allegations prompted a formal congressional inquiry, and in October 2007 Erik Prince, Blackwater's CEO, was compelled to testify in front of the House Committee on Oversight and Government Reform. Prince did neither himself nor his company much good when he stonewalled the committee, saying that Blackwater's financial information was beyond the purview of the government. He later retracted this statement, saying that such information would be provided upon a "written request." Blackwater then struggled under a pall of suspicion, and multiple investigations were soon under way involving the incident in Iraq, incidents in Afghanistan, and the allegations of illegal weapons smuggling by company employees. In the meantime, Congress considered legislation that would significantly tighten government control and oversight of private contractors, especially those involved in sensitive areas such as military security.

In February 2009 Blackwater officials announced that the company would now operate under the name Xe, noting that the new name reflected a "change in company focus away from the business of providing private security." There was no meaning in the new name, which was decided upon after a yearlong internal search. Prince abruptly announced his resignation as CEO and left the company in December 2010, at which time its ownership and management were taken over by an unnamed group of private investors. The investors substantially reorganized the company, changed its name to Academi in 2011, and drastically changed its mission. It largely divested itself of overseas private security programs and added a division that deals strictly with corporate governance and ethics issues.

In June 2009 the Central Intelligence Agency disclosed to Congress that in 2004 it had hired members of Blackwater as part of a secret effort to locate and assassinate top Al Qaeda operatives. Reportedly, Blackwater employees assisted with planning, training, and surveillance, but no members of Al Qaeda were captured or killed by them. By 2008, most Blackwater employees had left Iraq; U.S. troops were withdrawn from the country in December 2011. For a time, Blackwater/Xe continued to operate in Afghanistan but in much reduced numbers and with a much lower profile. By 2014, the company no longer operated in Afghanistan.

On October 21, 2014, four Blackwater employees who were involved in the September 16, 2007, shootings of 17 Iraqis in Baghdad were found guilty of manslaughter, murder, and weapons charges in a U.S. federal district court. The defendants were Paul A. Slough, Dustin L. Heard, Nicholas A. Slatten, and Evan S. Liberty, all of whom were Blackwater security guards at the time of the shootings. Only Slatten was convicted of murder; the other three defendants were found guilty of manslaughter and improperly using a weapon to commit a violent crime. A fifth defendant, Jeremy Ridgeway, had previously pleaded guilty to manslaughter and was a witness for the prosecution. The Blackwater personnel argued that the shootings were inadvertent and an unfortunate example of collateral damage in an active war zone. U.S. prosecutors, however, portrayed the shootings as needless acts of recklessness that targeted innocent civilians who were not breaking the law. They also argued that the incident was not the result of an unintentional battlefield calamity but rather a criminal act. The case certainly highlights the potential problem of placing nonmilitary, private contractors into war zones when they do not technically fall under any U.S. military chain of command.

The trial was the culmination of a long, tortuous seven-year quest to bring the perpetrators of the massacre to justice. The trial was based chiefly on witness testimony, as there was little usable forensic evidence. The defendants claimed that the shootings had not been unprovoked and that they had genuinely feared for their lives and for the lives of the individuals they had been asked to protect. Lawyers for the defendants claimed that the verdicts were wrong and "incomprehensible." They also vowed to appeal the rulings. The U.S. government is empowered to prosecute crimes committed overseas by all government-employed contractors or other individuals who are acting at its behest. Some observers have lamented the fact that Blackwater founder Erik Prince, who is no longer involved with the company, was not in any way held legally accountable for the 2007 tragedy.

Paul G. Pierpaoli Jr.

See also: Bremer, Lewis Paul, III; Contractors: Private Security Firms; Fallujah, First Battle of; Iraq, History of, 1990–Present; Iraqi Freedom, Operation

References

Buzzell, Colby. *My War: Killing Time in Iraq.* New York: Putnam, 2005.

Engbrecht, Shawn. *America's Covert Warriors: Inside the World of Private Military Contractors.* Dulles, VA: Potomac Books, 2010.

U.S. Congress. *Private Security Firms: Standards, Cooperation, and Coordination on the Battlefield; Congressional Hearing.* Darby, PA: Diane Publishing, 2007.

Halliburton

A multinational corporation based in Houston, Texas, Halliburton provides specialty products and services to the oil and gas industries and also constructs oil fields, refineries, pipelines, and chemical plants through its main subsidiary KBR (Kellogg, Brown, and Root). Although the company conducts operations in more than 120 countries, controversy regarding Halliburton Energy Services has focused on U.S. government contracts awarded to the company following the Iraq War and allegations of conflict of interest involving former vice president Dick Cheney, who had been Halliburton's chief executive officer (CEO).

In 1919 during the midst of the oil boom in Texas and Oklahoma, Mr. and Mrs. Erle P. Halliburton began cementing oil wells in Burkburnett, Texas. That same year, the Halliburtons established their business in Dallas, Texas. They then moved the business to Ardmore, Oklahoma. In 1924, the Halliburton Oil Well Cementing Company was incorporated. A significant expansion of the company occurred in 1962 with the acquisition of Brown & Root, a construction and engineering firm that became a wholly owned subsidiary of Halliburton. Brown & Root had been established in 1919 by brothers George and Herman Brown along with their brother-in-law Dan Root. Employing political patronage with influential figures such as Lyndon B. Johnson, Brown & Root grew

Henry Bunting, former field buyer for Halliburton, testifies before the Senate Democratic Policy Committee on contracting abuses in Iraq. He holds a towel bearing the insignia of the Halliburton subsidiary "KBR" that was sold to the military. (Tom Williams/Roll Call/Getty Images)

from fulfilling small road-paving projects to garnering military contracts constructing military bases and naval warships. Brown & Root was part of a consortium responsible for providing approximately 85 percent of the infrastructure required by the U.S. military during the Vietnam War.

The relationship between Halliburton and the U.S. military establishment was enhanced in 1992 when the Pentagon, under the direction of Secretary of Defense Dick Cheney, offered the company a contract for the bulk of support services for U.S. military operations abroad. Three years later Cheney was elected chairman and CEO of Halliburton. One of Cheney's first initiatives at Halliburton was the acquisition of rival Dresser Industries for $7.7 billion. Halliburton, however, also inherited the legal liabilities of Dresser for asbestos poisoning claims. The asbestos settlement caused Halliburton's stock price to plummet 80 percent in 1999. Nevertheless, during Cheney's five-year tenure at Halliburton (1995–2000), government contracts awarded to the company rose to $1.5 billion. This contrasts with just $100 million in government contracts from 1990 to 1995.

Upon assuming the vice presidency in the George W. Bush administration in 2001, Cheney declared that he would be severing all ties with the company. He continued, however, to earn deferred compensation worth approximately $150,000 annually, along with stock options worth more than $18 million. Cheney assured critics that he would donate proceeds from the stock options to charity.

Even if Cheney did not personally profit, Halliburton secured several lucrative government contracts to rebuild Iraq and support the U.S. military presence in that nation following the U.S.-led invasion of Iraq in March 2003. By 2006, it was estimated that Halliburton's Iraq contracts alone were worth as much as $18 billion. Although the company enjoys relatively low profit margins from its military contracts, Halliburton stock hit a record high in August 2008 of $43.94 per share. In February 2003, one month before the invasion of Iraq, Halliburton stocks were selling for just $10.13 per share. By March 2010 as the Iraq War was winding down, the company's stock had retreated to $30.15 per share.

These profits, however, were subject to charges of corruption. For example, in 2003 a division of Halliburton overcharged the government by some $61 million for buying and transporting fuel from Kuwait into Iraq. Halliburton insisted that the high costs were the fault of a Kuwaiti subcontractor. Halliburton also received criticism for a $7 billion no-bid contract to rebuild Iraqi oil fields. Defenders of Halliburton insist that few companies have the resources and capital necessary to carry out the large-scale assignments given to Halliburton. Company executives also point out that if Halliburton had not provided support operations, far more combat troops would have been needed in Iraq. The controversies surrounding Halliburton's role in the Iraq War continue to raise questions as to the rationale for the initial March 2003 invasion.

More recently, Halliburton again came under fire for its involvement in the 2010 Deepwater Horizon oil spill in the Gulf of Mexico that released some 4.9 million barrels of crude oil into gulf waters. The oil well was owned by BP, but Halliburton had been a prime subcontractor on the project. In July 2013, Halliburton pleaded guilty to having deliberately destroyed evidence that BP had demanded once the leak was sealed. The company was forced to pay a $200,000 statutory fine for this action and continues to face other legal problems related to the spill.

Ron Briley

See also: Bush, George Walker; Cheney, Richard Bruce; Iraq, History of, 1990–Present; Iraqi Freedom, Operation

References

Briody, Dan. *The Halliburton Agenda: The Politics of Oil and Money.* Hoboken, NJ: Wiley, 2004.

Purdum, Todd S., and Will Shortz. *A Time of Our Choosing: America's War in Iraq.* New York: Times Books, 2003.

Private Security Firms

Private security firms are legally established for-profit enterprises contracted by government agencies to provide armed security or to engage in security assistance aid—advisers, training, equipment and weapons procurement, etc.—to foreign and U.S. military and nonmilitary forces. Although broadly falling into the category of government contractors, private security firms performing protective functions—providing armed guards whose duties may involve the use of deadly force—are set apart from the vast majority of government contractors, who provide only logistical, communications, administrative, and other service support. Indeed, the use of deadly force by some U.S.-contracted private security firms in Afghanistan and Iraq generated significant controversy.

The use of private contractors by governments to provide military support dates back to at least the 18th century, when armies hired civilian drivers and teams to move artillery cannon around the battlefield. During the American Civil War (1861–1865), civilian teamsters were hired to drive army supply wagons, and sutlers (businessmen selling food, drink, and other items to soldiers that are not available in the military supply system) contracted with the army for the privilege of accompanying units in the field. During the Vietnam War, U.S. military forces hired commercial firms such as Pacific Architects and Engineers (PA&E) to provide construction and other services that were beyond the military's capability to accomplish. Widespread contracting of services previously performed by military personnel (such as dining hall workers) began in earnest in the U.S. armed forces during the Jimmy Carter administration and increased since the military drawdown that began with the end of the Cold War in 1991. Government contractors were employed during Operation Desert Shield and Operation Desert Storm (1990–1991), and private security firms providing military assistance (advising, training, etc.) were used extensively in support of several Balkan nations since the collapse of Yugoslavia. Since 2001, the U.S. Department of Defense has employed private security firms to provide military training assistance and advisers to the Afghan and Iraqi military and security forces.

However, the Defense Department is only one U.S. government agency employing civilian contractors in general, and private security firms providing armed guards in particular are most often contracted by non–Defense Department agencies, such as the State Department. Private armed security guards contracted by the State Department normally work for the Regional Security Officer (a career U.S. Foreign Service officer) who is responsible for the security of a U.S. mission in a foreign country. Well-established American firms such as Halliburton, Blackwater (later renamed Academi), DynCorp, Kroll, Triple Canopy, Custer Battles, and Military Professional Resources, Inc., have all competed and won U.S. government contracts from various government agencies and for a wide range of services in Iraq and Afghanistan (although most were in Iraq).

In Iraq, Blackwater/Academi provided security guards and helicopters for the now-defunct Coalition Provisional Authority. Similarly, British firms such as ArmorGroup, Global Risk Strategies, and Aegis also won contracts to operate in these areas. Many private security firms recruit not only retired military and police personnel from their home country but also people with similar skills from all over the world. Many of these companies also recruited Iraqis or joined with upstart security companies in Iraq.

Critics of the use of private security firms claim that they have eroded national sovereignty by diminishing the nation's monopoly on the use of force and point to alleged instances of abuse of local nationals by private security firm personnel. Proponents of private security firms counter that the firms perform vital functions that would otherwise be difficult to accomplish, given scarce personnel and fiscal resources.

The lack of clarity surrounding the legal status of contractors has also posed concerns about their employees' accountability. Unlike military personnel, private security personnel working for the U.S. government are not subject to the Uniform Code of Military Justice (UCMJ)—indeed, they are security guards, not soldiers, and most do not even work for the Defense Department—and those who are not nationals of the hiring nation often are not subject to that nation's laws. In Iraq, for example, until the U.S.-Iraq security agreement signed in January 2009 stated that civilian contractors may face criminal charges in Iraqi courts, private security contractors were immune from legal prosecution under Coalition Provisional Authority Order 17, which effectively barred the Iraqi government from prosecuting contractor crimes in its own courts. There were also several reported incidences in which armed guard security contractors working for the U.S. State Department killed Iraqi civilians through the apparent use of excessive force. Such overly aggressive behavior is counterproductive, as it undermines U.S. efforts at nation building by alienating the Iraqi population in general. Indeed, the prevailing attitude among most U.S. military personnel toward private security guard contractors is overwhelmingly negative—a reaction that cannot simply be explained away by envy over the fact that private security firm employees may earn up to four times what uniformed military personnel are paid. U.S. military personnel tend to believe that those carrying weapons and authorized to exercise deadly force in the name of the United States should be limited to uniformed military personnel subject to the UCMJ, sworn and commissioned law enforcement officers, and designated and trained operations officers of official government intelligence agencies.

Yet despite the problems posed by the increasing use of private security firms, there is no indication that their influence seems likely to decrease.

Kristian P. Alexander, Jerry D. Morelock, and David T. Zabecki

See also: Contractors: Blackwater USA; Detention Operations, Coalition: Abu Ghraib

References

Avant, Deborah D. *The Market for Force: The Consequences of Privatizing Security.* Cambridge: Cambridge University Press, 2005.

Caparini, Marina, ed. *Private Military and Security Companies: Ethics, Policies and Civil-Military Relations.* New York: Taylor and Francis, 2008.

Chesterman, Simon, and Chia Lehnardt, eds. *From Mercenaries to Markets: The Rise and Regulation of Private Military Companies.* New York: Oxford University Press, 2007.

Engbrecht, Shawn. *America's Covert Warriors: Inside the World of Private Military Contractors.* Dulles, VA: Potomac Books, 2010.

Mandel, Robert. *Armies without States: The Privatization of Security.* Boulder, CO: Lynne Rienner, 2002.

Scahill, Jeremy. *Blackwater: The Rise of the World's Most Powerful Mercenary Army.* Saddle Brook, NJ: Avalon, 2007.

Singer, Peter W. *Corporate Warriors: The Rise of the Privatized Military Industry.* Ithaca, NY: Cornell University Press, 2003.

D

Detention Operations, Coalition

When an army occupies a country, it is inevitable that some individuals will rise up in opposition to that occupation and, in the process, break the law. The challenge in such circumstances is to have a complete system of governance in place that goes beyond mere apprehension and incarceration. The system must include judges and a manner of progressing people through the full process of judicial hearing and review to incarceration and release. If that process is not fully developed, as was the case in Iraq in the early period of the occupation, then what is the role and purpose of detention? Interrogation has a very relevant purpose in an occupation in that it provides information on those opposing the government. In this process it is important to consider whether or not everyone who needs interrogation also needs detention.

The United States established numerous detention facilities to deal with the Global War on Terrorism. The material below deals with the two most important sites in Iraq: Abu Ghraib Prison and Camp Bucca. Because it is always relevant to the discussion, there is an entry on Guantánamo Bay. The events and images associated with Abu Ghraib and the conduct of soldiers responsible for detainees solidified the narrative that the United States disrespected the Iraqi people. Camp Bucca can be argued to be one of the primary birthplaces of ISIS.

Abu Ghraib

Notorious Iraqi prison facility located about 20 miles west of the Iraqi capital of Baghdad. Known during the regime of Saddam Hussein as an infamous place of torture and execution, Abu Ghraib prison later drew international attention when photographs of inmate abuse and reports of torture at the hands of coalition troops were made public in 2004.

Abu Ghraib, officially called the Baghdad Central Confinement Facility under the Hussein regime, was built by British contractors hired by the Iraqi government in the 1960s. Covering an area of about one square mile, the prison housed five different types of prisoners during the Hussein regime: those with long sentences, those with short sentences, those imprisoned for capital crimes, those imprisoned for so-called special offenses, and foreign detainees. Cells, which are about 51 square feet in area, held as many as 40 people each.

During the 1980–1988 Iran-Iraq War, the Iraqi Baathist regime used the facility to imprison political dissidents and members of ethnic or religious groups seen as threats to the central government. In particular, hundreds of Arab and Kurdish Shiites and Iraqis of Iranian heritage were arrested and housed in the Baghdad Central Confinement Facility; torture and executions became routine. Among the tactics used by prison guards was the feeding of shredded plastic to inmates, and it has been speculated that prisoners were used as guinea pigs for biological and chemical weapons. Although the

Iraqi government kept its actions within the complex secret from Iraqi citizens and the international community alike, Amnesty International reported several specific incidents, including the 1996 execution of hundreds of political dissidents and the 1998 execution of many people who had been involved in the 1991 Shiite revolt. The prison, which contained thousands of inmates who were completely cut off from outside communication and held without conviction, was also used to house coalition prisoners of war during the 1991 Persian Gulf War.

With the 2003 U.S.-led Iraq War and subsequent fall of the Hussein government in Iraq, coalition troops took control of Abu Ghraib prison. The U.S. military used the complex for holding Iraqi insurgents and terrorists accused of anti-U.S. attacks, although by 2004 it had released several hundred prisoners and shared use of the facility with the Iraqi government. Because of the disarray in the Iraqi criminal system, many common criminals uninvolved in the war were held at the facility as well.

Abu Ghraib became a household name in April 2004 when the television program *60 Minutes II* aired photographs of prisoner abuse at the hands of U.S. troops. Just two days later, the photographs were posted online with Seymour Hersch's article in the *New Yorker* magazine. The photos, which showed prisoners wearing black hoods, attached to wires with which they were threatened with electrocution, and placed in humiliating sexual positions, sparked worldwide outrage and calls for the investigation and conviction of the military personnel involved.

The abuse was immediately decried by U.S. president George W. Bush and by Defense Secretary Donald Rumsfeld, who on May 7, 2004, took responsibility for the acts occurring during his tenure. The Pentagon, which had been investigating reports of abuse since 2003, launched a further investigation into the incidents documented in the photographs. Previously, detainee abuse had been investigated by U.S. Army Major General Antonio Taguba, who had been given digital images of the abuse by Sergeant Joseph Darby in January 2004. Major General Taguba concluded in his 53-page report that U.S. military personnel had violated international law. More than a dozen U.S. soldiers and officers were removed from the prison as a result of the internal investigation.

More details emerged following the *60 Minutes II* broadcast. Photographs that the U.S. government would not allow to be released earlier were circulated in 2006. Most important, it appeared that the senior U.S. military officer, Lieutenant General Ricardo Sanchez, had authorized treatment "close to" torture, such as the use of military dogs, temperature extremes, and sensory and sleep deprivation, thus making it more difficult to locate responsibility for the general environment leading to abuse. However, in addition to charging certain troops and contractors with torture, the United States made an effort to reduce the number of detainees—estimated at 7,000 prior to the scandal's outbreak—by several thousand. However, many argued that the measures taken were not harsh enough to fit the crime, and some demanded Rumsfeld's resignation. Meanwhile, in August 2004 a military panel confirmed 44 cases of prisoner abuse at the facility and identified 23 soldiers as being responsible. The so-called ringleader of the operation, U.S. Army specialist Charles Graner, was convicted and sentenced to 10 years in prison. In January 2005, Abu Ghraib was twice attacked by insurgents attempting to free prisoners held there.

The United States held detainees in the portion of the prison known as "Camp

Redemption," built in 2004. In September 2006, the United States handed over control of Abu Ghraib to the Iraqi government. The Iraqi government holds convicted criminals in the older area known as the "Hard Site," although efforts were made to release those who might be innocent.

The terrorist organization Islamic State of Iraq claimed responsibility for two coordinated assaults on July 23, 2013, that freed 500–600 militants being held at Abu Ghraib and Taji. This action greatly enhanced the organization's fortunes in Iraq and Syria. At least 26 members of the Iraqi Security Forces and more than a dozen prisoners died.

Jessica Britt

See also: Bush, George Walker; Hussein, Saddam; Iraq, History of, 1990–Present; Islamic State of Iraq and al-Sham (ISIS): Al Qaeda in Iraq; Kurds; Secretary of Defense, U.S.: Donald Rumsfeld

References

Danner, Mark. *Torture and Truth: America, Abu Ghraib, and the War on Terror.* New York: New York Review Books, 2004.

Graveline, Christopher, and Michael Clemens. *The Secrets of Abu Ghraib Revealed.* Dulles, VA: Potomac Books, 2010.

Greenberg, Karen J., and Joshua L. Dratel, eds. *The Torture Papers: The Road to Abu Ghraib.* Cambridge, MA: Cambridge University Press, 2005.

Strasser, Steven, ed. *The Abu Ghraib Investigations: The Official Independent Panel and Pentagon Reports on the Shocking Prisoner Abuse in Iraq.* New York: PublicAffairs, 2004.

Camp Bucca

A U.S. detention camp near Umm Qasr, Iraq. After the U.S. invasion of Iraq in 2003, the British military established a camp to house Iraqi prisoners of war. Camp Freddy, as this British installation became known, was eventually transferred to American control and renamed Camp Bucca after NYC fire marshal Ronald Bucca, who died in the terrorist attacks of September 11, 2001.

During the early stages of the U.S. involvement in Iraq, there were reports of detainee abuse at Camp Bucca, including physical violence during interrogation. After the Abu Ghraib prisoner abuse scandal, the U.S. Army moved many detainees from Abu Ghraib to Camp Bucca and sought to introduce key changes to turn the camp into an example of a model detention facility. The detainees were interned in 10 climate-controlled housing compounds and provided with access to health care, education, and entertainment; prisoners could also participate in a family visitation allowance program. Each compound held up to 800 prisoners, who chose their own leader who both maintained order within a compound and served as a liaison with the camp authorities.

In 2007–2008, Camp Bucca was the largest detention facility in the world, with a prisoner population of more than 20,000 men. In 2009 the camp authorities gradually released or transferred detainees before shutting down the camp. A year later the U.S. military handed the base to the government of Iraq.

There is evidence that Abu Bakr al-Baghdadi, the leader of ISIS, was an inmate in Camp Bucca in 2006. Some suggest that it was in Camp Bucca that al-Baghdadi created his network that he used to build what became the senior leadership of ISIS.

Alexander Mikaberidze

See also: Bush, George Walker; Hussein, Saddam; Iraq, History of, 1990–Present; Islamic State of Iraq and al-Sham (ISIS): Al Qaeda in

Iraq; Kurds; Secretary of Defense, U.S.: Donald Rumsfeld

References

Angell, Ami. *Terrorist Rehabilitation: The US Experience in Iraq.* Boca Raton, FL: CRC Press, 2012.

Khalil, Ashraf. "Camp Bucca Turns 180 Degrees from Abu Ghraib." *Los Angeles Times,* January 10, 2005.

Pryer, Douglas. "The Fight for the High Ground: The U.S. Army and Interrogation during Operation Iraqi Freedom I, May 2003–April 2004." MA in Military Art and Science thesis, U.S. Army Command and General Staff College, 2009, www.dtic.mil/get-tr-doc/pdf?AD=ADA502354.

Guantánamo Bay Detention Camp

Detention camp operated by the U.S. government to hold enemy combatants taken prisoner during the Global War on Terrorism, which began in late 2001 following the September 11, 2001, terror attacks against the United States. The Guantánamo Bay Detention Camp is situated on the Guantánamo Bay Naval Base, operated by the United States in southeastern Cuba. The base covers approximately 45 square miles. In one of the most controversial aspects of the Global War on Terrorism, prisoners held at the camp have been stripped of legal protections afforded to citizens of any nationality under U.S. and international law. Legally

U.S. military police escort a detainee to his cell at the naval base at Guantanamo Bay, Cuba, on January 11, 2002. (U.S. Department of Defense)

classified as "enemy combatants," prisoners may be detained indefinitely, without formal charges brought against them and without access to legal counsel. Hundreds of such detainees from more than 35 nations have been kept prisoner at the camp since 2002 without formal charges and beyond the legal protection of the Geneva Conventions. Guantánamo Bay detainees have also been denied access to lawyers or contact with their families, diplomats, or national government officials.

The U.S. military acquired Guantánamo Bay as a naval base as a consequence of the Spanish-American War of 1898. It has maintained the facility since 1903, despite tensions with the communist regime in Cuba led by Fidel Castro and his brother, Raul Castro. Until the terrorist attacks of September 11, 2001, the U.S. military had used the base primarily as a gathering place for Cuban and Haitian refugees. Although the facility is only 45 square miles in size, more than 9,000 U.S. personnel are permanently stationed there.

Guantánamo has come under intense international scrutiny since 2002. The U.S. military moved its first detainees of the Global War on Terrorism in Afghanistan there on January 11, 2002, and by late 2014, 779 individuals from more than 35 nations had been held there (some were later released or transferred).

Despite pressure both nationally and internationally, the administration of President George W. Bush refused to change its policies regarding the detainees. The Bush administration contended that detainees at Guantánamo Bay fell into a new legal category of "enemy combatants" and as such must be assumed to be guilty until proven innocent, although precisely what evidentiary or legal avenues remained open to detainees is unclear. Bush's successor, President Barack Obama, vowed to close the facility when he took office in 2009, but he was unable to win sufficient congressional support throughout his presidency, and the facility remained open as he left office.

Human rights organizations such as Amnesty International and the International Committee of the Red Cross, as well as former military officials working at Guantánamo Bay, have described the conditions of prison life there, and they are far from pleasant. Prisoners are alleged to have been kept in isolation cells for many days at a time; beaten and otherwise physically harmed; exposed to aggressive dogs, loud music, and strobe lights; and kept caged but exposed in outdoor cells during violent tropical weather. Prisoners are also alleged to have been subjected to extremely hot and cold temperatures, chained in uncomfortable or strenuous positions, denied food and water, and have been forced to defecate and urinate upon themselves. Other allegations claim that prisoners have been sexually harassed and abused and have had their religious beliefs ridiculed. The U.S. government refuses to grant the International Committee of the Red Cross access to prisoners.

One of the most controversial allegations is that foreign nationals have in recent years been abducted by U.S. forces (a process termed "extraordinary rendition"); tortured in their native countries with U.S. assistance and instruction, chiefly by the Central Intelligence Agency (CIA); and then sent to Guantánamo Bay for indefinite detention. Evidence has been presented to Amnesty International, the Red Cross, and the British government that nationals of Pakistani, Chinese, Afghan, Egyptian, Syrian, Canadian, and Iraqi descent, among others, have been detained in this way. A handful of missing people throughout the world have become "ghost detainees"; that is, they are believed by many to have been abducted in such fashion and then completely disappeared.

Those known to be held at Guantánamo Bay have been routinely denied access to lawyers, and non-U.S. detainees are not given the rights to have any levied charges tried in courts where appeals are possible. A variety of legal rulings by U.S. courts, including the Supreme Court, have asserted that Guantánamo Bay detainees have the right to military tribunals as prisoners of war, and even to U.S. military or criminal courts in some cases. Nevertheless, the Bush administration unilaterally declared that any trials of camp detainees would be conducted by a new body formed in June 2004 and known as the Combatant Status Review Board (CSRB). That board was directly responsible only to the executive branch of the government, and there was no appeals process. Moreover, its tribunals accept coerced testimony or admissions as evidence. Defense lawyers, if they are consulted at all, are not given access to any evidence presented by the government. Because of this, the CSRB violated both international law and generally accepted human rights law.

On January 22, 2009, two days after taking office, President Barack Obama signed an executive order that mandated a suspension of criminal proceedings at Guantánamo Bay and the closure of the facility by year's end. This drew the immediate ire and suspicion of a number of Americans, who believed that such a move would imperil national security. In May 2009, the U.S. Senate voted to deny funds that might be used for the transfer or release of Guantánamo Bay detainees. Nevertheless, in December 2009 Obama signed another executive order that would have transferred all prisoners to an Illinois prison. That move caused outrage in Illinois, Obama's adoptive home state. Early the next year, the Guantánamo Review Task Force concluded that 126 detainees were eligible for transfer but that 40 others were deemed too dangerous to move. Meanwhile, many U.S. states flatly refused to take any of the prisoners, so Guantánamo Bay remained open.

Realizing that he was losing the battle to close the facility, in 2011 Obama signed an order forbidding the transfer of certain prisoners to the U.S. mainland, effectively ensuring that Guantánamo Bay would remain open. Attempts to try some of the suspects held there in U.S. civilian courts have likewise been stymied.

Nancy L. Stockdale and Paul G. Pierpaoli Jr.

See also: Bush, George Walker; Global War on Terrorism; Interrogation, Coercive (Torture); Obama, Barack Hussein, II

References

"Bowe Berghdal Fast Facts." CNN, July 21, 2014, http://www.cnn.com/2014/01/19/us/bowe-bergdahl-fast-facts.

Epstein, Edward. "Guantanamo Is a Miniature America." *San Francisco Chronicle,* January 20, 2002, A6.

Hansen, Jonathan M. "Making the Law in Cuba." *New York Times,* April 20, 2004, A19.

Mendelsohn, Sarah E. *Closing Guantanamo: From Bumper Sticker to Blueprint.* Washington, DC: Center for Security and International Studies, 2008.

"Obama Calls on Congress to Do More on Guantánamo Bay." Reuters, December 26, 2013, http://www.reuters.com/article/2013/12/26/us-usa-obama-defense-idUSBRE9BP0H620131226.

Saar, Erik, and Viveca Novak. *Inside the Wire: A Military Intelligence Soldier's Eyewitness Account of Life at Guantanamo.* New York: Penguin, 2005.

Yee, John. *War by Other Means: An Insider's Account of the War on Terror.* New York: Atlantic Monthly, 2006.

Doctrine, Counterinsurgency

A warfare strategy employed to defeat an organized rebellion or revolutionary movement aimed at bringing down and replacing established governmental authority. Among the more confusing terms relating to the practice of warfare, the term "counterinsurgency" implies both the purpose of military operations and the methods selected. U.S. interest in counterinsurgency soared in 2005 as it became increasingly apparent that an insurgency was gravely undermining the efforts of the United States and its allies to establish a new regime in Iraq after the 2003 Anglo-American–led invasion and occupation.

Understanding the term "counterinsurgency" requires an appreciation of its logical opposite: insurgency. Counterinsurgency originated as a conceptual response to the spread of insurgencies, particularly as carried out by anticolonialist or communist movements during the Cold War from the late 1940s to the 1980s. Insurgents typically lacked key sources of power, such as financial wealth, a professional military, or advanced weaponry, that were available to established regimes or governments. Consequently, insurgents adopted asymmetric tactics and strategies that focused on avoidance of direct combat until such time as governmental power had been gravely weakened. Instead, skillful insurgents blended an array of methods including propaganda, attacks on public institutions and infrastructure, the creation of secret support networks, and use of unconventional or guerrilla combat tactics. By these means, insurgents could whittle away at the strength of existing regimes or occupying powers while slowly increasing their own capabilities.

U.S. interest in counterinsurgency, sometimes referred to as counterrevolutionary warfare, grew during the Vietnam War. Efforts to defeat the Viet Cong guerrillas in South Vietnam were considered important but more often than not took a backseat to the conduct of conventional military operations against the People's Army of Vietnam (North Vietnamese Army). With the American withdrawal from Vietnam in 1973, however, the U.S. military resumed focusing on conventional war, and the study of counterinsurgency by the U.S. Army waned. Even with the end of the Cold War in 1991, the U.S. military did not regard the study of counterinsurgency as equally important to the mastery of conventional combat.

To many, Operation Desert Storm in Iraq in 1991 justified the American focus on conventional combat. The Persian Gulf War provided an awesome demonstration of U.S. military proficiency and technology. Indeed, American dominance was so compelling that it may have dissuaded future potential opponents from attempting to challenge American might on any conventional battlefield. One result of this was perhaps to encourage adversaries to attack U.S. interests by asymmetric means, such as guerrilla insurgency tactics or terror. There was also a growing perception among enemies of the United States that American politicians and military leaders were extremely uncomfortable in situations in which they could not bring superior conventional military power to bear. The deaths of 18 U.S. Army soldiers on October 3–4, 1993, during a raid against a renegade warlord in Somalia may have been the exception that proved the rule. Largely a product of events in Somalia, Bill Clinton's casualty-averse posture of U.S. forces in subsequent peacekeeping missions in Haiti, Bosnia, and Kosovo during the 1990s tended to reinforce the view that Americans were reluctant to suffer any casualties in scenarios short of unconstrained conventional combat.

The startling terror attacks on U.S. soil on September 11, 2001, led to a swift reorientation in American military thinking. The immediate American response was to strike against the Taliban regime in Afghanistan that had provided refuge for Al Qaeda terrorists claiming responsibility for the attacks. Informed by its own support for the mujahideen guerrilla resistance to the Soviet occupation of Afghanistan during the 1980s, the United States decided to rely as much as possible on small teams of special operations forces, which would support allied indigenous forces with cutting-edge technologies, rather than on massed conventional forces. The fall of the Taliban regime within three months now placed American forces in the position of stabilizing a fledgling regime under Hamid Karzai.

Very soon the tools of counterinsurgency would prove most relevant in Afghanistan against surviving remnants of the Taliban that found sanctuary along the Pakistani frontier. One important measure taken was the creation and deployment of Provincial Reconstruction Teams beginning in 2003. These combined a small number of military specialists with representatives of various U.S. or other foreign governmental agencies possessing expertise in diplomacy, policing, agriculture, and other fields relevant to the process of fostering security and development. Found to be effective in Afghanistan in extending governmental reach to remote areas, the concept soon found application in Iraq as well.

In the meantime, the invasion of Iraq in March 2003, while initially marking another triumph of conventional operations, did not result in a smooth transition to a stable civilian government. Indeed, coalition forces in Iraq soon faced a formidable counterinsurgency challenge for which neither military nor civilian officials had fully prepared. In fact, many critics maintain that the early failure to establish public order, restore services, and identify local partners provided the insurgency, which Iraqis term "the resistance," with an interval of chaos that enabled it to organize and grow. Since Iraqi politics had consistently shown wave after wave of resistance, purges, and new coups, such a challenge could reasonably have been expected. Sectarian leaders and their militias began to assert influence, and Al Qaeda fighters infiltrated key provinces in anticipation of a new struggle to come.

By 2005, spreading ethnic and religious violence in Iraq resulted in the deaths of many civilians as well as local governmental and security personnel. Suicide bombings as well as the remote detonation of improvised explosive devices became signature tactics of the Iraqi insurgency. Furthermore, repeated attacks on United Nations personnel and foreign relief workers caused a virtual suspension of outside aid to the Iraqi people.

Recognition of the need to focus on counterinsurgency methods led to a vitally significant effort to publish a military doctrinal manual on the subject. An initial indicator of the official shift in U.S. military thinking was the release of Department of Defense Directive 3000-05 on November 28, 2005, which specifically acknowledged responsibility for planning and carrying out so-called support and stability operations essential to any counterinsurgency campaign. Under the leadership of Lieutenant General David Petraeus during his tenure as commander,

Combined Arms Center, and commandant of the U.S. Army Command and General Staff College at Fort Leavenworth, Kansas, in 2006–2007, a team of writers and practitioners with experience in Iraq and Afghanistan undertook a crash project to draft, revise, and publish the new manual.

In his opening address to the Combat Studies Institute Military History Symposium on August 8, 2006, Petraeus set forth several points of emphasis of the soon-to-be-published U.S. Army Field Manual 3–24 (also known as U.S. Marine Warfighting Publication No. 3-33.5), titled *Counterinsurgency*. Asserting that T. E. Lawrence (of Arabia) had figured out the essentials of counterinsurgency during World War I, Petraeus contended that any prospect of success depended on identifying capable local leaders, providing them necessary assistance without doing the hard work for them, fostering the development of public institutions, forming a partnership with existing security forces, and maintaining a flexible and patient outlook. In other words, counterinsurgency would require far more of military leaders than the performance of traditional and familiar combat tasks. Petraeus himself had practiced these principles in Iraq, where in late 2004 he served as the first commander of the Multi-National Security Transition Command–Iraq, which focused on the training of local personnel to become civilian and military leaders in Iraq.

Officially released in December 2006, *Counterinsurgency* attracted great attention in the press and conveyed the impression that the military was not stuck in an outmoded mind-set. Rather, U.S. Army and U.S. Marine Corps leaders on the ground in Afghanistan and Iraq became increasingly adaptive and creative in the search for improved solutions to the problem of combating insurgency where nation building was still very much in progress. *Counterinsurgency* devoted a majority of its eight chapters and five appendices to tasks other than war fighting. Lengthy sections also related to ethics, civilian and military cooperation, cultural analysis, linguistic support, the law of war, and ethical considerations.

Of course, the U.S. Army and the U.S. Marine Corps had not ignored the principles of counterinsurgency before the new doctrine was published. However, publication signaled to the American public and the U.S. Congress that the military was wholly committed to the implementation of counterinsurgency principles. Implementation of this new counterinsurgency doctrine began to bear fruit but could not overcome the political decisions of the Iraqi government headed by Prime Minister Nuri al-Maliki (in power from May 2006 to September 2014), which took a decidedly sectarian approach that favored the Shiite majority at the expense of the Sunni and Kurdish minorities. The insurgency therefore continued well after the withdrawal of U.S. forces at the end of 2011, although it is now sometimes referred to as the Iraq Crisis.

Robert F. Baumann

See also: Commanders, U.S. Central Command: David H. Petraeus; Doctrine, Insurgency; Iraqi Freedom, Operation: The Surge and the Awakening; Islamic State of Iraq and al-Sham (ISIS): Al Qaeda in Iraq; Weapons, Insurgency, and Opposition: Improvised Explosive Devices

References

Keegan, John. *The Iraq War: The Military Offensive, from Victory in 21 Days to the Insurgent Aftermath*. New York: Vintage, 2005.

Kitson, Frank. *Low Intensity Operations: Subversion, Insurgency and Peacekeeping*. London: Faber and Faber, 1971.

Nagl, John A. *Learning to Eat Soup with a Knife: Counterinsurgency Lessons from Malaya and Vietnam*. Chicago: University of Chicago Press, 2005.

Doctrine, Insurgency

There are two works produced during the period from the September 11, 2001, attacks and the U.S. invasion in Iraq in 2003. Both shaped the way practitioners of insurgency approached fighting against the United States specifically and the West, in general.

The first book was written by Abu Musab al-Suri, born Mustafa bin Abd al-Qadir Setmariam Nasar. He is considered one of the most influential writers about modern jihad. His analysis and recommendations of conducting jihad is captured in a massive work called *Call to Global Resistance* or sometimes translated as *The Call for Global Islamic Resistance*. This work is about 1,600 pages and was spread online in 2004. He was an influential strategist and writer before this book, but this book provides his recommended pattern for success.

Al-Suri explained why jihad worked in Afghanistan (1979–1989) and why it failed in Algeria (1990s). He made a pragmatic argument for conducting operations that work rather than ones focused on spectacular effect. This document is credited with changing the nature of jihadist activities in Iraq and around the world since its publication. He challenged the use of extreme tactics as counterproductive to the overall struggle. He is one of the first to advocate for what has been called "lone wolf" or "stray dog" terrorism.

The second book is the *Management of Savagery: The Most Critical Stage through Which the Islamic Nation Will Pass*. It is a manifesto written by a salafi-jihadi thinker named Abu Bakr Naji that was published on the Internet in 2004. Based on its publication date, it is clear that this was written for the broader salafi-jihadi community though its author, Abu Bakr Naji, is a known Al Qaeda strategist, and the book was certainly intended to inform Al Qaeda's strategic thought. The recommendations in the book are significant when viewing the actions of Al Qaeda and ISIS over time and how they view the violence they perform.

Though the book and its thinking have been described as "Al Qaeda's Playbook," this is probably not true. It looks to be more influential in terms of shaping the actions of other groups like ISIS. Naji advocated for numerous small attacks rather than spectacular Hollywood-style or 9/11-style attacks. Al Qaeda always seemed to be looking for another big attack while ISIS was content with consistent smaller ones as described and advocated for by Naji. That said, this work describes the thinking and behavior regarding how to use violence in the fight between salafi-jihadis and their opponents.

The first doctrinal point identified in the book is that the salafi-jihadi community is fighting a war of attrition or exhaustion where the intent is to drain the resources of the opponent powers such that they no longer have the will to continue the struggle. Second, violence is to be used as a means to generate both energy within the salafi-jihadi community and a sense of urgency within the broader Sunni Muslim community. The author of this work and other salafi-jihadi thinkers acknowledge that the vast majority of Sunni Muslims are not awake to the perils of the West with respect to their belief and their way of life. Thus, the violence will do three things simultaneously. One, it will wake the broader community to the perils facing it. Two, the violence will bring Western powers into the Muslim world where they will commit their own violence. This will further estrange the Sunnis from the West, causing them to hate the West and struggle against it. Three, the allies of the West within the Muslim world will be discredited. This will come about through the inability of the West to prevent ISIS from targeting Western powers. In addition, the Saudi, Egyptian, Jordanian, and other governments will look weak and wrong because of their reliance on and association with Western powers that would then be responsible for all of the damage in the Muslim world.

The main idea is that violence is not an end to itself. The salafi-jihadis are not killing people and destroying things for a material benefit. They are beheading, burning people alive, and conducting suicide bomb attacks as part of a program to create an environment of Sunni energy and outrage against the West in an attempt to inspire the Sunnis to rise up and support the caliphate.

Brian L. Steed

See also: Commanders, U.S. Central Command: David H. Petraeus; Doctrine, Counterinsurgency

References

Al-Suri, Abu Musab. *Call to Global Islamic Resistance*, translated and condensed into *A Terrorist's Call to Global Jihad: Deciphering Abu Musab al-Suri's Islamic Jihad Manifesto*, edited by Jim Lacey. Annapolis, MD: Naval Institute Press, 2008.

Cruickshank, Paul, and Mohannad Hage Ali. "Abu Musab Al Suri: Architect of the New Al Qaeda." *Studies in Conflict & Terrorism*, 30(1) (December 21, 2006): 1–14. doi:10.1080/10576100601049928 (accessed April 23, 2018).

Maher, Shiraz. *Salafi-Jihadism: The History of an Idea*. New York: Oxford University Press, 2016.

Naji, Abu Bakr. *The Management of Savagery: The Most Critical Stage through Which the Umma Will Pass*. Translated by William McCants. Cambridge, MA: John M. Olin Institute for Strategic Studies, May 23, 2006, 230–231, https://www.narrativespace.net/support-files/management_of_savagery.pdf (accessed November 25, 2017).

Fallujah, First Battle of (April 4–May 1, 2004)

A U.S. military operation, the principal goal of which was to retake the Iraqi city of Fallujah after insurgents had seized control. Code-named Vigilant Resolve, it occurred during April 4–May 1, 2004. Sunni insurgents, including Al Qaeda fighters, had steadily destabilized Anbar Province in Iraq in the aftermath of the 2003 U.S.-led invasion. Fallujah, located some 42 miles west of Baghdad in the so-called Sunni Triangle, emerged as a focal point for anticoalition attacks. The town was dominated by Salafist groups who were extremely suspicious of all outsiders, particularly foreigners; family and clan ties dominated personal relationships. The collapse of Iraqi president Saddam Hussein's regime had left some 70,000 male inhabitants in the city unemployed, providing a major source of recruits for the Iraqi insurgency movement.

Growing violence in Fallujah in March 2004 led the U.S. military to withdraw forces from the city and conduct only armed patrols. On March 31 insurgents ambushed four contractors working for Blackwater USA, a private contracting company that provided security personnel to the Coalition Provisional Authority (CPA). The insurgents dragged the bodies through the streets and then hanged them from a bridge. Television cameras transmitted the grisly images around the world, prompting a strong response to offset the perception that coalition forces had lost control of the area.

In an effort to regain control of the city and the surrounding province, the U.S. military launched a series of operations against suspected insurgent groups and their bases. The lead unit was the I Marine Expeditionary Force, which had been deployed to Anbar in March. The ground forces were supported by coalition aircraft and helicopter units. U.S. lieutenant general James Conway had overall command of the operation. On April 4 some 2,200 marines surrounded Fallujah. They blockaded the main roads in and out of the city in an effort to allow only civilians to escape the fighting. The commanders on the ground believed that the marines should remain outside of the city because they lacked the troops to effectively control the area and the population; nevertheless, they were ordered to seize the city.

In the opening days of the operation, U.S. forces conducted air strikes on suspected targets and undertook limited incursions into Fallujah, including a strike to take control of its main radio station. At least one-quarter of the civilian population fled the city as insurgents used homes, schools, and mosques to attack the marines, who responded with devastating firepower that often produced high collateral damage and civilian casualties.

Within the city there were an estimated 15,000–20,000 insurgent fighters divided among more than a dozen insurgent groups of various origins. Some were former members of Hussein's security forces. They were armed with a variety of weapons, including light arms, rocket-propelled grenades, mortars, and improvised explosive devices

(IEDs). The insurgents used guerrilla tactics against the marines, including ambushes, mortar attacks, and mines and IEDs. Sniper fire was common throughout the operation. U.S. forces responded with artillery and air strikes, including the use of heavily armed Lockheed AC-130 gunships. Support from Bell AH-1W Super Cobra attack helicopters, however, was limited because of significant ground fire. Meanwhile, the marines attempted to secure neighborhoods one or two blocks at a time using air support and tanks.

There were problems coordinating movements in the dense urban environment, especially because maps were not standardized between the various units. Meanwhile, many of the remaining Iraqi Security Forces within the city either joined the insurgents or simply fled their posts. After three days of intense fighting, the marines had secured only about one-quarter of Fallujah.

In response to the escalating violence, the failure of the marines to make significant progress in the city, growing pressure from Iraqi political leaders, and increasing domestic pressure on the George W. Bush administration that was largely the result of media coverage, the U.S.-led CPA ordered a unilateral cease-fire on April 9 and initiated negotiations with the insurgent groups. The marines allowed humanitarian aid into the city; however, in spite of the cease-fire, sporadic fighting continued. Throughout the negotiations, it was decided that the United States would turn over security for the city to a newly formed ad hoc Iraqi militia force, the Fallujah Brigade. The United States agreed to provide arms and equipment for the brigade, which included former soldiers and police officers of the Hussein regime.

On May 1 U.S. forces completely withdrew from Fallujah, but they maintained a presence outside of the city at an observation base. More than 700 Iraqis had been killed in the fighting (the majority of these, perhaps as many as 600, were civilians), while 27 U.S. marines were killed and 90 were wounded.

The Fallujah Brigade failed to maintain security and began to disintegrate during the summer of 2004. Many of its members joined or rejoined the insurgency, and the military announced that Abu Musab al-Zarqawi, the leader of Al Qaeda in Iraq, was headquartered in Fallujah. The coalition undertook a second campaign in Fallujah in the autumn of 2004, code-named Operation Phantom Fury.

Tom Lansford

See also: Commanders, U.S. Central Command: James Mattis; Fallujah, Second Battle of

References

Afong, Milo. *Hogs in the Shadows: Combat Stories from Marine Snipers in Iraq.* New York: Berkley, 2007.

Cockburn, Patrick. *The Occupation: War and Resistance in Iraq.* New York: Verso, 2007.

O'Donnell, Patrick K. *We Were One: Shoulder to Shoulder with the Marines Who Took Fallujah.* New York: Da Capo, 2007.

West, Bing. *No True Glory: A Frontline Account of the Battle for Fallujah.* New York: Bantam, 2006.

Fallujah, Second Battle of (November 7–December 23, 2004)

Major battle fought in and around the city of Fallujah, some 42 miles west of Baghdad, between U.S., Iraqi, and British forces and Iraqi insurgents (chiefly Al Qaeda in Iraq but also other militias). Following the decision to halt the coalition assault on Fallujah in

U.S. Army soldiers clear houses of insurgent fighters during fighting in the Iraqi insurgent stronghold of Fallujah, November 10, 2004. (Scott Nelson/Getty Images)

Operation Vigilant Resolve (First Battle of Fallujah, April 4–May 1, 2004), the U.S. marines had withdrawn from the city and turned over security to the so-called Fallujah Brigade, an ad hoc force of local men who had formerly served in the Iraqi Army. The Fallujah Brigade failed dismally in this task, giving the insurgents another chance to claim victory and attract additional recruits. During the summer and autumn months, the Fallujah police turned a blind eye as the insurgents fortified positions inside Fallujah and stockpiled supplies. The Iraqi Interim Government, formed on June 28, 2004, then requested new efforts to capture and secure Fallujah.

In preparation for the ground assault, coalition artillery and aircraft began selective strikes on the city on October 30, 2004. Coalition ground forces (American, Iraqi, and British) cut off electric power to the city on November 5 and distributed leaflets warning people to stay in their homes and not use their cars. This was a response to insurgent suicide bombers who had been detonating cars packed with explosives. On November 7 the Iraqi government announced a 60-day state of emergency throughout most of Iraq. Because of all these warnings, between 75 and 90 percent of Fallujah's civilian population abandoned the city before the coalition ground offensive began. Many of them fled to Syria, where they remain as refugees.

The Americans initially labeled the assault Operation Phantom Fury. Iraqi prime minister Ayad Allawi, however, renamed it Al-Fajr (New Dawn). The operation's main objective was to demonstrate the ability of the Iraqi government to control its own territory, thereby bolstering its prestige. The American military focused on the important secondary objective of killing as many insurgents as possible while keeping coalition casualties low. About 10,000 American soldiers and marines and 2,000 Iraqi troops participated in Operation Al-Fajr. Some Royal Marines also took part. The American forces involved had considerable experience in urban combat.

The assault plan called for a concentration of forces north of Fallujah. Spearheaded by the army's heavy armor, army and marine units would attack due south along precisely defined sectors. The infantry would methodically clear buildings, leaving the trailing Iraqi forces to search for insurgents and assault the city's 200 mosques, which coalition tacticians suspected would be used as defensive insurgent strongpoints. Intelligence estimates suggested that some 3,000 insurgents defended the city, one-fifth of whom were foreign jihadists. Intelligence estimates also predicted fanatical resistance.

Ground operations associated with the Second Battle of Fallujah commenced on November 7, 2004, when an Iraqi commando unit and the U.S. Marine Corps 3rd Light Armored Reconnaissance Battalion conducted a preliminary assault. The objective was to secure the Fallujah General Hospital to the west of the city and capture two bridges over the Euphrates River, thereby isolating the insurgent forces inside the city. This preliminary assault was successful, allowing the main assault to commence after dark the following evening. The American military chose this time because it knew that its various night-vision devices would provide it a tactical advantage over the insurgents. Four marine infantry and two army mechanized battalions attacked in the first wave. M-1A2 Abrams tanks and M-2A3 Bradley infantry fighting vehicles provided mobile firepower for which the insurgents had no answer. The M-1A2 Abrams tanks exhibited the ability to absorb enormous punishment and keep operating. The speed and shock of the massed armor overwhelmed the insurgents, enabling the American soldiers to drive deep into Fallujah. Iraqi forces also performed surprisingly well. After four days of operations, coalition forces had secured about half the city.

By November 11, the methodical American advance had driven most of the insurgents into the southern part of Fallujah. Three days of intense street fighting ensued, during which time the Americans reached the southern limits of the city. On November 15 the Americans reversed direction and attacked north to eliminate any insurgents who had been missed in the first pass and to search more thoroughly for insurgent weapons and supplies. For this part of the operation, the ground forces broke down into squad-sized elements to conduct their searches. By November 16 American commanders judged Fallujah secured, although the operation would not end officially until December 23, by which time many residents had been allowed to return to their homes.

U.S. casualties in the Second Battle of Fallujah were 95 killed and 560 wounded; Iraqi Army losses were 11 killed and 43 wounded. Insurgent losses were estimated at between 1,200 and 2,000 killed, with another 1,000 to 1,500 captured. The disparity in the casualties indicated the extent of the coalition's tactical advantage. Indeed, postbattle army and marine assessments lauded the tremendous tactical skill in urban warfare displayed by American forces. However, the intense house-to-house fighting had caused the destruction of an estimated 20 percent of the city's buildings, while another 60 percent of the city's structures were damaged. The tremendous damage, including that to 60 mosques, enraged Iraq's Sunni minority. Widespread civilian demonstrations and increased insurgent attacks followed the Second Battle of Fallujah. Although the 2005 Iraqi elections were held on schedule, Sunni participation was very low partially because of the Sunnis' sense of grievance over the destruction in Fallujah.

James Arnold

See also: Commanders, U.S. Central Command: James Mattis; Fallujah, First Battle of; Islamic State of Iraq and al-Sham (ISIS): Al Qaeda in Iraq; Prime Minister, Iraq: Ayad Allawi; Sunni Islam

References

Ballard, John R. *Fighting for Fallujah: A New Dawn for Iraq.* Westport, CT: Praeger Security International, 2006.

Bellavia, David. *House to House: An Epic Memoir of War.* New York: Free Press, 2007.

Gott, Kendall D., ed. *Eyewitness to War: The U.S. Army in Operation Al Fajr; An Oral History,* 2 vols. Fort Leavenworth, KS: Combat Studies Institute Press, 2006.

G

Garner, Jay Montgomery (1938–)

U.S. Army general who, after retirement from active duty, in 2003 served as the first civilian director of the Office for Reconstruction and Humanitarian Assistance (ORHA) for Iraq. Jay Montgomery Garner was born on April 15, 1938, in Arcadia, Florida. After service in the U.S. Marine Corps, he earned a degree in history from Florida State University and secured a commission in the army. He later earned a master's degree from Shippensburg University in Pennsylvania.

Garner rose steadily through the ranks, holding a series of commands in the United States and in Germany and rising to major general by the time of the Persian Gulf War (Operation Desert Storm) in 1991. Garner helped develop the Patriot antimissile system and oversaw the deployment of Patriot batteries in Saudi Arabia and Israel during the Persian Gulf War. Garner subsequently managed efforts to improve the Patriot systems and to finalize and deploy the joint U.S.-Israeli Arrow theater antiballistic missile systems. He also worked with Israel, Kuwait, and Saudi Arabia on the sale of the Patriot system. Garner next commanded Operation Provide Comfort, the coalition effort to provide humanitarian assistance to Kurds in northern Iraq. He directed international forces that included U.S., British, French, and Italian troops in the delivery of food, medicine, and other supplies and in efforts to prevent reprisals by Iraqi government forces. Garner was subsequently named to command the U.S. Space and Strategic Defense Command.

Garner retired in 1997 as a lieutenant general and assistant vice chief of staff of the army. In September 1997 he was named president of SY Technology, a defense contractor, and he served on a variety of advisory boards on security issues, including the Commission to Assess United States National Security Space Management and Organization.

In March 2003 Garner was named head of ORHA for the Coalition Provisional Authority of Iraq, to coincide with Operation Iraqi Freedom and the allied postwar occupation. In this post, Garner was the senior civilian official during the initial period after the overthrow of Saddam Hussein in April 2003. Garner reported directly to the U.S. military commander in Iraq, General Tommy Franks. Garner's previous service in the region and work during Operation Provide Comfort made him an attractive candidate for the position, and the George W. Bush administration hoped that he would be able to integrate civilian and military occupation efforts in Iraq.

Garner's occupation strategy emphasized a quick turnover of appropriate authority to the Iraqis and a withdrawal of U.S. and coalition forces to protected bases outside of major urban areas. He also advocated early elections to create an interim Iraqi government with widespread popular legitimacy. Senior defense officials opposed his plans, however, and argued that too rapid a withdrawal of coalition forces would create a power vacuum and might lead to increased sectarian strife. U.S. officials also sought to ensure that former political and military officials linked to Hussein's Baath Party would be purged from their positions (a policy known as de-Baathification). Meanwhile, Garner's status as a former general and his close ties to Secretary of Defense Donald Rumsfeld undermined his ability to work with nongovernmental organizations and non-U.S. officials. Both groups saw him as an indication that the United States was not committed to democratic reform in Iraq.

Garner was confronted with a range of challenges. There was a growing insurgency being waged by Hussein loyalists and foreign fighters, and the country's infrastructure was in worse condition than anticipated as a result of the international sanctions of the 1990s, coalition military action, and a scorched-earth policy carried out by the former regime to deny assets to the invading forces. As a result, Garner was unable to restore basic services in a timely manner.

After initially dismissing the nation's security forces, Garner recalled policemen and initiated a new recruitment and screening process to expedite both the return of former police officers without close ties to the regime and the hiring of new officers. This was part of a broader effort to counter growing lawlessness in major cities, such as Baghdad. Garner also made the initial Iraqi appointments to various ministries as part of the foundation of a transitional government.

Garner was critical of the failure of the United Nations to immediately end sanctions on Iraq, and he called for the world body to act quickly to facilitate economic redevelopment and the rebuilding of the country's oil-producing infrastructure. Nevertheless, the blunt and plainspoken Garner faced increasing criticism for the deteriorating conditions in Iraq. He was replaced on May 11, 2003, by career diplomat L. Paul Bremer, who reported directly to Rumsfeld instead of to the coalition's military commander. Most members of Garner's senior staff were also replaced. Garner returned to the United States to work in the defense industry. He has remained largely silent on his short and tumultuous tenure in Iraq.

Tom Lansford

See also: Bremer, Lewis Paul, III; Iraq, History of, 1990–Present; Iraqi Freedom, Operation; Secretary of Defense, U.S.: Donald Rumsfeld

References

Allawi, Ali A. *The Occupation of Iraq: Winning the War, Losing the Peace.* New Haven, CT: Yale University Press, 2007.

Bremer, L. Paul, with Malcolm McConnell. *My Year in Iraq: The Struggle to Build a Future of Hope.* New York: Simon and Schuster, 2006.

Global War on Terrorism

"Global War on Terrorism" is the term used to describe the military, political, diplomatic, and economic measures employed by the United States and other allied governments against individuals, organizations, and countries that are committing terrorist acts, might be inclined to engage in terrorism, or support those who do commit such acts. The Global War on Terrorism is an amorphous concept and a somewhat indistinct term, yet its use emphasizes the difficulty in classifying the type of nontraditional warfare being waged against U.S. and Western interests by various terrorist groups that do not represent any nation. The term was coined by President George W. Bush in a September 20, 2001, televised address to a joint session of the U.S. Congress and has been presented in official White House pronouncements, fact sheets, State of the Union messages, and such National Security Council position papers as the *National Security Strategy* (March 2006) and the *National Strategy for Combating Terrorism* (February 2003 and September 2006 editions).

Bush administration objectives in what became formally known as the Global War on Terror included the destruction of terrorist organizations such as Al Qaeda, denying state sponsorship of terrorist activities, working with other nations to create an antiterrorist network, and seeking to diminish conditions in states that terrorists are able to exploit. Although the Global War on Terrorism was truly global and included operations as far flung as the Philippines, its centerpiece was the U.S.-led military intervention in Afghanistan.

Since 2001, the Global War on Terrorism has been directed primarily at Islamic terrorist groups but has also been expanded to include actions against all types of terrorism. During the Bush administration, Secretary of Defense Robert Gates also called it the "Long War." As with the Cold War, the Global War on Terrorism is being waged on numerous fronts against many individuals and nations and involves both military and nonmilitary tactics.

President Bush's announcement of the Global War on Terrorism was in response to the September 11, 2001, terror attacks against the United States, which led to the deaths of nearly 3,000 civilians, mostly Americans but representing civilians of 90 different countries.

Although the fight against terrorism constitutes a global effort, stretching into Asia, Africa, Europe, and the Americas, the Middle East remains a focal point. The ongoing conflict and the manner in which it has been waged has been the source of much debate. There is no widely agreed-on estimate regarding the number of casualties during the Global War on Terrorism, because it includes the invasion of Afghanistan in 2001 and the war in Iraq as well as many acts of terrorism around the world. Some estimates, which include the U.S.-led coalition invasion of Afghanistan in 2001 and the invasion of Iraq in March 2003, claim that well more than 2 million people have died in the struggle.

Following the September 11, 2001, terror attacks, the United States responded quickly and with overwhelming force against the organizations and governments that supported the terrorists. Evidence gathered by the U.S. government pointed to the Al Qaeda terrorist organization. Al Qaeda at the time was being given aid and shelter by the Taliban regime in Afghanistan. On September 20, 2001, President George W. Bush announced to a joint session of Congress that the Global War on Terrorism would not end simply with the defeat of Al Qaeda or the overthrow of the Taliban. "Our 'war on terror,'" he said, "begins with Al Qaeda, but it does not end there. It will not end until every terrorist group of global reach has been found, stopped, and defeated." These broad aims implied attacks on countries known to support terrorism, such as Iran and Syria. Bush further assured the American people that every means of intelligence, tool of diplomacy, financial pressure, and weapon of war would be used to defeat terrorism. He told the American people to expect a lengthy campaign. Bush also put down an ultimatum to every other nation, stating that each had to choose whether it was with or against the United States. There would be no middle ground. Clearly Bush's pronouncements were far-reaching, yet the enemies were difficult to identify and find.

Less than 24 hours after the September 11 attacks, the North Atlantic Treaty Organization (NATO) declared them to be against all member nations, the first time the organization had made such a pronouncement since its inception in 1949. Within a few weeks France, Great Britain, and other NATO members—including Turkey, Canada, New Zealand, and Australia—became part of an American-led antiterrorist coalition.

On October 7, 2001, U.S. and coalition forces (chiefly British) invaded Afghanistan to capture Osama bin Laden, the head of Al Qaeda, to destroy his organization and to overthrow the Taliban government that supported him. Eventually Canada, Australia, France, and Germany, among other nations, joined that effort. However, when a U.S.-led coalition invaded Iraq in March 2003, there was considerable international opposition to this campaign being included under the rubric of the Global War on Terrorism. One problem for national leaders who supported President Bush's policies was that many of their citizens did not believe that the overthrow of Iraqi dictator Saddam Hussein was really part of the Global War on Terrorism and questioned other reasons stated by the Bush administration to justify the U.S.-led invasion. International opinion polls have shown that support for the Global War on Terrorism has consistently declined since 2003, likely the result of opposition to the Bush administration's preemptive invasion of Iraq in 2003 and later revelations that Iraq possessed neither ties to Al Qaeda nor weapons of mass destruction.

The Global War on Terrorism has also been a sporadic and clandestine effort since its inception in September 2001. U.S. forces were sent to Yemen and the Horn of Africa to disrupt terrorist activities, while Operation Active Endeavor is a naval operation intended to prevent terror attacks and limit the movement of terrorists in the Mediterranean. Terrorist attacks in Pakistan, Indonesia, and the Philippines led to the insertion of coalition forces into these countries as well and concerns about the situation in other Southeast Asian countries. In the United States, Congress has also passed legislation intended to help increase the effectiveness of law enforcement agencies in their search for terrorist activities. In the process, however, critics claim that Americans' civil liberties have been steadily eroded, and government admissions that the Federal Bureau of Investigation and other agencies have engaged in wiretapping of international phone calls without requisite court orders and probable cause have caused a storm of controversy, as have the methods used to question foreign nationals.

The Bush administration also greatly increased the role of the federal government in the attempt to fight terrorism at home and abroad. Among the many new government bureaucracies formed was the Department of Homeland Security, a cabinet-level agency that counts at least 210,000 employees. The increase in the size of the government combined with huge military expenditures, most going to the Iraq War, added to the massive U.S. budget deficit.

Proponents of the Global War on Terrorism believe that proactive measures must be taken against terrorist organizations to effectively defeat global terrorism. They believe that in order to meet the diverse security challenges of the 21st century, a larger global military presence is needed. Without such a force, they argue, terrorist organizations will continue to launch strikes against innocent civilians. Many believe that the United States, Great Britain, Spain, and other countries, which have been the victims of large-scale attacks, must go on the offensive against such rogue groups and that not doing so will only embolden the attackers and invite more attacks. Allowing such organizations to gain more strength may allow them to achieve their goal of imposing militant Islamist rule.

Critics of the Global War on Terrorism claim that there is no tangible enemy to defeat, as there is no single group whose defeat will bring about an end to the conflict. Thus, it is virtually impossible to know if progress is being made. They also argue that terrorism, a tactic whose goal is to instill fear into people through violent actions, can never be truly defeated. There are also those who argue against the justification for preemptive strikes, because such action invites counter responses and brings about the deaths of many innocent people. Many believe that the Iraqi military posed no imminent threat to the United States when coalition forces entered Iraq in 2003, but the resultant war has been disastrous for both the Iraqi and American people. Civil rights activists contend that measures meant to crack down on terrorist activities have infringed on the rights of American citizens as well as the rights of foreign detainees. Furthermore, critics argue that the war and the amount of spending apportioned to military endeavors negatively affects the national and world economies. Others argue that the United States should be spending time and resources on resolving the Arab-Israeli problem and trying to eradicate the desperate conditions that feed terrorism.

As support for the Global War on Terrorism effort has diminished, the debate over its effectiveness has grown. Terrorist attacks have continued, and the deliberation over the best way to ensure the safety of civilian populations around the world continues.

Barack Obama was sworn in as president in January 2009. His administration eschewed the terms "Global War on Terrorism" and "Long War" in defense fact sheets. Rather, U.S. government agencies were instructed to use the term "overseas contingency operations." One phrase of particular importance was countering violent extremism. Former White House press secretary Robert Gibbs explained that Obama was "using different words and phrases in order to denote a reaching out to many moderate parts of the world that we believe can be important in a battle against extremists." However, the term "Global War on Terrorism" continued to be used, particularly in the media.

On May 1, 2011, the Global War on Terrorism reached a milestone of sorts with the killing of Osama bin Laden. After intelligence information suggested that bin Laden was in Abbottabad, Pakistan, Central Intelligence Agency (CIA) operatives and American military forces raided a compound at which he was staying. According to reports, bin Laden was killed in an ensuing firefight. President Obama addressed the nation to announce bin Laden's death, declaring that "justice has been done" but admonishing Americans to "remain vigilant at home and abroad."

In a much-anticipated speech at the National Defense University on May 23, 2013, President Obama said that it was time to narrow the scope of the grinding battle against terrorists and begin the transition to a day when the country would no longer be on a war footing. Declaring that "America is at a crossroads," the president called for redefining what had been a global war into a more targeted assault on terrorist groups threatening the United States. As part of a realignment of counterterrorism policy, he said that he would diminish the use of drone strikes, which have taken out a number of terrorist leaders but also killed many innocent civilians; recommit to closing the prison for terror suspects at Guantánamo Bay, Cuba; and seek new limits on presidential war powers, including for himself. The president suggested that the United States return to the state of affairs that existed before Al Qaeda toppled the World Trade Center, when terrorism was a persistent but not existential danger. With Al Qaeda's core now "on the path to defeat," he argued, the nation must adapt to new realities.

Nearly simultaneous with Obama's far-ranging speech were revelations by U.S. whistle-blower and former CIA and National Security Agency (NSA) employee Edward Snowden about the extent to which these agencies engaged in snooping on American citizens as well as friendly and adversarial governments abroad. Snowden's information suggested that the NSA had been keeping data logs of phone calls as well as Internet activity of millions of innocent U.S. citizens, all in the name of the Global War on Terrorism. These revelations seemed to undergird Obama's point that the conventional Global War on Terrorism was becoming too costly and unwieldy.

Gregory Wayne Morgan

See also: Detention Operations, Coalition: Guantánamo Bay Detention Camp; Doctrine, Counterinsurgency; Iraqi Freedom, Operation; Islamic State of Iraq and al-Sham (ISIS): Al Qaeda in Iraq; Obama, Barack Hussein, II; Weapons Systems, Coalition: Unmanned Aerial Vehicles

References

Bacevich, Andrew J. *The New American Militarism: How Americans Are Seduced by War.* New York: Oxford University Press, 2005.

Mahajan, Rahul. *The New Crusade: America's War on Terrorism.* New York: Monthly Review, 2002.

Woodward, Bob. *Bush at War.* New York: Simon and Schuster, 2002.

Hussein, Qusay (1966–2003)

Iraqi government and military official and son of Iraqi dictator Saddam Hussein. At the time of the U.S.-led invasion of Iraq in March 2003, Qusay Hussein was considered the second most powerful man in Iraq and the likely successor to his father. Qusay Hussein was born in Tikrit, Iraq, on May 17, 1966, the second son of Saddam Hussein and Sajida Talfah. As Arab custom dictates, Saddam Hussein's elder son, Uday, was the most prominent and was raised as his father's successor. Although out of the limelight, Qusay Hussein remained loyal to his father to the point of even imitating his dress and trademark mustache.

While Uday Hussein proved to be mentally unstable and a flamboyant sexual sadist whose antics embarrassed the ruling family, Qusay was much more reserved. Complying with his father's wishes, in 1987 he married the daughter of Mahir Abd al-Rashid, an influential military commander. The marriage produced four children. Although possessing numerous mistresses, Qusay Hussein portrayed himself as a devoted family man.

Qusay Hussein's loyalty and patience eventually bore dividends. When Uday's behavior became more erratic in the late 1980s, Saddam Hussein began to turn more to his second son. For example, Qusay was granted broad authority in crushing the Shiite Muslim and Marsh Arab uprisings following Iraq's defeat in the 1991 Persian Gulf War. He responded ruthlessly, using torture and executing entire families believed to be disloyal to the regime.

As Uday's position declined, Qusay began to emerge as the likely successor to his father. For his role in crushing the 1991 rebellions, Saddam entrusted Qusay with command of the Special Security Organization, including Internal Security and the Presidential Guard. In his role as security head, Qusay oversaw Iraqi's chemical, biological, and nuclear programs. He was also responsible for the repression of opponents of his father's regime. It is believed that Qusay, with his father's approval, had a hand in the attempted assassination of Uday on December 12, 1996.

Clearly Saddam Hussein's favorite, Qusay was named "caretaker" in the event of Saddam's illness or death and given command of the elite Republican Guard. Possessing no formal military training, Qusay refused to accept advice from more experienced commanders. None dared to question his orders for fear of the consequences, however. The dismal performance of the Republican Guard in failing to slow the American-led invasion in 1991 is often blamed on the lack of military experience of Qusay and his advisers.

Following the terror attacks of September 11, 2001, foreign pressure on Iraq began to increase, and the United States began preparing for a second invasion of Iraq, this time to topple the Hussein regime. Saddam Hussein and his sons temporarily rallied in the face of the overwhelming military force gathering to confront them. On March 18, 2003, U.S. president George W. Bush called on Saddam Hussein and his sons to leave the country, a demand that was rebuffed.

Following the invasion on March 20, 2003, Qusay Hussein went into hiding. On July 22,

2003, Qusay, his 14-year-old son Mustapha, Uday, and their bodyguard were cornered in Mosul. During the course of a four-hour firefight, all were killed. Following identification, the bodies were buried in Awja.

Robert W. Malick

See also: Hussein, Saddam; Hussein, Uday; Iraq, History of, 1990–Present; Iraqi Freedom, Operation; Shia Islam

References

Balaghi, Shiva. *Saddam Hussein: A Biography.* Westport, CT: Greenwood, 2006.

Bengio, Ofra. "How Does Saddam Hold On?" *Foreign Affairs* (July–August 2000): 90–103.

Bennett, Brian, and Michael Weisskopf. "The Sum of Two Evils." *Time,* June 2, 2003, 34.

Thomas, Evan, and Christopher Dickey. "Saddam's Sons." *Newsweek,* October 21, 2002, 34.

Woods, Kevin, James Lacy, and Williamson Murray. "Saddam's Delusions." *Foreign Affairs* (May–June 2006): 2–16.

Hussein, Saddam (1937–2006)

Iraqi politician, leading figure in the Baath Party, and president of Iraq (1979–2003). Born on April 28, 1937, in the village of Awja, near Tikrit, to a family of sheepherders, Saddam Hussein attended a secular school in Baghdad and in 1957 joined the Baath Party, a socialist and Arab nationalist party. Iraqi Baathists supported General Abd al-Karim Qasim's ouster of the Iraqi monarchy in 1958 but were not favored by President Qasim.

Wounded in an unsuccessful attempt to assassinate Qasim in 1959, Hussein subsequently fled the country but returned after the 1963 Baathist coup and began his rise in the party, although he was again imprisoned in 1964. Escaping in 1966, Hussein continued to ascend through the party's ranks, becoming second in authority when the party took full and uncontested control of Iraq in 1968 under the leadership of General Ahmad Hassan al-Bakr, a relative of Hussein's. The elderly Bakr gradually relinquished power to him so that Hussein eventually controlled most of the government.

Hussein became president when Bakr resigned, allegedly because of illness, in July 1979. A week after taking power, Hussein led a meeting of Baath leaders during which the names of his potential challengers were read aloud. They were then escorted from the room and shot. Because Iraq was torn by ethnic and religious divisions, Hussein ruled through a tight web of relatives and associates from Tikrit, backed by the Sunni Muslim minority. He promoted economic development through Iraqi oil production, which accounted for 10 percent of known world reserves. Hussein's modernization was along Western lines, with expanded roles for women and a secular legal system based in part on sharia and Ottoman law. He also promoted the idea of Iraqi nationalism and emphasized Iraq's ancient past, glorifying such figures as Kings Hammurabi and Nebuchadnezzar.

Before assuming the presidency, Hussein had courted both the West and the Soviet Union, resulting in arms deals with the Soviets and close relations with the Soviet Union and France. He was also instrumental in convincing Mohammad Reza Shah Pahlavi of Iran to curb his support of Iraqi Kurds. Hussein's efforts to take advantage of the superpowers' Cold War rivalry, including rapprochement with Iran, fell apart with the overthrow of the shah in the 1979 Iranian Revolution. The shah's successor, Ayatollah Khomeini, a radical fundamentalist Muslim,

Iraqi president Saddam Hussein salutes the crowd during a military parade in Baghdad, November 20, 2000. He was president of Iraq from July 16, 1979, until he was overthrown by the U.S.-led coalition on or about April 9, 2003. (Karim Sahib/AFP/Getty Images)

bitterly opposed Hussein because of his Sunni background and secularism.

After a period of repeated border skirmishes, Iraq declared war on Iran in September 1980. Hussein's ostensible dispute concerned a contested border, but he also feared Iran's fundamentalism and its support for the Iraqi Shia Muslim majority. Initial success gave way to Iraqi defeats in the face of human-wave attacks and ultimately a stalemate. By 1982 Hussein was ready to end the war, but Iranian leaders desired that the fighting continue. In 1988 the United Nations (UN) finally brokered a cease-fire, but not before the war had devastated both nations. The war left Iraq heavily in debt, and Hussein requested relief from his major creditors, including the United States, Kuwait, and Saudi Arabia. He also sought to maintain high oil prices. His efforts were in vain; creditors refused to write off their debts, and Kuwait maintained a high oil output, forcing other oil-producing nations to follow suit.

Hussein responded by declaring Kuwait a "rogue province" of Iraq. He was also enraged by Kuwaiti slant drilling into Iraqi oil fields. Hussein's demands became more strident, and after securing what he believed to be U.S. acquiescence, he ordered Iraqi forces to attack and occupy Kuwait on August 2, 1990. Hussein miscalculated the U.S. reaction. President George H. W. Bush assembled an international military coalition, built up forces in Saudi Arabia (Operation Desert Shield), and then commenced a relentless bombing campaign against Iraq in January 1991. The ground war of February 24–28, 1991, resulted in a crushing defeat of Iraqi forces. Although Hussein withdrew from Kuwait, coalition forces did not seek his overthrow; he remained in power, ruling a nation devastated by two recent wars.

Hussein retained control of Iraq for another decade, during which he brutally suppressed Kurdish and Shia revolts, relinquished limited autonomy to the Kurds, acquiesced to the destruction of stockpiles of chemical weapons, and pursued a dilatory response to UN efforts to monitor his weapons programs. Convinced—wrongly as it turned out—that Hussein had been building and stockpiling weapons of mass destruction, President George W. Bush asked for and received authorization from Congress to wage war against Iraq. U.S. and coalition forces invaded Iraq in March 2003. Coalition forces took Baghdad on April 10, 2003, and captured Hussein on December 14, 2003, to be brought to trial on charges of war crimes and crimes against humanity.

On November 5, 2006, the Iraqi Special Tribunal found Hussein guilty for the deaths of 148 Shiite Muslims in 1982 whose murders he had ordered. That same day, he was sentenced to hang. Earlier, on August 21, 2006, a second trial had begun on charges that Hussein had committed genocide and other atrocities by ordering the systematic extermination of northern Iraqi Kurds during 1987–1988, resulting in as many as 180,000 deaths. Before the second trial moved into high gear, however, Hussein filed an appeal, which was rejected by the Iraqi Supreme Court on December 26, 2006. Four days later on December 30, 2006, the Muslim holiday of Eid al-Adha, Hussein was executed by hanging in Baghdad. Before his death, Hussein told U.S. Federal Bureau of Investigation interrogators that he had misled the world to give the impression that Iraq had weapons of mass destruction in order to make Iraq appear stronger in the face of its enemy, Iran.

Daniel E. Spector

See also: Iraq, History of, 1990–Present; Iraqi Freedom, Operation; Kurds

References

Bengio, Ofra. *Saddam's Word: Political Discourse in Iraq.* New York: Oxford University Press USA, 1998.

Karsh, Efraim. *Saddam Hussein: A Political Biography.* New York: Grove/Atlantic, 2002.

Miller, Judith, and Laurie Mylroie. *Saddam Hussein and the Crisis in the Gulf.* New York: Times Books, 1990.

Wingate, Brian. *Saddam Hussein: The Rise and Fall of a Dictator.* New York: Rosen, 2004.

Hussein, Uday (1964–2003)

Iraqi government official, commander of the Fedayeen Saddam, and eldest son of Iraqi president and dictator Saddam Hussein. Uday Hussein was born in Baghdad on June 18, 1964, and was initially groomed to succeed his father as dictator of Iraq. Uday's mental instability, cruelty, and alcoholism, however, resulted in his being passed over for his younger brother, Qusay Hussein. Uday's fall from favor began in 1988. During a dinner party that year, he murdered his father's favorite bodyguard and food taster, Kamil Hanna Jajjo. Jajjo had supposedly introduced Saddam to his most recent mistress, which Uday viewed as insulting to his own mother. Originally sentenced to death, Uday was instead imprisoned and tortured. Upon his release, he was exiled to Switzerland as an assistant to the Iraqi ambassador. After six months, however, Swiss authorities quietly expelled him after he threatened, while in a restaurant, to kill a Swiss citizen.

Upon his return to Iraq, Uday attempted to rebuild his power base but was unable to control his sadistic and volatile nature. As head of the Iraqi Olympic Committee, he ordered the torture of athletes whom he believed were not performing to the best of their ability. In one instance, a missed soccer goal resulted in the offending athlete being dragged though gravel and then submerged in raw sewage. Uday also began to dominate the state-owned media, controlling state radio and the youth magazine *Babel*. As minister of youth affairs, he headed the paramilitary organization Fedayeen Saddam.

In 1994 Saddam granted Uday control of Iraq's oil-smuggling operations, which were in violation of sanctions by the United Nations (UN) that had been imposed following the 1991 Persian Gulf War. Supervising up to 150,000 barrels of smuggled oil a day provided a vast income. With this revenue, Uday lived a life of ostentatious luxury. He purchased hundreds of foreign sports cars, storing them in underground garages throughout Baghdad. At his numerous palaces, staffs were maintained around the clock, including a personal shopper and two trainers for his pet lions. At the palaces Uday set up torture chambers, and he reportedly ordered the kidnapping, rape, and torture of scores of Iraqi women, including married women, even brides. Brides were sometimes taken from their wedding celebrations if Uday favored them sexually.

On December 12, 1996, a botched assassination attempt riddled Uday's sports car and two escort vehicles with bullets as they sped through the upper-class Baghdad neighborhood of Mansur. Although hit eight times in the arm, leg, and stomach, Uday survived the attack. Official blame for the attack centered on Iran, although some sources claim that Saddam or his other son, Qusay, were involved.

Following the terror attacks on the United States of September 11, 2001, foreign pressure on Iraq began to mount. President Hussein and his sons rallied in the face of the overwhelming military force gathering to confront them, however. On March 18, 2003, on the eve of the Iraq War, U.S. president George W. Bush demanded that Saddam Hussein and his sons leave the country immediately or face an invasion. After they refused this ultimatum, coalition forces invaded Iraq on March 20. Uday went into hiding following the invasion, but on July 22, 2003, he and Qusay were cornered by Special Operations Task Force 20 and elements of the U.S. Army's 101st Airborne Division in Mosul, Iraq. After a four-hour firefight, Uday, Qusay, Qusay's 14-year-old son, and a bodyguard were shot dead. Saddam Hussein was apprehended by American forces on December 13, 2003, and was executed for war crimes on December 30, 2006.

Robert W. Malick

See also: Hussein, Qusay; Hussein, Saddam; Iraq, History of, 1990–Present

References

Cockburn, Andrew, and Patrick Cockburn. *Out of the Ashes: The Resurrection of Saddam Hussein*. New York: HarperCollins, 2000.

Marr, Phebe. *The Modern History of Iraq*, 2nd ed. Boulder, CO: Westview, 2003.

I

Insurgency and Opposition

Insurgency and its tactics are as old as warfare itself. Joint doctrine defines an insurgency as an organized movement aimed at the overthrow of a constituted government through the use of subversion and armed conflict (JP 1-02). Stated another way, an insurgency is an organized, protracted politico-military struggle designed to weaken the control and legitimacy of an established government, occupying power, or other political authority while increasing insurgent control. (*Field Manual 3–24: Counterinsurgency*, 1-1)

The above quote gives the U.S. military definition of an insurgent. This definition is useful in understanding the nature of those fighting against the U.S.-led coalition in Iraq. Secretary of Defense Donald Rumsfeld infamously characterized those fighting against U.S. and coalition forces as "dead-enders." His reference was viewed as minimizing or even underestimating the opponent present in the country. Those fighting against the coalition were a varied group representing nationalist, ideological, and sectarian interests. They started out as offshoots of the official military and security force establishment. This then turned into an amalgamation of different, sometimes competing groups. The main opponents were initially linked with the fedayeen. The later groups included Al Qaeda in Iraq, the Badr Organization, and the Mahdi Army. Al Qaeda in Iraq is listed separately under the general entry for ISIS. The other three groups are discussed in greater detail below.

Because Saddam Hussein knew that his conventional forces could not stop the coalition from reaching Baghdad, he created a force (fedayeen) to conduct irregular warfare activities: attack logistics and rear area "soft" targets, conduct attacks in civilian clothes and using civilian vehicles, and continue the fight if the regime collapsed. These forces were joined by others once the security forces were disbanded and their pay and pensions ended. The fedayeen tended to be referred to as Baathists or Saddam loyalists. The primary interest of this group was restoring a Baathist-like governance structure in Iraq.

There were other "terrorist" organizations operating in Iraq who existed to promote various ideological objectives. Once the U.S. invaded Iraq those groups tended to coalesce into a generic U.S. opposition. The group called ISIS or Al Qaeda in Iraq is one such group. They had a different name in 2003 when the U.S. invaded. This group and other similar groups tended to be Sunni. They were effectively weakened to the point of defeat by 2010, but they used the Syrian civil war and the vacuum of government control in Syria to regroup. Other groups sought security in the Sunni-dominated provinces waiting for the coalition withdrawal.

The last broad group formed later than the first two. They were Shia and tended to fall into one of two camps: Iranian-sponsored or coalition opposition. The Shia groups were happy to have the Baathists removed from power, but they were opposed to a prolonged

U.S. occupation. The longer the United States stayed in Iraq, the greater the Iranian influence on these groups, who often received equipment and training through Iranian networks. Both the Badr Organization and the Mahdi Army are from this third category. The Mahdi Army was effectively eliminated as a combat force in 2008. Other Shia opposition forces continued to attack coalition forces up through the withdrawal of all coalition forces in 2011.

Brian L. Steed

See also: Commanders, U.S. Central Command: David H. Petraeus; Doctrine, Counterinsurgency; Doctrine, Insurgency; Iraqi Freedom, Operation; Islamic State of Iraq and al-Sham (ISIS)

References

Cockburn, Patrick. *The Occupation: War and Resistance in Iraq.* New York: Verso, 2007.

Gordon, Michael R., and General Bernard E. Trainor. *Cobra II: The Inside Story of the Invasion and Occupation of Iraq.* New York: Pantheon Books, 2006.

Ricks, Thomas E. *Fiasco: The American Military Adventure in Iraq.* New York: Penguin, 2006.

U.S. Department of the Army. *Counterinsurgency. Field Manual 3–24.* Washington, DC: U.S. Department of the Army, December 15, 2006.

Badr Organization

Paramilitary wing of the Supreme Islamic Iraqi Council (SIIC), also referred to as the Supreme Islamic Council in Iraq, known for decades as the Supreme Council for the Islamic Revolution in Iraq (SCIRI), a Shia political party founded in Tehran, Iran, in November 1982 by Iraqi exiles led by Ayatollah Muhammad Baqir al-Hakim. The Badr Organization (Faylaq Badr), which is also commonly referred to as the Badr Corps, the Badr Brigade(s), and the Badr Army, was named after the Battle of Badr, fought between the Prophet Muhammad and the earliest Muslims against a larger and better-equipped armed force commanded by his Meccan opponents. The Badr Organization is led by Hadi al-Amiri, a high-ranking SIIC official and an ally of its political leaders, Abd al-Aziz al-Hakim and his son, Sayyid Ammar al-Hakim. Abd al-Aziz is the youngest brother of Muhammad Baqr, who was assassinated by a massive car bombing probably carried out by the organization headed by the Jordanian Abu Musab al-Zarqawi (1966–2006), and a son of Grand Ayatollah Sayyid Muhsin al-Hakim (1889–1970), the most influential and widely followed Shia religious leader in Iraq from 1955 until his death.

The Badr Organization's origins lay in armed units, numbering several thousand men at most, made up of Iraqi Arab exiles trained and equipped with assistance from the Iranian government. These units were originally named after Ayatollah Sayyid Muhammad Baqr al-Sadr (1935–1980), a prominent Iraqi Arab Shia religious scholar and opposition leader who was executed by the ruling Iraqi Baath Party along with his sister, Amina bint Haydar al-Sadr (also known as Bint al-Huda), in April 1980. Both Muhammad Baqr and Abd al-Aziz al-Hakim were students of Baqr al-Sadr, who was a student of their father, Muhsin al-Hakim. The two brothers along with their other brother, Muhammad Mahdi, were early members of the Islamic Dawa Party (Hizb al-Da'wa al-Islamiyya), which was originally founded by Shia religious scholars (*ulama*) in the southern Iraqi shrine city of Najaf.

The Iranian Revolutionary Guard Corps (IRGC), an armed force dedicated to the protection and preservation of the Iranian revolutionary system, was the key source of training and military equipment for SCIRI's paramilitary wing. This militia was renamed after the Battle of Badr (1982–1983) during the Iran-Iraq War (1980–1988). Badr drew its membership from the tens of thousands of Iraqi Arabs, the majority of them Shia political activists and anti-Baath operatives, who fled to Iran in the late 1970s and 1980s, particularly following the execution of Ayatollah Muhammad Baqr al-Sadr and his sister in April 1980.

After the start of the Iran-Iraq War following Iraq's invasion of western Iran in September 1980, Badr also recruited members from among Iraqi prisoners of war, since many Iraqi soldiers were Shia conscripts who had no love or loyalty for Iraqi president Saddam Hussein. Prisoners of war who wished to join Badr were first required to repent for their membership in the Iraqi Army because it was regarded as an instrument not of the Iraqi nation but of the Iraqi Baath Party. Abd al-Aziz al-Hakim served as Badr's commander from its founding in 1982–1983 until he and his brother Muhammad Baqr returned to Iraq in May 2003 following the collapse of the Iraqi Baathist regime in the wake of the U.S.- and British-led invasion of the country. Despite its Iraqi identity and membership, Badr's leadership was split between Iraqi Arabs such as Abd al-Aziz al-Hakim and IRGC officers, who were largely responsible for the military training of Badr's recruits. Badr included infantry, armor, artillery, antiaircraft, and commando units and maintained ties to activists and small units in Iraq.

The Badr Organization was actively involved in the Iran-Iraq War, primarily in northern Iraq (Iraqi Kurdistan). Following the capture of Haj Omran, a village in northeastern Iraq, by Iranian forces in 1983, Badr units were stationed there. Muhammad Baqr al-Hakim visited them and prayed on what was termed "freed Iraqi soil." The participation of Badr paramilitary fighters on the side of the Iranians during the war was not welcomed by all Iraqi Shias and was widely criticized by some of SCIRI's political rivals in the Iraqi Shia community.

Badr also carried out bombings and attacks on Iraqi Baath officials and offices during the 1980s and 1990s and sent units across the Iran-Iraq border in March–April 1991 to aid the uprisings in southern and northern Iraq among the Shia and Kurdish populations. These uprisings, encouraged by the U.S. government, were brutally crushed by Baath security forces and the Republican Guard after the United States refused to aid the rebels. The United States was reportedly fearful of empowering Iraq's Shia population. The United States heeded alarmist talk from its Sunni Arab allies and reacted warily to the appearance of Badr fighters in southern Iraq, many of whom carried portraits of Iran's late revolutionary leader, Grand Ayatollah Ruhollah Khomeini, and banners calling for the formation of an Islamic republic in Iraq.

Following the collapse of Saddam Hussein's Iraqi Baath government in April 2003, the SCIRI and Badr leaderships returned to Iraq from exile, mainly from Iran, in May 2003. Muhammad Baqir al-Hakim was welcomed in southern Iraq by tens of thousands of his supporters. According to the Hakims and SIIC/Badr officials, the Badr Organization fielded some 10,000 paramilitary fighters upon their return to Iraq. Abd al-Aziz al-Hakim subsequently claimed that Badr, in addition to its regular fighters, could call upon tens of thousands of other reservists, although this claim seems to be highly exaggerated.

The United Iraqi Alliance (UIA), a loose coalition of mainly Shia political parties, was swept into power in the December 2005 national elections. SCIRI and the Islamic Dawa Party were the two dominant political parties in the UIA. Bayan Jabr, a SCIRI official, was selected by Abd al-Aziz al-Hakim to head the Iraqi Ministry of the Interior in the 2005–2006 transitional government. Jabr oversaw the infiltration of the Iraqi Security Forces, police, and special commando units, all of which fall under the Interior Ministry. Badr members, both inside and outside of the national security forces, engaged in gun battles with rival Shia parties, particularly the Sadr Movement led by Muqtada al-Sadr, and in a series of operations in Basra and other southern Iraqi cities and towns in the spring and summer of 2008, which were aimed at weakening the Sadr Movement's political and paramilitary structure in southern Iraq before the 2009 elections. Badr members have also been blamed for carrying out sectarian killings and ethnic cleansing of Sunni Arabs in southern and central Iraq as well as in the capital city of Baghdad.

More recently, the Badr Organization separated itself from the armed militia units as it tried to gain more political support and legitimacy. Although the military units have continued to be active in certain areas of Iraq, their activity has diminished significantly since 2012. Beginning in early 2014, Badr militia units began battling Islamic extremists tied to the Islamic State of Iraq and Syria (ISIS).

Christopher Paul Anzalone

See also: Baath Party; Hussein, Saddam; Iraq, History of, 1990–Present; Political Parties, Iraq: Islamic Dawa Party, Supreme Iraqi Islamic Council; Sadr, Muqtada al-; Shia Islam; Sunni Islam

References

Jabar, Faleh A. *The Shi'ite Movement in Iraq.* London: Saqi Books, 2003.

Marr, Phebe. "Democracy in the Rough." *Current History* (January 2006): 27–33.

Samii, A. William. "Shia Political Alternatives in Postwar Iraq." *Middle East Policy* 10 (May 2003): 93–101.

Fedayeen

Term used to refer to various groups or civilians (usually Muslim) who have engaged in either armed struggle or guerrilla tactics against foreign armies. The term "fedayeen" is the English transliteration of the term *fida'iyuna,* which is the plural of the Arabic word meaning "one who is ready to sacrifice his life" (*fida'i*). Historically, the term has referred to different types of Muslim fighters, including Muslim forces waging war on the borders; freedom fighters; Egyptians who fought against the British in the Suez Canal Zone, culminating in a popular uprising in October 1951; Palestinians who waged attacks against Israelis from the 1950s until the present (including fighters of Christian background); Iranian guerrillas opposed to Mohammad Reza Shah Pahlavi's regime in the 1970s; Armenian fighters in Nagarno-Karabakh (also Christian); and a force loyal to Iraqi dictator Saddam Hussein (the Fedayeen Saddam) during the Iraq War that began in 2003.

The Fedayeen Saddam was so named to associate the force with patriotic self-sacrifice and anti-imperialism. Initially led by Hussein's son Uday in 1995, the group's leadership was handed over to his other son, Qusay, when it was discovered that Uday was diverting Iranian weaponry to the group. Participants were selected from the Baath Party based on perceived loyalty to Iraq and Saddam Hussein. They were organized in 2003 leading up to the U.S.-led invasion so that they could conduct irregular warfare against the technically more advanced coalition. They allowed the armored formations to pass and then attacked logistics convoys. They fought in cities and used the cities as staging grounds for their attacks on the convoys moving through the deserts. They used military supplies stockpiled throughout Iraq in the months leading to the fighting so that they regularly had supplies to continue to fight. They proved to be effective in temporarily disrupting the American invasion plan. Their attacks forced diversions of forces to clearing cities rather than simply bypassing cities.

After the fall of Baghdad, many of the Fedayeen Saddam became part of the Iraqi resistance, or *muqawamah,* who, following the March 2003 U.S.- and British-led invasion, used rocket-propelled grenades, machine guns, and mortars to attack coalition forces, forces of the new Iraqi government, and Sadrists. In January 2007 the group recognized Izzat Ibrahim al-Duri as the rightful leader of Iraq and secretary-general of the Iraqi Baath Party following the execution of Saddam Hussein.

Jessica Britt and Sherifa Zuhur

See also: Hussein, Qusay; Hussein, Saddam; Hussein, Uday; Iraq, History of, 1990–Present

References

Abdullah, Daud. *A History of Palestinian Resistance.* Leicester, UK: Al-Aqsa Publishers, 2005.

Khoury, Elias. *Gate of the Sun.* Translated by Humphrey Davies from *Bab al-Shams.* New York: St. Martin's, 2006.

Mahdi Army

Paramilitary wing of the Iraqi political movement Tayyar al-Sadr (Sadr Movement) led by Iraqi junior Shiite cleric Muqtada al-Sadr. He is the son of Ayatollah Muhammad Sadiq al-Sadr, a prominent and outspoken critic of the Iraqi Baath Party and of President Saddam Hussein's regime during the 1990s. The elder Sadr was assassinated along with two of his other sons, Mustafa and Muammal, on February 18, 1999. Sadiq al-Sadr was a cousin of both Grand Ayatollah Muhammad Baqir al-Sadr, a prominent Iraqi Shiite activist cleric in the 1960s and 1970s, and Musa al-Sadr, the prominent cleric who oversaw the political mobilization of Lebanese Shias from the late 1950s until his disappearance on a trip to Libya in 1978.

Sadiq al-Sadr received his religious education in the seminary of Najaf and studied with his cousin, Baqir al-Sadr, and Iranian grand ayatollah Ruhollah Khomeini, who lived in exile in Najaf from 1965 to 1978. Sadiq al-Sadr's popularity among Iraqi Shias began to grow beginning in the mid-1980s, and by the end of that decade, despite debates among clerical circles about his qualifications for the rank, he had come to be recognized by many as an elevated religious leader, or *marja' al-taqlid,* meaning a source of authority whom a follower might emulate.

Sadr was a rising star in the 1990s because of his vocal criticism of the Baathists and his belief in an active seminary. He challenged the silent seminary, which was represented by the politically quietist Grand Ayatollah Ali al-Husayn al-Sistani and the other members of the *marjaiyya,* the council of Iraq's resident grand ayatollahs that sits in Najaf. Sadr took advantage of government crackdowns on the traditional Shiite seminaries in southern Iraqi cities, such as Najaf, Karbala, and Kufa, following the suppression of the 1991 Shiite and Kurdish rebellions in Iraq.

While senior clerics such as Sistani came under increasing government scrutiny and were basically placed under house arrest, Hussein's regime initially tolerated Sadr

Iraqi militiamen of the Mahdi Army, loyal to Shiite cleric Muqtada al-Sadr, carry their guns during a parade to mark the second anniversary of Najaf fighting between the militia and U.S military on August 5, 2006, in the Sadr City area of Baghdad, Iraq. The ceremony, which was attended by Lebanon's ambassador to Iraq, was used also to show support for Lebanon's Hezbollah. (Wathiq Khuzaie/Getty Images)

because he was seen as a potential counterweight to Sistani. A divided Iraqi Shiite community was more advantageous to the ruling Baathists than a unified one. However, by the mid-1990s Sadr had begun to take more confrontational positions vis-à-vis the government, issuing a *fatwa* (juridical opinion) forbidding his followers from joining the Baath Party, holding Friday prayers in defiance of a government ban, and calling for the implementation of a clerically governed Islamic state in Iraq.

Sadr was also critical of Sistani and the *marjaiyya* for remaining politically disengaged in the face of government suppression. An Iraqi native and Arab, Sadr presented himself as the native alternative for Iraqi Shiites to follow in opposition to the Iranian-born Sistani and the other members of the *marjaiyya,* all of whom were foreign born. Sadr's speeches and sermons drew tens of thousands of people. In addition, his representatives successfully took over thousands of mosques, local religious centers, and Husseiniyyas (buildings used to commemorate the lives and martyrdom of the Shiite imams, such as the Third Imam, Hussein).

After the assassination of Sadr in February 1999, control of his grassroots movement in Iraq was assumed by his son Muqtada al-Sadr, a low-ranking seminary student, although most of his followers took as their *marja' al-taqlid* Ayatollah Kadhim Hairi, one of Sadiq al-Sadr's best students. Hairi, however, resided in Qum, Iran, where he remains today, and thus was not well placed to assume control of Sadiq al-Sadr's movement in Iraq. For a time, Muqtada al-Sadr recognized Hairi as the spiritual guide of the Sadr Movement; however, the two had a falling out in late 2003 after Hairi declined to return to Iraq.

In early April 2003, following the March U.S.- and British-led invasion of Iraq, Muqtada al-Sadr's representatives and clerical allies reopened mosques and religious centers in Sadrist strongholds in places such as the southern city of Kufa and the sprawling Shiite district known as Sadr City in eastern Baghdad. These mosques and centers form the social support base for the Sadr Movement and remain key elements of Sadr's influence and authority. Sadr City and large swaths of southern Iraq are Sadrist strongholds, giving the movement significant popular support among the Iraqi Shiite population, which makes up an estimated 60–65 percent of Iraq's 28 million people. Despite its continued prominence, the Sadr Movement began to splinter in 2005. Ayatollah Muhammad Yaqubi and Mahmoud Sarkhi al-Hassani, two former students of Sadiq al-Sadr, broke away from the movement and formed their own sociopolitical groups. Yaqubi created the Fadhila (Islamic Virtue) Party, and Hassani formed a smaller movement popular among more messianic Iraqi Shiites who await the return of the Twelfth Imam, Muhammad al-Mahdi.

The Mahdi Army was formed soon after the collapse of the Iraqi government in the spring of 2003. By the spring of 2004 its membership had swelled to an estimated 6,000–10,000 fighters, with a core group of 500–1,000 who were highly trained. Muqtada al-Sadr has been blamed for ordering the murder of Hujjat al-Islam Abd al-Majid al-Khoi, a midlevel cleric and son of the late prominent Iraq-based grand ayatollah Abu al-Qasim al-Khoi, who was a U.S. ally; the younger Khoi was stabbed to death in a crowd in Najaf on April 10, 2003. Sadr has repeatedly denied that he was involved in the murder. Later that month Mahdi Army fighters surrounded the Najaf homes of Sistani and other members of the *marjaiyya*, demanding that they leave Iraq. The Mahdi Army was forced to stand down when several thousand Shiite Arab tribesmen loyal to the *marjaiyya* came to Najaf to protect the grand ayatollahs. Sadr has maintained a tenuous relationship with the grand ayatollahs and has publicly recognized their authority, although he may simply be paying them lip service.

Sadr ordered the Mahdi Army into the streets in April 2004 after the Coalition Provisional Authority, the U.S.-dominated governing body headed by L. Paul Bremer that ran Iraq from 2003 to June 28, 2005, closed the offices of the main Sadrist newspaper, *al-Hawza*, and pressured an Iraqi court to indict Sadr and several of his aides for the murder of Khoi. Fighting between the Mahdi Army and coalition forces continued until early June, when a tenuous cease-fire was negotiated.

Heavy fighting between the two sides began again on August 3, 2005, when U.S. and Iraqi forces tried to arrest Sadr. The fighting lasted until August 25, when Sistani, who had recently returned to Iraq after undergoing medical treatment in Great Britain, brokered a cease-fire. During the height of the fighting, Sadr and several hundred of his supporters took over Najaf's Shrine of Imam Ali, a revered Shiite holy site where the first imam is buried. The old city of Najaf was heavily damaged in the fighting. After meeting with Sistani on August 25, Sadr and his armed supporters left the shrine compound and turned over its keys to Sistani's representatives.

Following the December 2005 national elections, the Sadr Movement gained control of four ministries and reportedly infiltrated branches of the security services with Mahdi Army militiamen, who were accused of carrying out attacks on Sadr's rivals and Sunni Arabs. Despite such allegations, Sadr remained the most popular Iraqi Shiite leader with Sunni Iraqis, many of whom respected and admired his resistance to continued U.S. and British occupation. His crossover popularity, however, was shattered following the February 22, 2006, bombing of the revered Shiite Askari shrine in Samarra. Mahdi Army militiamen and other rogue elements, some of them former members of his movement, ignored instructions from Sadr not to carry out random revenge attacks and instead attacked Sunni mosques and murdered Sunni religious leaders and random passersby in retaliation.

The ensuing descent of Iraq into a virtual civil war made it more difficult to determine which elements were truly a part of the Sadr Movement and the Mahdi Army, whose membership reportedly swelled to a peak of some 60,000 by late 2006, according to the Iraq Study Group report. Many groups that were carrying out sectarian killings were thought to be led by former Mahdi Army commanders who were expelled from the movement or even individuals who had never been Mahdi Army members but used its name to carry out extortion and kidnappings for ransom. The real Mahdi Army and the Sadr Movement, although initially supportive of Iraqi prime minister Nuri al-Maliki, began to face government-led attacks in April 2008 when Iraqi forces and U.S. aircraft attacked Mahdi Army positions in the southern port city of Basra. These assaults were reportedly spearheaded by Iraqi Army and police units dominated by the Supreme Islamic Iraqi Council, headed by Sadr's chief Shiite rival, Abd al-Aziz al-Hakim. The attacks are believed to have been an attempt to damage the Sadrists' political chances in provincial elections set for 2009.

The Mahdi Army and the Supreme Council's paramilitary wing, the Badr Corps, had engaged in running gun battles since 2005, with a large-scale battle between the two occurring in Karbala in January 2008 during Ashura religious processions. Despite these attacks, in early May 2008 Sadr announced the six-month renewal of a 2007 cease-fire agreement between the Sadr Movement and the Iraqi government. He also ordered his supporters not to engage in violence and instead requested that they focus on grassroots nonviolent political protests against the continued occupation of Iraq.

Although Sadr ostensibly suspended the Mahdi Army's military operations in late August 2008, he went on to form three new but smaller paramilitary organizations between the end of 2008 and the spring of 2010. In 2010, 40 former Mahdi Army participants or supporters gained seats in the Iraqi parliament, which may have obviated the need to resort to widespread armed conflict, although the renewed Iraqi insurgency since 2012 has likely been inspired, at least in part, by former Mahdi Army soldiers. In 2014, amid the Iraqi government's war against the Islamic State of Iraq and Syria (ISIS), the Mahdi Army appeared to have made a modest comeback, as numerous soldiers identifying themselves as Mahdi Army troops staged a parade in Sadr City, which had been the epicenter of the militia between 2003 and 2008. Whether Sadr himself had anything to do with the display remains uncertain.

Christopher Paul Anzalone

See also: Baath Party; Coalition Provisional Authority; Insurgency and Opposition: Badr Organization; Iraq, History of, 1990–Present;

Islamic State of Iraq and al-Sham (ISIS); Political Parties, Iraq: Supreme Iraqi Islamic Council; Prime Minister, Iraq: Nuri al-Maliki; Sadr, Muqtada al-; Shia Islam; Sunni Islam

References

Cockburn, Patrick. *Muqtada: Muqtada al-Sadr, the Shia Revival, and the Struggle for Iraq.* New York: Scribner, 2008.

Cole, Juan. "The United States and Shi'ite Religious Factions in Post-Ba'athist Iraq." *Middle East Journal* 57 (2003): 543–566.

Nakash, Yitzhak. *Reaching for Power: The Shi'a in the Modern Arab World.* Princeton, NJ: Princeton University Press, 2006.

Rahimi, Babak. "The Return of Moqtada Al-Sadr and the Revival of the Mahdi Army." Combatting Terrorism Center, June 3, 2010, https://www.ctc.usma.edu/posts/the-return-of-moqtada-al-sadr-and-the-revival-of-the-mahdi-army.

Visser, Reidar. *The Sadrists of Basra and the Far South of Iraq: The Most Unpredictable Political Force in the Gulf's Oil-Belt Region?* Oslo, Norway: Norwegian Institute of International Affairs, 2008.

Interrogation, Coercive (Torture)

Coercive interrogation involves methods of interrogation meant to compel a person to behave in an involuntary way or reveal information by use of threat, intimidation, or physical force or abuse. A wide variety of interrogation techniques commonly utilized during the Iraq War may be considered coercive. These include, but are not limited to: sleep deprivation, food deprivation, ceaseless noise, sexual abuse, forced nakedness, cultural humiliation, exposure to extreme cold, prolonged isolation, painful postures, beating, and waterboarding. Waterboarding is a particularly controversial interrogation method that involves positioning a victim on his back. The head is tilted back as water is poured over the face and head. Water enters the nasal passages and mouth, causing the victim to believe that drowning is imminent. Not surprisingly, waterboarding can be very effective in extracting confessions. The fact that it leaves no visible marks on the victim makes it a favored interrogation technique.

Coercive interrogation was used during the Iraq War and the greater Global War on Terrorism to obtain information from prisoners, especially those being held as terrorists. Coercive interrogation has many opponents. Many believe it to be ineffective and argue that it leads to false confessions. Others consider it an inhumane form of torture, contending that those who practice it should be charged as war criminals acting in violation of international law.

Torture has been an established part of judicial procedure for much of human history. In wartime, torture has historically been most commonly used to obtain intelligence information from prisoners of war in a rapid fashion. In other circumstances it has been used to extract a confession, or as a punishment and method of dehumanization. Torture has also been routinely employed to achieve a propaganda advantage by securing confessions or testimonials denouncing the policies of the victim's own government.

It is only in the past two centuries that concerted efforts have been made to ban torture and establish penalties for its use. Torture is banned by international law as a fundamental violation of human rights, whether inflicted on enemies or one's own population. It is specifically banned by the Third and Fourth Geneva Conventions (1929 and 1949) as well as the United Nations Convention against Torture (1987). There is an ongoing debate over what constitutes torture by nations that do not conform to international standards. Beyond wartime, the United Nations Convention against Torture regards capital punishment as well as many of the sanctioned legal punishments in Iran, Saudi Arabia, Libya, Pakistan, and under the Taliban to be torture.

Coercive interrogation became an issue during the George W. Bush administration after the Global War on Terrorism began in 2001. Although many international agreements signed by the United States forbid torture, President Bush and his administration supported the use of coercive interrogation in the Global War on Terrorism, the Afghanistan War, and the Iraq War. Bush believed that as commander in chief he could use the inherent powers given to him in the U.S. Constitution to stretch U.S. policy to best protect the citizens of the United States. The administration argued repeatedly that terrorism is a major threat that cannot be fought with conventional means. Also, the White House repeatedly stated that coercive interrogation is not torture in the strict sense of the word.

Beginning in 2004, accounts surfaced of Iraqi prisoners being abused by U.S. soldiers in the Abu Ghraib prison in Iraq. Pictures showing U.S. military personnel abusing and violating prisoners by various means proved highly incendiary. Some methods used included urinating on prisoners, punching prisoners excessively, pouring phosphoric acid on prisoners, rape, forcing prisoners to strip nude and attaching electrodes to their genitals, or photographing prisoners in compromising positions to humiliate them. Eventually, 17 soldiers and officers were removed from duty because of the Abu Ghraib scandal; some eventually faced criminal charges and trial.

The situation was compounded when the CIA was accused of having destroyed evidence of the torture of civilian detainees in 2005. There were apparently two videotapes (subsequently destroyed) that contained images of Al Qaeda suspects being tortured. By 2007, the CIA admitted to some use of coercive interrogation. However, the agency asserted that the use of such tactics (to include waterboarding) had been rare.

Despite public disapproval, the Bush administration stuck to its support of coercive interrogation techniques, arguing that they were not cruel and unusual and therefore did not constitute torture. Nevertheless, under considerable pressure, Bush signed an executive order in July 2007 forbidding the use of torture against terror suspects; it did not, however, specifically ban waterboarding.

In early 2008, waterboarding was again a hot topic as Congress considered an antitorture bill designed largely to limit the CIA's use of coercive interrogation. The bill, which was passed in February 2008, would have forced the CIA to abide by the rules found in the *Army Field Manual on Interrogation* (FM 34–52). The manual forbids the use of physical force and includes a list of approved interrogation methods; waterboarding is not among them. Bush vetoed the February 2008 bill, and its proponents did not have the requisite votes to override it. On January 29, 2009, President Barak Obama signed an executive order mandating that the CIA use only 19 interrogation methods as outlined in the *Army Field Manual on Interrogation* unless it obtained specific exemptions from the attorney general.

While the debate on the use of coercive interrogation and whether or not such tactics constitute torture has slipped into the shadows for the time being, it is by no means resolved. According to Amnesty International more than 150 nations routinely employed torture in the period 1997–2000. Clearly, it remains a prominent human rights issue into the 21st century.

Arthur M. Holst and
Paul Joseph Springer

See also: Bush, George Walker; Detention Operations, Coalition: Abu Ghraib, Guantánamo Bay Detention Camp; Obama, Barack Hussein, II

References

Bellamy, Alex J. "No Pain, No Gain? Torture and Ethics in the War on Terror." *International Affairs* 82 (2006): 121–148.

Danner, Mark. *Torture and Truth: America, Abu Ghraib, and the War on Terror.* New York: New York Review Books, 2004.

Dershowitz, Alan M. *Is There a Right to Remain Silent? Coercive Interrogation and the Fifth Amendment after 9/11.* Oxford: Oxford University Press, 2008.

Friedman, Lori, ed. *How Should the United States Treat Prisoners in the War on Terror?* Farmington Hills, MI: Greenhaven, 2005.

Guiora, Amos N. *Constitutional Limits on Coercive Interrogation.* New York: Oxford University Press, 2008.

Hersh, Seymour. *Chain of Command: The Road from 9/11 to Abu Ghraib.* New York: HarperCollins, 2004.

Meeropol, Rachel, and Reed Brody. *America's Disappeared: Secret Imprisonment, Detainees, and the "War on Terror."* New York: Seven Stories, 2005.

Posner, Eric A., and Adrian Vermeule. *Terror in the Balance? Security, Liberty, and the Courts.* New York: Oxford University Press, 2007.

Sampson, William. *Confessions of an Innocent Man: Torture and Survival in a Saudi Prison.* Toronto: McClelland and Stewart, 2005.

Zabecki, David T. "Torture: Lessons from Vietnam and Past Wars." *Vietnam* (October 2008): 32–35.

Iraq, Air Force

The Iraqi Air Force, initially created under the direction and guidance of the British mandate government in 1931, grew steadily through six decades by importing technology and hardware from multiple sources, most notably Great Britain, France, and the Soviet Union. Its expansion was largely driven by the aftermath of unsuccessful attacks on Israel, which often led to the destruction of significant numbers of Iraqi warplanes. In 1991 it was virtually destroyed by the combined air forces of the international coalition formed to evict Iraqi occupation units from Kuwait (Operation Desert Storm). Just prior to the 1991 Persian Gulf War, much of the pre-1991 Iraqi air fleet was flown to Iran in the hope of preserving the airplanes for future use. The government of Iran seized control of the warplanes, however, further degrading Iraq's aerial defense capability. In the years after the Persian Gulf War, Iraq's remaining warplanes slowly degenerated due to poor maintenance, a lack of trained aircraft technicians, and a shortage of vital repair parts. During the 2003 Anglo-American–led invasion of Iraq (Operation Iraqi Freedom), coalition forces reported virtually no aerial activity by the Iraqi Air Force.

In the period after the Persian Gulf War, coalition forces established a pair of no-fly zones over Iraq, prohibiting Iraqi warplanes from overflying all but the central third of the nation. Coalition aircraft frequently bombed targets in Iraq to enforce compliance with the terms of the 1991 ceasefire. As of 2002, Iraq owned only 5 serviceable MiG-29 fighters and fewer than 40 serviceable Mirage F1s, supplemented by fewer than 100 older warplanes. By the beginning of the Anglo-American–led coalition invasion of Iraq in March 2003 (Operation Iraqi Freedom), the Iraqi Air Force had virtually ceased to exist.

Coalition forces routinely found derelict aircraft as they captured Iraqi airfields. Some advanced Iraqi warplanes were found buried in the desert in an attempt to preserve them from enemy air strikes. After Iraqi president Saddam Hussein was deposed in April 2003, coalition forces began to slowly rebuild the Iraqi military as a key component of the establishment of a democratic Iraqi government. The resurgent air force now serves primarily in a transport capacity and has been outfitted with American-built C-130 Hercules transport planes and UH-1 helicopters. Iraq had not been able to import new aircraft since the 1991 Persian Gulf War, and thus its few remaining aircraft were becoming increasingly obsolete.

In August 2009, the Iraqi Defense Ministry revealed that Iraq owned 19 MiG-21 and MiG-23 fighter jets that were in storage in Serbia. Saddam Hussein had sent the aircraft to Serbia for repairs in the late 1980s during the Iran-Iraq War. The aircraft could not be returned to Iraq because of the subsequent international sanctions. Upon learning of the existence of the aircraft in 2009, the Iraqi government arranged with the Serbs to refurbish and return the aircraft on a priority basis.

In 2008, the United States agreed to provide Iraq with propeller-driven Hawker Beechcraft T-6A aircraft that would be used to train Iraqi jet pilots to fly the Lockheed Martin F-16 Fighting Falcon. In June 2014, the United States delivered the first of several F-16 jet fighters to Iraq. In May 2014, amid the growing Islamic State of Iraq and Syria (ISIS) insurgency, the U.S. government announced a $1 billion arms sale to the Iraqis, the vast majority of which will be composed of helicopters and various fixed-wing aircraft, including several more F-16s. Meanwhile, in the summer of 2014, the Iraqi government agreed to purchase 10–15 or so secondhand aircraft from Belarus and Russia with which to target ISIS insurgents. The first of those aircraft began arriving in Iraq in October 2014. In July, Iran dispatched seven Russian-made Sukhoi Su-25 aircraft (designed for close air support) to Iraq to be employed in the fight against ISIS. These jets had belonged to Iraq prior to the Persian Gulf War. The Iraqi government plans to have in its air force inventory 516 total aircraft by the end of 2015 and 550 by the end of 2018.

Paul Joseph Springer

See also: Iraq, Army; Iraqi Freedom, Operation; Islamic State of Iraq and al-Sham (ISIS)

References

Butler, Richard. *The Greatest Threat: Iraq, Weapons of Mass Destruction and the Growing Crisis in Global Security.* New York: PublicAffairs, 2000.

"Iraq Accepts Fist Lockheed Martin F-16 Aircraft." Lockheed Martin, June 5, 2014, http://www.lockheedmartin.com/us/news/press-releases/2014/june/140605ae_iraq-accepts-first-f-16.html.

Murray, Williamson, and Robert H. Scales Jr. *The Iraq War: A Military History.* Boston: Belknap, 2003.

Rubin, Barry, and Thomas A. Keaney, eds. *Armed Forces in the Middle East: Politics and Strategy.* Portland, OR: Frank Cass, 2002.

Iraq, Army

The Iraqi Army has historically been one of the most technologically advanced and aggressive military forces in the modern Middle East. Since the end of World War II, Iraq has joined three wars against Israel, launched invasions of Iran and Kuwait, and been attacked by two multinational forces under American leadership. The Iraqi Army has also frequently engaged in internal strife, fighting to put down repeated Kurdish and Shiite revolts against the government. In addition, the Iraqi Army has played a fundamental role in the Iraqi government, having participated in a series of coups d'état against the existing government beginning in the late 1950s. After the most recent invasion and occupation of Iraq, which began in 2003 with Operation Iraqi Freedom, the Iraqi Army was declared dissolved by the Coalition Provisional Authority (CPA), the interim occupation government. The CPA then began to rebuild the Iraqi military from the ground up, including its complete retraining.

The military history of Iraq stretches back several thousand years. The region of Mesopotamia, situated astride the Tigris and Euphrates Rivers, is often considered the cradle of civilization. The ancient Sumerian, Akkadian, and Babylonian Empires each dominated the region. By the ninth century CE, Baghdad was an economic and cultural center for the entire Muslim world. In 1638, the region was assimilated into the Ottoman Empire through military conquest. Iraq remained a part of Ottoman Turkey until World War I, when it was invaded and occupied by a British expeditionary force that landed at Basra and gradually moved northward. The British troops were assisted by Iraqi Arabs, emboldened by promises of independence at the end of the war. When World War I ended the Ottoman Empire was dissolved, but the modern state of Iraq was largely controlled by the British and remained a British mandate until 1947.

In the interwar period, a series of rebellions against British rule erupted in Iraq. The first began in May 1920, when Iraqi nationalists, angered at the creation of the British mandate, led a general Arab insurrection against the newly constituted government. In addition to feeling frustrated by their failure to obtain independence, the rebels also resented the actual composition of the mandate government. It consisted almost entirely of foreign bureaucrats, particularly British colonial officials transplanted from India. By February 1921 British military forces had successfully quelled the rebellion, only to see a Kurdish revolt begin the following year. The Kurdish attempt to form an independent Kurdish state was primarily stymied through the use of airpower, against which the Kurds had no defense. Iraqi Army units under British control assisted in the suppression of the Kurdish revolt. In the 1930s, two more major uprisings occurred. In August 1933 Assyrian Christians rebelled against the government, provoking a harsh retaliation by the Iraqi Army that left 600 dead. A religious-based revolt occurred again in 1935, when Shiite Muslims attempted to overthrow the reigning government and were brutally suppressed by British and Iraqi troops.

In 1941 with World War II raging in Europe, Iraqi politician Rashid Ali al-Gaylani and his military colleagues known as the Golden Square perceived an opportunity to overthrow British control. After they seized power, Ali proclaimed an independent Iraq. The Allied powers feared that he would align his government with the Axis nations of Germany and Italy because Germany had been directing propaganda efforts in neighboring Syria and Iran. British residents and officials took refuge in the British legation, and to rescue them the British sent in forces that quickly defeated the Iraqi Army and reestablished the mandate government. Three separate Kurdish revolts broke out in the 1940s, each led by Mullah Mustafa Barzani. All were quickly suppressed by the Iraqi Army, bolstered by British airpower.

On May 14, 1948, Jews in Palestine led by David Ben-Gurion proclaimed the state of Israel. The announcement provoked an immediate invasion by Egypt, Iraq, Lebanon, Syria, and Transjordan; thus began the Israeli War of Independence (1948–1949). Iraqi forces operated in conjunction with Syrian and Transjordanian troops and were occasionally aided by members of the Palestinian Arab Liberation Army. The Iraqi expeditionary force made small initial gains but could not withstand the eventual Israeli counterattack. The Iraqi troop contingent grew to more than 20,000 men during the war, including thousands of poorly trained recruits who volunteered for service in Palestine. Despite maintaining numerical superiority for the entire war, Iraqi troops made no progress in Israel after June 1948. By mid-1949 Iraqi troops had withdrawn from Israel, although the formal state of war remained through 2006.

In 1956, the Suez Crisis threatened to expand into a larger regional conflict. While Egyptian and Israeli units sparred for control of the Sinai Peninsula, Iraqi Army troops crossed into Jordan to prevent an Israeli attack there. Shortly after Iraqi troops returned home, Brigadier General Abd al-Karim Qasim led the Iraqi military in a coup against King Faisal II's government. Faisal had been installed as monarch in 1947, with British support. During the seizure of power, the king and Prime Minister Nuri al-Said were both killed.

The longest and most successful Kurdish revolt against Iraqi rule commenced in 1961. Mustafa Barzani led yet another uprising in the hope of gaining autonomy for the Kurdish people. The Iraqi Army proved incapable of quelling the rebellion, however, even when assisted by the Iraqi Air Force. By 1963, Syrian military forces moved into Iraq to assist in ending the rebellion, hoping to prevent an expansion of the uprising. With the exception of a one-year cease-fire that ended in April 1965, the conflict continued until 1970, when the Iraqi government finally admitted defeat and granted Kurdish autonomy without full independence.

In June 1967, the Six-Day War erupted between Israel and an Arab coalition. Israeli intelligence, detecting a massive Arab military buildup on its borders, compelled Israel to launch a series of preemptive strikes to prevent or delay the invasion. The majority of the Egyptian Air Force was destroyed in the first raids, and a similar raid against Iraqi airfields achieved modest success, destroying some aircraft and driving the rest to airfields in eastern Iraq, beyond the reach of Israeli attack aircraft. Although Iraq did not formally participate in the 1967 war, Iraqi troops again moved into defensive positions in Jordan, helping to deter a major Israeli advance across the Jordan River.

On October 6, 1973, Arab armies surprised Israel with a massive invasion on three fronts, sparking the Yom Kippur War. Although the Iraqi Army did not participate in the first days of the conflict, within a week Iraqi armor units were fighting the Israelis on the Golan Heights. More than 60,000 Iraqi troops were deployed in the war, supplemented by 700 tanks. The decision to attack Israel proved to be a debacle for the Iraqi Army, however. On October 13, an Israeli ambush destroyed 80 Iraqi tanks in a single day without the loss of any Israeli tanks. Iraqi military performance improved little throughout the war. The Iraqi military coordinated poorly with its Arab allies and was repeatedly mauled by the aggressive tactics of Israeli commanders. Although Iraq itself was never threatened with invasion, the Iraqi Army at the conclusion of the war showed the effects of devastating battlefield losses. During the spring of 1974, Barzani led another Kurdish revolt, this time supported by Mohammad Reza Shah Pahlavi of Iran. This rebellion was brutally put down by the Iraqi Army, forcing Pahlavi to withdraw his support. For the remainder of the decade, Iraq attempted to rebuild its army, relying primarily upon the Soviet Union for the supply of heavy weapons.

After five years of border disputes with Iran, Iraqi president Saddam Hussein ordered an invasion of Iran, beginning on September 22, 1980. At the time of the invasion, the Iraqi Army had grown to almost 200,000 troops, supplemented by 4,500 tanks, mostly of Soviet design. By gradually increasing tank imports while maintaining older designs in service, the Iraqi armored divisions fielded a very mixed force of vehicles, ranging from the T-55, designed in 1947, to the T-80 model of 1976. Initially, the army managed to advance into Iranian territory. However, the advance was soon halted by stronger than expected Iranian resistance. Eight years of bloody stalemate ensued, costing almost 1 million total casualties. In an effort to end the stalemate, Hussein ordered the use of chemical weapons on Iranian troops and the Iranian civilian population. The use of chemical weapons alarmed the entire region, particularly because the Iraqi government had a well-established nuclear weapons program in place and was actively seeking atomic weapons. On June 7, 1981, Israel launched an air raid to destroy Iraq's Osiraq nuclear reactor, decimating the bulk of the nuclear program in a single strike.

After eight years of combat, Iran and Iraq agreed to an armistice returning to the status quo antebellum. In 1988 Iraq possessed the largest army in the Middle East, capable of fielding 1 million troops from a population of only 17 million. In addition, imports of Soviet hardware made the Iraqi Army the most advanced in the region. Iraqi armored divisions relied on the Soviet T-80 main battle tank. The army contained 70 divisions of veteran troops, with a large number of artillery pieces. The Soviet Union also provided Iraq with tactical and strategic missiles capable of delivering biological and chemical weapons to Israel.

The Iraqi military did not remain idle for long after the Iran-Iraq War. Following two years of rebuilding, Iraq again looked to expand its territory along the Persian Gulf coast. After renewing claims that Kuwait was a renegade province of Iraq, the Iraqi government accused Kuwait of stealing oil reserves through illegal slant-drilling techniques and manipulating the price of oil. When Kuwait refused a series of Iraqi demands, Hussein ordered the invasion of Kuwait, beginning on August 2, 1990. The invasion quickly overwhelmed the small Kuwaiti military. The United States immediately deployed forces to Saudi Arabia to prevent further Iraqi aggression, and within four months 500,000 American troops defended Saudi Arabia, bolstered by detachments from dozens of nations (Operation Desert Shield). Included in the defensive forces were units from many of Iraq's Arabic neighbors. When Hussein ignored United Nations (UN) resolutions demanding the evacuation of Kuwait, the coalition forces launched a series of air strikes against targets in Iraq and Kuwait beginning in January 1991. Eventually during the Persian Gulf War (Operation Desert Storm), a massive ground assault forced Iraqi units to retreat from Kuwait.

Although Hussein threatened that coalition forces would face "the mother of all battles" if they dared to invade Iraq, the coalition ground attack quickly overwhelmed Iraqi units entrenched in prepared positions. The Iraqi military had no defense against coalition air supremacy, and thousands of destroyed Iraqi tanks and armored vehicles littered the retreat route. The vaunted Republican Guard divisions, elite units of the Iraqi Army, were eviscerated by coalition aircraft and tanks. Although the exact number of Iraqi soldiers killed remains unknown, estimates put the number at between 15,000 and 100,000, with a further 300,000 wounded in the fighting.

Even after Iraqi forces were driven from Kuwaiti soil, Iraq remained under tight economic sanctions in the decade after the Persian Gulf War. Because Hussein refused to account for the entire Iraqi biological and chemical weapons arsenal, UN weapons inspectors roamed the nation. Restrictions on imports into Iraq prevented Hussein from rebuilding the devastated Iraqi Army, and even vehicles that survived the coalition onslaught could not be maintained for want of spare parts.

On March 20, 2003, the United States led a thin coalition in a new invasion of Iraq (Operation Iraqi Freedom). Ostensibly, the invasion was triggered by Iraqi refusals to comply with UN weapons inspections. However, the new coalition did not include any of Iraq's Middle Eastern neighbors. Regardless of the much smaller size of the invading forces, the 2003 invasion conquered Iraq in only three weeks, deposing Hussein in April. Weapons inspectors did not find the expected stockpiles of chemical and biological weapons, although some small caches of illegal weapons were discovered in the aftermath of the fighting. At the time of the invasion, the Iraqi Army was a mere shadow of its 1990 size, with fewer than 400,000 poorly trained troops using obsolete equipment. Estimates for total Iraqi casualties in the 2003 war vary greatly, but U.S. general Tommy Franks reported in April 2003 that approximately 30,000 Iraqi soldiers died during the invasion.

After conquering Iraq, the Anglo-American–led forces established a provisional government. One of its earliest directives, proposed by Paul Bremer, head of the CPA, and announced on May 23, 2003, dissolved the Iraqi military, a move that in retrospect proved to be a disaster because occupying and pacifying the nation without the army proved impossible, especially considering that American forces in theater were only a fraction of what would have been needed. Rather, the provisional government planned to completely rebuild and retrain the Iraqi Army. This decision created a massive power vacuum in Iraqi society and contributed to the high unemployment, lawlessness, and insurgency that have characterized occupied Iraq. The Iraqi Army continues to operate Soviet-built tanks, but the vast majority of Iraq's top-quality armored vehicles were destroyed in 1991 and 2003, ensuring that most remaining Iraqi tanks are of long-obsolete designs, such as the T-62 and T-55. From the 70 divisions of 1988, the Iraqi Army was down to only 10 divisions by 2006, although by 2009 it encompassed 14 divisions and 56 brigades.

The Iraqi Army assumed complete control of Iraqi defenses when the last coalition troops withdrew from the country in December 2011. As of late 2014, the Iraqi Army had a total of about 800,000 personnel; approximately 283,000 were active duty, and the remainder were reserve forces. The army underwent a major restructuring between 2003 and 2007, and in 2008 it planned and executed its first high-profile, division-level combat operation.

Since 2003, the Iraqi Army has requisitioned much new weaponry, and after the United States withdrew its troops from Iraq, the Americans announced several major arms sales and transfers to Iraq; the latest one (May 2014), promised a $1 billion sale of warplanes, armored vehicles of varying types, and technology for surveillance purposes. Since 2008, the United States has sold a number of M1A1 Abrams main battle tanks to the Iraqis. The structure and size of the Iraqi Army has remained relatively constant since 2009, although the target of 350,000 active-duty soldiers has yet to be achieved.

Paul Joseph Springer

See also: Hussein, Saddam; Iraq, Air Force; Iraq, History of, 1990–Present; Iraqi Freedom, Operation; Islamic State of Iraq and al-Sham (ISIS); Kurds; Shia Islam; Sunni Islam

References

Butler, Richard. *The Greatest Threat: Iraq, Weapons of Mass Destruction and the Growing Crisis in Global Security.* New York: PublicAffairs, 2000.

Finnie, David H. *Shifting Lines in the Sand: Kuwait's Elusive Frontier with Iraq.* Cambridge, MA: Harvard University Press, 1992.

Herzog, Chaim. *The Arab-Israeli Wars: War and Peace in the Middle East from the War of Independence to Lebanon.* Westminster, MD: Random House, 1984.

Hiro, Dilip. *The Longest War: The Iran-Iraq Military Conflict.* London: Routledge, 1991.

Kirkpatrick, David D. "In Shake-Up, Iraqi Premier Replaces 36 Commanders." *New York Times,* November 12, 2014.

Murray, Williamson, and Robert H. Scales Jr. *The Iraq War: A Military History.* Boston: Belknap, 2003.

Rubin, Barry, and Thomas A. Keaney, eds. *Armed Forces in the Middle East: Politics and Strategy.* Portland, OR: Frank Cass, 2002.

Iraq, History of, 1990–Present

From 1990 until the U.S.-led coalition invasion of Iraq on March 20, 2003, which overthrew the government of President Saddam Hussein, Iraq was in perpetual crisis, and many of its citizens suffered from severe economic and military hardships. To make matters worse, Iraqi government policies during that period only exacerbated the chaos that defined the nation between 1990 and 2003. After Hussein was overthrown, Iraq was convulsed by violence due to sectarian strife and a potent Iraqi insurgency, and occupation forces had mixed success in dealing with the unrest. Reconstruction has proceeded slowly, and with no long-standing tradition of a freely elected democratic government, the new Iraqi government has proven to be not very adept at managing the nation's affairs. After coalition forces left Iraq in December 2011, the situation in Iraq steadily worsened, and by 2013 the country was being threatened by a potent insurgency spearheaded by Al Qaeda in Iraq as well as the Islamic State of Iraq and Syria (ISIS).

During much of the period Iraq was ruled by Saddam Hussein, who was president of Iraq from July 16, 1979, until April 9, 2003. On April 9, 2003, coalition forces captured Baghdad and established the Coalition Provisional Authority (CPA) to govern Iraq, which was later formed into the Iraqi Interim Government. The permanent government was elected in 2005. Large numbers of coalition forces—most of them American—remained in the country as part of an effort to quell the violence and help the government gain control of the country.

Following the conclusion of the eight-year Iran-Iraq War in 1988, Iraq faced economic disaster. The nation's foreign debt was estimated to be between $100 billion and $120 billion, with recovery costs estimated at more than $450 billion. Iraq's estimated oil reserve of 100 billion barrels, however, continued to be a viable asset. Nevertheless, Iraq's economy was incapable of absorbing most of the nearly 500,000 soldiers who were still in active service in the Iraqi military.

Hussein had hoped that neighboring Saudi Arabia or Kuwait would write off Iraq's war debts or even offer funds for reconstruction. When this did not occur, he became angry and accused Kuwait of deliberately keeping oil prices low by overproducing in an effort to further injure the Iraqi economy. He also accused the Kuwaitis of illegally slant drilling oil from the Rumaila oil field, located in southeastern Iraq.

On August 2, 1990, Iraqi troops invaded Kuwait and quickly occupied it. Immediately following the invasion, Kuwaiti officials and much of the international community condemned the action and demanded the withdrawal of Iraqi troops. The United Nations (UN) also denounced the act and immediately passed UN Resolution 661, which imposed wide-ranging sanctions on Iraq. These sanctions provided for a trade embargo that excluded only medical supplies, food, and other essential items. The embargo further depressed the Iraq economy. The UN also authorized a naval blockade of Iraq. The United States, meanwhile, was deeply concerned about the occupation of Kuwait, a potential Iraqi incursion into Saudi Arabia, and a potential disruption to world oil supplies; what is more, it worried over Iraqi programs that had called for the production of weapons of mass destruction (WMD). U.S. officials feared that these developments would upset the balance of power in the region and might imperil Israel.

The United States and Great Britain soon spearheaded a military coalition of 34 countries, including many Arab nations, to face down the Iraqi aggression. When diplomatic negotiations yielded no progress, coalition forces began a massive aerial campaign against Iraq on January 17, 1991. Nearly a month of aerial attacks against Iraq destroyed much of its entire infrastructure and killed an estimated 12,000 to 15,000 Iraqi soldiers and civilians. The aerial bombardment was followed by a quick ground assault in February 1991 in which coalition forces advanced into Kuwait and southern Iraq. Kuwait was liberated and Iraq resoundingly defeated in just 100 hours of ground combat. Some 60,000 Iraqi troops surrendered without a fight. On February 27, 1991, U.S. president George H. W. Bush ordered coalition forces to stand down. Estimates of Iraqi deaths during Operation Desert Storm, including civilian casualties, range from 20,000 to 281,000 people. Meanwhile, Iraq's military had been badly mauled, the economy was in tatters, and the nation's infrastructure was badly damaged.

Despite the destruction caused by the Persian Gulf War, Hussein's government survived. Bush called for the Iraqi people to force Hussein to step aside, and uprisings occurred among various groups, including Iraqi Army troops returning from their defeat. These began in March 1991 and soon engulfed much of the country. Shiite Muslims in southern Iraq and Kurds in northern Iraq, two religious sects that had been violently persecuted throughout Hussein's presidency, also rebelled against the Iraqi government. The refusal of the coalition governments to support the insurgents, however, allowed the government to suppress the rebellions with brutal force. Unfortunately for the opponents of Hussein, the Iraqi government was allowed under the terms of the agreements ending the war to employ helicopters, which it used with devastating effectiveness against the insurgents. Many Kurds fled north to Turkey to avoid the violent suppression that followed, and Shiite Muslims and Kurds continued to face persecution throughout the rest of Hussein's presidency.

The brutal campaigns against the Shiites and Kurds—especially those against the Kurds in the north—received wide-ranging media coverage and garnered much sympathy for the Kurdish population. Partly because of such coverage, a no-fly zone, an area over which the Iraqi Air Force had to relinquish its control, was established in northern Iraq, followed by a similar zone in southern Iraq.

Following the successful suppression of the uprisings, the Iraqi government set out to strengthen its hold on power. Hussein favored his most loyal supporters, Arab Sunnis from the area of his hometown of Tikrit. With the economy in shambles, many Iraqi people had begun seeking old institutions, such as Arab tribes, for support. At the same time, Hussein shrewdly sought backing from tribal leaders within Iraq. The government thus established the Assembly of Tribes, and Hussein made a public apology for past land reforms that had hurt tribal leaders. Tribalism and favoritism soon led to violence and ruthless competition among the various groups, however. In 1994, in order to quell such unrest, the government responded by implementing harsh new laws designed to limit the power of tribal groups. However, because of selective enforcement of such laws, there was little reduction in violence.

At the same time, UN sanctions devastated the Iraqi economy. Also, government policies supported large military and internal security forces at the expense of other sectors. The sanctions had declared that 30 percent of Iraqi oil exports had to be set aside for war reparations, but the Iraqi economy had grown to depend on its oil exports at the expense of other industries, especially agriculture. Thus, when money from the oil trade was diminished, many Iraqis suffered from malnourishment and grinding poverty. The effects of the sanctions combined with the large debts incurred during the war with Iran brought on hyperinflation, which nearly wiped out the Iraqi middle class. The value of the Iraqi currency, the dinar, plummeted, and food prices rose rapidly after the war. Cancer rates also increased, reportedly a result of the 300 to 800 tons of depleted uranium used in Iraq during the war.

Medical supplies were scarce in Iraq as a result of the sanctions, and the government hoarded them. Mortality rates in children under the age of five increased steeply. The Iraqi government implemented food rationing, but that did little to improve the situation. Illiteracy rates in Iraq also rose because many roads and schools had been damaged or destroyed. To add to the problem, the government withdrew much of its support for teachers and other salaried professionals. Power shortages caused widespread problems in homes and industries throughout Iraq, and many modern manufacturing facilities were forced to shut down.

In 1991, the Iraqi government had rejected UN proposals to trade its oil for food and other humanitarian supplies. On May 20, 1996, however, a Memorandum of Understanding was signed between the UN and the Iraqi government. The memorandum stated that the Iraqi government could sell oil to purchase food and other humanitarian supplies. The first shipments of food arrived in Iraq in March 1997. Unfortunately, the program suffered from rampant corruption and did little to improve the lot of average Iraqis, who continued to suffer from extreme poverty. By the late 1990s, the People's Republic of China and Russia were calling for a significant easing of UN sanctions. Such calls went unheeded, however, as the United States and other Western powers refused to grant any leniency to the Iraqi regime. By 2000, as many as 16 million Iraqis depended on some form of government assistance for survival.

Following the Persian Gulf War, the United States and its allies continued to limit

Hussein's power through numerous punitive military operations. These operations, mostly air and missile strikes, damaged infrastructure and put even more of a strain on the Iraqi economy. On October 8, 1994, Operation Vigilant Warrior began as a response to the deployment of Iraqi troops toward the Kuwaiti border. After some 170 aircraft and 6,500 military personnel were deployed to southern Iraq, Hussein recalled his troops, and the crisis passed. On September 3, 1996, Operation Desert Strike was launched in response to the movement of 40,000 Iraqi troops into northern Iraq, which threatened the Kurdish population. More than two years later on December 16, 1998, the United States and Great Britain began Operation Desert Fox, a four-day bombing campaign against select Iraqi targets. The operation was in response to the Iraqi government's refusal to comply with UN Security Council resolutions that called for the dismantling of certain weapons and the government's interference with UN weapons inspectors, whose goal was to ensure that the Iraqi government was complying with UN resolutions. The stated goal of Desert Fox was to destroy any hidden WMD and the Iraqi government's ability to produce and deploy them. The bombing targeted research and development installations.

On February 16, 2001, the United States and Great Britain launched a bombing campaign to damage Iraq's air defense network. Throughout the interwar period, bombing efforts meant to force Iraq's compliance with UN mandates caused much destruction while doing little to weaken Hussein's hold on power.

In response to such attacks, the Iraqi government, which had essentially been controlled by the decidedly secular Baath Party, began using Islam as a way to rally its citizens. The struggle against the United States was depicted as a jihad, or holy war, against the Western world. In 1994, the government encouraged the building of mosques as part of a new "faith campaign." Large murals portraying Hussein in prayer were exhibited, and government money was set aside to construct the largest mosque in the world. Hussein and his government also encouraged loyalty to the regime, and Hussein was depicted as a hero in his conflict against the United States.

In northern Iraq the Kurds were now separated from the rest of the country, and self-rule was largely implemented. Kurdish political parties allowed cable television from outside Iraq to be broadcast into their region. The UN and international aid groups with access to the north were able to distribute aid to the region. On the eve of the March 2003 invasion of Iraq, the Kurdish economy was performing much better than the rest of the country. Many Kurdish villages had been resettled, medical facilities were restored, and the infant mortality rate had improved dramatically.

Following the terror attacks on the United States of September 11, 2001, the George W. Bush administration took a more assertive stance with Iraq. Bush and his closest advisers believed that Iraq posed a threat to the United States and its allies, including Israel. Many of Bush's advisers mistakenly believed that Iraq possessed WMD and suggested an attack against Iraq, which would at once remove Hussein from power, secure the alleged WMD, and serve as a warning to other rogue states. Beyond that, they hoped that a democratic Iraq might be a force for change in the entire region.

Bush hoped to secure approval from the UN before proceeding with an attack. On September 12, 2002, he addressed the UN Security Council and attempted to make his case for an invasion of Iraq. Much of the international community was critical of such a move, however. Other world leaders did not believe that Iraq posed a threat or had links to such terrorist organizations as Al Qaeda, which the Bush administration alleged. On November 8, 2002, the UN Security Council passed Resolution 1441, which offered Iraq a final chance to comply with its disarmament agreements. The resolution required that the Iraqi government destroy all chemical, biological, and nuclear weapons as well as the means to deliver them and provide complete documentation of such.

On February 5, 2003, U.S. secretary of state Colin Powell addressed the UN General Assembly and presented evidence, some of which was later proven to be false, that Iraqi officials were impeding the work of the weapons inspectors, continuing to develop WMD, and directly supporting Al Qaeda, which had carried out the 9/11 attacks. Following the presentation, the United States and Great Britain, among others, proposed a UN resolution calling for the use of force against Iraq. Other countries, such as Canada, France, Germany, and Russia, urged continued diplomacy. Although the American effort failed, the United States decided to pursue an invasion without UN authorization.

On March 20, 2003, a U.S.-led coalition invaded Iraq with the objectives of disarming Iraq, ending Hussein's reign as president, and freeing the Iraqi people. Coalition forces were able to advance quickly through Iraq. On April 9 they captured Baghdad and officially toppled the Iraqi government, forcing Hussein to go into hiding.

On May 1, 2003, Bush declared that major combat operations in Iraq were over and that the postinvasion reconstruction phase had begun. However, the postinvasion period would prove very difficult for coalition forces. With the absence of government authority and social order, the country soon experienced widespread civil disorder, with many people looting palaces, museums, and even armories that the Iraqi government had once controlled. To complicate things, the coalition did not have enough troops on the ground to prevent such disorder and keep an insurgency at bay.

In an attempt to bring order in Iraq, the United States established the Coalition Provisional Authority (CPA) to govern Iraq and put it in place on April 20, 2003. While many of Hussein's palaces were looted, their physical structures remained intact. It was from these palaces that the CPA governed Iraq. On May 11, 2003, President Bush selected diplomat Lewis Paul Bremer III to head the CPA. On June 3, 2003, as part of the first act of the CPA, Bremer ordered the de-Baathification of Iraq. Senior officials within the Baath Party were removed from their positions and banned from future employment in the public sector. In all, about 30,000 party members became instantly unemployed. The next day, Bremer dissolved Iraq's 500,000-member army. This order left Iraq without a military or police force to stop the widespread looting. It also ensured a huge number of disgruntled, unemployed dissidents who viewed the CPA with great enmity. Violence against the occupation armies steadily increased. Notwithstanding the apparent early successes of the coalition forces, individuals opposed to the coalition presence in Iraq engaged in acts of violence, such as the use of ambush tactics, improvised explosive devices, and suicide bombings against coalition forces. Despite a quick military victory, coalition forces faced a long battle with Iraqi insurgents in their attempt to bring peace to Iraq.

Sectarian strife was also increasing, and by mid-2004 some analysts claimed that Iraq was perched on the edge of a full-blown civil war. The Arab Sunni leadership capitalized on Sunni fears of Shiite dominance of a new government. Sunni extremists routinely employed bombing and suicide-bombing attacks against Shiite civilians. Also, Shiite members of the new Iraqi Army used extralegal means to execute Sunni civilians. Shiites organized death squads, which killed many Iraqi civilians.

In the face of such violence, on June 28, 2004, governing authority was transferred to the Iraqi Interim Government, which was led by Prime Minister Iyad Allawi. The generally pro-Western Allawi launched a campaign to weaken the rebel forces of Muqtada al-Sadr, who had spoken out against the CPA. On September 1, 2004, Allawi pulled out of peace negotiations with Sadr. Eventually, however, Sadr agreed to a cease-fire and took part in the legislative elections, which were held on January 30, 2005.

As part of the January 2005 elections, the Iraqi people chose representatives for the 275-member Iraqi National Assembly. With 58.4 percent voter turnout, a total of 8.4 million people cast their ballots. At least every third candidate on the candidate lists was female. There were nine separate attacks in Iraq on election day that killed 44 people, although these numbers were less than most experts had expected.

Two parties supported largely by Shiite Muslims won a majority of the seats, and 85 of the 275 members were women. Many Sunni Arabs, who had largely supported Hussein and held power in the previous government, boycotted the elections, leading some observers to challenge the legitimacy of the elections. The assembly was immediately charged with writing a constitution for Iraq and approved the Iraqi Transitional Government on April 28, 2005. The transitional government gained authority on May 3, 2005. The Iraqi Constitution was approved on October 15, 2005, and described Iraq as a democratic, federal, representative republic.

On December 15, 2005, a second general election was held to elect a permanent Iraqi Council of Representatives. Following approval from the members of the National Assembly, a permanent government of Iraq was formed on May 16, 2006. Turnout for this election was high, at 79.4 percent, and the level of violence was lower than during the previous election. The United Iraqi Alliance, a coalition of Arab Shiite parties, won the most votes, with 41.2 percent. Ibrahim al-Jafari was nominated for the post of prime minister, but he was passed over after growing criticism by Nuri al-Maliki, a member of the Islamic Dawa Party, a conservative Shiite group. As prime minister, Maliki successfully negotiated a peace treaty with Sadr's rebel forces in August 2007.

Meanwhile, on December 13, 2003, U.S. forces captured Saddam Hussein in Dawr, a small town north of Baghdad and near Tikrit, his birthplace. An Iraqi Special Tribunal charged Hussein with crimes committed against the inhabitants of the town of Dujail in 1982. Dujail had been the site of an unsuccessful assassination attempt against Hussein. The former Iraqi president was charged with the murder of 148 people, with having ordered the torture of women and children, and with illegally arresting 399 others. On November 5, 2006, he was found guilty and sentenced to death by hanging. On December 30, Hussein was executed by Iraqi authorities.

In January 2007, President Bush presented his plan for "a new way forward" in Iraq. This was a new U.S. military strategy whose stated goal was to reduce the sectarian violence in Iraq and help the Iraqi people provide security and stability for themselves. Five additional U.S. Army brigades were deployed to Iraq between January and May 2007, totaling about 40,000 troops. Operations to secure Baghdad began immediately. The U.S. troop surge, as many commentators called the plan, continued into 2009 before most of the additional forces were gradually withdrawn.

The interpretations of the results of the surge were mixed. Many U.S. media outlets, including CNN, reported that violence had dropped anywhere from 40 to 80 percent in Iraq following the surge. ABC ran many reports on its nightly news show that highlighted the progress in Iraq. *New York Times* writer David Brooks argued that even President Bush's harshest critics would have to concede that he finally got one right. Barack Obama, who was elected president of the United States in November 2008 and was once a harsh critic of the surge, later asserted that the new military strategy had led to an improved security situation in Iraq, although he was quick to point out that the war should not have been launched in the first place.

Critics have argued that while violence may have fallen in Iraq following the surge, such evidence did not indicate that the surge was truly successful. A 2008 study of satellite imagery suggested that Shiite ethnic cleansing of Sunni neighborhoods had been largely responsible for the decrease in violence in Sunni areas. Some independent journalists argued that violence was down because the Shiites had won the battles of Baghdad in 2006–2007 and had controlled nearly three-fourths of the capital city. Others praised Maliki's government, not the U.S. government, for its efforts to stop the violence. Still others attributed it to deals struck by the occupying troops with the Sunnis to turn against Al Qaeda and other extremists.

Public opinion in Iraq seemed to suggest that Iraqis did not believe that the surge had led to any reduction in violence. A multi–news agency poll conducted in March 2008 showed that only 4 percent of Iraqis gave the U.S. surge any credit for any reduction in violence following the surge. Instead, many Iraqi people gave Iraqi institutions credit for the lowering of violence. Despite the reduction in violence, 50 percent of Iraqis still viewed security as the nation's main concern.

On December 4, 2008, the U.S. and Iraqi governments concluded a status of forces agreement, which stipulated that U.S. troops would depart from all Iraqi cities by June 30, 2009, and would leave Iraq entirely by December 31, 2011. U.S. forces were no longer allowed to hold Iraqi citizens without charges for more than 24 hours. Also, immunity from prosecution in Iraqi courts was taken away from U.S. contractors. Maliki, however, was faced by detractors who called for the immediate removal of foreign troops from Iraq. They believed that the agreement only prolonged an illegal occupation. Iraq's grand ayatollah, Sayyid Ali Husayn al-Sistani, led many of these protests and contended that Maliki was ceding too much control to the Americans. Such dissent forced the government to promise to hold a referendum on the agreement no later than June 20, 2009. If Iraqi citizens voted down the agreement, the Iraqi government would inform the United States that its troops would have to leave by June 2010, and the U.S. government would be forced to accept the referendum. The referendum was ultimately never held.

In the end Obama, who had pledged to remove all U.S. troops from Iraq before 2012, made good on his promise, and the last U.S. troops left the country on December 18,

2011, two weeks ahead of the schedule provided by the status of forces agreement. Prior to that date, the last coalition nation to withdraw from Iraq was the United Kingdom (in May 2011).

During the occupation years, the Iraqi economy improved largely due to an influx of money pouring in from abroad. Wages rose over 100 percent between 2003 and 2008, and taxes were cut by 15–45 percent, allowing many Iraqi citizens to increase their spending power. However, despite such successes, Iraq faced many economic problems as well. Unemployment remained high; the Iraq government estimated that unemployment was between 60 and 70 percent in 2008. At the same time, the Iraqi foreign debt rose as high as $125 billion. Since the withdrawal of coalition troops in late 2011, however, the Iraqi economy failed to make any major gains, and in many sectors it has steadily deteriorated. Much of this is the result of a growing insurgency and sectarian violence, combined with the ineffective and graft-ridden Maliki government.

In the years since coalition forces withdrew from Iraq, that nation witnessed an alarming reemergence of an antigovernment insurgency. This has included sectarian violence and the rise to prominence of Islamic extremist groups, including most notably the Islamic State of Iraq and al-Sham (ISIS). By early 2014, these groups seized control of virtually all of Iraq's Anbar Province. Meanwhile, the Iraqi government under Maliki was unable to stem the rising tide of deadly violence. Indeed, Mailiki's policies, which included a brutal crackdown on Iraq's Sunni population, had largely set the stage for the renewed insurgency. By the midsummer of 2014 the situation in Iraq was dire, and ISIS had advanced within 90 miles of Baghdad. Until then, the Iraqi Army had performed abysmally in its fight against ISIS; indeed, many soldiers simply deserted or fled in the face of ISIS military operations. In August, Maliki was under great domestic and international pressure to step down. Even those in his own party believed that he must go. In the meantime, the United States began dispatching small deployments of military advisers to Iraq even as U.S. aircraft began bombing raids against ISIS targets in northern and western Iraq. Maliki finally agreed to relinquish his office on September 8, 2014. He was succeeded by Haider al-Abadi, also of the Dawa Party. Abadi, who is a Shiite, vowed to reinvigorate Iraq's army and work closely with the new international coalition formed to stop and eventually eradicate ISIS. He also pledged more governmental transparency and efforts to bridge the gaping chasm between Iraq's Sunni and Shiite populations.

The fight against ISIS lasted until the end of 2017 when Prime Minister Abadi claimed that ISIS was defeated. Attacks still continue in the country though ISIS no longer claims to control cities or regions of the country. The fight against ISIS spurred greater claims of sovereignty from the Kurds, which included a referendum on independence in September 2017. The vote was overwhelmingly in favor of independence, but the Kurdish Regional Government failed to achieve any real effect as the region was cut off from outside travel and assistance by the Iraqi government in Bagdad. Tensions are still high though the sides have come to some level of accommodation.

Iraq is a mess. The economy is rife with corruption and unemployment is high. The 2018 parliamentary elections produced the Sadrist party with the largest block of seats, but no clear majority. As of this writing the parties are still in negotiations over how to form a government. Violence is still common though much reduced. Most of the areas controlled by ISIS are not being rebuilt in a timely fashion. More than 15 years after the U.S.-led invasion, very few of the goals and positive possibilities for Iraq and its people have been realized.

Gregory Wayne Morgan
and Paul G. Pierpaoli Jr.

See also: Baath Party; Bremer, Lewis Paul, III; Hussein, Saddam; Iraqi Freedom, Operation: The Surge and the Awakening; Islamic State of Iraq and al-Sham (ISIS): Al Qaeda in Iraq; Political Parties, Iraq: Islamic Dawa Party; Sadr, Muqtada al-; Shia Islam; Sistani, Sayyid Ali Husayn al-; Sunni Islam

References

Abdullah, Thabit. *A Short History of Iraq.* London: Pearson, 2003.

Allawi, Ali A. *The Occupation of Iraq: Winning the War, Losing the Peace.* New Haven, CT: Yale University Press, 2007.

Inati, Shams Constantine. *Iraq: Its History, People, and Politics.* Amherst, MA: Humanity Books, 2003.

"Iraq, Three Years Later." *The Week,* May 16, 2014, 11.

Marr, Phebe. *The Modern History of Iraq,* 2nd ed. Boulder, CO: Westview, 2003.

Tripp, Charles. *A History of Iraq.* Cambridge: Cambridge University Press, 2007.

Iraq, Navy

Prior to the 1991 Persian Gulf War, the Iraqi Navy was primarily a coastal defense force that could not operate far beyond its territorial waters. The U.S. Central Command estimated that the Iraqi Navy had poor overall operational capabilities. The force's readiness and training levels were low, and its ships were aging and in disrepair after the 1980–1988 Iran-Iraq War; it also suffered from poor maintenance programs. The main Iraqi naval base was in Basra, but access to the Persian Gulf was essentially blocked by remnants from the war with Iran. Other naval facilities were located in Az-Zubayr and Umm Qasr.

At the beginning of Operation Desert Storm, the Iraqi Navy had 13 missile boats, 9 mine warfare ships, 6 amphibious warfare ships, 4 Exocet-armed helicopters, and several patrol boats and auxiliary vessels.

By February 2, 1991, any threat posed by the Iraqi Navy had been removed. The Iraqi Navy lost 19 ships sunk and 6 others damaged. In all more than 100 Iraqi vessels of all types were destroyed in the war. The few Iraqi ships that survived the war were in poor condition and were thereafter rarely operated.

By 1993, the Iraqi Navy had only 1 operational Osa II missile patrol boat, 1 torpedo boat, a few small boats, and a few Silkworm missiles. In 1995 the navy had 2,000 personnel, 1 former Yugoslav frigate, 2 Assad-class corvettes, 1 Osa I missile fast patrol boat, and 11 patrol boats (3 Thornycroft types and 2 Bogomol-class, 1 Poluchat I–class, 2 Zhuk-class, and 3 PB-90–class vessels). After 1991, the subsequent United Nations–imposed arms, trade, and economic sanctions crippled the Iraqis' ability to repair their fleet and rebuild their naval force.

In 2002, Iraqi general Ali Hassan al-Majid al Tikriti (also known as "Chemical Ali") commanded military forces in the southern region of Iraq (one of four military commands), including the Iraqi Navy. The navy operated from bases at Basra, Umm Qasr, and Az-Zubayr. Personnel still numbered about 2,000 men.

Just prior to the start of the Iraq War, the Iraqi Navy consisted of seven patrol and coastal combat vessels as well as other auxiliary ships and small boats. It included one Bogomol-class large patrol craft (PCF), one

Osa I–class fast-attack missile craft (PTFG) equipped with Styx missiles, two 90-class inshore coastal patrol craft (PC), and three mine warfare craft (one Soviet Yevgenya-class and two Nestin-class minesweepers). The navy also operated a yacht with a helicopter deck for President Saddam Hussein.

There were many nonoperational craft in the Iraqi Navy, including an Osa I–class fast-attack missile boat and three mine warfare craft reportedly nonoperational since 1991. The presidential yacht was also nonoperational. There were many small patrol boats that were not heavily armed but could be used for mining or raiding missions. By some estimates, Iraq had more than 150 of these vessels.

The Iraqi Navy played little role in Operation Iraqi Freedom. On March 20, 2003, the first day of the war, coalition forces conducted an air and amphibious assault on the Faw Peninsula to secure oil wells located nearby. The Iraqi Navy had sent forces to guard the oil terminals, but coalition forces quickly took control of them. British forces took Umm Qasr and moved to Basra within the first two weeks of the war. The Iraqi Navy was decimated by coalition air strikes during the first days of the invasion.

The Iraqi Navy was reconstituted after 2003, and in 2014 it numbered about 1,500 active-duty sailors and a battalion of some 800 active-duty marines. The precise number of navy reservists is not known for certain but is estimated at about 2,500.

Alison Lawlor

See also: Iraqi Freedom, Operation

References

Marolda, Edward, and Robert Schneller. *Shield and Sword: The United States Navy and the Persian Gulf War*. Annapolis, MD: U.S. Naval Institute Press, 2001.

Pokrant, Marvin. *Desert Shield at Sea: What the Navy Really Did*. Westport, CT: Greenwood, 1999.

Iraq, Sanctions on

The international community imposed sanctions on Iraq beginning on August 6, 1990, four days after the Iraqi invasion of Kuwait. Various sanctions remained in place until May 22, 2003, at which time the Saddam Hussein government had been overthrown by the Anglo-American–led invasion of Iraq in March 2003. This was one of the longest and hardest sanction regimes ever imposed by the international community and the United Nations (UN) on one of its member states.

On August 2, 1990, Iraq's armed forces occupied Kuwait. Four days later UN Security Council Resolution 661 imposed comprehensive trade sanctions on Iraq. The sanctions prohibited the importation of any Iraqi commodities or products into all UN member states as well as the sale or supply of any products to Iraq. The resolution excluded the sale of medical supplies to Iraq as well as foodstuffs for humanitarian purposes.

Although the Persian Gulf War officially ended on February 28, 1991, the Security Council continued to employ sanctions against Iraq. Security Council Resolution 687 of April 3, 1991, instructed the government of Iraq to destroy, remove, and render harmless all its weapons of mass destruction (WMD) and medium-range missiles. The UN also decided to send to Iraq a team of international inspectors to supervise the implementation of the resolution. Continuing economic sanctions were supposed to maintain international pressure on Iraq to cooperate with the inspectors.

Because the 1991 war caused major damage to Iraq's infrastructure, including power plants, oil refineries, pumping stations, and water treatment facilities, the sanctions crippled Iraqi efforts to revive the economy and created a humanitarian crisis. In response to the plight of Iraqi civilians, UN secretary-general Javier Pérez de Cuéllar submitted a report to the Security Council on March 20, 1991, describing in detail the humanitarian crisis existing in Iraq after the war. In its conclusions, the report recommended that the international community work rapidly to reconstruct Iraq to improve the humanitarian situation there.

As a means of improving the humanitarian situation in Iraq, the Security Council passed Resolutions 706 and 712 in August and September of 1991, respectively. These resolutions allowed for the limited sale of Iraqi crude oil for the strict purpose of purchasing basic humanitarian goods for the Iraqi population. The government of Iraq rejected the offer, however, and demanded that all sanctions be immediately abolished.

The sanctions inflicted much more damage on Iraqi society during the 1990s. United Nations Children's Fund (UNICEF) surveys revealed that in the southern and central regions of Iraq, home to approximately 85 percent of the country's population, the mortality rate of children under the age of five had nearly tripled, from 56 deaths per 1,000 live births during 1984–1989 to 131 deaths per 1,000 live births during 1994–1999. Infant mortality (defined as children in their first year) increased from 47 per 1,000 live births to 108 per 1,000 live births within the same time frame.

The harsh conditions in Iraq soon caused a rift among the Security Council's permanent members. The United States and the United Kingdom advocated continuing the sanctions until the Iraqi government fulfilled all its obligations in compliance with Security Council Resolution 687. Their stance, however, was challenged by China, France, and Russia, which claimed that the sanctions only enhanced the suffering of the Iraqi people without influencing the Iraqi government to comply with Resolution 687.

On April 14, 1995, the UN Security Council suggested in Resolution 986 that the Iraqi government accept international supervision of the sale of Iraq's crude oil in return for humanitarian aid and basic needs such as food, medicine, and other essential civilian supplies. This diplomatic initiative finally bore fruit in May 1996 when the UN and Iraq signed a Memorandum of Understanding (MOU). Iraq began exporting crude oil under UN supervision in December 1996.

The MOU began the Oil-for-Food Programme, which operated until the invasion of Iraq by American- and British-led forces on March 20, 2003. The program was officially terminated on November 21, 2003, when authority was handed to the Coalition Provisional Authority, the entity that assumed the governance of Iraq headed by an American. On May 22, 2003, the Security Council abolished all sanctions against Iraq.

When the Oil-for-Food Programme began, Iraq was permitted to sell $2 billion of oil every six months. Two-thirds of the profits were channeled to humanitarian needs. In 1999 the Security Council decided to abolish the ceiling.

Under the program, the government of Iraq sold oil worth $64.2 billion. Of that amount, $38.7 billion was spent on humanitarian aid. Another $18 billion was given as compensation for lawsuits stemming from the occupation of Kuwait by Iraq. Finally, $1.2 billion was used to fund the program itself.

A total of $31 billion in humanitarian aid and equipment was transferred to Iraq under the program. Additional supplies and equipment totaling $8.2 billion were planned to be delivered to Iraq when the war broke out in March 2003. The program also helped to minimize the damage wrought by severe droughts in Iraq during 1999–2001.

During its seven years of operation, the program had a positive impact on civilian nutrition and health. It raised the average daily caloric intake for every Iraqi from 1,200 calories to 2,200 calories per day. The spread of contagious diseases such as cholera was also contained. The sewage system improved slowly during the 1990s, as did the delivery of medicine, particularly after the Oil-for-Food Programme was launched.

While the Oil-for-Food Programme succeeded in improving humanitarian conditions in Iraq, the diet quality was still poor. This caused malnutrition because of deficiencies in vitamins and minerals, which led to the spread of anemia, diarrhea, and respiratory infections, especially among young children. Furthermore, the program was criticized for restricting aid to food rather than also allowing the repair of infrastructure and the generation of employment. Because the aid was distributed through the government of Iraq, it actually helped the government maintain its hold over the people.

The full deficiencies of the aid plan became known after the occupation of Iraq began in 2003. In 2004 following complaints from U.S. senators and congressional representatives regarding irregularities in the UN-managed Oil-for-Food Programme, the UN created an independent inquiry committee (IIC) led by American banker Paul A. Volcker. The IIC completed its work at the end of 2005. The committee report pointed to mismanagement by the UN, corruption and bribery by top UN officials, and manipulation of the aid scheme by the government of Iraq, which received $1.8 billion in illegal aid. Also, IIC experts estimated that the government of Iraq was able to illicitly smuggle approximately $11 billion of oil outside Iraq, thereby circumventing the Oil-for-Food Programme.

Chen Kertcher

See also: Iraq, History of, 1990–Present; Iraqi Freedom, Operation; United Nations Weapons Inspectors

References

Alexander, Kern. *Economic Sanctions: Law and Public Policy.* London: Palgrave Macmillan, 2009.

Arnove, Anthony. *Iraq under Siege: The Deadly Impact of Sanctions and War.* London: Pluto, 2000.

Lopez George A., and David Cortright. "Containing Iraq: The Sanctions Worked." *Foreign Affairs* 83(4) (2004): 90–103.

Malone, David M. *The International Struggle over Iraq: Politics in the UN Security Council, 1980–2005.* Oxford: Oxford University Press, 2006.

Iraq Study Group

A bipartisan commission empowered by the U.S. Congress on March 15, 2006, to examine and analyze the situation in Iraq following the March 2003 invasion of that country and to recommend courses of action to curb the insurgency and end sectarian strife there. The Iraq Study Group was chaired by former secretary of state James Baker III and former U.S. representative Lee Hamilton. Also known as the Baker-Hamilton Commission, the group consisted of five Democrats and five Republicans and was aided in its work by the United States Institute of Peace. In addition to Baker, the other Republicans on the commission included Edwin Meese III,

James Baker (left) and Lee Hamilton, co-chairmen of the Iraq Study Group, prepare for a continuing hearing on alternative plans for Iraq, on January 30, 2007. (Tom Williams/Roll Call/Getty Images)

former U.S. attorney general; Lawrence Eagleburger, former secretary of state; Sandra Day O'Connor, former U.S. Supreme Court justice; and Alan K. Simpson, former U.S. senator from Wyoming. The Democrats, in addition to Hamilton, included Leon Panetta, former chief of staff to President Bill Clinton as well as future director of the Central Intelligence Agency and secretary of defense under President Barack Obama; Charles Robb, former U.S. senator from Virginia; Vernon Jordan, informal adviser to Bill Clinton; and William J. Perry, former secretary of defense. The group's final report was issued on December 6, 2006. During its deliberations, however, it maintained contact with the George W. Bush administration and in particular with National Security Advisor Stephen Hadley.

Creation of the Baker-Hamilton Commission was prompted by the steadily increasing violence in Iraq, which had continued to result in casualties and deaths to U.S. soldiers and Iraqi military personnel as well as civilians. By early 2006 the situation on the ground was growing ever more dire, and it was clear that U.S. public support for the war was eroding at an alarming rate. Although much congressional disapproval toward the war came from the Democratic ranks, an increasing number of Republicans were also questioning the conflict and the Bush administration's handling of it. With critical midterm congressional elections in the offing, many in Congress believed that the time had come to reassess the situation in Iraq and assert congressional authority over the conduct of the war there.

In public, the Bush White House voiced its approval of the commission, welcoming its bipartisanship, and appeared reassured that the group was being cochaired by James Baker. At the same time, the Bush administration stated that it would not be beholden to the commission's recommendations if these were deemed antithetical to American interests. Privately, however, there was considerably more consternation about the Iraq Study Group, and on several occasions White House officials allegedly clashed with commission members over their recommendations. In mid-November about three weeks before the commission's report was released, President Bush and key members of his national security team met with the group so that it could question them about specific details and give them a preview of the report to come. Just prior to that, the commission had also met with British prime minister Tony Blair, the Bush administration's primary foreign ally in the war in Iraq.

Several U.S. news magazines and other media outlets reported that there was considerable contention among the members of the Baker-Hamilton Commission. Some of these conflicts centered on different philosophies toward national security policy and the implementation of Middle East policy, while others involved the Bush administration's opposition to key recommendations. Among the recommendations was the group's position that the United States should engage in discussions with Iran and Syria to stem the external influences on the Iraqi insurgency. The White House was adamantly opposed to this idea, and squabbling among the commission's members on this point nearly led to a deadlocked conclusion. Nevertheless, consensus was reached, and the commission's report was issued on December 6, 2006. It offered 79 specific recommendations. The timing was crucial, as the Republicans had just lost control of Congress in the November elections, and Secretary of Defense Donald Rumsfeld, a chief architect of the Iraq War, had been recently forced to resign. The Bush administration stated, for the first time, that new approaches to the war were needed but also let it be known that the administration would not implement all of the commission's recommendations.

The report stated clearly that the situation in Iraq was grave and deteriorating rapidly. It also criticized the Pentagon for having underreported the sectarian violence in Iraq and underreporting the number of Iraqi casualties. It went on to suggest that the Iraqi government must quickly ramp up the number of Iraqi soldiers and accelerate their training. During this time, the United States should increase significantly its troop presence in Iraq to enable the Iraqis to take over their own affairs. Once that was accomplished, U.S. troops should be withdrawn rapidly from the country. The report was careful not to suggest a timetable for these developments, however, which the Bush administration had been on record as strongly opposing. The report also called for the United States to engage in a dialogue with the Syrians, Iranians, and other regional groups that might lead to their assistance in curbing the Iraqi insurgency. The commission hoped to see gradual, phased U.S. troop withdrawals beginning in 2007 and a complete withdrawal by the end of 2008. Overall, the commission's report was well received both in the United States and abroad.

In the end, the Bush administration did not follow many of the report's prescriptions. In early 2007 the administration announced its surge strategy, which saw the insertion of as many as 30,000 additional U.S. troops in Iraq. In the short and intermediate terms, the troop surge paid handsome dividends, as terrorist, sectarian, and antigovernment violence in Iraq was down substantially by early 2008. However, after the final withdrawal of coalition troops from Iraq in 2011, a renewed insurgency threatened the Iraqi government and led to increased terror attacks against civilians and government forces alike. The outbreak of the Syrian Civil War that same year also further complicated the situation in Iraq, as some antigovernment Syrian rebels joined forces with the Islamic State of Iraq and Syria (ISIS) and began launching raids and offensive operations into Iraq.

Paul G. Pierpaoli Jr.

See also: Bush, George Walker; Iraq, History of, 1990–Present; Iraqi Freedom, Operation: The Surge and the Awakening; Islamic State of Iraq and al-Sham (ISIS); Secretary of Defense, U.S.: Leon E. Panetta

References

Baker, James A., III, and Lee Hamilton. *The Iraq Study Group: The Way Forward, a New Approach.* New York: Vintage Books, 2006.

Gates, Robert M. *Duty: Memoirs of a Secretary at War.* New York: Knopf, 2014.

Stiglitz, Joseph E., and Linda J. Bilmes. *The Three Trillion Dollar War: The True Cost of the Iraq Conflict.* New York: Norton, 2008.

Iraqi Freedom, Operation (2003–2010)

Planning for Operations

On September 15, 2001, U.S. president George W. Bush and his national security team met to discuss how to respond to the September 11 terrorist attacks on the United States. Secretary of Defense Donald Rumsfeld and his aides offered three targets for retaliation: Al Qaeda, Afghanistan's Taliban regime, and Iraq. In November, Pentagon planners began to ponder formally how to attack Iraq. From the outset Rumsfeld and his circle of civilian planners argued with senior military officers over whether to attack Iraq and how many ground troops to employ. As pressure built for a U.S. invasion, based on the premise that Iraq possessed weapons of mass destruction (WMD), the U.S. Central Command (CENTCOM), commanded by General Tommy Franks, assumed responsibility for planning and executing the invasion of Iraq. For a variety of reasons, particularly civilian pressure from Rumsfeld and his aides, a perceived urgency that imposed undue haste, an overburdened staff that also had to address Afghanistan, and Franks's command style that squashed dissent, war planners focused on the relatively easy task of defeating the Iraqi military and gave less attention to what would come afterward.

During the years following the 1991 Persian Gulf War, military planners had prepared a plan for a second war against Iraq. Dubbed Operation Desert Crossing, it envisioned a large invasion force of about 350,000 men, with some variants involving a force of upwards of 500,000 men. The Rumsfeld circle argued that this was far too many ground forces. They pointed to the tremendous improvement in the U.S. military's ability to deliver precision-guided weapons as well as technical advances in reconnaissance systems and command and control networks and asserted that the military was now more mobile and more lethal than during the Persian Gulf War. Proponents of a smaller invasion force argued that these changes, coupled with the deterioration of the Iraqi military that had begun during the Persian

Gulf War, implied that a second war against Iraq would not be a difficult undertaking. The Rumsfeld circle also wanted the flexibility to launch the ground invasion without a long prewar buildup of forces.

The demand for a lean force that could attack without a long logistical buildup constrained military planners. CENTCOM created a list of things that it wanted to be able to affect or influence, including the Iraqi leadership, internal security, its WMD, and the Republican Guard. They then matched this list against such U.S. military capabilities as special operations forces, airpower, and conventional ground forces.

Meanwhile, a group of military planners, notably retired four-star general secretary of state Colin Powell, warned the Bush administration that the Iraqi Army was the glue holding Iraq together. If the United States dissolved that bond by destroying the army, it would inherit the responsibility for occupying and governing Iraq for a very long time. However, this minority viewpoint had little influence on the development of war plans.

During his 2002 State of the Union Address President Bush identified Iraq, Iran, and North Korea as hostile nations, part of an "axis of evil." He asserted that the United States would not stand idle while these nations threatened American interests with WMD. In June 2002 Bush spoke at the U.S. Military Academy, West Point, and formally announced the adoption of a strategy of preemption, known as the Bush Doctrine. These two speeches provided the intellectual rationale for the March 2003 invasion of Iraq.

In August 2002 the Bush administration drafted a secret document titled "Iraq: Goals, Objectives and Strategy." It was an ambitious statement that sought to eliminate the Iraqi WMD threat once and for all, end the Iraqi threat to its neighbors, liberate the Iraqi people from Saddam Hussein's tyranny, and end Iraqi support for international terrorism. The intention was that a stable democracy would be planted in Iraq that would grow and spread throughout the Middle East. In addition, the stupendous show of U.S. force would overawe potential future adversaries.

In its final form, the war plan called for army special operations helicopters and air force aircraft to begin operations on the evening of March 19 against Iraqi observation posts along the Saudi and Jordanian borders. Then, coalition special operations units would infiltrate western Iraq to eliminate missile sites that threatened Israel. Two days later, at 9:00 p.m. on March 21, Tomahawk cruise missiles, F-117 Nighthawk stealth fighters, and B-2 Spirit stealth bombers would strike targets in and around Baghdad. The next morning, Cobra II, the ground invasion, would begin. The army's V Corps, built around the tank-heavy 3rd Infantry Division, along with the 101st Airborne Division, would conduct the main thrust toward Baghdad. Simultaneously, the 1st Marine Division would seize the Rumaila oil fields, drive north across the Euphrates River, and protect the V Corps flank. The converging army and marine units would then form a cordon around Baghdad to prevent senior Iraqi leaders or WMD from escaping. British forces would seize the largely Shiite city of Basra in southeastern Iraq.

Plans had also called for an attack south from Turkey, mounted by the 4th Infantry Division. Last-minute Turkish obstinacy, despite financial incentives offered by the United States, blocked this part of the plan, forcing the 4th Infantry Division to become a follow-on force and allowing the Iraqis to concentrate their forces to the south. The northern front consisted of the 173rd Airborne Brigade working with lightly armed Kurdish forces to secure the key oil production center of Mosul. In total, the invading ground force was to number about 145,000 men, which was enough to provide a breakthrough force but insufficient to pacify conquered territory.

Planners thought that the ground invasion coming so soon after the air strike would surprise Iraqi military leaders. Air attacks began ahead of schedule, however, when intelligence reports indicated a meeting of Hussein and his senior leaders. The intelligence proved wrong.

Cobra II began on March 21 (local time), 2003. Conventional operations proceeded relatively smoothly, reaching an apparent high-water mark on April 9, when a live television broadcast showed U.S. troops helping a jubilant Iraqi crowd topple a giant statue of Saddam Hussein in downtown Baghdad. Thereafter, the failure to plan adequately for the subsequent occupation led to an insurgency that persisted for years.

James Arnold

See also: Iraqi Freedom, Operation: Air Campaign, Coalition Ground Forces, Coalition Naval Forces, Ground Campaign

References

Cordesman, Anthony H. *The Iraq War: Strategy, Tactics, and Military Lessons.* Westport, CT: Praeger, 2003.

Gordon, Michael R., and Bernard E. Trainor. *Cobra II: The Inside Story of the Invasion and Occupation of Iraq.* New York: Pantheon Books, 2006.

Gordon, Michael R., and Bernard E. Trainor. *The Endgame: The Inside Story of the Struggle for Iraq, from George W. Bush to Barack Obama.* New York: Vintage, 2013.

Record, Jeffrey. *Wanting War: Why the Bush Administration Invaded Iraq.* Dulles, VA: Potomac Books, 2009.

Ricks, Thomas E. *Fiasco: The American Military Adventure in Iraq.* New York: Penguin, 2006.

Air Campaign (March 20–April 7, 2003)

The air campaign was an important part of the Anglo-American invasion of Iraq (Operation Iraqi Freedom) and contributed enormously to its rapid success. For Iraqi Freedom, the U.S.-led coalition assembled a formidable array of airpower. The United States contributed 64,246 air personnel, including reserve and National Guard, and 1,663 aircraft. The latter included 293 fighters, 51 bombers, 182 tankers, and 337 aircraft of other types operated by the U.S. Air Force; 232 fighters, 52 tankers, and 124 aircraft of other types operated by the U.S. Navy; 130 fighters, 22 tankers, and 220 aircraft of other types operated by the U.S. Marine Corps; and 20 aircraft operated by the U.S. Army.

Aircraft participating in the operation included almost all models in the U.S. inventory: the B-1B Lancer, B-2 Spirit, and B-52H Stratofortress bombers; A-10A Thunderbolt II and AC-130 Spectre combat support aircraft; F-15 Eagle, F-16 Fighting Falcon, F/A-18 Hornet, and F-117 Nighthawk fighters; KC-130 Hercules transports; and KC-10 Extender and KC-135 Stratotanker tankers.

The Royal Air Force contributed some 8,000 personnel and 113 aircraft, including 66 fighters, 12 tankers, and 35 aircraft of other types. The Royal Australian Air Force contributed 22 aircraft, including 14 fighters, and 250 airmen. Canada contributed 3 transport aircraft.

Iraqi Freedom, Operation

Smoke billows from an explosion in President Saddam Hussein's presidential palace in Baghdad during a coalition air raid on April 2, 2003. The most intense period of the air war in Iraq, called "Shock and Awe," started on March 21, 2003. (Karim Sahib/AFP/Getty Images)

The Iraqi side at the beginning of the hostilities had 20,000 air force personnel, 325 combat aircraft, and 210 surface-to-air missiles.

The air campaign was designed as an integral part of a joint military operation, serving as a force multiplier to supplement the firepower of a relatively light land component. The allied air campaign was able to take advantage of Operations Northern Watch and Southern Watch, which the U.S. Air Force and Royal Air Force had been conducting since 1991, effectively transforming the United Nations–sanctioned policing of no-fly zones over northern and southern Iraq into a de facto sustained air campaign to conduct reconnaissance and suppress Iraqi air defenses. Thus, the coalition was able to prepare for battle well before the start of Operation Iraqi Freedom.

The air campaign of Operation Iraqi Freedom began early on the morning of March 20, 2003, with an unsuccessful air strike near Baghdad involving two F-117A stealth fighter-bombers, aimed at killing top Iraqi leaders, including President Saddam Hussein. The strike was followed by massive cruise missile attacks on key Iraqi command and control centers in and around Baghdad. By March 23–25, the air assault developed into the strategic phase of a so-called shock-and-awe campaign aimed to prevent the use of weapons of mass destruction by the Iraqis and disorganize the enemy, forcing its rapid defeat.

Afterward, the coalition air campaign changed its focus to aiding ground forces moving into Iraq from Kuwait; at this point, more than half of the new targets were not preplanned targets of opportunity. The Iraqis

A U.S. Air Force crew chief is protected from dust on an air base in Kuwait, on March 27, 2003. The mother of all sandstorms hampered combat operations from March 25 to March 27, 2003. (Paula Bronstein/Getty Images)

returned fire with sporadic and highly ineffective antiaircraft fire and random launches of surface-to-air missiles. They also managed to launch seven Ababil-100 tactical ballistic missiles, five of which were destroyed by U.S. Patriot batteries; two others missed their targets.

The growing flexibility of allied targeting reflected the proliferation of precision-guided munitions (smart bombs) in the coalition air force, which allowed more options in strike capabilities, redirecting of aircraft, performing close air support, and striking targets of opportunity. The air campaign also demonstrated the impressive global-reach capabilities of allied airpower. Indeed, bombers were flying in from bases as far away as Missouri, Diego Garcia in the Indian Ocean, and Great Britain. Others were operating from aircraft carriers in the Persian Gulf and the Mediterranean and from bases across the Middle East. The allies enjoyed uncontested air supremacy, as the remnants of the Iraqi air defense system were unable to operate effectively, and the enemy was unable to master a single sortie during the war. The coalition also benefited from the use of unmanned aerial vehicles (UAVs) as sensors and decoys to confuse the Iraqis.

The arrival of a major sandstorm on March 25–26 canceled about 65 percent of all sorties. Nevertheless, the coalition was able to adjust its reconnaissance and surveillance missions to harsh weather using the Joint Surveillance and Target Reader System (JSTARS) aircraft and long-range UAVs, which provided high-flying bombers with necessary information and data.

With the resumption of the ground march toward Baghdad, the allied air campaign shifted its focus to providing ground support, particularly targeting Iraqi Republican Guard units and militia formations, which were defending road approaches to the Iraqi capital. Finally, the air and ground assault on Baghdad merged into one coordinated effort.

Coalition airpower was able to destroy or significantly degrade the Republican Guard formations and to open a new dimension in the urban warfare, providing constant surveillance, reconnaissance, intelligence, and fire support to allied ground forces. Coalition airpower was also instrumental in the opening of the second front in northern Iraq. Major air operations in Iraq effectively ended with one final unsuccessful attempt on April 7 to eliminate Hussein when a B-1 bomber attacked a palace in Baghdad where the dictator was allegedly staying.

The aerial campaign during the Iraq War again demonstrated that there is no substitute for air dominance in modern warfare, a lesson that was gleaned from the 1991 Persian Gulf War. Additionally, the technological superiority and application of airpower in joint warfare operation allowed the coalition to enjoy unprecedented efficiency in reconnaissance, surveillance, and flexible real-time targeting while combining centralized control with decentralized execution of air operations. This also provided the coalition air force with almost instant capability to evaluate its performance as ground forces rapidly advanced into Iraq.

At the same time, however, the operation also witnessed an insufficiency in allied intelligence, particularly in regard to so-called decapitation air strikes. Some observers have noted that the planners of the operation displayed overconfidence that a massive initial air assault on limited command and control targets would lead to the quick collapse of the regime. The campaign also revealed a shortage of aerial tankers, as the prosecution of combat missions deep inside Iraq put serious pressure on the allied tanker fleet.

Overall, coalition air forces conducted 41,404 sorties in the skies over Iraq. The overall breakdown of sorties is as follows: the U.S. Air Force contributed 24,196 sorties, the U.S. Navy conducted 8,945 sorties, the U.S. Marine Corps contributed 4,948 sorties, the U.S. Army contributed 269 sorties, the Royal Air Force conducted 2,481 sorties, and the Royal Australian Air Force flew 565 sorties. Of 29,199 munitions used, 68 percent were precision-guided. The coalition lost just seven aircraft to enemy fire (six helicopters and one combat/support aircraft A-10A) and two pilots. One Royal Air Force fighter was lost due to friendly fire.

Peter J. Rainow

See also: Iraqi Freedom, Operation

References

Boyne, Walter J. *Operation Iraqi Freedom: What Went Right, What Went Wrong and Why.* New York: Forge Books, 2003.

Keegan, John. *The Iraq War: The Military Offensive, from Victory in 21 Days to the Insurgent Aftermath.* New York: Vintage, 2005.

Murray, Williamson, and Robert H. Scales Jr. *The Iraq War: A Military History.* Cambridge, MA: Belknap, 2005.

Coalition Ground Forces

During Operation Iraqi Freedom, the 2003 invasion of Iraq, U.S. forces led a small coalition of allied states to overthrow the regime of Saddam Hussein. The coalition was officially designated Combined and Joint Task Force 7 (CJTF-7), with "combined" meaning more than one nation and "joint" meaning more than one military service.

In an effort to avoid past problems in coalition warfare, including political interference and a lack of unity in the chain of command, and in light of limited potential contributions to the invading force, the United States developed an invasion plan that emphasized U.S. forces and those of the nation's close ally, the United Kingdom. When the government of Turkey refused to grant the United States permission to launch a second front from its territory, the invasion plan was revised to call for the major ground assault to occur from Kuwait, supported by airborne assaults and action by special operations forces in the north.

The coalition consisted of 248,000 U.S. personnel along with 45,000 British, 2,000 Australian, 1,300 Spanish, and 200 Polish troops. The majority of the Australian and Polish troops were special operations forces. The main British ground unit was the 1st Armoured Division. Prior to the invasion, the U.S. Army provided command and control gear to some of the British units to facilitate interoperability (the U.S. Army had to provide similar equipment to U.S. Marine Corps units). The equipment allowed the allied forces to communicate and exchange information through satellite systems and to employ tactical Internet capabilities. Nonetheless, national liaison officers had to be stationed among the units to coordinate air support and ground fire.

Coalition units were under the overall operational command of U.S. Army Lieutenant General David McKiernan, who was appointed as the head of Coalition Forces Land Component Command. McKiernan was second-in-command to the overall operation commander, U.S. general Tommy Franks. The senior British military officer was Air Chief Marshal Brian Burridge.

Additional countries contributed troops to the coalition war effort following initial operations. In September 2003 Iraq was divided into zones of occupation. The British took charge of the multinational forces in the four southern provinces, designated the South Zone. Coalition forces in the South Central Zone, consisting of four provinces and parts of two others, came under Polish command. Poland maintained elements of either an armored or a mechanized division as its core contribution, rotating units such as the 12th Mechanized Division or the 11th Lubusz Armored Cavalry Division through multiple tours in Iraq beginning in May 2003. Poland's peak contribution to the coalition was 2,500 troops, but the country withdrew its forces in October 2008.

A number of other countries also had significant deployments of more than 1,000 troops. In 2004 South Korea dispatched 3,600 troops, mainly medical, construction, and engineering units, but all forces were withdrawn in December 2008. The South Korean units were formed into the Zaytun Division (*zaytun* is Arabic for "olive"). Italy deployed 3,200 soldiers in 2003; however, these troops were withdrawn in November 2006. Georgia contributed 2,000 troops but withdrew the bulk of its forces during the brief Russo-Georgian War of August 2008. Ukraine deployed the 5th, 6th, and 7th Mechanized Brigades in succession, beginning in 2003, with a top commitment of about 1,800 troops. Ukraine withdrew its troops in December 2005. Australia deployed about 1,400 ground troops, including units from the Royal Australian Regiment, the 2nd Cavalry Regiment, and the Light Horse Regiment (Queensland Mounted Infantry). Australian forces left Iraq in July 2009. The Netherlands provided approximately 1,350 troops in July 2003 and withdrew its forces two years later. Spain contributed 1,300 troops in 2003 but withdrew its forces in 2004. By 2008, 40 countries had deployed forces at some point to support the CJTF-7, which was renamed the Multi-National Force–Iraq on May 15, 2004. However, the cost in both economic terms and loss of life led to growing antiwar sentiment in coalition states, leading many to draw down or completely withdraw their forces.

In addition to the larger troop contingents, the following countries contributed at least 100 soldiers (mostly support, medical, or engineering units): Albania, Azerbaijan, Bulgaria, the Czech Republic, Denmark, the Dominican Republic, El Salvador, Honduras, Hungary, Japan, Latvia, Lithuania, Mongolia, Norway, Nicaragua, Portugal, Romania, Slovakia, and Thailand.

The following countries contributed fewer than 100 troops: Armenia, Bosnia-Herzegovina, Estonia, Iceland, Kazakhstan, Macedonia, Moldova, New Zealand, the Philippines, Singapore, and Tonga. Several of these deployments were symbolic; for instance, Iceland deployed only two soldiers. In addition, Fiji deployed 150 troops in support of the United Nations mission in Iraq.

Between January 12, 2008, and December 31, 2011, 25 nations withdrew their contingents from Iraq. The last of the British troops left in May 2011, and the last U.S. troops were withdrawn in December 2011. A total of 318 non-U.S. coalition soldiers died in Iraq between March 2003 and December 2011; the United States suffered 4,488 deaths during that same period.

Tom Lansford

See also: Iraqi Freedom, Operation

References

Cockburn, Patrick. *The Occupation: War and Resistance in Iraq.* New York: Verso, 2007.

Gordon, Michael R., and Bernard E. Trainor. *The Endgame: The Inside Story of the Struggle for Iraq, from George W. Bush to Barack Obama.* New York: Vintage, 2013.

Keegan, John. *The Iraq War: The Military Offensive, from Victory in 21 Days to the Insurgent Aftermath.* New York: Vintage, 2005.

Murray, Williamson, and Robert H. Scales Jr. *The Iraq War: A Military History.* Cambridge, MA: Belknap, 2005.

Coalition Naval Forces

Naval forces from the United States and other nations played an important role in Operation Iraqi Freedom. Military operations opened on March 20, 2003, with the firing of 40 Tomahawk cruise missiles by British and American warships and air strikes by both U.S. Air Force and U.S. Navy fixed-wing aircraft; meanwhile, U.S. Navy EA-6 Prowlers jammed Iraqi radar systems. This was followed by the seizure of two offshore gas and oil platforms by Navy SEALs.

When coalition ground forces invaded Iraq, carrier aircraft provided close air support and struck targets in support of the bombing campaigns. The five U.S. Navy carrier battle groups operating in the Persian Gulf, the Indian Ocean, and the eastern Mediterranean Sea flew more than 7,000 sorties during the first three weeks of operations. Marines landed from two amphibious ready groups and joined army troops in the invasion of Iraq. The campaign was swift, and only a week after the Iraqi capital at Baghdad fell on April 10, 2003, Vice Admiral Timothy Keating, commander of the 140 U.S. warships in the region, suggested the return home or redeployment elsewhere of naval units. By the end of operations on April 30, 35 coalition ships had fired 1,900 Tomahawks, one-third of them from submarines.

There were no significant naval surface engagements because Iraqi leader Saddam Hussein did not possess naval forces capable of posing a credible threat to coalition naval operations. After British and American marines captured the Iraqi port of Umm Qasr 30 miles south of Basra on March 30, four U.S. and six British minesweepers (operating with the mother ship RFA *Sir Belvedere*) began clearing the narrow Khor Abd Allah waterway that linked the port to the Persian Gulf. Working with unmanned underwater vehicles and with more than 20 trained dolphins of the navy's Marine Mammals System, a Navy Very Shallow Water detachment consisting of Navy SEALs, Marine Force Reconnaissance divers, and Explosive Ordnance Disposal divers opened the waterway so that supplies could be funneled through the city to troops advancing inland.

President George W. Bush consistently referred to the Iraq War as "the central front in the War on Terror," contributing to the difficulty in distinguishing between naval forces involved in operations in Operation Iraqi Freedom (OIF), Operation Enduring Freedom–Afghanistan (OEF-A), and Operation Enduring Freedom–Horn of Africa (OEF-HOA). Warships of Great Britain's Royal Navy joined U.S. Navy forces in OIF, and the two navies often shifted forces between bilateral operations in the Persian Gulf and multinational operations farther afield. The invasion phase of the war was declared over on April 30, 2003, after which time the line between operations was further blurred with the establishment of Combined Task Force 150 (CTF-150) to support OIF, OEF-A, and OEF-HOA by monitoring shipping and countering piracy in the northern Persian Gulf.

Australia, Canada, Denmark, France, Germany, Italy, the Netherlands, New Zealand, Pakistan, Turkey, the United Kingdom, and the United States assigned warships to CTF-150 at varying times. CTF-150 usually contains about 15 ships, the command of which rotates among the participating navies in four- to six-month intervals. Commanders have included Spanish rear admiral Juan Moreno, British commodore Tony Rix, French vice admiral Jacques Mazars, Dutch commodore Hank Ort, Pakistani rear admiral Shahid Iqbal, German rear admiral Heinrich Lange, and British commodore Bruce Williams.

In 2003, Combined Task Force 158 was formed by U.S., British, Australian, and Iraqi naval forces to operate jointly with units of the Iraqi armed forces to train Iraqi naval personnel, protect Iraqi assets such as the Khawr al Amayah and Al Basrah oil terminals located on platforms off the coast of the Faw (Fao) Peninsula in southern Iraq, operate jointly with Kuwaiti naval patrol boats, and patrol international waters in a cone-shaped area extending into the Persian Gulf beyond the territorial waters of Iraq. Its commanders have included British commodore Duncan Potts and U.S. rear admiral Kendall Card.

James C. Bradford

See also: Iraqi Freedom, Operation

References

Boyne, Walter J. *Operation Iraqi Freedom: What Went Right, What Went Wrong and Why.* New York: Forge Books, 2003.

Holmes, Tony. *US Navy Hornet Units in Operation Iraqi Freedom,* 2 vols. Oxford, UK: Osprey, 2004–2005.

Lambeth, Benjamin S. *American Carrier Air Power at the Dawn of a New Century.* Santa Monica, CA: RAND Corporation, 2005.

Miller, Richard F. *A Carrier at War: On Board the USS Kitty Hawk in the Iraq War.* Washington, DC: Potomac Books, 2003.

Ground Campaign (March 20–May 1, 2003)

For some time, the United States and its coalition partners had been building up their forces in Kuwait. More than 300,000 personnel were deployed in the theater under U.S. Army Central Command (CENTCOM) commander general Tommy Franks. Actual coalition combat strength on the ground to implement Operation Cobra II, the ground invasion of Iraq, numbered some 125,000 U.S. troops, 45,000 British troops, 2,000 Australian troops, and 200 Polish troops. Other nations supplied support or occupation troops. Unlike the 1991 Persian Gulf War, there was no broad-based coalition helping to bear the cost of the war. Although Kuwait and Qatar supported the United States, Saudi Arabia refused the use of its bases for air strikes against Iraq. The United States also experienced a major setback when the Turkish parliament, despite pledges of up to $30 billion in financial assistance, refused to allow the United States to use its territory to open up a northern front, a key component of the U.S. military plan. Three dozen ships laden with equipment for the 30,000-man U.S. 4th Infantry Division lay off Turkish ports. Only after the war began were they redirected through the Suez Canal and around the Arabian Peninsula to Kuwait. The Turkish government's decision meant that the 4th Infantry Division would have to be part of the follow-on force and that Iraq could concentrate its military efforts to the south.

President George W. Bush, still in his flight suit, stands among crew members on the flight deck of the aircraft carrier *Abraham Lincoln* on May 1, 2003. On that day, Bush declared major military operations in Iraq to be over while a banner stating "Mission Accomplished" hung nearby. (U. S. Navy)

Iraqi Freedom, Operation | 143

A U.S. Army MIAI Abrams main battle tank and personnel from A Company, Task Force 1st Battalion, 35th Armor Regiment, 2nd Brigade Combat Team, 1st Armored Division, pose for a photo under the Hands of Victory monument in Ceremony Square, Baghdad, Iraq, during Operation Iraqi Freedom. The Hands of Victory monument, built at the end of the Iran-Iraq War, marks the entrance to a large parade ground in central Baghdad. The hand and arm are modeled after former dictator Saddam Hussein's, and are surrounded with thousands of Iranian helmets taken from the battlefield. (PJF Military Collection/Alamy Stock Photo)

The Iraq War began at 5:34 a.m. Baghdad time on March 20, 2003 (9:34 p.m., March 19 EST), although some air strikes were launched on the night of March 19. One, the Dora Farms Strike, was an unsuccessful effort to kill Saddam Hussein and his sons, but most or the March 19 strikes were directed against Iraqi air defense and missile systems threatening coalition forces in Kuwait as well as leaflet drops with capitulation instructions. Initially known as Operation Iraqi Liberation, it was later renamed Operation Iraqi Freedom (the British code name was Operation Telic, while the Australian forces knew it as Operation Falconer). The war commenced just hours after the expiration of U.S. president George W. Bush's 48-hour ultimatum to Saddam Hussein to step aside.

Baghdad was repeatedly hit with cruise missile attacks and air strikes by B-1, B-2, and B-52 bombers against key headquarters and command and control targets. This shock-and-awe campaign did not appear to be on the massive scale that CENTCOM had suggested. Part of this was the use of 70 percent smart bombs (guided) and 30 percent dumb aerial munitions (unguided), as opposed to only 10 percent smart weapons during the Persian Gulf War. Also, a good many of the air strikes occurred away from the capital.

As the air attacks unfolded, the ground war also began. The coalition advance from Kuwait was along two main axes northwest toward Baghdad by U.S. Army and U.S. Marine Corps units and one supporting thrust due north toward Basra. British forces on the far right under 1st Armoured Division commander major general Robin Brims were assigned the task of securing the Shatt al-Arab waterway and the important Shiite city of Basra, Iraq's second largest. At the same time, Lieutenant General James Conway's I Marine Expeditionary Force in the center and Lieutenant General William Scott Wallace's U.S. Army's V Corps to the west would drive on the Iraqi capital of Baghdad, 300 miles to the north. Major General Buford Blount's 3rd Infantry Division, with the 7th Armored Cavalry Regiment leading, made the most rapid progress, largely because it moved through more sparsely populated areas.

In the center part of the front, the I Marine Expeditionary Force, carrying out the longest march in its storied history, skirted to the west of the Euphrates River through the cities of Nasiriyah and on to Najaf and Karbala. Key factors in the allied success were coalition airpower (Iraqi aircraft and helicopters never got off the ground), including Apache helicopter gunships and the highly resilient tank-busting A-10 Thunderbolt; the rapidity of the advance; and the ability of coalition troops to fight at night.

The marines were successful in seizing by coup de main the oil fields north of Basra, some 60 percent of the nation's total, including key refineries. Having secured the Shatt al-Arab and wishing to spare civilians, the British were hopeful of an internal uprising and did not move into Basra itself. They were not actually encamped in the city until the night of April 2. In the meantime, they imposed a loose blockade and carried out a series of raids into Basra to destroy symbols of the regime in an effort to demoralize the defenders and convince them that coalition forces could move at will. At the same time, British forces distributed food and water to convince the inhabitants that they came as liberators rather than conquerors.

U.S. special forces secured airfields in western Iraq, and on the night of March 26, 1,000 members of the 173rd Airborne Brigade dropped into Kurdish-held territory in northern Iraq. Working in conjunction with lightly armed Kurdish forces, the brigade opened a northern front and secured the key oil-production center of Mosul. U.S. special forces also directed air strikes against the Islamic Ansar al-Islam camp in far northeastern Iraq, on the Iranian border.

A number of Iraqi divisions moved into position to block the coalition drive north. These troops largely evaporated, however, with many of their personnel simply deserting. Meanwhile, so-called Saddam Fedayeen, or "technicals"—irregulars often wearing civilian clothes—carried out attacks using civilian vehicles with mounted machine guns and rocket-propelled grenades on supply convoys along the lines of communication from Kuwait north, which came to be dubbed "Ambush Alley." Indeed, on March 23 the 507th Maintenance Company, part of a convoy moving north near the Euphrates, took a wrong turn, was ambushed, and in an ensuing firefight lost nine killed, five wounded, and six captured.

On March 26, U.S. 7th Cavalry Regiment and 3rd Infantry Division elements defeated an Iraqi force near Najaf in the largest battle of the war, killing some 450 Iraqis. On March 28 with U.S. forces some 100 miles south of Baghdad, there was an operational pause because of a fierce sandstorm extending over March 25–26 and the need for some army units to resupply.

The Iraqi leadership, meanwhile, repositioned its six Republican Guard divisions around Baghdad for a defense of the capital. As some of these divisions moved to take up new positions south of the city, they came under heavy air attack and lost much of their equipment. The coalition advance quickened again during April 1–2, following the serious degrading of the Baghdad and Medina divisions.

On April 3, U.S. forces reached the outskirts of Baghdad and over the next two days secured Saddam International Airport, some 12 miles from the city center. The speed of their advance allowed U.S. forces to take the airport with minimal damage to its facilities, and it soon became a staging area. By that date too, the Iraqi people sensed the shift of momentum and an imminent coalition victory. Advancing U.S. troops reported friendly receptions from civilians and increasing surrenders of Iraqi troops, including a reported 2,500 Republican Guards north of Kut on April 4.

By April 5, the 3rd Infantry Division was closing on Baghdad from the southwest, the marines were moving in from the southeast, and the 101st Airborne Division was preparing to move in from the north. Baghdad was in effect under a loose blockade, with civilians allowed to depart. On that day also, the 3rd Infantry Division's 2nd Brigade, commanded by Colonel David Perkins, pushed through downtown Baghdad in a three-hour operation, called a "Thunder Run," inflicting an estimated 1,000 Iraqi casualties. This proved to be a powerful psychological blow to the Iraqi regime, which had claimed that U.S. forces were nowhere near the city and that it still controlled the international airport. The operation also led to an exodus of many Baath Party officials and Iraqi military personnel.

This process was repeated on April 6 and 7. In a fierce firefight on April 6, U.S. forces killed an estimated 2,000–3,000 Iraqi soldiers and lost only one killed of their own. On April 7, three battalions of the 3rd Infantry Division remained in the city. The next day marine elements moved into southeastern Baghdad. With the 101st Airborne closing on the city from the northwest and the 3rd Infantry Division from the southeast, the ring around the capital was closed. On April 9, resistance collapsed in Baghdad as Iraqi civilians assisted by U.S. marines toppled a large statue of Saddam Hussein. There was still fighting in parts of the city as diehard Baath loyalists sniped at U.S. troops, but Iraqi government central command and control had collapsed by April 10.

Elsewhere on April 10 following the collapse of resistance in Baghdad, a small number of Kurdish fighters, U.S. special forces, and the 173rd Airborne Brigade liberated Kirkuk. The next day Mosul, Iraq's third-largest city, fell when the Iraqi V Corps commander surrendered some 30,000 men. Apart from some sporadic shooting in Baghdad and massive looting there and in other cities, the one remaining center of resistance was Hussein's ancestral home of Tikrit.

On April 12 the 101st Airborne relieved the marines and the 3rd Infantry Division in Baghdad, allowing them to deploy northwest to Tikrit. Meanwhile, the 173rd Airborne Brigade took control of the northern oil fields from the Kurds in order to prevent any possibility of Turkish intervention. The battle for Tikrit failed to materialize. Hussein's stronghold collapsed, and on April 14 allied forces entered the city. That same day the Pentagon announced that major military operations in Iraq were at an end; all that remained was mopping up. Through the end of April, the coalition suffered 139 U.S. and 31 British dead. The coalition reported that 9,200 Iraqi military personnel had also been slain, along with 7,299 civilians, the latter figure believed by many critics of the war to be far too low.

On May 1, 2003, President Bush visited the U.S. aircraft carrier *Abraham Lincoln* off San Diego, the carrier having just returned from a deployment to the Persian Gulf. There the president delivered his "Mission Accomplished" speech, broadcast live to the American public. Bush's characterization that the war was won proved premature. The administration had given insufficient thought to the postwar occupation of Iraq, and long-simmering tensions between Sunni, Shiite, and Kurds erupted into sectarian violence. A series of ill-considered policy decisions, including disbanding the Iraqi Army, abetted the poor security situation, as angry Sunnis, supported by volunteers from other Arab states, took up arms and launched suicide attacks against Iraqi civilians and the U.S. occupiers. A long insurgency ensued. Unguarded ammunition dumps provided plentiful supplies for the improvised explosive devices that claimed growing numbers of allied troops.

Spencer C. Tucker

See also: Bush, George Walker; Commanders, U.S. Central Command: Tommy Franks; Hussein, Saddam; Nasiriyah, Battle of; Weapons, Insurgency, and Opposition: Improvised Explosive Devices

References

Atkinson, Rick. *In the Company of Soldiers: A Chronicle of Combat.* New York: Henry Holt, 2005.

Franks, Tommy, with Malcolm McConnell. *American Soldier.* New York: Regan Books, 2004.

Murray, Williamson, and Robert H. Scales Jr. *The Iraq War: A Military History.* Cambridge, MA: Belknap, 2005.

Purdum, Todd S., and the Staff of *The New York Times. A Time of Our Choosing: America's War in Iraq.* New York: Times Books/Henry Holt, 2003.

Tucker-Jones, Anthony. *The Iraq War: Operation IRAQI FREEDOM 2003.* Barnsley, South Yorkshire, UK: Pen and Sword, 2014.

West, Bing, and Ray L. Smith. *The March Up: Taking Baghdad with the 1st Marine Division.* New York: Bantam, 2003.

Major Battles

Specific battles are explained in specific entries elsewhere in this work.

| | Coalition | | Opposition | | Civilians |
Dates	Forces	Killed	Forces	Killed	Killed
2003					
Battle of al-Faw March 20–24, 2003	3,500	19	1,000+	150+	
Battle of Umm Qasr March 21–25, 2003	Unknown	14	Unknown	30–40	
Battle of Basra March 23–April 7, 2003	Unknown	11	Unknown	295–515	
Battle of Nasiriyah March 23–29, 2003	~5,000	32	Unknown	~400	

(continued)

Dates	Coalition		Opposition		Civilians Killed
	Forces	Killed	Forces	Killed	
First Battle of Najaf March 24–April 4, 2003	Unknown	4	Unknown	590–780	
Operation Viking Hammer (Kurdistan) March 28–30, 2003	~7,000	30	600–800	250–300	
Battle of Samawah March 30–April 4, 2003	Unknown	1	Unknown	46	
Battle of Hillah March 31–April 2, 2003	Unknown	1	Unknown	1,200+	19
Battle of Karbala March 31–April 6, 2003	~5,000	21	Unknown	~200	
Battle of Karbala Gap April 1–4, 2003	Unknown	1	Unknown	680–940	
Battle of al-Kut April 3–4, 2003	~2,000	1	2,5–3,000	150–250+	
Battle of Baghdad April 5–10, 2003	30,000	34	40,000	2,300+	
Operation Planet X May 15, 2003	500	0	Unknown	0	
Ramadan Insurgency October 26–November 24, 2003	30,000	34	40,000	~2,000	
2004					
First Battle of Fallujah (Operation Vigilant Resolve) April 4–May 1, 2004	2,200	27	3,600	~200	~600
Battle of al-Kut April 5–7, 2004	Unknown	1	Unknown	180–200	
First Battle of Ramadi April 6–10, 2004	1,500	16	2,000	~250	
Battle of Husaybah April 17, 2004	150	5	300	150	
Second Battle of Najaf August 5–27, 2004	3,800	53	~14,000	1,594	
Battle of Samarra October 1–3, 2004	5,000	1	~750	127	20
Second Battle of Fallujah (Operation al-Fajr and Operation Phantom Fury) November 7–December 23, 2004	13,350	~107	~3,800	~1,700	~650
Battle of Mosul November 8–16, 2004	2,000	129	Unknown	71	Unknown

(continued)

	Coalition		Opposition		Civilians
Dates	Forces	Killed	Forces	Killed	Killed
2005					
Battle of Abu Ghraib April 2, 2005	Unknown	2	Unknown	70	
Battle of al-Qaim May 8–19, 2005	~1,000	9	Unknown	125+	
Battle of Haditha August 1–4, 2005	~1,000	21	Unknown	400	
Battle of Tal Afar (Operation Restoring Rights) September 1–18, 2005	8,500	19	Unknown	163	
Operation Steel Curtain November 5–22, 2005	Unknown	10	Unknown	139	97+
2006					
Second Battle of Ramadi June 17–November 15, 2006	7,500	~110	~5,000	~750	
Operation Together Forward July 9–October 24, 2006	~75,000	101	Unknown	400+	
Battle of Diwaniya August 28, 2006	Unknown	23	Unknown	20	7
Battle of Amarah October 19–20, 2006	Unknown	10	800	15	2
Battle of Turki November 15–16, 2006	50	2	Unknown	72	
Diyala Campaign December 25, 2006–October 1, 2007	26,200	428	2,000	1,070	
2007					
Diyala Campaign December 25, 2006–October 1, 2007	26,200	428	2,000	1,070	
Battle of Haifa Street January 6–9, 2007	1,000	21	Unknown	133	
Third Battle of Najaf January 28–29, 2007	800	27	1,000	250–400	
Operation Imposing Law (Operation Fardh al-Qanoon) February 14–November 24, 2007	90,000	872	Unknown	1,219	7,482
Battle of Baqubah (Operation Arrowhead Ripper) June 19–August 19, 2007	11,000	30	1,000+	100+	~350
Operation Black Eagle April 6–10, 2007	Unknown	36	Unknown	25	
Operation Phantom Thunder June 16–August 14, 2007	~30,100	380	Unknown	1,196	

(continued)

	Coalition		Opposition		Civilians
Dates	Forces	Killed	Forces	Killed	Killed
Operation Phantom Strike August 13–January 2008	28,000+	11	Unknown	330+	
2008					
Operation Phantom Phoenix January 8–July 28, 2008	168,000	839	Unknown	890	
2008 Iraqi Day of Ashura Fighting January 18–19, 2008	Unknown	18	200+	58	4
Ninewa Campaign January 23–July 28, 2008	Unknown	337	Unknown	224	548
Battle of Basra March 25–31, 2008	30,000	30	16,000	400	50
Iraq Spring Fighting of 2008 (Includes Battle of Sadr City) March 25–May 15, 2008	400,000	231	60,000	~1,500	1,116
Operation Augurs of Prosperity July 29–August 11, 2008	53,000	58	Unknown	15	70

The Surge and the Awakening

Much has been said about the success or failure of the period of the Iraq War known as the surge. To truly understand this portion of the Iraq War and its significance, one must examine the events leading up to the surge and the specific intent behind it. From a logistics standpoint, the surge involved the deployment of an additional approximately 30,000 U.S. ground forces to Iraq. This meant that five additional brigade combat teams came into the country. In addition, many of the already deployed brigades were extended to stay 15 months rather than the 12 months they were originally tasked to serve. From a tactical perspective, the intent of the surge was to quell the rising insurgency that had overtaken the Anbar Province of Iraq and was threatening the rest of the country. Those insurgents included both Al Qaeda terrorists and rival Sunni and Shiite sectarian militias.

The impetus for the troop surge was the November 2006 U.S. midterm election, in which the Republican Party lost control of both houses of Congress largely because of growing public opposition to the Iraq War and dismay with the level of casualties among U.S. soldiers. With the Democrats having made opposition to the Iraq War the central issue of the 2006 election and calling for a withdrawal of U.S. troops from Iraq, Bush announced a change in strategy to reduce violence and improve security in Iraq. This followed the resignation of Secretary of Defense Donald Rumsfeld, a key architect of the Iraq War, in December 2006. Referring to a "new way forward" in a televised national speech on January 10, 2007, the president announced a plan to secure the capital city, Baghdad, from both Al Qaeda and sectarian militias and rid Anbar Province (stretching west from Baghdad to the Syrian and Jordanian borders) of Al Qaeda fighters. Approximately 16,000 additional

U.S. troops were deployed to secure Baghdad, and another 4,000 troops were sent to Anbar Province.

U.S. Army General David Petraeus, commander Multi-National Forces–Iraq (MNF-I), is credited with the surge strategy. General Petraeus often spoke of a surge of ideas that was espoused primarily in the new U.S. Army and USMC field manual titled *Counterinsurgency*. General Petraeus's assumption of command of MNF-I was in fact part of this surge. His plan was to get soldiers off the large forward-operating bases to be and live among the Iraqi people and provide security to the populace. He was convinced that winning the trust of the Iraqi people was essential to the success of coalition efforts in Iraq. If the people believed the United States was working and fighting in their behalf they would be more inclined to support the military in its purpose there. By June 15, 2007, with these additional troops in place, the surge began in earnest. Instead of simply launching raids against Al Qaeda and sectarian militias, U.S. and Iraqi forces in Baghdad established posts within neighborhoods controlled by these groups.

Outside of Baghdad, the surge focused mainly on Anbar Province, which at that time had become the most violent region of Iraq. Anbar, the largest of Iraq's 18 provinces with its predominantly Sunni population, became a hotspot of insurgent activity following the fall of Baghdad in 2003. Disaffected sheikhs and their tribal followers gravitated to the insurgency, driven by anger at seeing their lands occupied by foreign soldiers, resentment over the loss of jobs and prestige, and distrust of the new Shiite-dominated political order, among other things. The porous border that Anbar shared with Syria at the far western end of the province also provided an easy point of entry for fighters from other nations, who filtered into Fallujah, Ramadi, and the smaller population centers along the upper Euphrates River. Many joined the organization founded by Jordanian extremist Abu Musab al-Zarqawi, which evolved into AQI.

Tribal insurgents had formed an alliance of convenience with AQI jihadists in Anbar, and AQI itself was actually an overwhelmingly Iraqi, not foreign, organization. By the middle of 2006, the insurgency had grown so strong that Anbar outpaced even Baghdad in terms of the number of violent incidents, with 30–40 attacks occurring daily in the province. Conditions in Ramadi were particularly grim: public services were negligible, and the Iraqi security presence was almost nonexistent, enabling insurgent fighters to operate freely in most sections of the city. A classified assessment completed by the U.S. Marine Corps in August 2006 concluded that the province was all but lost to the insurgency.

Yet AQI laid the groundwork for its own demise by demanding control of the insurgency and reducing Anbar's tribal chiefs to subordinate status. AQI operatives punished in brutal fashion any who opposed them, with bombings and murders that targeted not only the sheikhs but also their family members and supporters. The vicious tactics used by AQI to cow the tribes also alienated them and opened up a rift within the insurgency. In what in retrospect can be seen as a precursor to the Anbar Awakening movement, several tribes around Ramadi in January 2006 formed the al-Anbar People's Council, a breakaway group that sought to distance itself from AQI while continuing to resist the coalition. The council collapsed soon thereafter after seven of its members were assassinated and a suicide bomber killed dozens at a police recruiting event.

The demise of the al-Anbar People's Council demonstrated that the Ramadi tribes lacked the strength and cohesion to stand up against AQI on their own. A few months later, the sheikhs gained a powerful new benefactor when Colonel Sean MacFarland arrived with the U.S. Army's 1st Brigade Combat Team to take charge of Ramadi's security. MacFarland and his brigade had deployed first in January 2006 to Tal Afar, the city in northern Iraq that had been pacified the previous year by Colonel H. R. McMaster in what was widely hailed as a textbook counterinsurgency operation. Moving to Ramadi in June 2006, MacFarland was determined to apply some of the same counterinsurgency practices that had proven so effective at Tal Afar.

As one of the first steps in his plan to win back the city, MacFarland launched an outreach program aimed at gaining the trust and support of Ramadi's leaders. Among the earliest to respond was a charismatic young sheikh of relatively junior stature named Abd al-Sattar Buzaigh al-Rishawi. His record was far from clean, however: he was reputed to be a smuggler and highway bandit who had cooperated with AQI in the past. More recently, however, he had lost his father and three brothers to AQI's campaign of terror against the tribes, so he was receptive to American overtures. With Sattar's help in gathering recruits, MacFarland was able to begin the process of rebuilding Ramadi's embattled police force, which numbered only about 400 at the beginning of his tour. The sheikh also assisted with MacFarland's efforts to persuade other tribal leaders to shift their allegiance from AQI to the coalition.

Sattar expanded his opposition to AQI into a full-fledged movement after AQI agents bombed one of the new Iraqi police stations that had been set up in the city and murdered the sheikh whose tribesmen were staffing the post. In response, Sattar convened a meeting of more than 50 sheikhs and MacFarland at his home on September 9, 2006. At the gathering, Sattar announced the launching of the Anbar Awakening, an alliance of tribes dedicated to expelling AQI from the region. Initially, only a handful of tribes signed on to the movement. However, over the next few months the movement acquired new converts in and around Ramadi once those related to Sattar saw that MacFarland was committed to using his troops to protect the tribes that rejected AQI. The American commander also supported the tribes' efforts to defend themselves through the organization of armed tribal auxiliary groups, later known as Concerned Local Citizens or Sons of Iraq. MacFarland arranged for militia members to receive training and ensured that as many as possible were incorporated into the Iraqi police force. By the end of 2006, some 4,000 recruits had been added to police ranks.

AQI did not allow itself to be swept aside by the Anbar Awakening movement without a fight. Violence levels in Anbar peaked in October 2006 and remained high through March 2007. But the movement acquired its own momentum, spreading from Ramadi and gaining adherents in Fallujah and other parts of the province throughout 2007. Insurgent activity dropped sharply after March, a trend that reflected not only the diminishing strength of AQI but also the fact that once sheikhs joined the Anbar Awakening, they directed their followers to cease all attacks on American troops. Sattar himself was killed in a bombing outside his Ramadi home on September 13, 2007, a mere 10 days after he had met with President George W. Bush at a military base in Anbar. Nonetheless, Sattar's death did not reverse or slow the progress that had been made in the province, nor did it diminish local support for the Awakening Councils and their militia offshoots, which had sprouted up in Sunni areas outside of Anbar.

On September 1, 2008, Anbar completed its own remarkable turnaround from the most volatile region in Iraq to a more stable environment, and security for the province was officially transferred to the Iraqi government.

The results of the troop surge could be seen in the statistical decline in both Iraqi and U.S. casualties. According to a June 2008 Pentagon report, violence in Iraq dropped 40–80 percent from presurge levels, while the number of violent incidents fell to their lowest point in more than four years. In addition, fewer U.S. troops were killed in May 2008, when 19 died (compared to 126 in May 2007), than in any other month since the invasion of Iraq in March 2003; 29 U.S. troops were killed in June 2008 compared to 101 in June 2007. The Iraqi Body Count, a group that keeps a tally of Iraqi casualties from media reports, noted that 712 Iraqi civilian deaths occurred in June 2008, less than a third of the average during the summer of 2007.

Expanding revenues from the export of Iraqi oil and continued growth in the Iraqi economy (4 percent in 2007) also contributed to a decline in violence in the country as unemployment dropped. The June 2008 Pentagon report, however, warned that security gains could not be preserved without continued progress in economic development and reconstruction; increasing government services, such as electricity (currently available for a national daily average of only 14.9 hours, including just 13 hours in Baghdad); health care; water and sewage treatment; and national political reconciliation among Iraq's rival religious and political groups. An important step in political reconciliation was taken with the passage of a long-awaited and needed Amnesty Law on February 26, 2008, for Iraqis accused or convicted of crimes of terrorism. In addition, Iraq's largest Sunni Arab bloc, the Iraqi Accord Front, prepared to rejoin Prime Minister Maliki's cabinet after a yearlong boycott protesting the government's alleged policies of excluding and marginalizing Sunnis. The inclusion of Sunnis into Iraq's government was cited by both the United States and Iraq as a major factor in bringing about national unity. Sunni Arabs had a great deal of power during Saddam Hussein's regime but became marginalized after he was toppled in 2003. Since then, the Iraqi government has been dominated by Shiites and Kurds.

Despite these developments, however, it was acknowledged that the Iraqi government remained corrupt and inefficient and that it lacked sufficiently qualified personnel to effectively govern and execute policies and programs. In sum, the surge proved to be successful, but as Petraeus remarked, "we can't kill ourselves out of this endeavor." Ultimately, it is only the Iraqi government that can build a stable, secure, prosperous, and united nation.

Stefan Brooks, Jeff Seiken, and Brian L. Steed

See also: Commanders, U.S. Central Command: David H. Petraeus; Insurgency and Opposition: Mahdi Army; Iraq, History of, 1990–Present; Islamic State of Iraq and al-Sham (ISIS): Al Qaeda in Iraq; Obama, Barack Hussein, II; Prime Minister, Iraq: Nuri al-Maliki; Sadr, Muqtada al-; Secretary of Defense, U.S.: Donald Rumsfeld

References

Engel, Richard. *War Journal: My Five Years in Iraq.* New York: Simon and Schuster, 2008.

Galbraith, Peter. *The End of Iraq: How American Incompetence Created a War without End.* New York: Simon and Schuster, 2007.

Isikoff, Michael, and David Corn. *Hubris: The Inside Story of Spin, Scandal, and the Selling of the Iraq War.* New York: Three Rivers/Random House, 2007.

Lubin, Andrew. "Ramadi: From the Caliphate to Capitalism." *Proceedings* 134 (April 2008): 54–61.

McCary, John A. "The Anbar Awakening: An Alliance of Incentives." *Washington Quarterly* 32 (January 2009): 43–59.

Smith, Major Niel, and Colonel Sean MacFarland. "Anbar Awakens: The Tipping Point." *Military Review* (March–April 2008): 41–52.

West, Bing. *The Strongest Tribe: War, Politics, and the Endgame in Iraq.* New York: Random House, 2008.

Islamic State of Iraq and al-Sham (ISIS)

The Islamic State of Iraq and al-Sham (analogous to the modern concept of Syria or greater Syria) (ISIS), variously known as the Islamic State of Iraq and the Levant as well as the Islamic State, is a radical Sunni jihadist organization currently active in Iraq and Syria. ISIS is a successor organization of Al Qaeda in Iraq and was formally established in 2006, at which time it became known as the Islamic State of Iraq (ISI). ISIS is currently led by Abu Bakr al-Baghdadi, an Iraqi born in Samara in 1971 who took part in the post-2003 Iraqi insurgency following the Anglo-American–led invasion of Iraq in March 2003; he was also a member of Al Qaeda in Iraq. Baghdadi has been the acknowledged leader of ISIS since 2010.

As with Al Qaeda in Iraq, ISIS sought to expel all foreign troops and personnel from Iraq and wage war against the Shia-dominated secular government of Iraq. These organizations have not only battled coalition and Iraqi armed forces but have also engaged in myriad acts of terrorism and war crimes that have frequently involved civilians. ISIS, however, had ambitions beyond these activities. It sought to establish an Islamic regime, based on strict interpretations of Islamic law or sharia, within Iraq and Syria. It even hoped to eventually extend its reach into the Levant, which encompasses Lebanon, Israel, Palestine, and Jordan.

By 2010, Baghdadi had emerged as a top leader of Al Qaeda in Iraq. He co-opted several other jihadist organizations, most notably the Mujahideen Shura Council, and began recruiting followers who shared his more expansive vision. Observers believed that Baghdadi enjoyed success in recruiting fighters (many are foreigners, and some even hailed from Western Europe and the United States) because he was a charismatic military strategist and battlefield commander as well as a theologian.

By the spring of 2013, ISIS had become a potent force in both Iraq and Syria. In Syria, ISIS has taken full advantage of the bloody civil war there that had been raging since early 2011. ISIS rebels have been battling Syrian government forces defending the regime of President Bashar al-Assad as well as other antigovernment rebel groups. Many Syrians have come to despise ISIS because of its violence toward civilians, attacks on other rebel groups, and uncompromising positions, which include the subjugation of women and enslavement of captured women prisoners. In early 2014, Western-backed Syrian rebels and even other Islamist groups launched a major campaign to expel ISIS from Syria. It met with only modest success, however, and ISIS extended its reach within Syria to include areas populated by the Kurds.

ISIS had an even greater impact in Iraq, however, and by the summer of 2014 it was threatening the very existence of the Iraqi government of President Nuri al-Maliki.

Throughout 2013, ISIS made major advances in northern and western Iraq. By late January 2014, ISIS and affiliated groups had managed to seize control of the key cities of Fallujah and Ramadi and virtually all of Anbar Province. In early June 2014 the group enjoyed even bigger gains, taking Mosul (Iraq's third-largest city) as well as Tikrit. ISIS forces reached to only some 60 miles north of Baghdad and were attempting to drive farther south.

The fall of Mosul stunned the Iraqi government and much of the international community. By mid-June, the United States and other Western nations were involved in urgent negotiations to determine how they should aid Maliki's government and prevent all of Iraq from falling into the hands of the ISIS. Unfortunately, the corrupt, ineffectual, and anti-Sunni Maliki regime proved virtually incapable of halting ISIS's advance, and many components of the Iraqi Army simply bolted and fled in the face of ISIS offensives.

During the summer of 2014, the Barack Obama administration began implementing a strategy to reverse ISIS's advances. This included cobbling together a multinational coalition, including a number of Arab states, to participate in air strikes against ISIS targets, arming moderate Syrian rebel groups combating ISIS fighters, sending more military hardware to the Iraqi government, dispatching some 3,000 military "advisers" to Iraq, and commencing air strikes against ISIS. These began on August 8, 2014, and the U.S.-coalition air campaign against ISIS in Syria commenced on September 23. Those operations, code-named Operation Inherent Resolve since October 15, 2014, continued into 2018. At the same time that the Obama administration had announced its intent to defeat ISIS, it was lobbying for Maliki to be replaced as Iraqi prime minister. Under great internal and international pressure, he finally resigned on September 8 and was succeeded by Haider al-Abadi, who pledged to pursue conciliatory policies in Iraq and work cooperatively with the United States and its coalition partners in order to subdue the ISIS insurgency. The rise of ISIS has certainly proven to be the worst crisis to hit Iraq since the beginning of the postinvasion insurgency during 2003–2004 and has also greatly complicated the internecine Syrian Civil War.

By late December 2014, there were indications that the anti-ISIS effort was beginning to show some incipient signs of progress. Although Syrian officials reported that ISIS had killed 1,878 people (the vast majority of them civilians) between June 2014 and January 2015, Kurdish fighters announced in late December 2014 that they had made sizable inroads against ISIS in the Syrian border town of Kobanî; by then the Kurds, who have been aided by U.S. and coalition air strikes against ISIS, reportedly controlled more than 60 percent of Kobanî and the surrounding area. They also pushed ISIS out of the Iraqi city of Sinjar, a development that was hailed by some as a possible turning point in the war against ISIS. In May 2015, ISIS was defeated in Tikrit. Over late 2015 and throughout 2016 ISIS suffered a series of defeats in Ramadi and Fallujah. By late 2016, ISIS was under siege and later attack in Mosul. Mosul was returned to Iraqi government control in July 2017 after a battle of nearly seven months.

The threat from ISIS was considerably larger than its military operations in Iraq and Syria might suggest. Indeed, the group routinely violated basic international law and human rights by kidnapping innocent foreign civilians, beheading them, and then releasing the videos of the executions on the Internet. In addition to targeting innocent civilians, ISIS also engaged in the severe repression of women in areas under its control; the group has also engaged in the sexual exploitation and enslavement of women and even young girls.

Beginning in the late summer of 2014, ISIS began publicly executing foreigners. As part of its strategy of conquest, ISIS began to employ terror tactics such as public beheadings to vanquish its opponents, frighten local populations into submission, and attract new recruits. The first public beheading occurred on August 19, 2014, when American journalist James Foley was executed. The video recording was immediately made available on the Internet, which shocked and offended most Americans as well as the international community.

The ISIS campaign of beheading seemed to have backfired, at least in its effect on Western public opinion. After James Foley was killed in August, U.S. public support for a military campaign against ISIS rose dramatically. The same phenomenon occurred in Britain after David Haines's beheading. The French were outraged by the killings, and President François Hollande promptly decided to take military action against ISIS. The beheadings also spurred many Arab and Islamic nations into action. A number of high-profile Islamic scholars and leaders (including Sunnis) condemned ISIS and its deplorable tactics, and Iran also vowed to defeat ISIS.

There have been many reports of ISIS engaging in the sexual enslavement of women, particularly among the Christian and Yazidi minority groups residing in the border areas of Iraq and Syria. In December 2014, the Yazidis asserted that ISIS currently had some 3,500 women and girls imprisoned as sex slaves. In June 2014 as ISIS made more territorial gains in Iraq, it engaged in the kidnapping and rape of women and girls in several Iraqi towns and cities. There are also reports that ISIS operatives kidnapped women and then sold them into slavery to third parties. Indeed, in places such as Mosul, Iraq, and Raqqa, Syria, there were reportedly women and girls on display bearing price tags.

From 2015 to 2018 ISIS lost effectively all of the territory it controlled in Iraq and nearly all of the territory in Syria. Iraqi prime minister Haidar al-Abadi declared victory over ISIS at the end of 2017. The enclaves of ISIS in Syria are limited to a handful of villages and neighborhoods in larger cities in 2018.

The final fate of ISIS is uncertain. As their physical self-declared caliphate shrunk, they encouraged attacks outside of Syria and Iraq. They launched or inspired attacks in Paris, Marseilles, Nice, London, Berlin, Orlando, San Bernardino, and possibly Las Vegas. They have also inspired affiliates across the globe from Nigeria to Afghanistan to Indonesia and the Philippines. ISIS has influenced people through an innovative approach to social media and mass communications. They have promulgated their message with videos, online magazines, and twitter accounts. Some have dubbed this the virtual caliphate and have suggested that so long as this exists then the organization may continue to exist.

Paul G. Pierpaoli Jr.

See also: Baghdadi, Abu Bakr al-; Iraq, History of, 1990–Present; Prime Minister, Iraq: Nuri al-Maliki

References

Brisard, Jean-Charles, and Damien Martinez. *Zarqawi: The New Face of Al Qaeda.* New York: Other Press, 2005.

"Indianapolis Native Peter Kassig Named Next ISIS Target." *Indianapolis Star,* October 12, 2014, http://www.indystar.com/story/news/2014/10/03/reports-indianapolis-man-named-next-isis-target/16667489.

"Inside Kobane: United against ISIS." Al Jazeera, December 22, 2014, http://www.aljazeera.com/news/middleeast/2014/12/inside-kobane-united-against-isil-201412225408474476.html.

"Iraqi Kurdish Fighters Push into ISIS-held Sinjar." CTV News, December 21, 2014, http://www.ctvnews.ca/world/iraqi-kurdish-fighters-push-into-isis-held-sinjar-1.2157491.

"The Slow Backlash: Sunni Religious Authorities Turn against the Islamic State." *Economist,* September 6, 2014, http://www.economist.com/news/middle-east-and-africa/21615634-sunni-religious-authorities-turn-against-islamic-state-slow-backlash.

"Syria Iraq: The Islamic State Militant Group." BBC News, August 2, 2014, http://www.bbc.com/news/world-middle-east-24179084.

Al Qaeda in Iraq

Al Qaeda in Iraq (al-Qa'ida fi Bilad al-Rafhidayn, AQI—literally "the base in the land of the two rivers") is a violent Sunni jihadist organization that has taken root in Iraq since the 2003 Anglo-American–led invasion of that nation. This group is the root organization for what became the Islamic State in Iraq, the Islamic State of Iraq and al-Sham (ISIS), and the Islamic State. For the purposes of this entry it will be referred to as AQI. The U.S. government has characterized AQI, sometimes referred to as Al Qaeda in Mesopotamia, as the deadliest Sunni jihadist insurgent force now in Iraq. Other sources and experts argue that this designation is exaggerated, as the group is among more than 40 similar organizations, and the claim was made symbolically to rationalize the idea that coalition forces are fighting terrorism in Iraq and thus should not withdraw precipitously.

Opponents of the continuing U.S. presence in Iraq have argued that the 2003 invasion sparked the growth of Salafi jihadism and suicide terrorism in Iraq and its export to other parts of the Islamic world. AQI first formed under the name Jama'at al-Tawhid wa-l Jihad (Group of Monotheism and Jihad) under Abu Musab al-Zarqawi in 1999.

Zarqawi fought in Afghanistan in the 1980s and 1990s, and when he returned to his native Jordan, he organized a group called Bayt al-Imam with the noted Islamist ideologue Abu Muhammad al-Maqdisi (Muhammad Tahir al-Barqawi) and other veterans of the war in Afghanistan. Zarqawi was arrested and imprisoned but was released in 1999. He returned to Afghanistan and set up camp in Herat. Following the U.S. invasion of Afghanistan, he fled to the Kurdish region of northern Iraq by way of Iran and Syria. Once Mullah Krekar, the leader of the Kurdish group Islamist Ansar al-Islam, was deported to the Netherlands in 2003, certain sources claim that Zarqawi led some 600 Arab fighters in Syria.

Following the U.S. invasion of Iraq in 2003, Jama'at al-Tawhid wa-l Jihad was blamed for, or took credit for, numerous attacks, including bombings of the Jordanian embassy, the Canal Hotel that killed 23 at the United Nations headquarters, and the Imam Ali mosque in Najaf. Jama'at al-Tawhid wa-l Jihad is also credited with the killing of Italian paramilitary police and civilians at Nasiriyah and numerous suicide attacks that continued through 2005. The group also seized hostages and beheaded them. A video of the savage execution of U.S. businessman Nicholas Berg, murdered in Iraq on May 7, 2004, reportedly by Zarqawi himself, was followed by other killings of civilians.

AQI has targeted Iraqi governmental and military personnel and police because of their cooperation with the American occupying force. AQI's recruitment videos have highlighted American attacks and home searches of defenseless Iraqis and promised martyrdom. Estimates of AQI members have ranged from 850 to several thousand. Also under dispute have been the numbers of foreign fighters in relation to Iraqi fighters. Foreign fighters' roles were first emphasized, but it became clear that a much higher percentage (probably 90 percent) of fighters were Iraqi: members of the Salafi jihadist, or quasi-nationalist jihadist, groups.

In October 2004 Zarqawi's group issued a statement acknowledging the leadership of Al Qaeda under Osama bin Laden and adopted the name al-Qa'ida fi Bilad al-Rafhidayn. The Iraqi city of Fallujah, in western Anbar Province, became an AQI stronghold. U.S. forces twice tried to capture the city, first in the prematurely terminated Operation Vigilant Resolve from April 4 to May 1, 2004. The Fallujah Guard then controlled the city. U.S. military and Iraqi forces conquered the city in Operation Phantom Fury (Fajr) during November 7–December 23, 2004, in extremely bloody fighting.

Zarqawi formed relationships with other Salafist jihad organizations, announcing an umbrella group, the Mujahideen Shura Council, in 2006. After Zarqawi was reportedly at a safe house in June 2006, the new AQI leader, Abu Ayyub al-Masri, announced a new coalition, the Islamic State of Iraq, that included the Mujahideen Shura Council.

Al Qaeda, along with other Sunni Salafist and nationalist groups, strongly resisted Iraqi and coalition forces in Baghdad, Ramadi, and Baqubah and continued staging very damaging attacks into 2007. However, by mid-2008 U.S. commanders claimed dominance over these areas. Nevertheless, AQI was acknowledged to still be operative southeast of Baghdad in Jabour, Mosul, Samarra, Hawijah, and Miqdadiyah. The United States believed that AQI's diminished presence was attributable to the Anbar Awakening, which enlisted numerous tribes, including some former AQI members, to fight Al Qaeda. The Americans further believed that AQI had been diminished because of the troop surge strategy that began in early 2007. From then until his death on May 1, 2011, bin Laden had urged the mujahideen to unify in the face of these setbacks.

AQI has strongly influenced other jihadist groups and actors, particularly through its Internet presence. In sparking intersectarian strife in Iraq, the group has also badly damaged Iraq's postwar reconstruction efforts and tapped into the intolerance of many Salafi groups as well as other Sunni Iraqis and Sunni Muslims outside of Iraq who have been threatened by the emergence of Shia political parties and institutions that had suffered under the Baathist regime of Saddam Hussein. Iraq's Al Qaeda affiliate claimed responsibility for the July 23, 2013, jailbreak from the infamous Abu Ghraib prison that unleashed 500 to 600 militants into an already unstable region and boosted the group's resurgent fortunes in Iraq and Syria. The prisoners were freed in two coordinated assaults in which fighters used suicide bombs and mortars to storm the two top security prisons on Baghdad's outskirts at Abu Ghraib and Taji. Both were once run by the U.S. military and housed the country's most senior Al Qaeda detainees. At least 26 members of the Iraqi Security Forces and more than a dozen prisoners were killed.

The scale of the attacks against the heavily guarded facilities reinforced an impression building among many Iraqis that their security forces are struggling to cope with a resurgent Al Qaeda since U.S. forces withdrew in

December 2011, taking with them much of the expertise and technology that had been used to hold extremists at bay. Iraqis' fears about a resurgent Al Qaeda were further vindicated when the group took control of Fallujah and Ramadi and much of Anbar Province by January 2014. Meanwhile, car bombings, kidnappings, and other violence perpetrated by Al Qaeda and allied groups accelerated rapidly during 2013 and into 2014.

Sherifa Zuhur

See also: Fallujah, Second Battle of; Zarqawi, Abu Musab al-

References

Brisard, Jean-Charles, and Damien Martinez. *Zarqawi: The New Face of al-Qaeda.* New York: Other Press, 2005.

Burns, John, and Melissa Rubin. "U.S. Arming Sunnis in Iraq to Battle Old Qaeda Allies." *New York Times,* June 11, 2007.

Congressional Research Service. *Iraq: Post-Saddam Governance and Security, September 6, 2007.* Report to Congress. Washington, DC: U.S. Government Printing Office, 2007.

"In Motley Array of Iraqi Foes, Why Does U.S. Spotlight al-Qaida?" *International Herald Tribune,* June 8, 2007.

K

Karbala, First Battle of (March 31–April 6, 2003)

Located in central Iraq some 60 miles southwest of Baghdad, Karbala is regarded as one of the holiest cities in Shia Islam. Three notable battles have occurred there: one in October 680 CE among Islamic factions, one during Operation Iraqi Freedom in 2003, and one between Iraqi factions in 2007. The March 31–April 6, 2003, battle occurred during the Iraq War when U.S. forces attempted to evict Iraqi forces from Karbala. Units involved in the fight included those from the U.S. 3rd Infantry Division, the 1st Armored Division, and the 101st Airborne Division; Iraqi forces consisted of members of the Fedayeen Saddam and Syrian mercenaries.

During the initial phase of the 2003 invasion of Iraq, advance units of the U.S. 3rd Infantry Division, having pushed their way through Republican Guard forces southeast of Karbala, arrived in the area on March 31. While some troops kept a watchful eye on the Iraqis in Karbala, the main body bypassed the city and attacked Baghdad through the Karbala Gap. This meant that U.S. forces would have to clear the Iraqis out of Karbala later.

This task fell principally to the 101st Airborne Division, supported by the 2nd Battalion, 70th Armored Regiment, 1st Armored Division. On April 2, 2003, a U.S. Army Sikorsky UH-60 Black Hawk helicopter was shot down near Karbala, killing seven soldiers and wounding four others. This event appeared to indicate a significant enemy presence in the city.

The 101st Airborne Division decided to insert three battalions via helicopter at three landing zones (LZs) on the outskirts of the city, designated LZ Sparrow, LZ Finch, and LZ Robin. M-1 Abrams tanks and M-2 Bradley fighting vehicles of the 2nd Battalion, 70th Armored Regiment, were to support these forces.

On the morning of April 5, 23 UH-60 Black Hawks escorted five CH-47 Boeing Chinook helicopters ferrying three battalions of the 502nd Infantry Regiment to their LZs. The 3rd Battalion landed at LZ Sparrow and met heavy but uncoordinated resistance. The 2nd Battalion landed to the south at LZ Robin and found numerous arms caches hidden in schools as well as a suspected terrorist training camp. As night fell, the battalion had cleared 13 of its 30 assigned sectors.

The 1st Battalion landed at LZ Finch in the southeast, where it captured a large store of weapons. As the infantry moved forward, it was constantly supported by helicopters and artillery. While the soldiers went house to house, armored vehicles from the 2nd Battalion, 70th Armored Regiment, arrived and engaged the enemy.

The following morning, April 6, the Americans continued operations until 5:00 p.m., when all sectors were secured. Symbolic of the victory, members of the 2nd Battalion, 70th Armored Regiment, tore down a large statue of Iraqi dictator Saddam Hussein in the middle of the city. Reported casualties were as many as 260 for the Iraqis;

the Americans suffered 8 killed. One UH-60 helicopter was also lost. One U.S. M1 Abrams tank was disabled but not destroyed.

William P. Head

See also: Iraqi Freedom, Operation: Major Battles

References

Atkinson, Rick. *In the Company of Soldiers: A Chronicle of Combat.* New York: Henry Holt, 2005.

NBC Enterprises. *Operation Iraqi Freedom: The Insider Story.* Kansas City, MO: Andrews McMeel, 2003.

Kurds

People of Indo-European origin who inhabit the upcountry and mountainous areas chiefly in Iran, Iraq, Syria, and Turkey. Their primary area of concentration in southern Turkey and the northern parts of Iran and Iraq is known as Kurdistan, although this is not an autonomous region. There are also small enclaves of Kurds in southwestern Armenia, Azerbaijan, and Lebanon. The total Kurdish population worldwide is estimated at between 30 million and 35 million people, making the Kurds perhaps the largest ethnic group in the world not enjoying their own autonomous homeland. Today they constitute some 19 percent of the population of Turkey, 17 percent of Iraq's population, 9 percent of that of Syria, and 7–10 percent of the Iranian population.

The Kurds, whose language is of Indo-European background, are not Arabs. However, numerous Kurds have intermarried with Arabs and have played an important role in Arab and Muslim history. Salah al-Din al-Ayyubi (Saladin), one of the greatest of Muslim leaders, was of Kurdish origin.

Kurdish refugees in the United Nations–administered Makhmur Refugee Camp in Kurdistan, northern Iraq, on January 26, 2007. (Sadık Güleç/Dreamstime.com)

There have also been numerous Kurdish dynasties, such as the Ziyarids, the Jastanids, and the Kakuyids.

The great majority of Kurds are Sunni Muslims, and their language is related to Persian (which is spoken chiefly in Iran, Afghanistan, and Tajikistan). There are numerous dialects of Kurdish divided into two primary dialect groups: Sorani and Kumanji. Just as they have their own language, the Kurds maintain their own unique culture and traditions.

Until the first few decades of the 20th century, most Kurds lived a pastoral, nomadic existence and divided themselves into tribes. For centuries, they led a somewhat isolated lifestyle that clung to tradition and was well ordered by tribal hierarchy and customs. The mountain Kurds' principal means of subsistence was herding goats and sheep, which was migratory in nature. In this sense, they were not unlike the Bedouins to the south. However, when the Ottoman Empire broke apart as a result of World War I, the Kurds found themselves circumscribed within newly created states, none of which was interested in allowing them to continue their centuries-old lifestyle and customs.

As new nations such as Iraq and Turkey organized themselves into nationalistic nation-states, the Kurds came under great pressure to abandon their tribal ways and assimilate into the majority culture. They were also greatly limited in their migratory patterns, which served only to further marginalize them.

At the end of World War I, Kurds called for their own nation, Kurdistan. They expected support in this endeavor from the United States. But as an Associated Power in World War I rather than an Entente Power, the United States had not declared war on the Ottoman Empire; therefore, after the war it had no voice in its dismemberment and the subsequent League of Nations mandates. Beyond that, however, the American public had little interest in such an undertaking.

While the British gave some lip service to the establishment of a Kurdish state, the Turks effectively quashed the idea, with Iraq and Iran agreeing that they would recognize no Kurdish state encompassing any part of their territory. The Kurds were now subjected to discrimination and oppression in general. This situation was particularly bad in Turkey. The Turkish government refused to recognize the Kurds as a distinct ethnic group (a state of affairs that continues today), forced them to abandon their language, banned their traditional garb, and lured them into urban areas to curtail their pastoral life. This brought more discrimination and resulted in high unemployment and poverty rates for urbanized Kurds.

In Turkey, the Kurds have periodically risen up against the government and demanded greater freedoms, only to be crushed by the Turkish Army. However, an underground Kurdish guerrilla group, formed out of the Kurdistan Workers' Party in the 1980s, continued to pursue the dream of an independent Kurdish state and engaged Turkish, Iranian, and Syrian troops in an ongoing insurgency. In the late 1940s and again in the late 1970s, Kurds attempted to form their own autonomous region in Iran. These efforts were both put down by the Iranians.

For decades, Kurds were subjected to brutal oppression by the Iraqi government. From 1960 to 1975, Iraqi Kurds, under the leadership of Mustafa Barzani, waged a guerrilla-style war with Iraqi regular forces. This brought significant casualties to the Iraqis and forced them in 1970 to enter into talks with the rebelling Kurds. That same year, the Iraqi government offered a peace deal to the Kurds that would have brought them their own autonomous region (but not sovereignty) by 1974. Meanwhile, Barzani continued his campaign, and the peace offer never took hold. In 1975 the Iraqis began moving thousands of people into northern Iraq in an attempt to Arabize the region while simultaneously exiling close to 200,000 Kurds.

The Iran-Iraq War (1980–1988) brought great misery and many fatalities to Iraqi Kurds. Saddam Hussein's government was extraordinarily brutal in its treatment of the minority, and in 1988 Hussein launched his so-called Anfal (Spoils of War) Campaign. During a period of several months, Iraqi forces killed perhaps as many as 100,000 Kurds and destroyed some 2,000 villages, often employing chemical weapons. In 1991 in the immediate aftermath of the Persian

Gulf War, Iraqi Kurds rebelled again and were again crushed. Finally, to protect the Kurds the United States established a safe haven and imposed a northern no-fly zone on the Iraqi military. Following a number of military clashes between the Iraqi Army and Kurdish forces, an autonomous Kurdish region was established, ruled by the Kurdistan Democratic Party (KDP), headed by Massoud Barzani, and the Patriotic Union of Kurdistan (PUK), led by Jalal Talabani. Economic advances occurred, and the Kurds created an infrastructure independent of that of the Iraqi government. Although there was fighting between the KDP and the PUK during 1994–1998, Kurdish autonomy was undisturbed, and the economy was stable.

Following the Anglo-American invasion of Iraq in March 2003, the Kurds expanded the area under their control southward, securing control of Kirkuk and part of Mosul. This gave Kurds more access to water and oil resources, bringing improved relations with Turkey, which imported the oil. The Kurdish region of northern Iraq, comprising three provinces, sees continued infighting between the KDP and PUK, but their goals and programs are remarkably similar, and they have been able to work together effectively. Indeed, the Kurdish fighting groups known as the Peshmerga have fought for decades in Iraq, Iran, and Turkey. Some have fought alongside U.S. troops in a joint effort to defeat Kurdish Islamic extremist groups, such as Ansar al-Islam and now the Islamic State of Iraq and Syria (ISIS).

Ironically, while the United States and its allies have been unable to build a stable democratic regime in central and southern Iraq, the Kurds in the north have been far more successful in creating a stable environment. The Kurds are strongly prodemocratic and somewhat more pro-American than other Iraqis. Northern Iraq has experienced some attacks and bombings, and Mosul and Kirkuk were key problem areas as of 2009, but other areas of historic Iraqi Kurdistan have been less dangerous for coalition forces.

The Kurdish area of Iraq saw considerable fighting in 2014 when it came under military attack from ISIS, which enjoyed a considerable advantage in heavy weapons captured from the Syrian and Iraqi Armies. ISIS captured Mosul in June 2014, but the Kurds, supported by U.S. air strikes and weapons deliveries, retook strategic Mosul Dam from ISIS and in late 2014 resisted an all-out ISIS effort to capture the large Kurdish city of Kobanî on the Turkish border.

The major Kurdish political parties decry Islamic extremism and do not support a theocratic government, although many smaller Kurdish groups do. There is still a great deal of support for the creation of a separate Kurdish nation among Kurds. Such a move, however, would be vociferously opposed by the Turks and Iranians. There is as yet no resolution over the status of Kirkuk, where Arabs and Turkomen dispute Kurdish claims. However, if this issue and some other matters can be resolved and the Kurds continue to exercise effective government in their region, they will have a nation in everything but name.

Paul G. Pierpaoli Jr.

See also: Hussein, Saddam; Iraq, History of, 1990–Present; Islamic State of Iraq and al-Sham (ISIS); Political Parties, Iraq: Kurdistan Democratic Party, Patriotic Union of Kurdistan

References

Bulloch, John, and Harvey Morris. *No Friends but the Mountains: The Tragic History of the Kurds.* New York: Oxford University Press, 1993.

Ciment, James. *The Kurds: State and Minority in Turkey, Iraq, and Iran.* New York: Facts on File, 1996.

Izady, Mehrdad R. *The Kurds: A Concise Handbook.* Washington, DC: Crane Russak, Taylor and Francis, 1992.

Lawrence, Quil. *Invisible Nation: How the Kurds' Quest for Statehood Is Shaping Iraq and the Middle East.* New York: Walker, 2008.

McDowall, David. *A Modern History of the Kurds.* New York: I. B. Tauris, 2000.

Mosul, Battle of (November 8–16, 2004)

Pitched battle fought in the city of Mosul, located in northern Iraq some 250 miles northwest of Baghdad, during November 8–16, 2004. The battle involved the U.S. Army 1st Battalion, 24th Infantry Regiment; Iraqi Security Forces (Iraqi police, Iraqi Army, Iraqi National Guard, and Iraqi Border Patrol); and Kurdish Peshmerga fighting Iraqi insurgents (former Baath Party members, fundamentalist factions with ties to the Al Qaeda in Iraq organization, and fighters from other extremist groups). The Battle of Mosul was brought on as much by political expediency as it was by the need to protect civilians from harassment by the insurgents. It ended in a clear-cut victory for coalition forces.

The Battle of Mosul occurred simultaneously with another furious battle between coalition forces and insurgents in Fallujah. The Second Battle of Fallujah (November 7–23, 2004) drew insurgents and foreign fighters in droves. The coalition responded to the insurgent attacks with overwhelming force, which included recalling then major general David Petraeus and the 101st Airborne Division to Fallujah. The 101st Airborne Division had been maintaining a peaceful occupation of the primarily Sunni Mosul for the preceding year. Coalition troops took little time to rout the insurgency, and the surviving insurgents fled Fallujah. A number of them then went to Mosul.

The 25th Infantry Division was deployed to Mosul in mid-October 2004 to replace the 101st Airborne Division. This was approximately the same time that displaced insurgents began arriving from Fallujah. The insurgents announced their arrival with an enormous wave of kidnappings and beheadings that left more than 200 of Mosul's residents dead in the streets for resisting the insurgents.

On November 8, 2004, Iraqi insurgents began to carry out coordinated attacks within Mosul. It was on this day also that the 1st Battalion, 24th Infantry Regiment, reported the first major engagement of what would become the Battle of Mosul, near the Yarmuk traffic circle in the western part of the city. Soldiers of the regiment were pinned down by coordinated mortar fire from the north and were being pounded from the other three directions by rocket-propelled grenades and machine-gun fire in a daylong firefight.

The insurgents also used this opening day of the battle to overrun two Iraqi police stations. The insurgents then cleaned out the station armories, taking weapons and flak jackets, and killed a dozen Iraqi policemen. The Western media reported that the majority of the policemen had deserted their posts after reporting attacks by "hundreds" of insurgents against their stations. However, when the Americans retook the stations, they estimated that only 20–30 insurgents had taken each station.

On November 9, insurgents successfully attacked a forward operating base in Mosul, killing two American army officers. By November 10, Iraqi insurgents were openly taking to the streets in defiance of coalition forces, and by November 11 they had taken another Iraqi police station and destroyed two others. The time had come for a coalition counteroffensive.

Members of the U.S. 24th Infantry Regiment were sent out in an effort to crush the insurgents between two companies. The blow was aimed, again, at the strategically critical Yarmuk traffic circle. The 24th Infantry Regiment encountered fierce resistance as it pushed from house to house in close-quarter urban fighting. Yet with air support, the regiment was able to regain control of four of the five bridges over the Tigris River.

In the meantime, the insurgents sacked nine more police stations, destroying eight and occupying the ninth. On November 12, additional insurgent reinforcements arrived, and despite U.S. Air Force bombing, by November 13 insurgent forces held as much as 70 percent of Mosul. The insurgents became so secure in their military superiority that they began seeking out members of the Iraqi Security Forces to behead.

Coalition reinforcements began to arrive by November 13, including a battalion of the U.S. 25th Infantry Regiment, a group of Kurdish Peshmerga fighters, and elements of the Iraqi Special Forces and National Guard. On November 16 U.S. forces retook the fifth insurgent-held bridge over the Tigris and began to sweep through all of Mosul except for the western sector. The Americans met little resistance, but the insurgents burned many of the police stations they had occupied. By November 16, the major fighting was over. The western sector of Mosul, however, would remain in insurgent hands until another coalition surge involving an influx of 12,000 troops arrived in December and January 2005. This was timed to secure Mosul for Iraq's first democratic elections in January.

The coalition official casualty report for the Battle of Mosul was 4 U.S. soldiers killed, 9 Peshmerga fighters killed, and 116 Iraqi Security Forces killed (as many as 5,000 are believed to have deserted). Total losses for insurgents are unknown, although 71 were confirmed killed. Also, 5 civilians were reported killed, as were 2 contractors (1 British and 1 Turkish). Precise casualty figures, including the number of wounded, remain unknown, and some estimates claim much higher death tolls for both the civilians and insurgents.

The importance of the battle could be measured by the fact that although there were mass desertions of Iraqi police and security forces targeted by insurgents, a sense of esprit de corps and pride among Iraqi forces developed, which had been sorely lacking before the event. In turn, the police and the security forces became better equipped to handle the insurgency, and the Iraqi citizenry gained trust in them, which led to the citizenry providing more information to coalition forces regarding insurgent activity. The terrorist tactics employed by the insurgents in the battle backfired. However, Mosul remained one of the most violent and unstable places in Iraq through 2014.

In June 2014 forces from the Islamic State of Iraq and Syria (ISIS) captured Mosul, creating a potential humanitarian crisis for the city's Christian, Kurdish, and Yazidi populations. The fall of Mosul triggered a U.S. air campaign against ISIS in August.

Keith Murphy

See also: Commanders, U.S. Central Command: David H. Petraeus; Fallujah, Second

Battle of; Islamic State of Iraq and al-Sham (ISIS)

References

Allawi, Ali A. *The Occupation of Iraq: Winning the War, Losing the Peace.* New Haven, CT: Yale University Press, 2007.

"Iraqis Prepare ISIS Offensive, with U.S. Help." *New York Times,* November 2, 2014, http://www.nytimes.com/2014/11/03/world/middleeast/iraqis-prepare-isis-offensive-with-us-help.html?_r=2.

Tucker, Mike. *Among Warriors in Iraq: True Grit, Special Ops, and Raiding in Mosul and Fallujah.* Guilford, CT: Lyons, 2005.

Nasiriyah, Battle of (March 23–29, 2003)

The Shiite-dominated town of Nasiriyah occupies an important location in southern Iraq. Situated some 225 miles southeast of the capital of Baghdad, Nasiriyah is the fourth most populous city of Iraq after Baghdad, Basra, and Mosul. In 2003 Nasiriyah had a population of some 560,000 people. It is also an important transportation hub, with key bridges spanning the Euphrates River on either side of the city. Located close to Tallil Airfield and the headquarters of the Iraqi Army III Corps of three divisions, Nasiriyah was thus a key objective in the first phases of the Iraq War. During the 1991 Persian Gulf War, Nasiriyah had been the most northerly point in Iraq for U.S. forces, with the 82nd Airborne having reached the city's outskirts.

In 2003 the task of taking Nasiriyah and the bridges over the Euphrates fell to U.S. Marine Corps Task Force Tarawa (TF Tarawa), commanded by Brigadier General Richard Natonski. TF Tarawa was the code name for the 2nd Marine Expeditionary Brigade, centered on the 2nd Marine Regiment, Marine Aircraft Group 29, Company A of the 8th Tank Battalion (with M-1 Abrams tanks), and Combat Service Support Battalion 22. TF Tarawa was the vanguard of the I Marine Expeditionary Force (I MEF), commanded by Lieutenant General James Conway, which was centered on the 1st Marine Division led by Major General James Mattis.

TF Tarawa's assignments were to first secure Jalibah Air Base and then secure the bridges across the Euphrates and the Saddam Canal. Taking and holding these crossing points were essential for enabling the 1st Marine Division to continue its drive northward on Highway 7 toward Kut. With this accomplished, TF Tarawa was to keep open the supply corridor that would enable the 1st Marine Division to continue north and engage and defeat the Republican Guard divisions defending the southern approaches to Baghdad.

In its drive north into Iraq from Kuwait, TF Tarawa was obliged to move through the desert to get to Jalibah Air Base because the supply vehicles of the U.S. Army's 3rd Infantry Division, which had movement priority, occupied the roads. Meanwhile, the 3rd Infantry Division also advanced toward Baghdad, taking a crossing over the Euphrates west of Nasiriyah. As the 3rd Infantry Division defeated Iraqi forces in and around Tallil Airfield and bypassed Nasiriyah to the west, TF Tarawa moved on that city.

TF Tarawa departed Jalibah Air Base for Nasiriyah early on March 23, but taking the city did not go according to plan. Natonski had planned for the 1st Battalion, 2nd Marine Regiment, to move through the eastern part of Nasiriyah and seize one of the northern bridges, after which another battalion was to secure the city, thereby allowing the three regimental combat teams of the I MEF to continue the drive north on Route 7.

The marines had anticipated fighting at Nasiriyah but not the level of resistance encountered. One thing did go according to plan: much of the Iraqi 11th Division simply deserted. What the marines had also

A U.S. marine assists displaced Iraqi civilians caught in a firefight north of Nasiriyah, Iraq, on March 26, 2003. (U.S. Department of Defense)

expected did not occur, however: an uprising by the population of Nasiriyah against the regime. The inhabitants had done so in 1991, and many had been massacred by the Saddam Hussein regime. The survivors had learned their lesson. Indeed, they now prepared to defend the city. The composition of those fighting is still disputed; some of the fighters certainly were members of the Fedayeen Saddam who began arriving in the city on March 22 in private vehicles and commandeered buses. Although poorly trained, they were fanatical fighters and willing to die in a jihad. Under the command of ruthless Iraqi general Al Hassan al-Majid, a relative of Hussein who had charge of the south, the defenders of Nasiriyah prepared to do battle with the marines.

Fighting began as soon as the leading marine element, the 1st Battalion, 2nd Marine Regiment, supported by some armor, arrived at the city outskirts. The marines quickly destroyed nine stationary T-72 tanks—a number of them bereft of engines—that had been dug in to defend a railroad bridge south of the river.

At about 7:30 a.m., marines of A Company were startled to make contact with an American military truck belonging to the army's 507th Maintenance Company. The men in it informed the marines that their 18 trucks had been part of a 3rd Infantry Division supply column. The 507th Maintenance Company, which included female soldiers Jessica Lynch and Lori Piestewa, had taken a wrong turn on Route 7 and proceeded into Nasiriyah, where it had been ambushed. In the ensuing fighting 11 American soldiers had been killed, and 6 others, including Lynch and Piestewa, were taken prisoner.

Piestewa died of her wounds shortly after capture, while the remaining 5 prisoners, including Lynch, were later rescued. Piestewa was a member of the Hopi tribe and is thus believed to have been the first Native American woman killed in combat in a foreign war. On learning of the plight of the 507th Maintenance Company, the marines immediately headed north and rescued a dozen wounded members of that unit.

Unfortunately for the marines, the appearance of the 507th Maintenance Company trucks had alerted the defenders of Nasiriyah to the imminent arrival of other American forces. The ensuing firefight and the desperate effort of the members of the maintenance company to escape also served to give the defenders a false sense of their ability to stop the Americans.

After a pause to refuel, the marines then drove to the Euphrates. The Iraqis had not blown the bridge, but a major firefight soon erupted. One company took a wrong approach to another bridge over the Saddam Canal, and a number of its vehicles became bogged down in soft sand. The marines resumed their advance to the canal down the city's main road, which they soon dubbed "Ambush Alley."

Supported by tank fire, the marines succeeded in getting across the canal, but one of their amphibious assault vehicles took a hit from a rocket-propelled grenade (RPG) on the bridge. Four marines were wounded, and the amphibious assault vehicles barely made it across the span. Worse, a Fairchild-Republic A-10 Warthog aircraft, supporting the marines, attacked marines on the north side of the bridge, mistaking them for Iraqis and killing six. Two other marine vehicles sent south of the river back down Ambush Alley as part of a convoy to remove wounded were struck and destroyed by RPG and small-arms fire that killed most of those inside. Heavy fighting for the bridgehead raged during the night, with the marines supported by Bell AH-1S Cobra attack helicopters. By the morning of March 24, the marines had control of both bridges and had suppressed some of the resistance along Ambush Alley. Determined to press on as quickly as possible in order to threaten Kut and thereby present the Iraqis with two threats to Baghdad, Conway, Mattis, and Natonski decided to push the 1st Marnie Regiment up Ambush Alley through Nasiriyah and up Highway 7. At the same time, the 5th and 7th Marine Regiments were able to secure the bridge outside the urban area and reach Highway 1.

The 5th and 7th Marine Regiments had a relatively easy time of it, but it was a different story for the members of the 1st Marine Regiment, pushing up Highway 8 on the evening of March 24. They came under heavy small-arms fire, including RPGs and mortar fire. Sustaining relatively few casualties, however, the 1st Marine Regiment passed through the city on the night of March 24–25 and was soon on its way to Kut.

TF Tarawa now was faced with the difficult task of clearing Nasiriyah in order to protect the marine supply line north to Routes 1 and 7. These efforts were severely impacted by the arrival of a *shamal*. This fierce sandstorm lasted several days and not only reduced air support available to the marines but also made the efforts to clear out snipers and fighters more difficult, complicating fighting conditions. Artillery proved to be the only all-weather continuous fire support asset for TF Tarawa. On March 26 high-explosive rounds with concrete-piercing fuses were fired against a hospital that was serving as a paramilitary strongpoint and was then seized by the marines. A concentrated artillery fire mission against an estimated 2,000 fedayeen at a railroad station in the southern part of the city reported to be preparing to launch a counterattack not only ended that threat but also killed some 200 of the fedayeen.

A number of marine vehicles were lost to RPGs, but the situation was eased by a cordon around the city that cut off resupply to the Iraqi fighters. With the end of the *shamal* and the arrival of unmanned aerial vehicles over Nasiriyah, more accurate targeting information was soon available. Marine aircraft also took part. Also, some residents began to come forward to identify Iraqi sniper nests and command centers, and special forces units also assisted in the targeting.

Intelligence provided by friendly Iraqis also enabled a team of marines, Navy SEALs, and Army Rangers to rescue Private Lynch and the other Americans who had been captured earlier. The fighting was largely over by March 29, but it was not until early April that Nasiriyah was completely secure. The fighting for the city had claimed 18 marines killed and more than 150 wounded.

Spencer C. Tucker

See also: Insurgency and Opposition: Fedayeen; Iraqi Freedom, Operation: Ground Campaign

References

Cordesman, Anthony H. *The Iraq War: Strategy, Tactics, and Military Lessons.* Westport, CT: Praeger, 2003.

Keegan, John. *The Iraq War: The Military Offensive, from Victory in 21 Days to the Insurgent Aftermath.* New York: Vintage, 2005.

Livingston, Gary. *An Nasiriyah: The Fight for the Bridges.* North Topsail Island, NC: Caisson, 2004.

Lowry, Richard S. *Marines in the Garden of Eden: The Battle for An Nasiriyah.* New York: Berkley, 2006.

Murray, Williamson, and Robert H. Scales Jr. *The Iraq War: A Military History.* Cambridge, MA: Belknap, 2005.

Pritchard, Tim. *Ambush Alley: The Most Extraordinary Battle of the Iraq War.* New York: Ballatine Books, 2007.

New Dawn, Operation (2010–2011)

Operation New Dawn was the name given to the advise and assist phase of United States Forces–Iraq (USF-I) activities within Iraq. The "last" combat brigade departed Iraq on August 19, 2010. Operation New Dawn began, officially, on September 1, 2010. After August 19, 2010, about 50,000 soldiers in USF-I remained in Iraq. Sometimes the remaining units are characterized as being advise and assist brigades as if there was a different formation within the U.S. military. In 2010 and 2011 there was no difference between the brigades that left before August 19 and the ones that remained; they were exactly the same kind of forces. The departure of the brigades prior to September 1 allowed political leaders to claim that combat officially ended by September 1, 2010.

One of the primary responsibilities for USF-I during Operation New Dawn was to help Iraqi Security Forces (ISF) close the capability gap between their current performance and that required to conduct operations independent of U.S. assistance. Such an effort was intended to create competent ISF so that once all U.S. forces departed country the ISF could conduct all necessary operations. Another effort was on the political front, and it focused on getting the Iraqi government to agree to a U.S. residual force. The senior U.S. military leadership believed that the ISF would not be capable to conduct the necessary security tasks absent U.S. assistance. The recommended residual force varied in size from thousands to 30,000. The political pressure on the Iraqi government from the United States to accept such a force came primarily from senior leaders serving in Iraq as the White House was not in favor of the idea. This idea failed to materialize and all U.S. forces left Iraq by mid-December 2011. The failure to secure a residual force was blamed as a precipitating factor for the rise and successful offensive actions of ISIS in 2013 and 2014.

It may be reasonable to consider why such a force was needed. Why wasn't the ISF ready to conduct their own internal and external defense after more than eight years of U.S. training and investment? This is not a simple question to answer. Operation Iraqi Freedom was not initially envisioned as a training mission. It took years for MNF-I to get the training system operating at anything like a proper capacity. Then, Lieutenant General Petraeus complained about not having his complete staff as he commanded Multi-National Security Transition Command–Iraq (MNSTC-I) more than a year after the invasion. MNSTC-I and all of its predecessors and successors was always manned through ad hoc personnel assignments. The U.S. military had not created a complete foreign military from scratch in its history, and it required a difficult learning curve. Additionally, the insurgency in Iraq was raging in 2005 to 2008, and so the ISF forces were thrown immediately into the fight. There was no time to establish institutional or even organizational capacity to maintain personnel records, develop professional military education, or create national level defense capabilities. The ISF only purchased F-16s, their first air defense aircraft system in 2011 with deliveries slated for years in the future.

There were many reasons for the problems still needing a solution in 2011. The full scope of the unsolved problems was not revealed until the successful ISIS offensives in 2014.

Brian L. Steed

See also: Commanders, Multi-National Force–Iraq: David H. Petraeus, Raymond T. Odierno, Lloyd J. Austin III; Commands, U.S. and Coalition Military: Multi-National Force–Iraq, Multi-National Security Transition Command–Iraq

References

Rayburn, Joel. *Iraq after America: Strongmen, Sectarians, Resistance*. Stanford, CA: Hoover Institution Press, 2014.

Sky, Emma. *The Unravelling: High Hopes and Missed Opportunities in Iraq*. New York: PublicAffairs, 2015.

Stern, Jessica, and J. M. Berger. *ISIS: The State of Terror*. New York: HarperCollins, 2015.

Weiss, Michael, and Hassan Hassan. *ISIS: Inside the Army of Terror*. New York: Regan Arts, 2015.

Obama, Barack Hussein, II (1961–)

Attorney, Democratic Party politician, U.S. senator (2005–2008), and president of the United States (2009–2017). Barack Hussein Obama II was born on August 4, 1961, in Honolulu, Hawaii, the son of a white American woman and an African from Kenya. Obama's parents separated when he was just two years old in 1964. Obama's father returned to Kenya and had limited contact with his son after that time; Obama saw his father, who died in a car accident in 1982, only once after he left for Kenya. Obama's maternal grandparents were a major force in his life and in many ways served as his surrogate parents.

Obama's mother subsequently married a man from Indonesia, and Obama moved to Jakarta, Indonesia, where he attended several schools until he returned to live with his grandparents in Hawaii in 1971. In 1979 Obama entered Occidental College before transferring to Columbia University, from which he graduated in 1983. From 1985 to 1988 he worked as a community organizer on the South Side of Chicago; his experiences there led to his adoption of Chicago as his home city.

In 1988 Obama entered Harvard Law School, where he became president of the *Harvard Law Review;* he was the first African American ever to hold that position. In 1991 he secured his law degree and returned to Chicago; the following year he led a successful voter registration drive in Illinois that registered as many as 150,000 previously unregistered African American voters. In 1992 Obama joined the faculty of the University of Chicago School of Law, serving in various teaching capacities until 2004. From 1993 to 2004 he was also a member of a small Chicago law firm that specialized in civil rights issues and local economic development. In 1997 Obama became an Illinois state senator, a post he held until 2004. As a state senator, he garnered much praise for his grasp of important issues and his ability to sponsor and guide bipartisan-backed legislation through the Senate.

In 2004 Obama, a gifted orator, made a run for the U.S. Senate, winning by the largest landslide in Illinois electoral history. He campaigned on a platform that was sharply critical of the Iraq War and promised to reorder America's social and economic priorities. He also vowed to help unite Americans and heal racial, social, and economic divisions.

In July 2004 Obama delivered the keynote address at the Democratic National Convention, as a result of which he became a national phenomenon. His electrifying speech caught the attention of many and helped prepare the way for his run for the White House in 2008. Obama was sworn in as a U.S. senator in January 2005. He worked closely with Republican senator Richard Lugar, chairman of the Senate Committee on Foreign Relations; the two visited nuclear missile launch sites in Russia in an effort to ensure the safety of the armaments. Obama also continued his criticism of the Iraq War, arguing that it had been an unnecessary operation and was badly managed by the George W. Bush administration.

In February 2007 Obama announced his intention to run for the U.S. presidency on the 2008 Democratic ticket. At the time many dismissed his intentions, pointing to his relative inexperience and the likely candidacies of such heavy-hitters as Senators Hillary Clinton, Joseph Biden, Christopher Dodd, and John Edwards, among others. But Obama ran an impressively earnest and well-executed primary campaign, and by the midwinter of 2008 his many rivals had all dropped out of the race except for Senator Clinton. Meanwhile, the Obama campaign's brilliant use of the Internet to raise money and get out his message paid handsome dividends; in early June 2008 Obama became the presumptive Democratic nominee when Clinton conceded the race. From then on Obama, who eschewed public funding of his campaign, continued to raise massive sums of money and garnered an impressive list of endorsements from both Democrats and Republicans, including former secretary of state and Republican Party stalwart Colin L. Powell. By the early fall, Obama had raised more money by far than any other presidential candidate in history.

In the general election Obama faced off against Republican senator John S. McCain, a war hero and prisoner of war during the Vietnam War and the son and grandson of U.S. Navy admirals. Until September the tenor of the race focused chiefly on Obama's insistence that U.S. troops be withdrawn from Iraq as expeditiously as possible, his calls for energy independence, his desire to implement universal and affordable health care for all, and his hope to lessen the power of Washington lobbyists and special interests. He traveled to the Middle East and several European nations in July 2008 amid much fanfare in an attempt to bolster his foreign policy bona fides. The McCain camp sought to portray Obama as too inexperienced and naive to be president, and McCain argued that the troop surge in Iraq, begun in early 2007, had made a quantifiable difference in the course of the conflict. He suggested that Obama's plan for a specific timetable for the withdrawal of U.S. troops from Iraq represented a "cut and run" mentality that would play into the hands of the insurgents. Obama's suggested timetable ended up being embraced by the Iraqi government and became the basis for the U.S.-Iraqi status of forces agreement, finalized in late 2008.

Obama continued to argue that the Iraq War had been unnecessary from the start and was based on flimsy intelligence and poor judgment on the part of the Bush administration. Obama also asserted that the conflict had caused the United States to dilute its efforts in the Afghanistan War, resulting in the increasingly deadly Taliban insurgency there. Obama promised to redouble U.S. efforts in Afghanistan and dispatch significantly more troops there.

In August, Obama named Senator Joseph Biden, from Delaware, to be his vice-presidential running mate. Biden added his many years of governmental experience to the ticket, and the choice was generally hailed as a wise move. In September the focus of the campaign shifted dramatically as the U.S. economy plunged into a downward spiral. By midmonth, the Iraq War had taken a distant second place to the struggling economy. Each day brought more bad news: the financial system was paralyzed by a series of spectacular bank and investment house failures, the stock market gyrated wildly but in a persistently downward trajectory, unemployment rose dramatically, and the housing market was in full-fledged crisis. Obama made the most of the situation, asserting that a vote for McCain would be a vote for more economic chaos. By election day Obama enjoyed a comfortable lead over McCain and went on to win the presidency, winning 52.9 percent of the popular vote and 365 electoral votes.

Obama's transition to power went smoothly, although Republicans, in the now well-established pattern of U.S. partisan politics, consistently challenged both his appointees and his statements. His nomination of former rival Hillary Clinton for secretary of state proved an adroit move, and she won easy Senate confirmation. Choosing stability over change, Obama chose to keep Robert M. Gates, a holdover from the Bush administration, in the key post of secretary of defense.

Obama's early efforts to solve the financial crisis through massive government bailouts to the financial and auto industries generated some opposition but nothing like the opposition to his health care plan, the Patient Protection and Affordable Care Act, which passed in March 2010 amid much acrimony among the Republicans, who rejected it entirely. Indeed, the legislation, soon dubbed "Obamacare," did not receive even one Republican vote in either house of Congress. In the years that followed, the Obama White House came under some criticism for having implemented a major piece of social welfare legislation without any support from the opposition party. Obama's public approval ratings began to sag late in 2009 and continued to fall into 2010 before moving higher during 2011 and 2012.

Internationally, Obama's assumption of the presidency was initially well received, particularly his apparent willingness to reach out to European and other allies, reset deteriorating relations with Russia, and undertake new diplomatic initiatives and approaches to the Muslim world. In October 2009, Obama was awarded the Nobel Peace Prize. The oddity of this award was that the deadline for the nomination was within weeks of his inauguration, and thus he was not really recognized for any action as much as for his promise to promote international cooperation and stability.

In December 2009 after much study and internal debate, the Obama administration announced a troop surge in Afghanistan. The surge deployed some 33,000 additional troops to deal with the worsening Taliban insurgency and would occur over a 6-month period, from January to June 2010. Obama, however, stipulated that troop withdrawals from Afghanistan would begin 18 months after the surge ended in June 2010. Obama's strategy met some opposition. Many Democrats disagreed with the surge, and many Republicans found a mandated timetable for troop withdrawals ill-advised and shortsighted. Nevertheless, the last of the additional troops were withdrawn on schedule from Afghanistan in September 2012.

The Republican assault on Obamacare combined with a still-struggling economy resulted in the Democrats losing control of the House of Representatives in the November 2010 midterm elections, although they retained control of the Senate by a narrow margin. This created a badly divided government that precipitated repeated crises and showdowns over fiscal and tax policies between the White House and Congress, including a government shutdown in the fall of 2013. These developments tended to work more against the Republicans, who were perceived as do-nothing obstructionists, but also significantly reduced Obama's ability to marshal other items on his political agenda through Congress.

On May 1, 2011, acting on intelligence information, Obama issued an order for U.S.

Navy SEALs to raid a compound in Abbottabad, Pakistan, housing Osama bin Laden, leader of the Al Qaeda terrorist network. Bin Laden and four others, including one of bin Laden's wives and one of his sons, were killed in the raid, and computers were seized. There were no U.S. causalities during the operation. The death of bin Laden fulfilled what had been a priority for U.S. forces in the invasion of Afghanistan that began in October 2001 following the terror attacks of September 11, 2001, masterminded by bin Laden. Obama was widely lauded for the handling of the raid but not in Pakistan, where the government had not been consulted and saw the raid as an invasion of Pakistani sovereignty.

During his 2012 reelection campaign Obama cited sustained job growth, the auto industry bailout, and Obamacare among his greatest domestic policy achievements and the end of the Iraq War (which occurred in December 2011) and the death of bin Laden among his most noteworthy foreign policy accomplishments. Following a tight race against the Republican nominee, former Massachusetts governor Mitt Romney, Obama won reelection to a second term in office in November 2012 by a fairly comfortable margin, garnering 51.1 percent of the popular vote and 332 electoral votes.

Meanwhile, Obama's troop surge strategy in Afghanistan had yielded few lasting results, and since 2013 the Afghan insurgency led by the Taliban had grown more threatening. By 2014 U.S.-Afghan relations had plummeted, with Afghan president Hamid Karzai blaming the United States for increasing violence in his country. The Obama administration threatened to withdraw all U.S. forces from Afghanistan by December 31, 2014, unless the Afghan government signed the status of forces agreement that Karzai had already negotiated and that had been approved by a *loya jirga* (Afghan assembly of notables). Karzai's successor, Ashraf Ghani, signed the agreement on September 30, 2014. The active combat phase of the Afghanistan War ended officially on December 31, 2014, but as many as 10,800 U.S. troops, along with 4,000 North Atlantic Treaty Organization troops, remained in Afghanistan during 2015 in recognition of the vulnerability of that country to Taliban attacks.

In February 2013, John F. Kerry was sworn in as U.S. secretary of state; he succeeded Hillary Clinton, who had planned to serve only one term. Kerry immediately set the stage for new peace talks between the Palestinians and Israelis, an effort that nevertheless foundered in less than a year. He also sought to reinvigorate negotiations with Iran over its alleged nuclear weapons program, an endeavor that received a major boost in late 2013 by Iran's newly elected moderate president, Hassan Rouhani.

Obama's second term was marred by several foreign policy crises, including the ongoing Syrian Civil War, the Russian seizure of Crimea in March 2014 and military intervention in eastern Ukraine, and the rise of the Islamic State of Iraq and Syria (ISIS). Obama resisted calls to become directly involved in the Syrian Civil War, although in the summer of 2014, with ISIS on the march in both Syria and Iraq, he agreed to begin arming select moderate Syrian rebel groups who were battling ISIS forces. In July, Obama reluctantly dispatched several thousand U.S. military personnel to help Iraq stem the tide of the ISIS advance, which was within 60 miles of Baghdad. By August he also turned up the pressure against sectarian and ineffectual Iraqi premier Nuri al-Maliki, who finally resigned under domestic and international pressure in September. At the same time, Obama and Kerry were cobbling together a broad international coalition of nations, including several Arab countries, in order to defeat ISIS. With that coalition in place, and with American air strikes in Iraq under way since early August, the coalition campaign against ISIS in Syria commenced in late September 2014. By the end of his presidency, the anti-ISIS air campaign had begun to yield results, as the extremist group suffered a series of military defeats in northern Syria and northwestern Iraq. Obama was quick to point out, however, that the struggle against ISIS would not likely end quickly.

In the meantime, the Obama administration was stung by the Democrats' loss of the House of Representatives in the November 2014 elections, which handed control of both houses of Congress to the Republicans. By the fall of 2014 Obama's approval rating had dipped markedly, in part a result of his perceived hesitancy to deal quickly and decisively with the recent foreign policy challenges and his administration's less than confident reaction to an Ebola epidemic sweeping across West Africa. Oddly enough, the U.S. economy by late 2014 was more robust than it had been since the Bill Clinton administration, a situation aided by plummeting oil prices, but these developments did not seem to affect voters' overall perception of the Democrats or of their president. Prior to the 2014 elections the Obama White House did a poor job, however, of touting the improving economy or pointing out that Obamacare was working better than even its supporters had hoped.

Some of Obama's problems were the result of his aloof, professional leadership style; his perceived hesitancy while making major decisions; and his inability or unwillingness to engage more directly with Congress, even when his own party controlled it. On the other hand, Obama's struggles during his second term are not unlike those of his recent predecessors, all of whom suffered political and/or personal reversals after their reelection. Indeed, almost every president since Franklin D. Roosevelt experienced a period of growing public ennui with his leadership after being elected to another term in office.

Despite the historic nature of the Obama presidency, it ended like every other presidency since George H. W. Bush, with a handoff to the opposing party. In January of 2017 the Obama administration surrendered the White House to the Republicans as Donald J. Trump took office following a controversial campaign and election. According to Gallup, Obama's average approval rating upon exiting the White House was 47.9 percent, ranking him ninth among the last 12 presidents. Only Gerald Ford, Jimmy Carter, and Harry Truman had a lower average approval rating during their presidencies. This is perhaps to be expected given the expanding divisions that continue to exist in American politics.

Paul G. Pierpaoli Jr.

See also: Bush, George Walker; Consequences of the Iraq War; Secretary of Defense, U.S.: Robert M. Gates; Secretary of State, U.S.: Hillary R. Clinton

References

Maraniss, David. *Barack Obama: The Story.* New York: Simon and Schuster, 2012.

Obama, Barack. *Dreams from My Father: A Story of Race and Inheritance.* New York: Three Rivers, 2004.

Obama, Barack. *The Audacity of Hope: Thoughts on Reclaiming the American Dream.* New York: Three Rivers, 2007.

Obama for America. *Change We Can Believe In: Barack Obama's Plan to Renew America's Promise.* New York: Three Rivers, 2008.

Sides, John, and Lynn Vavreck. *The Gamble: Choice and Chance in the 2012 Presidential Election. Princeton, NJ:* Princeton University Press, 2013.

Woodward, Bob. *Obama's Wars.* New York: Simon and Schuster, 2010.

Oil

A strategic nonrenewable energy resource at the center of debates regarding the U.S. role in international politics and economics, particularly in the Middle East. Oil from the Middle East has long been an essential security priority of the United States and other industrialized nations and a major source of energy for the world economy. Strategic concerns about access to petroleum reserves played a key role in virtually all regional Middle East conflicts after World War II, including the Iran-Iraq War (1980–1988), the Persian Gulf War (1991), and the Iraq War (2003–2011).

In Paris at the end of 1968, the director of the U.S. State Department Office of Fuels and Energy informed delegates of the Oil Committee of the Organization of Economic Cooperation and Development that American oil production would soon reach capacity. Until very recently, growing oil demand caused U.S. economic and military dependence on foreign petroleum production to be an important part of national and international political and economic debates.

The Persian Gulf basin is the source of approximately two-thirds of all known global petroleum reserves. Of the major oil producers, Saudi Arabia has the largest proven reserve, with 264 billion barrels. Iraq has the third-largest reserve of conventional oil in the world, with a total of 115 billion barrels. Middle East oil production played a central role in the 1991 Persian Gulf War, the Global War on Terrorism that began in 2001, and the Iraq War that began in 2003. The geopolitical importance of oil is clear in the international dialogue regarding these conflicts. Indeed, a conflict between Iraq and Kuwait, largely over the price of oil and a disputed oil field, led Iraqi dictator Saddam Hussein to invade Kuwait in August 1990, which served as the principal catalyst for the Persian Gulf War. An American-led international coalition evicted Hussein's troops from Kuwait in February 1991.

While retreating from Kuwait, Iraqi Army troops set many Kuwaiti oil fields on fire, causing a significant short-term oil shortage in the world market and a major spike in oil prices. The shortage was quickly remedied by increased production within the Organization of Petroleum Exporting Countries (OPEC) and the utilization of U.S. and International Energy Agency strategic petroleum reserves. Despite these measures, the instability of the global oil supply caused the international price of oil to rise to a record of $40.42 per barrel in late winter of 1991. Following the war, Iraq received heavy economic sanctions but was later permitted by the United Nations to import certain products under the Oil-for-Food Programme.

Despite the fact that Iraqi oil output was severely limited, world oil supplies became plentiful by the mid-1990s, and by 1999 an oil glut caused prices to drop to as low as $22 per barrel. In the United States, gasoline was selling in most places for less than 99 cents per gallon.

After the terrorist attacks of September 11, 2001, the fact that 15 of the 19 Islamist terrorists who hijacked the airliners used to carry out the attacks were Saudis initiated a close examination of the political and economic relationship between the United States and Saudi Arabia, the country's largest supplier of foreign oil.

The resultant Global War on Terrorism also sharply increased U.S. military involvement in the Middle East. The United States invaded Afghanistan in October 2001 (Operation Enduring Freedom) with a considerable amount of world support. In March 2003 the United States, the United Kingdom, and a small international coalition extended the war by invading Iraq (Operation Iraq Freedom) with the stated goal of ending the international threat posed by the regime of Saddam Hussein, which allegedly sponsored international terrorism and possessed weapons of mass destruction (WMD). Coalition forces quickly defeated the Iraqi Army, but they were unable to establish a stable government, and no active WMD program was found.

The inability to achieve political stability had a profoundly negative effect on Iraqi oil production. In 2003 Iraqi production ceased, causing a loss of 2 million barrels a day. This affected the global oil market and sent prices higher. In 2006 Iraq's oil production was still down 600,000 barrels per day from prewar production levels. By the end of 2007, however, production had reached prewar levels.

The Iraqi production lapse had a profound impact on the international oil market. The lack of excess production capacity in addition to refinery shortages and individual production problems in the OPEC nations only exacerbated the effects of the Iraqi shortage on the global economy. The United States also decided not to tap oil from its strategic petroleum reserve. Because of continuing growth in world demand in a time of relative oil scarcity and instability, petroleum prices increased dramatically, reaching $80–$90 per barrel at the beginning of 2007 and $140 per barrel by mid-2008. From that high, however, oil prices dropped substantially by the end of 2008 and early 2009, a result of the global economic recession that began in late 2007.

The Iraq War effort faced domestic and international criticism from both popular and official sources. Many of the protests against the war have centered around the themes of U.S. dependency on foreign oil, control of oil production, and rising oil prices. Among other nations, the war enhanced tensions among the United States, Iran, and Venezuela, also major international oil producers.

As early as 2003, international commentators alleged that the Bush administration had used military force in Iraq because the country had the potential to destabilize the international oil market. In 2003 the White House and the Department of Defense denied that oil was part of the motivation for the Iraq War. However, in the summer of 2005 President George W. Bush argued that U.S. troops needed to continue fighting in Iraq to prevent the country's oil fields from coming under the control of terrorist extremists. The Energy Task Force, headed by Vice President Richard Cheney, also noted the fundamental importance of the region, especially considering the dependence of the United States on oil imports. By 2008 thanks to the situation in Iraq, disruptions due to unrest in Nigeria, and growing demand in such nations as China and India, oil prices had reached historic highs, hitting more than $140 per barrel.

In the United States, the surging fuel prices spiked inflation to its highest level in 17 years and, along with depreciating home prices, a major slump in homes sales, and the subprime mortgage crisis, threatened to tilt the economy into a full-blown recession. By the summer of 2008 gasoline prices were averaging more than $4 per gallon, drying up demand for large vehicles such as light trucks and sport-utility vehicles and hammering the domestic car industry. Skyrocketing gas prices hit all sectors of the economy and reined in consumer spending as a whole.

The resulting sharp economic retraction once again forced oil prices down, but when an economic recovery commenced in 2010, oil prices recovered, approaching $95–$105 per barrel.

Since 2009, a revolution in oil extraction in Canada and the United States involving hydraulic fracking and the exploitation of vast oil tar sands has greatly increased oil production in those countries. By late 2014 this revolution had resulted in a dramatic drop in world oil prices and made the United States, the world's largest oil consumer, much less dependent on foreign oil supplies. It also began to erode the primacy of OPEC. Indeed, the United States became the world's largest oil producer in 2014, outproducing even Saudi Arabia.

Christopher R. W. Dietrich

See also: Bush, George Walker; Cheney, Richard Bruce; Iraq, History of, 1990–Present; Iraqi Freedom, Operation

References

Klare, Michael T. *Blood and Oil: The Dangers and Consequences of America's Growing Dependency on Imported Petroleum.* New York: Owl Books, 2005.

Roberts, Paul. *The End of Oil: On the Edge of a Perilous New World.* Boston: Houghton Mifflin, 2004.

"U.S. Seen as Biggest Oil Producer after Overtaking Saudi Arabia." Bloomberg, July 4, 2014, http://www.bloomberg.com/news/2014-07-04/u-s-seen-as-biggest-oil-producer-after-overtaking-saudi.html.

Yergin, Daniel. *The Prize: The Epic Quest for Oil, Money, and Power.* New York: Simon and Schuster, 1993.

Phantom Strike, Operation (August 13, 2007)

A Multi-National Force–Iraqi Army offensive launched on August 13, 2007. The attackers numbered some 28,000 troops, many of whom were present as a result of the George W. Bush administration's troop surge, which had begun earlier in the year. Following on the heels of recent coalition offensive operations, which began in June 2007, including Fardh al-Qanoon (Baghdad Security Plan) and Phantom Thunder (a nationwide counteroffensive), Operation Phantom Strike was designed to root out remaining Al Qaeda in Iraq terrorists and Iranian-backed extremist elements (including the Mahdi Army) and to reduce sectarian violence—with the goal of restoring law and order for the Iraqi people. Phantom Strike was led by U.S. Army Lieutenant General Ray Odierno, then commander of the Multi-National Corps–Iraq. It was a joint mission conducted with the Iraqi Security Force. Opposing them were Abu Omar al-Baghdadi and Abu Ayyub al-Masri, leaders of Al Qaeda in Iraq. Phantom Strike was begun one month before General David Petraeus, commander of all coalition forces in Iraq, was to report to the U.S. Congress on progress in Iraq.

During the operation, coalition and Iraqi security forces went into previously unsecured regions and attempted to eliminate terrorist groups from safe havens in the capital city of Baghdad and the provinces of northern Babil, eastern Anbar, Salahuddin, and Diyala. Considerable emphasis was placed on destroying the terror cells in Baghdad, Diyala, and central and northern Iraq. Largely an intelligence-driven operation, Phantom Strike had coalition forces move into previous no-go zones and establish local security forces and intelligence networks designed to pinpoint the exact makeup and location of Sunni and Shia extremist groups while also rooting out Al Qaeda operatives in outlying regions of Baghdad and the more violent provinces. Both the Baghdad Security Plan and Phantom Thunder shaped the culminating operations for Phantom Strike.

Coalition and Iraqi security forces launched dozens of raids in and around Baghdad. These included units of varying sizes and composition. Among those American and Iraqi units participating in the total operation were troops of the 3rd Stryker Brigade Combat Team, the 2nd Infantry Division, the 3rd Brigade Combat Team, the 1st Cavalry Division, the 25th Combat Aviation Brigade, and the Iraqi Army 1st and 4th Divisions. Strike forces went into action by land and air. In some of the attacks, it was a matter of getting in and out quickly. In others, the forces remained for an extended period in order to keep the insurgents on the defensive and thus turn former "safe" insurgent areas into places too risky for them to return. Commanders of the surge forces were told only to take territory they could hold. As part of General Petraeus's new counterinsurgency strategy, Phantom Strike resulted in coalition forces moving out of their bases and into neighborhoods all across Baghdad and other major urban centers in the country in order to establish a security area based on the doctrine of clear, control, and retain.

Phantom Strike marked the last military offensive of Operation Phantom Thunder and lasted until January 2008. From June 16 to August 19, 2007, alone, some 1,196 insurgents were killed and 6,702 captured. The precise number of killed or captured during the entire effort is uncertain. Eleven U.S. military personnel died during the operation; the number of Iraqi government casualties is unknown. The operation was termed a success in that insurgent groups were ejected from their strongholds in northern Babil, eastern Anbar, and Diyala Provinces and the southern outskirts of Baghdad. Furthermore, the raids conducted during Phantom Strike gathered valuable information on Al Qaeda and Iranian-backed terror cells countrywide.

Charles Francis Howlett

See also: Commanders, Multi-National Force–Iraq: David H. Petraeus, Raymond T. Odierno

References

Filkins, Dexter. *The Forever War.* New York: Knopf, 2008.

Roggio, Bill. "Coalition, Iraqi Forces Launch Operation Phantom Strike." *The Long War Journal,* August 13, 2007, http://longwarjournal.org/archives.

West, Bing. *The Strongest Tribe: War, Politics, and the Endgame in Iraq.* New York: Random House, 2008.

Phantom Thunder, Operation (June 16–August 14, 2007)

Corps-size operation carried out by coalition forces in Iraq (American and Iraq Security Forces) that commenced on June 16, 2007, under the command of General David Petraeus (Multi-National Force–Iraq, overall headquarters) and Lieutenant General Raymond Odierno (Multi-National Corps–Iraq, major troop force). Operation Phantom Thunder was part of the U.S. troop surge strategy implemented in January 2007 and was designed to root out extremist groups, including Al Qaeda, from Iraq. Phantom Thunder involved several subordinate operations, including Operations Arrowhead Ripper in Diyala Province, Marne Torch and Commando Eagle in Babil Province, Fardh al-Qanoon in Baghdad, Alljah in Anbar Province, and special forces attacks against the Mahdi Army in southern Iraq. In preparation for this campaign against the so-called Baghdad Belt, an additional five American brigades were deployed to Iraq between January and June 2007.

As the buildup began, Operation Law and Order started on February 14, 2007, in an effort to resecure Baghdad, with estimates running as high as almost 70 percent of the city under insurgent control. It became part of Operation Phantom Thunder when American and Iraqi forces moved to clear Sunni insurgents, Al Qaeda fighters, and Shiite militiamen from Baghdad's northern and southern flanks. The United States wanted to take quick advantage of the arrival of 30,000 additional troops, so the offensive was begun as soon as possible. During Operation Law and Order, 311 insurgents were killed.

Operation Marne Torch began on June 16 in Arab Jabour and Salman Pak, major transit points for insurgent forces in and out of Baghdad. By August 14, some 2,500 allied troops had killed 88 insurgents, captured more than 60 suspected terrorists, destroyed 51 boats, and destroyed 51 weapons caches.

On June 18, Operation Arrowhead Ripper commenced when multinational troops assaulted Al Qaeda forces in the city of

Baquba in Diyala Province with nighttime air strikes. As the ground forces moved in, intense street fighting engulfed the center of the city near the main market. By August 19, U.S. and Iraqi forces had killed 227 insurgents.

Multinational forces began Operation Commando Eagle on June 21 in the Mahmudiyyah region southwest of Baghdad. The area was known as the "Triangle of Death" because three U.S. soldiers had been kidnapped and killed there in mid-May 2007. Employing Humvee-based attacks supported by helicopter gunships, the operation resulted in roughly 100 insurgents killed and more than 50 captured.

Operations Fardh al-Quanoon and Alljah were also conducted by multinational forces, this time west of Baghdad. The primary targets were Fallujah (Alljah), Karma, and Thar Thar. Allied planners developed a concept of attack similar to the one that took Ramadi in 2003. On June 17 a raid near Karma killed a known Libyan Al Qaeda fighter and six of his aides. Four days later, six Al Qaeda leaders were killed and five were captured near Karma. By the end of July, ground commanders reported that Karma and Thar Thar had been secured.

Throughout the summer, U.S. air strikes also proved effective against insurgents in Fallujah. However, on June 22 insurgents retaliated with two suicide bombing attacks on off-duty police officers that left four dead. On June 29 U.S. forces killed Abu Abd al-Rahman al-Masri, a senior Egyptian Al Qaeda leader, east of Fallujah. They also captured and killed many others in the ensuing weeks. Fallujah proved hard to secure, and while officials declared it secure in late August, periodic incidents continued to occur well into 2008.

The final part of Phantom Thunder was the action against the Mahdi Army. In June, Iraqi special forces, the core of the joint Iraqi-American operation, killed and captured dozens of Mahdi Army troops.

Several lesser operations were also conducted against retreating insurgent forces in which an additional 234 were killed by August 14, when the operation officially came to an end and Operation Phantom Strike began. Operation Arrowhead Ripper continued for another five days until street fighting in Baquba ended. This action blended into Operation Phantom Strike.

Official reports of the action stated that coalition and Iraqi security forces had pushed into areas previously not under their control and had killed or expelled insurgent forces from northern Babil, eastern Anbar, and Diyala Provinces as well as from the southern outskirts of Baghdad. During the operation, Iraqi and coalition forces conducted intelligence raids against Al Qaeda in Iraq and the Iranian-backed cells nationwide.

Iraqi and coalition forces conducted 142 battalion-level joint operations, detaining 6,702 insurgents, killing 1,196, and wounding 419. Of this number, 382 were high-value targets. They captured 1,113 weapons caches and neutralized more than 2,000 improvised explosive devices (IEDs) and vehicle-borne IEDs. Of the approximately 28,000 U.S. and Iraqi military personnel who took part in Phantom Thunder, 140 American soldiers died; the number of wounded has not been determined. Of the Iraqi security forces who fought with the Americans, 220 died; the number of wounded is not known. An additional 20 Iraqis died fighting in U.S.-allied militia units.

William P. Head

See also: Arrowhead Ripper, Operation; Insurgency and Opposition: Mahdi Army; Iraqi Freedom, Operation: The Surge and the

Awakening; Islamic State of Iraq and al-Sham (ISIS): Al Qaeda in Iraq; Phantom Strike, Operation

References

"Operation Phantom Thunder." Institute for the Study of War, http://www.understandingwar.org/operation/operation-phantom-thunder.

Roggio, Bill. "Operation Phantom Thunder: The Battle of Iraq." *The Long War Journal*, June 21, 2007, http://www.longwarjournal.org/archives/2007/06/operation_phantom_fu.php.

Political Parties, Iraq

Under the regime of Saddam Hussein there was only one allowed political party in Iraq—the Baath Party. In the entries below, it is clear that parties existed as a form of social and political organization, but they were not allowed to participate in the process of governance. Following the toppling of the regime and the establishment of the Coalition Provisional Authority, political parties became the norm in Iraq. The first parliamentary election was held in January 2005 with another in December 2005 and the last during the U.S. occupation happening in 2010. Iraq, under the post-Saddam constitution formed a parliamentary system that requires a majority of seats to form a government. This has regularly required a coalition of parties to rule. The parties have also tended to form themselves into alliances to gain greater influence in the system. Kurdish parties, for example, which often have significant disagreements on the conduct of politics in the Kurdish region of Iraq, typically combine to form an alliance in the national elections and therefore they have a larger share of seats in the national parliament than if they were to have campaigned as separate parties.

Influence of political parties grew throughout the U.S. occupation as this was the way for average people to express their opinions at a national level. The entries below represent several of the most influential parties with respect to U.S. decisions during the Iraq War.

Islamic Dawa Party

Iraqi Shia political party founded in 1958 by junior Islamic clerics (*ulama*), merchants, and religious intellectuals in the Shiite holy city of Najaf. The party sought to achieve a staged implementation of an Islamic governing system based on Islamic law. The party's name in Arabic, Hizb al-Da'wa al-Islamiyya, translates roughly as the "Islamic Call Party." The Arabic word *dawa* in this context refers to "call" or "invitation" in the religious missionary sense. The party's founding council included several Shiite clerics who would rise to prominence in later decades, including Muhammad Mahdi al-Hakim and Muhammad Baqir al-Hakim, sons of Grand Ayatollah Muhsin al-Hakim, the preeminent Shiite religious scholar in Iraq from 1955 until his death in 1970.

Baqir al-Hakim founded the Supreme Council for Islamic Revolution in Iraq (recently renamed the Supreme Islamic Iraqi Council) in 1982 while in exile in Tehran, Iran, with the support of Grand Ayatollah Ruhollah Khomeini and the Iranian revolutionary government. The Dawa Party's unofficial religious guide was Ayatollah Muhammad Baqir al-Sadr (1935–1980), an activist Iraqi cleric, a noted Islamic thinker and author, and a student of Muhsin al-Hakim. Subsequently, many Dawa Party members were arrested, imprisoned, and killed by Iraqi Baathists, and hundreds of others went into self-imposed exile in Iran, the Persian Gulf states, and Europe. Some returned to Iraq in 2003 following the overthrow of Iraqi dictator Saddam Hussein and his Baath Party in the spring of 2003.

Baqir al-Sadr was a prolific writer who penned numerous books on subjects ranging from Islamic economics and philosophy to the establishment of an Islamic state and is probably best known for an early two-volume work on Islamic economics. His ideas influenced the formation of the Islamic state in Iran, and he was known as the "Khomeini of Iraq." He also wrote several textbooks on Islamic jurisprudence and Koranic hermeneutics, which remain classics in modern Shiite thought and are still used in Shiite and even Sunni seminaries today. His theory of *wilayat al-ummah* (governance or authority of the people) and proposals for a four-stage implementation of an Islamic system of governance were the basis of the Dawa Party's founding political platform.

In the first stage of this process, Islamic principles and ideas would be spread by Dawa members to build party membership and create a viable political constituency. In the second stage, once it had laid this groundwork, the party would enter the political realm and seek to build up its power and influence. The third stage would witness the party removing the ruling secular elite from power. In the final stage, triumphant Dawa members would establish an Islamic system of government in which clerics would play a substantial role but would not govern day-to-day affairs.

Baqir al-Sadr broke formal ties with the party in 1961 at the insistence of his teacher, Grand Ayatollah Hakim, because affiliation with the party would have compromised Sadr's scholarly status; clerics were to remain at least somewhat separate from political parties. However, he reportedly maintained ties to the party and continued to serve as a *marja,* or spiritual leader, to Dawa members. Sadr was executed because of his political activism in April 1980, along with his sister Amina bint Haydar al-Sadr (also known as Bint al-Huda), on the direct orders of Saddam Hussein.

The Dawa Party expanded its membership between 1958 and 1963, taking advantage of a series of military coups beginning with the overthrow of the Hashemite monarchy in 1958 by Abd al-Karim Qasim. During his tenure of office, the Dawa Party competed with secular Iraqi political parties, such as the Iraqi Communist Party, which were gaining ground among Iraqi youths, including many Shias. The growing number of Iraqi Shiite activists came under increasing pressure during the 1960s, and the detachment of the senior Shiite *ulama* from politics convinced these activists that an alternative to the religious elite was needed to achieve their political goals. The party recruited in Najaf, at Baghdad University, and in the Thawra slum of Baghdad, later known as Saddam City (and now Sadr City).

The Baath Party's seizure of power in July 1968 marked a new chapter in the relationship between the Dawa Party and the central Iraqi government. In April 1969 Grand Ayatollah Hakim refused to issue a fatwa (juridical opinion) in support of Iraqi president and Baath Party chief Ahmad Hassan al-Bakr in his dispute with Mohammad Reza Shah Pahlavi of Iran over control of the Shatt al-Arab waterway. Angered, Bakr cracked down on Shiite political, social, and religious institutions. In response, Hakim issued a fatwa prohibiting Muslims from joining the Baath Party. Hakim's death in 1970 led to a split within the Iraqi Shias, with political activists looking to Baqir al-Sadr and political quietists following Ayatollah Abu al-Qasim al-Khoi, another student of Hakim's.

Baath suppression of the Dawa Party continued in the 1970s. Hundreds of party members were arrested, imprisoned, tortured, and even executed. Despite increasing government pressure, Baqir al-Sadr continued to call for activism against the ruling Baath regime. In 1977 the government banned religious processions commemorating Ashura, a 10-day period of mourning that commemorates the martyrdom of the third Shiite imam, Hussein bin Ali, and his companions at Karbala in October 680 during the Islamic month of Muharram. Hundreds of Shias were arrested for ignoring the ban. Shortly before the arrest of Baqir al-Sadr and his sister Amina, a decree was issued by new Iraqi president Saddam Hussein that sentenced all members of the Dawa Party to death for treason. Following Baqir al-Sadr's execution, hundreds of Dawa members fled abroad to escape Baathist suppression. During their two decades in exile, party members participated in the Committee for Collection Action and the Iraqi National Congress, two major Iraqi exile political coalitions.

The exiled Dawa Party leadership and many members returned to Iraq following the U.S.- and British-led invasion during the spring of 2003. Along with the Supreme Islamic Iraqi Council, the Dawa Party was a key ally of the American, British, and coalition forces and held seats on the Iraqi Governing Council, an advisory body set up following the collapse of the Baath Party government. Dawa Party secretary-general Ibrahim al-Jafari served as the interim prime minister from April 2005 to May 2006.

After losing the political backing of the U.S. government and, more important, key Iraqi Shia leaders including Grand Ayatollah Ali al-Sistani, Jafari was replaced as prime minister and Dawa secretary-general by Nuri al-Maliki, also a Dawa adherent, in May 2006. In the 2010 parliamentary elections, the Dawa Party was part of the larger State Law of Coalition, established by Maliki. It won 89 seats, giving it just two fewer seats than the Iraqi National Movement. Maliki nevertheless remained prime minister. Maliki's coalition picked up 3 additional seats in the April 2014 parliamentary elections, giving it the largest bloc of any other coalition or party.

By the summer of 2014, Maliki was under great pressure to step aside. Even Iran, a staunch and longtime supporter of the Dawa Party, believed that Maliki's government had become untenable. In the face of a growing threat by the Islamic State of Iraq and Syria (ISIS), increased sectarian violence, and a spectacular surge in suicide and terrorist bombings, Maliki finally stepped down in September 2014. He was succeeded by Haider al-Abadi, also of the Dawa Party. Haider pledged to pursue conciliatory policies within Iraq and to work with the international coalition that was cobbled together to combat and eradicate ISIS. In July 2018 Haider al-Abadi was replaced as president of Iraq by Kurdish politician Muhammad Fuad Masum.

Christopher Paul Anzalone

See also: Baath Party; Iraq, History of, 1990–Present; Political Parties, Iraq: Supreme Iraqi Islamic Council; Prime Minister, Iraq: Ibrahim al-Jaafari, Nuri al-Maliki; Shia Islam; Sunni Islam

References

Alawi, Ali A. *The Occupation of Iraq: Winning the War, Losing the Peace.* New Haven, CT: Yale University Press, 2007.

Baram, Amatzia. "Two Roads to Revolutionary Shi'i Fundamentalism in Iraq: Hizb al-Da'wa Islamiyya and the Supreme Council of the Islamic Revolution of Iraq." In *Accounting for Fundamentalisms,* edited by Martin E. Marty and R. Schott Appleby, 531–588. Chicago: University of Chicago Press, 1994.

Jabar, Faleh A. *The Shi'ite Movement in Iraq.* London: Saqi Books, 2003.

"Prime Minister Haider al-Abadi Pledges to Unify Iraq in Fight against Islamic State." *Wall Street Journal,* September 25, 2014, http://online.wsj.com/articles/prime-mini ster-haider-al-abadi-pledges-to-unify-iraq -in-fight-against-islamic-state-1411688702.

Ruhaimi, Abdul-Halim al-. "The Da'wa Islamic Party: Origins, Actors and Ideology." In *Ayatollahs, Sufis and Ideologues: State, Religion, and Social Movements in Iraq,* edited by Faleh A. Jabar, 149–155. London: Saqi Books, 2002.

Shanahan, Rodger. "Shi'a Political Development in Iraq: The Case of the Islamic Da'wa Party." *Third World Quarterly* 25 (2004): 943–954.

Kurdistan Democratic Party

Kurdish political party operating in Kurdish-dominated northern Iraq. The Kurdistan Democratic Party (KDP) was founded in Baghdad in 1946. Mustafa Barzani, tribal chief, fervent Kurdish nationalist, and Naqshbandi sheikh, was its elected president in exile. The KDP, which generally embraces a social democratic ideology and has consistently fought for a Kurdish state, finds its support base in northern Kurdistan (i.e., Irbil, about 50 miles east of Mosul). Most members belong to the Naqshbandi Sufi order and speak the Kurmanji dialect. There are also KDPs in Iran, Syria, and Armenia as well as a KDP-Bakur in Turkey. This entry describes only the KDP operating in and around Iraq.

In 1958 Barzani returned to Iraq from exile in the Soviet Union, claiming that he could unify all Kurdish groups under his control. His return coincided with the overthrow of the Iraqi monarchy that same year. When Iraqi prime minister Abd al-Karim Qasim began forcibly deporting Kurds from Kirkuk, Barzani responded in 1961 by leading a rebellion against the Iraqi regime that lasted on and off until 1975. The Baathists controlling Iraq committed the full strength of their army and air force to destroy the Kurds and drive them into the Zagros and Taurus mountains.

Barzani, along with thousands of Kurds, fled to neighboring Iran, for Iran provided the KDP with weapons, supplies, and sanctuary. Barzani and the KDP would thus become a permanent enemy of successive Iraqi governments. In 1979 on the death of Mustafa Barzani, his son, Masud Barzani, became the leader of the KDP. He served as president of the Kurdistan Regional Government (KRG) from June 2005–November 2017.

In the late 1980s Iraqi dictator Saddam Hussein tried to eradicate the Kurds during the Anfal Campaign. As many as 4,000 Kurdish villages were destroyed, and more than 100,000 Kurds were killed. A number of members of the Barzani family, tribe, and associated relatives were among those murdered. This campaign caused the Kurds to change their strategy prior to Operation Desert Storm, which included union with competing political groups.

The KDP, the Patriotic Union of Kurdistan (PUK), and other Kurdish groups formed the Iraqi Kurdistan Front (IKF) to combine forces to fight Hussein. Once Desert Storm began in January 1991, 50 percent of the Kurdish soldiers in the Iraqi Army deserted, and some fought in conjunction with coalition troops. After Iraq's defeat in the Persian Gulf War, Kurds from all walks of life joined the IKF. Barzani and Jalal Talabani, leader of the PUK, jointly directed IKF attacks, using Peshmerga (Kurdish fighters). They seized Kirkuk and 75 percent of Kurdistan and added many Iraqi Army deserters to their ranks, thereby obtaining large numbers of heavy weapons. However, immediately after the Persian Gulf War cease-fire, the Iraqi Republican Guard destroyed many Kurdish irregular units, and by March 1991 nearly 1.5 million Kurds had become refugees.

On April 5, 1991, the United Nations (UN) passed Resolution 688, which codified the no-fly zones in northern and southern Iraq and provided for the air-dropping of food and medicine to the Kurds. At the same time, the United States and several of its allies implemented Operation Provide Comfort, a major humanitarian mission to help the embattled Kurds. On April 10, 1991, the United States established the northern no-fly zone at the 36th Parallel. On April 18, 1991, the UN created a Kurdish-controlled enclave in northern Iraq. However, because there was no political support for a long-term occupation of the region, the UN withdrew all forces on July 5, 1991.

The KDP and PUK now established control in the UN-mandated Kurdish zone. In May 1992 the Kurds founded the KRG, which is composed of, among other groups, the KDP, the PUK, and the Iraqi Communist Party. The Kurds held elections and established a joint legislative assembly with a cabinet. However, the KDP and PUK each tried to seize control of the autonomous region. Amnesty International later reported that in 1994 and 1995 both groups committed scores of killings during their battle for power.

In August 1996, 2,000 Iranian Revolutionary Guard Corps soldiers entered Iraq and attacked the KDP on behalf of the PUK. Barzani turned to Hussein for help. Soon a force of as many as 60,000 Iraqi Republican Guards entered the autonomous Kurdish region and drove the PUK from Irbil. The KDP then pushed the remnants of the PUK to the Iranian border. Hussein and the KDP now controlled all of northern Iraq.

On February 5, 1999, U.S. president Bill Clinton issued Presidential Decision Directive 99-13, which authorized the KDP and the PUK to receive U.S. military assistance through the Iraq Liberation Act (Public Law 105–338). During the 2003 invasion of Iraq, the PUK and KDP cooperated with the Anglo-American–led coalition and sent soldiers into the fight. They also removed Ansar al-Islam from the Kurdish region.

The Kurdistan Brigades, led by Dilshad Kalari (Dilshad Garmyani), publicly called for jihad against the KDP and PUK. The Kurdistan Brigades considers both Masud and PUK leader Talabani apostate politicians. Among other things, the Kurdistan Brigade decries the cooperation between the Peshmerga and the Nuri al-Maliki administration in Baghdad and has criticized the loss of control over certain areas in Kurdistan.

Many Iraqi Kurds have fully assimilated into Iraq and do not support Kurdish separatism. The Kurdish region has few resources with which to develop a viable economy, which is one reason why Kurdish nationalists want control of the Kirkuk oil fields. Since 2003 the KDP and PUK have once again united to form the Democratic Patriotic Alliance of Kurdistan in an attempt to realize a Kurdish state.

In recent years the KDP has come under considerable criticism both from within Kurdistan and from international nongovernmental agencies, including Human Rights Watch and Amnesty International, which have charged the KDP with corruption, nepotism, and violence against dissidents. KDP leaders, especially Barzani, and PUK leaders are said to have personally benefited substantially from the sale of Iraqi oil.

Calls during the 2011 Arab Spring for reform and the disbanding of the Kurdistan Regional Government led to a government crackdown and several deaths among the protesters. This in turn brought the burning of some government buildings. Its critics charge that the KDP is a group of clans, operating similarly to the Mafia.

Donald Redmond Dunne

See also: Arab Spring; Kurds; Political Parties, Iraq: Patriotic Union of Kurdistan

References

Batatu, Hanna. *The Old Social Classes and the Revolutionary Movement of Iraq: A Study of Iraq's Old Landed and Commercial Classes and of Its Communists, Ba'athists, and Free Officers.* Princeton, NJ: Princeton University Press, 1978.

Bengio, Ofra. *Saddam's Word: Political Discourse in Iraq.* New York: Oxford University Press, 1998.

Marcus, Aliza. *Blood and Belief: The PKK and the Kurdish Fight for Independence.* New York: New York University Press, 2007.

Natali, Denise. *International Aid, Regional Politics, and the Kurdish Issue in Iraq after the Gulf War.* Abu Dhabi, United Arab Emirates: Emirates Center for Strategic Studies and Research, 1999.

O'Leary, Brendan, John McGarry, and Khaled Smith. *The Future of Kurdistan in Iraq.* Philadelphia: University of Pennsylvania Press, 2005.

Stansfield, Gareth R. V. *Iraqi Kurdistan: Political Development and Emergent Democracy.* New York: Routledge, 2003.

Patriotic Union of Kurdistan

Kurdish nationalist party in northern Iraq founded and led by Jalal Talabani. The Patriotic Union of Kurdistan (PUK) split from the Kurdistan Democratic Party (KDP) during the early 1960s and existed as a coalition of several Kurdish political groups before it was officially founded in June 1975, following the collapse of the Kurdish revolt against the Iraqi government. Talabani, who died in October 2017, served as the president of Iraq from April 7, 2005, until July 24, 2014. The PUK's base of support is principally in southern Kurdistan (i.e., in Sulamaniyah), and since the 1980s it has courted rural Kurds to broaden its appeal. Most of its adherents speak the Sorani dialect, and some belong to the Qadiri Sufi order.

Talabani broke with the KDP chiefly over his refusal to serve under Massoud Barzani, son of the founder of the KDP and head of the party until November 2017. Talabani tried to consolidate his control of the entire Kurdish movement by marginalizing Barzani. Over the next several decades, the PUK and KDP fought for control of the Kurdish nationalist movement. But they also fought for and against the Iraqi and Iranian governments.

Because of the KDP's increasing support from Iran, in 1979 Talabani made overtures to Iraqi president Saddam Hussein, indicating that the PUK would cease its antigovernment activity for certain concessions. Hussein, however, was unwilling to meet these, which included giving the PUK control of the Kirkuk oil fields, allowing Kurdish forces to provide local security, and developing independent financial systems. During the 1980–1988 Iran-Iraq War, the PUK formed guerrilla units and established links with Iran to obtain financial and military support.

As mentioned in the previous entry, Saddam Hussein attempted to eradicate the Kurds during the Iran-Iraq War through the use of chemical weapons. He succeeded in killing more than 100,000, but his actions did something that would never have happened otherwise: they unified the Kurds against a common enemy. In 1988 the KDP and PUK united to form the Iraqi Kurdistan Front (IKF), which Talabani and Barzani directed jointly. In the wake of Hussein's defeat in the 1991 Persian Gulf War, and with the assistance of Kurdish soldiers who had deserted from the Iraqi Army during that conflict, the IKF launched a revolt against the Iraqi government (see previous entry). During the international relief efforts that followed, the KDP and PUK parted ways, each striving for control of the Kurdish region.

In May 1992, the Kurds founded the Kurdistan Regional Government (KRG). Elections were held, and a joint legislative assembly was established. Ultimately, a civil war broke out in which both the KDP and the PUK committed countless murders in an attempt to gain power. In 1996, the PUK sought the assistance of the Iranian Revolutionary Guard Corps in attacking the KDP, and the KDP sought the assistance of Saddam Hussein's government in attacking the PUK. In 1999 U.S. president Bill Clinton issued a directive authorizing U.S. military assistance to the Kurds through the Iraq Liberation Act (Public Law 105–338). Both the PUK and the KDP supported the 2003 Anglo-American invasion of Iraq.

At present, the prospect of a truly unified administration within the KRG seems remote. The PUK continues to demand progress toward Kurdish autonomy in exchange for its continued support of all the KRG initiatives, but many Kurds believe they would be better off building their region and are therefore opposed to immediate Kurdish separatism.

The PUK is organized into eight bureaus, each designed to administer to a particular need of the party and of Kurds more generally. They include the Bureau of Organization, the Bureau of Information, the Bureau for Culture and Democratic Organization, the Bureau of Finance and Management, the Bureau for Human Rights, the Bureau for Social Affairs, the Bureau for Martyrs and Veterans' Affairs, and the Bureau for International Relations. The party is divided into 36 branches, each with its own head and two deputies. Depending on the number of PUK members in each branch, the number of assistant deputies ranges from four to eight. There are also 2 party branches that include Peshmerga.

During the Iraqi Kurdistan legislative election of 2009, the PUK suffered a major setback when it narrowly lost the city of Sulaymaniyah, a stronghold for the party. Observers believed that the PUK lost the city because of reports of widespread corruption and nepotism within the PUK hierarchy.

Donald Redmond Dunne

See also: Kurds; Political Parties, Iraq: Kurdistan Democratic Party

References

Batatu, Hanna. *The Old Social Classes and the Revolutionary Movement of Iraq: A Study of Iraq's Old Landed and Commercial Classes and of Its Communists, Ba'athists, and Free Officers.* Princeton, NJ: Princeton University Press, 1978.

Bengio, Ofra. *Saddam's Word: Political Discourse in Iraq.* New York: Oxford University Press USA, 1998.

Marcus, Aliza. *Blood and Belief: The PKK and the Kurdish Fight for Independence.* New York: New York University Press, 2007.

Natali, Denise. *International Aid, Regional Politics, and the Kurdish Issue in Iraq after the Gulf War.* Abu Dhabi, United Arab Emirates: Emirates Center for Strategic Studies and Research, 1999.

O'Leary, Brendan, John McGarry, and Khaled Smith. *The Future of Kurdistan in Iraq.* Philadelphia: University of Pennsylvania Press, 2005.

Stansfield, Gareth R. V. *Iraqi Kurdistan: Political Development and Emergent Democracy.* New York: Routledge, 2003.

Supreme Iraqi Islamic Council

Shia resistance group founded in 1982 and a powerful political party in post-2003 Iraq. The Supreme Iraqi Islamic Council (SIIC) was created and known for decades as the Supreme Council for the Islamic Revolution in Iraq (SCIRI). It is an Islamist-oriented organization whose goal has been the creation of an Islamic-based regime in Iraq. The group advocates a decentralized Iraqi government and the establishment of an autonomous zone reserved for Shiites in the south of Iraq. The party's name was changed in 2007 to remove the term "Islamic Revolution" from the official title. This move also seemed to signal a concern on the part of the SIIC to eschew the advocacy of civil and sectarian violence in Iraq, and to draw more Iraqis into its ranks.

SCIRI was formed in 1982 during the Iran-Iraq War. At that time, the Islamic Dawa Party, Iraq's principal Islamist group, was severely repressed by the Saddam Hussein regime. SCIRI was formed as a party in exile in Iran, with the backing of the Iranian regime, and contrasted with the Islamic Dawa Party, many of whose members left Iran because they did not wish to fight Iraqis in the Iran-Iraq War. Muhammad Baqir al-Hakim, a member of one of Iraq's most prominent Shia clerical families, came to lead the group. Upon the creation of the party, Hakim made it clear that the primary and immediate goal of the organization was to overthrow Hussein's Baathist regime and establish an Islamic state in Iraq, along the lines of the regime in Iran. But SCIRI also became an umbrella organization, allowing other Shia groups to ally with it.

SCIRI espoused the belief that ideally an Islamist regime must be controlled by Islamic scholars (*ulema*), the system that is in operation in Iran. Other Shia Islamist groups, however, did not subscribe to that framework, believing instead that the government should be guided by the whole of the Muslim community (*ummah*). Until the fall of the Hussein regime in 2003, SCIRI operated largely in exile and along the fringes of Iraqi politics.

That all changed after the Anglo-American–led invasion of Iraq in March 2003, which ousted Hussein from power. Working in tandem with other Shia groups, SCIRI moved to solidify its base and influence in a nation that had been dominated for many years by the Sunnis. Taking its cues from Islamist organizations in other countries, especially the Muslim Brotherhood and Hamas, SCIRI gained many adherents by providing humanitarian aid and basic services to displaced and poor Shia Iraqis. The United States became closer to SCIRI than to any of the other Shia parties, for despite its Islamism, the group was well organized, promised to control other Shia militias, and had English-speaking leaders, whom the Americans preferred to Ibrahim al-Jafari of the Islamic Dawa Party. However, other American and British officials sometimes viewed the party with a wary eye, as the SIIC has likely received financial support and, allegedly, weapons from Iran. In an attempt to make itself more credible, the party has soft-pedaled its devotion to revolution and the imposition of an Islamic state in Iraq since the 2003 invasion. Instead, it has stated its commitment to democratic processes and has demonstrated a willingness to cooperate with rival political parties.

Not surprisingly, the SIIC's power base is located in the center and south of Iraq. It has competed with other Shia parties, particularly Fadhila in the city of Basra, which has a heavily Shia population. The party maintains an armed militia. The first was known as the Badr Brigades, which has since separated from the SIIC. It is believed that those forces contained 5,000 to 10,000 well-armed men, the weapons of which came largely from the Iranians. After the withdrawal of coalition troops from Iraq in late 2011 and the resumption of the Iraqi insurgency, the SIIC formed another armed militia, known as the Knights of Hope. It is believed that this group has been responsible for the repression and violence against Iraqi Sunnis in recent years.

The party suffered a setback in August 2003 when its leader, Ayatollah Hakim, was killed in Najaf in a car bombing. It has been posited that Al Qaeda in Iraq was behind the murder. Hakim's brother, Abd al-Aziz al-Hakim, then took control of the organization. He died in a Tehran hospital in August 2009 of lung cancer and was succeeded by his son, Ammar al-Hakim.

In January 2005 the SIIC joined forces with the United Iraqi Alliance and captured six of the eight Shia-majority governorates and garnered 40 percent of the votes in Baghdad. Numerous SIIC members have held both official and unofficial positions with the Iraqi government. Hakim was a member of the Iraqi Governing Council, created by the United States, and served as that body's president briefly in late 2003. Hakim adeptly walked a political tightrope and managed to maintain relatively cordial relations with the United States. Indeed, he met with numerous high-level U.S. officials, including Secretary of Defense Donald Rumsfeld, and had a one-on-one meeting with President George W. Bush at the White House in December 2006.

In the 2009 Iraqi governorate elections, the SIIC coalition captured 6.6 percent of the total votes that included 14 districts. It won 52 of 440 seats, placing it second overall in the elections. The results surprised and discouraged the SIIC leadership. After the 2010 national elections and the 2013 provincial elections, the SIIC held only 12 of 325 seats in the Council of Representatives and 54 of 440 seats in Iraq's local governate councils. The SIIC's control of the southern Iraqi governorates has more recently come under fire for alleged corruption and the misdeeds of its Badr organization and the Knights of Hope militia.

Paul G. Pierpaoli Jr.

See also: Bush, George Walker; Iraq, History of, 1990–Present; Secretary of Defense, U.S.: Donald Rumsfeld

References

Nasr, Vali. *The Shia Revival: How Conflicts within Islam Will Shape the Future.* New York: Norton, 2006.

Packer, George. *The Assassins' Gate: America in Iraq.* New York: Farrar, Straus and Giroux, 2005.

Stansfield, Gareth. *Iraq: People, History, Politics.* Cambridge, UK: Polity, 2007.

Prime Minister, Iraq (Selected) (Chronological Order)

Under the Iraqi monarchy and the Baath Party rule, the prime minister of Iraq was an appointed position as the leader of parliament. According to the Iraqi Constitution accepted under the Coalition Provisional

Iraqi Governing Council (2003–2004)

• Ibrahim al-Jaafari	Islamic Dawa Party	August 1, 2003–August 31, 2003
• Ahmed al-Chalabi	Iraqi National Congress	September 1, 2003–September 30, 2003
• Ayad Allawi	Iraqi National Accord	October 1, 2003– October 31, 2003
• Jalal Talabani	Patriotic Union of Kurdistan	November 1, 2003– November 30, 2003
• Abdul Aziz al-Hakim	Supreme Council for the Islamic Revolution in Iraq	December 1, 2003–December 31, 2003
• Adnan al-Pachachi	Assembly of Independent Democrats	January 1, 2004–January 31, 2004
• Mohsen Abdel Hamid	Iraqi Islamic Party	February 1, 2004–February 29, 2004
• Mohammad Bahr al-Ulloum	Independent	March 1, 2004–March 31, 2004
• Massoud Barzani	Kurdistan Democratic Party	April 1, 2004–April 30, 2004
• Ezzedine Salim	Islamic Dawa Party	May 1, 2004–May 17, 2004 (died in office)
• Ghazi Mashal Ajil al-Yawer	Independent	May 17, 2004–June 1, 2004

Republic of Iraq (2004–Present)

• Ayad Allawi Acting Prime Minister	Iraqi National Accord	June 1, 2004–May 3, 2005
• Ibrahim al-Jaafari	Islamic Dawa Party	May 3, 2005–May 20, 2006
• Nuri al-Maliki	Islamic Dawa Party	May 20, 2006–September 8, 2014
• Haider al-Abadi	Islamic Dawa Party	September 2014–July 2018
• Adil Abd al-Mahdi	Independent	October 2018–Incumbent

Authority period the prime minister is the executive authority of the Iraqi government. The Iraqi system is parliamentary and the prime minister comes from the majority party. Absent a majority, then the prime minister comes from the party of plurality within the governing coalition. The president of Iraq has the authority to designate the party who will form a coalition government. This was a point of significance in the 2009/2010 time period when one party had two more seats, but the sitting prime minister was from a party with two fewer seats in the election, and he was designated to form the government.

Under the Iraqi Governing Council, which was the Iraqi face during the Coalition Provisional Authority period, prime ministers only served for a single month (beginning on the first and ending on the last calendar day of the month). The first parliamentary elections occurred in 2005; that election produced the first democratically elected prime minister in Iraqi history. The following table includes the names and dates of prime ministers from both the Iraqi Governing Council and the Republic of Iraq periods. The entries that follow include those for all of the appointed or elected prime ministers in the Republic of Iraq until July 2018.

Ibrahim al-Jaafari (1947–) (from August 1, 2003, to August 31, 2003, and from May 3, 2005, to May 20, 2006)

Iraqi politician who served as prime minister under the Interim Governing Council, the first elected prime minister of Iraq, and the foreign minister of Iraq from September 2014 to October 2018. He has also served as vice president. He has regularly been the spokesperson for the Islamic Dawa Party. He was born in the city of Karbala, Iraq, on March 25, 1947. He received his degree as a medical doctor from Mosul University. His family left Iraq for Iran where he remained until 1989 when he moved to London. He opposed the U.S.-led invasion in 2003, but he returned soon after to actively participate in Iraqi politics.

He brought the Islamic Dawa Party into the United Iraqi Alliance for the January 2005 election. The alliance had the plurality of seats and al-Jaafari became prime minister after nearly four months of negotiating the details of the governing coalition. He was approved as prime minister on April 28, 2005. In December 2005 elections were held again. Though his party again had the plurality of seats, the growing violence in Iraq tainted his role as prime minister. The Kurdish and Sunni parties opposed him resuming his position. After significant political maneuvering and the intervention of Grand Ayatollah Ali al-Sistani, al-Jaafari stepped aside and Nuri al-Maliki became prime minister.

In 2008, al-Jaafari started a new party, the National Reform Trend. From September 2014 to October 2018, he was the minister of foreign affairs for Prime Minister Haider al-Abadi.

Brian L. Steed

See also: Bush, George Walker; Obama, Barack Hussein, II

References

Al-Ali, Zaid. *The Struggle for Iraq's Future: How Corruption, Incompetence and Sectarianism Have Undermined Democracy.* New Haven, CT: Yale University Press, 2014.

Allawi, Ali. *The Occupation of Iraq: Winning the War.* New Haven, CT: Yale University Press, 2007.

Mansoor, Peter R. *Surge: My Journey with General David Petraeus and the Remaking of the Iraq War.* New Haven, CT: Yale University Press, 2013.

Ahmed Abd al-Hadi Chalabi (1944–2015) (from September 1, 2003, to September 30, 2003)

Prominent Iraqi dissident and founder and leader of the U.S.-funded Iraqi National Congress (INC) from 1992 to 1999. Born on October 30, 1944, in Baghdad, Iraq, Ahmed Abd al-Hadi Chalabi, a liberal Shiite Muslim, was a member of one of Iraq's wealthiest and most influential families. Prior to the 1958 revolution that overthrew the Iraqi monarchy, Chalabi's father, a prominent banker, was president of the Senate and an adviser to King Faisal II.

Although the entire royal family and many of its supporters were murdered by the revolutionaries, Chalabi's family managed to escape into exile, living primarily in England and the United States. Chalabi earned a BS degree in mathematics from the Massachusetts Institute of Technology in 1965. In 1969 he obtained a PhD in mathematics from the University of Chicago and subsequently taught mathematics at the American University in Beirut until 1977.

In 1977 Chalabi relocated to Jordan, where he established the Petra Bank. Within two years, Petra Bank had become the second-largest bank in Jordan. In 1989, Jordanian Central Bank governor Mohammad Said Nabulsi ordered the 20 banks operating in Jordan to deposit 30 percent of their foreign exchange holdings with the Central Bank. When Petra Bank refused to comply with the order, the Jordanian government launched an investigation of the bank's holdings, which revealed that most of the bank's stated assets in fact did not exist. Chalabi then fled to the United Kingdom. Although Chalabi later claimed that the entire situation was the result of Iraqi dictator Saddam Hussein's chicanery, the Jordanian government was forced to pay

$200 million to depositors to avert the complete collapse of the Jordanian banking system. In 1992, the Jordanian government sentenced Chalabi in absentia to 22 years in prison for bank fraud. Chalabi continues to proclaim his innocence in the affair.

In 1991 immediately following the Persian Gulf War, Chalabi began lobbying influential members of the U.S. Congress, the Central Intelligence Agency (CIA), and the Pentagon for funding to sponsor a coup against Hussein's government. In 1992 Chalabi formed the INC. Between 1992 and 2004 he and the INC received more than $30 million from U.S. government sources.

Many within the CIA and the U.S. State Department eventually became suspicious of Chalabi's ability to deliver on promises made concerning the opposition and attacked his veracity. But his close ties with former defense secretary vice president Dick Cheney and Deputy Secretary of Defense Paul Wolfowitz enabled Chalabi to continue to receive funding until the eve of the 2003 Anglo-American invasion of Iraq. In 1999 Chalabi broke with the INC and established the National Congress Coalition, a group that considered itself a less Islamist alternative to other Iraqi opposition groups. During the U.S. occupation of Iraq, Chalabi served as one of the deputy prime ministers in Ibrahim al-Jafari's cabinet.

When it had become patently clear that there was no active program of weapons of mass destruction in Iraq, the existence of which had been a major pretext of the 2003 war, the George W. Bush administration became more concerned about its connections with Chalabi. The information that he had been giving the administration since at least mid-2001 was either falsified or unintentionally erroneous. Be that as it may, Chalabi steadfastly stood by the top-secret reports, much of which pointed to an illicit Iraqi program to build nuclear, chemical, and biological weapons.

On May 20, 2004, U.S. and Iraqi forces raided Chalabi's residence to determine the extent of his duplicity in his dealings with American officials. Charges were briefly drawn up against him, but these were later dropped. Nevertheless, in November 2005 Chalabi flew to Washington, DC, to meet with high-level Bush administration officials.

From December 2005 to January 2006 Chalabi was Iraq's oil minister, and in April 2005 he was appointed deputy prime minister, a post he held from May 2005 to May 2006. In the December 15, 2005, elections, Chalabi suffered a humiliating defeat in his quest to become Iraqi prime minister. Allegations that he was bolstering his relations with Iranians and supposedly passed secret information to them in 2004 further tarnished his reputation in Washington. Paradoxically, his reputation in Iraq was troubled by his close relationship with the Americans.

In October 2007, Iraqi prime minister Nuri al-Maliki appointed Chalabi to head the Iraq Services Committee, a group that linked eight government service ministries and several Baghdad municipal agencies that were at the forefront of the recovery and modernization effort in postwar Iraq. In 2012, the French government asserted that Chalabi was indeed an Iranian agent. Chalabi remained a divisive and distrusted figure in much of the West, and in recent years he had remained out of the Iraqi political scene. Chalabi died of a heart attack in Baghdad on November 3, 2015.

Michael R. Hall

See also: Bush, George Walker; Cheney, Richard Bruce; Hussein, Saddam; Prime Minister,

Iraq: Ibrahim al-Jaafari, Nuri al-Maliki; Wolfowitz, Paul Dundes

References

Fox, Robert. *Peace and War in Iraq, 2003–2005.* Barnsley, UK: Leo Cooper, 2005.

Packer, George. *The Assassins' Gate: America in Iraq.* New York: Farrar, Straus and Giroux, 2005.

Ricks, Thomas E. *Fiasco: The American Military Adventure in Iraq.* New York: Penguin, 2006.

Ayad Allawi (1944–) (from October 1, 2003, to October 31, 2003, and from June 1, 2004, to May 3, 2005)

Iraqi politician who served as prime minister of Iraq's appointed interim government that assumed the governance of Iraq on June 28, 2004. He held the premiership until April 7, 2005. Allawi was born into a well-to-do family in Baghdad on May 31, 1944. His father and uncle were physicians. His father was also a member of Iraq's parliament, and his grandfather had participated in the negotiations that granted Iraq its independence in 1932. The family had commercial and political ties to both the British and the Americans.

Allawi graduated from the American Jesuits' Baghdad College, an intermediate and senior-level preparatory school, and entered the Baghdad University College of Medicine in 1961, the same year he joined the Baath Party, met future Iraqi dictator Saddam Hussein, and became active in the Iraqi National Students' Union. Allawi organized strikes and other activities against the government of Abd al-Karim Qasim. On February 8, 1963, Qassim was overthrown in a Baathist coup, which resulted in General Ahmed Hassan al-Bakr becoming prime minister. Allawi was eventually placed in charge of the central security office at the presidential palace and was given the nickname "palace doctor."

Although unproven, there are charges that Allawi participated in intense interrogations and torture that led to the deaths of trade union officials, students, and political leaders. Allawi was arrested on these charges but was released after Bakr intervened. Allawi participated in the July 17, 1968, coup that made Bakr president and excluded all but Baathists from government positions. Bakr then pressured the minister of health Ezzat Mustafa to expedite Allawi's graduation from the college of medicine.

Opposition to Allawi grew within the government, and he was sent to Beirut in 1971 before moving to London in 1972 to head the Baath National Students Union and to pursue advanced medical studies. Allawi left the Baath Party in 1975 and supposedly began working for MI6, the British foreign intelligence service. In 1976, he earned a master's of science in medicine from London University. Allawi's name was placed on an assassination list in 1978 after Iraqi president Saddam Hussein failed to convince him to rejoin the Baathists. In February 1978, Allawi and his wife were attacked by an ax-bearing intruder in their Surrey home but escaped serious injury. Allawi earned a doctorate in medicine in 1979 from London University before being certified as a neurologist in 1982.

In 1979, Allawi had begun gathering alienated former Iraqi Baathists together into a group that grew into a Hussein opposition party. It was formalized in December 1990 as the Iraqi National Accord (INA). The INA received backing from Britain, the United States, Jordan, Saudi Arabia, and Turkey. It fomented dissent among the disaffected in Iraq and committed acts of terror and sabotage in that country in an attempt to bring down the Hussein regime. Allawi and the INA were recruited by the U.S. Central Intelligence Agency (CIA) after the Persian Gulf War (1990–1991) and paid $5 million in 1995 and $6 million in 1996. The CIA supported the INA's 1996 failed military coup, code-named Dbachilles, which led to the execution of many Iraqis and to the confiscation or destruction of approximately $250 million of Allawi family assets.

The INA and Allawi gathered intelligence establishing the alleged existence of weapons of mass destruction in Iraq that formed the core of the MI6 dossier released in September 2002. This dossier formed a major part of the rationale for the 2003 U.S.- and British-led coalition invasion of Iraq in March 2003. On July 13, 2003, Allawi was appointed by Coalition Provisional Authority administrator Paul Bremer to the 25-member Iraqi Governing Council (IGC), where he served as minister of defense and assumed the rotating presidency for October 2003. Allawi resigned as head of the IGC security committee in April 2004 over alleged concerns about U.S. tactics used to subdue the 2004 Fallujah insurgency.

The coalition-led IGC transferred authority to the Iraqi Interim Government, with Allawi as the appointed interim prime minister, on June 28, 2004. During his tenure in this position, he created a domestic spy agency named the General Security Directorate to counter the Iraqi insurgency, closed the Iraqi office of the television network Al Jazeera, attempted to marginalize radical Shiite cleric Muqtada al-Sadr and his militia, and assumed the power to declare martial law. Allawi tried to draw Baathists who had not committed criminal acts during Hussein's rule into the government and considered pardoning insurgents who surrendered their weapons. Allawi stepped down as premier on April 7, 2005, the day Islamic Dawa Party leader Ibrahim al-Jaafari was elected to lead the transitional Iraqi National Assembly.

Allawi's INA won just 25 seats in the December 2005 elections establishing the permanent Iraqi National Assembly. This placed the party a distant third in the assembly, with only 14 percent of the vote. His party fared far better in the 2010 elections, however, capturing the largest plurality of votes (24.7 percent), giving it more seats than any other bloc or party. Allawi retains his dual British citizenship, and his wife and children reside in the United Kingdom for security reasons.

Richard M. Edwards

See also: Bremer, Lewis Paul, III; Iraq, History of, 1990–Present

References

Allawi, Ali. *Winning the War, Losing the Peace: The Occupation of Iraq.* New Haven, CT: Yale University Press, 2006.

Keegan, John. *The Iraq War: The Military Offensive, from Victory in 21 Days to the Insurgent Aftermath.* New York: Vintage, 2005.

Polk, William R. *Understanding Iraq: The Whole Sweep of Iraqi History, from Genghis Khan's Mongols to the Ottoman Turks to the British Mandate to the American Occupation.* New York: Harper Perennial, 2006.

Nuri al-Maliki (1950–) (from May 20, 2006, to September 8, 2014)

Iraqi political leader, prime minister (May 20, 2006–September 8, 2014), and vice president of Iraq (September 9–present). For many years, Nuri Muhammed Kamil Hasan al-Maliki was a leader of the Islamic Dawa Party, an Islamist organization that was ruthlessly suppressed by former Iraqi president

Iraqi prime minister Nuri al-Maliki served from May 20, 2006, to September 8, 2014. He represented the Islamic Dawa Party and was criticized for being too sectarian in his approach to governing. (Markwaters/Dreamstime.com)

Saddam Hussein. Until 2006 Maliki was known by the pseudonym "Jawad," which he adopted while in exile in Syria.

Maliki was born in Abi Gharq, Iraq, near Karbala, on June 20, 1950. He received a bachelor's degree at the Usul al-Din College in Baghdad and a master's degree in Arabic literature at Salahaddin University in Sulamaniyah. It was during his college years that he became politically active and joined the Islamic Dawa Party in 1968, steadily rising in the organization's hierarchy. Maliki represents the jihadist faction within the party.

When Iraqi president Saddam Hussein cracked down on the Dawa Party in the 1970s, its members were sentenced to death, even in absentia. Maliki was forced to leave Iraq in October 1979. Fleeing through Jordan, he first traveled to Syria and remained there until 1982, when he moved to Iran. He resided for a year in Ahwaz and then moved to Tehran. In September 1989, he returned to Damascus. He remained in Syria until the fall of Hussein's government in April 2003.

While in Syria, Maliki supervised the Dawa Party's publication, *Al-Mawqif,* and became head of the organization in Damascus and in Lebanon, participating in the Iraqi opposition coalition known as the Joint Action Committee in 1990. He toured the Middle East and Europe to solicit support for the Iraqi opposition movement and convened an important conference representing the various Iraqi opposition groups held in Beirut in 1991.

On his return to Iraq in 2003, Maliki served in various positions in the new Iraqi Interim Government; he was named to the National Council, headed the security committee of the transitional Iraqi National Assembly, and was then elected to the new National Assembly, where he served on the National Sovereignty Committee. He also became the chief spokesperson and negotiator for the alliance of the various Shia parties and groups known as the United Islamic Alliance during the drafting of the new Iraqi Constitution.

When Ibrahim al-Jaafari, Iraq's first prime minister, was unable to obtain support from the United States and certain Iraqi groups, Maliki was nominated as prime minister. He took office on May 20, 2006; he also served as the acting minister of the interior until June 2006.

Maliki was described by Iraq experts as a pragmatic individual who represented the Arab-Iraqi–centered orientation of the Dawa Party and was not overly influenced by Iran. However, it remained difficult for Iraqi officials to steer clear of pressure from the United States and to deal with sectarian and party loyalties in the context of intersectarian fighting, which further delayed reestablishing stability in Iraq. U.S. senator Carl Levin (D-MI), chairman of the Senate Armed Services Committee, attacked the Maliki government in August 2007 for being "too beholden to religious and sectarian leaders." At the same time, Senator Hillary Clinton (D-NY) charged that Maliki was too "divisive" a figure. Yet his political skills were demonstrated, certainly prior to his assuming the office of prime minister, in his generally good working relationships with various opposition parties. These relationships were strained later, in part because of the tension between Washington's and Baghdad's differing goals and priorities.

Under the Maliki government, the U.S. military forged new alliances with Sunni tribal elements to defeat Al Qaeda in Iraq and other Sunni insurgency groups and urged measures to reverse de-Baathification, causing concerns among Iraqi Shiites. A point of controversy was legislation regarding the sharing of oil revenues, resisted by Sunni and Kurdish leaders. A major Maliki triumph, however, was passage of the status of forces agreement of December 2008. U.S. forces, the last contingent of the international military coalition to leave Iraq, were withdrawn in December 2011.

In the 2010 parliamentary elections, the Dawa Party was part of the larger State Law of Coalition, established by Maliki. It won 89 seats, giving it just 2 fewer seats than the Iraqi National Movement. Maliki nevertheless remained prime minister. His coalition picked up 3 additional seats in the April 2014 parliamentary elections, giving it the largest bloc of any other coalition or party.

Since the departure of coalition forces in 2011, the political and security situation in Iraq steadily worsened, with Maliki becoming involved in an increasingly vitriolic and bloody crackdown against Iraq's minority Sunni population. When he secured reelection in 2010, he promised a broadly representative government that would involve Sunnis. Instead, once coalition forces vacated Iraq, he reversed course and purged his government of Sunnis and ordered the arrests of thousands of political dissidents, most of them Sunnis. Iraq's Sunnis were now effectively shut out of the governing process. These policies emboldened antigovernment militants and extremists and alienated many rank-and-file Iraqis. As time went on, Maliki became more dictatorial while his regime fostered cronyism, endemic corruption, and political and religious-based repression.

Maliki's regime fanned the flames of a potent, radical Sunni insurgency and permitted other extremist groups, such as Al Qaeda in Iraq and the Islamic State of Iraq and Syria (ISIS), to gain significant footholds in Iraq. At the same time, Maliki had permitted the Iraqi Army to languish; morale was low, training was subpar, and leadership was weak and preferential toward Shiites. By early 2014 much of Anbar Province, including Fallujah and Ramadi, had been taken over by these extremist groups, and the Iraqi Army was ill-prepared to counter the growing threat. In January 2014, the Barack Obama administration announced an emergency sale of Hellfire missiles to Iraq to help Maliki fend off ISIS gains. In May 2014, the U.S. government announced a $1 billion sale of warplanes, armored vehicles, and surveillance equipment to the Iraqi government. Meanwhile, civilian casualties sharply escalated, and in April 2014 alone at least 750 Iraqis had died in sectarian- and insurgency-based attacks.

In the summer of 2014 ISIS made major gains in Iraq, seizing Mosul and threatening to unleash a genocide against Iraq's Yazidi and Christian populations. The radical group also threatened to kill en masse any Muslims who did not subscribe to their extremist Islamic tenets. In June 2014 with ISIS units less than 100 miles from Baghdad, pressure on Maliki to step down increased substantially. By then, the Barack Obama administration had publicly rebuked the prime minister and suggested that he resign. Even Iran, a heretofore strong supporter of the Maliki government, had lost confidence in the embattled prime minister. By early August 2014, calls for Maliki to step aside grew even stronger. Indeed, even many of his allies and those in his own party urged him to resign for the good of the country. He resisted as long as he could, but on August 15 he announced that he would relinquish his post, allowing Haider al-Abadi, also of the Dawa Party, to assume the premiership. Maliki formally stepped down on September 8, 2014, at which time he became Iraq's vice president, a largely ceremonial post. The change in leadership was welcome news to U.S. policy makers, who vowed more aid in the fight against ISIS.

Sherifa Zuhur

See also: Insurgency and Opposition: Badr Organization, Mahdi Army; Iraq, History of, 1990–Present; Islamic State of Iraq and al-Sham (ISIS); Political Parties, Iraq: Islamic Dawa Party; Sadr, Muqtada al-

References

"Prime Minister Haider al-Abadi Pledges to Unify Iraq in Fight against Islamic State." *Wall Street Journal,* September 25, 2014, http://online.wsj.com/articles/prime-minister-haider-al-abadi-pledges-to-unify-iraq-in-fight-against-islamic-state-1411688702.

Raghvan, Sudarsan. "Maliki's Impact Blunted by Own Party's Fears: Hussein-Era Secrecy Persists, Analysts Say." *Washington Post,* August 3, 2007, A-01.

Shanahan, Rodger. "The Islamic Da'wa Party: Past Development and Future Prospects." *Middle East Review of International Affairs* 8(2) (June 2004): 112–125.

Woodward, Bob. *The War Within: A Secret White House History, 2006–2008.* New York: Simon and Schuster, 2008.

R

Reconstruction

When the U.S.-led coalition invaded Iraq in 2003, there was little expectation of the need to rebuild Iraq. In part, this was because the war was sold to the American people as being focused solely on regime change and that the oil wealth of Iraq would quickly pay for the cost of the war and any necessary reconstruction. It was accepted that "if we break it, we buy it," meaning that once we invade then we own the problems of Iraq. Iraq was also in worse shape than was expected. Most of this was the result of failure to maintain infrastructure caused, in part, by the sanctions imposed on Iraq from 1990 until 2003. Some of the problems were a result of the bombing campaigns directed, in part, against Iraqi infrastructure in both 1991 and 2003. When the U.S.-led coalition took control of Iraq, there was a significant need for reconstruction.

The first organization tasked to manage this was the Office for Reconstruction and Humanitarian Assistance (ORHA) led by retired marine Lieutenant General Jay Garner. This later morphed into several other primarily U.S. organizations. These have included the Iraq Construction and Management Office, the Project and Contracting Office, the U.S. Army Corps of Engineers Gulf Region Division, and the U.S. Agency for International Development (USAID). The largest of several funds for reconstruction was the Iraq Relief and Reconstruction Fund (IRRF).

A popular program with soldiers was the Commander's Emergency Response Program (CERP). These funds allowed commanders direct funding for immediate need and usually immediate results projects like removing trash from a neighborhood. The actions and results associated with this fund gave the impression of support and commitment to a community.

Madrid, Spain, hosted an Iraq donor's conference in October 2003. In preparation for this conference, the expected need for reconstruction was estimated at slightly less than $36 billion. Over the course of the occupation, the U.S. alone spent about $60 billion, and the entire global community and Iraqi government spent a total of $213 billion in reconstruction. There were certainly inaccuracies in the original understanding of the problems and the assessment. There were also significant problems in oversight and project management. In 2005, the U.S. Congress created the Special Inspector General for Iraq Reconstruction (SIGIR). The SIGIR conducted investigations of U.S. use of reconstruction funds for the remainder of the U.S. occupation of Iraq and postoccupation. The final accounting was provided to the U.S. Congress in 2013. Over the eight years of oversight the SIGIR reported on numerous cases of fraud and mismanagement. Much of the reconstruction money went to provide security as Iraq was inherently unstable and violent and the Iraqi government was unable to provide a secure work environment for construction.

Despite these problems, the reconstruction effort still built power plants that increased the production of power from a prewar capacity of about 3,400 megawatts to 8,400 megawatts by 2012. Another focus was on the improvement of sanitation and potable water. The ability to compare is difficult; however, significant investment did result in marked improvements in availability and water quality. Oil production improved from a prewar average of 2.4 million barrels a day to a 2012 average of 2.6 million barrels a day. Reconstruction programs built or repaired more than 2,900 schools and increased school attendance across the country by 27 percent. Part of reconstruction also included the creation and training of the Iraq Security Forces and the improvement of governance that included a new constitution and democratic elections.

Though rife with problems, corruption, mismanagement, and security issues, the reconstruction of Iraq did demonstrate improvement in every field of endeavor. That improvement was almost always overpriced and poorly delivered with tremendous waste. As is true with almost everything associated with the war in Iraq, reconstruction is a story of good with lots of bad.

Brian L. Steed

See also: Garner, Jay Montgomery; Secretary of Defense, U.S.: Donald Rumsfeld; U.S. Agency for International Development, Iraq; Wolfowitz, Paul Dundes

References

"Learning from Iraq: A Final Report from the Special Inspector General for Iraq Reconstruction." Washington, DC: Office of SIGIR, March 2013.

Lutz, Catherine. "Reconstructing Iraq: The Last Year and the Last Decade." Watson Institute for International Studies, Brown University, March 8, 2013, http://watson.brown.edu/costsofwar/files/cow/imce/papers/2013/Reconstructing%20Iraq.pdf (accessed May 20, 2018).

Rudd, Gordon W. *Reconstructing Iraq: Regime Change, Jay Garner, and the ORHA Story.* Lawrence: University Press of Kansas, 2011.

S

Sadr, Muqtada al- (1973–)

Influential religious figure in the Iraqi Shia community, leader of the Sadriyun that included the Mahdi Army militias, and considered by many to be the most populist of Iraqi Shiite leaders. In the 2018 parliamentary elections, his party won the plurality of seats. The fourth son of the famous Iraqi cleric Muhammad Sadiq al-Sadr, Muqtada al-Sadr was born on August 12, 1973, in Baghdad. He is also the son-in-law and nephew of the extremely influential Shiite cleric and activist, Mohamed Baqir al-Sadr. Sadr became a political leader with an enhanced following as a consequence of his nationalist stance against the coalition presence in Iraq, beginning in 2003. He acquired a loyal following of his own and, during a period of political truce with the Iraqi government, sought to enhance his standing by continuing his own religious training. Like his father and Iraq's highest Shiite religious authority, Grand Ayatollah Sayyid Ali Husayn al-Sistani, Sadr drew support from a network of mosques but also from extensive charitable and social services provided to impoverished Shia communities in various areas of Baghdad. He also has followers in many other cities and areas of southern and central Iraq. Sadr became especially popular in the large slum areas in Baghdad including the Thawra area, which became known as Sadr City from the strength of his followers there.

The elder Sadr was a revered member of the Iraqi Shiite clergy who was assassinated, along with his two elder sons, in 1999. It is widely believed that the assassination was ordered by Iraqi leader Saddam Hussein.

Muqtada al-Sadr spoke out fiercely against the actions of the U.S.-led coalition in Iraq despite his opposition, and that of his followers, to Hussein's dictatorial government. Sadr's opposition to the coalition presence was based on both political and religious considerations. After the U.S. Coalition Provisional Authority (CPA) closed Sadr's newspaper *al-Hawza* on March 28, 2004, there were numerous attacks against him in the American-funded Iraqi press. Sadr thus mobilized his militia, known as the Mahdi Army. This was to protest what he perceived as the CPA's attempt to eliminate his organization prior to the transfer of authority to Iraqi officials, scheduled for June 30, 2004. The subsequent protests turned violent when a key Sadr aide was arrested on April 3, 2004. The situation was further enflamed two days later when CPA administrator L. Paul Bremer issued a warrant for Sadr's arrest and essentially declared him an outlaw. Sadr's Mahdi Army subsequently seized control of several cities in southern Iraq, provoking the worst crisis for the U.S.-led occupation since the spring of 2003, especially as the Mahdi Army held the loyalty of the most fiercely anti-Baathist groups in the country.

During the ensuing week of violence, Sadr sought refuge in the Imam Ali Mosque in Najaf, the holiest shrine in Shia Islam. Sadr's popularity soared during this period because he appeared to be the only Iraqi leader willing to actively resist the occupation. All others, even Ayatollah Sistani, appeared to be passively silent or even acquiescent to the Western authorities. Sadr declared a cease-fire on April 10, 2004, ostensibly to observe a three-day religious holiday, but momentum had also shifted as the CPA retook certain key bases in southern cities. In subsequent negotiations, the CPA called for Sadr to surrender but refrained from overt attempts to arrest him.

In late August 2004 following more than three weeks of renewed fighting between Mahdi Army fighters and U.S. forces, Sadr's forces withdrew from the Imam Ali Mosque. Sadr issued a statement urging his fighters to lay down their arms in line with an agreement he had reached with Ayatollah Sistani. On August 27, 2004, members of the Mahdi Army began surrendering their arms to Iraqi police. But Iraqi prime minister Iyad Allawi renewed the violence when he refused to honor the tenuous truce; fighting ensued, especially in Sadr City. Sadr, in an attempt to distance himself from the acrimony, was thereafter careful not to involve himself directly in Iraqi politics.

In October 2006 the Mahdi Army seized control of Amarah in southern Iraq. A pitched battle ensued between Iraqi security forces and the militiamen. Sadr implored the Mahdi soldiers to lay down their arms, and some have speculated that he had not authorized the Amarah offensive and had lost control over Mahdi Army groups in that area. Sadr's plea was largely ignored. In February 2007 the U.S. media reported that Sadr had fled to Iran in anticipation of the security crackdown attendant with the U.S. troop surge strategy. Sadr, however, had merely gone into seclusion in Iraq, and during his two-month hiatus he sharply condemned the U.S.-led occupation and called for Iraqi security forces not to cooperate with occupation forces. In 2008 in response to myriad negotiations with Iranian and Iraqi leaders following several months of brutal fighting between the Mahdi Army and Iraqi government forces, Sadr called for a truce and implored the Mahdi Army to lay down its arms. He continued to condemn the presence of U.S. and coalition occupation forces in Iraq, as that was the primary concern of his followers. In late 2008 he called for attacks against U.S. troops in Iraq in retaliation for the Israeli incursion into the Gaza Strip, seeking to defeat the radical Palestinian group Hamas. However, this was largely a rhetorical gesture, as his followers continued to observe the truce in place.

In 2010, Sadr urged all Iraqis to participate in that year's national elections. He also continued to call for the withdrawal of all foreign forces from Iraq. The next year, Sadr reached an uneasy agreement with Prime Minister Nuri al-Maliki; meanwhile, Sadr's followers controlled a sizable bloc in Iraq's parliament. After the withdrawal of U.S. troops from Iraq in December 2011, Sadr took a more moderate stance, eschewing violence and urging peace in an increasingly unstable Iraq. In February 2014, Sadr stunned many by officially withdrawing from Iraqi politics and disbanding his party's structure. This move was seen as a boost to Maliki's reelection bid in the April 2014 elections.

Paul G. Pierpaoli Jr.

See also: Bremer, Lewis Paul, III; Hussein, Saddam; Insurgency and Opposition: Mahdi Army; Prime Minister, Iraq: Ayad Allawi; Sistani, Sayyid Ali Husayn al-

References

Cockburn, Patrick. *Muqtada: Muqtada al-Sadr, the Shia Revival, and the Struggle for Iraq.* New York: Scribner, 2008.

Nasr, Vali. *The Shia Revival: How Conflicts within Islam Will Shape the Future.* New York: Norton, 2006.

"The New Maqtada al-Sadr Seeks Moderate Image." *Iraq-Business News,* March 13, 2013, http://www.iraq-businessnews.com/2013/03/13/the-new-muqtada-al-sadr-seeks-moderate-image.

Sadr City, Battle of (March 26–May 11, 2008)

A battle during the Iraq War that occurred during March 26–May 11, 2008. In the Battle of Sadr City, coalition forces principally fought elements of the Mahdi Army. Sadr City is one of nine administrative districts of Baghdad. It is home to more than 1 million Shia Muslims, many of them poor. Part of the district had been known as Thawra and was termed "Saddam City" by the Americans in 2003. American forces in the coalition then began to call the area "Sadr City" from the strength there of Muqtada al-Sadr's followers, known as the Sadriyuns.

The coalition forces in Iraq had long sought permission from Iraqi prime minister Nuri al-Maliki to subdue the Jaysh al-Mahdi militias, which they called the Mahdi Army. The Sadriyuns, or Sadrists, possessed militias just as did the Dawa Party and the Supreme Council of the Islamic Revolution in Iran (SCIRI). However, these militias also clashed with them, and therefore the coalition had to some degree been influenced by the competition of the various Shia political forces. The Americans claimed that certain elements from the Jaysh al-Mahdi were obtaining arms from Iran, although their competitors, such as the Badr Brigades, were more clearly linked with Iranian support or at least had been in the past. Maliki was reluctant to approve coalition operations against fellow Shiites, particularly as he might not have been elected had it not been for his good relations with Muqtada al-Sadr and his followers. Also, the largest Shia party in the country had been even closer to Iran than the Sadriyuns, who were seen as an Iraqi-based party. Another concern was the vulnerability of the poor civilian population of Sadr City. However, under pressure from Washington, when 12 rockets were launched from the Sadr City area into the Green Zone on March 25, 2008, Maliki approved a joint Iraqi-American response.

Forces of the Iraqi Army 11th Division entered Sadr City on March 26, supported by the U.S. Army 3rd Brigade Combat Team, 4th Infantry Division, commanded by Colonel John Hort. As the Iraqis moved in, American combat engineers began construction of a concrete barrier across the southern one-third of Sadr City in order to push insurgent forces back beyond rocket range of the coalition-controlled Green Zone. An American Stryker brigade and other supporting coalition units, including troops from the 2nd Stryker Cavalry Regiment, succeeded over the course of a month in building a three-mile-long wall across the southern third of the neighborhood. The concrete Gold Wall was constructed from sections 12 feet high by 5 feet wide, placed individually by crane. The "Gold Wall" and the construction of barriers has been highly criticized by Iraqis and others who believe that defense of perimeters or the erection of "sanitized zones" is untenable in the long run.

The fighting in Sadr City was some of the heaviest in the Iraq War. Significantly, for the first time an unmanned aerial vehicle (UAV), or drone, was placed under the direct control of a battlefield commander. Utilizing helicopters and armed and unarmed UAVs and leveraging the persistent surveillance ability of the surveillance drones—which could follow a target on the ground for hours—American forces were able to strike insurgent targets deep within Sadr City.

Precision attacks directed or conducted by UAVs killed numerous insurgent mortar and rocket teams.

The heaviest fighting took place on April 28 as militia forces, emboldened by the lack of American air support during a heavy sandstorm, attacked along the heavily contested area of al-Quds Street, known to allied forces as Route Gold. Dozens of militia fighters were killed in ensuing firefights. Mahdi Army forces marshaled heavy firepower to oppose the construction of the concrete wall. Although they employed .50-caliber sniper rifles and RPG-29 rockets and detonated more than 120 Iranian-made mines with explosively forged projectiles against coalition forces, the militias nevertheless failed to prevent construction of the wall.

Of the 2,000 or so American troops in the battle, 6 were killed. Some 5,000 men of the Iraqi Army took part in the battle; their casualty figures were not reported. The Mahdi militia numbered perhaps between 2,000 and 4,000 members; they are believed to have suffered 700–1,000 casualties.

The forces of the Supreme Islamic Iraqi Council (Majlis al-'A'la al-Islami al-'Iraqu), formerly known as the Supreme Council of the Islamic Revolution in Iran, are heavily represented in the new Iraqi Army; consequently, the action was understood as one of intrasectarian and political warfare. Muqtada al-Sadr went into seclusion but called for his fighters to adhere to a truce, or this campaign could have led to a much wider popular rebellion against the new Iraqi government. Unfortunately, violence continued in Baghdad with numerous large-scale suicide bombings there and in other cities in the spring of 2009. These, however, were primarily Sunni attacks on Shia or Iraqi and coalition forces.

The Battle of Sadr City was seen as a significant victory for coalition forces; however, it came at the expense of Prime Minister Maliki's impartiality and credibility to some degree, making him appear to be a creature of the coalition. Sadrist forces and Maliki reached a cease-fire agreement on May 11, 2008, bringing an end to the major fighting in Sadr City.

Shawn Fisher and Sherifa Zuhur

See also: Insurgency and Opposition: Mahdi Army; Prime Minister, Iraq: Nuri al-Maliki; Sadr, Muqtada al-

References

Gordon, Michael R., and Stephen Farrell. "Iraqi Troops Take Charge of Sadr City in Swift Push." *New York Times*, May 21, 2008.

Gordon, Michael R., and Alissa J. Rubin. "Operation in Sadr City Is an Iraqi Success, So Far." *New York Times*, May 22, 2008.

Gordon, Michael R., and Bernard E. Trainor. *The Endgame: The Inside Story of the Struggle for Iraq, from George W. Bush to Barack Obama.* New York: Vintage, 2013.

Secretary of Defense, U.S. (Chronological Order)

The secretary of defense is a cabinet level position in the United States executive branch of government. The position serves as the chief executive for the Department of Defense and is sixth in line of succession in case of the death or incapacitation of the president. The position is appointed by the president and is approved by the vote of the U.S. Senate. The position is designated in U.S. law to be the principal adviser to the president on all matter of defense. This position generally corresponds to foreign ministers of defense.

During the fighting in Iraq there were three secretaries of defense. Donald Rumsfeld was brought in to the position to improve the business practices of the Pentagon, notorious for its convoluted and inefficient bureaucracy. Robert Gates was brought in to the position following the 2006 midterm electoral defeat of the Republicans. The general perception was that Iraq was spinning out of control and that a new approach was necessary—Gates was to provide that new approach. Gates was kept on when the administrations changed hands in 2009. Leon Panetta replaced Gates and oversaw the complete withdrawal of U.S. forces from Iraq.

- Donald Rumsfeld, Republican, January 20, 2001–December 18, 2006
- Robert M. Gates, Republican, December 18, 2006–June 30, 2011
- Leon Panetta, Democrat, July 1, 2011–February 26, 2013

Donald Rumsfeld (1932–)
(Secretary from January 20, 2001, to December 18, 2006)

U.S. secretary of defense (1975–1977, 2001–2006). Born in Chicago, Illinois, on July 9, 1932, Donald Rumsfeld graduated from Princeton University in 1954. He was commissioned in the navy through the Naval Reserve Officers' Training Corps and served during 1954–1957 as a pilot and flight instructor. Rumsfeld remained in the reserves, retiring as a navy captain in 1989.

Rumsfeld began his long association with Washington, DC, as an administrative assistant to Representative David S. Dennison Jr. of Ohio during 1957–1959, then joined the staff of Representative Robert Griffen of Michigan. During 1960–1962, Rumsfeld

Defense Secretary Donald Rumsfeld responds to questions from the troops during a town hall meeting in Baghdad, Iraq, on April 12, 2005. Rumsfeld was in Iraq to visit with U.S. and coalition forces and to meet with the newly elected members of the Iraqi government. (U.S. Department of Defense)

worked for an investment banking firm. In 1962 he was elected to the U.S. House of Representatives as a Republican from Illinois and served until 1969 when he resigned to accept appointment as director of the Office of Economic Opportunity and assistant to President Richard M. Nixon (1969–1970). Rumsfeld was then counselor to the president and director of the Economic Stabilization Program (1971–1973). During 1973–1974 he was U.S. ambassador to the North Atlantic Treaty Organization and thus avoided any involvement with the Watergate Scandal.

When Nixon resigned and was succeeded by Gerald Ford, Rumsfeld returned to Washington in August 1974 to serve as chair of the new president's transition team. He was then Ford's chief of staff. During 1975–1977, Rumsfeld served as secretary of defense. At age 43, he was the youngest person to hold that position. During Rumsfeld's 14 months in office, he oversaw the transformation of the military to an all-volunteer force and other post–Vietnam War reforms. He also actively campaigned for additional defense appropriations and the development of weapons systems such as the B-1 bomber, the Trident missile system, and the MX missile. Ford honored Rumsfeld for his government service in 1977 with the Presidential Medal of Freedom, the nation's highest civilian award.

Rumsfeld left government service when President James (Jimmy) E. Carter took office in January 1977. Following a brief period as a university lecturer, Rumsfeld entered private business. He was chief executive officer and then chairman of G. D. Searle, a pharmaceutical company (1977–1985). From 1990 until 1993, Rumsfeld served as chairman and chief executive officer of General Instrument Corporation. During 1997–2001 he was chairman of Gilead Sciences, Inc. Concurrent with his work in the private sector, Rumsfeld served on numerous federal boards. He also served in the Ronald Reagan administration as special presidential envoy to the Middle East during 1983–1984.

In January 2001, newly elected president George W. Bush appointed Rumsfeld to be secretary of defense for a second time. Rumsfeld was then the oldest individual to hold the post. Bush charged him with transforming the military from its Cold War emphasis on major conventional warfare into a lighter, more efficient force capable of rapid deployment around the world. Rumsfeld worked to develop network-centric warfare, an approach to military operations that relies on technological innovation and integration of weapons and information systems to produce more firepower with fewer personnel. In addition, Rumsfeld initiated the restructuring of the U.S. military presence throughout the world and the closure and consolidation of bases. He also refocused the strategic forces of the United States by emphasizing missile defense and space systems following the 2002 U.S. withdrawal from the Anti-Ballistic Missile Treaty. Rumsfeld angered a number of congressional representatives when he canceled such weapons systems as the Comanche helicopter and Crusader self-propelled artillery system.

Rumsfeld's reform efforts and his restructuring of the military were overshadowed by his role in the post–September 11, 2001, Global War on Terrorism. As secretary of defense, Rumsfeld oversaw the military operation that overthrew the Taliban regime in Afghanistan (Operation Enduring Freedom), although the failure to capture Osama bin Laden tarnished the otherwise successful military campaign.

Rumsfeld was one of the foremost proponents of military action against Iraq, teaming up with President Bush and Vice President Richard Cheney to overcome opposition from within the cabinet by Secretary of State Colin Powell. Rumsfeld then directed the 2003 invasion of Iraq (Operation Iraqi Freedom). In the campaign, he employed a strategy that relied on firepower and smaller numbers of ground troops.

While the overthrow of the Iraqi regime of Saddam Hussein was highly successful, the subsequent occupation of Iraq did not go well. Within the Pentagon, there were complaints of Rumsfeld running roughshod over those who disagreed with him. He was much criticized for his outspoken, combative management style, such as when he pointedly referred to the French and British governments, which had opposed the war, as "Old Europe." But there was good reason to criticize his military decisions and specifically his overly optimistic assessment of the situation that would follow the overthrow of Hussein. Disbanding the Iraqi Army to rebuild it from scratch came to be seen in retrospect as a major blunder. Rumsfeld had also ignored previous recommendations that 400,000 U.S. troops would be required for any occupation of Iraq. The actual number of troops involved was only about a third that number. As a consequence, Iraqi arms depots, oil production facilities, and even the national museum were looted in the immediate aftermath of the invasion.

Occupation troops were unable to halt a growing insurgency. As U.S. casualties escalated and Iraq descended into sectarian violence, mounting calls for Rumsfeld's ouster came from Republicans as well as Democrats and even a number of prominent retired generals. Just prior to the 2006 midterm elections, an editorial in the *Military Times* newspaper demanded his removal.

Rumsfeld resigned on November 8, 2006. This came a week after President Bush had expressed confidence in his defense secretary and said that he would remain until the end of his term, but it was also one day after the midterm elections in which the Republican Party lost its majorities in both the House of Representatives and the Senate. The election was widely seen as a referendum on the Iraq War and, by extension, Rumsfeld's leadership in it. President Bush named former Central Intelligence Agency director Robert Gates to succeed Rumsfeld. In early 2011 Rumsfeld published his autobiography, *Known and Unknown: A Memoir,* a spirited defense of his policies in the George W. Bush administration.

Tom Lansford and Spencer C. Tucker

See also: Bush, George Walker; Cheney, Richard Bruce; Global War on Terrorism; Secretary of Defense, U.S.: Robert M. Gates; Secretary of State, U.S.: Colin L. Powell

References

Scarborough, Rowan. *Rumsfeld's War: The Untold Story of America's Anti-Terrorist Commander.* Washington, DC: Regnery, 2004.

Woodward, Bob. *Bush at War.* New York: Simon and Schuster, 2003.

Woodward, Bob. *Plan of Attack.* New York: Simon and Schuster, 2004.

Woodward, Bob. *State of Denial: Bush at War, Part III.* New York: Simon and Schuster, 2006.

Robert M. Gates (1943–) (Secretary from December 18, 2006, to June 30, 2011)

U.S. Air Force officer, president of Texas A&M University, director of the Central Intelligence Agency (CIA), and secretary of defense from December 18, 2006, until July 1, 2011. Robert Michael Gates was born in Wichita, Kansas, on September 25, 1943. He graduated in 1965 from the College of

William and Mary with a bachelor's degree in history, then earned a master's degree in history from Indiana University in 1966 and a PhD in Russian and Soviet history from Georgetown University in 1974.

Gates served as an officer in the U.S. Air Force's Strategic Air Command (1967–1969) before joining the CIA in 1969 as an intelligence analyst, a post he held until 1974. He was on the staff of the National Security Council from 1974 to 1979, before returning to the CIA as director of the Strategic Evaluation Center in 1979. Gates rose through the ranks to become the director of central intelligence/deputy director of central intelligence executive staff (1981), deputy director for intelligence (1982), and deputy director of central intelligence (1986–1989).

Nominated to become director of the CIA in 1987, Gates withdrew his nomination when it appeared that his connection with the Iran Contra Affair might hamper his Senate confirmation. He then served as deputy assistant to the president for national security affairs (March–August 1989) and as assistant to the president and deputy national security adviser from August 1989 to November 1991.

The Iran Contra Affair erupted in 1987 when it was revealed that members of President Ronald Reagan's administration had sold weapons to Iran and illegally diverted the funds to the Nicaraguan Contras, the rightist anti-Sandinista rebels. Gates's political enemies assumed that he was guilty because of his senior status at the CIA, but an exhaustive investigation by an independent counsel determined that Gates had done nothing illegal, and on September 3, 1991, the investigating committee stated that Gates's involvement in the scandal did not warrant prosecution. The independent counsel's final 1993 report came to the same conclusion. In May 1991 President George H. W. Bush renominated Gates to head the CIA, and the Senate confirmed Gates on November 5, 1991.

Gates retired from the CIA in 1993 and entered academia. He also served as a member of the Board of Visitors of the University of Oklahoma International Programs Center, and as an endowment fund trustee for the College of William and Mary. In 1999 he became the interim dean of the George Bush School of Government and Public Service at Texas A&M University, and in 2002 he became president of Texas A&M University, a post he held until 2006.

Gates remained active in public service during his presidency, cochairing in January 2004 a Council on Foreign Relations task force on U.S.-Iran relations, which suggested that the United States engage Iran diplomatically concerning that nation's pursuit of nuclear weapons. Gates was a member of the Iraq Study Group (March 15, 2006–December 6, 2006), also known as the Baker-Hamilton Commission, a bipartisan commission charged with studying the Iraq War, when he was nominated to succeed the controversial and discredited Donald Rumsfeld as defense secretary. Gates assumed the post on December 18, 2006.

In addition to the challenges of the Iraq War, Gates was faced in February 2007 with a scandal concerning inadequate and neglectful care of returning veterans by Walter Reed Army Medical Center. In response, he removed both Secretary of the Army Francis J. Harvey and U.S. Army surgeon general Kevin C. Kiley from their posts. Gates further tightened his control of the Pentagon when he did not recommend the renomination of U.S. Marine Corps general Peter Pace as chairman of the Joint Chiefs of Staff that June. Pace would have certainly faced tough questioning by Congress. It was also Gates's job to implement the so-called troop surge initiated by Bush in January 2007.

In March 2008 Gates accepted the resignation of Admiral William Joseph "Fox" Fallon, commander of the U.S. Central Command, a departure that was due in part to the controversy surrounding an article by Thomas P. M. Barnett titled "The Man between War and Peace," published in *Esquire* magazine on March 11, 2008. The article asserted policy disagreements between Fallon and the Bush administration on the prosecution of the war in Iraq and potential conflict with Iran over that nation's nuclear arms program. Gates rejected any suggestion that Fallon's resignation indicated a U.S. willingness to attack Iran in order to stop its nuclear weapons development.

Unlike his abrasive predecessor, Gates brought an era of calm and focus to the Pentagon and was far more willing to engage in discussion and compromise over matters of defense and military policy. In April 2009 Gates proposed a major reorientation in the U.S. defense budget, which would entail deep cuts in more traditional programs that provide for conventional warfare with such major military powers as Russia and China, and shift assets to those programs that would aid in fighting the insurgencies in both Iraq and Afghanistan. At the same time, the new budget would provide for a sharp increase in funding for surveillance and intelligence-gathering equipment, to include the Predator-class unmanned aerial vehicles, and increase manpower in the army to include special forces and the U.S. Marine Corps. These decisions triggered major debate in Congress over defense spending and priorities.

Although Gates had been looking forward to leaving the Pentagon at the end of Bush's administration (he kept a countdown timer in his briefcase), he agreed to stay on as defense secretary in the new Barack Obama administration, which took office in January 2009. Some questioned the choice because Obama had been a vocal critic of the Iraq War during his 2008 presidential campaign, but others saw the choice as a smart bipartisan move, as Gates had support on both sides of the aisle in Congress. Gates also agreed with Obama on key matters, including the need to reduce the number of U.S. troops in Iraq as soon as practical. Obama advisers also noted that with the country fighting two wars, keeping Gates on was a way of maintaining stability during a time of significant transition in the executive branch. Because he already held the position, Gates did not have to be confirmed by the Senate. In December 2009 Gates was the first senior U.S. official to visit Afghanistan after President Obama announced his intention to deploy 30,000 additional military personnel to that country.

On July 1, 2011, Secretary of Defense Gates voluntarily stepped down and was replaced by Leon Panetta. At his retirement ceremony President Obama presented Gates with the Presidential Medal of Freedom for his 40-year career in the intelligence services and the Pentagon.

On February 3, 2012, Gates became the chancellor of the College of William and Mary in Williamsburg, Virginia. He has also served on the board of directors of several companies, including Starbucks. In January 2014 Gates's memoir, *Duty: Memoirs of a Secretary at War,* created controversy because in it he criticized President Obama's approach to the war in Afghanistan. Gates suggested that Obama was not entirely sold on the troop surge strategy his administration implemented in Afghanistan during 2010–2012, writing that "I never doubted [his] support for the troops, only his support for their mission."

Richard M. Edwards

See also: Bush, George Walker; Commanders, U.S. Central Command: William J. Fallon; Iraq Study Group; Iraqi Freedom, Operation; Obama, Barack Hussein, II; Secretary of Defense, U.S.: Donald Rumsfeld

References

Barnett, Thomas P. M. "The Man between War and Peace." *Esquire,* March 11, 2008, 1–4.

Gates, Robert M. *From the Shadows: The Ultimate Insider's Story of Five Presidents and How They Won the Cold War.* New York: Simon and Schuster, 1996.

Gates, Robert M. *Understanding the New U.S. Defense Policy through the Speeches of Robert M. Gates, Secretary of Defense.* Rockville, MD: Arc Manor, 2008.

Gates, Robert M. *Duty: Memoirs of a Secretary at War.* New York: Knopf, 2014.

Oliphant, Thomas. *Utter Incompetents: Ego and Ideology in the Age of Bush.* New York: Thomas Dunne Books, 2007.

Leon E. Panetta (1938–) (Secretary from July 1, 2011, to February 26, 2013)

Democratic congressman, chief of staff to President Bill Clinton, director of the Central Intelligence Agency (2009–2011), and U.S. secretary of defense (2011–2013). Leon Edward Panetta was born in Monterey, California, on June 28, 1938, the son of Italian immigrants. He graduated magna cum laude in political science from the University of Santa Clara and received his law degree from the same school, where he was editor of the law review. He entered private practice in 1963 and during 1964–1965 served in the U.S. Army as a commissioned officer.

Panetta was initially a Republican but was fired from his post as director of civil rights at what was then the federal Department of Health, Education, and Welfare in 1970 after proceeding with plans to resolve more than 600 school desegregation cases; the Richard Nixon administration wanted to see the cases postponed in an effort to attract support from southern Democrats. Although Panetta continued to embrace fiscal conservatism, the events spurred a change in his political allegiance, and he became Democratic New York City mayor John Lindsay's coordinator of state and federal aid.

In 1971, Panetta returned to private legal practice in California. He ran for Congress as a Democrat in 1976 and won the seat representing central California. During his tenure in Congress, Panetta served as the chair of the House Budget Committee and as a member of the Agriculture Committee. Despite his reputation for frugality and honesty, he was caught up in the House banking scandal of 1992 after he was found to have written two overdrafts on his account at the House bank. He attributed the checks to sloppy bookkeeping.

Panetta remained in Congress until January 23, 1993, when he was confirmed as director of the Office of Management and Budget (OMB). During his short tenure at the OMB, he focused his attention on efforts to cut the federal budget deficit. Clinton later moved Panetta to the White House Chief of Staff post in the hope that his position as a Washington insider would enhance administration relationships with the legislative branch. Panetta assumed his new post on July 17, 1994, and was credited with bringing more order and discipline to the daily operations of the White House. He stepped down in January 1997, choosing not to serve a second term, and was replaced by Erskine Bowles. From 2000 to 2003, Panetta served as chair of the Pew Oceans Commission. In 2006, he was selected to serve on the bipartisan Iraq Study Group. Panetta has also codirected the Leon & Sylvia Panetta Institute for Public Policy with his wife, Sylvia.

On January 9, 2009, President-elect Barack Obama named Panetta as his choice to head the Central Intelligence Agency (CIA). The announcement initially sparked some concerns because Panetta had no background in intelligence; however, his advocates believed that he was well qualified for the position, citing his policy management skills and his foreign policy experiences during his time in the Clinton White House and with the Iraq Study Group. At his Senate confirmation hearing, Panetta said that he would not be involved in the everyday intelligence operations at the CIA, although he made it clear that his would be the final word at the agency. Panetta was confirmed by the Senate on February 12 and was sworn into office on February 13.

When Panetta took the helm at the CIA, the organization was on shaky ground after reports detailing its use of coercive interrogation techniques and extraordinary rendition in pursuit of the Global War on Terrorism. Panetta said at his Senate confirmation hearings that he would continue the rendition practice but would consider enhanced interrogation techniques only in "a ticking bomb situation." When the Department of Justice (DOJ) sought in 2009 to determine whether CIA agents' interrogation techniques had broken the law, Panetta worked to curb the DOJ's investigation, citing previous investigations into the matter and legal flaws in some of the cases against the agents. Panetta had previously argued in his Senate confirmation hearing that CIA agents should not be prosecuted for using interrogation methods that the DOJ had previously authorized. Although the DOJ was ultimately allowed to pursue its investigation, Panetta's efforts helped narrow the scope of the investigation.

As director, Panetta worked to build trust with Congress by sharing more information with the body and increased the CIA's use of predator drones in bombing missions in Afghanistan, Pakistan, Yemen, and elsewhere. Shortly after taking office, Obama instructed Panetta to make tracking and capturing or killing Osama bin Laden his top priority, and Panetta ultimately supervised the May 1, 2011, operation that resulted in Navy SEALs killing bin Laden at a compound in Abbottabad, Pakistan. On May 1 Obama announced that bin Laden had been killed, just days after announcing that Panetta was his pick to replace retiring secretary of defense Robert Gates. On June 21, the U.S. Senate unanimously confirmed Panetta for the post. He stepped down as CIA head on June 30 and was sworn in as Obama's second secretary of defense the following day.

One of Panetta's primary objectives as head of the Pentagon was to pave the way for the repeal of the "Don't Ask, Don't Tell" policy regarding gays and lesbians in the U.S. military. Within months the policy was rescinded, and gays and lesbians were permitted to serve openly in all branches of the armed services. He also repeatedly warned during his tenure in office that the U.S. defense budget should not be cut by more than $400 billion over a 10-year period, asserting that an amount exceeding that figure would precipitate problems in the military and weaken America's ability to respond to a variety of military threats. He largely succeeded in holding the line on such cuts. In 2012, Panetta warned that Iran must not be permitted to develop nuclear weapons and that any attempt to close the strategic Strait of Hormuz would elicit a military response by the United States. In January 2013, Panetta also set in motion plans to allow women to hold combat positions "at all levels" within the U.S. armed forces. This initiative was later codified into policy.

Panetta decided to leave government service on February 27, 2013, with the advent of the second Obama administration. Exhausted after years of dedicated service in stressful high-level posts, he longed to return to his home in California. In retirement, Panetta has given a number of speeches and has been involved in numerous academic and environmental organizations. Panetta's memoir *Worthy Fights,* released in October 2014, created quite a stir. In it, the former defense secretary criticized President Barack Obama, claiming that he tended to be reactive instead of proactive and shied away from confrontation. Panetta also faulted the president for not having developed better relations with Congress, for having ignored pleas to leave a small troop deployment in Iraq beyond 2011, and for having failed to respond aggressively enough to Syrian president Bashar al-Assad's use of chemical weapons in 2013.

Paul G. Pierpaoli Jr.

See also: Global War on Terrorism; Interrogation, Coercive (Torture); Iraq Study Group; Obama, Barack Hussein, II; Secretary of Defense, U.S.: Robert M. Gates

References

Panetta, Leon, with Jim Newton. *Worthy Fights: A Memoir of Leadership in War and Peace.* New York: Penguin, 2014.

"Panetta's Memoir Blasts Obama on His Leadership, Blames for State of Iraq and Syria." *Newsweek,* October 10, 2014, http://www.newsweek.com/panettas-memoir-blasts-obama-his-leadership-blames-him-state-iraq-and-syria-276582.

Secretary of State, U.S. (Chronological Order)

The secretary of state is a cabinet-level position in the U.S. executive branch of government. The position serves as the chief executive for the Department of State and is fourth in line of succession in case of the death or incapacitation of the president. The position is appointed by the president and is approved by the vote of the U.S. Senate. The position is generally considered to be the chief diplomat for the United States and is responsible for diplomatic missions globally. This position generally corresponds to foreign ministers for foreign affairs.

During the fighting in Iraq there were three secretaries of state. Colin Powell was considered to be one of the most experienced people to hold the position. He was notorious for his testimony before the United Nations Security Council justifying the invasion of Iraq to stop its programs for weapons of mass destruction. He served for the entirety of President George W. Bush's first term, and Condoleezza Rice served for the entirety of his second term. Hillary Clinton served in the position for the entirety of President Barack Obama's first term.

- Colin Powell, Republican, January 20, 2001–January 26, 2005
- Condoleezza Rice, Republican, January 26, 2005–January 20, 2009
- Hillary Clinton, Democrat, January 21, 2009–February 1, 2013

Colin L. Powell (1937–) (Secretary from January 20, 2001, to January 26, 2005)

U.S. Army general, chairman of the Joint Chiefs of Staff, and secretary of state. Colin Luther Powell was born in New York City on April 5, 1937, the child of Jamaican immigrants. While pursuing a geology degree at the City College of New York, Powell received his commission as a 2nd lieutenant through the Reserve Officers' Training

Corps in 1958. After paratrooper and ranger training, Powell was deployed as a military adviser to Vietnam. Even though he was wounded and received a Purple Heart during his first tour, he chose to volunteer for a second tour before earning a master's degree in business administration at George Washington University in 1971. He earned a White House fellowship in 1972 before returning to the military to command at the battalion and division levels.

Powell returned to civilian government as an executive assistant to the Energy and Defense Departments during the administration of President Jimmy Carter. Under President Ronald Reagan, Powell quickly moved up the ranks from senior military assistant to Secretary of Defense Casper Weinberger, whom Powell assisted during both the 1983 invasion of Grenada and the 1987 raid on Libya. That same year Powell, now a lieutenant general, became Reagan's national security adviser. In 1989, Powell became the youngest person and the first African American to serve as chairman of the Joint Chiefs of Staff.

By 1991 Powell was a four-star general, and the onus had fallen on him to develop the strategy that would allow a coalition of nations to push Iraqi president Saddam Hussein's invasion force out of Kuwait. Powell's strategy was a simple one: when the American military is to be used, it should be used to win a conflict quickly and decisively. The central tenet of the coalition strategy was that overwhelming force should be brought to bear against the enemy. This approach led to a rapid and decisive victory over Iraqi forces in Operation Desert Storm. The victory came so quickly that, some argued, it left the job unfinished because Hussein was left in power. However, neither President George H. W. Bush nor Powell was eager to prosecute the war beyond the coalition's mandate or to make it appear as if the West was intent on punishing the Iraqi people.

The use of overwhelming force was one of the three tenets of the Powell Doctrine, which guided U.S. military strategy in the immediate aftermath of the Cold War. The doctrine also held that the United States should use its military only when the country's vital interests were at stake and only when there was a clear goal and a clearly defined exit strategy.

Powell served as secretary of state under President George W. Bush, beginning in 2001. It was clear from the start, however, that Powell would play a rather subservient role to Vice President Richard Cheney, Secretary of Defense Donald Rumsfeld, Deputy Secretary of Defense Paul Wolfowitz, and National Security Adviser Condoleezza Rice. Except perhaps for Rice, all were considered rightists who adhered to the gospel of neoconservativism, particularly in matters of national security and warfare. Powell, who did not subscribe to the rigid ideology of neoconservativism, found himself in the difficult position of having to rally the international community around the war on terror after the September 11 terrorist attacks. His job was not an easy one, because he walked a diplomatic tightrope between the Bush administration neoconservatives and the exigencies of the post-9/11 environment. Powell traveled less than any secretary of state in 30 years, demonstrating the demands that the Global War on Terrorism and the Iraq War exacted on his time.

Soon after September 11, 2001, Powell was given the responsibility of building the case for a second invasion of Iraq to topple the Hussein regime and ensure that the nation did not harbor or use weapons of mass destruction (WMD). Powell was opposed to the forcible overthrow of Hussein, arguing that it was better to contain him, which the international community had effectively done since 1991. Nevertheless, he agreed to work with the administration if it sought an international coalition to effect regime change in Iraq. Powell did convince Bush to take the case for war before the United Nations (UN); however, he had to serve as the point man for these actions.

As the United States moved toward war with Iraq, Powell addressed a plenary session of the UN on February 5, 2003, carefully building a case for international military action. He emphatically stated that the Iraqis had biological weapons in hand and that Hussein had many of the key components for the construction of a nuclear weapon. Powell's speech was immediately controversial; many claimed that his statements concerning Iraqi WMD were unsubstantiated. Powell was himself skeptical about some of the intelligence presented to him but nevertheless presented it as irrefutable. He would later refer to his UN speech as a blot on his record.

Powell must have been disappointed when the Iraq War was waged with insufficient numbers of troops to secure the peace in Iraq (a cardinal violation of the Powell Doctrine). The coalition that did invade Iraq in 2003 was not nearly as large, diverse, or unified as the 1991 coalition, another disappointment for Powell. Once Hussein had been toppled, Powell had the unenviable task of building international support for the rebuilding of Iraq, which was made far more difficult when a nearly two-year search failed to find the active WMD program that Powell and others had claimed were in Iraq.

As the war in Iraq began to deteriorate, Powell was even more marginalized within the administration. Realizing that his voice had been muted, he announced his intention to resign only days after Bush's November 2004 reelection. Powell left office in January 2005. He has since joined the venture capital firm of Kleiner, Perkins, Caulfield & Byers; embarked on an extended speaking tour; and stayed active in moderate Republican political circles. In the summer of 2007, Powell revealed that he had spent much time attempting to persuade George W. Bush not to invade Iraq. Powell also stated his belief that Iraq had descended into a civil war, the outcome of which could not be determined by the United States.

In 2007 Powell made a significant monetary contribution to Republican senator John McCain's 2008 presidential campaign and reportedly advised McCain on both military and foreign policy matters. However, in the run-up to the 2008 election, Powell publicly endorsed the candidacy of McCain's Democratic Party opponent, Barack Obama. In October 2012, Powell endorsed Obama's 2012 reelection bid and expressed chagrin that some leaders in the Republican Party were unfairly demonizing Obama, which he believed was hurting the Republican Party. Powell has remained busy speaking, consulting, and teaching. He has embraced the repeal of the "Don't Ask, Don't Tell" policy for the U.S. military and in May 2012 publicly supported the legalization of same-sex marriage.

Keith Murphy and Paul G. Pierpaoli Jr.

See also: Bush, George Walker; Obama, Barack Hussein, II

References

Adler, Bill. *The Generals: The New American Heroes.* New York: Avon Books, 1991.

Cummings, Judith, and Stefan Rudnicki. *Colin Powell and the American Dream.* Beverly Hills, CA: Dove Books, 1995.

Powell, Colin L., with Joseph E. Perisco. *My American Journey*. New York: Random House, 1995.

Woodward, Bob. *The Commanders*. New York: Simon and Schuster, 1991.

Condoleezza Rice (1954–) (Secretary from January 26, 2005, to January 20, 2009)

First woman to hold the post of national security adviser (2001–2005) to the president of the United States and only the second female U.S. secretary of state (2005–2009). Condoleezza Rice was born on November 14, 1954, in Birmingham, Alabama. Rice grew up in the segregated South in a prominent African American family. Her family moved to Denver in 1967 when her father accepted a position as vice chancellor at the University of Denver. Rice's intellectual abilities were evident at an early age, and she graduated from the University of Denver at age 19 and went on to earn a master's degree from Notre Dame in 1975. After working in the State Department during the Jimmy Carter administration, Rice returned to the University of Denver and earned a doctorate in international studies in 1981. Her specialty was the Soviet Union and Cold War security issues. She joined the faculty at Stanford University and became a tenured professor of political science and a fellow at the Hoover Institute.

During her years as an academic, Rice held a variety of government positions or posts on advisory boards. In 1989 she joined the administration of President George H. W. Bush, where she worked closely with Secretary of State James Baker on policy toward the Soviet Union in the waning days of the Cold War. Rice was the director of Soviet and East European affairs on the National Security Council and a special assistant to the president on national security affairs. During this period, Rice became known for her intelligence and work ethic. She impressed the elder Bush, who subsequently recommended her to George W. Bush when the Texas governor began to prepare his presidential campaign.

In 1993, Rice became the provost of Stanford University. In addition to her duties at Stanford, she became a fellow at the Council on Foreign Relations and continued to serve as an adviser during the Bill Clinton administration. In 1996 she was appointed as an adviser to the Joint Chiefs of Staff, and the following year she served on a board examining gender and military training. Rice was also invited to join a number of corporate boards. She left her post at Stanford in 1999 to advise George W. Bush during his presidential campaign.

In 2001, Bush appointed Rice as the nation's first female and second African American national security adviser. Following the September 11, 2001, terrorist attacks on the United States, Rice emerged as a central figure in crafting the U.S. military and diplomatic response and in advocating war with Iraq. She also worked with Secretary of State Colin Powell to ensure that the U.S. response to the attacks included nonmilitary actions such as increased international law enforcement cooperation and the development of a comprehensive homeland security policy.

Rice helped develop the 2002 U.S. national security strategy, commonly referred to as the Bush Doctrine, that emphasized preemptive military strikes to prevent the use of weapons of mass destruction. She was also instrumental in the administration's hardline policy toward the Iraqi regime of Saddam Hussein, including the effort to isolate Iraq and formulate an international coalition. She was also identified as one of the main proponents of the 2003 U.S.-led invasion of Iraq, Operation Iraqi Freedom. In March 2004, Rice was asked to testify before a commission investigating the September 11, 2001, terrorist attacks in contravention of a long-standing informal policy that members of the White House staff did not testify before congressional committees. A compromise was reached since the 9/11 Commission was not a congressional body, and Rice became the first national security adviser to publicly testify on policy issues.

During the 2004 presidential campaign, Rice became the first national security adviser to openly campaign on behalf of a candidate. She faced domestic criticism by Democrats for her hardline security policies and for her advocacy against affirmative action policies. After the election Rice was appointed secretary of state, becoming the second female and second African American to occupy the post. She handpicked her successor as national security adviser: Stephen Hadley, her former deputy. Once in office in 2005, Rice worked to repair relations with major allies such as France and Germany, which were opposed to the U.S.-led invasion of Iraq. She also endeavored to increase international support for the continuing U.S. efforts in Iraq. The sound working relationship between Rice and Hadley ensured that the State Department and the security establishment had a high degree of cooperation. Rice's closeness with Bush provided her with greater access, and therefore more influence, than her predecessor. One result was that during Bush's second term, Secretary of Defense Donald Rumsfeld had less influence in broad security policy, while Rice increased, or restored, the role of the State Department in formulating such policy. Rice's diplomacy was generally less dogmatic than what neoconservatives might have preferred, and she worked hard, but with little success, to foster democratic movements around the world, particularly in the Middle East.

After leaving office in January 2009, Rice returned to Stanford University as a professor and fellow in political science, and since 2010 she has directed the school's Global Center for Business and the Economy.

Tom Lansford

See also: Bush, George Walker; Bush Doctrine; Global War on Terrorism; Secretary of Defense, U.S.: Donald Rumsfeld; Secretary of State, U.S.: Colin L. Powell

References

Kessler, Glenn. *The Confidante: Condoleezza Rice and the Creation of the Bush Legacy.* New York: St. Martin's, 2007.

Woodward, Bob. *Plan of Attack.* New York: Simon and Schuster, 2004.

Hillary R. Clinton (1947–) (Secretary from January 21, 2009, to February 1, 2013)

Attorney, former first lady (1993–2001), U.S. senator (2001–2009), presidential candidate in 2008 and 2016, and secretary of state (2009–2013). Hillary Diane Rodham was born on October 26, 1947, in Chicago and was raised in Park Ridge, a prosperous Chicago suburb. Her family was staunchly Republican, and during the 1964 presidential campaign, while still a high school student, she actively campaigned for Republican nominee Barry Goldwater. She entered Wellesley College in 1965, and by 1968 she had become disenchanted with Republican politics and the Vietnam War. By 1968 she supported the Democratic antiwar presidential candidate Eugene McCarthy; the following year she graduated with a degree in political science.

Rodham enrolled at Yale Law School, where she met fellow student Bill Clinton, whom she would later marry. Graduating in 1973, she took a position with a child advocacy group. The next year she served as a staff attorney for the House Committee on the Judiciary during the Watergate Scandal that caused President Richard Nixon to resign in 1974. In 1975, she wed Bill Clinton.

In 1976, Bill Clinton launched his political career when he was elected attorney general of Arkansas. The next year, Hillary Clinton joined the Rose Law Firm, the premier legal firm in Arkansas, where she specialized in intellectual property law and continued pro bono child advocacy legal work. Bill became governor of Arkansas in January 1979, the same year that Hillary Clinton became a full partner in the Rose Law Firm, the first woman to achieve such status. In 1981 Bill lost a reelection bid but was reelected in 1982; Hillary was again the first lady of Arkansas, an informal post that she would hold until her husband became president in January 1993. She continued her legal work and was active on several boards, including those of Arkansas-based Wal-Mart as well as Lafarge and TCBY.

Taking a leave of absence from the Rose Law Firm to help her husband campaign for the presidency in 1992, Clinton proved to be a formidable campaigner, repeatedly weathering allegations that her husband had engaged in extramarital affairs. After Bill Clinton upset incumbent president George H. W. Bush in the November 1992 elections, Hillary Clinton became first lady in January 1993. She was an activist first lady, certainly more so than any of her immediate predecessors. Some pundits likened her to Eleanor Roosevelt.

Hillary Clinton's role in White House policy making was derided by the right wing of the Republican Party, and even some mainstream Democrats openly questioned her central role in decision making. In 1993 her husband named her chairperson of the Task Force on National Health Care Reform. Many questioned Hillary Clinton's motives, and the secrecy in which she conducted much of the task force's business only added to the public's skepticism. In the end, her health care plan was deemed too bureaucratic and too burdensome for business. The plan died in Congress and became a major campaign boon to the Republicans in the 1994 elections, which saw the Democrats lose their control of Congress. Despite the setback, Clinton actively promoted certain national legislation, including the State Children's Health Insurance Program in 1997. She traveled widely, ultimately visiting 79 nations.

Clinton was at the epicenter of the fruitless Whitewater investigation, a Republican-inspired inquiry into a decade-old land deal in which the Clintons had been involved in Arkansas. As such, she became the only first lady to be subpoenaed by a federal grand jury. Although years of probing and $50 million of taxpayers' money went into the Whitewater inquiry, neither Clinton was found to have engaged in any illegal activity. Unfortunately, however, Whitewater revealed a sexual dalliance between Bill Clinton and a White House intern, Monica Lewinsky, which mortified Hillary Clinton and led to the president's impeachment in December 1998. While Mrs. Clinton's allegation that the persecution of her and her husband was the result of a "vast right-wing conspiracy" may have been hyperbole, there can be little doubt that the Clintons were subjected to endlessly harsh scrutiny and criticism, particularly by Republicans and other detractors.

In 2000 the Clintons purchased a home in New York, and Hillary Clinton ran for the state's senatorial seat being vacated by retiring U.S. senator Daniel Patrick Moynihan. Clinton was at first running against popular New York City mayor Rudolph Giuliani, and many believed that her chances of winning were not good. But after Giuliani dropped out of the race because of health problems, Clinton—now running against Rick Lazio, a relatively unknown congressman—was virtually assured a win. Clinton won the election by an impressive 12-point margin and took office in January 2001.

During her first term Clinton maintained a relatively low profile but garnered high marks for her intellect, excellent grasp of issues, and willingness to work in a bipartisan manner. Following the September 11, 2001, terror attacks on the United States, Clinton strongly backed the George W. Bush administration's response, including Operation Enduring Freedom in Afghanistan and the 2001 Patriot Act. In October 2002 Clinton voted with the majority to grant the Bush administration authority to wage war in Iraq to enforce United Nations resolutions should diplomacy fail. She did not support an amendment that would have required another congressional resolution to invade Iraq. Meanwhile, Clinton visited both Afghanistan and Iraq to gauge the effectiveness of the U.S. war efforts there.

By 2005, already planning a run for the presidency in 2008, Clinton began to publicly criticize the Iraq War effort, noting the growing insurgency and the absence of firm plans to either extricate the United States from Iraq or quash the insurgents. She was careful to state, however, that a precipitous withdrawal was unwise if not dangerous, a position that chagrined many antiwar Democrats. Clinton did not back any of the Bush tax cuts, viewing them as economic grenades that would derail the economy, nor did she vote for Bush's two Supreme Court nominees, John Roberts and Samuel Alito.

In November 2006 Clinton, now quite popular with New York voters, won a landslide reelection. In early 2007 she began transferring leftover funds from her Senate race to her presidential campaign. On January 20, 2007, she announced her intention to form an exploratory committee for the 2008 presidential contest. That same year, she refused to support the Bush administration's troop surge in Iraq and backed unsuccessful legislation that would have forced the president to withdraw troops from Iraq based on a predetermined timeline. Forced to deal with her affirmative vote for the Iraq War, Clinton now had to explain that she probably would have voted against the 2002 resolution had she been privy to accurate and reliable intelligence. Her position change left many wondering why she had taken so long to come to such a conclusion.

By the autumn of 2007, Clinton seemed the person to beat amid a large Democratic presidential field. Following a mediocre performance in a debate in October, Clinton's momentum began to slip. After placing third in the January 2008 Iowa caucus, Clinton's campaign began to slowly unravel as Senator Barack Obama made significant inroads with Democratic voters. Clinton dropped out of the race on June 7, 2008, and endorsed Obama's candidacy. President Obama subsequently nominated Clinton as secretary of state, and she was confirmed in that position by the Senate on January 21, 2009, by a vote of 94 to 2.

Clinton was sworn into office on January 21, making her the third female secretary of state. As the nation's top diplomat, Clinton attempted to repair relations with Europe, which had become tense during the George W. Bush administration, and sought to reset U.S.-Russian relations, which had also deteriorated under Bush. While her efforts to reengage U.S. partners in Europe paid dividends, her overtures to the Russians were decidedly less successful.

Clinton supported Obama's troop surge in Afghanistan in 2010 and tried to forge a pragmatic, largely nonideological foreign policy. She counseled caution during the Arab Spring movement, which began in early 2011 and witnessed major uprisings in Egypt, Libya, and Syria, among other nations. To her detractors, however, this initial caution appeared to be weakness. Nevertheless, as the Libyan Civil War unfolded, Clinton came to favor limited U.S. military aid to the rebels in the way of air support in conjunction with other nations, which helped topple Libya's government under Muammar Qadaffi. In 2012, Clinton supported a plan by which the U.S. government would train and equip select rebel groups fighting in the Syrian Civil War, but the White House rejected the scheme. Clinton was also supportive of engaging in diplomacy and employing sanctions in order to convince Iran to abandon its suspected nuclear weapons program. Meanwhile, in late 2010 and early 2011, the secretary of state spearheaded the effort to limit the damage resulting from WikiLeaks documents that were critical of various foreign leaders and diplomats.

Perhaps Clinton's greatest test came after the September 11, 2012, terror attack against the U.S. consulate in Benghazi, Libya, in which three Americans, including the ambassador to Libya, were killed. She accepted full responsibility for the outcome of the debacle but flatly rejected Republicans' claims that she had been involved in a cover-up attempt after the attack.

Clinton left office on February 1, 2013, and was succeeded by John F. Kerry. Clinton maintained a fairly low profile, but in the early autumn of 2014 she criticized President Obama's approach to the Syrian Civil War, intimating that his overly cautious policies toward Syria had enabled the rise of the Islamic State of Iraq and Syria (ISIS). In the summer of 2014, Obama was compelled to take military action against ISIS in Iraq; in the fall, he expanded that effort to include air strikes against ISIS in Syria. Clinton failed to attain the presidency in 2016 in the midst of a combative campaign where she won the majority of the popular vote but lost in the electoral college.

Paul G. Pierpaoli Jr.

See also: Arab Spring; Iraqi Freedom, Operation: The Surge and the Awakening; Islamic State of Iraq and al-Sham (ISIS); Obama, Barack Hussein, II; WikiLeaks

References

Bernstein, Carl. *A Woman in Charge: The Life of Hillary Rodham Clinton.* New York: Knopf, 2007.

Clinton, Hillary Rodham. *Living History.* New York: Simon and Schuster, 2003.

Shia Islam

The smaller of the two predominant branches of Islam, the larger being Sunni Islam. The name "Shia" derives from the Arabic term "Shiat Ali" (Party or Partisans of Ali), whereas the name "Sunni" derives from the term "Ahl al-Sunnah wa al-Jama'ah" (People of the Prophet's Practice and Unified Community). Adherents to Shia Islam account for 12–15 percent of all Muslims worldwide.

Shia Islam grew out of political struggles against the Umayyad caliphs. As a result of its political and theological evolution, it came to incorporate the descendants of several different trends: activists, moderates, and extremists. In addition, Shiite leadership is divided into different positions and differs in the degree of approved activism by clerics. The Ithna Ashariyya, called Twelvers by Westerners and Jafariyya by adherents for their school of Islamic law, were historically moderates; the Ismailiyya (Seveners) were labeled extremists, or *ghulat,* by their enemies; and the Zaydiyya (Fivers) were activists (in their support of Zayd in his jihad against the caliph). The three groups are named according to the prominent figures in the chain of religious leaders (*a'imah,* or imams) whom each recognizes as constituting the proper line of religious authority passed down to them from the Prophet Muhammad. The Ithna Ashariyya, or Twelvers, are the dominant form of Shiism in Iran and Iraq.

Shiism is the dominant branch of Islam in Iran (90 percent of the population), Iraq, Lebanon, Bahrain, and Azerbaijan. Shiism also has adherents in Syria, Yemen, East Africa, India, Pakistan, Afghanistan, Tajikistan, Turkey, Qatar, Kuwait, the United Arab Emirates, the Eastern Province of Saudi Arabia, and many areas outside the Middle East, such as the United States, Canada, South Asia, the United Kingdom, Europe, Australia, and East Africa.

The Shiat Ali (Party or Partisans of Ali) were those who preferred the succession of Ali ibn Abi Talib as *khalifa* (caliph) when the Prophet Muhammad died. Ali ibn Abi Talib was the son-in-law of Muhammad by marriage to Muhammad's only surviving daughter, Fatima.

Ali accepted Abu Bakr as caliph, or political leader of the Muslims, even though Ali's supporters preferred Ali, and he also accepted the caliph Umar. The caliphate was then offered to him, but he was told that he would have to follow the precedents of Abu Bakr and Umar, and Ali refused to do this.

His supporters agitated again when Uthman became the third caliph. Uthman was so disliked for nepotism and the enrichment of his Umayyad relatives that a revolt occurred in which he was killed. Ali's followers recognized him as the fourth caliph in 656 CE. However, the Umayyads claimed the caliphate for Muawiya, cousin of Uthman, and this led to two civil wars in Islam and Ali's assassination in 661. Following Ali's death, his son Hasan was forced to abdicate, and his other son Husayn fought the Umayyads and was killed at Karbala. These events are commemorated in Shiism and given a deeply symbolic meaning.

While all Muslims revere the Prophet and his family (known as Ahl al-Bayt, or People of the House), Sunni Muslims recognize a large number of the Prophet's early companions at Medina as transmitters of hadith, the short texts relating Muhammad's words, actions, or preferences. In contrast, Shias do not recognize the authority of certain companions and teach the traditions (hadith) transmitted by others or the Ahl al-Bayt from the Prophet, his daughter Fatima, and Ali on to Ali's sons Hasan and Husayn and also the succession of imams who followed them. More important, because Ali had rejected the injunction to follow the precedents of the first two caliphs rather than the sunna (traditions or practices) of the Prophet, the foundational logic for Shiism to develop its own *fiqh,* or legal school, was set.

In the Umayyad period, the followers of Ali began to develop their own attitudes and worldview in contrast to other Muslims. The Battle of Karbala in October 680 between the supporters and relatives of Muhammad's grandson Husayn ibn Ali and forces of Yazid I, the Umayyad caliph, reinforced the Shia belief in *walaya,* or devotion to the Prophet's family, and also provided a reason for rebellion. A movement called the *tawabbun* (penitents) rose up to fight the Umayyads a year after the Battle of Karbala because they had not defended Husayn then, and 3,000 of them were killed.

Shiites believe that Ali was the first imam, thereby inheriting the *nass,* or spiritual legitimacy, of the Prophet. The imam is the sole legitimate religious successor of the Prophet, and each imam designates his own successor. In Shia Islam, each imam is held to have special knowledge of the inner truth of the Koran, Muhammad's sunna, and Islam. This institution is called the imamate in English (*a'imah*). Those in the *a'imah,* or chain of imams, are believed to be infallible, sinless, and personally guided by Allah (God) and are also believed to possess the divine authority over Islam and humanity granted to Ali by the Prophet Muhammad.

Shiites and Sunnis have the same beliefs about Allah, who has omnipotence over all beings and is also perceived as merciful and beneficent, closer to man than his own jugular vein and one who cares deeply about his creation. In both branches of Islam there is also a dynamic between faith and the acceptance of divine will along with the responsibility of the human believer. Indeed, apart from the differences in the Shia view of leadership, the two sects are very similar in many aspects. They diverge, however, in their legal systems. The Shias recognize all the same religious duties as the Sunnis, which are described in the study of Islam in the West as the Five Pillars with two additional duties.

The Shias stress the unicity or oneness (*tawhid*) of Allah, a strict monotheism, and the avoidance of any trace of polytheism. They support social justice (*'adalah*), which means equity within society, and aid to the oppressed and the needy. As with Sunni Muslims, the Shias adhere to the principle of the *hisba,* or commanding the good and forbidding the reprehensible. This refers to all that is licit or recommended in Islamic law as opposed to sins that are forbidden. Entrance into Paradise is based on doing more good than evil or on martyrdom. All Muslims, Shia as well as Sunni, respect the prophets, including Abraham, Moses, Jesus, and Muhammad, whom they believe revealed to humans the true religion of Allah.

The concept of the *a'imah*—that specific leaders are appointed by Allah and then designated by other imams (*nass*)—grew in strength thanks to the sixth imam, Jafar al-Sadiq. His followers developed the Twelver legal and theological tradition. The last of these 12 imams, Muhammad al-Mahdi, did not make himself known at the death of the 11th imam, al-Hasan al-Askari; however, texts revealed his presence. Mahdi is believed to be hiding on Earth, neither alive nor dead but in a state of occultation and will return at the Day of Judgment and the Resurrection (*qiyamah*) when Allah will decide the fate of all humanity, Muslim and non-Muslim alike.

The Twelvers believe that Mahdi, born in 689, was the son of Hasan. The Shias believe that Mahdi was in hiding from the caliph and that between the years 874 and 941 he communicated by letters with his people. During this period, called the Lesser Occultation, the community recognized four regents for Mahdi. In his last letter, he wrote that he would no longer communicate with humanity. Thus, the period from 941 to the present is known as the Greater Occultation.

In Twelver Islam, every human is held accountable for his or her deeds. The deeds of each individual are judged by Allah and weighed on a scale. If the good outweighs the evil, then the individual gains entrance into Paradise. If the evil outweighs the good, the individual spends eternity in Hell. The Shias, like the Sunnis, also believe that the prophets, imams, and martyrs can intercede with Allah for a soul on the Day of Judgment and may seek this intercession (*shafa'a*) if possible through prayer, religious rituals, or appeals to the Fourteen Infallibles: the Prophet Muhammad, his daughter Fatima, and the Twelve Imams, or martyrs. They also seek redemption through the ritual of repentance performed on the Day of Ashura, the commemoration of Imam Husayn's death.

Shiism's Twelvers, the largest Shia group, proclaim the necessity of obligatory religious duties or acts of outward worship. The first is the *shahada,* or testimony that there is no God but God and that Muhammad is his prophet and Ali his imam. The next is prayer (*salat*), recited five or more times a day. The third is fasting (*sawm*) during the daylight hours for all of the month of Ramadan, the ninth month of the Islamic calendar. The fourth religious practice is the pilgrimage (*hajj*), a journey to the holy city of Mecca that should be made at least once during a person's life if he or she is physically and financially able to undertake it. The fifth religious practice is the paying of *zakat,* a voluntary tax that is used to support the poor, to spread Islam or sometimes for other purposes, such as aid to travelers and the funding of jihad. The assessment of *zakat* should be 2.5 percent of one's income and assets in any given year. (All Muslims also give gifts of money during and at the end of Ramadan and the Eid al-Adha, but these are in addition to *zakat*.) Another form of tithing, the *khums,* is a 20 percent tax on all annual profits from any source levied on all adult males and is used to support the mosque and the clerics. Jihad is also a commanded duty in Shiism and refers to the struggle of the faithful to please Allah as well as to defend Islam by waging war against those who attack Muslims. The idea of the *walaya* is important in Shiism (but also in Sufi Islam), as is the *tabarra*. These mean a special reverence for all members, past and descended, of the Ahl al-Bayt; the guardianship of the imamate; and the disassociation from all enemies of the Ahl al-Bayt.

In addition to the Shia groups mentioned above, there are others. The Shaykhiyya of Basra and Bahrain are a subsect of Twelver Shia, influenced by Akhbari thought. The Druze (who call themselves *muwahiddun,* or unitarians) are an offshoot of the Ismailiyya sect, and the Alawites found in Syria and Turkey are a distinct subsect of Shiism. Sunni Muslims and some Shias, however, consider the Alawi sect extreme because of some of its syncretic practices. Nonetheless, it was declared a licit school of Islam in a fatwa issued by Imam Musa al-Sadr in order to legitimate the rule of President Hafiz al-Assad, an Alawi, in Syria. Although all branches of Islam believe in a divine savior, the Mahdi (the Guided One) who will come at the Day of Judgment, the Twelver branch of Shiism holds that the Twelfth Imam, or Hidden Imam since he is in occultation, is the Mahdi and call him the Imam Mahdi.

In Iran, many believe that the Imam Mahdi will reappear from a well at the mosque in Jamkaran just outside of the holy city of Qum, Iran. The site is frequently visited by Shiite pilgrims who drop messages into the well hoping that the Hidden Imam will hear them and grant their requests. Along with the Imam Mahdi's return at the Day of Judgment, there are various beliefs about other millenarian events and wars that will occur before this period.

Since the disappearance of the Twelfth Imam, the Shia *ulama* (clerics) have served as his deputies, interpreting the law and leading the Shiite faithful under the authority of the Hidden Imam. In Twelver Shiism it is believed that four persons acted as the deputies or special vice-regents (*wakala al-khassa*) of the Hidden Imam during the Lesser Occultation. These persons were called the *bab* (gate) or *na'ib* (deputy) for the imam. From 941 there have been no overt claims of a *bab* except for Sayyid Ali Muhammad (known as "The Bab"), who established Babism in the 19th century, and the Shaykhi Shia, who put forth the idea of the perfect Shia who lives in each age. Generally, in this period, the idea is that there is a *wakala al-'amma,* or a general vice-regency, that has been delegated to the Shia clerics. When Iran's Ayatollah Ruhollah Khomeini and his government established the system of rule of the cleric (*vilayat-e faqih* or wilayat al-faqih in Arabic, which can be translated as the rule of the jurisprudent—the one authorized to interpret the law) in Iran, there were disputes about whether he was to be considered the *na'ib al-imam,* or deputy of the Hidden Imam. The idea of rule of the cleric was and is still controversial throughout Shia Islam.

Khomeini's official title became "Supreme Faqih" (Jurist), and he governed the Council of Guardians as its supreme religio-political authority. There had been several clerics more senior to Khomeini who were, however, marginalized or even assassinated after the Islamic Revolution. Khomeini's successor, Ali Husayni Khamenei, was not the most senior of the clerics who might potentially have followed Khomeini in power. Khamenei was granted the title of ayatollah to ensure his authority. Some described him as a political appointee.

While there was never a concept of Sunni Islam as a sect as it is described today, the non-Alid Muslims (those who did not insist on Ali gaining political leadership) accepted the institution of the caliphate even though the caliph was not a spiritual descendant of the Prophet. Still, the caliph received an oath of allegiance from his people and had to be pious and promote and protect Islam. Alids (supporters of Ali), later called Shias, accepted their temporal rulers but did not regard them as being spiritually legitimate in the manner of the imams. For purposes of survival, they could deny their Shia beliefs if need be in the practice known as *taqqiya* (dissimulation). There are major legal and philosophical differences in Shia Islam, such as the theme of the oppressed Muslims who act out their penitence for their inability to defend Husayn at Karbala, the imamate, the concept of the Occultation and the Return, and the concept of *marjaiyya,* the idea that a believer should follow a particular cleric as a guide. Minor differences pertain to aspects of daily prayer and the commencement of holidays, which often begin on one day in Iran and, typically, a day earlier in Saudi Arabia and other Sunni centers.

Shiite Islamic education is centered in Najaf and Karbala in Iraq and in Qum and Mashhad in Iran, with other religious authorities in Tehran and additional centers of learning elsewhere. Shia clerics from Lebanon typically studied in Iraq or Iran. One of the most influential Shia theorists in Iran following the Islamic Revolution was probably Abd al-Karim Sorush, who is famous for his idea of the expansion and contraction of Islamic law (*qabz va bast-e shari'at*). The most senior cleric in Iraq today is the Shia Grand Ayatollah Sistani. The clerical establishment in Iraq is referred to as the *hawzah,* and its duty is to train the future clerics of Shiism, provide judgments, and officiate over pilgrimages and those who wish to be buried at the holy sites. Other important cities of Shia learning are Qum, Mashhad, and Tehran, all in Iran.

The last great single *marja' al-mutlaq* (the absolute source of emulation), Ayatollah Burujerdi, died in 1961. Debate then began between different reformist leaders about the degree of activism in which clerics should engage. In the 1960s a more radical, or activist, Shiism began to develop. Informal gatherings and new publications began to spread new radical Shiite thought. Ayatollah Khomeini's resistance to Mohammad Reza Shah Pahlavi was significant, but so too was the work of Dr. Ali Shariati (1933–1977).

Educated in Mashhad and Paris, Shariati challenged the quietism of many religious scholars, writing essays and giving lectures to galvanize a new activism in Shiism that combined with existentialism and Third Worldist views. Another major influence on radical Shiism in this period was Murtaza Mutahari (1920–1979).

Sunnis and Shiites have different approaches to jurisprudence, or the making of Islamic law, and therefore also in the issuance of fatwas to broader religious questions of Muslims. The different Sunni schools of law use as sources (*usul al-fiqh*) the Koran, the hadith, analogy (*qiyas*), and *ijma*, or the consensus of the community at Medina or of the jurists. In earlier periods, these legal schools also used *ray* (opinion of the jurist) or *ijtihad*, a particular technique of intellectual problem solving. In the 10th century, the Sunni jurists decided to stop using *ijtihad* so as to avoid the introduction of too many innovations into sharia (Islamic law). However, the Shia legal school of the Twelvers retained this principle. Consequently, Shia cleric-jurists who train in this technique and qualify receive the title of *mujtahid*, or one who can enact *ijtihad*.

Ijtihad has come to mean more than a principle of Islamic jurisprudence. As contemporary activist Shiism was developing, Ali Shariati began to apply *ijtihad* to Muslim life, including a vibrant definition of monotheism and the application of Muslim principles.

There are various ranks of clerics in Shia Islam in addition to the *mujtahid*, such as the elevated designations of ayatollah and grand ayatollah that other clerics should agree on. In addition, a Shia may follow his or her own preferred *marja' al-taqlid* (source of emulation). Above all of these clerics, there may be one agreed-upon *marja' al-mutlaq*, or source of emulation of the age.

These are not the only differences between Sunni and Shia Islam. Shias constituted minorities in such countries as Lebanon and Saudi Arabia, where they were an underclass socially and economically. In the modern period, leaders such as Ali Shariati and Imam Musa Sadr in Lebanon supported populism and addressed the discrimination against and suffering of the Shiite masses.

While at times some Sunni groups have expressed both discrimination and hatred toward Shia Muslims, there have also been efforts at ecumenism and more cooperation between the sects. Al-Azhar University in Egypt teaches about the Jafariyya (Twelver) *madhhab*, or legal school of Islam, in spite of the government of Egypt having outlawed Shiism. It should also be noted that Shia and Sunni Muslims had coexisted peacefully and have frequently intermarried in Iraq. Shia Muslims were often members of the Communist Party or the Baath Party, and just like the Iranian clerics responding to the inroads made by secular ideologies in that country, the clerics in Iraq began an Islamic movement in part to encourage youths to reengage with Islamic education. When this movement developed from a clerical organization into an activist one, Iraqi president Saddam Hussein ruthlessly suppressed it. Sadly, the end of Hussein's rule brought Shia-Sunni sectarian conflict to Iraq, fueled in part by Sunni Islamists and nationalists who viewed the new Shia-dominated majority as conspirators with the Americans and call the Shias apostates or renegades. After the withdrawal of U.S. and coalition troops from Iraq in late 2011, the Shia-dominated government of Nuri al-Maliki engaged in wholesale repression and even violence against Iraq's Sunni population, which led to a renewed insurgency and even more sectarian violence.

Richard M. Edwards and Sherifa Zuhur

See also: Iraq, History of, 1990–Present; Political Parties, Iraq: Islamic Dawa Party; Prime Minister, Iraq: Nuri al-Maliki; Sunni Islam

References

Daftari, Farhad. *The Isma'ilis: Their History and Doctrines.* Cambridge: Cambridge University Press, 1990.

Fuller, Graham E., and Rend Rahim Francke. *The Arab Shi'a: The Forgotten Muslims.* Hampshire, UK: Palgrave Macmillan, 2001.

Gregorian, Vartan. *Islam: A Mosaic, Not a Monolith.* Baltimore: Brookings Institute Press, 2004.

Sobhani, Ayatollah Jafar, and Reza Shah Kazemi. *Doctrines of Shi'i Islam: A Compendium of Imami Beliefs and Practices.* London: I. B. Tauris, 2001.

Sistani, Sayyid Ali Husayn al- (1930–)

Islamic cleric and the most imposing traditional religious authority in Iraq, a prolific author (38 books), and a key presence in post-2003 Iraq. Sayyid Ali Husayn al-Sistani was born in Mashhad, Iran, on August 4, 1930, into a sayyid family that traced its lineage to the Prophet Muhammad. Sistani began his religious training in Mashhad and then moved to Qum, Iran, to study Islamic jurisprudence and theory when the supreme and only *marja'-e mutlaq* (source of emulation) of his time, Muhammad Husayn Burujerdi, taught there.

Sistani moved to Najaf, Iraq, in 1951. There he attended lectures by Grand Ayatollahs Abu al-Qassim Khoi and Sheikh Hussayn Hilli. Upon his return to Mashhad, Sistani received the certificate of *ijtihad* by both Khoi and Hilli. *Ijtihad* is a source of law in Jafari jurisprudence involving independent deductive and creative reasoning attainable only after sufficient study and with acknowledgment by certain clerics.

Sistani later returned to Najaf to teach, remaining a quietist during the Islamic revival and rise of activist parties, such as the Islamic Dawa Party, and surviving when other Shiite clerics were persecuted by the Baathist government. Sistani served as the prayer imam in Khoi's own mosque from 1987 to 1993 and announced his status as a *marja' al-taqlid* (religious source of emulation) after Khoi's death. This led to challenges to his authority by clerics in Qum, but Sistani shrugged them off thanks largely to responses of his *wakil* (agent) and son-in-law Javad Shahrastani. Sistani's mosque was closed in 1994, and he was placed under house arrest. Sistani rarely traveled except for pilgrimages, but he went to London in 2004 to be treated for a heart condition.

Grand Ayatollah Sistani and his *wakils,* including Shahrastani, built and continue to maintain a vast network of adherents and centers of learning and charity. This includes a main office in Qum, which manages his mosques, as well as scholarly libraries, charities, schools, hospitals, seminaries, the publishing of Islamic legal codes, and the distribution of preachers' and students' salaries. The main office also manages the transfers to other agents of his international network, which consists of mosques, charitable organizations, Internet sites, and seminaries, all of which operate on a multimillion-dollar budget. Sistani's activities in Najaf further the *hawzah* (scholarly establishment) there, shaping the future role of clerics, supporting pilgrims and other religious traffic to Iraq's holy cities, and managing educational, Internet, and publishing outlets.

Beyond his religious reach, since 2003 Sistani has significantly impacted the political life of Iraqis, facilitating the integration of clerical influence in the country with government agencies, for the dominant political parties are Islamist and have been extremely powerful within the various ministries. Indeed, he helped move the Iraqi polity more toward an Islamic democratic system than the secular, liberal democracy envisioned by American administrators during 2003–2011.

From the beginning of the Iraqi occupation, the Americans realized that Sistani was an important contact point for them in postinvasion Iraq, but they did not fully understand his beliefs or stances vis-à-vis Islamic life and government, Iraqi sovereignty, Iran's role in the country, or Shiism. He refused to meet with them, as he did not support a lengthy occupation of Iraq and did not wish to be compromised. Communications were thus carried on through intermediaries.

With his thick Iranian accent and his image as a cleric steeped in the Iranian tradition, Sistani has garnered ire from those who oppose Islamic clerics, the Shias, and Iran in general. He could have initially more forcefully opposed the American occupation, but he instead urged Iraqi cooperation to build stability and independence. However, on June 26, 2003, Sistani's office called for an immediate general election instead of the formation by the Coalition Provisional Authority (CPA) of a transitional government. He then opposed the CPA-supported plan for caucuses that would precede an election. His followers staged protests throughout Iraq and ultimately defeated the plan. Sistani, however, was sustaining his legacy as a quietist scholar who had to preserve clerical independence from politicians and the media. At the same time, he had to oppose undue Western interference in Iraqi affairs.

Sistani nevertheless encouraged all Iraqis to participate in the 2005 elections as their Islamic duty. The result was the emergence of a democratically elected coalition of Shiite parties with an Islamist agenda. One may conclude that Sistani's interpretation of the role of the cleric (*ulama*) differs from that of the late Ayatollah Ruhollah Khomeini's in that Sistani does not argue for *vilayat al-faqih* (or wilayat al-faqih in Arabic meaning rule of the cleric or rule of the jurisprudent—the one authorized to interpret the law) and opposes authoritarianism. Instead, he holds that the cleric's role in Muslim society is a holistic defense of Islam.

Sistani has decried the civil and sectarian violence that has convulsed Iraq since 2005, calling for restraint in revenge attacks against Sunni Iraqis, although his ability to moderate these conflicts, or inter-Shiite conflicts, in central and southern Iraq is limited. He opposed the Iraqi government's 2008 attacks on the Mahdi Army, the militia controlled by cleric Muqtada al-Sadr, because of the need for Iraqi unity. Sistani did not favor the proposed mutual security agreement between Iraq and the United States, which became operational after the United Nations Security Council's authorization of U.S. troop presence in Iraq ended in December 2008.

In more recent years, Sistani has urged Iraqis to unify in the face of threats from militant Islamists, most notably appealing directly to Iraqis to fight the Islamic State of Iraq and Syria (ISIS) in June 2014. He has also decried violence against Iraqi Christians. In the spring of 2014, Sistani was mentioned as a possible recipient of the Nobel Peace Prize.

Sherifa Zuhur

See also: Insurgency and Opposition: Mahdi Army; Iraq, History of, 1990–Present; Islamic State of Iraq and al-Sham (ISIS); Political Parties, Iraq: Islamic Dawa Party; Sadr, Muqtada al-; Shia Islam

References

"Iraqi MPs Launch Move to Nominate Ayatollah Sistani for Nobel Peace Prize." *Tehran Times,* March 8, 2014, http://www.tehrantimes.com/middle-east/114569-iraqi-mps-launch-move-to-nominate-ayatollah-sistani-for-nobel-peace-prize.

Khalaji, Mehdi. *The Last Marja: Sistani and the End of Traditional Religious Authority in Shiism.* Policy Focus #59. Washington, DC: Washington Institute for Middle Eastern Affairs, September 2006.

Rahimi, Babak. *Ayatollah Sistani and the Democratization of Post-Ba'thist Iraq.* Special Report No. 187. Washington, DC: U.S. Institute of Peace, June 2007.

Sunni Islam

Largest of the two predominant branches of Islam. Approximately 85 percent of Muslims worldwide are adherents of Sunni Islam, although the exact proportions of the two branches are disputed. Muslims themselves seldom use the word "Sunni." The term "Sunni" derives from a medieval Arabic phrase, *ahl al-sunnah wa al-jama'a,* meaning those who live according to the Prophet's model, unified in a community. In the early period, this term did not refer to all Muslims but rather to those who were engaged in Islamic scholarship and learning. The sunna (way) of the Prophet Muhammad refers to his tradition, or practice, of Islam during his 23 years of life following the initial revelation of Allah's words to him. However, sunna generally referred to any tradition of the ancient Arabs.

It is mostly in the West that Muslims are differentiated as Sunnis or Shias. If asked, a Muslim may instead identify himself by a school of Islamic law or jurisprudence, such as the Hanafi school, which was the official legal doctrine of the Ottoman Empire, or of a particular movement. Since the most recent Islamic revival (*sahwa islamiyya*) began in the 1970s, the term *sunniyyun* (plural of *sunni* used interchangeably with *Islamiyyun*) has acquired the meaning of a very devout Muslim, or a Salafi.

In contrast with the more institutionalized clerics, courts, and systems of Sunni Muslim learning, Sufi Islam is a mystical movement within Islam, the goal of which is the spiritual development of the individual. Sufis seek out personal guides (*shaykhs* or *pirs*) and are organized into brotherhoods (*tariqats*). There are Shia as well as Sunni Sufi orders. Sufism can be highly ascetic, while mainstream Islam is not. In contemporary times, sometimes even official clerics are also Sufis; however, the Salafists oppose Sufism.

Sunni Muslims do not adhere to the doctrine of the imams, as do several sects of Shia Muslims (excluding the Zaydiyyas). In the past, they generally judged the validity of the caliph (the temporal political and military leader) or the caliphate (Islamic government) itself by his or its adherence to the faith and the order and harmony that he or it maintained. In contrast with the Shias, Sunni Muslims believe that Abu Bakr, Umar, and Uthman—the first three Rashidun caliphs following Muhammad—were legitimate successors of Muhammad and that they are of equal standing with the fourth caliph, Ali, Muhammad's son-in-law. Ali became the fourth caliph in 656 CE after the murder of Caliph Uthman and was himself assassinated in 661. However, there were other Muslims, not Ali's supporters, who also opposed the Umayyads, so the political divisions over leadership were complex.

It was not a requirement that the political and religious leadership in Sunni Islam trace its lineage through Ali, although the requirements of a caliph as defined by the scholar Abu al-Hasan Ali Ibn Muhammad Ibn Habib al-Mawardi (972–1058) indicated that he must be of the Prophet Muhammad's Quraysh tribe, male, not physically impaired, and pious. Any link to the Ahl al-Bayt, the immediate family members of the Prophet, was, however, highly regarded. The caliphs lost their real authority in 1055 with the arrival of the Seljuk Turks as a governing force. They retained an element of religious authority only in name, as the caliph was mentioned in the Friday prayers. With the Mongol sack of Baghdad in 1258, the caliphs lost all power. For Sunni Muslims, other political leaders were acceptable, though they were supposed to uphold Islamic law. When the Ottoman sultans declared themselves to be caliphs in order to wage jihad, other Muslims questioned their religious claim. By the 20th century, some Muslims understood the caliphate as an ideal structure but one that could be replaced by other forms of authority. Others supported attempts to restore the caliphate.

In the absence of the caliphate, Muslim politics continued under the precept that other rulers, sultans, or emirs would rule to the best of their ability in accordance with sharia (Islamic law) and uphold the *hisba,* the principle of "commanding the good and forbidding the evil," a key principle in Islam. Clerics, or *ulama* (those who possess *'ilm,* or religious knowledge), were to be consulted by the ruler, issue fatwas, and help to guide the believers.

To justify Islamic rule, the Ottomans, who were Sunni Muslims, later governed under a particular theory called the circle of equity, in which mutual responsibilities were to provide equity, security, and justice. In the 20th century both Sunni and Shia politicized Islamic movements argued for a more intensely Islamic government. The Muslim Brotherhood, Hamas, Hezbollah, Jamaat Islamiya, and Al Qaeda have all taken this position. These groups draw on very important arguments about governance and the state that have developed in Islamic history. The Muslim Brotherhood relinquished jihad as armed struggle and sought to change society through *dawa,* a program involving recruitment, education, and social support. Hezbollah and Hamas argue for both armed struggle and *dawa.* Islamic Jihad (in Egypt), Jamaat Islamiya, and Al Qaeda all argue that the groups who only conducted *dawa* are not supporting Muslims and that jihad as armed struggle is necessary. However, Jamaat Islamiya and Egyptian Islamic Jihad (in Egypt, excluding those members who joined Al Qaeda) recanted their use of jihad beginning in 1997 and reached a truce with the Egyptian government in 1999.

In general, individual interpretations of Islamic law by scholars may vary. There is no pope or central authority in Sunni Islam. In Sunni Islam, unlike Shia Islam, there is no *marjaiyya,* or formal policy of choosing a cleric as a source of emulation. However, there are today many very popular Sunni clerics and preachers whose followers are loyal to their various positions.

The Sunni legal schools employ a principle of lawmaking known as *ijma,* or consensus, that is not employed by the Shia legal schools. However, there are differences in the legal definitions of that consensus. Additionally, a Sunni Muslim could resort to a cleric of one school to obtain a ruling, or fatwa, and is generally expected to adhere to the commonly acknowledged features of his own school. But Muslims may also seek advice from other clerics or authorities, and advice columns in newspapers and on the Internet provide differing opinions, sometimes based on the positions of other legal schools.

Muslims believe that the Koran is the literal word of God delivered in Arabic by the angel Gabriel to Muhammad over a period of 23 years. Any desecration of the Koran is therefore a desecration of the very words of Allah. Although the Koran is the final statement of Allah to humanity, when it does not offer explicit advice on a particular matter, a Muslim may appeal to a jurist to look to the Prophet's sunna, as recorded in the hadith, or collected materials concerning the tradition, behavior, practices, and sayings of the Prophet. They may also use *qiyas,* or a type of analogy, in determining the licitness of any action or behavior, or the principle of *ijma.*

The hadith are always introduced by listing the chain of their transmitters. Ideally, the first transmitter of the text was a companion (*sahabah*) of Muhammad. An important companion was Abu Bakr, also known as "The Most Truthful" (*al-Siddiq*), the first caliph. The next companions in level of importance are the next two caliphs, Umar and Uthman. The Shias reject the hadith transmitted by those they call "unjust companions," who repudiated the leadership of Ali ibn abi Talib. Although these 3 are important companions, there are 10 who are thought to warrant paradise. A much longer list of *sahabah* exists because Sunnis consider anyone who knew or even saw Muhammad, accepted his teachings, and died as a Muslim to be a companion. Early Sunni scholars identified these companions, wrote their biographies, and listed them in various reference texts. This identification was essential, because their testimonies and their reputation for veracity affirm and determine the content of the hadith and therefore the sunna.

There are many collections of these original oral traditions, but they are graded according to their soundness with six respected collections, two of which—that of Muslim and Bukhari—are considered most reliable. However, many Muslims repeat and believe in hadith that are not necessarily the most sound, and since the reform movement of the 19th century, some Muslims believe that the hadith brought many unwanted innovations or, conversely, too much imitation of tradition (*taqlid*) into Islam. Shia Islamic law generally uses hadith that pertain to Muhammad as told to members of Ali's family. These variations lead to some differences in Sunni Islamic law and Shia Islamic law.

Muslims must practice their faith through demonstrated religious rituals and obligations. Many sources speak of five religious practices or duties, often referred to as the Five Pillars. The first pillar is called bearing witness (*shahadah*) and is the recitation of the creed or confession of faith, called the Testimony of Faith: "There is no God, but Allah; and Muhammad is His prophet." The *shahadah* is also uttered as part of the Muslim call (*adhan*) to prayer and is part of the Tashahud, which follows each set of two prayer sequences, when they are recited at least five times daily (at different times two, three, or four sequences are the minimum required). The second pillar is prayer (*salat*), performed at least five times a day (dawn, noon, midafternoon, sunset, and evening). Muslims purify themselves before prayer by washing their hands, face, mouth, nose, ears, and feet. During prayer, all Muslims face Mecca. The third pillar is fasting (*sawm*) during the daylight hours for all of the month of Ramadan, the ninth month of the Islamic lunar calendar. This fasting means that no food or beverages are consumed and that there is no smoking or sexual intercourse. Those who are sick are excused from fasting and make up their fast. Other days of fasting may be observed, but it is obligatory during Ramadan. The fourth pillar is almsgiving, effectively a tax (*zakat*) of 2.5 percent calculated on one's income and assets. But unlike a tax, it is supposed to be voluntary. It is used for the community's poor, the promotion of Islam, and the maintenance of the mosque and other religious institutions. The fifth pillar is the required pilgrimage (hajj) once in a lifetime to the holy city of Mecca, as commanded in the Koran in *surah* XXII, al-Hajj, 22–33.

The responsibility for performing these duties falls on the individual, but stricter Muslims and Muslim governments hold that it is the duty of the state to command the good and thus to enforce their performance. There are other strictures as well. For example, Muslims must not drink alcohol, not simply as a forbidden substance but because it clouds alertness and judgment and makes it impossible to pray. Pork is forbidden, as are games of chance. Many Muslim women believe that covering their heads is a required individual duty, but others do not. Modest behavior is, however, required of both men and women.

Ethical behavior is very important to Islamic belief, including the commitment to social justice, as in protection of the weak and aid to the poor and socially disadvantaged. Islam seeks to promote an ethical life lived within a community. It is more difficult in many ways to be a good Muslim while fulfilling one's obligations to family and community than to live as a hermit, and the Prophet Muhammad is said to have promoted marriage and discouraged celibacy or an extreme ascetic lifestyle. Many of the rules regarding relations between men and women, which non-Muslims find very strict and hard to understand, are indeed intended to provide a moral and ethical grounding for the community.

Muslims are concerned with *iman,* or faith, as well as acts of submission (*islam*) and rightful intentions (*ihsan*), and many religio-philosophical principles guide them. The most basic aspect of Islam is belief in Allah and the Oneness (*tawhid*) of Allah. This monotheism is expressed in many ways. Muslims believe in the prophets and believe that they brought important messages to mankind, but Muhammad is considered the Seal of Prophecy, or the last prophet. Nonetheless, Jesus, Moses, Abraham, and others are revered. However, Muslims believe that some Jews did not heed the word of God in his divine message to them. Muslims, who believe that Jesus was only a prophet, also argue that Christians wrongly recognize Christ as Father and Divine Spirit. The doctrine of the Trinity violates the idea of the Oneness of Allah.

Muslims recognize the scriptures as revelations of Allah. Allah was the creator, but he did not simply create the world and humankind and leave humanity to fend for itself. Rather, Allah provided revelations for the guidance of men. The Koran is the transcending revelation of Allah that cannot be contradicted by any other revelations of Allah. Still, Muslims recognize other revelations, which include the Jewish and Christian holy scriptures as well as the Zoroastrian texts.

Muslims believe in the angels (*malaika*), who are the servants of Allah. Angels were not given the free will that Allah granted to humans. Their duties include recording all human deeds, ensouling the fetus at 120 days of gestation (although some Islamic scholars believe that ensoulment occurs on the 40th or 80th day), watching over and caring for creation, gathering souls at death, and much more.

All Muslims also believe in the Day of Judgment and in the Resurrection (*qiyama*), when Allah will return to judge all of humanity, Muslim and non-Muslim, including the dead. After the Resurrection, every human is held accountable for his or her deeds. The deeds of each individual are judged by Allah and weighed on a scale. If the good outweighs the evil, then the individual gains entrance into Paradise. If the evil outweighs the good, the individual spends eternity in Hell.

In the pre-Islamic era, referred to as the *jahiliyya* (time of barbarity), people believed entirely in preordination. Islam rejects this passivity because people possess free will and can thus choose to do good or evil and are held accountable for their decisions. At the same time, it is difficult to retain faith in the face of tragedy, poverty, or disaster. The Muslim belief in the omnipotence of God, his transcendence and simultaneous immanence, is meant to solace the believer.

The application of reason, in the form of Hellenic philosophical arguments to theology, philosophy, and the sciences, was prominent in the golden age of Islam. Reacting to the philosophers and those who used logical reasoning (*kalam*) were Traditionists, the scholars who focused on hadith to determine the sunna and rejected the methodology of logical reasoning.

Multiple Sunni traditions, or schools of law and theology, arose over time. Not all survive today. These schools share the basic theology described above and assert the primacy of the Koranic revelation, but there are notable differences.

Sunni Islamic law is based on the Koran and the sunna, as nuanced by the particular hadith collector and his interpretation. Different scholars using different assumptions, reasoning, hermeneutics (guiding interpretive principles), and source materials arrived at different applications of Islamic law, which were organized into schools known as *madhahib*. Muslims assert that sharia never changes but that the understanding and application of it into jurisprudence (*fiqh*) does change, since jurisprudence is carried out by human beings. Muslims generally seek to avoid illicit innovation (*bidah*), but many "innovations" have to be considered. The Koran predates the telegraph. Thus, the application of *fiqh* to adjudicate the use of the telegraph was a matter of interpretation. In addition to the usual sources of law, jurists took into account *maslaha,* public benefit or the common good, in considering new technology.

There are four surviving major schools of law in Sunni Islam. The various schools predominate in different regions. These dominant Sunni schools of law are Hanbali, Hanafi, Maliki, and Shafi, and all use the Koran as their primary source.

Hanbali law is the strictest tradition and was practiced by Muslims in Saudi Arabia, Qatar, Syria, Palestine, and elsewhere; with the growth of Salafism and neo-Salafism, it has expanded. It was founded by Ahmad ibn Hanbal and is the dominant tradition on the Arabian Peninsula, although it has adherents in Iraq, Syria, Jerusalem, and Egypt as well.

The Hanafi *madhhab* may be the largest school. It was founded by Abu Hanifa and encompasses 30 percent of Sunnis. Its adherents are mainly in Turkey, Central Asia, the Balkans, Iraq, Afghanistan, Pakistan, India, Bangladesh, lower Egypt, and former states of the Soviet Union. Both the Mongol Empire and the Ottoman Empire promoted the Hanafi tradition. When the Ottoman sultan Selim the Grim (1512–1520) captured Palestine, he imposed Hanafi law on the region. The official judicial traditions and systems in contemporary Syria, Jordan, and Palestine are derived from the Hanafi tradition.

The Maliki school has approximately 15 percent of Sunnis as adherents. It was founded by Malik ibn Anas and has adherents in North Africa and West Africa, particularly upper Egypt, Algeria, Tunisia, Morocco, Mauritania, and Libya, as well as in the Sudan, Kuwait, Dubai, and Abu Dhabi. The Maliki school derives its *fiqh* through consensus more than do any of the other traditions. The Maliki system of lawmaking is built on the Koran and hadith, supplemented by an interpretation of *ijma* (consensus), as being the consensus or agreed opinion of the People of Medina, and analogy (*qiyas*). In addition, Malik considered the statements of the Prophet's companions and referred to the public good (*maslahah*), customary law (*urf*), common practice (*adat*), and several other legal principles.

The Shafi school was founded by Muhammad ibn Idris al-Shafi and has adherents in the southern Arabian Peninsula, the Hejaz, Palestine, Indonesia, Malaysia, Thailand, Cambodia, parts of India, the Philippines, Sudan, Ethiopia, Somalia, North Yemen, Kurdistan, Sri Lanka, and lower Egypt. The Shafi school utilizes the *usul al-fiqh* (roots of lawmaking) in a way that places *ijma* ahead of analogy.

Salafism, a reform movement in Islam, actually developed in two different contexts in the 18th century in Arabia and in the 19th century in Egypt and the Ottoman Empire. The 19th- to early 20th-century reformers Jamal al-Din al-Afghani, Muhammad Abduh, Qasim Amin, and Rashid Rida initiated a discussion about the decline of the Muslim world and the reforms it should carry out to overcome the negative influence of Western colonialism and imperialism. While Afghani looked for an Islamic ruler who would stand up to the West and believed that Pan-Islam could solve the problem, Muhammad Abduh, an Egyptian jurist, recommended reform of Islamic education and the methodology of Islamic law in which blind imitation of the past would cease. He thought that Sunni Muslims should consider a return to *ijtihad* (a Shia methodology of lawmaking) to meet contemporary requirements, and he wanted Western sciences introduced into the educational curriculum. Qasim Amin argued for an end to enforced marriages, female seclusion, and lack of education for women, while Rashid Rida pursued a somewhat stricter and more Islamist approach to the proper way of life for Muslims.

Earlier, Muhammad abd al-Wahhab in Arabia promoted a strict monotheism, which he claimed would cleanse Islam of many syncretic traditions that constituted *shirk,* or polytheism. This tradition is referred to by his enemies as Wahhabism, which is the general term used today in the West. The *muwahiddun,* or Unitarians, as they call themselves, who fought as warriors for the Saud tribe were known as the Ikhwan (brethren). In general, the *muwahiddun* are considered Salafis because they wanted to cleanse Islamic practice and society of un-Islamic accretions and innovations (*bida*) that had arisen through cultural synthesis. However, this cleansing is a matter of gradation, so not all Wahhabis, as the West calls them, are either violent purists or ardent Salafists. The Wahhabis adhere to the Hanbali school of law, although some modern Salafis speak of rejecting all legal tradition and utilizing only the Koran and the sunna. The Salafis were anti-Ottoman, anti-Shia, and anti-Sufi and opposed such practices as Sufi ceremonies and visiting tombs, even at Mecca. These Salafis called for jihad in its active form with which they, in alliance with the Saud family, drove out first the Ottomans and then, in a later historical period, the Rashids and the Hashimites.

Terrorist and Al Qaeda leader Osama bin Laden was a neo-Salafi and a Wahhabi. He believed that the Saudi Arabian royal family does not strictly uphold Wahhabi or Salafi values and should be militantly opposed for its alliance with the West. Other Salafis have been part of the resistance to U.S. occupation and the new Iraqi government in post-2003 Iraq.

Some Salafis consider the Shias to be renegades (this refers to a specific denigrating legal epithet given them during the civil wars in Islamic history) or apostates, apostasy being a capital crime in Islam. The Shias had come to fear and hate the Wahhabis because of their raids on Shia areas historically, but this animosity is not true of all Sunnis and Shias who, in general, lived peacefully alongside each other in prewar Iraq. Some charge that the United States and Israel, as well as certain Arab countries, are heightening fears in the region of a Shia crescent of influence, running from Iran to the Shias of Iraq and the Persian Gulf states and then to the Shias of Lebanon. Such discourse could create more problems among Muslims in the region. Therefore, King Abdullah of Saudi Arabia spoke out against sectarian discord. Elsewhere leaders such as at al-Azhar try to represent the Jafari *madhhab* as a legitimate legal school of Islam.

Richard M. Edwards and Sherifa Zuhur

See also: Shia Islam

References

Ahmed, Akbar S. *Islam Today: A Short Introduction to the Muslim World,* rev. ed. London: I. B. Tauris, 1999.

Esposito, John L. *The Oxford History of Islam.* New York: Oxford University Press, 2000.

Gregorian, Vartan. *Islam: A Mosaic, Not a Monolith.* Baltimore: Brookings Institute Press, 2004.

Sachiko, Muratam, and William C. Chittick. *The Vision of Islam.* New York: Paragon House, 1994.

U

United Nations Weapons Inspectors

Following the Persian Gulf War of 1991, the United Nations (UN) Security Council authorized a team of weapons inspectors to rid Iraq of all its weapons of mass destruction (WMD), which included biological and chemical weapons as well as all materials related to nuclear weapons development. As a condition for the cessation of hostilities against Iraq in the Persian Gulf War after the international coalition forces' liberation of Kuwait, the UN Security Council passed Resolution 687 on April 3, 1991. This called for the creation of the United Nations Special Commission (UNSCOM) to inspect and disarm Iraq's WMD as well as all its missiles with a range greater than 90 miles.

From 1991 to 1999, UNSCOM was charged with enforcing UN Resolution 687. In 1999 a successor to UNSCOM came into being. It was known as the United Nations Monitoring, Verification and Inspection Committee (UNMOVIC) and was in Iraq from December 2002 to March 2003. Although Iraq repeatedly sought to conceal the extent of its WMD program and also resisted cooperating fully with UNSCOM by, for example, denying inspectors access to certain sites, UNSCOM nevertheless engaged in significant disarmament activities. However, the sheer size of the country of Iraq, the technically complex nature of disarmament, and repeated Iraqi deception and resistance to UNSCOM efforts make it hard to know precisely the extent of success. For its part, Iraq accused UNSCOM of spying and of being a puppet of the United States and Israel.

In late 1998 UNSCOM withdrew from Iraq in the face of renewed Iraqi resistance and imminent punitive American and British air strikes in December. For the next four years, there were no weapons inspectors operating inside Iraq. This, of course, prompted concerns that Iraqi dictator Saddam Hussein had secretly renewed his WMD program.

Beginning in 2002, U.S. president George W. Bush demanded that Iraq comply with UN resolutions and disarm once and for all or face an invasion. On November 8, 2002, UN Security Council Resolution 1441 declared that Iraq was in violation of Resolution 687. It denounced Iraq's "omissions or false statements" with respect to its WMD stockpiles and offered Iraq "a final opportunity to comply with its disarmament obligations." In December 2002 in the face of an imminent American and British invasion of Iraq, Hussein agreed to allow UN weapons inspectors back into the country; however, they were withdrawn in March 2003 just before the beginning of the Iraq invasion (Operation Iraqi Freedom) on March 20, 2003.

The head of UNMOVIC, Hans Blix, a Swedish diplomat, reported to the UN on March 7, 2003, that Iraq had not provided sufficient documentary evidence to account for its WMD stockpiles and missiles. He expressed doubt as to whether Iraq had fully agreed to disarm. Unlike the United States, Britain, and Spain, however, a majority of members of the Security Council, including France, China, and Russia, opposed any resolution authorizing an attack or invasion

United Nations (UN) inspectors leave a site after conducting an inspection for weapons of mass destruction in Baghdad, Iraq, on February 14, 2003. Chief UN weapons inspector Hans Blix stated that banned Iraqi weapons were still unaccounted for. (Oleg Nikishin/Getty Images)

of Iraq on this basis. The Americans, supported by Britain and Spain, denied that any additional UN resolution was necessary to authorize the use of force against Iraq. Indeed, they cited UN Security Council Resolution 686 of November 29, 1990, which authorized any UN member to use "all necessary means" to "restore international peace and security to the Persian Gulf Region." The three nations also pointed out that the Iraqis had violated 16 UN resolutions and in 12 years had failed to disarm. Based on the October 11, 2002, authorization by the U.S. Congress to use force against Iraq, the Anglo-American invasion of Iraq commenced on March 20, 2003.

In the aftermath of the invasion, the Iraqi Survey Group was unable to find any active WMD program. Several reasons have been advanced for this. The most obvious explanation is that Iraq had ceased its program sometime before 2003. Indeed, one of Saddam Hussein's sons-in-law, Hussein Kamal, who had charge of Iraq's WMD program, made this claim repeatedly and with extensive detail upon defecting to Jordan in 1995, but U.S. and British intelligence agents doubted his veracity even though he, unlike other defectors, did not make efforts to secure personal financial gain. Indeed, he returned to Iraq and was killed. Upon being captured in December 2004, Saddam Hussein also told American interrogators that Iraq no longer had WMD. U.S. officials also considered the veracity of his comments problematic.

Other explanations for the absence of WMD rest on sheer speculation and have never been verified but remain popular in certain political circles. For example, although no evidence exists to prove this claim, some critics of Operation Iraqi Freedom claim that the Bush administration knew Iraq had halted its WMD program but lied to the American people to justify the invasion and regime change. Other critics of the war, mostly Democrats but some Republicans as well (most of whom had voted for the war), have since argued that Bush was misled by faulty intelligence, which was driven by the need to provide evidence to support the war rather than by a balanced appraisal of the true situation on the ground. They have concluded that the Bush administration presented only that evidence that supported its own conclusions. The U.S. Senate Intelligence Committee issued two reports in 2004 and 2006 documenting Bush administration intelligence failures regarding Iraq.

Finally, some observers believe that Iraq hid its remaining WMD stockpiles or shipped them to Iran and/or Syria. It is highly unlikely that Iraq would ever ship such stockpiles to Iran. Although no conclusive evidence has been put forth to support this claim, its supporters cite the fact that Russian truck convoys left Iraq for Syria and other countries as coalition forces invaded. Those who support this theory also make the claim that Russia was assisting Hussein's WMD program development.

Many in the UN and the international community did not support the March 2003 invasion of Iraq. They further believed that the United States and Great Britain had purposely tried to sabotage and discredit UNMOVIC to help justify the war against Iraq. Blix was absolutely furious over the contretemps, and in a February 2004 report to the Security Council he admitted that Iraq should have been more forthcoming with weapons inspectors since 1991 but also maintained that UNSCOM and UNMOVIC had accomplished the task of ridding Iraq of WMD. That same month during a television interview in Great Britain, Blix pointedly asserted that the United States and Britain had purposely overemphasized the threat of Iraqi WMD to justify their invasion. In the end no active WMD program was located in Iraq, even after years of searching by perhaps thousands of members of the occupation forces in Iraq. Blix claims that the United States so mistrusted him that his home and office were bugged.

Stefan Brooks

See also: Bush, George Walker; Hussein, Saddam; Iraqi Freedom, Operation; Weapons of Mass Destruction

References

Blix, Hans. *Disarming Iraq.* New York: Pantheon, 2004.

Butler, Richard. *The Greatest Threat: Iraq, Weapons of Mass Destruction and the Growing Crisis in Global Security.* New York: PublicAffairs, 2000.

Pearson, Graham S. *The UNSCOM Saga: Chemical and Biological Weapons Non-Proliferation.* New York: Palgrave Macmillan, 2000.

Ritter, Scott. *Endgame: Solving the Iraqi Crisis.* New York: Simon and Schuster, 2002.

Trevan, Tim. *Saddam's Secrets: The Hunt for Iraq's Weapons.* New York: HarperCollins, 1999.

Whitney, Craig. *The WMD Mirage: Iraq's Decade of Deception and America's False Premise for War.* New York: PublicAffairs, 2005.

U.S. Agency for International Development, Iraq

The United States Agency for International Development (USAID) is the principal U.S.

government organization that supervises and distributes American foreign aid to Iraq. This assistance began in 2003 shortly after the Anglo-American invasion overthrew the regime of President Saddam Hussein. The genesis of USAID can be found in the 1947 Marshall Plan and President Harry S. Truman's 1949 Point Four Program. Both of those programs systematized U.S. foreign assistance in the post–World War II era.

The U.S. Congress created USAID with the passage of the 1961 Foreign Assistance Act. The act mandated the establishment of an umbrella organization for U.S. foreign economic assistance, which led to the creation of USAID on November 3, 1963. Since then, it has distributed hundreds of billions of dollars in assistance around the world and has served as a unifying organization that brings together almost all U.S. financial, technical, and economic development programs under one broad banner.

USAID has weathered periodic reform initiatives and considerable criticism that it is a bureaucratic leviathan that wastes money that could be channeled to other purposes. Nevertheless, it continues on more than 55 years after its creation as the premier U.S. foreign assistance agency. USAID receives its guidance from the U.S. secretary of state, whose job it is to ensure that its aims and programs are consonant with American foreign policy goals and mandates established by the U.S. Congress.

The postwar reconstruction of Iraq, a primary mandate for USAID, represents the single largest U.S. foreign aid initiative since the Marshall Plan. Among USAID's chief missions in Iraq are economic reconstruction and growth, the reinvigoration of health care and educational systems, the support of democratic institutions, the provisioning of humanitarian aid to homeless and displaced persons, and the rebuilding and upgrading of critical infrastructure, to include sewage treatment plants, electrical generation facilities, and water treatment systems. All of these activities are meant to foster representative democracy, internal security, and economic independence. Clearly, the ongoing Iraqi insurgency has made it quite difficult for USAID to achieve its goals; the continuing presence of large numbers of U.S. and coalition troops in the country has also been a challenge for USAID officials.

USAID workers have been working with former Iraqi government officials, retraining and readying them to assume various governmental functions. USAID has also been working with provincial and municipal government officials in an attempt to ensure that basic services are met at the local and regional level. USAID works closely with the Central Bank of Iraq and the Ministry of Finance in implementing effective budgetary and cost-tracking measures.

From 2003 to 2006, USAID helped add 1,292 megawatts of electricity to Iraq's electric grid, bringing electrical service to hundreds of thousands of people. Still, there are considerable shortages, and current production is only about two-thirds of the stated goals. The effort to rebuild Iraq's electrical infrastructure has been hampered by the inability to construct or restore transmission lines in hostile territories.

USAID has also made possible the rebuilding or expansion of 19 water treatment plants, bringing potable water to 3.1 million Iraqis who heretofore had no access to clean water. USAID improvements to sewage treatment facilities have brought modern sewage service to at least 5.1 million Iraqis. In health care, USAID has also provided many improvements. In 2005 alone, almost 98 percent of all Iraqi children were vaccinated against childhood diseases.

In education, USAID has built, rebuilt, or refurbished thousands of schools and has developed programs to ensure that all Iraqis have access to educational institutions from elementary to university levels. In cities and towns hard hit by fighting, USAID works in tandem with other international agencies and multinational corporations to revitalize local economies.

Clearly, the continuing insurgency in Iraq hampered USAID efforts to reconstruct the country, and it is anyone's guess how much money has been wasted trying to rebuild a nation that remains at war with itself.

Paul G. Pierpaoli Jr.

See also: Iraq, History of, 1990–Present

References

Agresto, John. *Mugged by Reality: The Liberation of Iraq and the Failure of Good Intentions.* New York: Encounter Books, 2007.

Glantz, Aaron. *How America Lost Iraq.* New York: Jeremy P. Tarcher, 2005.

Stephenson, James. *Losing the Golden Hour: An Insider's View of Iraq's Reconstruction.* Dulles, VA: Potomac Books, 2007.

V

Viking Hammer, Operation (March 28–30, 2003)

Part of the March 2003 Anglo-American–led invasion of Iraq (Operation Iraqi Freedom), Operation Viking Hammer was an offensive waged from March 28 to March 30, 2003, in northern Iraq by anti–Saddam Hussein Kurds with the assistance of coalition special operations forces against the Islamic terrorist group Ansar al-Islam.

The original planning for Operation Iraqi Freedom had called for a northern front, but when the Turkish government denied the coalition the use of its territory, planners had to shift strategy. Instead, they hoped to utilize pro-American militias of the Kurdish Regional Government. The latter was dominated by two groups, the Patriotic Union of Kurdistan (PUK), led by Jalal Talabani, and the Kurdistan Democratic Party (KDP), led by Masoud Barzani. The PUK's Peshmerga militias were the largest and best trained of the Kurdish forces.

In the months prior to the invasion, the United States had inserted special operations forces to train and coordinate with the Kurds. Coalition planners believed that a Kurdish military campaign would keep Iraqi units tied down in the northern regions of the country and therefore render them unavailable to fight the two main prongs of the invading forces, which would advance from the south. To support the Kurds, the coalition planned to deploy additional special operations forces. Later, airborne units would be dropped in to fight alongside the Peshmerga and KDP fighters in attacks on Iraqi targets, including the important cities of Mosul and Kirkuk. The plan was a bold endeavor that asked a small number of special operations forces, airborne troops, and Kurdish fighters to accomplish the same goals as 60,000 U.S. ground troops, namely tying down 13 Iraqi divisions.

Kurdish Peshmerga fighters and U.S. Special Forces advance toward the road between Kirkuk and Mosul on April 6, 2003, in Abushita, northern Iraq. Special Forces, who were in the north in small numbers for weeks, supplied logistical support to the Kurds, calling in air strikes as the militia advanced. Kurds have long sought to regain control of the oil-rich area around Kirkuk. (Patrick Barth/Getty Images)

The Kurds were apprehensive that they would be vulnerable to attacks by Islamic terrorist groups, located along the border with Iran, if they deployed their forces to the south. Viking Hammer was designed essentially to neutralize the threat to the Kurdish heartland. Viking Hammer and subsequent offensives were also an effort by the United States to demonstrate the country's commitment to the Kurds and ensure support from the Kurdish Regional Government in a postwar Iraq. However, the United States was concurrently trying to avoid further straining relations with Turkey, which faced an ongoing Kurdish separatist insurgency. Consequently, the United States chose not to supply the Peshmerga with extensive weaponry for fear that some might be used against Turkish forces.

Before the Peshmerga could engage the Iraqi forces, they had to first secure their own territory and suppress Ansar al-Islam, a Kurdish Sunni Islamist group. Ansar al-Islam was originally formed in 2001 by Islamist Kurdish factions. The group was dominated by Kurds who had fought against the Soviets in Afghanistan. Led by Mullah Krekar, Ansar al-Islam sought to impose a strict version of sharia (Islamic law) on towns near the border with Iran, including Halabja, Biyara, and Tawela. It also worked with other smaller Islamist groups against the Kurdish Regional Government and was blamed for a number of terrorist attacks against rival Kurdish groups. Ansar al-Islam had approximately 500–600 fighters and controlled more than 100 square miles of territory. Its allies in the other small Islamist groups provided an additional 100–300 fighters to Ansar al-Islam. U.S. defense officials were especially concerned about Ansar al-Islam because of intelligence that the group was harboring senior Al Qaeda figures, which was unfounded. The Peshmerga and KDP militias in Viking Hammer numbered approximately 7,000 troops of varying quality with an assortment of mainly Soviet-era weaponry, including mortars, some artillery, and a limited number of armored vehicles. Most were armed with AK-47s and had about 150–200 rounds apiece. Many lacked uniforms, boots, or helmets and instead wore tennis shoes and red scarves. However, the Kurds were highly motivated, and U.S. special operations forces provided the heavy firepower, including mortars, grenade launchers, and machine guns. They also had charge of communications between units. Most important, the U.S. personnel were able to coordinate ground support from coalition aircraft and cruise missiles.

There were approximately 600 U.S. soldiers from the 10th Special Forces Group with the PUK and KDP, organized into 12-member teams. U.S. colonel Charlie Cleveland was the operational commander of the covert U.S. troops. The special operations forces had previously staged in Romania and been given the code name Task Force Viking (which led in turn to the offensive's title, Viking Hammer). In Viking Hammer, the Kurdish offensive was led by 40 soldiers of the 3rd Battalion of the 10th Special Forces Group, commanded by Lieutenant Colonel Ken Tovo. Tovo divided his men into split teams; each 6-member group worked with a Kurdish unit of 150–800 troops.

Ansar al-Islam and its allies had constructed a series of complexes on mountains and hilltops overlooking the surrounding valleys near Halabja, Iraq. The Kurds were apprehensive that any attack would leave them vulnerable to mortar and machine-gun fire from the heights. U.S. personnel scouted the positions and pretargeted them for air strikes.

On March 21, 2003, 64 cruise missiles hit Ansar al-Islam bunkers in a three-hour period. The pro-U.S. Kurds were impressed by the precision and power of the attack. About 100 members of the radical Islamic Group of Kurdistan, an ally of Ansar al-Islam, were killed in the strikes, and the remainder of the group surrendered the following morning. Another small Islamic group also surrendered before the main offensive commenced.

On March 28, the U.S.-Kurdish force began its attack at 6:00 a.m. The allies were divided into four groups, each led by a special forces team. The Ansar al-Islam fighters proved to be a tough and experienced foe, for they had the routes into the mountains covered with mortars and would fire a limited number of rounds and then move in an effort to avoid being targeted by U.S. spotters. Peshmerga artillery and mortars provided the opening salvos from the coalition forces. When the advance encountered its first organized resistance, air strikes were called in, and two U.S. Navy F-18s dropped precision-guided 500-pound bombs on the Iraqi position. By 9:00 a.m. the Kurds had captured Gulp, the first significant village. Coalition forces found various weapons, including explosive suicide vests and bomb-making materials. The four teams had to assault and capture a series of bunkers and complexes under mortar fire and incoming rounds from Katyusha rockets. Slowly they moved into the mountains, using the heavy weapons and sniper fire of the special operations forces to engage enemy positions. The mountainous terrain impeded the ability of the U.S. troops to radio for air strikes, and the coalition forces had to rely on their own weapons and capabilities. U.S. snipers proved especially effective because of their long-range capabilities. By the afternoon, the combined forces had taken the strategic town of Sagrat, which had served as the headquarters of the senior Ansar al-Islam leaders. Around 5:00 p.m., the U.S. forces were able to regain radio contact and arrange air strikes on enemy positions. Once again, 500-pound precision-guided bombs were used.

Over the next two days, the U.S.-Kurdish force continued its advance. Much of the fighting involved attacks on enemy cave complexes. The coalition forces endeavored unsuccessfully to use tear gas to force the fighters from the caves. When that tactic failed, the U.S. forces used grenades and antitank missiles to destroy the cave bunkers. The Peshmerga forces did not have equipment to engage in night fighting, which limited the ability of the coalition forces to pursue Ansar al-Islam fighters. After the first day of combat, an increasing number of the Islamic fighters had fled across the border into Iran. The Iranians reportedly disarmed the fighters but did not detain them. Some were forcibly returned across the border.

The U.S. forces were able to collect a considerable amount of intelligence on Ansar al-Islam and its links with Al Qaeda. In addition, the coalition forces found that almost half of the fighters killed or captured were foreign born and had come to Iraq to train for terrorist missions. On March 29, a U.S. team explored a suspected chemical weapons manufacturing and training facility in Sagrat. The team discovered instructions on the manufacture of chemical weapons; they also found chemical suits and traces of the highly toxic ricin.

Sporadic fighting continued until March 30, the day Viking Hammer officially ended. During the operation, 3 Peshmerga soldiers were killed and 23 were wounded. No U.S. personnel were killed or seriously wounded. Approximately 150–250 Ansar al-Islam fighters were killed, in addition to the 100 killed among the Islamic Group of Kurdistan. After Viking Hammer, the Kurdish forces moved south as part of the broader coalition northern offensive against the regular Iraqi Army. Ansar al-Islam reemerged after the fall of Saddam Hussein as one of the numerous groups in the anti-U.S. insurgency.

Tom Lansford

See also: Iraqi Freedom, Operation; Iraqi Freedom, Operation: Coalition Ground Forces; Islamic State of Iraq and al-Sham (ISIS): Al Qaeda in Iraq; Kurds; Political Parties, Iraq: Kurdistan Democratic Party, Patriotic Union of Kurdistan

References

Gunter, Michael M. *The Kurds Ascending: The Evolving Solution to the Kurdish Problem in Iraq and Turkey.* New York: Palgrave Macmillan, 2008.

McKiernan, Kevin. *The Kurds: A People in Search of Their Homeland.* New York: St. Martin's, 2006.

O'Leary, Brendan, John McGarry, and Khaled Salih, eds. *The Future of Kurdistan in Iraq.* Philadelphia: University of Pennsylvania Press, 2005.

Tucker, Mike. *Among Warriors in Iraq.* New York: Lyons, 2005.

Yildiz, Kerim, and Tom Blass. *The Kurds in Iraq: The Past, Present and Future.* London: Pluto, 2004.

Weapons, Insurgency, and Opposition

The nature of the fighting in Iraq after the defeat of the formal Iraqi military was such that it was dominated by small arms weapons. That is with one exception: the innocuously named weapon—improvised explosive device (explained below). Because of the lack of importance of any other specific weapon system, this is the only entry.

It is important to note that rifles, mortars, grenades, rockets, and missiles all were regularly present on the battlefield. In this, the fighting throughout the eight plus years resembled that of hundreds of conflicts in the modern era where nonstate actors fought against states. In all of these conflicts, it was a lightly armed and equipped fighter wearing civilian clothes fighting against the industrially equipped and regularly armed and uniformed state forces.

Improvised Explosive Devices

Improvised explosive devices (IEDs) have been employed in warfare almost since the introduction of gunpowder. They remain the weapon of choice for insurgent and resistance groups that lack the numerical strength and firepower to conduct conventional operations against an opponent. IEDs are the contemporary form of booby traps employed in World War II and the Vietnam War. Traditionally, they are used primarily against enemy armor and thin-skinned vehicles.

A water cart filled with explosives was employed in a futile effort to assassinate Napoleon Bonaparte in Paris as he traveled to the opera on Christmas Eve in 1800. The emperor escaped injury, but the blast killed the little girl the conspirators paid to hold the horse's bridle and killed or maimed a dozen other people. In more recent times, IEDs have been employed against civilian targets by Basque separatists and the Irish Republican Army. Molotov cocktails, or gasoline bombs, are one form of IED. The largest, most deadly IEDs in history were the U.S. jetliners hijacked by members of the terrorist organization Al Qaeda on September 11, 2001, and used to attack the World Trade Center in New York City and the Pentagon in Washington, DC.

IEDs became one of the chief weapons employed by insurgents during the Iraq War (2003–2011) and its aftermath to attack U.S. forces and Iraqi police and carry out sectarian and antigovernment violence. The simplest type of IED is a hand grenade, rigged artillery shell, or bomb triggered by a trip-wire or simple movement. It might be as simple as a grenade with its pin pulled and handle held down by the weight of a corpse; once the corpse is raised, the grenade explodes. Bombs and artillery shells are also used as IEDs. Such weapons can be exploded remotely by wireless detonators in the form of garage door openers and two-way radios or infrared motion sensors. More powerful explosives and even shaped charges can be used to attack armored vehicles. Casualty totals are one way to judge the effectiveness of a military operation, and growing casualties from IEDs in the 1980s and 1990s induced the Israeli Army to withdraw from southern Lebanon. More recently, the perpetrators of

U.S. Marines find what they believe to be a vehicle-borne improvised explosive device (VBIED) factory and weapons cache in Anbar Province, Iraq, on April 26, 2005. (U.S. Department of Defense)

the Boston Marathon Bombing (April 15, 2013) employed two crude IEDs—low-yield explosives contained in enclosed pressure cookers detonated remotely with a handheld device. They were packed with metal shards, perhaps ball bearings and nails, to increase their lethality. That attack killed 4 and injured more than 260 others.

Spencer C. Tucker

See also: Iraqi Freedom, Operation

References

Crippen, James B. *Improvised Explosive Devices (IED)*. New York: CRC Press, 2007.

DeForest, M. J. *Principles of Improvised Explosive Devices*. Boulder, CO: Paladin, 1984.

"Terrorism Strikes Boston Marathon as Bombs Kill 3; Scores Wounded." CNN, April 16, 2013, http://www.cnn.com/2013/04/15/us/boston-marathon-explosions.

Tucker, Stephen. *Terrorist Explosive Sourcebook: Countering Terrorist Use of Improvised Explosive Devices*. Boulder, CO: Paladin, 2005.

Weapons of Mass Destruction

Weapons of mass destruction (WMD) are biological, chemical, and nuclear weapons capable of inflicting mass casualties. Use of these weapons is viewed as not only immoral but contrary to international law and the laws of war because WMD have the ability to kill indiscriminately, meaning that their destructive nature is not limited to just combatants or military assets. During the Cold War, fears about nuclear weapons and their

U.S. secretary of state Colin Powell holds up a vial that he claims could contain anthrax as he presents evidence of Iraq's alleged weapons programs to the United Nations Security Council in New York, on February 5, 2003. (Timothy A. Clary/AFP/Getty Images)

use were commonplace. Nevertheless, these weapons were under tight control, and neither side dared employ them for fear of the total destruction that a retaliatory strike would bring. With the end of the Cold War, however, nuclear proliferation has become a significant problem, and the likelihood of a rogue state or terrorist group attaining WMD, including nuclear weapons, has increased substantially.

During the Iran-Iraq War (1980–1988), Iraq employed chemical weapons on Iranian troops, something that Iraqi dictator Saddam Hussein publicly admitted to in December 2006 during his trial for war crimes. It remains in dispute whether Iran employed them as well. The Iran-Iraq War was also the first conflict since World War I in which chemical weapons, apart from tear gas, had been employed. In 1988 as part of an operation to suppress a revolt by Iraqi Kurds, the Hussein government unleashed a chemical attack on the northern Iraqi town of Halabja, killing at least 5,000 people in the first recorded event of such weapons used against civilians. The terrorist bombings in Japan in 1994 and 1995 in which chemical weapons were released in a Tokyo neighborhood and subway reminded the world of the destructive capability of WMD.

Since the terror attacks of September 11, 2001, the fear of and danger posed by WMD has increased significantly, owing to the desire of terrorist groups such as Al Qaeda and their affiliates to acquire and employ such weapons against the United States and other countries. The September 11 terrorist attacks on the United States and the 2004 Madrid bombings and 2005 London bombings clearly demonstrated the ability and willingness of Al Qaeda to engage in terrorism to inflict mass casualties, leaving no doubt about their willingness to use WMD in future terrorist attacks. In March and April 2006 in Iraq, Al Qaeda is believed to have been responsible for a series of terrorist chemical attacks using chlorine gas that killed dozens and sickened hundreds.

Because of the instability and recurrence of war and conflict in the Middle East, the presence of WMD has only heightened the arms race between Arab states and Israel and also among Arab states themselves. Egypt, Syria, Algeria, and Iran were believed to have significant stockpiles of biological and chemical weapons. In 2003 Libya, seeking to normalize relations with the United States and Europe and end its international isolation and reputation as a sponsor of terrorism, announced that it was abandoning its WMD programs. Some observers have suggested that President George W. Bush's decision to invade Iraq in 2003 and Libya's failure to end its isolation and convince the United Nations (UN) to lift its sanctions prompted this change of behavior.

Egypt was the first country in the Middle East to develop chemical weapons, which may have been prompted, at least in part, by Israel's construction of a nuclear reactor in 1958. The size of Egypt's chemical weapons arsenal is thought to be perhaps as extensive as Iraq's prior to the 1991 Persian Gulf War, although the end of hostilities between Egypt and Israel since the 1978 Camp David Accords may have obviated the need for maintaining the same quantities of such weapons.

In 1993 as part of the Arab campaign against Israel's nuclear weapons program, Egypt and Syria (along with Iraq) refused to sign the Chemical Weapons Convention, which bans the acquisition, development, stockpiling, transfer, retention, and use of chemical weapons. These states also refused to sign the Biological Weapons Convention of 1975, which prohibits the development, production, acquisition, transfer, retention, stockpiling, and use of biological and toxin weapons. Iraq later signed the Biological Weapons Convention. The extent of Egypt's biological weapons program is unknown, but it clearly has the ability to develop such weapons if it already does not have weaponized stockpiles.

With respect to nuclear weapons, Israel is believed to possess at least 100 nuclear warheads, although the Israeli government has never overtly confirmed possessing such weapons. On December 12, 2006, Israeli prime minister Ehud Olmert admitted in an interview that Israel possessed nuclear weapons, only to be contradicted by a government spokesman the next day denying that Olmert had made such an admission. In the meantime, Israel has refused to sign the Nuclear Non-Proliferation Treaty and has not allowed UN International Atomic Energy Agency (IAEA) inspectors to inspect its suspected nuclear sites.

Israel has repeatedly shown its willingness to use force to maintain its suspected nuclear monopoly and deny any Arab state the ability to acquire or develop nuclear weapons. In 1981, the Israeli Air Force destroyed the Osiraq nuclear reactor site under construction in Iraq.

It was believed that Iraq had an active weapons of mass destruction program in 2001 and 2002, and this was used as justification for the U.S.-led invasion of Iraq in

2003. It was learned that no active program existed though thousands of older chemical artillery rounds and rockets were found and destroyed by coalition forces.

Iran enriched uranium for what it claims were peaceful purposes, but the United States and much of Western Europe accused Iran of aspiring to build nuclear weapons. That state's refusal to cooperate with the IAEA led the UN in December 2006 and March 2007 to impose sanctions on Iran as punishment for its defiance. Those sanctions were broadened and made more potent beginning in 2009. The Joint Comprehensive Plan of Action was signed between Iran, the United States, China, France, Germany, Russia, and the United Kingdom on July 14, 2015.

Stefan Brooks

See also: Iraq, History of, 1990–Present

References

Hayes, Stephen F. *The Connection: How al Qaeda's Collaboration with Saddam Hussein Has Endangered America.* New York: HarperCollins, 2004.

Hutchinson, Robert. *Weapons of Mass Destruction: The No-Nonsense Guide to Nuclear, Chemical and Biological Weapons Today.* London: Weidenfeld and Nicholson, 2003.

Langford, R. Everett. *Introduction to Weapons of Mass Destruction: Radiological, Chemical, and Biological.* Hoboken, NJ: Wiley-Interscience, 2004.

Woodward, Bob. *Plan of Attack.* New York: Simon and Schuster. 2004.

Weapons Systems, Coalition

The U.S.-led coalition featured every modern weapon of war from tanks to artillery to aircraft and ships. Weapons were fired from every modern platform over the course of the more than eight years of war. There is not sufficient space in this book to address the variety of weapons present. There isn't space to even address the critical systems. What appears below are two weapons that were new to the fighting and existed as a result of the action-reaction dynamic of war. As improvised explosive devices became more and more important, it became clear that a new vehicle was needed to protect soldiers as they moved through the theater of war. That vehicle was the mine-resistant ambush-protected (MRAP) vehicle. As explained in the entry below, this was not a single vehicle but a series of different vehicles across the spectrum of mobility needs.

The second new weapon system first made its appearance in the fighting in Afghanistan, but it was still new and developing during the fighting in Iraq. This is the armed unmanned aerial vehicle or UAV. Like with the MRAP, UAV is a single name for an entire spectrum of capabilities.

These are neither the only two weapons systems used, nor were they necessarily the most important for the soldiers, sailors, airmen, and marines who deployed to fight in Iraq. However, they were new and specific to the fighting in Iraq.

Mine-Resistant Ambush-Protected Vehicles

The mine-resistant ambush-protected (MRAP) vehicle is an armored truck developed by the U.S. military in Operation Iraqi Freedom in Iraq and Operation Enduring Freedom in Afghanistan to protect troops from improvised explosive devices (IEDs) (see IED entry). IEDs were the cause of almost half the fatalities suffered by U.S.

forces in Iraq, while about half the fatalities in Afghanistan have been from IEDs.

While IEDs can sometimes be effective against the Abrams tank and the Bradley Fighting Vehicle, they are very highly effective against unarmored transport vehicles. These include the high mobility multipurpose wheeled vehicle (Humvee), the modern equivalent of the World War II–era jeep, and the 2.5- and 5-ton trucks and tanker trucks used to move personnel, ammunition, provisions, and fuel over the extensive roadways of Afghanistan and Iraq. These vehicles were not designed as armored combat vehicles; rather, they were specially designed and reinforced versions of commercial transports for military logistics purposes.

The threat from IEDs led to a program to armor Humvees and other transport vehicles, a program that continued throughout the fighting. The basic problem of refitting such vehicles is how to cope with the added weight of the armor without making major modifications to engine power, transmissions, engine cooling, and suspension systems. This has to be balanced with the differences between up-armoring vehicles in the theater of war versus the extended choices of doing so at depots in the United States.

A parallel approach to retrofitting existing vehicles has been the development and fielding of MRAPs to provide better protection for vehicles and crews. MRAPs are wheeled vehicles with a V-shaped hull and armored plating designed to deflect the impact of IEDs. They were used in small numbers in Iraq and Afghanistan in 2003 for route clearance and explosive ordnance disposal (EOD). The protection they provided led to the U.S. Department of Defense decision in 2007 to make deployment of MRAPs a high priority.

The resulting program involves three categories of MRAPs based on size and mission. Category I MRAPs are 7 to 15 tons, carrying a crew of two plus four passengers, mainly for urban transportation. Category II vehicles weigh between 15 and 25 tons, carry a crew of two and eight passengers, and are designed for road escort, ambulance, and EOD missions. Category III vehicles weigh 25 tons or more, carry a crew of two plus four passengers, and are designed for EOD missions that require more equipment than can be carried in Category II vehicles. The dimensions and missions changed during the war, and refinements followed to meet the newly presented needs.

Several companies, both domestic and foreign, have had various types of vehicles under development or in production, and as the U.S. military began to invest in armored vehicles, many companies competed for the new market, potentially worth several billion dollars. The vehicles are called Cougar, Buffalo, MaxxPro, Caiman, and Alpha. The Defense Department continues to prefer referencing the vehicles as Category I, II, and III MRAPs, but the commercial names have also remained, leading to some confusion, as the Cougar and Caiman come in both 4×4 and 6×6 versions. Domestic production companies have included Force Protection Industries, BAE Systems of North America, Navistar subsidiary International Military and Government LLC, Armor Holdings LLC, Oshkosh Truck, General Dynamics, Textron, and Protected Vehicles. Companies in Canada, Germany, Israel, and South Africa have also been involved because they have also been developing new armored wheeled vehicles.

The designs of the vehicles vary. Some have a one-piece hull and chassis. Others have the hull bolted to the chassis. Some have the V-shaped armor covering the entire vehicle, while others have that protection only for the crew and passengers. There are variations in mobility both on and off the road, engine size, and dimensions. All have been through extensive tests at Aberdeen Proving Ground and elsewhere and were evaluated by infield performance in Iraq and Afghanistan.

By the end of 2007, the Defense Department had placed orders for 7,774 MRAPs and projected a total requirement of 23,000 in Iraq. By April 2008 there were about 5,000 MRAPs in Iraq, with projections of having about 6,000 by December 2008. Costs through fiscal year 2009 were estimated at $25 billion. Costs were based on the actual cost of the various vehicles, which vary widely even within category, and mode of shipment. The military prefers air transport to bring the vehicles into the war zone, but doing so costs $135,000 for each vehicle, compared with just $18,000 by ship.

In October 2012, the Pentagon ordered the production of MRAPs to stop; by then, 27,740 had been produced. By the end of 2014, an estimated 20,000 MRAPs were in service. As many as 12,000 of these vehicles are slated to go into storage, a result of the end of the Iraq War in December 2011 and the drawdown of U.S. troops from Afghanistan by the end of December 2014. Some will be sold to Iraq or Afghanistan as well as select law enforcement departments in the United States.

Although several vehicle models have been used in Iraq and Afghanistan, there are three that represent the categories well. Their characteristics demonstrate the flux in the scope of the Defense Department categories in a very short time. For Category I, the Navistar MaxxPro, a model that dominates that category with $3.5 billion in orders, has an 8.7-liter six-cylinder diesel engine that produces 330 horsepower. It is 21 feet long, 8.5 feet wide, and 10 feet high. It weighs 40,000 pounds, has a ground clearance of 11 inches, and carries a 2-man crew and up to 10 passengers. The cost is $549,000.

For Category II, the Force Protection Cougar 6×6 has a 7.2-liter diesel engine that produces 330 horsepower. It is 23 feet long, 8.5 feet wide, and 8.8 feet high. Weighing in at 39,000 pounds, it has a 15-inch ground clearance. It carries a crew of two and eight passengers. Unit cost is $649,000.

The Force Protection Buffalo represents Category III. Its 12-liter six-cylinder diesel engine produces 400 horsepower. It is 27 feet long, 8.25 feet wide, and 13 feet high. The weight is 45,320 pounds, ground clearance is 16 inches, and it has a crew of two plus four passengers. The $855,000 cost includes a remote-controlled external arm to help with EOD. Its large size allows more EOD equipment.

The armored Humvee has a 6.5-liter diesel V-8 engine producing 190 horsepower. It is 16 feet long, 7.5 feet wide, and 6.25 feet high. It weighs 12,000 pounds and has a ground clearance of 16.8 inches. Carrying four people, its unit cost is $150,000.

It is impossible to determine what the U.S. military, particularly the U.S. Army and U.S. Marine Corps, will eventually choose for transport vehicles, both wheeled and tracked, armored or not. It is clear that the decisions will be based not only on testing in the United States but also on performance of the many versions of transport vehicles. They will be expected to perform in the varied terrain presented by Iraq and Afghanistan, which ranges from desert to densely populated urban areas and from sea level to mountain ranges higher than any in the continental United States, with climates of intense heat to below-zero temperatures and widely different challenges posed by rain, snow, drought, and blinding sandstorms. Ground clearance will be a critical factor for off-road travel. Size will be important not only for maneuverability in crowded urban areas but also for transport to the field of battle, especially by air. The height of the vehicles will be important, as bigger targets are more vulnerable to attack from armor-piercing rounds from rocket-propelled grenades and other weapons. If applied with thought, the lessons learned from actual combat in Iraq and Afghanistan should lead to a U.S. military equipped with the best possible range of transport vehicles for future challenges.

Daniel E. Spector

See also: Weapons, Insurgency, and Opposition: Improvised Explosive Devices

References

Dixon, Chris. "Blast Proof Wheels for the Mean Streets of War Zones." *New York Times,* February 24, 2008.

Feickert, Andrew. *Mine-Resistant, Ambush-Protected (MRAP) Vehicles: Background and Issues for Congress.* Washington, DC: Congressional Research Service, Library of Congress, 2007.

Schwartz, General Norton A. *Statement before the Senate Homeland Security and Government Affairs Committee.* Washington, DC: U.S. Government Printing Office, September 27, 2007.

Unmanned Aerial Vehicles

Unmanned aerial vehicles (UAVs), also known as drones, are unmanned aircraft flown by remote control. They were formerly known as remotely piloted vehicles (RPVs). UAVs have evolved into powerful aerial reconnaissance, surveillance, and strike platforms. Although the U.S. Air Force employed AQM-34 drones for high-risk aerial reconnaissance missions during the Vietnam War, those units were quickly retired after the

A Predator unmanned aerial vehicle (UAV) flies on a simulated U.S. Navy aerial reconnaissance mission off the coast of California. This model of UAV drone was commonly used during the conflict with Iraq. (U.S. Department of Defense)

conflict, and postwar funding cuts prevented any new unmanned aerial reconnaissance systems from entering service. Israel subsequently pioneered RPV development, and the U.S. government became interested in using them by the late 1980s. Today they are an integral part of the battlefield environment.

The success of Israeli UAV operations over Lebanon in the early 1980s convinced the U.S. Navy to examine unmanned aircraft for artillery spotting and to provide a UAV capability for the U.S. Marine Corps. UAVs were then acquired and embarked first aboard the Iowa-class battleship Iowa. Pioneer short-range UAVs flew more than 300 combat reconnaissance missions preceding and during the 1991 Persian Gulf War, demonstrating the advantages of such aircraft over manned aircraft and space-based reconnaissance systems. The foremost of these advantages is their ability to linger over a target, providing comparatively long-term surveillance. They are also far less expensive than manned aircraft, and their loss to accident or enemy fire does not imperil a pilot and aircrew. During the next decade, Pioneers flew some 14,000 flights and supported every major U.S. military operation.

Buoyed by the success of UAVs in the Persian Gulf War, the Central Intelligence Agency and the military accelerated the development of far more capable unmanned aerial platforms. As these entered operational testing, their greater capabilities and expense drove their sponsors to introduce the designation "UAV" to distinguish them from their earlier, more primitive counterparts. The primary difference is in the control system. RPVs are radio-controlled from within line of sight of the vehicle, while UAVs can be programmed to fly autonomously along a planned route and utilize satellite links that enable their operators to control them from thousands of miles away. They can also fly a mix of manual and autonomous operations. Stealthy and equipped to provide instantaneous and nearly continuous transmission of their collected information, UAVs have been a critical component of all major U.S. military operations since 1994 but most especially during the Global War on Terrorism.

All U.S. military services now operate UAVs, and their missions have expanded from reconnaissance and strike to communications relay and even tactical logistics support to units in the field. The Pioneer has been replaced by a vast array of UAVs, ranging from the hand-launched RQ-11 Raven to the long-range Global Hawk. The RQ-1 Predator is the best known of the UAVs. First entering service in 1995, the Predator has a loaded weight of 2,250 pounds and 40-hour endurance. It is equipped to provide near real reporting from a wide variety of sensor packages, including elecro-optical, infrared, and radar imaging to electronic signals monitoring. Flying at an operational altitude above 26,000 feet, its sensors can monitor an area the size of New York City. The Predator is most famous for its use in Hellfire missile strikes on terrorist leaders and their compounds as part of the Global War on Terrorism. The first of these was in Afghanistan in 2001, and they increased significantly throughout the wars in Afghanistan and Iraq.

The United States conducted numerous lethal UAV attacks in Yemen and Somalia but primarily in the border area of Afghanistan and Pakistan. These increased markedly under the Barack Obama administration, with more than 390 attacks in a five-year span through January 2014 that have killed some 2,400 people. This is four times the number of attacks during the eight years of the George W. Bush administration. Indeed, some commentators have referred to the UAV as Obama's "weapon of choice."

UAVs now constitute an integral component of all U.S. security operations, from the military through to the Coast Guard and Border Patrol. The U.S. Navy is testing the use of UAVs from aircraft carriers down to patrol craft and submarines, including those that are submerged. The United States does not have a monopoly on UAVs, however. U.S. allies as well as China, Iran, and Russia have UAVs in service, and the Lebanese militant group Hezbollah employs them extensively. It is apparent that UAV employment in conflicts will only grow as the 21st century advances.

Microminiaturization and high-tech data links and computer systems promise to give the smallest tactical units reconnaissance capabilities beyond that imagined for major field forces 100 years ago. Some UAVs in testing are so small that they have been disguised to look like birds as small as hummingbirds and even insects. It is only a matter of time before the development of an attack variant of these microminiature UAVs. Science fiction's reconnaissance probes have become a battlefield reality.

Carl Otis Schuster

See also: Global War on Terrorism; Iraqi Freedom, Operation: Air Campaign

References

Munson, Kenneth, ed. *World Unmanned Aircraft*. London: Jane's, 1988.

Munson, Kenneth, ed. *Jane's Unmanned Aerial Vehicles and Targets, 1995–1996*. London: Jane's, 1996.

Office of the Secretary of Defense. *Unmanned Aerial Vehicles (UAVs): Roadmap; 2002–2027, Progressive Management*. Washington, DC: Department of Defense, 2008.

Taylor, John William Ransom. *Jane's Pocket Book of Remotely Piloted Vehicles*. New York: Collier, 1977.

WikiLeaks

A whistle-blowing website dedicated to covertly acquiring classified information and posting it on the Internet. Founded in 2006 by Julian Assange, an Australian, WikiLeaks posted its first document in December of that year. Assange and WikiLeaks were primarily known only within a few technology and journalism circles until over the course of 2010 WikiLeaks began posting classified material taken from U.S. military and diplomatic reports.

In early April 2010, WikiLeaks posted a video of a 2007 U.S. Apache helicopter attack in Baghdad, Iraq, that killed 12 people, including civilians, and injured 2 children. In July, the website shared tens of thousands of classified military reports about operations in Afghanistan with the *New York Times,* Britain's *The Guardian,* and Germany's *Der Spiegel.* And in October of that year, WikiLeaks released several hundred thousand classified documents pertaining to the war in Iraq. On November 28, 2010, WikiLeaks posted 220 cables written by U.S. diplomats stationed around the world. The collection was only a fraction of the nearly 250,000 transmissions to and from the U.S. State Department that WikiLeaks had acquired, many of which have been released to the *New York Times* and other prominent news organizations. A number of the cables contained blunt—and sometimes unflattering—assessments and statements about foreign leaders and governments that caused much embarrassment for the U.S. government.

While the American government maintained that documents regarding the Afghanistan War and the Iraq War did not unveil anything that was not already generally known, officials in the Pentagon criticized and denounced WikiLeaks for publicly sharing sensitive information, some of it not censored to protect confidential sources. Assange nevertheless defended his actions, likening the war logs to the Pentagon Papers and arguing that the United States should be transparent in and accountable for its dealings with the Middle East. In printing selections from the leaked documents, the *New York Times* assured readers that it had taken care to redact information that might endanger national security, but the paper maintained that the war reports were of significant public interest and deserved to be published.

WikiLeaks and Assange have been praised by people who agree with the organization's stance that the United States should be more transparent in its foreign policy. Criticism, on the other hand, has ranged from disappointment in WikiLeaks's insensitivity about the delicate nature of diplomatic relations to vilification of Assange as a traitor to U.S. interests. The controversy has only been inflamed by the divisive figure of Assange himself, who remained hidden until, on December 7, 2010, he appeared in a British court to fight extradition to Sweden, where he faces questioning for alleged sex crimes.

Since 2010 WikiLeaks has published many other sensitive, top-secret documents relating to the Guantánamo Bay Detention Camp, e-mails and other correspondence of Syrian government officials, and correspondence between European leaders and private surveillance companies.

American officials wishing to hold WikiLeaks accountable for the release of classified documents face a number of serious dilemmas. First, Assange is not an American citizen, making charges of treason virtually moot. Second, WikiLeaks is based in Sweden, and its volunteers and employees hail from many different nations, meaning that the United States does not have clear jurisdiction over the organization's operations. Third, Assange himself has resided in Ecuador's London embassy since June 2012, and the Ecuadoran government has steadfastly refused to extradite him to Sweden to answer to sex crime charges there or to the United States. Finally, the fact that WikiLeaks publishes its documents online and is not a traditional news outlet like the *New York Times* makes stifling the organization all the more complicated.

Since 2013, the WikiLeaks imbroglio has been superseded by the Edward Snowden affair. Snowden, an American citizen, is a former Central Intelligence Agency employee and a contractor for the National Security Agency who stole hundreds of thousands of top-secret electronic government records and began leaking them to international press outlets. Snowden was most assuredly inspired by WikiLeaks and has received help from Assange's organization. Indeed, after Snowden fled the United States for Hong Kong in May 2013, he reportedly received help in relocating to Moscow on June 23, 2013. Snowden has remained in Moscow since that time.

Jessica Ramsay and Paul G. Pierpaoli Jr.

See also: Detention Operations, Coalition: Guantánamo Bay Detention Camp; Global War on Terrorism; Obama, Barack Hussein, II

References

Khatchadourian, Raffi. "No Secrets: Julian Assange's Mission for Total Transparency." *New Yorker,* June 7, 2010.

Lagan, Bernard. "International Man of Mystery." *Sydney Morning Herald,* April 10, 2010.

"Profile: Julian Assange, the Man behind Wikileaks." *Sunday Times,* April 11, 2010.

Star, Alexander. *Open Secrets: Wikileaks, War, and American Diplomacy.* New York: New York Times, 2011.

Wolfowitz, Paul Dundes (1943–)

Neoconservative academic, U.S. assistant secretary of state for East Asian and Pacific affairs (1982–1986), and deputy secretary of defense (2001–2005). Paul Wolfowitz was the chief architect of the Bush Doctrine that advocated preemptive strikes against potential threats to U.S. interests. Wolfowitz first proposed preemptive strikes against Iraq during Ronald Reagan's presidency (1981–1989) and strongly advocated for the Iraq War. Wolfowitz was born in Ithaca, New York, on December 22, 1943. He graduated from Cornell University in 1965 and earned a doctorate in political science from the University of Chicago in 1972. His dissertation focused on the potential for nuclear proliferation in the Middle East.

Wolfowitz taught political science at Yale University from 1970 to 1972 and became an aide in U.S. Democratic senator Henry "Scoop" M. Jackson's 1972 and 1976 presidential campaigns. Wolfowitz began working in the U.S. Arms Control and Disarmament Agency (ACDA) in 1972 and studied policies related to the SALT I strategic arms limitation talks and the Henry Kissinger/Richard Nixon policy of détente. George H. W. Bush, then director of the Central Intelligence Agency, formed a committee to which Wolfowitz, in his continuing capacity at the ACDA, was assigned as a member of a team that discredited both détente and SALT II. This work brought Wolfowitz's ideas to the attention of U.S. secretary of defense Donald Rumsfeld and Governor Ronald Reagan of California.

U.S. deputy defense secretary Paul Wolfowitz talks with Colonel James Hickey of the 4th Infantry Division as he visits the soldiers, October 24, 2003. Wolfowitz was an advocate for the war in Iraq. (Joe Raedle/Getty Images)

In 1977 Wolfowitz became deputy assistant secretary of defense for regional programs in President Jimmy Carter's administration and continued to develop his theory that the best way to prevent nuclear war was to stop conventional war. It was also during this time that Wolfowitz became convinced that the highly petroleum-dependent West was extremely vulnerable to disruptions in Persian Gulf oil. In studying the issue, he envisioned the possibility that Iraq might someday threaten Kuwait or Saudi Arabia, a scenario that was realized when Iraqi president Saddam Hussein ordered the invasion and annexation of Kuwait in August 1990. Wolfowitz determined that the United States had to be able to quickly project force into the region. His studies formed the rationale for the creation of the U.S. Central Command, responsible for the U.S. rapid deployment forces that proved so important to the successful prosecution of the 1991 Persian Gulf War and the Iraq War (2003–2011).

Wolfowitz left the Defense Department in 1980 for a visiting professorship at the Paul H. Nitze School of Advanced International Studies (SAIS) at Johns Hopkins University. He reentered public service in 1981, becoming the director of policy planning for the State Department, tasked with conceptualizing President Reagan's long-term foreign policy. Wolfowitz's distrust of Hussein resurfaced when he disagreed with the administration's policy of covertly supporting Iraq in the Iran-Iraq War (1980–1988). Wolfowitz also disagreed with the administration's sale of airborne warning and control system aircraft to Saudi Arabia and its incipient dialogue with the Palestine Liberation Organization.

U.S. secretary of state George P. Schultz appointed Wolfowitz assistant secretary for East Asian and Pacific affairs in 1982, and in that capacity, Wolfowitz urged the Reagan administration to support democracy in the Philippines. Wolfowitz believed that a healthy democracy was the best defense against communism or totalitarianism, a view that would again be reflected as part of the rationale for the Iraq War. He then served as U.S. ambassador to the Republic of Indonesia (1986–1989).

President George H. W. Bush named Wolfowitz undersecretary of defense for policy (1989–1993). In this post, Wolfowitz was responsible for U.S. military strategy in the post–Cold War era and reported to U.S. defense secretary Dick Cheney. Wolfowitz disagreed with the decision not to overthrow Hussein in the 1991 Persian Gulf War (Operation Desert Storm). He saw the decision as poor strategy, believing that this task would then have to be undertaken in the future. He also saw it as a betrayal of the Iraqi Shiites and Kurds, whom the United States had encouraged to revolt and then largely abandoned.

Wolfowitz left public service during the William J. Clinton presidency, returning to Johns Hopkins as dean of the SAIS from 1993 to 2001. He did not forgo politics, however, and in 1997 became a charter member of the Project for the New American Century (PNAC), a neoconservative think tank. Fellow charter members included Rumsfeld, Cheney, and Richard Perle. In 1998, Wolfowitz signed an open PNAC letter to Clinton urging a policy shift away from containing Iraq to a preemptive attack against Iraq. Wolfowitz later joined a group that advised the 2000 Republican Party presidential candidate George W. Bush on foreign policy matters.

Wolfowitz became U.S. deputy secretary of defense in 2001 and served in that capacity until 2005. It was in this capacity that he urged Bush to mount a preemptive strike on Iraq following the September 11, 2001, terrorist attacks. This idea of preemptive strikes against potential threats, which Wolfowitz had first conceived during the Reagan era, came to be known as the Bush Doctrine. An American- and British-led military coalition invaded Iraq in March 2003, asserting in part that Iraq's alleged weapons of mass destruction (WMD) were an imminent threat worthy of preemptive intervention. As the war dragged on and settled into a bloody stalemate and no active WMD program was found in Iraq, Wolfowitz and his neoconservative cohorts were gradually shunted aside. Bush subsequently nominated Wolfowitz to be the 10th president of the World Bank Group, and he assumed the post on June 1, 2005.

Wolfowitz generated controversy in April 2007 when he admitted that in 2005, he had approved a pay raise and promotion to his companion, who was at the time a World Bank employee. The woman, Shaha Ali Riza, was transferred to the U.S. State Department but remained on the bank's payroll. While he apologized for his actions, Wolfowitz resisted any suggestion that he resign as president of the World Bank. Nevertheless, the following month he announced his resignation after a special panel determined that he had violated the bank's conflict of interest rules when approving the compensation package for Riza. Wolfowitz resigned effective June 30, 2007, and was succeeded by Robert Zoellick on July 1. Wolfowitz subsequently became involved in several international organizations, served as a consultant to the U.S. State Department, and has worked for the American Enterprise Institute.

Richard M. Edwards

See also: Bush, George Walker; Bush Doctrine; Cheney, Richard Bruce; Commands, U.S. and Coalition Military: U.S. Central Command; Hussein, Saddam; Iraqi Freedom, Operation; Kurds; Secretary of Defense, U.S.: Donald Rumsfeld; Secretary of State, U.S.: Condoleezza Rice; Weapons of Mass Destruction

References

Chernus, Ira. *Monsters to Destroy: The Neoconservative War on Terror and Sin.* Boulder, CO: Paradigm, 2006.

Crane, Les, ed. *Wolfowitz on Point.* Philadelphia: Pavillion, 2003.

Solomon, Lewis D. *Paul D. Wolfowitz: Visionary Intellectual, Policymaker, and Strategist.* Westport, CT: Praeger Security International, 2007.

Women, Role of in Afghanistan and Iraq Wars

While American women have always participated in military operations, few routinely deployed to active theaters of operations. This limitation reflected not only societal norms and expectations but also legislative and policy restrictions. In 1993, U.S. secretary of defense Les Aspin removed policy restrictions that barred women from training for combat aviation missions, following legislative action by the U.S. Congress. Female aviators flew combat missions in 1998 for the first time over the no-fly zone in Iraq. Moreover, by 1994 the Department of Defense had abolished the so-called risk rule, which prohibited women from serving in ground combat support groups. This action opened the bulk of all military occupational specialties to female personnel.

Women's participation in military operations greatly expanded in scope and experience during Operation Enduring Freedom (the coalition effort in Afghanistan, 2001–2014) and Operation Iraqi Freedom (the Iraq War, 2003–2011). More women deployed, performed a greater variety of occupational specialties, and were dispersed more widely across active theaters of operations than ever before in U.S. military history. According to figures produced by the Defense Manpower Data System and other sources, as of September 2014, nearly 300,000 women had deployed to these two operations, representing more than 11 percent of the active-duty personnel. This figure is almost double the just more than 6 percent female personnel who deployed to the Persian Gulf region earlier in Operation Desert Storm (1991) and is nearly six times higher than the number of women who served in the Vietnam War (about 2 percent).

The U.S. Air Force deployed the largest percentage of women, roughly 16 percent, trailed closely by the U.S. Army and the U.S. Navy at 12.5 percent and 12 percent, respectively. The U.S. Marine Corps claimed just 3.6 percent. Although the prohibition of women in direct ground combat remained in effect for all of the Iraq War and much of the Afghanistan War, many women found themselves under fire while in transportation convoys, returning fire in defensive combat roles, and performing the majority of all available military duties. Military necessity dispersed women to geographically diverse positions throughout the theater of operations.

The increase of women in combat situations has, not surprisingly, resulted in numerous casualties among women in the military. Of the 4,411 military personnel who lost their lives in Operation Iraqi Freedom, 110 of them were women. Additionally, 627 women were wounded in the Iraq War.

On a more positive note, several women distinguished themselves in combat during the Iraq War. Of particular note are Army Sergeant Leigh Ann Hester and Chief Warrant Officer 3 Lori Hill. Sergeant Hester was awarded the Silver Star (the U.S. Armed Forces' third highest personal decoration for valor in combat) for her role in the counterattack against insurgents who ambushed her convoy in March 2005. She was the first women since World War II to earn the prestigious award. Chief Hill became the first woman to be awarded the Distinguished Flying Cross for her actions in March 2006. While piloting an OH-58 Kiowa helicopter, she drew enemy fire away from the lead helicopter, provided suppressive fire for ground troops until they reached safety, and piloted her damaged helicopter safely back to base with a gunshot wound to the ankle.

The role of women in the military in general and combat in particular continues to expand. In response to the increased strain on forces brought about by the extended deployments in Iraq and Afghanistan, policy makers reviewed the prohibition of women in units engaged in direct ground combat missions. In January 2014, the Defense Department announced that 33,000 combat-prone positions formerly open only to men would be open to women by the spring of 2014.

Deborah Kidwell and Sheri Steed

See also: Casualties, Operation Iraqi Freedom; Iraqi Freedom, Operation

References

Biddle, Stephen. *Afghanistan and the Future of Warfare: Implications for Army and Defense Policy.* Carlisle Barracks, PA: U.S. Army War College Strategic Studies Institute, 2002.

Bowman, Steven R. *Iraq: U.S. Military Operations.* Electronic resource. Washington, DC: Library of Congress, Congressional Research Service, 2006.

Brower, J. Michael. *The Officer* 81(2) (March 2005): 38–42.

DeBruyne, Nese F. "American War and Military Operations Casualties: Lists and

Statistics." Washington, DC: Congressional Research Service, April 26, 2017.

Maitra, Sumantra. "Women in War: Women in Combat and the Internal Debate in the Field of Gender Studies." *Global Policy,* April 22, 2013, http://www.globalpolicyjournal.com/blog/22/04/2013/women-and-war-women-combat-and-internal-debate-field-gender-studies.

Woodward, Robert Upshur (1943–)

American journalist, acclaimed investigative reporter, and chronicler of the George W. Bush administration following the September 11, 2001, terror attacks on the United States. Robert (Bob) Upshur Woodward was born in Geneva, Illinois, on March 26, 1943, but spent his childhood in nearby Wheaton, Illinois. He graduated from Yale University in 1965 and was commissioned an ensign in the U.S. Navy. During his service, he served as a communications officer and as aide to Admiral Thomas H. Moorer. Woodword left the navy in 1970.

Instead of attending law school as his father wished, Woodward went to work as a reporter for the *Montgomery Sentinel* before moving on to the much more prestigious *Washington Post* in 1971. Woodward and fellow *Washington Post* reporter Carl Bernstein's investigative work on the June 1972 Watergate break-in ultimately led to revelations about President Richard M. Nixon's use of slush funds, obstruction of justice, and various dirty tricks that resulted in congressional investigations and the president's resignation in August 1974.

The Watergate scandal made Woodward a household name and one of the most sought-after investigative reporters in the nation. He and Bernstein later wrote *All the President's Men,* which was subsequently made into a movie starring Robert Redford and Dustin Hoffman, and *The Final Days,* covering their Watergate reporting. Woodward's work on the Watergate story garnered him a Pulitzer Prize. In 1979 the *Washington Post* promoted him to assistant managing editor of the metro section, and in 1982 he became assistant managing editor for investigative news. He received a second Pulitzer Prize for his reporting on the September 11, 2001, attacks and their aftermath.

Woodward's books are written in the voice of an omniscient narrator and are compiled from in-depth research, but they rely most heavily on extensive interviews with important principals. Most often, the subjects of these works have a natural interest in cooperating with Woodward. Without their input, they are more likely to be portrayed poorly in the product. All of Woodward's books have received criticism from some commentators, who usually point to inconsistencies or contest the factuality of the interviews.

Woodward's *The Commanders* (1991) covers President George H. W. Bush's handling of the December 1989–January 1990 Panama invasion and the Persian Gulf War of 1991. In *The Agenda* (1994), Woodward examined the passing of President Bill Clinton's first budget. In *The Choice* (1996), Woodward covered the 1996 presidential election contest. In *Shadow* (1999), he examined the ways in which the legacy of Watergate has affected how five presidents have dealt with scandal since 1974. In *Maestro* (2000), he analyzed the Federal Reserve Board; its chairman, Alan Greenspan; and the American economy. In 2005 following the death of Marc Felt (the anonymous Watergate source "Deep Throat"), Woodward and Bernstein produced the *Secret Man,* giving new revelations about their Watergate experience.

Woodward has also written four books on President George W. Bush's administration following the terrorist attacks of September 11, 2001: *Bush at War* (2002), *Plan of Attack* (2004), *State of Denial* (2006), and *The War Within* (2008). Woodward received criticism for being allegedly excessively friendly to Bush and his agenda after the publication of both *Bush at War* and *Plan of Attack*. The third book, however, *State of Denial*, was far more critical of the Bush administration and its failings in the war in Iraq. *The War Within* was seen by some as too deferential to the Bush administration's troop surge strategy in Iraq, and its sales have paled in comparison to Woodward's earlier books. Nevertheless, all of the books illustrate well the divisions within the White House and the Pentagon and the manner in which decisions were made within the Bush administration.

Woodward's *Plan of Attack* chronicles the Bush administration's reaction to September 11, the opening salvos in the so-called Global War on Terrorism, and the planning and implementation of Operation Enduring Freedom, which saw U.S. and coalition forces topple the Taliban regime in Afghanistan. *Plan of Attack* takes a more controversial slant by examining how, when, and why Bush decided to go to war against Iraq in 2003 and remove Saddam Hussein from power. Woodward's main contention is that the Bush administration had planned on regime change in Iraq from the very early days of Bush's tenure in office, just weeks after the 9/11 attacks, even though there was no evidence linking Hussein to the attacks. In *State of Denial,* Woodward's most damaging indictment of the Bush White House, the journalist chronicled the many missteps, mistakes, and gaffes that turned the U.S.-led war in Iraq into an embarrassing quagmire. The book also showed how many of the neoconservatives in the administration were in denial about their role in the debacle and refused to see the seriousness of the situation. The book came out less than a month before the November 2006 congressional elections, which swept the Republicans from power in both houses and brought about the forced resignation of Secretary of Defense Donald Rumsfeld.

The War Within: A Secret White House History examines the Bush administration's decision to implement a significant troop surge in Iraq beginning in early 2007. The book also examines how the Bush White House changed the way in which it formulated military and national security policy in the aftermath of the November 2006 midterm elections. The book claims that Bush's troop surge was postponed until after the 2006 midterm elections for purely political reasons. The Republicans would go on to lose control of both houses of Congress in that election.

In 2010 Woodward published *Obama's Wars,* which details the struggles within the Obama administration as it sought to deal with the Iraq and Afghanistan Wars. Among other things, it chronicles the decision making that resulted in the final withdrawal of U.S. troops from Iraq in late 2011 and the Obama troop surge in Afghanistan, which began in 2010. Although he was not as critical of Obama as he had been of George W. Bush, Woodward has nevertheless pointed out the Obama administration's foibles and mistakes when necessary. In 2013, Woodward claimed that the budget sequester that would soon take effect had been an idea initially floated by the White House. White House officials, however, insisted that the sequester had originated with the Republicans. This resulted in a brief war of words between Woodward and the White House.

Woodward is such a part of the Washington establishment that it is sometimes difficult to say to what extent his interpretations are affected by conventional wisdom, as he is one of the primary shapers of conventional wisdom. On the other hand, his painstaking interviews and investigative research make it difficult for anyone to mount a serious challenge to the veracity of his books.

Michael K. Beauchamp and Paul G. Pierpaoli Jr.

See also: Bush, George Walker; Global War on Terrorism; Iraqi Freedom, Operation; Obama, Barack Hussein, II; Secretary of Defense, U.S.: Donald Rumsfeld

References

Shephard, Alicia P. *Woodward and Bernstein: Life in the Shadow of Watergate.* Indianapolis: Wiley, 2006.

Woodward, Bob. *Bush at War.* New York: Simon and Schuster, 2003.

Woodward, Bob. *Plan of Attack.* New York: Simon and Schuster. 2004.

Woodward, Bob. *State of Denial: Bush at War, Part III.* New York: Simon and Schuster, 2006.

Woodward, Bob. *The War Within: A Secret White House History, 2006–2008.* New York: Simon and Schuster, 2008.

Woodward, Bob. *Obama's Wars.* New York: Simon and Schuster, 2010.

Z

Zarqawi, Abu Musab al- (1966–2006)

Leader of Al Qaeda in Iraq and arguably the founder of ISIS and its ideology and one of the world's most wanted terrorists until his death in June 2006 during a U.S. air strike in Iraq. Abu Musab al-Zarqawi, whose given name may have been Ahmad Fadeel al-Nazal al-Khalayleh, was born on October 20, 1966, in Zarqa, Jordan. "Zarqawi" means "from Zarqa." Although little is known about his childhood, he was reportedly a thug, drug dealer, and is believed to have dropped out of school when he was 17 years old. After serving a short time in prison for petty crimes, he traveled to Afghanistan in 1989. He remained there only briefly, but it is suspected that during this time Zarqawi became acquainted with Osama bin Laden.

Zarqawi returned to Jordan, where in 1992 he was imprisoned for plotting to replace the monarchy with an Islamic regime. After his release in 1999 he again traveled from his homeland, spending time in Europe in addition to the Middle East and South Asia. While traveling, Zarqawi reportedly raised funds and gathered members for a new organization—Jama'at al-Tawhid wa-l Jihad—aimed at establishing an Islamic caliphate in Jordan. Although some reports indicate that he may have received $200,000 from bin Laden in support of the group, captured members reportedly told German government officials that the organization was designed for militants who were looking for an alternative to Al Qaeda. It was at this time that Zarqawi was charged in absentia in Jordan for his role in a plot to use explosives at the Radisson Hotel, a popular hotel for U.S. and Israeli tourists in the Jordanian capital, Amman. The judge hearing the charges sentenced Zarqawi to death in absentia.

Back in Afghanistan, Zarqawi established a militant training camp in Herat near the Iranian border using money obtained from bin Laden. Following the September 11, 2001, terrorist attacks on the United States and subsequent U.S. attacks on Afghanistan, Zarqawi fled to Iraq following a missile strike on the camp. Once in Iraq, he joined with a militant Kurdish group in the northern part of the country where he reportedly continued to mastermind attacks in his Jordanian homeland in addition to plotting violence in Morocco, Turkey, and Iraq. The U.S. government attributed the October 2002 assassination of Laurence Foley, a U.S. Agency for International Development official who worked in Amman, to Zarqawi. Again, Zarqawi was charged in absentia in Jordan, and again he was sentenced to death in absentia.

Zarqawi attained notoriety in the United States in February 2003 when U.S. secretary of state Colin Powell claimed that Zarqawi's presence (and possible medical treatment for injuries sustained in the missile attack in Afghanistan) in Iraq was evidence of Saddam Hussein's connection to Al Qaeda. This Iraq–Al Qaeda connection—since disproved—was considered by some to be a substantial justification for the U.S. invasion of Iraq and the subsequent Iraq War (2003–2011).

After the Iraq War began, Zarqawi instigated a variety of attacks on U.S. targets and was the first proponent of widespread sectarian conflict in the country. By the time of his death in June 2006, Shiite civilians in Iraq were his Sunni supporters' primary target. Over a period of time, the United States accused him of more than 700 killings, the U.S. State Department named him as the person primarily responsible for the bombing of a United Nations hotel in August 2003, and the Central Intelligence Agency claimed that he was the man who beheaded American communications worker Nicholas Berg in a videotape released in May 2004. Indicative of the contradictory accounts that surrounded Zarqawi, many reports had claimed that he lost a leg in the 2001 Afghan missile attack, although the videotape proved this claim to be false. Although Zarqawi was accused of planning a series of bombings in November 2005 that killed 70 people in Amman, a Shiite cleric in Iraq went so far as to claim that Zarqawi himself was fictitious and possibly a creation of U.S. propagandists.

Although possibly captured by Iraqi forces in 2004 and released due to Iraqi officials' failure to recognize him (a claim that the United States never confirmed but acknowledged as possible), Zarqawi remained on the loose until his death. Despite an April 2006 report that he had resigned as the leader of a coalition of Iraqi militant groups, it was believed that he still led Al Qaeda in Iraq, which was established in 2004 when his Tawhid and Jihad organization merged with bin Laden's Al Qaeda. Zarqawi was considered the number two man in Al Qaeda, and the U.S. offer of $25 million for information leading to his capture was the same amount that the U.S. government offered for bin Laden. Zarqawi was killed on June 7, 2006, when a U.S. warplane bombed a safe house north of Baghdad where he was attending a meeting.

Jessica Britt

See also: Iraqi Freedom, Operation; Islamic State of Iraq and al-Sham (ISIS): Al Qaeda in Iraq

References

"At Site of Attack on Zarqawi, All's That Left Are Questions." *New York Times,* June 11, 2006, http://www.nytimes.com/2006/06/11/world/middleeast/11scene.html?pagewanted=all&_r=0.

Brisard, Jean-Charles, and Daniel Martinez. *Zarqawi: The New Face of Al-Qaeda.* New York: Other Press, 2005.

Napoleoni, Loretta. *Insurgent Iraq: Al-Zarqawi and the New Generation.* New York: Seven Stories, 2005.

Primary Source Documents

Excerpt from Congressional Resolution Supporting the Use of Force against Iraq, October 16, 2002

Explanation

Following the attacks of September 11, 2001, the U.S. Congress voted for an Authorization for Use of Military Force (AUMF) for "all necessary and appropriate force against those nations, organizations, or persons he determines planned, authorized, committed, or aided the terrorist attacks that occurred on September 11, 2001, or harbored such organizations or persons, in order to prevent any future acts of international terrorism against the United States by such nations, organizations or persons" (Public Law 107-40). Operations against Al Qaeda and other organizations including the Taliban government of Afghanistan began on October 7, 2001.

None of these places—Afghanistan, Philippines, Horn of Africa (mostly Somalia)—seemed capable of generating a serious threat to the United States. Of all the possible places where terrorists operated or trained, the biggest threat was deemed to come from belligerent and capable states. The state that seemed the biggest threat was Iraq. As previously stated, Saddam Hussein had demonstrated a precedent for behavior in opposition to the world order and a desire to harm the United States. Unlike the other places Iraq was an industrialized and moderately modern country against which the technological might of the coalition of countries could more effectively be used. So Iraq became the focus of planning for the next phase of the Global War on Terrorism.

That is the way many in the U.S. government looked at the events in 2002. The vote on the following resolution was moderately contentious.

Document

Resolved by the Senate and House of Representatives of the United States of America in Congress assembled,

(a) Authorization.—The President is authorized to use the Armed Forces of the United States as he determines to be necessary and appropriate in order to—

(1) defend the national security of the United States against the continuing threat posed by Iraq; and
(2) enforce all relevant United Nations Security Council resolutions regarding Iraq.

(b) Presidential Determination.—In connection with the exercise of the authority granted in subsection (a) to use force the President shall, prior to such exercise or as soon thereafter as may be feasible, but no later than 48 hours after exercising such authority, make available to the Speaker of the House of Representatives and the President pro tempore of the Senate his determination that—

(1) reliance by the United States on further diplomatic or other peaceful means alone either (A) will not adequately protect the national security of the United States against the continuing threat posed by Iraq or (B) is not likely to lead to enforcement of all relevant United Nations Security Council resolutions regarding Iraq; and

(2) acting pursuant to this joint resolution is consistent with the United States and other countries continuing to take the necessary actions against international terrorist and terrorist organizations, including those nations, organizations, or persons who planned, authorized, committed or aided the terrorist attacks that occurred on September 11, 2001.

(c) War Powers Resolution Requirements.—

(1) Specific statutory authorization.— Consistent with section 8(a)(1) of the War Powers Resolution, the Congress declares that this section is intended to constitute specific statutory authorization within the meaning of section 5(b) of the War Powers Resolution.

Source: United States Congress Joint Resolution. Public Law 107–243, 107th Congress. Washington, DC: Government Printing Office, 2002. Available at http://www.gpo.gov/fdsys/pkg/PLAW-107publ243/html/PLAW-107publ243.htm.

Excerpt of the State of the Union Address, January 28, 2003

Explanation

On September 18, 2001, the U.S. Congress passed the Authorization for use of Military Force in response to the attacks of September 11, 2001, and oriented against Al Qaeda and the Taliban government of Afghanistan. On October 16, 2002, the Congress again passed an Authorization for Use of Military Force, this time directed against Iraq. On November 8, 2002, the United Nations passed UN Security Council Resolution 1441, which strengthened UN inspectors and threatened additional action if support of those inspectors was not forthcoming. In less than a week after this address the U.S. secretary of state went before the UN Security Council to make a legal case for military action against Iraq. The case laid out by the president of the United States in this speech is the definitive U.S. position and argument for conducting a war against the state of Iraq and the regime of Saddam Hussein.

Document

Our nation and the world must learn the lessons of the Korean Peninsula and not allow an even greater threat to rise up in Iraq. A brutal dictator, with a history of reckless aggression, with ties to terrorism, with great potential wealth, will not be permitted to dominate a vital region and threaten the United States. (Applause.)

Twelve years ago, Saddam Hussein faced the prospect of being the last casualty in a war he had started and lost. To spare himself, he agreed to disarm of all weapons of mass destruction. For the next 12 years, he systematically violated that agreement. He pursued chemical, biological, and nuclear weapons, even while inspectors were in his country. Nothing to date has restrained him from his pursuit of these weapons—not economic sanctions, not isolation from the civilized world, not even cruise missile strikes on his military facilities.

Almost three months ago, the United Nations Security Council gave Saddam Hussein his final chance to disarm. He has shown instead utter contempt for the United Nations, and for the opinion of the world. The 108 U.N. inspectors were sent to conduct—were not sent to conduct a scavenger hunt for hidden materials across a country the size of California. The job of the inspectors is to verify that Iraq's regime is disarming. It is up to Iraq to show exactly where it is hiding its banned weapons, lay those weapons out for the world to see, and destroy them as directed. Nothing like this has happened.

The United Nations concluded in 1999 that Saddam Hussein had biological weapons sufficient to produce over 25,000 liters of anthrax—enough doses to kill several million people. He hasn't accounted for that material. He's given no evidence that he has destroyed it.

The United Nations concluded that Saddam Hussein had materials sufficient to produce more than 38,000 liters of botulinum toxin—enough to subject millions of people to death by respiratory failure. He hadn't accounted for that material. He's given no evidence that he has destroyed it.

Our intelligence officials estimate that Saddam Hussein had the materials to produce as much as 500 tons of sarin, mustard and VX nerve agent. In such quantities, these chemical agents could also kill untold thousands. He's not accounted for these materials. He has given no evidence that he has destroyed them.

U.S. intelligence indicates that Saddam Hussein had upwards of 30,000 munitions capable of delivering chemical agents. Inspectors recently turned up 16 of them—despite Iraq's recent declaration denying their existence. Saddam Hussein has not accounted for the remaining 29,984 of these prohibited munitions. He's given no evidence that he has destroyed them.

From three Iraqi defectors we know that Iraq, in the late 1990s, had several mobile biological weapons labs. These are designed to produce germ warfare agents, and can be moved from place to a place to evade inspectors. Saddam Hussein has not disclosed these facilities. He's given no evidence that he has destroyed them.

The International Atomic Energy Agency confirmed in the 1990s that Saddam Hussein had an advanced nuclear weapons development program, had a design for a nuclear weapon and was working on five different methods of enriching uranium for a bomb. The British government has learned that Saddam Hussein recently sought significant quantities of uranium from Africa. Our intelligence sources tell us that he has attempted to purchase high-strength aluminum tubes suitable for nuclear weapons production. Saddam Hussein has not credibly explained these activities. He clearly has much to hide.

The dictator of Iraq is not disarming. To the contrary; he is deceiving. From intelligence sources we know, for instance, that thousands of Iraqi security personnel are at work hiding documents and materials from the U.N. inspectors, sanitizing inspection sites and monitoring the inspectors themselves. Iraqi officials accompany the inspectors in order to intimidate witnesses.

Iraq is blocking U-2 surveillance flights requested by the United Nations. Iraqi intelligence officers are posing as the scientists inspectors are supposed to interview. Real scientists have been coached by Iraqi officials on what to say. Intelligence sources indicate that Saddam Hussein has ordered that scientists who cooperate with U.N. inspectors in disarming Iraq will be killed, along with their families.

Year after year, Saddam Hussein has gone to elaborate lengths, spent enormous sums, taken great risks to build and keep weapons of mass destruction. But why? The only possible explanation, the only possible use he could have for those weapons, is to dominate, intimidate, or attack.

With nuclear arms or a full arsenal of chemical and biological weapons, Saddam Hussein could resume his ambitions of conquest in the Middle East and create deadly havoc in that region. And this Congress and the America people must recognize another threat. Evidence from intelligence sources, secret communications, and statements by people now in custody reveal that Saddam Hussein aids and protects terrorists, including members of al Qaeda. Secretly, and without fingerprints, he could provide one of his hidden weapons to terrorists, or help them develop their own.

Before September the 11th, many in the world believed that Saddam Hussein could be contained. But chemical agents, lethal viruses and shadowy terrorist networks are not easily contained. Imagine those 19 hijackers with other weapons and other plans—this time armed by Saddam Hussein. It would take one vial, one canister, one crate slipped into this country to bring a day of horror like none we have ever known. We will do everything in our power to make sure that that day never comes. (Applause.)

Some have said we must not act until the threat is imminent. Since when have terrorists and tyrants announced their intentions, politely putting us on notice before they strike? If this threat is permitted to fully and suddenly emerge, all actions, all words, and all recriminations would come too late. Trusting in the sanity and restraint of Saddam Hussein is not a strategy, and it is not an option. (Applause.)

The dictator who is assembling the world's most dangerous weapons has already used them on whole villages—leaving thousands of his own citizens dead, blind, or disfigured. Iraqi refugees tell us how forced confessions are obtained—by torturing children while their parents are made to watch. International human rights groups have catalogued other methods used in the torture chambers of Iraq: electric shock, burning with hot irons, dripping acid on the skin, mutilation with electric drills, cutting out tongues, and rape. If this is not evil, then evil has no meaning. (Applause.)

And tonight I have a message for the brave and oppressed people of Iraq: Your enemy is not surrounding your country—your enemy is ruling your country. (Applause.) And the day he and his regime are removed from power will be the day of your liberation. (Applause.)

The world has waited 12 years for Iraq to disarm. America will not accept a serious and mounting threat to our country, and our friends and our allies. The United States will ask the U.N. Security Council to convene on February the 5th to consider the facts of Iraq's ongoing defiance of the world. Secretary of State Powell will present information and intelligence about Iraqi's legal—Iraq's illegal weapons programs, its attempt to hide those weapons from inspectors, and its links to terrorist groups.

We will consult. But let there be no misunderstanding: If Saddam Hussein does not fully disarm, for the safety of our people and for the peace of the world, we will lead a coalition to disarm him.

Source: Bush, George W. "Address before a Joint Session of the Congress on the State of the Union."

January 28, 2003. *Public Papers of the Presidents of the United States. George W. Bush, 2003, Book 1.* Washington, DC: Government Printing Office, 2006, 82–90.

President Bush's Address to the Nation at the Start of Hostilities, March 19, 2003

Explanation

President George W. Bush spoke to the American people and to the world on the night that hostilities began between the U.S.-led coalition and the regime of Saddam Hussein. In this speech justification for the war had shifted dramatically. The administration had initially argued that Saddam Hussein's WMD programs and his alleged ties to terrorist organizations posed an immediate threat to security that must be removed. These arguments had, however, been effectively challenged. In this speech he shifted his emphasis to liberating the Iraqi people from the tyranny of Saddam Hussein, a goal reflected in the name of the mission, Operation Iraqi Freedom. This final justification came closest to a core reason for the invasion. President Bush and the neocons who supported him saw Iraq as the hub of a new Middle East. A regime in Baghdad loyal to Washington would counterbalance Iran, cease to threaten Israel, provide another secure source of oil, and serve as a shining example of the efficacy of American democracy for the entire region.

Thomas R. Mockaitis

Document

My fellow citizens, at this hour, American and coalition forces are in the early stages of military operations to disarm Iraq, to free its people and to defend the world from grave danger.

On my orders, coalition forces have begun striking selected targets of military importance to undermine Saddam Hussein's ability to wage war. These are opening stages of what will be a broad and concerted campaign. More than 35 countries are giving crucial support—from the use of naval and air bases, to help with intelligence and logistics, to the deployment of combat units. Every nation in this coalition has chosen to bear the duty and share the honor of serving in our common defense.

To all the men and women of the United States Armed Forces now in the Middle East, the peace of a troubled world and the hopes of an oppressed people now depend on you. That trust is well placed.

The enemies you confront will come to know your skill and bravery. The people you liberate will witness the honorable and decent spirit of the American military. In this conflict, America faces an enemy who has no regard for conventions of war or rules of morality. Saddam Hussein has placed Iraqi troops and equipment in civilian areas, attempting to use innocent men, women and children as shields for his own military—a final atrocity against his people.

I want Americans and all the world to know that coalition forces will make every effort to spare innocent civilians from harm. A campaign on the harsh terrain of a nation as large as California could be longer and more difficult than some predict. And helping Iraqis achieve a united, stable and free country will require our sustained commitment.

We come to Iraq with respect for its citizens, for their great civilization and for the religious faiths they practice. We have no ambition in Iraq, except to remove a threat and restore control of that country to its own people.

I know that the families of our military are praying that all those who serve will return safely and soon. Millions of Americans are praying with you for the safety of your loved ones and for the protection of the innocent. For your sacrifice, you have the gratitude and respect of the American people. And you can know that our forces will be coming home as soon as their work is done.

Our nation enters this conflict reluctantly—yet, our purpose is sure. The people of the United States and our friends and allies will not live at the mercy of an outlaw regime that threatens the peace with weapons of mass murder. We will meet that threat now, with our Army, Air Force, Navy, Coast Guard and Marines, so that we do not have to meet it later with armies of fire fighters and police and doctors on the streets of our cities.

Now that conflict has come, the only way to limit its duration is to apply decisive force. And I assure you, this will not be a campaign of half measures, and we will accept no outcome but victory.

My fellow citizens, the dangers to our country and the world will be overcome. We will pass through this time of peril and carry on the work of peace. We will defend our freedom. We will bring freedom to others and we will prevail.

May God bless our country and all who defend her.

Source: Bush, George W. "Address to the Nation on Iraq." March 19, 2003. *Public Papers of the Presidents of the United States. George W. Bush, 2003, Book 1.* Washington, DC: Government Printing Office, 2006, 281–282.

Excerpt of President Bush's Remarks to the Crew of the USS Abraham Lincoln, May 1, 2003

Explanation

President George W. Bush was a pilot in the Air National Guard, and on May 1, 2003, he became the first sitting president to make an arrested landing on an aircraft carrier. Of note, his father had been a navy carrier pilot in World War II and thus had made numerous arrested landings. President Bush arrived on an S-3 Viking as a passenger in the plane using the call sign *Navy One*. President Bush arrived on the USS Abraham Lincoln off the coast of San Diego to welcome the crew home after a 10-month deployment—one of the longest carrier deployments since the end of the Vietnam War. The ship bore a banner that said "Mission Accomplished." The banner was to celebrate the crew's end of mission, and the White House said that it was not to state that the war was over or that the fighting was complete in Iraq.

The fighting in Iraq was changing in tone and character from an invasion to an occupation and preferably a transition to Iraqi sovereignty and American and coalition departure. Looting was ending and the transition was beginning. The intent was to transition to Iraqi elections in a matter of months—something like 90 days—and depart Iraq by the end of 2003.

The official part of the transition within Iraq could be considered to have begun on April 15, 2003, with a conference held in Nasariyah attended by something like 100 Iraqi political leaders. A follow-up meeting was held on April 28 with about 250 Iraqi leaders. In this second meeting leaders of various political parties were designated, and it looked as if the process was moving forward according to plans.

Document

Thank you all very much. Admiral Kelly, Captain Card, officers and sailors of the USS Abraham Lincoln, my fellow Americans: Major combat operations in Iraq have ended. In the battle of Iraq, the United States and our allies have prevailed. (Applause.) And now our coalition is engaged in securing and reconstructing that country.

In this battle, we have fought for the cause of liberty, and for the peace of the world. Our nation and our coalition are proud of this accomplishment—yet, it is you, the members of the United States military, who achieved it. Your courage, your willingness to face danger for your country and for each other, made this day possible. Because of you, our nation is more secure. Because of you, the tyrant has fallen, and Iraq is free. (Applause.)

Operation Iraqi Freedom was carried out with a combination of precision and speed and boldness the enemy did not expect, and the world had not seen before. From distant bases or ships at sea, we sent planes and missiles that could destroy an enemy division, or strike a single bunker. Marines and soldiers charged to Baghdad across 350 miles of hostile ground, in one of the swiftest advances of heavy arms in history. You have shown the world the skill and the might of the American Armed Forces.

This nation thanks all the members of our coalition who joined in a noble cause. We thank the Armed Forces of the United Kingdom, Australia, and Poland, who shared in the hardships of war. We thank all the citizens of Iraq who welcomed our troops and joined in the liberation of their own country. And tonight, I have a special word for Secretary Rumsfeld, for General Franks, and for all the men and women who wear the uniform of the United States: America is grateful for a job well done. (Applause.)

The character of our military through history—the daring of Normandy, the fierce courage of Iwo Jima, the decency and idealism that turned enemies into allies—is fully present in this generation. When Iraqi civilians looked into the faces of our servicemen and women, they saw strength and kindness and goodwill. When I look at the members of the United States military, I see the best of our country, and I'm honored to be your Commander-in-Chief. (Applause.)

In the images of falling statues, we have witnessed the arrival of a new era. For a hundred of years of war, culminating in the nuclear age, military technology was designed and deployed to inflict casualties on an ever-growing scale. In defeating Nazi Germany and Imperial Japan, Allied forces destroyed entire cities, while enemy leaders who started the conflict were safe until the final days. Military power was used to end a regime by breaking a nation.

Today, we have the greater power to free a nation by breaking a dangerous and aggressive regime. With new tactics and precision weapons, we can achieve military objectives without directing violence against civilians. No device of man can remove the tragedy from war; yet it is a great moral advance when the guilty have far more to fear from war than the innocent. (Applause.)

In the images of celebrating Iraqis, we have also seen the ageless appeal of human freedom. Decades of lies and intimidation could not make the Iraqi people love their oppressors or desire their own enslavement. Men and women in every culture need liberty like they need food and water and air. Everywhere that freedom arrives, humanity rejoices; and everywhere that freedom stirs, let tyrants fear. (Applause.)

We have difficult work to do in Iraq. We're bringing order to parts of that country that remain dangerous. We're pursuing and finding leaders of the old regime, who will be held to account for their crimes. We've begun the search for hidden chemical and biological weapons and already know of hundreds of sites that will be investigated. We're helping to rebuild Iraq, where the dictator built palaces for himself, instead of hospitals and schools. And we will stand with the new leaders of Iraq as they establish a government of, by, and for the Iraqi people. (Applause.)

The transition from dictatorship to democracy will take time, but it is worth every effort. Our coalition will stay until our work is done. Then we will leave, and we will leave behind a free Iraq. (Applause.)

The battle of Iraq is one victory in a war on terror that began on September the 11, 2001—and still goes on. That terrible morning, 19 evil men—the shock troops of a hateful ideology—gave America and the civilized world a glimpse of their ambitions. They imagined, in the words of one terrorist, that September the 11th would be the "beginning of the end of America." By seeking to turn our cities into killing fields, terrorists and their allies believed that they could destroy this nation's resolve, and force our retreat from the world. They have failed. (Applause.)

In the battle of Afghanistan, we destroyed the Taliban, many terrorists, and the camps where they trained. We continue to help the Afghan people lay roads, restore hospitals, and educate all of their children. Yet we also have dangerous work to complete. As I speak, a Special Operations task force, led by the 82nd Airborne, is on the trail of the terrorists and those who seek to undermine the free government of Afghanistan. America and our coalition will finish what we have begun. (Applause.)

From Pakistan to the Philippines to the Horn of Africa, we are hunting down al Qaeda killers. Nineteen months ago, I pledged that the terrorists would not escape the patient justice of the United States. And as of tonight, nearly one-half of al Qaeda's senior operatives have been captured or killed. (Applause.)

The liberation of Iraq is a crucial advance in the campaign against terror. We've removed an ally of al Qaeda, and cut off a source of terrorist funding. And this much is certain: No terrorist network will gain weapons of mass destruction from the Iraqi regime, because the regime is no more. (Applause.)

In these 19 months that changed the world, our actions have been focused and deliberate and proportionate to the offense. We have not forgotten the victims of September the 11th—the last phone calls, the cold murder of children, the searches in the rubble. With those attacks, the terrorists and their supporters declared war on the United States. And war is what they got. (Applause.)

Our war against terror is proceeding according to principles that I have made clear to all: Any person involved in committing or planning terrorist attacks against the American people becomes an enemy of this country, and a target of American justice. (Applause.)

Any person, organization, or government that supports, protects, or harbors terrorists is complicit in the murder of the innocent, and equally guilty of terrorist crimes.

Any outlaw regime that has ties to terrorist groups and seeks or possesses weapons of mass destruction is a grave danger to the civilized world—and will be confronted. (Applause.)

And anyone in the world, including the Arab world, who works and sacrifices for freedom has a loyal friend in the United States of America. (Applause.)

Our commitment to liberty is America's tradition—declared at our founding; affirmed in Franklin Roosevelt's Four Freedoms; asserted in the Truman Doctrine and in Ronald Reagan's challenge to an evil empire. We are committed to freedom in Afghanistan, in Iraq, and in a peaceful Palestine.

The advance of freedom is the surest strategy to undermine the appeal of terror in the world. Where freedom takes hold, hatred gives way to hope. When freedom takes hold, men and women turn to the peaceful pursuit of a better life. American values and American interests lead in the same direction: We stand for human liberty. (Applause.)

The United States upholds these principles of security and freedom in many ways—with all the tools of diplomacy, law enforcement, intelligence, and finance. We're working with a broad coalition of nations that understand the threat and our shared responsibility to meet it. The use of force has been—and remains—our last resort. Yet all can know, friend and foe alike, that our nation has a mission: We will answer threats to our security, and we will defend the peace. (Applause.)

Our mission continues. Al Qaeda is wounded, not destroyed. The scattered cells of the terrorist network still operate in many nations, and we know from daily intelligence that they continue to plot against free people. The proliferation of deadly weapons remains a serious danger. The enemies of freedom are not idle, and neither are we. Our government has taken unprecedented measures to defend the homeland. And we will continue to hunt down the enemy before he can strike. (Applause.)

The war on terror is not over; yet it is not endless. We do not know the day of final victory, but we have seen the turning of the tide. No act of the terrorists will change our purpose, or weaken our resolve, or alter their fate. Their cause is lost. Free nations will press on to victory. (Applause.)

Other nations in history have fought in foreign lands and remained to occupy and exploit. Americans, following a battle, want nothing more than to return home. And that is your direction tonight. (Applause.) After service in the Afghan—and Iraqi theaters of war—after 100,000 miles, on the longest carrier deployment in recent history, you are homeward bound. (Applause.) Some of you will see new family members for the first time—150 babies were born while their fathers were on the Lincoln. Your families are proud of you, and your nation will welcome you. (Applause.)

We are mindful, as well, that some good men and women are not making the journey home. One of those who fell, Corporal Jason Mileo, spoke to his parents five days before his death. Jason's father said, "He called us from the center of Baghdad, not to brag, but to tell us he loved us. Our son was a soldier."

Every name, every life is a loss to our military, to our nation, and to the loved ones who grieve. There's no homecoming for these families. Yet we pray, in God's time, their reunion will come.

Those we lost were last seen on duty. Their final act on this Earth was to fight a great evil and bring liberty to others. All of you—all in this generation of our military—have taken up the highest calling of history. You're defending your country, and protecting the innocent from harm. And wherever you go, you carry a message of hope—a message that is ancient and ever new. In the words of the prophet Isaiah, "To the captives, 'come out,'—and to those in darkness, 'be free.'"

Thank you for serving our country and our cause. May God bless you all, and may God continue to bless America. (Applause.)

Source: Bush, George W. "Address to the Nation on Iraq from the U.S.S. Abraham Lincoln." May 1, 2003. *Public Papers of the Presidents of the United States. George W. Bush, 2003, Book 1.* Washington, DC: Government Printing Office, 2006, 410–413.

Excerpt of Coalition Provisional Order Number 1, May 16, 2003

Explanation

Jay Garner was designated to be the director of the Office for Reconstruction and Humanitarian Assistance (OHRA) for Iraq in January 2003. The intent was that this organization would serve as a caretaker administration until a democratically elected Iraqi government could take over. This organization only lasted less than a month as retired lieutenant general Garner arrived in Baghdad on April 21, 2003, and he was replaced on May 11, 2003, by L. Paul Bremer. There are differing accounts of the reasons for this abrupt transition. One of the arguments offered is that Garner was not moving quickly enough to remove Baath Party members from positions of authority.

When Bremer arrived in country he was the U.S. presidential envoy and administrator in Iraq and the chief executive for the Coalition Provisional Authority (CPA). In this position he worked directly for the U.S. Department of Defense.

The CPA was headquartered in Saddam Hussein's palaces in and around Baghdad.

If the criticism of Garner was that he did not move fast enough for de-Baathification, then the CPA under Bremer did the opposite. CPA Order 1 was the order to remove all employees from the Baath Party from the public sector and ban them from future public sector employment. This order was issued on May 16, 2003. Garner approached de-Baathification much as had the U.S. occupation of Germany approached de-Nazification.

Document

COALITON PROVISIONAL AUTHORITY ORDER NUMBER 1 DE-BA'ATHIFICATION OF IRAQI SOCIETY

Pursuant to my authority as Administrator of the Coalition Provisional Authority (CPA), relevant U.N. Security Council resolutions, and the laws and usages of war, Recognizing that the Iraqi people have suffered large scale human rights abuses and depravations over many years at the hands of the Ba'ath Party, Noting the grave concern of Iraqi society regarding the threat posed by the continuation of Ba'ath Party networks and personnel in the administration of Iraq, and the intimidation of the people of Iraq by Ba'ath Party officials, Concerned by the continuing threat to the security of the Coalition Forces posed by the Iraqi Ba'ath Party, I hereby promulgate the following:

Section 1

Disestablishment of the Ba'ath Party

1) On April 16, 2003 the Coalition Provisional Authority disestablished the Ba'ath Party of Iraq. This order implements the declaration by eliminating the party's structures and removing its leadership from positions of authority and responsibility in Iraqi society. By this means, the Coalition Provisional Authority will ensure that representative government in Iraq is not threatened by Ba'athist elements returning to power ant that those in positions of authority in the future are acceptable to the people of Iraq.

2) Full members of the Ba'ath Party holding the ranks of 'Udw Qutriyya (Regional Command Member), 'Udw Far' (Branch Member). 'Udw Shu'bah (Section Member), and 'Udw Firqah (Group Member) (together, "Senior Party Members") are [hereby] removed from their positions and banned from future employment in the public sector. These Senior Party Members shall be evaluated for criminal conduct or threat to the

security of the Coalition. Those suspected of criminal conduct shall be investigated and, if deemed a threat to security or a flight risk, detained or placed under house arrest.

3) Individuals holding positions in the top three layers of management in every national government ministry, affiliated corporations and other government institutions (e.g., universities and hospitals) shall be interviewed for possible affiliation with the Ba'ath Party, and subject to investigation for criminal conduct and risk to security. Any such persons detained to be full members of the Ba'ath Party shall be removed from their employment. This includes those holding the more junior ranks of 'Udw (Member) and 'Udw 'Amil (Active Member), as well as those determined to be Senior Party Members.

4) Displays in government buildings or public spaces of the image or likeness of Saddam Hussein or other readily identifiable members of the former regime or of symbols of the Baath Party or the former regime are hereby prohibited.

5) Rewards shall be made available for information leading to the capture of senior members of the Baath party and individuals complicit in the crimes of the former regime.

6) The Administrator of the Coalition Provisional Authority or his designees may grant exceptions to the above guidance on a case-by-case basis.

Section 2

Entry into Force

This Order shall enter into force on the date of signature.

Source: Coalition Provisional Authority. "Order Number 1: De-Ba'athification of Iraqi Society." May 16, 2003. National Security Archives. Available at https://nsarchive2.gwu.edu/NSAEBB/NSAEBB418/docs/9a%20-%20Coalition%20Provisional%20Authority%20Order%20No%201%20-%205-16-03.pdf.

Excerpt of Coalition Provisional Order Number 2, May 23, 2003

Explanation

Jay Garner was accused of not moving fast enough with respect to de-Baathification. L. Paul Bremer rectified that problem with the issuance of CPA Order Number 1 (see previous entry). Garner also recommended using the existing Iraqi security forces to provide basic policing functions. This served as another point of contention and was also rectified by Bremer by this order a week after the de-Baathification order and less than two weeks after arriving in country.

This order, disbanding the Iraqi Army, all military personnel, and revoking all pensions and benefits, along with CPA Order 1, has been given the distinction of doing more than anything else to generate the opposition to the occupation and to fuel the sectarian violence to come. If there was going to be a spark for revolution and opposition, then this order provided the fuel that the spark would light and turn into an inferno.

Document

COALITION PROVISONAL AUTHORITY ORDER NUMBER 2 DISSOULUTION OF ENTITIES

Pursuant to my authority as Administrator of the Coalition Provisional Authority (CPA), relevant U.N. Security Council resolutions, including Resolution 1483 (2003), and the laws and usages of war, Reconfirming all of the provisions of General Franks' Freedom Message to the Iraqi People of April 16, 2003, Recognizing that the prior Iraqi regime used certain government entities to oppress the Iraqi people and as instruments of torture, repression and corruption, Reaffirming the Instructions to the Citizens of Iraq regarding Ministry of Youth and Sport of May 8, 2003, I hereby promulgate the following:

Section 1

Dissolved Entities

The entities (the "Dissolved Entities") listed in the attached Annex are hereby dissolved. Additional entities may be added to this list in the future.

Section 2

Assets and Financial Obligations

1) All assets, including records and data, in whatever from maintained and wherever located, of the Dissolved Entities shall be held by the Administrator of the CPA ("the Administrator") on behalf of and for the benefit of the Iraqi people and shall be used to assist the Iraqi people and to support the recovery of Iraq.

2) All financial obligations of the Dissolved Entities are suspended. The Administrator of the CPA will establish procedures whereby persons claiming to be the beneficiaries of such obligations may apply for payment.

3) Persons in possession of assets of the Dissolved Entities shall preserve those assets, promptly inform local Coalition authorities, and immediately turn them over, as directed by those authorities. Continued possession, transfer, sale, use, conversion, or concealment of such assets following the date of this Order is prohibited and may be punished.

Section 3

Employees and Service Members

1) Any military or other rank, title, or status granted to a former employee or functionary of a Dissolved Entity by the former Regime is hereby cancelled.

2) All conscripts are released from their service obligations. Conscriptions is suspended indefinitely, subject to decisions by future Iraq governments concerning whether a free Iraq should have conscription.

3) Any person employed by a Dissolved Entity in any form or capacity, is dismissed effective as of April 16, 2003. Any person employed by a Dissolved Entity, in any from or capacity remains accountable for acts committed during such employment.

4) A termination payment in an amount to be determined by the Administrator will be paid to employees so dismissed, except those who are Senior Party Members as defined in the Administrator's May 16, 2003 Order of the Coalition Provisional Authority De-Ba`athification of Iraqi Society, ("Senior Party Members") (See Section 3.6).

5) Pensions being paid by, or on account of service to, a Dissolved Entity before April 16, 2003 will continue to be paid, including to war widows and disabled veterans, provided that no pension payments will be made to any person who is a Senior Party Member (see Section 3.6) and that the power is reserved to the Administrator and to future Iraqi governments to revoke or reduce pensions as a penalty for past or future illegal conduct or to modify pension arrangements to eliminate improper privileges granted by the Ba`athist regime or for similar reasons.

6) Notwithstanding any provision of this Order, or any other Order, law, or regulation, and consistent with the Administrator's May 16, 2003 Order of the Coalition Provisional Authority De-Ba`athification of Iraqi Society, no payment, including a termination or pension payment, will be made to any

person who is or was a Senior Party Member. Any person holding the rank under the former regime of Colonel or above, or its equivalent, will be deemed a Senior Party Member, provided that such persons may seek, under procedures to be prescribed, to establish to the satisfaction of the Administrator, that they were not a Senior Party Member.

Source: Coalition Provisional Authority. "Order Number 2: Dissolution of Entities." May 23, 2003. National Security Archives. Available at https://nsarchive2.gwu.edu/NSAEBB/NSAEBB418/docs/9b%20-%20Coalition%20Provisional%20Authority%20Order%20No%202%20-%208-23-03.pdf.

Excerpt of Iraqi Constitution: Preamble and Basic Rights, October 15, 2005

Explanation

The creation of an Iraqi Constitution by Iraqis was deemed to be one of the most important aspects of establishing sovereignty in Iraq. The process took longer than expected. It began with the establishment of the Iraqi Governing Council (or nearly at the beginning) on or about July 13, 2003, and concluded with the publishing of the final document on October 15, 2005. As will be noted there is a lot of compromise captured in the document.

This excerpt includes parts of the rights that make clear some of the trauma experienced in the past and the desire to legally preempt a recurrence of that trauma in the future.

Document

THE PREAMBLE

In the name of God, the most merciful, the most compassionate. We have honored the sons of Adam.

We are the people of the land between two rivers, the homeland of the apostles and prophets, abode of the virtuous imams, pioneers of civilization, crafters of writing and cradle of numeration. Upon our land the first law made by man was passed, the most ancient just pact for homelands policy was inscribed, and upon our soil, companions of the Prophet and saints prayed, philosophers and scientists theorized and writers and poets excelled. Acknowledging God's right over us, and in fulfillment of the call of our homeland and citizens, and in response to the call of our religious and national leaderships and the determination of our great (religious) authorities and of our leaders and reformers, and in the midst of an international support from our friends and those who love us, marched for the first time in our history toward the ballot boxes by the millions, men and women, young and old, on the 30th of January, 2005, invoking the pains of sectarian oppression sufferings inflicted by the autocratic clique and inspired by the tragedies of Iraq's martyrs, Shiite and Sunni, Arabs and Kurds and Turkmen and from all the other components of the people and recollecting the darkness of the ravage of the holy cities and the South in the Sha'abaniyya uprising and burnt by the flames of grief of the mass graves, the marshes, Dujail and others and articulating the sufferings of racial oppression in the massacres of Halabja, Barzan, Anfal and the Fayli Kurds and inspired by the ordeals of the Turkmen in Bashir and as is the case in the remaining areas of Iraq where the people of the west suffered from the assassinations of their leaders, symbols and elderly and from the displacement of their skilled individuals and from the drying out of their cultural and intellectual wells, so we sought hand in hand and shoulder to shoulder to create our new Iraq, the

Iraq of the future free from sectarianism, racism, locality complex, discrimination and exclusion.

Accusations of being infidels, and terrorism did not stop us from marching forward to build a nation of law. Sectarianism and racism have not stopped us from marching together to strengthen our national unity, and to follow the path of peaceful transfer of power and adopt the course of the just distribution of resources and providing equal opportunity for all.

We the people of Iraq who have just risen from our stumble, and who are looking with confidence to the future through a republican, federal, democratic, pluralistic system, have resolved with the determination of our men, women, the elderly and youth, to respect the rules of law, to establish justice and equality to cast aside the politics of aggression, and to tend to the concerns of women and their rights, and to the elderly and their concerns, and to children and their affairs and to spread a culture of diversity and defusing terrorism. We the people of Iraq of all components and shades have taken upon ourselves to decide freely and with our choice to unite our future and to take lessons from yesterday for tomorrow, to draft, through the values and ideals of the heavenly messages and the findings of science and man's civilization, this lasting constitution. The adherence to this constitution preserves for Iraq its free union, its people, its land and its sovereignty.

Section One: Fundamental Principles
Article 1:

The Republic of Iraq is a single federal, independent and fully sovereign state in which the system of government is republican, representative, parliamentary, and democratic, and this Constitution is a guarantor of the unity of Iraq.

Article 2:

First: Islam is the official religion of the State and is a foundation source of legislation:

A. No law may be enacted that contradicts the established provisions of Islam.
B. No law may be enacted that contradicts the principles of democracy.
C. No law may be enacted that contradicts the rights and basic freedoms stipulated in this Constitution.

Second: This Constitution guarantees the Islamic identity of the majority of the Iraqi people and guarantees the full religious rights to freedom of religious belief and practice of all individuals such as Christians, Yazidis, and Mandean Sabeans.

Article 3:

Iraq is a country of multiple nationalities, religions, and sects. It is a founding and active member in the Arab League and is committed to its charter, and it is part of the Islamic world.

Article 4:

First: The Arabic language and the Kurdish language are the two official languages of Iraq. The right of Iraqis to educate their children in their mother tongue, such as Turkmen, Syriac, and Armenian shall be guaranteed in government educational institutions in accordance with educational guidelines, or in any other language in private educational institutions.

Second: The scope of the term "official language" and the means of applying the provisions of this article shall be defined by a law and shall include:

A. Publication of the Official Gazette, in the two languages;

B. Speech, conversation, and expression in official domains, such as the Council of Representatives, the Council of Ministers, courts, and official conferences, in either of the two languages;
C. Recognition and publication of official documents and correspondence in the two languages;
D. Opening schools that teach the two languages, in accordance with the educational guidelines;
E. Use of both languages in any matter enjoined by the principle of equality such as bank notes, passports, and stamps.

Third: The federal and official institutions and agencies in the Kurdistan region shall use both languages.

Fourth: The Turkomen language and the Syriac language are two other official languages in the administrative units in which they constitute density of population.

Fifth: Each region or governorate may adopt any other local language as an additional official language if the majority of its population so decides in a general referendum.

Article 5:

The law is sovereign. The people are the source of authority and legitimacy, which they shall exercise in a direct, general, secret ballot and through their constitutional institutions.

Article 6:

Transfer of authority shall be made peacefully through democratic means as stipulated in this Constitution.

Article 7:

First: Any entity or program that adopts, incites, facilitates, glorifies, promotes, or justifies racism or terrorism or accusations of being an infidel (takfir) or ethnic cleansing, especially the Saddamist Ba'ath in Iraq and its symbols, under any name whatsoever, shall be prohibited. Such entities may not be part of political pluralism in Iraq. This shall be regulated by law.

Second: The State shall undertake to combat terrorism in all its forms, and shall work to protect its territories from being a base, pathway, or field for terrorist activities.

Article 8:

Iraq shall observe the principles of good neighborliness, adhere to the principle of noninterference in the internal affairs of other states, seek to settle disputes by peaceful means, establish relations on the basis of mutual interests and reciprocity, and respect its international obligations.

Article 9:

First:

A- The Iraqi armed forces and security services will be composed of the components of the Iraqi people with due consideration given to their balance and representation without discrimination or exclusion. They shall be subject to the control of the civilian authority, shall defend Iraq, shall not be used as an instrument to oppress the Iraqi people, shall not interfere in the political affairs, and shall have no role in the transfer of authority.

B- The formation of military militias outside the framework of the armed forces is prohibited.

C- The Iraqi armed forces and their personnel, including military personnel working in the Ministry of Defense or any subordinate departments or organizations, may not stand for election to political office, campaign for candidates, or participate in other activities prohibited by Ministry of Defense regulations. This ban includes the activities of the personnel mentioned above acting in their personal or professional capacities, but shall not infringe upon the right of these personnel to cast their vote in the elections.

D- The Iraqi National Intelligence Service shall collect information, assess threats to national security, and advise the Iraqi government. This Service shall be under civilian control, shall be subject to legislative oversight, and shall operate in accordance with the law and pursuant to the recognized principles of human rights.

E- The Iraqi Government shall respect and implement Iraq's international obligations regarding the non-proliferation, non-development, nonproduction, and non-use of nuclear, chemical, and biological weapons, and shall prohibit associated equipment, materiel, technologies, and delivery systems for use in the development, manufacture, production, and use of such weapons.

Second: Military service shall be regulated by law.

Article 10:

The holy shrines and religious sites in Iraq are religious and civilizational entities. The State is committed to assuring and maintaining their sanctity, and to guaranteeing the free practice of rituals in them.

Article 11:

Baghdad is the capital of the Republic of Iraq.

Article 12:

First: The flag, national anthem, and emblem of Iraq shall be regulated by law in a way that symbolizes the components of the Iraqi people.

Second: A law shall regulate honors, official holidays, religious and national occasions and the Hijri and Gregorian calendar.

Article 13:

First: This Constitution is the preeminent and supreme law in Iraq and shall be binding in all parts of Iraq without exception.

Second: No law that contradicts this Constitution shall be enacted. Any text in any regional constitutions or any other legal text that contradicts this Constitution shall be considered void.

Section Two: Rights and Liberties
Chapter One: [Rights]
First: Civil and Political Rights
Article 14:

Iraqis are equal before the law without discrimination based on gender, race, ethnicity, nationality, origin, color, religion, sect, belief or opinion, or economic or social status.

Article 15:

Every individual has the right to enjoy life, security and liberty. Deprivation or restriction of these rights is prohibited except in accordance with the law and based on a decision issued by a competent judicial authority.

Article 16:

Equal opportunities shall be guaranteed to all Iraqis, and the state shall ensure that the necessary measures to achieve this are taken.

Article 17:

First: Every individual shall have the right to personal privacy so long as it does not contradict the rights of others and public morals.

Second: The sanctity of the homes shall be protected. Homes may not be entered, searched, or violated, except by a judicial decision in accordance with the law.

Article 18:

First: Iraqi citizenship is a right for every Iraqi and is the basis of his nationality.

Second: Anyone who is born to an Iraqi father or to an Iraqi mother shall be considered an Iraqi. This shall be regulated by law.

Third:

F. An Iraqi citizen by birth may not have his citizenship withdrawn for any reason. Any person who had his citizenship withdrawn shall have the right to demand its reinstatement. This shall be regulated by a law.
G. Iraqi citizenship shall be withdrawn from naturalized citizens in cases regulated by law.

Fourth: An Iraqi may have multiple citizenships. Everyone who assumes a senior, security or sovereign position must abandon any other acquired citizenship. This shall be regulated by law.

Fifth: Iraqi citizenship shall not be granted for the purposes of the policy of population settlement that disrupts the demographic composition of Iraq.

Sixth: Citizenship provisions shall be regulated by law. The competent courts shall consider the suits arising from those provisions.

Article 19:

First: The judiciary is independent and no power is above the judiciary except the law.

Second: There is no crime or punishment except by law. The punishment shall only be for an act that the law considers a crime when perpetrated. A harsher punishment than the applicable punishment at the time of the offense may not be imposed.

Third: Litigation shall be a protected and guaranteed right for all.

Fourth: The right to a defense shall be sacred and guaranteed in all phases of investigation and the trial.

Fifth: The accused is innocent until proven guilty in a fair legal trial. The accused may not be tried for the same crime for a second time after acquittal unless new evidence is produced.

Sixth: Every person shall have the right to be treated with justice in judicial and administrative proceedings.

Seventh: The proceedings of a trial are public unless the court decides to make it secret.

Eighth: Punishment shall be personal.

Ninth: Laws shall not have retroactive effect unless stipulated otherwise. This exclusion shall not include laws on taxes and fees.

Tenth: Criminal laws shall not have retroactive effect, unless it is to the benefit of the accused.

Eleventh: The court shall appoint a lawyer at the expense of the state for an accused of a felony or misdemeanor who does not have a defense lawyer.

Twelfth:

H. Unlawful detention shall be prohibited.
I. Imprisonment or detention shall be prohibited in places not designed for these purposes, pursuant to prison laws covering health and social care, and subject to the authorities of the State.

Thirteenth: The preliminary investigative documents shall be submitted to the competent judge in a period not to exceed twenty-four hours from the time of the arrest of the accused, which may be extended only once and for the same period.

Article 20:

Iraqi citizens, men and women, shall have the right to participate in public affairs and to enjoy political rights including the right to vote, elect, and run for office.

Article 21:

First: No Iraqi shall be surrendered to foreign entities and authorities.

Second: A law shall regulate the right of political asylum in Iraq. No political refugee shall be surrendered to a foreign entity or returned forcibly to the country from which he fled.

Third: Political asylum shall not be granted to a person accused of committing international or terrorist crimes or to any person who inflicted damage on Iraq.

Second: Economic, Social and Cultural Liberties
Article 22:

First: Work is a right for all Iraqis in a way that guarantees a dignified life for them.

Second: The law shall regulate the relationship between employees and employers on economic bases and while observing the rules of social justice.

Third: The State shall guarantee the right to form and join unions and professional associations, and this shall be regulated by law.

Article 23:

First: Private property is protected. The owner shall have the right to benefit, exploit and dispose of private property within the limits of the law.

Second: Expropriation is not permissible except for the purposes of public benefit in return for just compensation, and this shall be regulated by law.

Third:

J. Every Iraqi shall have the right to own property anywhere in Iraq. No others may possess immovable assets, except as exempted by law.

K. Ownership of property for the purposes of demographic change is prohibited.

Article 24:

The State shall guarantee freedom of movement of Iraqi manpower, goods, and capital between regions and governorates, and this shall be regulated by law.

Article 25:

The State shall guarantee the reform of the Iraqi economy in accordance with modern economic principles to insure the full investment of its resources, diversification of its sources, and the encouragement and development of the private sector.

Article 26:

The State shall guarantee the encouragement of investment in the various sectors, and this shall be regulated by law.

Article 27:

First: Public assets are sacrosanct, and their protection is the duty of each citizen.

Second: The provisions related to the preservation of State properties, their management, the conditions for their disposal, and the limits for these assets not to be relinquished shall all be regulated by law.

Article 28:

First: No taxes or fees shall be levied, amended, collected, or exempted, except by law.

Second: Low income earners shall be exempted from taxes in a way that guarantees the preservation of the minimum income required for living. This shall be regulated by law.

Article 29:

First:

L. The family is the foundation of society; the State shall preserve it and its religious, moral, and national values.
M. The State shall guarantee the protection of motherhood, childhood and old age, shall care for children and youth, and shall provide them with the appropriate conditions to develop their talents and abilities.

Second: Children have the right to upbringing, care and education from their parents. Parents have the right to respect and care from their children, especially in times of need, disability, and old age.

Third: Economic exploitation of children in all of its forms shall be prohibited, and the State shall take the necessary measures for their protection.

Fourth: All forms of violence and abuse in the family, school, and society shall be prohibited.

Article 30:

First: The State shall guarantee to the individual and the family—especially children and women—social and health security, the basic requirements for living a free and decent life, and shall secure for them suitable income and appropriate housing.

Second: The State shall guarantee social and health security to Iraqis in cases of old age, sickness, employment disability, homelessness, orphanhood, or unemployment, shall work to protect them from ignorance, fear and poverty, and shall provide them housing and special programs of care and rehabilitation, and this shall be regulated by law.

Article 31:

First: Every citizen has the right to health care. The State shall maintain public health and provide the means of prevention and treatment by building different types of hospitals and health institutions.

Second: Individuals and entities have the right to build hospitals, clinics, or private health care centers under the supervision of the State, and this shall be regulated by law.

Article 32:

The State shall care for the handicapped and those with special needs, and shall ensure their rehabilitation in order to reintegrate them into society, and this shall be regulated by law.

Article 33:

First: Every individual has the right to live in safe environmental conditions.

Second: The State shall undertake the protection and preservation of the environment and its biological diversity.

Article 34:

First: Education is a fundamental factor for the progress of society and is a right guaranteed by the state. Primary education is mandatory and the state guarantees that it shall combat illiteracy.

Second: Free education in all its stages is a right for all Iraqis.

Third: The State shall encourage scientific research for peaceful purposes that serve humanity and shall support excellence, creativity, invention, and different aspects of ingenuity.

Fourth: Private and public education shall be guaranteed, and this shall be regulated by law.

Article 35:

The state shall promote cultural activities and institutions in a manner that befits the civilizational and cultural history of Iraq, and it shall seek to support indigenous Iraqi cultural orientations.

Article 36:

Practicing sports is a right of every Iraqi and the state shall encourage and care for such activities and shall provide for their requirements.

Chapter Two: [Liberties]

Article 37:

First:

N. The liberty and dignity of man shall be protected.
O. No person may be kept in custody or investigated except according to a judicial decision.
P. All forms of psychological and physical torture and inhumane treatment are prohibited. Any confession made under force, threat, or torture shall not be relied on, and the victim shall have the right to seek compensation for material and moral damages incurred in accordance with the law.

Second: The State shall guarantee protection of the individual from intellectual, political and religious coercion.

Third: Forced labor, slavery, slave trade, trafficking in women or children, and sex trade shall be prohibited.

Article 38:

The State shall guarantee in a way that does not violate public order and morality:

Q. Freedom of expression using all means.
R. Freedom of press, printing, advertisement, media and publication.
S. Freedom of assembly and peaceful demonstration, and this shall be regulated by law.

Article 39:

First: The freedom to form and join associations and political parties shall be guaranteed, and this shall be regulated by law.

Second: It is not permissible to force any person to join any party, society, or political entity, or force him to continue his membership in it.

Article 40:

The freedom of communication and correspondence, postal, telegraphic, electronic, and telephonic, shall be guaranteed and may not be monitored, wiretapped, or disclosed except for legal and security necessity and by a judicial decision.

Article 41:

Iraqis are free in their commitment to their personal status according to their religions, sects, beliefs, or choices, and this shall be regulated by law.

Article 42:

Each individual shall have the freedom of thought, conscience, and belief.

Article 43:

First: The followers of all religions and sects are free in the:

A- Practice of religious rites, including the Husseini rituals.
B- Management of religious endowments (waqf), their affairs, and their religious institutions, and this shall be regulated by law.

Second: The State shall guarantee freedom of worship and the protection of places of worship.

Article 44:
First: Each Iraqi has freedom of movement, travel, and residence inside and outside Iraq.
Second: No Iraqi may be exiled, displaced, or deprived from returning to the homeland.

Article 45:
First: The State shall seek to strengthen the role of civil society institutions, and to support, develop and preserve their independence in a way that is consistent with peaceful means to achieve their legitimate goals, and this shall be regulated by law.
Second: The State shall seek the advancement of the Iraqi clans and tribes, shall attend to their affairs in a manner that is consistent with religion and the law, and shall uphold their noble human values in a way that contributes to the development of society. The State shall prohibit the tribal traditions that are in contradiction with human rights.

Article 46:
Restricting or limiting the practice of any of the rights or liberties stipulated in this Constitution is prohibited, except by a law or on the basis of a law, and insofar as that limitation or restriction does not violate the essence of the right or freedom.

Source: Government of Iraq. Final Draft of Iraqi Constitution: Baghdad, Iraq, October 15, 2005. Available at WIPO, http://www.wipo.int/wipolex/en/details.jsp?id=10027.

Joint Statement by President George W. Bush and Prime Minister Nuri al-Maliki of Iraq, November 30, 2006

Explanation
Throughout 2005 there was only one month with fewer than 1,000 people killed in Iraq. In 2006 the numbers became worse with regular deaths in excess of 2,000 or even 3,000 per month. These numbers are civilian deaths. The first month under 1,000 was December 2007 and then not regularly under 1,000 until May 2008. The news was filled with scenes of death and destruction and explosions. For comparison the average per month deaths in 2001 was about 350. In 2004, 2005, 2006, and 2007 the annual coalition deaths were about 900 per year with the highest being 961 in 2007.

On November 8, 2006, President Bush announced the resignation of Donald Rumsfeld as secretary of defense and the nomination of Robert Gates.

Document
We were pleased to continue our consultations on building security and stability in Iraq. We are grateful to His Majesty King Abdullah II of Jordan for hosting these meetings here in Amman.

Our discussions reviewed developments in Iraq, focusing on the security situation and our common concern about sectarian violence targeting innocent Iraqis. In this regard, the Prime Minister affirms the commitment of his government to advance efforts toward national reconciliation and the need for all Iraqis and political forces in Iraq to work against armed elements responsible for violence and intimidation. The Prime Minister also affirms his determination with help from the United States and the international community to improve the efficiency of government operations, particularly in confronting corruption and strengthening the rule of law.

We discussed the plague of terrorism in Iraq which is being fomented and fueled by Al Qaeda. The people of Iraq, like the people of the United States and the entire civilized world, must stand together to face this common threat. The Prime Minister affirmed that Iraq is a partner in the fight against Al Qaeda. We agreed that defeating Al Qaeda and the terrorists is vital to ensuring the success of Iraq's democracy. We discussed the means by which the United States will enhance Iraq's capabilities to further isolate extremists and bring all who choose violence and terror to full justice under Iraqi law.

We agreed in particular to take all necessary measures to track down and bring to justice those responsible for the cowardly attacks last week in Sadr City. The Prime Minister has also pledged to bring to justice those responsible for crimes committed in the wake of this attack.

We discussed accelerating the transfer of security responsibilities to the Government of Iraq; our hopes for strengthening the future relationship between our two nations; and joint efforts to achieve greater cooperation from governments in the region and to counter those elements that are fueling the conflict.

We received an interim report from the high-level Joint Committee on Accelerating the Transferring of Security Responsibility, and encouraged the Committee to continue its good work. We agreed that reform of the Iraqi security ministries and agencies and addressing the issue of militias should be accelerated. The ultimate solution to stabilizing Iraq and reducing violence is true national reconciliation and capable and loyal Iraqi forces dedicated to protecting all the Iraqi people.

We are committed to continuing to build the partnership between our two countries as we work together to strengthen a stable, democratic, and unified Iraq.

Source: Joint Statement by President George W. Bush and Prime Minister Nuri al-Maliki of Iraq. November 30, 2016. *Public Papers of the Presidents of the United States: George W. Bush, 2006, Book 2*. Washington, DC: Government Printing Office, 2010, 2141–2142.

Excerpt of Field Manual 3–24: Counterinsurgency, 2006

Explanation

During World War II and the Cold War it was common to hear about German or Soviet officers who would say that the U.S. military does not follow its own doctrine. Many of these "quotes" are suspect and probably not true. Despite this, there has been a perception that the United States is nondoctrinal. Since the creation of the all-volunteer force and the U.S. Army Training and Doctrine Command (TRADOC) in 1973, there has been an invigoration of the importance of doctrine. By the time of the fighting in Iraq, doctrine was a critical component of training and education in the U.S. military.

Doctrine serves as the foundational concepts and principles for military action. It is not designed to communicate what to do in a specific circumstance, but rather the general guides and principles to shape thinking and promote good decision making in preparation for and execution of military operations. As such, doctrine serves an important role in providing the context for thought.

Within TRADOC is the Combined Arms Center at Fort Leavenworth, Kansas. This command is responsible for overseeing the actions and activities of numerous schools within the U.S. Army. It also serves and served as the place for thinking about how to fight the, then current, war in Iraq. It was here that General Petraeus was assigned to command and took the responsibility for completing the doctrine for counterinsurgency, or COIN.

Document

1–159. COIN [counterinsurgency] is an extremely complex form of warfare. At its core, COIN is a struggle for the population's support. The protection, welfare, and support of the people are vital to success. Gaining and maintaining that support is a formidable challenge. Achieving these aims requires synchronizing the efforts of many nonmilitary and HN agencies in a comprehensive approach.

160. Designing operations that achieve the desired end state requires counterinsurgents to understand the culture and the problems they face. Both insurgents and counterinsurgents are fighting for the support of the populace. However, insurgents are constrained by neither the law of war nor the bounds of human decency as Western nations understand them. In fact, some insurgents are willing to commit suicide and kill innocent civilians in carrying out their operations—and deem this a legitimate option. They also will do anything to preserve their greatest advantage, the ability to hide among the people. These amoral and often barbaric enemies survive by their wits, constantly adapting to the situation. Defeating them requires counterinsurgents to develop the ability to learn and adapt rapidly and continuously. This manual emphasizes this "Learn and Adapt" imperative as it discusses ways to gain and maintain the support of the people.

1–161. Popular support allows counterinsurgents to develop the intelligence necessary to identify and defeat insurgents. Designing and executing a comprehensive campaign to secure the populace and then gain its support requires carefully coordinating actions along several LLOs over time to produce success. One of these LLOs is developing HN security forces that can assume primary responsibility for combating the insurgency. COIN operations also place distinct burdens on leaders and logisticians. All of these aspects of COIN are described and analyzed in the chapters that follow.

Successful and Unsuccessful Counterinsurgency Operational Practices

Successful Practices	Unsuccessful Practices
• Emphasize intelligence. • Focus on the population, its needs, and its security. • Establish and expand secure areas. • Isolate insurgents from the populace (population control). • Conduct effective, pervasive, and continuous information operations.	• Overemphasize killing and capturing the enemy rather than securing and engaging the populace. • Conduct large-scale operations as the norm. • Concentrate military forces in large bases for protection. • Focus special forces primarily on raiding.

(continued)

Successful and Unsuccessful Counterinsurgency Operational Practices (continued)

Successful Practices	Unsuccessful Practices
• Provide amnesty and rehabilitation for those willing to support the new government. • Place host-nation police in the lead with military support as soon as the security situation permits. • Expand and diversify the host-nation police force. • Train military forces to conduct counterinsurgency operations. • Embed quality advisors and special forces with host-nation forces. • Deny sanctuary to insurgents. • Encourage strong political and military cooperation and information sharing. • Secure host-nation borders. • Protect key infrastructure.	• Place low priority on assigning quality advisors to host-nation forces. • Build and train host-nation security forces in the U.S. military image. • Ignore peacetime government processes, including legal procedures. • Allow open borders, airspace, and coastlines.

Source: U.S. Department of the Army. *Counterinsurgency*. Field Manual 3–24. Washington, DC: U.S. Department of the Army, December 15, 2006. Available at http://usacac.army.mil/cac2/Repository/Materials/COIN-FM3-24.pdf.

Excerpt of Testimony of General David Petraeus to Congress, September 10, 2007

Explanation

On September 10, 2007, General David Petraeus and Ambassador Ryan Crocker went to Capitol Hill to brief a joint session of the U.S. Congress House Armed Services and Senate Foreign Relations committees on the situation in Iraq. These events were more than a commander giving accountability, but it also became high-stakes theater as the testimony was part of a larger political debate happening in Washington, DC, about the nature of the Iraq War and the potential for further action in the country.

In addition to the testimony a written report was released that included the assessment of both the general and the ambassador. The excerpts below are from that report.

Document

Current Situation and Trends

The most significant development in the past six months likely has been the increasing emergence of tribes and local citizens rejecting Al Qaeda and other extremists. This has, of course, been most visible in Anbar Province. A year ago the province was assessed as "lost" politically. Today, it is a model of what happens when local leaders and citizens decide to oppose Al Qaeda and reject its Taliban-like ideology. While Anbar is unique and the model it provides cannot be replicated everywhere in Iraq, it does demonstrate the dramatic change in security that is possible with the support and participation of local citizens . . . other tribes have been inspired by the actions of those in Anbar and have volunteered to fight extremists as well. We have, in coordination with the Iraqi government's National Reconciliation

Committee, been engaging these tribes and groups of local citizens who want to oppose extremists and to contribute to local security. Some 20,000 such individuals are already being hired for the Iraqi Police, thousands of others are being assimilated into the Iraqi Army, and thousands more are vying for a spot in Iraq's Security Forces.

Iraqi Security Forces
Iraqi Security Forces have continued to grow, to develop their capabilities, and to shoulder more of the burden of providing security for their country . . . there are now nearly 140 Iraqi Army, National Police, and Special Operations Forces Battalions in the fight, with about 95 of those capable of taking the lead in operations, albeit with some coalition support. Beyond that, all of Iraq's battalions have been heavily involved in combat operations that often result in the loss of leaders, soldiers, and equipment. These losses are among the shortcomings identified by operational readiness assessments, but we should not take from these assessments the impression that Iraqi forces are not in the fight and contributing. Indeed, despite their shortages, many Iraqi units across Iraq now operate with minimal coalition assistance.

As counterinsurgency operations require substantial numbers of boots on the ground, we are helping the Iraqis expand the size of their security forces. Currently, there are some 445,000 individuals on the payrolls of Iraq's Interior and Defense Ministries. Based on recent decisions by Prime Minister Maliki, the number of Iraq's security forces will grow further by the end of this year, possibly by as much as 40,000. Given the security challenges Iraq faces, we support this decision, and we will work with the two security ministries as they continue their efforts to expand their basic training capacity, leader development programs, logistical structures and elements, and various other institutional capabilities to support the substantial growth in Iraqi forces.

Significantly, in 2007, Iraq will, as in 2006, spend more on its security forces than it will receive in security assistance from the United States. In fact, Iraq is becoming one of the United States' larger foreign military sales customers, committing some $1.6 billion to FMS already, with the possibility of up to $1.8 billion more being committed before the end of this year . . .

To summarize, the security situation in Iraq is improving, and Iraqis elements are slowly taking on more of the responsibility for protecting their citizens. Innumerable challenges lie ahead; however, Coalition and Iraqi Security Forces have made progress toward achieving sustainable security. As a result, the United States will be in a position to reduce its forces in Iraq in the months ahead.

Recommendations
One may argue that the best way to speed the process in Iraq is to change the MNF-I mission from one that emphasizes population security, counter-terrorism, and transition, to one that is strictly focused on transition and counter-terrorism. Making that change now would, in our view, be premature. We have learned before that there is a real danger in handing over tasks to the Iraqi Security Forces before their capacity and local conditions warrant. In fact, the drafters of the recently released National Intelligence Estimate on Iraq recognized this danger when they wrote, and I quote, "We assess that changing the mission of Coalition forces from a primarily counterinsurgency and stabilization role to a primary combat support role for Iraqi forces and counterterrorist operations to prevent AQI from establishing

a safe haven would erode security gains achieved thus far."

In describing the recommendations I have made, I should note again that, like Ambassador Crocker, I believe Iraq's problems will require a long-term effort. There are no easy answers or quick solutions. And though we both believe this effort can succeed, it will take time. Our assessments underscore, in fact, the importance of recognizing that a premature drawdown of our forces would likely have devastating consequences.

That assessment is supported by the findings of a 16 August Defense Intelligence Agency report on the implications of a rapid withdrawal of US forces from Iraq. Summarizing it in an unclassified fashion, it concludes that a rapid withdrawal would result in the further release of the strong centrifugal forces in Iraq and produce a number of dangerous results, including a high risk of disintegration of the Iraqi Security Forces; rapid deterioration of local security initiatives; Al Qaeda-Iraq regaining lost ground and freedom of maneuver; a marked increase in violence and further ethno-sectarian displacement and refugee flows; alliances of convenience by Iraqi groups with internal and external forces to gain advantages over their rivals; and exacerbation of already challenging regional dynamics, especially with respect to Iran.

Lieutenant General Odierno and I share this assessment and believe that the best way to secure our national interests and avoid an unfavorable outcome in Iraq is to continue to focus our operations on securing the Iraqi people while targeting terrorist groups and militia extremists and, as quickly as conditions are met, transitioning security tasks to Iraqi elements.

Source: Petraeus, David H. *Report to Congress on the Situation in Iraq.* Headquarters, Multi-National Force–Iraq, Baghdad, Iraq, September 10–11, 2007. Available at http://www.dtic.mil/dtic/tr/fulltext/u2/a473579.pdf.

Excerpt of "Agreement between the United States of America and the Republic of Iraq on the Withdrawal of United States Forces from Iraq and the Organization of Their Activities during Their Temporary Presence in Iraq," November 17, 2008

Explanation

A Status of Forces Agreement (SOFA) is a common framework to discuss the rules associated with the stationing of foreign forces on foreign sovereign soil. The U.S. government typically views a SOFA as necessary to protect the legal rights of its citizens serving in foreign countries. The agreement is designed to establish ground rules for prosecution of crimes committed by U.S. forces and who has jurisdiction. This can make a SOFA controversial as it can be seen as placing U.S. law above that of local law and it also can be perceived as treating U.S. lives and interests as more important than those of the host nation.

This particular SOFA also placed time limitations on U.S. presence in Iraq and U.S. presence in specific places in Iraq, which make the document more than a SOFA. In this last sense it also served as a roadmap for operational behavior. U.S. forces are directed to pull out of cities by June 2009 (only about seven months from the signing of the document) and depart the country by the end of 2011.

The document was signed by Iraqi foreign minister Hoshiyar Zebari and U.S. ambassador Ryan Crocker in an official ceremony on November 17, 2008. It was ratified by the

Iraqi Parliament on November 27, 2008, and later signed by President Bush.

This is a heavily edited document because of the legal tone and technical language. Some articles are entirely omitted due to technical language and specific issues: definition of terms, tax exempt status, claims, etc.

Document

Preamble

The United States of America and the Republic of Iraq, referred to hereafter as "the Parties":

Recognizing the importance of: strengthening their joint security, contributing to world peace and stability, combating terrorism in Iraq, and cooperating in the security and defense spheres, thereby deterring aggression and threats against the sovereignty, security, and territorial integrity of Iraq and against its democratic, federal, and constitutional system;

Affirming that such cooperation is based on full respect for the sovereignty of each of them in accordance with the purposes and principles of the United Nations Charter;

Out of a desire to reach a common understanding that strengthens cooperation between them;

Without prejudice to Iraqi sovereignty over its territory, waters, and airspace; and

Pursuant to joint undertakings as two sovereign, independent, and coequal countries;

Have agreed to the following:

Article 1: Scope and Purpose

This Agreement shall determine the principal provisions and requirements that regulate the temporary presence, activities, and withdrawal of the United States Forces from Iraq....

Article 3: Laws

1. While conducting military operations pursuant to this Agreement, it is the duty of members of the United States Forces and of the civilian component to respect Iraqi laws, customs, traditions, and conventions and to refrain from any activities that are inconsistent with the letter and spirit of this Agreement. It is the duty of the United States to take all necessary measures for this purpose....

Article 4: Missions

1. The Government of Iraq requests the temporary assistance of the United States Forces for the purposes of supporting Iraq in its efforts to maintain security and stability in Iraq, including cooperation in the conduct of operations against al-Qaeda and other terrorist groups, outlaw groups, and remnants of the former regime.

2. All such military operations that are carried out pursuant to this Agreement shall be conducted with the agreement of the Government of Iraq. Such operations shall be fully coordinated with Iraqi authorities....

3. All such operations shall be conducted with full respect for the Iraqi Constitution and the laws of Iraq. Execution of such operations shall not infringe upon the sovereignty of Iraq and its national interests, as defined by the Government of Iraq. It is the duty of the United States Forces to respect the laws, customs, and traditions of Iraq and applicable international law.

4. The Parties shall continue their efforts to cooperate to strengthen Iraq's security capabilities including, as may be mutually agreed, on training, equipping, supporting, supplying, and establishing and upgrading logistical systems, including transportation, housing, and supplies for Iraqi Security Forces.

5. The Parties retain the right to legitimate self defense within Iraq, as defined in applicable international law.

Article 5: Property Ownership

1. Iraq owns all buildings, non-relocatable structures, and assemblies connected to the soil that exist on agreed facilities and areas, including those that are used, constructed, altered, or improved by the United States Forces.

2. Upon their withdrawal, the United States Forces shall return to the Government of Iraq all the facilities and areas provided for the use of the combat forces of the United States, based on two lists. The first list of agreed facilities and areas shall take effect upon the entry into force of the Agreement. The second list shall take effect no later than June 30, 2009, the date for the withdrawal of combat forces from the cities, villages, and localities. The Government of Iraq may agree to allow the United States Forces the use of some necessary facilities for the purposes of this Agreement on withdrawal. . . .

Article 6: Use of Agreed Facilities and Areas

1. With full respect for the sovereignty of Iraq, and as part of exchanging views between the Parties pursuant to this Agreement, Iraq grants access and use of agreed facilities and areas to the United States Forces, United States contractors, United States contractor employees, and other individuals or entities as agreed upon by the Parties.

2. In accordance with this Agreement, Iraq authorizes the United States Forces to exercise within the agreed facilities and areas all rights and powers that may be necessary to establish, use, maintain, and secure such agreed facilities and areas. . . .

3. The United States Forces shall assume control of entry to agreed facilities and areas that have been provided for its exclusive use. . . .

Article 9: Movement of Vehicles, Vessels and Aircraft

1. With full respect for the relevant rules of land and maritime safety and movement, vessels and vehicles operated by or at the time exclusively for the United States Forces may enter, exit, and move within the territory of Iraq for the purposes of implementing this Agreement. . . .

2. With full respect for relevant rules of safety in aviation and air navigation, United States Government aircraft and civil aircraft that are at the time operating exclusively under a contract with the United States Department of Defense are authorized to over-fly, conduct airborne refueling exclusively for the purposes of implementing this Agreement over, and land and take off within, the territory of Iraq for the purposes of implementing this Agreement. The Iraqi authorities shall grant the aforementioned aircraft permission every year to land in and take off from Iraqi territory exclusively for the purposes of implementing this Agreement. United States Government aircraft and civil aircraft that are at the time operating exclusively under a contract with the United States Department of Defense, vessels, and vehicles shall not have any party boarding them without the consent of the authorities of the United States Forces. . . .

3. Surveillance and control over Iraqi airspace shall transfer to Iraqi authority immediately upon entry into force of this Agreement.

4. Iraq may request from the United States Forces temporary support for the Iraqi authorities in the mission of surveillance and control of Iraqi air space.

5. United States Government aircraft and civil aircraft . . . shall not be subject to payment of any taxes, duties, fees, or similar charges, including overflight or navigation fees, landing, and parking fees at government airfields. Vehicles and vessels owned or operated by or at the time exclusively for the United States Forces shall not be subject to payment of any taxes, duties, fees, or similar charges, including for vessels at government ports. Such vehicles, vessels, and aircraft shall be free from registration requirements within Iraq.

6. The United States Forces shall pay fees for services requested and received.

7. Each Party shall provide the other with maps and other available information on the location of mine fields and other obstacles that can hamper or jeopardize movement within the territory and waters of Iraq. . . .

Article 12: Jurisdiction

Recognizing Iraq's sovereign right to determine and enforce the rules of criminal and civil law in its territory, in light of Iraq's request for temporary assistance from the United States Forces set forth in Article 4, and consistent with the duty of the members of the United States Forces and the civilian component to respect Iraqi laws, customs, traditions, and conventions, the Parties have agreed as follows:

1. Iraq shall have the primary right to exercise jurisdiction over members of the United States Forces and of the civilian component for the grave premeditated felonies enumerated pursuant to paragraph 8, when such crimes are committed outside agreed facilities and areas and outside duty status.

2. Iraq shall have the primary right to exercise jurisdiction over United States contractors and United States contractor employees.

3. The United States shall have the primary right to exercise jurisdiction over members of the United States Forces and of the civilian component for matters arising inside agreed facilities and areas; during duty status outside agreed facilities and areas; and in circumstances not covered by paragraph 1.

4. At the request of either Party, the Parties shall assist each other in the investigation of incidents and the collection and exchange of evidence to ensure the due course of justice.

5. Members of the United States Forces and of the civilian component arrested or detained by Iraqi authorities shall be notified immediately to United States Forces authorities and handed over to them within 24 hours from the time of detention or arrest. Where Iraq exercises jurisdiction pursuant to paragraph 1 of this Article, custody of an accused member of the United States Forces or of the civilian component shall reside with United States Forces authorities. United States Forces authorities shall make such accused persons available to the Iraqi authorities for purposes of investigation and trial.

6. The authorities of either Party may request the authorities of the other Party to waive its primary right to jurisdiction in a particular case. The Government of Iraq agrees to exercise jurisdiction under paragraph 1 above, only after it has determined and notifies the United States in writing within 21 days of the discovery of an alleged offense, that it is of particular importance that such jurisdiction be exercised.

7. Where the United States exercises jurisdiction pursuant to paragraph 3 of this Article, members of the United States Forces and of the civilian component shall be entitled to due process standards and protections pursuant to the Constitution and laws of the United States. Where the offense arising

under paragraph 3 of this Article may involve a victim who is not a member of the United States Forces or of the civilian component, the Parties shall establish procedures through the Joint Committee to keep such persons informed as appropriate of: the status of the investigation of the crime; the bringing of charges against a suspected offender; the scheduling of court proceedings and the results of plea negotiations; opportunity to be heard at public sentencing proceedings, and to confer with the attorney for the prosecution in the case; and, assistance with filing a claim under Article 21 of this Agreement. As mutually agreed by the Parties, United States Forces authorities shall seek to hold the trials of such cases inside Iraq. If the trial of such cases is to be conducted in the United States, efforts will be undertaken to facilitate the personal attendance of the victim at the trial.

8. Where Iraq exercises jurisdiction pursuant to paragraph 1 of this Article, members of the United States Forces and of the civilian component shall be entitled to due process standards and protections consistent with those available under United States and Iraqi law. . . .

9. Pursuant to paragraphs 1 and 3 of this Article, United States Forces authorities shall certify whether an alleged offense arose during duty status. In those cases where Iraqi authorities believe the circumstances require a review of this determination, the Parties shall consult immediately through the Joint Committee, and United States Forces authorities shall take full account of the facts and circumstances and any information Iraqi authorities may present bearing on the determination by United States Forces authorities.

10. The Parties shall review the provisions of this Article every 6 months including by considering any proposed amendments to this Article taking into account the security situation in Iraq, the extent to which the United States Forces in Iraq are engaged in military operations, the growth and development of the Iraqi judicial system, and changes in United States and Iraqi law.

Article 13: Carrying Weapons and Apparel

Members of the United States Forces and of the civilian component may possess and carry weapons that are owned by the United States while in Iraq according to the authority granted to them under orders and according to their requirements and duties. Members of the United States Forces may also wear uniforms during duty in Iraq. . . .

Article 24: Withdrawal of United States Forces from Iraq

Recognizing the performance and increasing capacity of the Iraqi Security Forces, the assumption of full security responsibility by those Forces, and based upon the strong relationship between the Parties, an agreement on the following has been reached:

1. All the United States Forces shall withdraw from all Iraqi territory no later than December 31, 2011.

2. All United States combat forces shall withdraw from Iraqi cities, villages, and localities no later than the time at which Iraqi Security Forces assume full responsibility for security in an Iraqi province, provided that such withdrawal is completed no later than June 30, 2009. . . .

4. The United States recognizes the sovereign right of the Government of Iraq to request the departure of the United States Forces from Iraq at any time. The Government of Iraq recognizes the sovereign right

of the United States to withdraw the United States Forces from Iraq at any time.

5. The Parties agree to establish mechanisms and arrangements to reduce the number of the United States Forces during the periods of time that have been determined, and they shall agree on the locations where the United States Forces will be present.

Article 25: Measures to Terminate the Application of Chapter VII to Iraq

Acknowledging the right of the Government of Iraq not to request renewal of the Chapter VII authorization for and mandate of the multinational forces contained in United Nations Security Council Resolution 1790 (2007) that ends on December 31, 2008;

Taking note of the letters to the UN Security Council from the Prime Minister of Iraq and the Secretary of State of the United States dated December 7 and December 10, 2007, respectively, which are annexed to Resolution 1790;

Taking note of section 3 of the Declaration of Principles for a Long-Term Relationship of Cooperation and Friendship, signed by the President of the United States and the Prime Minister of Iraq on November 26, 2007, which memorialized Iraq's call for extension of the above-mentioned mandate for a final period, to end not later than December 31, 2008:

Recognizing also the dramatic and positive developments in Iraq, and noting that the situation in Iraq is fundamentally different than that which existed when the UN Security Council adopted Resolution 661 in 1990, and in particular that the threat to international peace and security posed by the Government of Iraq no longer exists, the Parties affirm in this regard that with the termination on December 31, 2008 of the Chapter VII mandate and authorization for the multinational force contained in Resolution 1790, Iraq should return to the legal and international standing that it enjoyed prior to the adoption of UN Security Council Resolution 661 (1990), and that the United States shall use its best efforts to help Iraq take the steps necessary to achieve this by December 31, 2008.

Article 26: Iraqi Assets

1. To enable Iraq to continue to develop its national economy through the rehabilitation of its economic infrastructure, as well as providing necessary essential services to the Iraqi people, and to continue to safeguard Iraq's revenues from oil and gas and other Iraqi resources and its financial and economic assets located abroad, including the Development Fund for Iraq, the United States shall ensure maximum efforts to:

a. Support Iraq to obtain forgiveness of international debt resulting from the policies of the former regime.
b. Support Iraq to achieve a comprehensive and final resolution of outstanding reparation claims inherited from the previous regime, including compensation requirements imposed by the UN Security Council on Iraq.

2. Recognizing and understanding Iraq's concern with claims based on actions perpetrated by the former regime, the President of the United States has exercised his authority to protect from United States judicial process the Development Fund for Iraq and certain other property in which Iraq has an interest. The United States shall remain fully and actively engaged with the Government of Iraq with respect to continuation of such protections and with respect to such claims.

3. Consistent with a letter from the President of the United States to be sent to the Prime Minister of Iraq, the United States remains committed to assist Iraq in connection with its request that the UN Security Council extend the protections and other arrangements established in Resolution 1483 (2003) and Resolution 1546 (2004) for petroleum, petroleum products, and natural gas originating in Iraq, proceeds and obligations from sale thereof, and the Development Fund for Iraq.

Article 27: Deterrence of Security Threats

In order to strengthen security and stability in Iraq and to contribute to the maintenance of international peace and stability, the Parties shall work actively to strengthen the political and military capabilities of the Republic of Iraq to deter threats against its sovereignty, political independence, territorial integrity, and its constitutional federal democratic system. To that end, the Parties agree as follows:

1. In the event of any external or internal threat or aggression against Iraq that would violate its sovereignty, political independence, or territorial integrity, waters, airspace, its democratic system or its elected institutions, and upon request by the Government of Iraq, the Parties shall immediately initiate strategic deliberations and, as may be mutually agreed, the United States shall take appropriate measures, including diplomatic, economic, or military measures, or any other measure, to deter such a threat.

2. The Parties agree to continue close cooperation in strengthening and maintaining military and security institutions and democratic political institutions in Iraq, including, as may be mutually agreed, cooperation in training, equipping, and arming the Iraqi Security Forces, in order to combat domestic and international terrorism and outlaw groups, upon request by the Government of Iraq.

3. Iraqi land, sea, and air shall not be used as a launching or transit point for attacks against other countries.

Article 28: The Green Zone

Upon entry into force of this Agreement the Government of Iraq shall have full responsibility for the Green Zone. The Government of Iraq may request from the United States Forces limited and temporary support for the Iraqi authorities in the mission of security for the Green Zone. Upon such request, relevant Iraqi authorities shall work jointly with the United States Forces authorities on security for the Green Zone during the period determined by the Government of Iraq. . . .

Article 30: The Period for which the Agreement is Effective

This Agreement shall be effective for a period of three years, unless terminated sooner by either Party pursuant to paragraph 3 of this Article.

Source: U.S. Department of State. Agreement between the United States of America and the Republic of Iraq on the Withdrawal of United States Forces from Iraq and the Organization of Their Activities during Their Temporary Presence in Iraq. Available at http://www.state.gov/documents/organization/122074.pdf.

Excerpt of President Obama's Speech at Camp Lejeune, February 27, 2009

Explanation

President Barack Obama won the election in 2008 running on a platform of ending the wars in Iraq and Afghanistan. He assumed office on January 20, 2009. On February 27,

2009, he traveled to Camp Lejeune, North Carolina, where he addressed members of the U.S. Marine Corps, and there provided his vision for accomplishing his campaign promises with respect to the wars he inherited from his predecessor.

It is important to note what he does and does not promise in this endeavor. As with his predecessor he does not suggest rapid change. This speech serves as the point of transition from one administration to the next.

Document

Next month will mark the sixth anniversary of the war in Iraq. . . .

Today, I have come to speak to you about how the war in Iraq will end.

To understand where we need to go in Iraq, it is important for the American people to understand where we now stand. Thanks in great measure to your service, the situation in Iraq has improved. Violence has been reduced substantially from the horrific sectarian killing of 2006 and 2007. Al Qaeda in Iraq has been dealt a serious blow by our troops and Iraq's Security Forces, and through our partnership with Sunni Arabs. The capacity of Iraq's Security Forces has improved, and Iraq's leaders have taken steps toward political accommodation. The relative peace and strong participation in January's provincial elections sent a powerful message to the world about how far Iraqis have come in pursuing their aspirations through a peaceful political process.

But let there be no doubt: Iraq is not yet secure, and there will be difficult days ahead. Violence will continue to be a part of life in Iraq. Too many fundamental political questions about Iraq's future remain unresolved. Too many Iraqis are still displaced or destitute. Declining oil revenues will put an added strain on a government that has had difficulty delivering basic services. Not all of Iraq's neighbors are contributing to its security. Some are working at times to undermine it. And even as Iraq's government is on a surer footing, it is not yet a full partner—politically and economically—in the region, or with the international community

In short, today there is a renewed cause for hope in Iraq, but that hope rests upon an emerging foundation.

On my first full day in office, I directed my national security team to undertake a comprehensive review of our strategy in Iraq to determine the best way to strengthen that foundation, while strengthening American national security. I have listened to my Secretary of Defense, the Joint Chiefs of Staff, and commanders on the ground. We have acted with careful consideration of events on the ground; with respect for the security agreements between the United States and Iraq; and with a critical recognition that the long-term solution in Iraq must be political—not military. Because the most important decisions that have to be made about Iraq's future must now be made by Iraqis.

We have also taken into account the simple reality that America can no longer afford to see Iraq in isolation from other priorities: we face the challenge of refocusing on Afghanistan and Pakistan; of relieving the burden on our military; and of rebuilding our struggling economy—and these are challenges that we will meet.

Today, I can announce that our review is complete, and that the United States will pursue a new strategy to end the war in Iraq through a transition to full Iraqi responsibility.

This strategy is grounded in a clear and achievable goal shared by the Iraqi people and the American people: an Iraq that is sovereign, stable, and self-reliant. To achieve that goal, we will work to promote an Iraqi government that is just, representative, and accountable, and that provides neither support nor safe-haven to terrorists. We will help Iraq build new ties of trade and commerce with the world. And we will forge a partnership with the people and government of Iraq that contributes to the peace and security of the region.

What we will not do is let the pursuit of the perfect stand in the way of achievable goals. We cannot rid Iraq of all who oppose America or sympathize with our adversaries. We cannot police Iraq's streets until they are completely safe, nor stay until Iraq's union is perfected. We cannot sustain indefinitely a commitment that has put a strain on our military, and will cost the American people nearly a trillion dollars. America's men and women in uniform have fought block by block, province by province, year after year, to give the Iraqis this chance to choose a better future. Now, we must ask the Iraqi people to seize it.

The first part of this strategy is therefore the responsible removal of our combat brigades from Iraq.

As a candidate for President, I made clear my support for a timeline of 16 months to carry out this drawdown, while pledging to consult closely with our military commanders upon taking office to ensure that we preserve the gains we've made and protect our troops. Those consultations are now complete, and I have chosen a timeline that will remove our combat brigades over the next 18 months.

Let me say this as plainly as I can: by August 31, 2010, our combat mission in Iraq will end.

As we carry out this drawdown, my highest priority will be the safety and security of our troops and civilians in Iraq. We will proceed carefully, and I will consult closely with my military commanders on the ground and with the Iraqi government. There will surely be difficult periods and tactical adjustments. But our enemies should be left with no doubt: this plan gives our military the forces and the flexibility they need to support our Iraqi partners, and to succeed.

After we remove our combat brigades, our mission will change from combat to supporting the Iraqi government and its Security Forces as they take the absolute lead in securing their country. As I have long said, we will retain a transitional force to carry out three distinct functions: training, equipping, and advising Iraqi Security Forces as long as they remain non-sectarian; conducting targeted counter-terrorism missions; and protecting our ongoing civilian and military efforts within Iraq. Initially, this force will likely be made up of 35–50,000 U.S. troops.

Through this period of transition, we will carry out further redeployments. And under the Status of Forces Agreement with the Iraqi government, I intend to remove all U.S. troops from Iraq by the end of 2011. We will complete this transition to Iraqi responsibility, and we will bring our troops home with the honor that they have earned. . . .

Source: Obama, Barack. "Remarks on Military Operations in Iraq at Camp Lejeune, North Carolina." February 27, 2009. *Public Papers of the Presidents of the United States: Barack Obama, 2009, Book 1.* Washington, DC: Government Printing Office, 2010, 158–163.

Presidential Address on the End of Combat Operations in Iraq, August 31, 2010

Explanation

The Iraq War did not end on August 31, 2010. This became a transition from Operation Iraqi Freedom to Operation New Dawn. In this new operation the intent was to train and advise the Iraqi security forces and to move the remainder of U.S. forces out of Iraq. This was a herculean task as it meant closing more than a hundred bases, transferring equipment to the Iraqis or removing it from the country, and moving the remaining approximately 50,000 personnel out of the country. With the change in the operation one of the primary tasks for the United States Forces–Iraq was to get out of Iraq.

Document

Good evening. Tonight, I'd like to talk to you about the end of our combat mission in Iraq, the ongoing security challenges we face, and the need to rebuild our nation here at home.

I know this historic moment comes at a time of great uncertainty for many Americans. We've now been through nearly a decade of war. We've endured a long and painful recession. And sometimes in the midst of these storms, the future that we're trying to build for our nation—a future of lasting peace and long-term prosperity—may seem beyond our reach.

But this milestone should serve as a reminder to all Americans that the future is ours to shape if we move forward with confidence and commitment. It should also serve as a message to the world that the United States of America intends to sustain and strengthen our leadership in this young century.

From this desk, seven and a half years ago, President Bush announced the beginning of military operations in Iraq. Much has changed since that night. A war to disarm a state became a fight against an insurgency. Terrorism and sectarian warfare threatened to tear Iraq apart. Thousands of Americans gave their lives; tens of thousands have been wounded. Our relations abroad were strained. Our unity at home was tested.

These are the rough waters encountered during the course of one of America's longest wars. Yet there has been one constant amidst these shifting tides. At every turn, America's men and women in uniform have served with courage and resolve. As Commander-in-Chief, I am incredibly proud of their service. And like all Americans, I'm awed by their sacrifice, and by the sacrifices of their families.

The Americans who have served in Iraq completed every mission they were given. They defeated a regime that had terrorized its people. Together with Iraqis and coalition partners who made huge sacrifices of their own, our troops fought block by block to help Iraq seize the chance for a better future. They shifted tactics to protect the Iraqi people, trained Iraqi Security Forces, and took out terrorist leaders. Because of our troops and civilians—and because of the resilience of the Iraqi people—Iraq has the opportunity to embrace a new destiny, even though many challenges remain.

So tonight, I am announcing that the American combat mission in Iraq has ended. Operation Iraqi Freedom is over, and the Iraqi people now have lead responsibility for the security of their country.

This was my pledge to the American people as a candidate for this office. Last February, I announced a plan that would bring our combat brigades out of Iraq, while redoubling our efforts to strengthen Iraq's Security Forces and support its government and people.

That's what we've done. We've removed nearly 100,000 U.S. troops from Iraq. We've closed or transferred to the Iraqis hundreds of bases. And we have moved millions of pieces of equipment out of Iraq.

This completes a transition to Iraqi responsibility for their own security. U.S. troops pulled out of Iraq's cities last summer, and Iraqi forces have moved into the lead with considerable skill and commitment to their fellow citizens. Even as Iraq continues to suffer terrorist attacks, security incidents have been near the lowest on record since the war began. And Iraqi forces have taken the fight to al Qaeda, removing much of its leadership in Iraqi-led operations.

This year also saw Iraq hold credible elections that drew a strong turnout. A caretaker administration is in place as Iraqis form a government based on the results of that election. Tonight, I encourage Iraq's leaders to move forward with a sense of urgency to form an inclusive government that is just, representative, and accountable to the Iraqi people. And when that government is in place, there should be no doubt: The Iraqi people will have a strong partner in the United States. Our combat mission is ending, but our commitment to Iraq's future is not. . . .

Ending this war is not only in Iraq's interest—it's in our own. The United States has paid a huge price to put the future of Iraq in the hands of its people. We have sent our young men and women to make enormous sacrifices in Iraq, and spent vast resources abroad at a time of tight budgets at home. We've persevered because of a belief we share with the Iraqi people—a belief that out of the ashes of war, a new beginning could be born in this cradle of civilization. Through this remarkable chapter in the history of the United States and Iraq, we have met our responsibility. Now, it's time to turn the page.

As we do, I'm mindful that the Iraq war has been a contentious issue at home. Here, too, it's time to turn the page. This afternoon, I spoke to former President George W. Bush. It's well known that he and I disagreed about the war from its outset. Yet no one can doubt President Bush's support for our troops, or his love of country and commitment to our security. As I've said, there were patriots who supported this war, and patriots who opposed it. And all of us are united in appreciation for our servicemen and women, and our hopes for Iraqis' future. . . .

Indeed, one of the lessons of our effort in Iraq is that American influence around the world is not a function of military force alone. We must use all elements of our power—including our diplomacy, our economic strength, and the power of America's example—to secure our interests and stand by our allies. And we must project a vision of the future that's based not just on our fears, but also on our hopes—a vision that recognizes the real dangers that exist around the world, but also the limitless possibilities of our time. . . .

Part of that responsibility is making sure that we honor our commitments to those who have served our country with such valor. As long as I am President, we will maintain the finest fighting force that the world has ever known, and we will do whatever it takes to serve our veterans as well as they have served us. This is a sacred trust. That's why we've already made one of the largest increases in funding for veterans in decades. We're treating the signature wounds of today's wars—post-traumatic stress disorder and traumatic brain injury—while providing the health care and benefits that all of our veterans have earned. And we're funding a Post-9/11 GI Bill that helps our veterans and their families pursue the dream of a college education. Just as the GI Bill helped those who fought World War II—including my grandfather—become the backbone of our middle class, so today's servicemen and women must have the chance to apply their gifts to expand the American economy. Because part of ending a war responsibly is standing by those who have fought it.

Two weeks ago, America's final combat brigade in Iraq—the Army's Fourth Stryker Brigade—journeyed home in the pre-dawn darkness. Thousands of soldiers and hundreds of vehicles made the trip from Baghdad, the last of them passing into Kuwait in the early morning hours. Over seven years before, American troops and coalition partners had fought their way across similar highways, but this time no shots were fired. It was just a convoy of brave Americans, making their way home.

Of course, the soldiers left much behind. Some were teenagers when the war began. Many have served multiple tours of duty, far from families who bore a heroic burden of their own, enduring the absence of a husband's embrace or a mother's kiss. Most painfully, since the war began, 55 members of the Fourth Stryker Brigade made the ultimate sacrifice—part of over 4,400 Americans who have given their lives in Iraq. As one staff sergeant said, "I know that to my brothers in arms who fought and died, this day would probably mean a lot."

Those Americans gave their lives for the values that have lived in the hearts of our people for over two centuries. Along with nearly 1.5 million Americans who have served in Iraq, they fought in a faraway place for people they never knew. They stared into the darkest of human creations—war—and helped the Iraqi people seek the light of peace.

In an age without surrender ceremonies, we must earn victory through the success of our partners and the strength of our own nation. Every American who serves joins an unbroken line of heroes that stretches from Lexington to Gettysburg; from Iwo Jima to Inchon; from Khe Sanh to Kandahar—Americans who have fought to see that the lives of our children are better than our own. Our troops are the steel in our ship of state. And though our nation may be travelling through rough waters, they give us confidence that our course is true, and that beyond the pre-dawn darkness, better days lie ahead.

Thank you. May God bless you. And may God bless the United States of America, and all who serve her.

Source: Obama, Barack. "Address to the Nation on the End of Combat Operations in Iraq." August 31, 2010. *Public Papers of the Presidents of the United States: Barack Obama, 2010, Book 2.* Washington, DC: Government Printing Office, 2013, 1260–1264.

Chronology of the Iraq War

1990
August 2: Iraq invades Kuwait.
August 7: United States begins Operation Desert Shield to protect Saudi Arabia.
November 29: UN Security Council passes resolution (UNSCR) 678 setting a deadline for Iraq to withdraw from Kuwait before January 15, 1991, or face military action.

1991
January 12: U.S. Congress passes joint resolution authorizing use of military force to drive Iraq from Kuwait.
January 17: Operation Desert Storm begins with air campaign.
January 29: Iraqi forces attack into Saudi Arabia to the town of Khafji.
February 1: Iraqi forces driven out of Saudi Arabia.
February 24: Operation Desert Storm ground campaign begins.
February 27: Coalition forces enter and liberate Kuwait City.
February 28: Operation Desert Storm ceasefire declared.
March 3: Iraq accepts ceasefire terms from the UN.
March 20: United States shoots down Iraqi warplane over Kurdish territory and thus unofficially begins Operation Provide Comfort, which was a relief and protection effort, including a no-fly zone, for Iraqi Kurds. This operation ended on December 31, 1996.
April 5: UNSCR 688 passed, which required Iraq cease the repression of the Iraqi people and allow international humanitarian organizations access.

1992
August 27: Operation Southern Watch established. This was a no-fly zone patrolled by aircraft from the United States, United Kingdom, and France. UNSCR 688 was used as the justification. This was initially established at the 32nd parallel and then later moved north to the 33rd parallel. The no-fly zone ended on March 19, 2003, with the beginning of Operation Iraqi Freedom.

1993
April 13: Kuwaiti officials foil a plan to bomb President George H. W. Bush during a visit to Kuwait following his departure from office.

1997
January 1: Operation Northern Watch begins. This was the northern no-fly zone and the continuation of the no-fly zone protection that began with Operation Provide Comfort. This extended down to the 36th parallel. This operation ended on March 17, 2003, with the beginning of Operation Iraqi Freedom.

1998

December 16–19: Operation Desert Fox conducted. This was a four-day bombing campaign of Iraqi targets with the justification of obstruction of UN Special Commission inspectors.

2001

February 16–17: United States and United Kingdom conduct bombing raids of Iraqi targets, attempting to disable Iraqi air defenses.
September 11: Attacks by Al Qaeda on the World Trade Center and Pentagon. Saddam Hussein immediately declares that Iraq played no part in the attacks.
October 7: Operation Enduring Freedom begins with attacks on Afghanistan.
December 6–17: Battle of Tora Bora in Afghanistan to defeat remnants of Al Qaeda.
December 7: The Taliban lose their last major stronghold in Afghanistan.

2002

March 1–18: Operation Anaconda attempts to destroy last remnants of Al Qaeda and the Taliban in Afghanistan.
July 5: Saddam rejects new UN weapons inspectors.
August 2: Saddam meets with chief weapons inspector Hans Blix.
September 12: President Bush addresses UN and challenges the organization to confront "grave and gathering danger" of Iraq or allow the United States and likeminded nations to act.
October 2: U.S. Congress passes joint resolution authorizing use of military force against Iraq.
October 16: President Bush signs authorization for use of force against Iraq.
November 8: UNSCR 1441 passed, which requires Saddam Hussein to disarm or face "serious consequences."
November 18: UN weapons inspectors arrive in Iraq.
December 7: Iraq submits a 12,000-page weapons declaration as required by UNSCR 1441. This document is seen as incomplete and insufficient to meet the requirement.

2003

January 3: UN Monitoring, Verification and Inspection Commission (UNMOVIC) inspectors have established a base of operations in Mosul to speed the inspection process.
January 9: UN chief weapons inspector Hans Blix and International Atomic Energy Agency head Mohammed El Baradei give a report to the UN Security Council that they are making progress, but the Iraqi government is not forthcoming.
January 16: UN weapons inspectors find empty rocket warheads designed to carry chemical weapons.
January 18: Global protests against the Iraq War occur in cities around the world, including Tokyo, Moscow, Paris, London, Montreal, Ottawa, Toronto, Cologne, Bonn, Göteborg, Istanbul, Cairo, Washington, DC, and San Francisco, California.
January 20: U.K. government announces the deployment of British forces to Kuwait.
January 23: Australian forces begin deployment to Kuwait and the Gulf region.
January 28: U.S. State of the Union Address by President Bush.
January 30: Eight nations (Britain, Spain, Italy, Portugal, Hungary, Poland, Denmark, and the Czech Republic) release a statement in support of U.S. efforts to invade Iraq.
February 5: U.S. secretary of state Colin Powell presents the U.S. case against Saddam Hussein to the UN Security Council to gain international support for military action against Iraq.

February 12: Al-Jazeera releases an audio tape purporting to include a statement from Osama bin Laden recounting the Battle of Tora Bra and urges Muslims to overthrow the regime of Saddam Hussein.

February 14: UNMOVIC chief weapons inspector Hans Blix reports to the UNSC that the Iraqis had been cooperating and that no weapons of mass destruction had been found though the government had to account for many banned weapons believed to be in the Iraqi arsenal. He also calls into question some of the information presented by Secretary Powell on February 5.

Tariq Aziz met with Pope John Paul II.

February 15: Largest international war protest with an estimated 6 million people in more than 600 cities.

February 16: A missile larger than allowed by UN sanctions is found in Iraq.

February 24: Colin Powell states in a meeting in Beijing that "We are reaching a point where serious consequences must flow."

February 26: Hans Blix states there is no evidence that Iraq has weapons of mass destruction.

Saddam appears in a televised interview with CBS News Anchor Dan Rather and rules out exile as an option.

February 28: Iraq begins the destruction of banned missiles. The White House questions the validity of the effort.

March 1: Several countries call for Saddam Hussein to step down.

Turkey votes against allowing U.S. forces to enter Turkey.

March 7: Hans Blix reports increased but still qualified cooperation from Iraq.

March 12: Possible additional UNSCRs have been scuttled by various members of the council threatening vetoes.

March 16: Leaders from the United States, United Kingdom, Portugal, and Spain meet in the Azores to discuss the invasion timing.

March 17: President Bush gives a final ultimatum to Saddam Hussein for him to leave Iraq with his sons in 48 hours.

UN secretary general orders all UN personnel to leave Iraq.

March 18: Colin Powell announces a 30-nation "Coalition of the Willing."

March 20: Operation Iraqi Freedom begins.

March 21: "Shock and Awe" aerial bombardment campaign begins.

March 26: Elements of 173rd Airborne Brigade parachute into Bashur Drop Zone in northern Iraq.

April 2–4: Battle of the Karbala Gap.

April 4–9: "Thunder Run" into Baghdad by 2nd Brigade, 3rd Infantry Division.

April 10: Baghdad is secured by coalition forces.

Kurdish forces capture Kirkuk.

April 15: Coalition forces control Tikrit, Saddam's hometown.

April 21: Retired lieutenant general Jay Garner becomes the civilian leader of Iraq with the establishment of the Office for Reconstruction and Humanitarian Assistance (ORHA).

April 23: Coalition forces enter Fallujah.

April 28: 200 protesters defy the coalition-imposed curfew in Fallujah and organize a protest. During the protest soldiers occupying a schoolhouse claim to have been fired upon, and kill 15 in returning fire. No U.S. casualties were reported.

May 1: President Bush announces an end to major combat operations.

May 12: Paul Bremer arrives in Iraq as the head of the newly formed Coalition Provisional Authority (CPA) and replaces General Jay Garner as the civil leader of Iraq.

May 15: U.S forces launch Operation Planet X, capturing hundreds of people.

May 23: L. Paul Bremer issues CPA Order Number 2 disbanding the Iraqi Army.

June 15: Operation Desert Scorpion begins. It consisted of a series of raids across Iraq intended to find resistance members and heavy weapons.

June 24: Six British soldiers killed by a mob in Southern Iraq.

July 2: President Bush says, "My answer is, bring 'em on," in responding to the growing violence in Iraq.

July 6: Joseph C. Wilson IV refutes the evidence of yellow cake uranium used to justify the invasion of Iraq in the *New York Times*' editorial page.

July 7: General John Abizaid replaces General Tommy Franks as CENTCOM commander.

July 13: The Iraqi Governing Council is established under the authority of the U.S. Coalition Provisional Authority.

July 22: Uday and Qusay Hussein are killed during a three-hour battle in Mosul, Iraq, by elements of the 101st Airborne Division.

August 7: The first car bomb of Operation Iraqi Freedom explodes outside the Jordanian embassy in Baghdad, killing 17.

August 19: Truck bomb explodes outside the UN headquarters killing the top UN envoy, Sergio Vieira de Mello, and 21 others and leading to the withdrawal of the UN from Iraq due to security concerns.

August 29: The Imam Ali Mosque in Najaf, Iraq, is attacked by a suicide car bomb resulting in at least 85 killed.

September 3: First post-Saddam government.

September 20: Aquila al-Hashimi, a member of the Iraq Interim Governing Council, is shot. She dies five days later.

September 23: Gallup poll shows majority of Iraqis expect better life in five years. Around two-thirds of Baghdad residents state the Iraqi dictator's removal was worth the hardships they've been forced to endure.

October 2: David Kay's Iraq Survey Group report finds little evidence of WMD in Iraq.

October 16: UNSCR passed, which envisions a multinational force and preserves Washington's quasi-absolute control of Iraq.

October 27: Baghdad bombings, beginning of the Ramadan Offensive.

November 2: Heaviest single loss for the coalition troops up to that time—two U.S. Chinook helicopters are fired on by two surface-to-air missiles, and one crashed near Fallujah on its way to Baghdad airport; soldiers are killed and 20 wounded.

November 12: A suicide truck bomb blows up the Italian headquarters in Nasiriyah, killing 19 Italians (17 of them soldiers) and 14 Iraqis.

November 15: The Governing Council unveils an accelerated timetable for transferring the country to Iraqi control.

November 22: An Airbus A-300 freighter belonging to German courier firm DHL is forced to make an emergency landing with a wing fire after being struck by a shoulder-fired SA-14 missile.

November 26: Abed Hamed Mowhoush, Iraqi general, dies in U.S. custody. U.S. soldiers accused of torturing him to death.

November 27: President Bush surprises U.S. troops and accompanies them for Thanksgiving dinner.

November 30: The U.S. military reports killing 46 militants and wounding 18 in clashes in the central city of Samarra. The reports are later called into question as reporters interview residents of the city. Hospital staff only reports eight dead—most or all of them civilians, including an elderly Iranian pilgrim. No bodies of dead guerrillas are found.

December 13: Saddam Hussein is captured by soldiers from the 1st Brigade, 4th Infantry Division. He was hiding in a hole in a barn in al-Dawr, near Tikrit, Iraq. Saddam stated, "I am Saddam Hussein. I am the president of Iraq. I want to negotiate." The U.S. soldier responded, "President Bush sends his regards."

December 17: The U.S. 4th Infantry Division launches Operation Ivy Blizzard, lasting from dawn until midmorning. The operation resulted in the arrest of several guerrilla fighters and possible terrorists.

2004

January 18: Suicide truck bomb detonates with 1,000 pounds of explosives outside the headquarters of the U.S.-led coalition, killing about 20 people and injuring more than 60.

January 26: Japanese Iraq Reconstruction and Support Group: Japanese troops begin participation in most risky military expedition since World War II.

February 1: Two suicide bombers strike Kurdish political offices in the northern city of Irbil, killing 117 and injuring 133.

February 10: At least 50 people killed in a car bomb attack on a police recruitment center south of Baghdad.

March 2: Multiple bombings in Baghdad and Karbala at the climax of the Shi'a festival of Ashurah kill nearly 200, the deadliest attacks up to that time.

March 8: Provisional Iraqi government unanimously approves the country's new interim constitution.

March 11: Madrid bombings killing 191 on commuter trains.

March 31: Four Blackwater contractors ambushed and killed in Fallujah.

April 4–May 1: First Battle of Fallujah (Operation Vigilant Resolve)

April 8: Beginning of the kidnapping of foreign civilians in Iraq with the abduction of several Japanese.

The Jaysh al-Mahdi takes full control in Kut and partial control of Najaf, Karbala, and Kufa.

April 16: Kut is retaken by coalition forces, but Najaf, Karbala, and Kufa remain under control of Jaysh al-Mahdi.

April 18: Spain, led by newly elected José Luis Rodríguez Zapatero (Socialist Party), vows to withdraw its troops.

Beginning of release of Abu Ghraib prisoner abuse images.

April 20: Mortar rounds fired on Abu Ghraib Prison by insurgents; 22 detainees killed and 92 wounded.

April 21: Attacks on police stations in Basra and Az Zubayr kill at least 73 people, including 17 children, along with 94 wounded.

April 26: Iraq Interim Governing Council announces a new flag for post-Saddam Iraq. The flag is later abandoned; among sentiments that it looks too much like Israel's flag.

May 17: Ezzedine Salim, head of the Iraqi Governing Council, killed in a suicide attack.

May 19: U.S. forces bomb a wedding party killing 42 people.

May 28: Iyad Allawi is chosen as the prime minister for the Iraqi Interim Government.

June 8: UNSCR 1546 passed, which transfers sovereignty from the CPA to the Iraqi Interim Government.

June 21: Iranian seizure of Royal Navy personnel.

June 28: At 10:26 a.m., the U.S.-led CPA formally transferred sovereignty of Iraqi territory to the Iraqi Interim Government, two days ahead of schedule. L. Paul Bremer departed the country two hours later.

June 30: Saddam Hussein and 11 high ex-governmental figures are put under the Iraqi Interim Government's authority.

July 1: Saddam Hussein appears at his first hearing.

July 20: President of the Philippines confirms that hostage Angelo de la Cruz has been freed by his captors after their demands for a one-month-early withdrawal of all 51 Filipino troops from Iraq were met.

August 5–27: Battle of Najaf.

September 12: Haifa Street helicopter incident where 13 Iraqis are killed.

September 14: Baghdad car bomb near market and police station kills at least 47.

September 30: Insurgents detonate three car bombs killing 41 people (34 of them children) in the Shi'ite Amil area of southern Baghdad. The blasts, which wounded 139, occurred shortly after U.S. troops had celebrated opening a new sewage system and distributed candy to children.

October 1: Battle of Samarra.

October 17: Abu Musab al-Zarqawi changes his group's name to Tanzim Qaedat al Jihad fi Bilad al Rafidayn aka Al Qaeda in Iraq (AQI).

Late October: United States warned that more than 300 tons of high explosives from the al-Qaqaa facility were removed.

November 7–December 23: Second Battle of Fallujah (Operation Phantom Fury)

November 8–16: Battle of Mosul.

December 19: Suicide car bomb in Najaf, close to the Imam Ali shrine, kills 52 and wounds at least 140. On the same day, a car bomb exploded in Karbala, killing 14 and injuring at least 52.

December 21: Attack on Forward Operating Base Marez, kills 22, including 18 U.S. personnel.

2005

January 26: 31 U.S. soldiers die in a helicopter crash, deadliest day of the entire postwar period for the U.S. military.

January 30: Iraqi legislative election. Sunnis mostly boycott.

February 17: Full election results released.

February 28: Al-Hillah bombing: the deadliest single blast up to that time, a car bomb kills 127 in Hillah; the identity of the bomber as a Jordanian caused a diplomatic row between Iraq and Jordan.

March 4: Liberation of Italian journalist Giuliana Sgrena, during which secret Italian agent Nicola Calipari is killed by U.S. fire. Italian government announces a partial retreat of Italian troops from the coalition.

March 16: First meeting of the transitional National Assembly.

April 2: Battle of Abu Ghraib.

April 6: Jalal Talabani (Kurd) elected president of Iraq.

April 7: Ibrahim al-Jaafari is nominated as prime minister of Iraq.

April 9: Tens of thousands of demonstrators loyal to Shiite cleric Muqtada Sadr march through Baghdad denouncing the U.S. occupation of Iraq.

April 28: The parliament votes in support of the new government.

May 8: Battle of al-Qaim.

May 11: Suicide bombers kill at least 71 people and wound more than 160 in a crowded market and a line of security force recruits.

May 15: Formation of the parliamentary commission to draft the new constitution.

June 20: Suicide bomber kills 13 policemen and injures more than 100 people, in Irbil, northern Iraq.

July 3–8: Egyptian ambassador designee to Iraq abducted while buying a newspaper. He was killed while a captive.

July 16: Suicide bombing in Musayyib kills 100.

August 1–4: Battle of Haditha.

August 22: Draft of constitution presented to Iraqi parliament.

August 28: Full constitution presented to parliament.

August 31: Rumors of a suicide bomber lead to a stampede on the Al-Aaimmah bridge; about 1,000 people died.

September 1–18: Battle of Tal Afar.

September 7: American hostage Roy Hallums is rescued in Iraq. He was kidnapped in November 2004 and later appeared in a video released by militants.

September 14: Bombings in Baghdad kill more than 150 and injure more than 500. Deadliest day in the insurgency so far.

September 19: British forces conduct a raid on a Basra prison to free captive SAS soldiers.

September 26: U.S. Army PFC Lynndie England is found guilty of six of seven charges by a military court in connection with the Abu Ghraib prisoner abuse scandal.

September 29: Bombings in Balad kill more than 100.

October 15: Iraqi Constitutional Referendum. Voters approve new constitution.

October 19: Beginning of Saddam Hussein's trial.

October 24: Palestine and Sheraton hotels are hit with truck bombs.

November 5–22: Operation Steel Curtain. First large deployment of Iraqi Army in support of coalition operation to remove foreign fighters.

November 15: 173 prisoners are found in an Iraqi government bunker in Baghdad, having been starved, beaten, and tortured.

November 18: Suicide attacks on Shia mosques in Khanaqin, Iraq, kill dozens.

November 19: Haditha killings. U.S. soldiers kill 24 unarmed Iraqi civilians.

November 24: Khadim Sarhid al-Hemaiyim, one of the most important Sunni Arab tribal leaders in Iraq, killed with his three sons and a son-in-law in Baghdad. The gunman appeared to be a member of the new Iraqi Army.

November 26–March 23: Four human rights workers of Christian Peacemaker Teams held hostage. One is killed and the rest are freed on March 23, 2006.

December 14: President George W. Bush says that the decision to invade Iraq in 2003 was the result of faulty intelligence and accepts responsibility for that decision. He maintains that his decision was still justified.

December 15: Iraqi Legislative Election.

December 18: Primetime Oval Office from President Bush. He said, "Not only can we win the war in Iraq—we are winning the war in Iraq."

2006

January 5: Suicide bombers kill more than 100 people in separate attacks in Karbala and Ramadi.

January 15: Al Qaeda in Iraq forms Mujahideen Shura Council with other groups.

February 22: The al-Askari mosque in Samarra is bombed. No one is killed, but during retaliatory violence more than a thousand die. This is considered the start of the Iraqi Civil War.

March 12: Abeer Qassim Hamza al-Janabi, a 14-year-old Iraqi girl raped and murdered together with her family by U.S. forces in the Mahmudiyah killings.

April 26: Hamdania incident. Marines abduct an Iraqi civilian from a house, kill him, and place components and spent AK-47 cartridges near his body to make it appear he was planting an IED.

May 5: Iraq was listed fourth on the 2006 Failed States Index compiled by the American Foreign Policy magazine and the Fund for Peace think tank.

May 20: New Iraqi government begins to function.

June 7: Abu Musab al-Zarqawi is killed by a U.S. air strike. It was hoped that his death will ease the sectarian killings rampant in Iraq.

June 14–October 24: Operation Together Forward. Security plan designed to reduce the sectarian violence in Baghdad since the al-Askari mosque bombing. This was deemed a failure.
June 17–November 15: Battle of Ramadi.
July 25–27: Operation River Falcon. Designed to remove insurgents from a region of southeast Baghdad.
September 27–February 18: Operation Sinbad to remove corrupt police in Basra and restore law and order.
October 15: Al Qaeda in Iraq changes its name to the Islamic State of Iraq (ISI).
October 19–20: Battle of Amarah between members of the Jaysh al-Mahdi and the Badr Corps—competing Shia militias.
November 7: U.S. congressional midterm elections. Democratic Party wins both chambers.
November 23: Multiple suicide car bombs kill hundreds and wound hundreds more in Sadr City. Shiites retaliate with mortar attacks on a Sunni shrine in Baghdad and other Sunni targets.
December 6: Iraq Study Group releases their final report.
December 21: U.S. forces raid a building believed to contain insurgents, and they instead turn out to be Iranian diplomats.
December 25–October 1, 2007: Diyala Campaign. A coalition series of operations to secure the province.
December 30: Execution of Saddam Hussein.

2007

January 6–9: Battle of Haifa Street rages to control a road in downtown Baghdad.
January 10: The Iraq War troop surge of 2007 is announced.
January 11: U.S. raid on Iranian Liaison Office in Irbil.
January 15: Awad Hamed al-Bandar, former head of Iraq's Revolutionary Court; and Barzan Ibrahim, Saddam's half-brother and former intelligence chief, were both executed by hanging before dawn in Baghdad.
January 16: Series of car bombs across Baghdad kill more than 100 people.
January 20: The third deadliest day for U.S. troops in Iraq occurred, with at least 25 U.S. soldiers killed in a helicopter shootdown, in Anbar province, and in roadside bombings.
January 21: Moqtada al-Sadr announces his block will return to parliament after two months of boycott.
January 23: Five Blackwater contractors are killed in a helicopter shootdown.
January 28–29: Battle of Najaf.
February 3: Baghdad market bomb kills 135.
February 6: Chinook helicopter crashes in western Iraq. This is the fifth U.S. helicopter to crash in two weeks.
February 14–November 24: Operation Law and Order is a joint coalition–Iraqi security plan for Baghdad.
February 15: Operation Shurta Nasir (Operation Police Victory) to remove Al Qaeda from Hit.
February 27–September 3: Siege of U.K. bases in Basra.
March 6: Al-Hillah bombing kills 115.
March 23: Iranian naval personnel seize 15 Royal Navy personnel conducting a search of merchant vessels in the Persian Gulf. The sailors were released on April 4.
March 27: Tal Afar bombings kill 152.
March 30: U.S. Senate approved a goal, not a requirement, of getting all combat soldiers out of Iraq by March 31, 2008.
March 10–August 19: Battle of Baqubah.
April 6–10: Operation Black Eagle in al-Diwaniyah.
April 11: Secretary of Defense Robert Gates announces U.S. Army units will remain in Iraq for 15 months rather than 12.

April 16: Moqtada al-Sadr's party resigns from parliament over a lack of a timeline for U.S. withdrawal.
April 18: Series of bombings across Baghdad kill nearly 200.
May: Iraq oil law submitted to Iraqi Council of Representatives.
May 8: 144 of 275 Iraqi parliament members sign a petition requiring the Iraqi government to seek parliamentary approval before it requests an extension of the UN mandate.
June 13: Al-Askari Mosque bombing blows up two of the mosque's minarets.
June 16–August 14: Operation Phantom Thunder focused on removing Al Qaeda in Iraq and other extremist organizations.
July 12: The Apache airstrikes associated with the WikiLeaks released and edited video "Collateral Murder" occurs.
July 17: Suicide car bomb attack in Amirli kills 156.
August 14: Four coordinated suicide bombs kill an estimated 796 Yazidis in multiple locations.
August 15–January 2008: Operation Phantom Strike focused on removing Al Qaeda in Iraq and Iranian-supported extremists.
September 3: British forces finish withdrawal from Basra leaving the city in the complete control of Iraqi security forces.
September 10: General Petraeus and Ambassador Ryan Crocker submit their report to Congress on the situation in Iraq.
September 16: Blackwater Security Consulting contractors kill 17 Iraqis during a protection mission at Nisour Square in Baghdad.
November 1: Statistics for October show a significant reduction in violence since the beginning of "the Surge."
December 16: British forces hand control of Basra over to Iraqi security forces.
December 18: UNSCR 1790 extends the UN mandate until December 31, 2008.

2008
January 8–July 28: Operation Phantom Phieonix is a continuation of Operations Phantom Thunder and Phantom Strike.
January 11: First snowfall in Baghdad in more than 50 years.
January 13: Iraqi government announced a law that allows former Baath Party members to have civil and military positions.
January 22: Iraqi Parliament approves a new flag which removes the three stars that symbolized the ideals of the Baath Party.
January 23–July 28: Ninewa Campaign was a series of offensives and counterattacks in the northern province.
February 1: Two suicide bombs kill 99 in the Baghdad animal market.
February 21–29: Turkey invades northern Iraq to combat Kurdish fighters from the PKK (Kurdistan Workers Party) who have launched attacks in Turkey.
March 20: Al-Jazeera releases Osama bin Laden recording where he states that "Iraq is the perfect base to set up the jihad to liberate Palestine."
March 23: U.S. soldiers killed in action in Global War on Terrorism exceeds 4,000.
March 25–31: Battle of Basra began with the Charge of the Knights led by Prime Minister Nuri al-Maliki to combat opposition attacks in Basra.
March 25–May 11: Battle of Sadr City.
April 8: General Petraeus and Ambassador Crocker testify before U.S. Senate.
April 9: General Petraeus and Ambassador Crocker testify before U.S. House.
May 8: Abu Ayyub al-Masri is arrested in Mosul. He is the suspected leader of Al Qaeda in Iraq.
June 14: Iraqi forces begin an offensive against Mahdi Army in Maysan Province.
July 29–August 11: Operation Augurs of Prosperity was intended to clear Diyala Province of opposition elements.

September 1: United States transfers security responsibility for Anbar Province to Iraq.
October 4: Polish forces complete mission in Iraq.
October 26: Abu Kemal raid into Syria by U.S. special operations forces.
October 29: United States transfers security responsibility for Wasit Province to Iraq.
November 4: Barack Obama elected president of the United States.
November 17: U.S.-Iraq Status of Forces Agreement signed by Iraqi foreign minister and U.S. ambassador to Iraq. This agreement requires U.S. forces to be out of cities in 2009 and out of Iraq by the end of 2011.
December 4: Czech Republic forces complete mission in Iraq.
December 5: South Korean forces complete mission in Iraq.
December 9: Ukrainian forces complete mission in Iraq.
December 14: President Bush signs status of forces agreement. This was the president's fourth and final trip to Baghdad. During the press conference one of the reporters hurled two shoes at the president in protest for the chaos in Iraq.
December 17: Moldovan, Bulgarian, and Albanian forces complete mission in Iraq.

2009

January 1: United States formally transfers security responsibility for Green Zone to Iraq. United States opens new embassy in Baghdad.
January 20: Barack Obama sworn in as 44th president of the United States.
January 22: Estonian and Salvadoran forces complete mission in Iraq.
January 31: Iraqi Provincial Elections.
February 27: President Obama announces Christopher Hill as the new ambassador to Iraq and that U.S. combat operations will end on August 31, 2010.

April 7: Obama visits Iraq for the first time as president.
June 4: Romanian forces complete mission in Iraq.
June 30: U.S. forces withdraw from cities and towns in Iraq.
July 28: United Kingdom, Australia, and Romania complete mission in Iraq. United States is the only foreign military force in Iraq.
August 19: Numerous bombs detonate in Baghdad killing more than 100 and wounding hundreds more.
October 25: Two large car bombs kill 155 in central Baghdad and wound hundreds more.
December 8: A series of car bombs kill at least 127 people in Baghdad.
December 18: Iran invades to seize East Maysan oil field.

2010

March 7: Parliamentary Election.
April 18: A joint U.S.-Iraqi operation near Tikrit, Iraq, kills Abu Ayyub al-Masri and Abu Omar al-Baghdadi. They are the leaders of the Islamic State of Iraq—the precursor group for the Islamic State of Iraq and al-Sham (ISIS).
August 18: Last U.S. combat brigade departs Iraq. More than 50,000 U.S. military forces remain in Iraq conducting mostly advice and assist missions.
August 31: Operation Iraqi Freedom formally ends.
September 1: Operation New Dawn begins.

2011

January 8: Moqtada al-Sadr returns to Iraq and urges the rejection of violence and peaceful resistance against the country's "occupiers" in his first public address.
January 15: Iraqi soldier kills two U.S. soldiers at a training center.
January 17: Car bombs kill 133 across Iraq.

April 8: Iraqi forces raid Camp Ashraf—the "refugee" camp for the People's Mujahedin of Iran—killing 34 and injuring hundreds.
December 18: Last U.S. troops leave Iraq.

2013
April 8: The Islamic State of Iraq changes its name to the Islamic State of Iraq and al-Sham (ISIS).
July 22: ISIS organizes a prison breakout from Taji and Abu Ghraib, Iraq.

2014
January 3: ISIS proclaims itself to be the Islamic State in Fallujah.
June 9: Mosul, Iraq, falls to ISIS.
June 10–11: Islamist extremist forces make huge gains in Iraq, seizing Mosul and much of Tikrit. These gains threaten to break Iraq apart; they also compel the United States to send more military aid to the Iraqi government.
June 15: Operation Inherent Resolve begins with a purpose of coordinating a regional response to ISIS.
June 29: ISIS changes its name to the Islamic State and claims to be a caliphate.
August 19: Kurdish and Iraqi forces, aided by dozens of American airstrikes, retake control of Mosul Dam, which had been seized by ISIS. This is seen as a key victory in the fight against ISIS in northern Iraq.
September 5: The United States announces the formation of an international coalition, including several Arab countries, which will help fight ISIS in both Iraq and Syria. Much of the aid will come in the form of airstrikes and military/financial aid.
September 8: Haider al-Abadi becomes Iraqi prime minister. He takes office after Nuri al-Maliki reluctantly resigns under great domestic and international pressure. Abadi promises to rid Iraq of graft and corruption and to reinvigorate Iraq's fight against ISIS.

2015
March 2: Second Battle of Tikrit commences. This is the first significant effort by the Iraqi government to retake territory captured by ISIS in northern Iraq.
April 2: Iraqi forces finally take control of Tikrit. This success compels the Iraqi government to announce a larger ground offensive that will aim to retake control of Anbar Province, which came under ISIS control in 2013.
June 10: The United States announces plans to establish a base of operations in Anbar Province and pledges to send several hundred more military trainers to Iraq in an effort to retake Ramadi and, eventually, all of Anbar Province.
December 27: The Iraqi government announces that all of Ramadi has been liberated from ISIS occupation.

2016
June 26: Iraqi forces retake Fallujah, which is heavily damaged by the ISIS occupation and the Iraqi effort to recapture it.
July 3: Two massive car bomb attacks in Baghdad kill as many as 324 civilians and injure scores more. ISIS claims responsibility, asserting the attacks were meant to kill Iraqi Shiites.
October 17: Iraqi government forces, aided by U.S. and coalition special forces as well as Kurdish and Sunni militias, begin their offensive to wrest Mosul from ISIS control.

2017
July 20: The Battle of Mosul ends with a decisive ISIS defeat.
December 8: The Iraqi government declares victory in its war against ISIS.

Recommended Bibliography

MEMOIRS

Baker, James A., III. *The Politics of Diplomacy: Revolution, War & Peace, 1989–1992.* New York: G. P. Putnam's Sons, 1995.

Blix, Hans. *Disarming Iraq.* New York: Pantheon, 2004.

Bolger, Daniel P. *Why We Lost: A General's Inside Account of the Iraq and Afghanistan Wars.* Boston: Houghton Mifflin Harcourt, 2014.

Bremer, L. Paul, with Malcolm McConnell. *My Year in Iraq: The Struggle to Build a Future of Hope.* New York: Simon and Schuster, 2006.

Bush, George, and Brent Scowcroft. *A World Transformed.* New York: Knopf, 1998.

Bush, George W. *Decision Points.* New York: Random House, 2010.

Casey, George. *Strategic Reflections: Operation Iraqi Freedom July 2004–February 2007.* Washington, DC: National Defense University Press, 2012.

Clinton, Hillary. *Hard Choices.* New York: Simon and Schuster, 2014.

Franks, Tommy, with Malcolm McConnell. *American Soldier.* New York: Regan Books, 2004.

Gates, Robert M. *Duty: Memoirs of a Secretary at War.* New York: Knopf, 2014.

Morrell, Michael. *The Great War of Our Time: The CIA's Fight against Terrorism—From al Qa'ida to ISIS.* New York: Hatchet Book Group, 2015.

Panetta, Leon, with Jim Newton. *Worthy Fights: A Memoir of Leadership in War and Peace.* New York: Penguin, 2014.

Powell, Colin L., with Joseph E. Perisco. *My American Journey.* New York: Random House, 1995.

Rumsfeld, Donald. *Known and Unknown: A Memoir.* New York: Penguin Group, 2011.

Sanchez, Ricardo S., and Donald T. Phillips. *Wiser in Battle: A Soldier's Story.* New York: Harper, 2008.

BOOKS

Abrams, David. *Fobbit.* New York: Grove Press, Black Cat, 2012.

Al-Ali, Zaid. *The Struggle for Iraq's Future: How Corruption, Incompetence and Sectarianism Have Undermined Democracy.* New Haven, CT: Yale University Press, 2014.

Allawi, Ali A. *The Occupation of Iraq: Winning the War, Losing the Peace.* New Haven, CT: Yale University Press, 2007.

Al-Suri, Abu Musab. *Call to Global Islamic Resistance*, translated and condensed into *A Terrorist's Call to Global Jihad: Deciphering Abu Musab al-Suri's Islamic Jihad Manifesto*, edited by Jim Lacey. Annapolis, MD: Naval Institute Press, 2008.

Atkinson, Rick. *In the Company of Soldiers: A Chronicle of Combat.* New York: Henry Holt, 2005.

Bacevich, Andrew J. *The New American Militarism: How Americans Are Seduced by War.* New York: Oxford University Press, 2005.

Baker, James A., III, and Lee Hamilton. *The Iraq Study Group: The Way Forward, a New Approach.* New York: Vintage Books, 2006.

Broadwell, Paula. *All In: The Education of General David Petraeus.* New York: Penguin Press, 2012.

Chandrasekaran, Rajiv. *Imperial Life in the Emerald City: Inside Iraq's Green Zone.* New York: Vintage Books, 2007.

Danner, Mark. *Torture and Truth: America, Abu Ghraib, and the War on Terror.* New York: New York Review of Books, 2004.

Drogin, Bob. *Curveball: Spies, Lies, and the Con Man Who Caused a War.* New York: Random House, 2007.

Fick, Nathan. *One Bullet Away: The Making of a Marine Officer.* New York: Mariner Books, 2006.

Filkins, Dexter. *The Forever War.* New York: Vintage, 2009.

Finkel, David. *The Good Soldiers.* New York: Picador, 2010.

Fontenot, Gregory, E. J. Degen, and David Tohn. *On Point: The United States Army in Operation Iraqi Freedom.* Fort Leavenworth, KS: U.S. Army Command and General Staff College Press, 2004.

Frederick, Jim. *Black Hearts: One Platoon's Descent into Madness in Iraq's Triangle of Death.* New York: Harmony Books, 2010.

Gentile, Gian. *Wrong Turn: America's Deadly Embrace of Counterinsurgency.* New York: New Press, 2013.

Gordon, Michael R., and General Bernard E. Trainor. *Cobra II: The Inside Story of the Invasion and Occupation of Iraq.* New York: Pantheon Books, 2006.

Gordon, Michael R., and Bernard E. Trainor. *The Endgame: The Inside Story of the Struggle for Iraq, from George W. Bush to Barack Obama.* New York: Vintage, 2013.

Hersh, Seymour. *Chain of Command: The Road from 9/11 to Abu Ghraib.* New York: HarperCollins, 2004.

Holmstedt, Kirsten. *Band of Sisters: American Women at War in Iraq.* Mechanicsburg, PA: Stackpole Books, 2008.

Holmstedt, Kirsten. *The Girls Come Marching Home: Stories of Women Warriors Returning from the War in Iraq.* Mechanicsburg, PA: Stackpole Books, 2011.

Hughes, Christopher P. *War on Two Fronts: An Infantry Commander's War in Iraq and the Pentagon.* Philadelphia: Casemate, 2007.

Isikoff, Michael. *Hubris: The Inside Story of Spin, Scandal, and the Selling of the Iraq War.* New York: Broadway, 2007.

Kagan, Kimberly. *The Surge: A Military History.* New York: Encounter Books, 2008.

Kaplan, Fred. *The Insurgents: David Petraeus and the Plot to Change the American Way of War.* New York: Simon and Schuster, 2014.

Kilcullen, David. *Counterinsurgency.* Oxford: Oxford University Press, 2010.

Kilcullen, David. *The Accidental Guerilla: Fighting Small Wars in the Midst of a Big One.* Oxford: Oxford University Press, 2011.

Kyle, Chris, and Scott McEwen. *American Sniper: The Autobiography of the Most Lethal Sniper in U.S. Military History.* New York: HarperCollins, 2013.

Lacey, James G. *Takedown: The 3rd Infantry Division's Twenty-One Day Assault on Baghdad.* Annapolis, MD: Naval Institute Press, 2007.

Ludwig, Konrad R. K. *Stryker: The Siege of Sadr City.* La Canada, Flintridge, CA: Roland-Kjos Publishing, 2013.

Maher, Shiraz. *Salafi-Jihadism: The History of an Idea.* New York: Oxford University Press, 2016.

Mansoor, Peter. *Surge: My Journey with General David Petraeus and the Remaking of the Iraq War.* New Haven, CT: Yale University Press, 2013.

Montalvan, Luis Carlos. *Until Tuesday: A Wounded Warrior and the Golden Retriever Who Saved Him.* New York: Hachette Books, 2011.

Murray, Williamson, and Robert H. Scales Jr. *The Iraq War: A Military History.* Cambridge, MA: Belknap, 2005.

Nagl, John A. *Learning to Eat Soup with a Knife: Counterinsurgency Lessons from Malaya and Vietnam.* Westport, CT: Praeger Publishers, 2002.

Nagl, John A. *Knife Fights: A Memoir of Modern War in Theory and Practice.* New York: Penguin Press, 2014.

Naji, Abu Bakr. *The Management of Savagery: The Most Critical Stage through Which the Umma Will Pass.* Translated by William McCants. Cambridge, MA: John M. Olin Institute for Strategic Studies, May 23, 2006. https://www.narrativespace.net/support-files/management_of_savagery.pdf (accessed 25 November 25, 2017).

Nasr, Vali. *The Shia Revival: How Conflicts within Islam Will Shape the Future.* New York: Norton, 2006.

Polk, William R. *Understanding Iraq: The Whole Sweep of Iraqi History, from Genghis Khan's Mongols to the Ottoman Turks to the British Mandate to the American Occupation.* New York: Harper Perennial, 2006.

Prince, Erik. *Civilian Warriors: The Inside Story of Blackwater and the Unsung Heroes of the War on Terror.* New York: Penguin Group, 2013.

Raddatz, Martha. *The Long Road Home: A Story of War and Family.* New York: Penguin Group, 2008.

Ricks, Thomas E. *Fiasco: The American Military Adventure in Iraq.* New York: Penguin, 2006.

Ricks, Thomas E. *The Gamble: General David Petraeus and the American Military Adventure in Iraq, 2006–2008.* New York: Penguin Press, 2009.

Robinson, Linda. *Tell Me How This Ends: General David Petraeus and the Search for a Way Out of Iraq.* New York: PublicAffairs, 2008.

Scahill, Jeremy. *Blackwater: The Rise of the World's Most Powerful Mercenary Army.* New York: Nation Books, 2007.

Shadid, Anthony. *Night Draws Near: Iraq's People in the Shadow of America's War.* New York: Henry Holt and Company, 2005.

Singer, Peter W. *Corporate Warriors: The Rise of the Privatized Military Industry.* Ithaca, NY: Cornell University Press, 2003.

Singer, P. W. *Wired for War: The Robotics Revolution and Conflict in the 21st Century.* New York: Penguin Press, 2009.

Sky, Emma. *The Unravelling: High Hopes and Missed Opportunities in Iraq.* New York: PublicAffairs, 2015.

Stern, Jessica, and J. M. Berger. *ISIS: The State of Terror.* New York: HarperCollins, 2015.

Stiglitz, Joseph E., and Linda J. Bilmes. *The Three Trillion Dollar War: The True Cost of the Iraq Conflict.* New York: Norton, 2008.

Tripp, Charles. *A History of Iraq.* Cambridge: Cambridge University Press, 2007.

Weiss, Michael, and Hassan Hassan. *ISIS: Inside the Army of Terror.* New York: Regan Arts, 2015.

West, Bing. *No True Glory: A Frontline Account of the Battle for Fallujah.* New York: Bantam Books, 2005.

West, Bing. *The Strongest Tribe: War, Politics, and the Endgame in Iraq.* New York: Random House, 2009.

Woodward, Bob. *Bush at War.* New York: Simon and Schuster, 2002.

Woodward, Bob. *Plan of Attack.* New York: Simon and Schuster, 2004.

Woodward, Bob. *State of Denial: Bush at War, Part III.* New York: Simon and Schuster, 2006.

Woodward, Bob. *The War Within: A Secret White House History, 2006–2008.* New York: Simon and Schuster, 2009.

Woodward, Bob. *Obama's Wars.* New York: Simon and Schuster, 2010.

Wright, Donald P., and Timothy R. Reese. *On Point II: Transition to the New Campaign: The United States Army in Operation Iraqi Freedom May 2003–January 2005.* Fort Leavenworth, KS: U.S. Army Command and General Staff College Press, 2008.

Wright, Evan. *Generation Kill.* New York: Berkley, 2008.

Zinsmeister, Karl. *Dawn over Baghdad: How the U.S. Military Is Using Bullets and Ballots to Remake Iraq.* New York: Encounter Books, 2004.

Zucchino, David. *Thunder Run: The Armored Strike to Capture Baghdad.* New York: Atlantic Monthly Press, 2004.

FILMS AND TELEVISION

Movies

The A Team. Director: Josh Carnahan. 20th Century Fox, 2010.

American Sniper. Director: Clint Eastwood. Warner Bros, 2014.

Green Zone. Director: Paul Greengrass. Universal Pictures, 2010.

The Hurt Locker. Director: Kathryn Bigelow. Voltage Pictures, 2009.

The Men Who Stare at Goats. Director: Grant Heslov. BBC Films, 2009.

Redacted. Director: Brian De Palma. Film Farm, 2007.

Saving Jessica Lynch. Director: Peter Markle. Daniel L. Paulson Productions, 2003.

Taking Chance. Director: Ross Katz. HBO Films, 2009.

Zero Dark Thirty. Director: Kathryn Bigelow. Columbia Pictures, 2012.

Documentaries

American War Generals. Executive producers: Peter Bergen, Tresha Mabile, Jonathan Towers. National Geographic Channel, 2014.

Control Room. Director: Jehane Noujaim. Noujaim Films, 2004.

Fahrenheit 9/11. Director: Michael Moore. Fellowship Adventure Group, 2004.

Ghosts of Abu Ghraib. Director: Rory Kennedy. HBO Documentary Film, 2007.

Television

Frontline: Blair's War. Director: Eamonn Matthews. PBS, 2003

Frontline: Beyond Baghdad. Executive Producer: David Fanning. PBS, 2004.

Frontline: Chasing Saddam's Weapons. Executive Producer: David Fanning. PBS, 2004.

Frontline: The Invasion of Iraq. Director: Richard Sanders. PBS, 2004.

Frontline: Al Qaeda's New Front. Director: Ruthie Calarco, Neil Docherty. PBS, 2005.

Frontline: Private Warriors. Producer: Martin Smith. PBS, 2005.

Frontline: The Torture Question. Director: Michael Kirk, 2005.

Frontline: Gangs of Iraq. Executive Producer: David Fanning. PBS, 2007.

Frontline: Bush's War. Director: Michael Kirk. PBS, 2008.

Frontline: Rules of Engagement. Executive Producer: David Fanning. PBS, 2008.

Frontline: Losing Iraq. Director: Michael Kirk. PBS, 2014.

Frontline: The Rise of ISIS. Director: Martin Smith. PBS, 2014.

Generation Kill. Director: Susanna White, Simon Cellan Jones. Blown Deadline Productions, 2008.

List of Contributors

VOLUME EDITOR

Brian L. Steed
Senior Fellow, Narrative Strategies
Assistant Professor of Military History
U.S. Army Command and General Staff College, Fort Leavenworth

CONTRIBUTORS

Dr. Rebecca Adelman
Assistant Professor
University of Maryland–Baltimore County

Kristian P. Alexander
Associate Instructor
University of Utah

Christopher Paul Anzalone
Independent Scholar

James Arnold
Independent Scholar

Dr. Robert F. Baumann
Professor of History
U.S. Army Command and General Staff College, Fort Leavenworth

Michael K. Beauchamp
Texas A&M University

Walter F. Bell
Information Services Librarian
Aurora University

James C. Bradford
Professor of History
Texas A&M University

Ron Briley
Assistant Headmaster
Sandia Preparatory School

Jessica Britt
Independent Scholar

Dr. Stefan Brooks
Assistant Professor of Political Science
Lindsey Wilson College

Gates Brown
Assistant Professor of Military History
U.S. Army Command and General Staff College, Fort Leavenworth

Tamar Burris
Independent Scholar

List of Contributors

Marcel A. Derosier
Independent Scholar

Christopher R. W. Dietrich
University of Texas at Austin

Dr. Paul William Doerr
Associate Professor
Acadia University
Canada

Colonel Donald Redmond Dunne
U.S. Army

Dr. Richard M. Edwards
Senior Lecturer
University of Wisconsin Colleges

Dr. Shawn Fisher
Assistant Professor
History and Social Sciences
Harding University

Major Benjamin D. Forest
Air Command and Staff College

Dr. Michael R. Hall
Associate Professor of History
Armstrong Atlantic State University

Dr. William P. Head
Historian/Chief, WR-ALC Office of History
U.S. Air Force

Dr. Arthur M. Holst
MPA Program Faculty
Widener University

Dr. Charles Francis Howlett
Associate Professor
Molloy College

Dr. Gary Lee Kerley
North Hall High School

Dr. Chen Kertcher
School of History
Tel Aviv University

Dr. Deborah Kidwell
U.S. Army Command and General Staff
College, Fort Leavenworth

Dr. Tom Lansford
Dean, Gulf Coast
University Southern Mississippi

Alison Lawlor
Independent Scholar

Keith A. Leitich
Independent Scholar

Robert W. Malick
Adjunct Professor of History
Harrisburg Area Community College

Alexander Mikaberidze
Professor of History
Louisiana State University (Shreveport)

Dr. Thomas R. Mockaitis
Professor of History
DePaul University

Dr. Jerry D. Morelock
Colonel
U.S. Army, Retired
Editor in Chief, Armchair General
Magazine

Gregory Wayne Morgan
Independent Scholar

List of Contributors

Dr. Keith Murphy
Associate Dean
Fort Valley State University

Dr. Paul G. Pierpaoli Jr.
Fellow
Military History, ABC-CLIO, Inc.

Dr. Peter J. Rainow
Independent Scholar

Jessica Ramsay
Independent Scholar

Karl Lee Rubis
University of Kansas

Captain Carl Otis Schuster (retired)
U.S. Navy
Hawaii Pacific University

Larry Schweikart
Independent Scholar

Dr. Jeff Seiken
Independent Scholar

James E. Shircliffe Jr.
Principal Research Analyst
CENTRA Technology, Inc.

Dr. Daniel E. Spector
Independent Scholar

Dr. Paul Joseph Springer
Professor of Comparative Military Studies
Chair of the Department of Research
Air Command and Staff College, Maxwell Air Force Base

Brian L. Steed
Senior Fellow, Narrative Strategies
Assistant Professor of Military History
U.S. Army Command and General Staff College, Fort Leavenworth

Sheri Steed
Independent Editor and Researcher

Dr. Nancy L. Stockdale
Assistant Professor, Middle Eastern history
University of North Texas

Randy Jack Taylor
Librarian
Howard Payne University

Dr. Spencer C. Tucker
Senior Fellow
Military History, ABC-CLIO, Inc.

Tim J. Watts
Subject Librarian
Kansas State University

Lori Weathers
Independent Scholar

Dr. David T. Zabecki
Major General
Army of the United States, Retired

Dr. Sherifa Zuhur
Visiting Professor of National Security Affairs
Regional Strategy and Planning Department
Strategic Studies Institute
U.S. Army War College

Index

Note: **Boldface** page numbers indicate main entries in the book.

Abadi, Haider al-, xviii, xxvi, 126, 155, 188, 196, 202
Abbas, Mahmoud, 28
Abdullah (Crown Prince of Saudi Arabia), 28, 237
Abizaid, John, 50–51, 52
Abrams tanks, 254. *See also* Tanks
Abu Bakr (caliph), 224, 231, 233
Abu Ghraib Prison, 12, 41, 43, 73–75, 112, 157
Academi, 67, 70. *See also* Blackwater USA
Active Endeavor, Operation, 94
Afghani, Jamal al-Din al-, 236
Afghanistan, xiv, 26–27, 29, 57, 80, 82, 133, 213, 270
  counterinsurgency in, 80
  Crocker's role in, 5
  Khalilzad's role in, 4
  Operation Enduring Freedom, 49
  sectarian violence in, 31
  security operations in, 64
  Soviet invasion of, 61
  Taliban in, 62, 178, 210
  troop surge in, 177
  U.S. invasion of, 31, 93, 94, 181
Afghanistan War, 112, 176
Aflaq, Michel, 19
Agenda, The (Woodward), 264
Ahl al-Bayt (People of the House), 224, 226, 232

Aircraft, 113–114, 135, 136–138, 140
Aircraft carriers, 137, 140
Al Basrah oil terminals, 141
Al Qaeda
  doctrines of, 82, 232
  Iraq's links to, 123, 272
  linked to Ansar al-Islam, 246, 247
  linked to Iraqi insurgency, xxv
  operations against, 10–12, 27, 62, 63, 67, 93, 94, 96, 112, 133, 183, 269, 290
  severing ties with ISIS, 22
  Taliban providing refuge for, 80, 93, 269, 270
  terrorist acts by, 16, 26, 158, 249, 251–252
  See also Bin Laden, Osama
Al Qaeda in Iraq (AQI), xvii, 21, 45, 94, 103, 119, 156–158, 165, 268, 294, 301
  executions staged by, 156, 194
  insurgency, 85–86, 149, 201
  operations against, 10–11, 86, 149–150, 183–184, 185, 201
  terrorist acts by, 1
  See also Zarqawi, Abu Musab al-
Al Qaeda in Mesopotamia, 156. *See also* Al Qaeda in Iraq (AQI)
Al-Askari Mosque (Golden Mosque) bombing, xvii, **1–2**, 110
Alawite Muslims, 226
Albania, 59, 140

Algeria, 82
Ali ibn Abi Talib, 224, 232, 233
All the President's Men (Woodward and Bernstein), 264
Allah, 225, 233, 234
Allawi, Ayad (Iyad), 87, 124, 198–199, 206
Allen, John R., 47, 56
Alljah, Operation, 184, 185
Almsgiving (*zakat*), 226, 233–234
Amarah offensive, 206
Ambassadors to Iraq, U.S., **2–7**
    Crocker, Ryan Clark, 5–6
    Hill, Christopher R., 6–7
    Jeffrey, James F., 7
    Khalilzad, Zalmay Mamozy, 3–5
    Negroponte, John Dimitri, 2–3
American Civil War, 70
American Enterprise Institute, 36
Amiri, Hadi al-, 104
Amnesty International, 77, 112, 190
Amnesty Law, 152
Anbar Awakening movement, xxvii, 150, 157
Anfal (Spoils of War) Campaign, 161
Angar People's Council, 150
Ansar al-Islam, 156, 162, 190, 246
    operation against (Viking Hammer), 245–248
Arab Baath Party. *See* Baath Party
Arab Socialist Baath Party. *See* Baath Party
Arab Spring, **7–9**, 32, 190, 223
Arab-Israeli conflict, 28
Armenia, 60, 106, 140
Army Field Manual on Interrogation (U.S. Department of the Army), 112
Arrow theater antiballistic missile system, 91
Arrowhead Ripper, Operation, **10–12**, 184–185
Arsuzi, Zaki al-, 19
Askari, al-Hasan al-, 225
Askari shrine bombing, xvii, 1–2, 110

Aspin, Les, 262
Assad, Bashar al-, 6, 9, 20, 22, 153, 216
Assad, Hafiz al-, 20, 226
Assange, Julian, 258–259
Atrocities, U.S., **12–17**, 28
    Haditha Incident, 12–16
    Mahmudiyah Incident, 16–17
Austin, Lloyd J., III, 46–47
Australia, xiv, 59, 94, 139, 141, 142, 275
Awakening Councils, 46
Axis of evil, xiii, xxiii, 134
Azerbaijan, 59, 140

Baath Party, xvi, **19–21**, 24, 61, 103, 104, 105, 107, 108, 122, 186
    Ayad Allawi and, 198
    campaign against the Kurds, 189
    Saddam Hussein's involvement in, 98
    suppression of Dawa Party by, 187–188
    See also De-Baathification
Baath Party of Iraq, 20
Baath Party of Syria, 20
Baathism. *See* Baath Party
Babism, 227
Badr, Battles of, 104, 105
Badr Brigades, 194, 207
Badr Corps, 110
Badr Organization, 104–106
Baghdad
    Al Qaeda in, 149, 157
    bombing of, xiv, xxiv, 136, 137–138, 143–144
    capture of, xv, xxvii, 27, 100, 119, 123, 125, 134–135, 138, 140, 145, 150, 159, 275
    civilian shootings by security personnel in, 63, 66, 67
    as economic and cultural center, 115
    effort to resecure, 184
    helicopter attack on, 258
    infrastructure in, 152
    insurgents in, 149–150, 183–184
    Iraqi defense of, 103, 145

Israeli destruction of nuclear reactor in, xxii
lawlessness in, 92
Mongol sack of, 232, 258
plan to capture, 134, 149–150
plan to secure, 149–150
as seat of government, 5, 7, 190, 194, 273, 278
Shiite victories in, 125
slum areas of, 187, 205, 207
terrorist groups in, 183–184
U.S. military police in, 24
U.S. withdrawal from, 305
Baghdad Belt, 184
Baghdad Central Confinement Facility. *See* Abu Ghraib Prison
Baghdad Security Plan (Fardh al-Qanoon), 10, 45, 183, 184, 185
Baghdadi, Abu Bakr al-, **21–23**, 75, 153
Baghdadi, Abu Omar al-, 183
Bahrain
and the Arab Spring, 8, 9
Baath Party in, 19, 21
Baker, James III, 130, 131, 132, 212
Baker-Hamilton Commission, 130–133, 212
Bakr, Ahmad Hassan al-, 98, 187, 198
Baqr, Muhammad, 104
Baquba, 10–12
Barbero, Michael, 60
Bargewell, Eldon, 13
Barker, James, 17
Barnett, Thomas P. M., 52, 213
Barqawi, Muhammad Tahir al- (Abu Muhammad al-Maqdisi), 156
Barzani, Massoud (Masoud; Masud), 162, 189, 190, 191, 245
Barzani, Mustafa, 115, 116, 161, 189
Basra, xiv, 144, 194
Bayt al-Imam, 156
Ben-Gurion, David, 115
Berg, Nicholas, 156, 268
Biden, Joseph, 176
Bin Laden, Osama, 24, 31, 94, 157
death of, 22, 95, 178, 215

Biological weapons, xiv, 30, 73, 97, 118, 123, 197, 218, 239, 250, 252, 270, 271, 272, 275, 284
Biological Weapons Convention, 252
Bitar, Salah al-Din al-, 19
Blackwater USA, 62, 64–68, 71, 85
Blair, Tony, xiii, xiv
Blix, Hans, xiii, 239, 241
Blount, Buford, 144
Bolton, John R., 4
Bosnia, 80
Bosnia-Herzegovina, 59, 140
Bouazizi, Mohamed, 8
Bradley Fighting Vehicles, 254
Bremer, Lewis Paul, III "Jerry," xv, 1, 20, **23–25**, 38–39, 1, 51, 92, 109, 118, 199, 205, 274
Bribery, 130
Brims, Robin, 144
Britain. *See* Great Britain
Brown, George, 68
Brown, Herman, 68
Brown & Root, 68–69
Bucca, Ronald, 75
Bulgaria, 59, 140
Bunting, Henry, 68
Burridge, Brian, 139
Burujerdi, Ayatollah, 227
Bush, George Herbert Walker, 25, 36, 62, 120, 212, 217, 260, 261
administration of, 3
and Operation Desert Shield, 99–100
Bush (George Walker) administration
aggressive foreign policy approach of, xxiii–xxiv
alliance with Blair, 132
approach to Iraq, 27, 122–123, 134, 181, 197
approach to national security, 27
on the Arab-Israeli conflict, 28
and the Baker-Hamilton commission, 131–132
battles over planning within, 4
Cheney's role in, 36, 69

Index

Bush (George Walker) administration (*cont.*)
  on coercive interrogation, 29, 112
  criticism of, 42, 176, 265
  Crocker's role in, 5
  dealing with the UN, 2
  dismissal of Baath Party, xvi
  easy victory promised by, xxvi
  Fallon's disagreements with, 52, 213
  Garner's appointment, 91
  Gates's role in, 177
  and the Global War on Terror, 93, 94, 265
  on Guantanamo Bay, 77–78
  Hillary Clinton and, 222
  on the invasion of Iraq, 31
  and the Iraq war, 43, 46, 55, 58–59, 60, 86, 132, 183, 241
  Khalilzad's role in, 3–4
  opponents of, 13, 94
  Powell's role in, 134, 217
  Rumsfeld's role in, 211
  view of developments in Iraq, xvii
Bush, George Walker, xiii–xiv, xxi, 4, 24, **25–30**, 52, 55, 56, 74, 77, 97, 101, 122, 142, 146, 151
  address to the nation at the start of hostilities (March 19, 2003), 273–274
  appointment of Cheney, 37
  appointment of Negroponte, 2
  appointment of Rice, 219
  appointment of Rumsfeld, 210
  and the Bush Doctrine, 27, 30–32
  and the Global War on Terrorism, 92–93, 112, 141
  Hakim's meeting with, 194
  invasion of Iraq, 100
  and the Iraq Study Group, 132
  joint statement with Maliki, 289–290
  on need to protect oil fields, 181
  remarks to the crew of USS *Abraham Lincoln* (May 1, 2003), 274–277
  State of the Union Address (January 28, 2003), 270–273
  2002 State of the Union Address, xxiii
  on weapons inspection in Iraq, 239
  Woodward's books about, 265
Bush Doctrine, 27, **30–32**, 134, 219, 260, 262

Caliphate, xviii, 22, 83, 155, 224, 227, 231, 232, 267
Call to Global Resistance (*The Call for Global Islamic Resistance*) (al-Suri), 82
Camp Bucca, 75–76
Camp David Accords, 252
Camp Freddy. *See* Camp Bucca
Canada, 94, 135, 141, 182
Card, Kendall, 141
Carter, James Earl "Jimmy," xxii
Carter administration, 70
Casey, George William, Jr., xvii, 42–44, 53, 55, 58
Casey, George William, Sr., 42
Casualties, Operation Iraqi Freedom, **33–35**
  Ansar al-Islam, 247–248
  Battle of Mosul, 166
  British, 33–35, 145
  civilian, 12–16, 34, 65, 71, 145–146, 152
  by coalition nation, 35
  insurgent, 184, 185
  Iraqi, xxviii, 152, 185
  journalist, 34
  Peshmerga, 247
  security employee, 65, 85
  U.S., xxviii, 33–35, 88, 145, 152, 184, 185, 208
  women, 263
Central Intelligence Agency (CIA), xiv, 27, 56, 67, 197, 199
  Gates as head of, 212
  Panetta as head of, 215
  use of coercive interrogation by, 112
  use of UAVs by, 257
Chalabi, Ahmed Abd al-Hadi, 196–198
Chemical weapons, xiv, 30, 123, 191, 197, 247, 250, 253, 275, 284
  use by Al Qaeda, 252
  destruction of by Iran, 100

use by Iraq, 73, 97, 117–118, 161, 251, 270, 271, 272
in the Middle East, 252
use by Syria, 32, 216
Chemical Weapons Convention, 252
Cheney, Richard Bruce "Dick," xxii, 29–30, **35–38**, 68–69, 181, 197, 210, 217
Chessani, Jeffrey R., 15
China, 181, 213
opposition to invasion of Iraq, 239–240
opposition to Iran, xxvi
use of UAVs by, 258
Choice, The (Woodward), 264
Christians, 155, 166, 201, 231
Citizens' militias, xiv
Civil rights, 284–286
Cleveland, Charlie, 246
Clinton, Hillary Rodham, 176, 177, 201, 216, 220–223
background and education, 220–221
political experience, 221–222
as secretary of state, 222–223
Clinton, William Jefferson "Bill," xiv, xxiii, 36, 79, 190, 192, 214
Clinton administration, xxiii
Clinton-Bush Haiti Fund, 30
Coalition Forces Land Command, 139
Coalition Military Assistance Training Team, 60
Coalition of the willing, xiv
Coalition Provisional Authority (CPA), xv, xvi, 23–24, **38–39**, 41, 51, 60, 109, 118, 119, 129, 194–195
Coalition Provisional Order Number 1, xvii, 61, 278–279
Coalition Provisional Order Number 2, xvii, 61, 279–281
and the Iraqi military, 115
and the Mahdi Army, 205–206
Cobra II, Operation, 134, 135, 142
Combatant Status Review Board (CSRB), 78
Combined and Joint Task Force 7 (CJTF-7), 138

Combined Forces Command Afghanistan, 62
Combined Joint Task Force–Horn of Africa, 62
Combined Task Force 150 (CTF-150), 141
Combined Task Force 158 (CTF-158), 141
Commanders, Multi-National Force–Iraq (or United States Forces–Iraq), **40–47**
Austin, Lloyd J., III, 46–47
Casey, George William, Jr., 42–44, 53, 55, 58
Odierno, Raymond T., 44–46, 56, 58, 183, 184
Petraeus, David Howell, 44, 45, 46, 58, 59, 150, 152
Sanchez, Ricardo S., 40–42, 43, 58, 74
Commanders, The (Woodward), 264
Commanders, U.S. Central Command (CENTCOM), **47–58**
Abizaid, John, 50–51, 52
Allen, John R., 47, 56
Dempsey, Martin, 53–54, 60
Fallon, William J., 51–53, 213
Franks, Tommy, 48–50, 91, 118, 133, 139, 142
Mattis, James, 15, 56–58, 169, 171
Petraeus, David Howell, 44, 54–56, 57
Commander's Emergency Response Program (CERP), 203
Commando Eagle, Operation, 184, 185
Commands, U.S. and Coalition Military, **58–62**
Joint Improvised Explosive Device Defeat Organization (JIEDDO), 58
Multi-National Force–Iraq (MNF-I), 58–60
Multi-National Security Transition Command–Iraq (MNSTC-I), 60–61
U.S. Central Command (CENTCOM), 61–62
Committee for Collective Action, 188
Concerned Local Citizens, 151

Contractors, **62–72**
   Blackwater USA, 62, 64–68, 71, 85
   Halliburton, 36–37, 68–70
   private security firms, 70–72
Conway, James, 144, 169, 171
Corruption, xvi, 8, 69, 121, 126, 130, 190, 192, 194, 201, 204, 280, 290
Cortez, Paul, 17
Counterinsurgency, doctrine of, 79–82
Counterinsurgency field manual, 81, 150, 290–292
Counterrevolutionary warfare, 79
Crimea, 178
Crimes against humanity, 9, 100
Crocker, Ryan Clark, 5–6
   testimony to Congress, 292–294
Cultural liberties, 284–289
Czech Republic, 59, 140

Damin, Abd al-Rahman al-, 19
Darby, Joseph, 74
Dawa Party. *See* Islamic Dawa Party (Hizb al-Da'wa al-Islamiyya)
Dayton Peace Accords, 6
De La Cruz, Sanick, 14
Death squads, 124
De-Baathification, 20, 39, 92, 201, 278–279. *See also* Baath Party
Deepwater Horizon oil spill, 69
Deliberate Force, Operation, 52
Democracy, xxiii, xxiv, xxvi, 7, 8, 9, 28, 31, 134, 230, 242, 261, 273, 276, 290
Democratic Patriotic Alliance of Kurdistan, 190
Dempsey, Martin, 53–54, 60
Denmark, 59, 140, 141
Department of Homeland Security, 27, 94
Desert Crossing, Operation, 133
Desert Fox, Operation, 122
Desert Shield, Operation, 36, 45, 52, 53, 61, 70
Desert Storm, Operation, xiii, 36, 45, 50, 52, 53, 57, 62, 70, 79, 91, 113, 117–118, 120, 189, 261, 263. *See also* Persian Gulf War
Desert Strike, Operation, 122
Detention Operations, Coalition, **73–79**
   Abu Ghraib Prison, 12, 41, 43, 73–75, 112, 157
   Camp Bucca, 75–76
   Guantánamo Bay Detention Camp, 28, 76–79, 95, 259
Did You Know (U.S. Army video), xxvii
Diyala Operations Center, 11
Doctrine, Counterinsurgency, **79–82**
Doctrine, Insurgency, **82–83**
Dominican Republic, 59, 140
"Don't Ask, Don't Tell" policy, 215, 218
Dora Farms Strike, xiv, 143
Dresser Industries, 69
Drone strikes, 95. *See also* Unmanned aerial vehicles (UAVs)
Druze Muslims, 226
Dubik, James, 60
Duri, Izzat Ibrahim al-, 107

Eagleburger, Lawrence, 131
Economic rights, 284–289
Education, 20, 243
Egypt
   and the Arab Spring, 8, 223
   fedayeen in, 106
   invasion of Israel by, 116
   Islamic Jihad in, 232
   use of chemical weapons by, 251–252
   and the Yom Kippur War, xxi
Egyptian Revolution, 8
Ehime Maru (Japanese fishing training ship), 52
El Abidine Ben Ali, Zine, 8
El Salvador, 59, 140
Emergency Plan for AIDS Relief, 29
Emergency Supplemental Appropriations Act for Defense, 38
Enduring Freedom, Operation, 31, 33, 49, 57, 62, 181, 210, 222, 253, 262

Enduring Freedom–Afghanistan, Operation (OEF-A), 141
Enduring Freedom–Horn of Africa, Operation (OEF-HOA), 141
Energy Task Force, 181
Enforcing the Law, Operation, 45
Estonia, 59, 140
Ethnic cleansing, 106, 125, 283. *See also* Genocide
European Command (EUCOM), 62
European Union, 28
Ewers, John, 15
Executions, 73, 74, 105, 107, 154, 156, 188, 199
Explosive Ordnance Disposal divers, 141
Extraordinary rendition, 77

Fadhila (Islamic Virtue) Party, 109, 194
Faisal II, 116
Falconer, Operation, 143
Fallon, William Joseph "Fox," 51–53, 213
Fallujah, 154
  as AQI stronghold, 157
  and Operation Alljah, 184, 185
  and Operation Fardh al-Quanoon, 185
Fallujah, First Battle of, 57, 65, **85–86**
Fallujah, Second Battle of, 57, **86–89**, 165
Fallujah Brigade, 86, 87
Fardh al-Qanoon (Baghdad Security Plan), 10, 45, 183, 184, 185
Fasting, 226, 233–234
Fatima (daughter of the Prophet), 224, 226
Faylaq Badr. *See* Badr Organization
Fedayeen Saddam, 100, 101, 103, 106–107, 144, 170
Federal Bureau of Investigation (FBI), 94, 100
Felt, Marc, 264
Ferriter, Michael, 60
Fieth, Douglas, 39
Fiji, 140
Final Days, The (Woodward and Bernstein), 264
Five Pillars, 225, 233–234

Fivers, 224
Foley, James, 155
Foley, Lawrence, 267
Folsom, Steve, 15
Force Protection Buffalo, 255
Force Protection Cougar, 255
Ford, Gerald, 36
Foreign Assistance Act, 242
Fourteen Infallibles, 226
France, 141, 239–240
Franks, Tommy, 48–50, 91, 118, 133, 139, 142
Freedom of press, 288
Freedom of religion, 288–289
Fukuyama, Francis, xxiii

Garner, Jay Montgomery, 24, 38, **91–92**, 203, 278
Gates, Robert Michael, 93, 177, 209, 211–214
  education and experience, 211–212
  as head of CIA, 212
  in public service, 212
  as secretary of defense, 212–213
Gaylani, Rashid Ali al-, 115
Gender equality, 20
General Association of Iraqi Women, 20
General Security Directorate, 199
Geneva Conventions, 77, 111
Genocide, 12, 100, 201. *See also* Ethnic cleansing
Georgia, 59, 139
Germany, 141
Ghani, Ashraf, 178
Ghost detainees, 78
Gibbs, Robert, 95
Glaspie, April, xxii
Global War on Terrorism, 2, 13, 27, 37, 51, 62, 73, 76, 77, **92–96**, 217, 265, 277
  role of oil in, 180–181
  Rumsfeld's role in, 210
  use of coercive interrogation techniques by, 111
  and the use of UAVs, 257

Golden Mosque. *See* Al-Askari Mosque (Golden Mosque) bombing
Golden Square, 115
Gore, Al, xxiii, 25
Graner, Charles, 74
Great Britain
  as member of coalition, 139, 142, 275
  and the multi-national command, 59
  Operation Desert Fox, 122
  Operation Iraqi Freedom casualties, 33–35
  participation in Iraq War, xiii, xiv
  support for invasion of Iraq, 239–240
  terrorist acts in, 94
Greater Occultation, 225
Green, Steven, 17
Greeneville (U.S. submarine), 52
Grenada, 50
Guantánamo Bay Detention Camp, 28, 76–79, 95, 259
Guantánamo Review Task Force, 78
Guerrilla insurgency attacks, 79
Gulf Region Division, 59

Haas, 206
Hadith, 224, 228, 233, 235, 236
Haditha Incident, 12–16
Hadley, Stephen, 131, 220
Haines, David, 155
Hairi, Ayatollah Kadhim, 108–109
Haiti, 80
Hajj (pilgrimage), 226, 234
Hakim, Abd al-Aziz al-, 104, 105, 106, 110, 194
Hakim, Ammar al-, 104, 194
Hakim, Muhammad Baqir al- (Ayatollah), 104, 186, 193
Hakim, Muhammad Mahdi al-, 186
Hakim, Muhsin al- (Grand Ayatollah), 104, 187, 194
Halliburton, Erle P., 68
Halliburton (Company), 36–37, 68–70
Hama massacre, 21
Hamas, 28, 193, 232

Hamilton, Lee, 130, 131, 212
Hanafi school of law, 235–236
Hanbali school of law, 235, 236
Hariri, Rafik al-, 4
Harvey, Francis J., 212
Hasan (son of the Prophet), 224, 225
Hassani, Mahmoud Sarkhi al-, 109
Heard, Dustin L., 67
Hellfire missiles, 201, 257
Helmick, Frank, 60
Hester, Leigh Ann, 263
Hezbollah, 232, 258
Hill, Christopher R., 6–7
Hill, Lori, 263
Holbrooke, Richard, 6
Hollande, François, 155
Homeland Security Advisory Council, 24
Honduras, 59, 140
Horn of Africa, 94
Human rights, 112
Human Rights Watch, 190
Humanitarian aid, 59, 86, 129–130, 193, 242
Humvees, 254, 255
Hungary, 59, 140
Hurricane Katrina, 65
Husayn (son of the Prophet), 224–225, 227
Husayn ibn Ali (grandson of the Prophet), 224–225
Hussein, Qusay, 41, **97–98**, 100, 106
Hussein, Saddam, **98–100**
  assassinations ordered by, 205
  and the Baath Party, 20, 39, 92, 198–199
  background, 98
  Bush's ultimatum to, xiv, 97, 101, 143
  capture of, 41, 45, 100, 101, 124
  and the Dawa Party, 187, 188, 193, 200
  decapitation strike against, xiv, 49, 135, 136, 143
  defense of Baghdad, 103
  evasion of weapons inspections by, xiii, 27, 239
  execution of, 100, 101, 124
  executions ordered by, 73, 98, 187, 188

and the Fedayeen Saddam, 103
George H. W. Bush's decision not to
 remove, 62, 100, 120, 217
in hiding, xv, 123
intent to remove, xxiv
and the invasion of Kuwait, xxii, 20,
 61–62, 99–100, 117–118, 120, 180, 261
and Iraqi aircraft, 114
and the Iraqi Baath Party, 20
Israeli distrust of, xxii
overthrow of, 9, 20, 27, 62, 94, 118, 119,
 123, 134, 193, 211, 218, 265
persecution of Kurds by, 120–121, 122,
 161, 189, 191
possession of WMDs by, xxi, xxiii, xxiv,
 27, 31, 100, 122, 181, 217, 239–241,
 271–272
as president of Iraq, 98–99, 119
Reagan's rapprochement with, xxii
removal of statue of, 135, 145, 159
troops loyal to, 106
UN instruction to disarm, xiii, 271
U.S. decision to remove, xxii–xxiii, xxiv,
 xxv, xxvi, 5
use of chemical weapons by, 117, 161,
 251
use of poison gas against Kurds, xxii
and the war with Iran, 20, 99, 117
Hussein, Uday, 41, **100–101**, 106
Hydraulic fracking, 182

Iceland, 60, 140
Ijtihad, 228, 229, 236
Imam Ali Mosque (Najaf), 205–206
Imamate, 225, 227
Improvised explosive devices (IEDs), 10,
 13, 14, 58, 85–86, 123, 146, 185,
 249–250
 vehicles protected against, 253–256
Independent inquiry committee (IIC), 130
India, 181
Indonesia, 94
Infant mortality, 129
Inherent Resolve, Operation, 154

Insurgency and opposition, **103–111**, 126,
 149, 150, 173, 211
 Badr Organization, 104–106
 Battle of Mosul, 165
 Fedayeen, 100, 101, 103, 106–107, 144,
  170
 and the International Atomic Energy
  Agency (IAEA), 252, 271
 Islamist, 31
 Mahdi Army, 104, 107–111, 183, 184,
  185, 205, 207–208, 230
 Shiite, xvi, xxv, 107, 115
 Sunni, xvi, xviii
International Committee of the Red
 Cross, 77
International Coordination Council, 38
Interrogation, coercive (torture), **111–113**,
 215
Iqbal, Shahid, 141
Iran
 and the Arab Spring, 9
 as enhanced threat, xxv
 fedayeen in, 106
 Iraq's invasion of, 114, 117
 Kurds in, 160, 161
 nuclear weapons in, 253
 opposition to ISIS, 155
 rulers of, 98
 support for Kurds by, 189
 UN sanctions against, 101
 use of UAVs by, 258
Iran Contra Affair, 212
Iran hostage crisis, xxii
Iranian Revolution, 98
Iranian Revolutionary Guard Corps
 (IRGC), 104–105, 189–190
Iran-Iraq War, 73, 99, 105, 117, 119, 161,
 191
 role of oil in, 180
 use of chemical weapons, 251
Iraq
 and the Arab Spring, 9
 as British mandate, 115
 changes to currency, 39

Iraq (*cont.*)
 civil war in, xvi, xvii, 110, 218
 education in, 20, 243
 elections in, 124
 infrastructure in, 129, 152, 203–204, 242–243
 internal conflict in, xxvi
 invasion of Iran by, 20, 114, 117
 invasion of Israel by, 116
 invasion of Kuwait by, xxii, 20, 36, 99–100, 114, 117, 120, 180
 and the Islamic World, 282
 Kurds in, 160, 161
 occupation of, xv, xvi, 50, 91, 103–104, 126, 130, 211
 official languages of, 282–283
 oil production in, 181, 204
 oil reserves in, xxii
 and regional security, xxv–xxvi
 removal of U.S. troops from, 125–126
 U.S. foreign aid to, 241–243
 U.S. invasion of, 20, 49, 60, 80, 100, 122–123, 181, 199, 240, 267
 See also Al Qaeda in Iraq (AQI); Baghdad; Iraq War; Reconstruction; Sectarian violence
Iraq, Air Force, **113–114**
Iraq, Army, xiv, **114–119**
 2nd Brigade, 10
 5th Division, 10
 and the Battle of Sadr City, 207
 desertion of Kurds from, 189–190
 disbanding of, xvi, 24, 39, 51, 61, 123, 211, 279–281
 surrender by troops, xv
Iraq, History of (1990–present), **119–127**
Iraq, Navy, **127–128**
Iraq, Sanctions on, **128–130**
Iraq Coalition Casualty Count, xxviii, 34–35
Iraq Construction and Management Office, 203
Iraq Family Health Survey (IFHS) Study Group, 34
Iraq Liberation Act, 190, 192
Iraq Memory Foundation, 20
Iraq Relief and Reconstruction Fund (IRRF), 203
Iraq Study Group, **130–133**, 214, 215
Iraq War
 Bush Doctrine as justification for, 31
 Bush's involvement with, 28–29
 causes of, xxi–xxiv
 consequences of, xxv–xxix
 H. Clinton's criticism of, 222
 major battles, 146–149
 Obama's criticism of, 175–176
 overview of, xiii–xviii
 role of oil in, 180
 start of the war, xiv–xv
 as two separate wars, xvi
 use of coercive interrogation techniques in, 112
 See also Casualties, Operation Iraqi Freedom
Iraqi Accord Front, 152
Iraqi Communist Party, 19, 187, 190
Iraqi Constitution, 124, 194–195, 200
 civil and political rights, 284–286
 economic, social, and cultural liberties, 284–289
 excerpt: preamble and basic rights, 281–289
 fundamental principles, 282–284
 liberties, 288–289
 preamble, 281–282
 social and cultural liberties, 286–288
Iraqi Council of Representatives, 124
Iraqi Freedom, Operation (OIF), xv, xvi, xxiv, xxvi, xxvii, xxix, 40–41, 46, 49, 55, 57, 62, 113, 115, 118, 129, **133–153**, 239, 253, 262, 275
 air campaign (March 20–April 7, 2003), 135–138
 casualties, 33–35
 coalition ground forces, 138–140
 coalition naval forces, 140–141
 ground campaign (March 20–May 1, 2003), 142–146

major battles, 146–149
planning for, 133–135
Rice's support for, 220
the Surge and the Awakening, 149–153
Iraqi Governing Council (IGC), 38–39, 194, 195, 199
Iraqi Interim Governing Council, 24
Iraqi Interim Government, 39, 87, 124, 200
Iraqi Kurdistan Front (IKF), 189, 192
Iraqi Liberation, Operation, 143. *See also* Iraqi Freedom, Operation
Iraqi National Accord (INA), 198–199
Iraqi National Assembly, 124, 199, 200
Iraqi National Congress, 188, 196, 197
Iraqi National Movement, 201
Iraqi Security Forces (ISF), 43, 51, 86, 106, 166, 172–173, 204, 293
and Operation Phantom Strike, 183
and Operation Phantom Thunder, 184
Iraqi Special Tribunal, 100, 124
Iraqi Survey Group, 240
Iraqi Transitional Government, 124
ISIS. *See* Islamic State of Iraq and al-Sham (ISIS); Islamic State of Iraq and Syria (ISIS)
Islam, as official religion of Iraq, 282. *See also* Alawite Muslims; Druze Muslims; Shia Islam; Sunni Islam
Islamic Dawa Party (Hizb al-Da'wa al-Islamiyya), 104, 106, 124, 126, 186–189, 193, 195–196, 200
Islamic extremists, 106, 162
Islamic Jihad, 232
Islamic Revolution (Iran), 61
Islamic State, 21, 156. *See also* Islamic State of Iraq and al-Sham (ISIS); Islamic State of Iraq and Syria (ISIS)
defeat of, xxvi
Islamic State in Iraq, 156. *See also* Islamic State of Iraq and al-Sham (ISIS); Islamic State of Iraq and Syria (ISIS)
Islamic State of Iraq and al-Sham (ISIS), xxv, xxviii–xxix, 126, **153–158**, 156. *See also* Al Qaeda in Iraq (AQI)

Al Qaeda in Iraq, 156–158
in Syria, 153–154
Islamic State of Iraq and Syria (ISIS), xv, xviii, xxvii, 6, 21, 22, 32, 75, 82, 106, 110, 119, 162, 173, 201
executions staged by, 154–155
in Mosul, 166
Sistani's opposition to, 230
U.S. campaign against, 178–179
Islamic State of Iraq and the Levant. *See* Islamic State of Iraq and al-Sham (ISIS)
Islamic State of Iraq (ISI), 21–22, 153
Islamist insurgency, 31
Ismailiyya (Seveners), 224, 226
Isolationism, xxvii
Israel, 91, 115–116, 206, 252
Arab-Israeli conflict, 28
and the Six-Day War, 116
use of UAVs by, 257
and the Yom Kippur War, xxi, 116
Israeli War of Independence, 116
Italy, 59, 139, 141
Ithna Ashariyya, 224

Jaafari, Ibrahim al-, xv, 124, 195–196, 197, 199, 200
Jabhat al-Nusra, 22
Jabr, Bayan, 106
Jafariyya (Twelvers), 224, 225
Jajjo, Kamil Hanna, 100
Jama'at al-Tawhid wa-I Jihad, 156
Jamaat Islamiya, 232
Jamaat Jaysh Ahl a-Sunnah wa-i-Jamaah (JJASJ), 21
Janabi, Abir Qasim Hamza al-, 16
Japan, 59, 140
Jaysh al-Mahdi militias. *See* Mahdi Army
Jeffrey, James F., 7
Jihad, 82–83, 170, 190, 226, 232, 236
Jihadist groups, 156–157
Joint Action Committee, 200
Joint Base Balad, 59

Joint Comprehensive Plan of Action, xxvi, 253
Joint Guardian, Operation, 50
Joint Improvised Explosive Device Defeat Organization (JIEDDO), 58
Joint Surveillance and Target Reader System (JSTARS) aircraft, 137
Joint Task Force Lebanon, 62
Jordan, 9, 19
Jordan, Vernon, 131

Kalari, Dilshad (Dilshad Garmyani), 190
Kallop, William, 14, 15
Kamal, Hussein, 240
Karbala, Battle of, 55, 159
Karbala, First Battle of, **159–160**, 224–225, 227
Karzai, Hamid, 4, 80, 178
Kazakhstan, 60, 140
KBR (Kellogg, Brown, and Root), 68
Keating, Timothy, 140
Kerry, John F., 178, 223
Khalf al-Mutayibin group, 10
Khalilzad, Zalmay Mamozy, 3–5
Khamenei, Ali Husayni (Ayatollah), 227
Khawr al Amlayah oil terminal, 141
Khoi, Abu al-Qasim al- (Grand Ayatollah), 109
Khoi, Hujjat al-Islam Abd al-Majid al-, 109
Khomeini, Ruhollah (Grand Ayatollah), 98, 105, 186, 227, 228
Khor Abd Allah waterway, 141
Khudayri, Agd al-Khaliq al-, 19
Kiley, Kevin C., 212
Kingston, Robert C., 61
Knights of Hope, 194
Koran, 233, 234, 235
Kosovo, 80
Krekar, Mullah, 156, 246
Kurdish forces, 144, 145. *See also* Peshmerga fighters
Kurdish rebellion, 107, 115, 116–117, 120–121, 189, 190, 192
Kurdish Regional Government, 126, 245, 246
Kurdistan, 160, 161
Kurdistan Brigades, 190
Kurdistan Democratic Party (KDP), 162, 189–191, 245, 246
Kurdistan Regional Government (KRG), 189, 190, 192
Kurdistan Workers' Party, 66, 161
Kurds, 81, 100, 122, **160–163**, 166, 245
Kuwait
 Iraq's invasion of, xxii, 20, 36, 99–100, 114, 117, 120, 180
 support for Operation Iraqi Freedom, 142

Lange, Heinrich, 141
Latvia, 59, 140
Law and Order, Operation, 184
Lebanon, 19, 21, 116
Lehr, John, 10
Leon & Sylvia Panetta Institute for Public Policy, 214
Lesser Occultation, 225, 227
Levin, Carl, 201
Libby, I. Lewis "Scooter," 37
Liberty, Evan S., 67
Libya, 251–252
 and the Arab Spring, 8, 223
Libyan Civil War, 32, 223
Literacy, 20
Lithuania, 59, 140
Long War, 93, 95
Looting, xv, 24, 27–28, 123, 145, 211, 274
Lynch, Jessica, 170, 172

Macedonia, 59, 140
MacFarland, Sean, 151
Maestro (Woodward), 264
Mahdi, Muhammad al-, 104, 225
Mahdi Army, 104, 107–111, 183, 184, 185, 205, 230
 and the Battle of Sadr City, 207–208
 See also Sadr Movement (Tayyar al-Sadr)

Mahmudiyah Incident, 16–17
Majid, Al Hassan al-, 170
Maliki, Nuri (Nouri) al-, xv, xviii, xxv, xxvi, 20, 81, 110, 124, 126, 152, 153, 154, 178, 188, 190, 196, 199–202
   joint statement with Bush, 289–290
   and the Mahdi Army, 207, 208
   and Muqtada al-Sadr, 206
Maliki school of law, 236
Management of Savagery: The Most Critical Stage through Which the Islamic Nation Will Pass (Abu Bakr Naji), 82
Maqdisi, Abu Muhammad al- (Muhammad Tahir al-Barqawi), 156
Marne Torch, Operation, 184
Marine Force Reconnaissance divers, 141
Marine Mammals System, 141
Marshall Plan, 242
Masri, Abu Abd al-Rahman al-, 185
Masri, Abu Ayyub al-, 183
Mattis, James, 15, 56–58, 169, 171
Mauritania, 19
Mawardi, Abu al-Hasan Ali Ibn Muhammad Ibn Habib al-, 232
Mazars, Jacques, 141
McCain, John S., 176–177, 218
McChrystal, Stanley A., 56, 57
McKiernan, David, 139
McMaster, H. R., 151
Meese, Edwin, III, 130
Meier, Golda, xxi
Memorandum of Understanding (MOU), 121, 129
Mine-resistant ambush protected (MRAP) vehicles, 253–256
Minesweepers, 141
Moldova, 60, 140
Mongolia, 59, 140
Moreno, Juan, 141
Morocco, 9
Mosul, Battle of, **165–167**
Mubarak, Hosni, 8
Muhammad (Prophet), 224, 234

Muhammad, Sayyid Ali ("The Bab"), 227
Muhammad Abduh, 236
Mujahideen Shura Council (MSC), 21, 153
Mujtahid, 228
Mullen, Michael, 53
Multi-National Division–Baghdad, 59
Multi-National Division–Center, 59
Multi-National Division–North, 59
Multi-National Division–Southeast, 59
Multi-National Division–West, 59
Multi-National Force–Iraq (MNF-I), xvii, 10, 58–60, 62, 140, 150, 183, 184
   commanders, 40–47
Multi-National Force–Iraqi Army, 183
Multi-National Security Transition Command–Iraq (MNSTC-I), 58, 59, 60–61, 62, 173
Murtha, John, 13, 51
Muslim Brotherhood, 193, 232
Mutahari, Murtaza, 228

Najaf, Battle of, 55
Naji, Abu Bakr, 82
Nasiriyah, Battle of, **169–172**
National Congress Coalition, 197
National Reform Trend, 196
National Security Agency (NSA), 96
National Sovereignty Committee, 200
Natonski, Richard, 169
Naval fleet, 127–128
Navistar MaxxPro, 255
Navy SEALs, 140, 141, 172, 178, 215
Negroponte, John Dimitri, 2–3, 24, 43
Neoconservatism, xxiii, 217
Nepotism, 190, 192, 224
Netherlands, 59, 139, 141
New Dawn, Operation, 46, **172–173**
New Zealand, 59, 94, 140, 141
Nicaragua, 59, 140
Nigeria, 181
Nixon, Richard M., 210, 221, 264
Nixon administration, 214
No Child Left Behind Act (U.S.), 26

No-fly zones
  in Iraq, xxii, xxiii, 62, 113, 121, 136, 162, 190, 262
  in Libya, 8
North Atlantic Treaty Organization (NATO), xxiii, 93–94
North Atlantic Treaty Organization (NATO) Training Mission–Iraq, 59
Northern Watch, Operation, 136
Norway, 59, 140
Nuclear Non-Proliferation Treaty, 252
Nuclear weapons
  and the Cold War, 250–251
  in Iran, xxvi, 4, 52, 178, 212, 213, 215, 223, 253
  in Iraq, xiv, xxii, xxiii, xxiv, 97, 117, 197, 218, 239, 270, 271, 272, 284
  in Israel, xxi, 252
  in North Korea, 6
  in Russia, 175
  use by terrorist groups, 251

Obama, Barack Hussein, II, xvii, 6, 12, 30, 54, 56, 77, 78, 112, **175–180**, 223
  address at the end of combat operations in Iraq, 302–305
  and the Bush Doctrine, 32
  combating ISIS, 154
  election of, 177, 178, 222
  family and education, 175
  first term as president, 177–178
  and the Global War on Terrorism, 95
  political career, 175–177
  Powell's support for, 218
  second term as president, 178–179
  speech at Camp Lejeune, 300–302
  use of UAVs by, 257–258
Obama administration, xviii, 12, 22, 31–32
  combating ISIS, 154
  criticism of Maliki government, 202
  Gates as secretary of defense, 213
  sale of missiles to Iraq, 201
Obamacare, 177, 178, 179
O'Connor, Sandra Day, 131

Odierno, Raymond T., 44–46, 56, 58, 183, 184
Office for Reconstruction and Humanitarian Assistance (ORHA), 38, 91, 203, 278
Oil, **180–182**
Oil-for-Food Programme, 129–130, 180
Organization of Economic Cooperation and Development (OECD), Oil Committee, 180
Organization of Petroleum Exporting Countries (OPEC), 180, 182
Ort, Hank, 141
Osiraq nuclear reactor, 117
Ottoman Empire, 115, 161, 232
Overseas contingency operations, 95

Pace, Peter, 212
Pahlavi, Mohammad Reza Shah, 98, 106, 116–117, 187, 228
Pakistan, 94, 141
Palestine, 19, 21, 106
Palestinian Arab Liberation Army, 116
Palestinian National Authority, 28
Panetta, Leon Edward, 131, 209, 213, 214–216
  under Clinton, 214
  education and experience, 214
  as head of CIA, 215
  under Obama, 215
  as secretary of defense, 215–216
Patient Protection and Affordable Care Act, 177. *See also* Obamacare
Patriot Act, 222
Patriot antimissile system, 91, 137
Patriotic Union of Kurdistan (PUK), 162, 189–193, 245
People's Army of Vietnam, 79
Perkins, David, 145
Perry, William J., 131
Persian Gulf crisis, 50
Persian Gulf War, xiii, xv, xxii–xxiii, 27, 33, 36, 48, 74, 79, 91, 117–118, 121, 261
  role of oil in, 180

use of UAVs in, 257
See also Desert Shield, Operation; Desert Storm, Operation
Peshmerga fighters, 162, 190, 192, 246
 in Operation Viking Hammer, 245–248
Petra Bank, 196
Petraeus, David Howell
 commanding CENTCOM, 44, 54–56, 57
 commanding MNF-I, 44, 45, 46, 58, 59, 150, 152
 commanding MNSTC-I, 40, 43, 60, 173
 counterinsurgency strategy, 80–81, 183, 291
 with the 101st Airborne Division, 165
 and Operation Phantom Thunder, 184
 testimony to Congress, 5–6, 292–294
Phantom Fury, Operation, 57, 86, 87
Phantom Strike, Operation, **183–184**
Phantom Thunder, Operation, 183, **184–186**
Philippines, 60, 94, 140, 261
Piestewa, Lori, 170
Pilgrimage, 226, 234
Piracy, 141
Poland, xiv, 59, 139, 142, 275
Political parties
 Kurdistan Democratic Party, 162, 189–191
 Patriotic Union of Kurdistan (PUK), 162, 189–193
 Syrian Socialist National Party, 19
Political parties, Iraq, **186–194**
 Baath Party, 19–21, 186
 Fadhila (Islamic Virtue) Party, 109, 194
 Iraqi Communist Party, 19, 187, 190
 Islamic Dawa Party (Hizb al-Da'wa al-Islamiyya), 124, 126, 186–189
 Supreme Iraqi Islamic Council, 193–194
Political rights, 284–286
Portugal, 59, 140
Potts, Duncan, 141
Powell, Colin Luther, xiv, 5, 28–29, 36, 123, 134, 176, 211, 216–218, 219, 251, 267
 family and education, 216–217
 under George H. W. Bush, 217

 under George W. Bush, 217
 military experience, 217
 Operation Desert Storm, 217
 political experience, 217
 under Reagan, 217
 and the second invasion of Iraq, 218
Powell Doctrine, 217, 218
Prayer, 226, 227, 233–234
Precision-guided (smart) bombs, xiv, 137, 143
Presidential Decision Directive, 99–13, 190
Presidential Study Directive on Mass Atrocities (PSD-10), 12
Prime Minister, Iraq (Selected), **194–202**
 Allawi, Ayad, 87, 124, 198–199, 206
 Chalabi, Ahmed Abd al-Hadi, 196–198
 Jaafari, Ibrahim al-, xv, 124, 195–196, 197, 199, 200
 Maliki, Nuri al-, 199–202 (*see also* Maliki, Nuri (Nouri) al-)
Prince, Eric, 64, 65, 66, 67
Prisoners of war, 74, 75, 105
Private security firms, 70–72
 British firms, 71
 U.S. firms, 70–71
Project for the New American Century, xxiii, 4
Provide Comfort, Operation, 50, 91, 190
Provincial Reconstruction Teams, 80

Qadaffi (Qaddafi), Muammar, 8, 223
Qadiri Sufi order, 191
Qasim, Abd al-Karim, 20, 98, 116, 187, 189, 198
Qasim Amin, 236
Qatar, 142

Ramadi, 154
Rashid Rida, 236
Reagan, Ronald, 217, 260, 261, 276
Reagan administration, xxii, 2, 61, 210, 212
Reconstruction, xv, xxviii, 5, 24, 38, 59, 80, 119–120, 123, 152, 157, **203–204**, 218, 242. *See also* U.S. Agency for International Development, Iraq

Reconstruction of Iraq and Afghanistan, 38
Republican Guard, 97, 105, 117, 134, 138, 145, 159, 169, 190
Rice, Condoleezza, 29, 216, 217, 219–220
  academic experience of, 219
  education and experience, 219
  as national security advisor, 219
  as secretary of state, 220
Ridgeway, Jeremy, 67
Rikabi, Fuad al-, 19
Rishawi, Abd al-Sattar Buzaigh al-, 151
Rix, Tony, 141
Riza, Shaha Ali, 262
Road Map to Peace, 28
Robb, Charles, 131
Romania, 59, 140
Romney, Mitt, 178
Root, Dan, 68
Royal Air Force, 135, 136, 138
Royal Australian Air Force, 135, 138
Royal Navy, 141
Rumsfeld, Donald, xiv, xxiii, 28, 42, 43, 51, 74, 92, 103, 132, 133–134, 149, 194, 208, 209–211, 217, 220
  directing Operation Iraqi Freedom, 211
  education and political experience, 209–210
  work in the private sector, 210
Russia, 213
  nuclear weapons in, 175
  opposition to invasion of Iraq, 239–240
  opposition to Iran, xxvi
  and the Road Map to Peace, 28
  seizure of Crimea, 178
  use of UAVs by, 258
  See also U.S.S.R.
Russo-Georgian War, 139

Saddam Fedayeen. *See* Fedayeen Saddam
Sadr, Amina bint Haydar al- (Bint al-Huda), 104, 105, 187
Sadr, Ayatollah Muhammad Sadiq al-, 107–108
Sadr, Muammal al-, 107
Sadr, Muhammad Baqir al- (Ayatollah), 104, 105, 107, 186–188
Sadr, Muhammad Saliq al-, 205
Sadr, Muqtada al-, 106, 107–110, 124, 199, **205–207**, 208, 230
Sadr, Musa al-, 107, 226
Sadr, Mustafa al-, 107
Sadr City, Battle of, **207–208**
Sadr Movement (Tayyar al-Sadr), 106, 107. *See also* Mahdi Army
Sadriyuns, 207
Said, Nuri al-, 116
Salafi jihadists, 82–83, 157, 236–237
Salafism, 236
Salah al-Din al-Ayyubi (Saladin), 160
Salih, Ali Abdallah, 8–9
Sanchez, Ricardo S., 40–42, 43, 58, 74
Sandstorms, 137, 144, 171, 208, 255
Saudi Arabia, xxvi, 61–62, 142, 180
Schwarzkopf, H. Norman, 61
Secret Man (Woodward and Bernstein), 264
Secretary of defense, U.S., **208–216**. *See also* Gates, Robert Michael; Panetta, Leon Edward; Rumsfeld, Donald
Secretary of state, U.S., **216–223**. *See also* Clinton, Hillary Rodham; Powell, Colin Luther; Rice, Condoleezza
Sectarian violence
  in Bahrain, 9
  civilian casualties from, 34, 132
  increase in, xvii, 1, 4, 126, 132, 188, 211, 229, 230, 279
  Kurdish involvement in, 146
  operations aimed at reducing, 124, 183, 193
  Shiite involvement, xvi, 146
  Sunni involvement, xvi, 146
Sectarianism, xxix, 282
September 11, 2001, attacks, xiii, xxi, 26, 28, 30, 37, 42–43, 49, 62, 80, 93, 122, 133, 180, 220, 222, 249, 252
Shadow (Woodward), 264
Shafi school of law, 236

Shah of Iran, xxi. *See also* Pahlavi, Mohammad Reza Shah
Shahrastani, 229
Sharia (Islamic law), 232, 235
Shariati, Ali, 228
Sharon, Ariel, 28
Sharrat, Justin, 14
Shatt al-Arab, 144
Shaykhi Shia, 227
Shaykhiyya Muslims, 226
Shia Islam, 81, 99, 100, 103, 104, 105, 106, 107, 108, 109, 115, 120, 124, 149, 157, **223–229**
  approach to jurisprudence, 228, 232–233
  in Bahrain, 9
  beliefs shared with Sunni Islam, 234–235
  centers of education, 227
  conflict with Sunni Islam, 1, 228–229
  considered apostasy by Salafis, 237
  development of, 223–224
  differences from Sunni Islam, 227, 228, 231–232, 232–233
  in Karbala, 159
  in Nasiriyah, 169
  subsects of, 226
  tenets of, 226
  See also Islamic Dawa Party (Hizb al-Da'wa al-Islamiyya); Sadr, Muqtada al-; Supreme Islamic Iraqi Council (SIIC)
Shiite insurgents, xvi, xxv, 107, 115
Shinseki, Eric, xiv
Shock-and-awe campaign, 49, 136, 143
Simpson, Alan K., 131
Singapore, 59, 140
Sistani, Sayyid Ali Husayn al- (Grand Ayatollah), 107, 108, 109, 125, 188, 196, 205, 206, 227, **229–231**
Six-Day War, 116
Slatten, Nicholas A., 67
Slough, Paul A., 67
Slovakia, 59, 140
Smart bombs, xiv, 143

Snowden, Edward, 96, 259
Social justice, 234
Social rights, 284–289
Somalia, 79, 257
Sons of Iraq, 151
Sorush, Abd al-Karim, 227
South Korea, 59, 139
Southern Watch, Operation, 136
Spain, 59, 94, 139, 203, 239–240
Special Inspector General for Iraq Reconstruction (SIGIR), 203
Spielman, Jesse, 17
State Department, use of private security firms by, 70
State Law of Coalition, 188, 201
Status of Forces Agreement (SOFA), 294
Stealth bombers, xiv
Stryker Brigade Combat Teams, xxvii
Sudan, 19, 21
Suez Crisis, 116
Sufi Islam, 231
Suicide bombings, 80, 83, 146, 150, 157, 208
Sunni Islam, 43, 81, 82–83, 98, 99, 103, 105, 121, 123–124, 126, 146, 149, 152, 157, 184, **231–237**
  approach to jurisprudence, 228, 232–233, 235–236
  in Bahrain, 9
  beliefs shared with Shia Islam, 234–235
  conflict with Shia Islam, 1, 228–229
  differences from Shia Islam, 227, 228, 231–233
  extremism in, xvii
  grievance over destruction of Fallujah, 89
  and the Kurds, 160
  See also Al Qaeda in Iraq (AQI)
Sunni rebels, xvi, xviii
Sunni Triangle, 45, 85
Supreme Council for Islamic Revolution, 186. *See also* Supreme Islamic Iraqi Council (SIIC)
Supreme Council for the Islamic Revolution in Iraq (SCIRI), 104–105, 106

Supreme Iraqi Islamic Council, 193–194
Supreme Islamic Iraqi Council (SIIC), 104, 110, 186, 188, 208
Suri, Abu Musab al-, 82
Sutherland, David, 10
Syria, 252
   and the Arab Spring, 8, 9, 223
   Baath Party in, 19–21
   invasion of Israel by, 116
   ISIS in, 153
   Kurds in, 160
   and the Yom Kippur War, xxi
   See also Islamic State of Iraq and al-Sham (ISIS); Syrian Civil War
Syrian Civil War, 9, 20, 21, 22, 32, 103, 133, 154, 178, 223
Syrian National Council, 9
Syrian Observatory for Human Rights, 9
Syrian Socialist National Party, 19

Taguba, Antonio, 74
Taji prison, 157
Talabani, Jalal, xv, 162, 189, 190, 191, 245
Taliban, xxiii, 26–27, 29, 62, 80, 94, 133, 176, 178, 210, 270
Tanks, 118–119, 143, 254
Tayyar al-Sadr. *See* Sadr Movement (Tayyar al-Sadr)
Telic, Operation, 143
Terrazas, Miguel, 13
Terrorist acts, 79, 82, 93
   in Africa, 94
   Al-Askari Mosque (Golden Mosque) bombing, 1–2, 110
   by AQI, 157–158
   in Benghazi, Libya, 223
   in Great Britain, 94, 252
   in Indonesia, 94
   by the Iraqi National Accord (INA), 198–199
   by ISIS, 155
   by Jama'at al-Tawhid wa-I Jihad, 156
   in Japan, 251
   in Pakistan, 94
   in the Philippines, 94
   September 11, 2001, attacks, xiii, xxi, 26, 28, 30, 37, 42–43, 49, 62, 80, 93, 122, 133, 180, 220, 222, 249, 252
   in Spain, 94, 252
   in the U.S., 94, 250
   by Zarqawi, 267–268
Thailand, 59, 140
Thunder Run, 145
Tierney, John F., 62
Tikrit, Battle of, xv
Tithing, 226
Tomahawk missiles, xiv, 134, 140
Tonga, 59, 140
Torture, 73–74, 77, 97, 101, 111–113, 124, 198, 215
Tovo, Ken, 246
Townsend, Steven, 10
Transjordan, 116
Triangle of Death, 185
Troop surge
   under George W. Bush, xvii, 1, 10, 11, 29, 43, 46, 55, 59, 125, 133, 149, 157, 183, 184, 206, 213, 222, 265
   under Obama, 31, 176, 177, 178, 213, 223, 265
Trump, Donald J., xxvi, 179
Trump administration, xviii
Tunisia, 8
Tunisian Revolution, 8
Turkey, 134, 139, 141, 142, 245
   Kurds in, 160, 161
   as part of antiterrorist coalition, 94
Twelver Shiism, 224, 225–227, 228

Ukraine, 59, 139, 178
Umar (caliph), 224, 231, 233
Umayyads, 224–225, 231–232
UN International Atomic Energy Agency (IAEA), 252
UN Security Council Resolutions
   Resolution 661, 120
   Resolution 686, 240
   Resolution 687, 128, 239

Resolution 688, 190
Resolution 706, 129
Resolution 712, 129
Resolution 986, 129
Resolution 1441, xiii, 23, 239, 270
Resolution 1483, 38
Resolution 1511, 38
Unemployment, 126, 152
Uniform Code of Military Justice (UCMJ), 71
United Arab Republic (UAR), 19
United Iraqi Alliance (UIA), 105–106, 124, 194, 196
United Islamic Alliance, 200
United Kingdom, 141, 181. *See also* Great Britain
United Nations (UN)
 and the Iran-Iraq War, 99
 opposition to Iraq War, xxiii
 and the Road Map to Peace, 28
 sanctions against Iraq, xiii, 118, 121, 128–130, 180
United Nations (UN) Assistance Mission–Iraq, 59
United Nations Children's Fund (UNICEF), 129
United Nations Convention against Torture, 112
United Nations Monitoring, Verification and Inspection Committee (UNMOVIC), xxiv, 239, 241
United Nations Special Commission (UNSCOM), 239, 241
United Nations Weapons Inspectors, **239–241**, 271
United States
 1992 presidential election, 221
 1996 presidential election, 264
 2000 presidential election, 25, 37
 2004 presidential election, 28, 218, 220
 2008 presidential election, 30, 176–177, 218, 222
 2012 presidential election, 178, 218
 2016 presidential election, 179, 223

atrocities committed by, 12–17, 28
Congressional Resolution Supporting the Use of Force against Iraq, 269–270
current role in Iraq, xviii
defense against terrorism, 270
defense spending by, xxviii
foreign policy in the Middle East, xxi–xxii
gasoline prices in, 181–182
invasion of Afghanistan by, 31, 93, 94, 181
invasion of Iraq by, 60, 80, 100, 122–123, 181, 199, 240, 267
involvement in Iraq's reconstruction, 203–204, 218
and the multi-national command, 59
naval involvement in Operation Iraqi Freedom, 140–141
occupation of Iraq by, 103–104, 126, 130, 211
oil extraction in, 182
oil production in, 182
opposition to Iran, xxvi
policy of containment toward Iraq, xxii–xxiii, xxviii
support for invasion of Iraq, 239–240
use of coercive interrogation techniques by, 29
withdrawal from Iraq, xxv
United States Forces–Iraq (USF-I), 172
Unmanned aerial vehicles (UAVs), 14–15, 137, 207–208, 256–258
U.S. Africa Command, 62
U.S. Agency for International Development, Iraq, **241–243**
U.S. Agency for International Development (USAID), 203, 241–242
U.S. Air Force, 138, 263
U.S. Army, 138
 abuse of prisoners by, 74, 75
 approach to counterinsurgency, 80–81, 183
 and coalition ground forces, 139
 at the Battle of Mosul, 165

U.S. Army (*cont.*)
  and the Battle of Sadr City, 207
  equipment used by, xxvii
  Field Manual 3-24: *Counterinsurgency*, 81, 290–292
  at the First Battle of Karbala, 159–160
  in Iraq, xxvi–xxvii, 144–145
  Mahmudiyah Incident, 16–17
  and Operation Phantom Strike, 183–184
  role of in the 21st century, xxvii–xxviii
  withdrawal from Iraq, xxvii, 30
  women serving in, 263
U.S. Army Field Manual 3-24: *Counterinsurgency*, 81, 290–292
U.S. Army Corps of Engineers, 59
U.S. Army Corps of Engineers Gulf Region Division, 203
U.S. Central Command (CENTCOM), 41, 46–47, 61–62, 133–134, 142
  commanders, 47–58
U.S. Department of Defense, use of private security firms by, 70
U.S. Marine Corps, xxviii, 138, 213
  approach to counterinsurgency, 81
  at the Battle of Nasiriyah, 169–171
  and coalition ground forces, 139
  Haditha Incident, 12–16
  in Iraq, xxvi–xxvii, 144
  at the Second Battle of Fallujah, 88
  use of UAVs by, 257
  women serving in, 263
U.S. Marine Warfighting Publication No. 3-33.5, 81
U.S. military, 294
  departure from Iraq, 125–126, 173, 201, 294–300
  high suicide rate, 35
  troop surge, xvii, 1, 10, 11, 29, 31, 43, 46, 55, 59, 125, 133, 152, 157, 176, 177, 178, 183, 184, 206, 213, 222, 223, 265
  See also U.S. Air Force; U.S. Army; U.S. Marine Corps; U.S. Navy
U.S. Navy, 257, 258, 263

USCENTCOM. *See* U.S. Central Command (CENTCOM)
U.S.S.R., in Afghanistan, xxii. *See also* Russia
Uthman (caliph), 224, 231, 232, 233

Vehicle-borne improvised explosive device (VBIED), 250
Vehicles, ambush-protected, 253–256
Vietnam War, 69, 70, 79
Vigilant Resolve, Operation, 57, 85, 87, 157
Vigilant Warrior, Operation, 122
Viking Hammer, Operation, **245–248**
Virtual caliphate, 155
Volcker, Paul A., 130

Wahhab, Muhammad abd al-, 236
Wahhabism, 236–237
Wallace, Scott, 144
War crimes, 15
War on Terrorism. *See* Global War on Terrorism
War Powers Resolution, 270
Waterboarding, 29, 111, 112
Watergate scandal, 264
Watt, Justin, 17
Waxman, Henry, 62
Weapons, Insurgency, and Opposition, **249–250**
  improvised explosive devices (IEDs), 249–250
Weapons of mass destruction (WMD), xiii, xxi, xxiii, xxiii–xxiv, xxiv, 27, 28, 31, 94, 100, 118, 120, 122, 123, 128, 133, 134, 181, 197, 199, 217, **250–253**, 262. *See also* Biological weapons; Chemical weapons; Nuclear weapons
  CIA reports, xiv
  search for, xv
  UN inspectors, 239–241
  use by terrorist groups, 251–252
Weapons systems, coalition, **253–258**
  Hellfire missiles, 201, 257

mine-resistant ambush protected (MRAP) vehicles, 253–256
precision-guided (smart) bombs, xiv, 137, 143
unmanned aerial vehicles (UAVs), 14–15, 137, 207–208, 256–258
Whitewater investigation, 221
WikiLeaks, **258–259**
Williams, Bruce, 141
Wilson, Joseph, 37
Wilson, Valerie Plame, 37
Wolfowitz, Paul Dundes, xiv, xxiii, 3, 197, 217, **260–262**
  under Carter, 261
  education and background, 260
  under George H. W. Bush, 261
  under George W. Bush, 261–262
  under Reagan, 261
  as secretary of defense, 261–262
Women
  in combat, 170–172, 262–264
  enslavement of, 153
  repression of by ISIS, 155
  sexual enslavement of, 155
  subjugation of, 153

Women, role of in Afghanistan and Iraq Wars, **262–264**
Woodward, Robert Upshur, **264–266**
  books on the George W. Bush administration, 265
  books on Iraq, 265
  books on the Obama administration, 265
  politics-themed books, 264
World Trade Center attacks. *See* September 11, 2001, attacks
Wuterich, Frank, 14, 15

Xe, 66–67. *See also* Blackwater USA

Yaqubi, Muhammad Sarkhi (Ayatollah), 109
Yazid I (caliph), 224
Yazidi people, 155, 166, 201
Yemen, 8–9, 19, 94, 257
Yom Kippur War, xxi, 116

Zakat (tax/alms), 226, 233–234
Zarqawi, Abu Musab al-, 86, 104, 150, 156, **267–268**
Zaydiyya (Fivers), 224, 231

About the Editor

Brian L. Steed is a retired U.S. Army lieutenant colonel with nearly 29 years of uniformed experience in artillery, armor, cavalry (reconnaissance and security), international engagement, and professional military education. He is a practitioner, student and writer of military theory, Middle East culture, and history in trying to communicate the importance of nonkinetic aspects of counterterrorism, defeating violent extremism, irregular warfare, large-scale conflict mediation, and peace building. His last U.S. Army assignment was as an assistant professor of military history at the U.S. Army Command and General Staff College where he was the 2018 military educator of the year. He was also a Middle East foreign area officer, which included eight and a half consecutive years in the Middle East including assignments in the Levant (Jordan and Israel), Mesopotamia, and the Arabian Peninsula. He served briefly in Iraq in 2005, a full year in 2010–2011, and again December 2014–February 2015. He has written numerous books, articles, and papers on military theory, military history, and cultural awareness. He previously wrote the ABC-CLIO book *ISIS: An Introduction and Guide to the Islamic State* and was the editor for the ABC-CLIO book *Voices of the Iraq War: Contemporary Accounts of Daily Life (Voices of an Era)*. Since returning from Iraq in March 2015, he has been an internationally acclaimed and much sought-after speaker on contemporary conflict, cross-cultural competency, and understanding ISIS in historical and cultural context.

www.ingramcontent.com/pod-product-compliance
Lightning Source LLC
Chambersburg PA
CBHW060506300426
44112CB00017B/2564